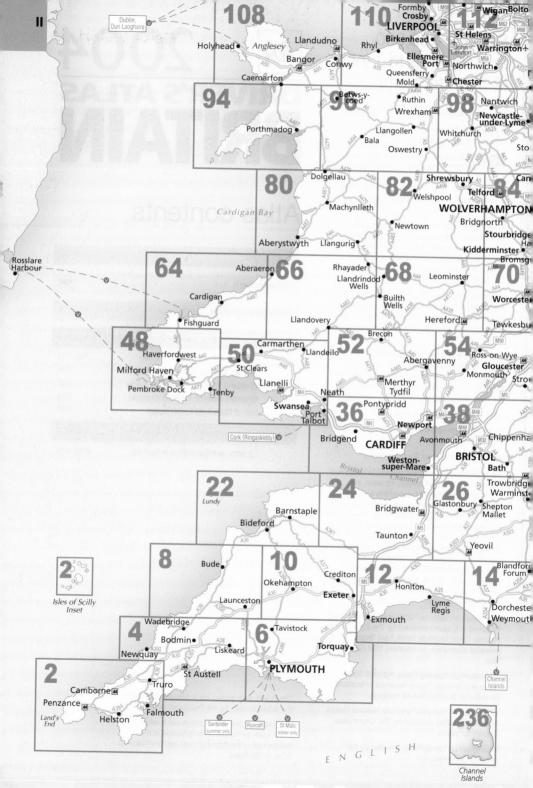

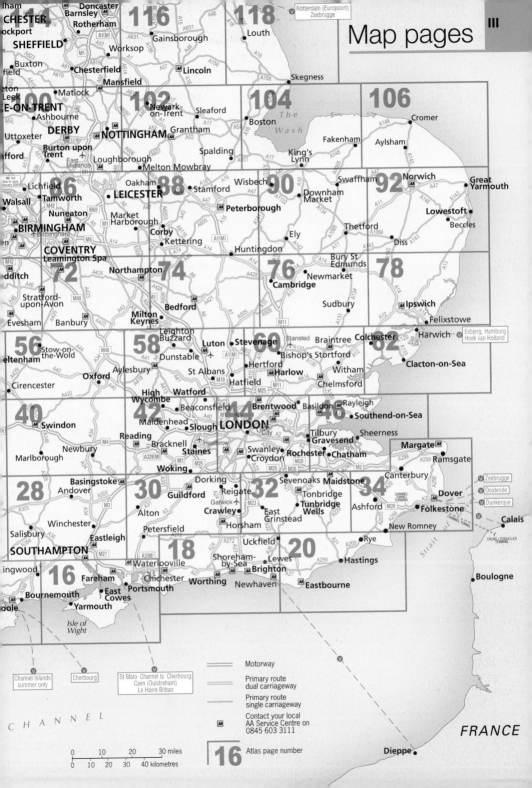

Map pages

III

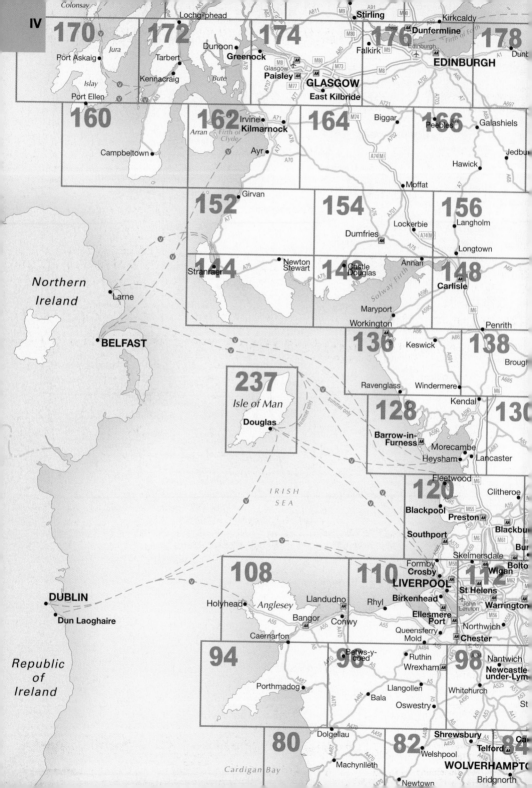

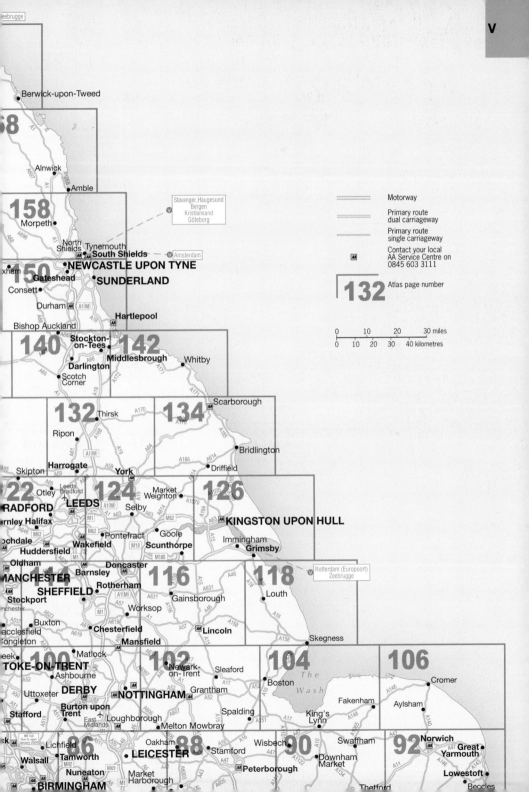

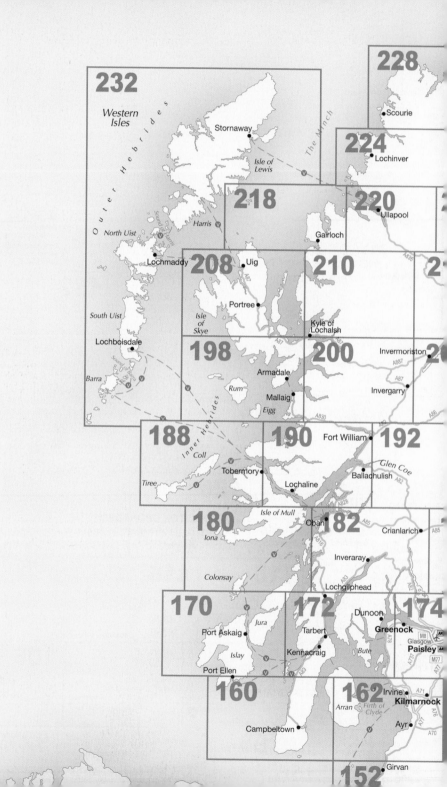

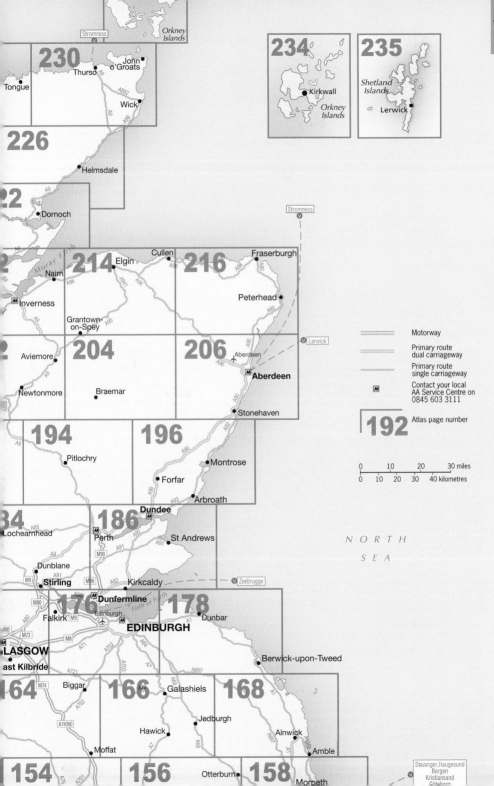

230
Stromness
Orkney Islands
Tongue
Thurso
John o'Groats
Wick

234
Kirkwall
Orkney Islands

235
Shetland Islands
Lerwick

226
Helmsdale

22
Dornoch

Stromness

214
Elgin
Cullen
Nairn
Moray Firth

216
Fraserburgh
Peterhead

Inverness
Grantown-on-Spey

Lerwick

204
Aviemore
Newtonmore
Braemar

206
Aberdeen
Stonehaven

194
Pitlochry

196
Montrose
Forfar
Arbroath

34
Lochearnhead

186
Dundee
Perth
St Andrews
Dunblane
Stirling
Kirkcaldy

176
Dunfermline
Falkirk
Edinburgh
EDINBURGH

178
Dunbar

Zeebrugge

LASGOW
ast Kilbride

Berwick-upon-Tweed

164
Biggar

166
Galashiels

168
Jedburgh
Hawick
Moffat
Alnwick
Amble

154

156
Otterburn

158
Morpeth

Motorway

Primary route
dual carriageway

Primary route
single carriageway

Contact your local
AA Service Centre on
0845 603 3111

192   Atlas page number

0   10   20   30 miles
0 10 20 30 40 kilometres

NORTH
SEA

Stavanger,Haugesund
Bergen
Kristiansand
Göteborg

Mileage chart

The mileage chart shows distances in miles between two towns along AA-recommended routes. Using motorways and other main roads this is normally the fastest route, though not necessarily the shortest.

The journey times, shown in hours and minutes, are average off-peak driving times along AA-recommended routes. These times should be used as a guide only and do not allow for unforeseen traffic delays, rest breaks or fuel stops.

For example, the 378 miles (608 km) journey between Glasgow and Norwich should take approximately 7 hours 28 minutes.

journey times

The chart lists distances in miles between the following towns (read along the diagonal):

Aberdeen · Aberystwyth · Barnstaple · Birmingham · Brighton · Bristol · Cambridge · Cardiff · Carlisle · Carmarthen · Dorchester · Dover · Edinburgh · Exeter · Fort William · Glasgow · Gloucester · Guildford · Hereford · Holyhead · Hull · Inverness · Kendal · Leeds · Lincoln · Liverpool · Maidstone · Manchester · Middlesbrough · Newcastle · Northampton · Norwich · Nottingham · Oxford · Penzance · Perth · Peterborough · Plymouth · Portsmouth · Preston · Salisbury · Sheffield · Shrewsbury · Southampton · Stoke-on-Trent · Stranraer · Taunton · Wick · York · LONDON

Distance matrix (lower triangle), reading each row left to right:

```
472
608 214
436 124 180
613 288 210 171
518 130 100 90 169
463 215 267 97 120 170
537 111 128 109 202 44 203
236 336 371 199 376 281 256 300
520 48 190 172 264 107 266 68 284
600 206 94 172 119 62 184 120 364 182
587 326 272 208 82 205 124 239 381 301 200
126 336 471 299 476 381 333 400 100 386 463 458
593 198 44 165 178 84 259 113 356 175 57 248 455
156 435 570 398 576 480 456 499 199 485 562 580 137 554
150 332 467 295 472 373 353 396 96 382 459 477 47 451 102
484 113 126 56 155 36 150 63 248 125 118 192 346 110 445 343
571 224 175 128 44 106 96 139 335 201 97 43 433 150 532 430 99
487 79 144 59 189 54 153 59 250 85 136 225 349 129 448 346 34 133
464 102 339 167 345 259 202 228 150 331 369 326 323 323 215 302 156
376 227 320 139 258 230 138 250 277 247 304 367 266 396 196 239 198 218
106 496 631 459 637 541 517 561 260 546 623 641 157 616 66 176 507 595 510 488 430
283 189 234 153 330 234 251 254 47 240 318 347 73 336 131 164 307
329 173 301 120 262 211 146 230 123 224 293 271 200 285 321 219 177 220 179 165 79 383 110
388 199 275 98 216 185 95 205 182 267 246 220 258 260 379 277 151 173 154 204 44 441 176 74
362 110 272 178 182 193 202 126 158 264 302 224 752 64 221 155 102 128 386 79 74 139
545 284 234 166 50 167 82 200 339 262 161 41 416 209 537 435 153 58 186 327 220 599 313 231 178 261
357 134 261 89 201 156 70 190 120 254 293 290 219 235 216 136 224 139 125 97 380 74 44 85 34 248
276 244 357 176 318 267 197 286 95 294 349 324 146 341 283 190 232 276 235 259 89 267 102 95 174 296 119 39
235 275 388 207 349 298 229 317 60 325 380 353 106 372 242 153 264 307 266 266 182 207 102 95 145 311 145 39
486 174 212 55 133 115 56 142 249 197 155 348 196 447 345 79 99 118 145 94 151 113 139 189 220
488 278 329 160 168 233 63 266 282 328 241 172 359 313 480 378 212 160 215 321 147 542 276 174 103 240 130 185 223 254 118
395 162 232 51 193 142 86 161 189 223 224 210 266 216 387 285 107 151 110 178 93 449 164 77 39 112 168 71 130 161 64 119
510 160 170 68 109 73 82 107 274 169 115 146 373 154 472 370 48 67 81 242 190 534 228 174 132 176 107 164 227 258 44 146 102
702 308 108 274 287 193 368 222 466 284 167 357 564 109 663 562 229 409 259 434 415 726 419 403 370 367 398 356 451 482 326 433 326 265
86 388 523 379 529 433 378 453 152 438 515 503 42 507 102 64 399 486 401 379 21 192 245 173 103 278 461 275 192 150 402 404 310 426 617
435 204 263 86 158 173 91 229 225 264 162 306 248 427 325 139 115 142 225 110 489 223 121 51 150 270 201 45 78 86 357 115 97 351
633 239 62 205 218 124 299 153 397 215 98 288 495 44 594 493 151 340 190 365 346 657 350 334 301 298 296 289 382 413 257 364 257 196 78 544 288
594 244 152 154 53 125 137 158 360 220 131 54 458 132 558 456 118 45 152 328 276 546 314 260 173 262 102 250 313 344 130 204 188 85 241 508 157 172
329 146 281 110 287 191 209 197 23 193 271 311 98 266 287 185 157 245 160 138 122 349 43 19 93 33 269 35 103 139 272 295 184 375 237 180 306 270
549 184 118 121 90 52 188 91 313 160 39 160 411 93 511 409 72 62 105 281 261 573 267 244 202 215 121 203 298 329 115 212 173 70 203 461 165 134 44 223
397 166 272 91 233 182 122 201 116 203 261 264 244 235 216 124 151 150 157 66 411 135 47 79 29 205 109 104 148 45 142 306 309 129 245 209 92 161 88
417 75 220 48 226 130 140 111 181 110 12 250 279 205 379 277 96 184 52 160 65 154 162 135 119 124 45 208 71 190 221 98 203 87 123 459 97 91 146
578 225 142 135 66 106 116 234 340 201 53 142 440 111 539 437 100 41 133 309 258 601 295 241 159 252 20 252 23 209 191 146 166 92 154 520 172 46 26 252 39
392 112 220 48 226 130 140 111 181 110 12 250 279 205 379 277 96 184 52 160 65 411 162 135 119 124 45 208 71 190 221 98 203 87 123 459 97 91 146 88 45 123
235 342 477 305 482 387 363 406 106 392 469 487 132 461 181 86 352 440 355 333 276 261 153 229 288 232 445 229 201 163 354 388 295 380 571 149 333 502 466 195 418 267 287 447 261
560 165 50 132 150 71 225 52 220 80 323 142 45 224 42 54 419 77 126 96 235 147 149 107 210 28 114 130 123 254 57 146 251 120 223 265 477
207 597 732 560 738 642 618 662 361 647 724 742 258 716 166 277 608 695 610 588 531 104 408 484 543 487 700 484 409 367 609 640 516 635 826 215 589 757 721 451 673 523 542 702 516 362 684
323 201 314 134 243 156 210 195 78 257 306 321 319 298 314 201 189 172 103 129 193 233 192 376 201 159 166 87 170 204 271 51 89 180 184 408 218 329 269 96 254 57 146 251 120 223 265 477
550 239 216 121 54 120 59 153 314 215 78 142 200 512 410 110 21 136 282 186 504 288 581 178 192 235 95 199 262 293 79 159 137 52 137 462 86 241 75 225 85 169 163 77 161 420 167 675 211
```

Road map symbols

M4	Motorway with number	
Toll T4 Toll	Toll motorway with toll station	
11	Motorway junction with and without number	
3	Restricted motorway junctions	
S Fleet	Motorway service area	
	Motorway and junction under construction	
A3	Primary route single/dual carriageway	
1	Primary route junction with and without number	
3	Restricted Primary route junctions	
S Grantham North	Primary route service area	
BATH	Primary route destination	
A1123	Other A road single/dual carriageway	

B2070	B road single/dual carriageway	
	Unclassified road single/dual carriageway	
	Roundabout	
	Interchange/junction	
	Narrow primary/other A/B road with passing places (Scotland)	
	Road under construction	
	Road tunnel	
	Steep gradient (arrows point downhill)	
Toll	Road toll	
5	Distance in miles between symbols	
	Railway station and level crossing	
	Tourist railway	

AA	AA Service Centre
V St Malo	Vehicle ferry
⊕ Ⓗ	Airport/Heliport
Ⓕ	International freight terminal
P·R	Park and Ride location (at least 6 days)
	City, town, village or other built-up area
628 ▲	Spot height in metres
	Sandy beach
	National boundary
	County, administrative boundary
23	Page continuation number

	Tourist Information Centre (all year/seasonal)		Country park		Viewpoint		Rugby Union national stadium
	Visitor or heritage centre		Agricultural showground		Picnic site		International athletics stadium
	Abbey, cathedral or priory		Theme park		Hill-fort		Horse racing/Show jumping
	Ruined abbey, cathedral or priory		Farm or animal centre		Roman antiquity		Motor-racing circuit
	Castle		Zoological or wildlife collection		Prehistoric monument		Air show venue
	Historic house or building		Bird collection	1066	Battle site with year		Ski slope (natural/artificial)
	Museum or art gallery		Aquarium		Steam centre (railway)	NT NTS	National Trust property (England & Wales/ Scotland)
	Industrial interest		RSPB site		Cave	★	Other place of interest
	Aqueduct or viaduct		National Nature Reserve (England, Scotland, Wales)		Windmill		Attraction within urban area
	Garden		Local nature reserve		Monument		Forest Park
	Arboretum	....	Forest drive		Golf course		National Park and National Scenic Areas
	Vineyard	---	National trail		County cricket ground		Heritage coast

8

A B C D E F

1
2
3
4
5
6
7
8

Higher Sharpn

Lower Sharpn

Ste

Bud
Bay

Wi

Dizzard Point P
St
Gennys Coxford T
Crackington Haven T
Cambeak T
Sweets Wainho
Corne

Witchcraft B3263 15 A39 Marshgate
Pentire Point - Widemouth Tresparrett Otte
Heritage Coast Boscastle Lesnewth
Trevalga B3266
Tintagel 6 B3263
TINTAGEL HEAD Trethevey B3383
Tintagel Bossiney Davidstow
Old Post Office NT Trewarmett
Penhallic Point British Cycling Tremail
Treknow Centre B3314 R I
Trebarwith Gaia Trefrew
Energy
Centre Crowdy
Delabole Camelford Reservoir
South West Coast Path Westdowns Pengelly
Port Isaac Lanteglos Watergate 34
Rumps Kelland Varley Bay Trewalder Helstone
Point Port Quin Head Head 419
Pentire Point Bay Port Port Port-Gaverne B3314 Treveighan BROWN
Padstow Bay Quin Isaac St Teath WILLY
Stepper Point Polzeath Long Treveighan B
Hayle Bay Cross Trelights Pendoggett Michaelstow BODM
Trevose A B 4 C St Endelli D relill E A39 F
He 0 1 2 3 4 miles B3314 Churchtown
TREVO 0 1 2 3 4 5 kilometres St Minver St Kew St Breward Jamaica Inn
Head Rock Tr Trequite St Kew
Bay Trevone St Kew

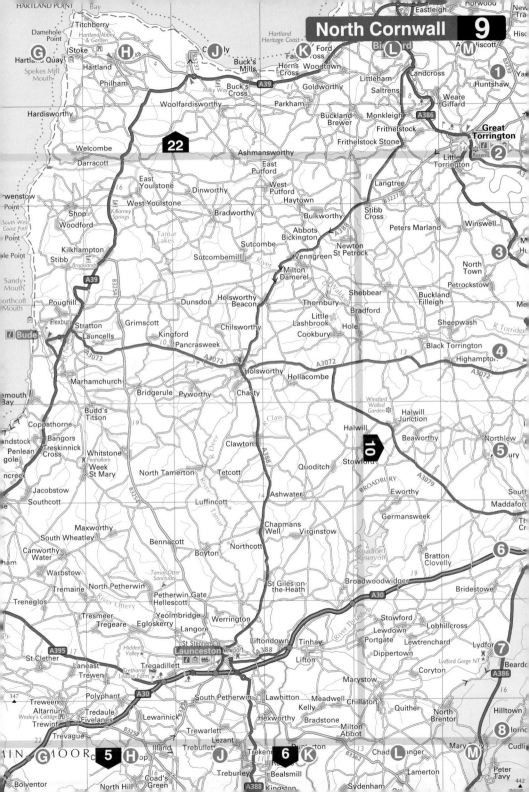

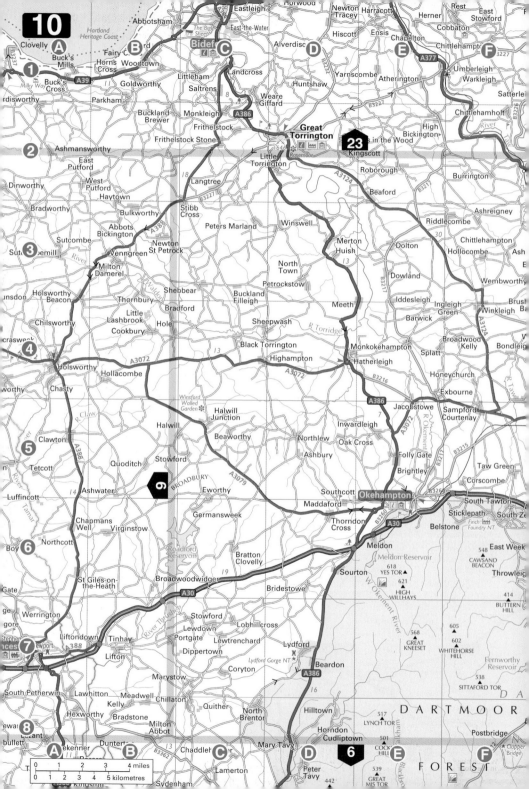

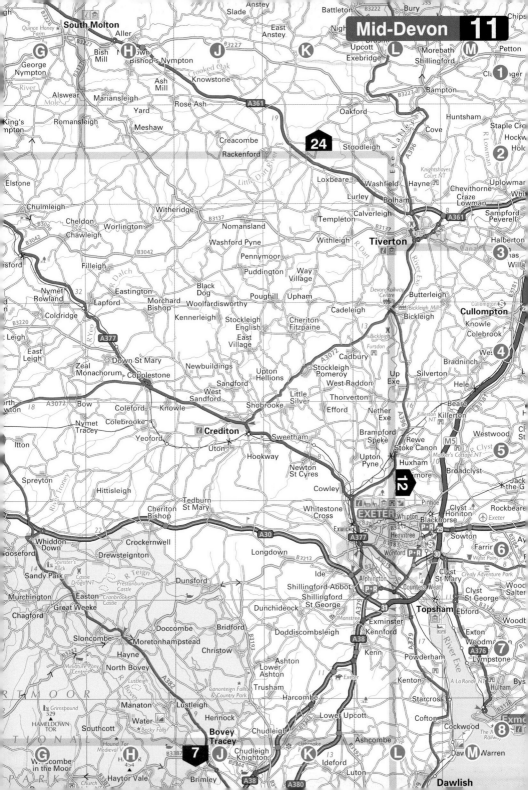

A B C D E F

1

2

3

North West Point

Lundy Heritage Coast

LUNDY

▲142

Marisco

Shutter Point

Surf Point

Baggy Point

Croyde B

4

Ne Heri

BARNSTAPLE

OR

5

BIDEFORD BAY

Westward

HARTLAND POINT

Shipload Bay

Titchberry

Abbotsham

Damehole Point

Hartland Abbey & Garden

Stoke

Clovelly

Hartland Heritage Coast

Ford

6

Hartland Quay

B3248

Buck's Mills

Fairy Cross

Spekes Mill Mouth

Hartland

Philham

B3237

Milky Way

Buck's Cross

A39

Horns Cross

Woodtown

Goldworthy

Parkham

Woolfardisworthy

Hardisworthy

Buckland Brewer

Frith

Welcombe

Ashmansworthy

East Putford

7

Darracott

9

East Youlstone

Dinworthy

West Putford

Haytown

Morwenstow

16

West Youlstone

Bradworthy

Bulkworthy

Higher Sharpnose Point

South West Coast Path

Shop

Killarney Springs

Tamar Lakes

Sutcombe

Abbots Bickington

8

Lower Sharpnose Point

Woodford

Sutcom ill

Ven Newt St Pet

Steeple Point

Kilkhampton

bb

Brocklanda

Milton Damerel

Sandy Mouth

A39

B3254

River

Holsworthy

Northcott

A388

A3

0 1 2 3 4 miles
0 1 2 3 4 5 kilometres

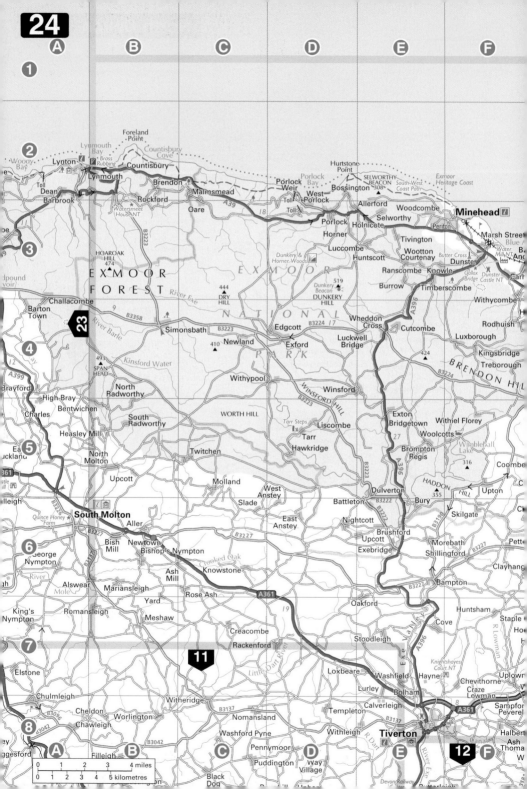

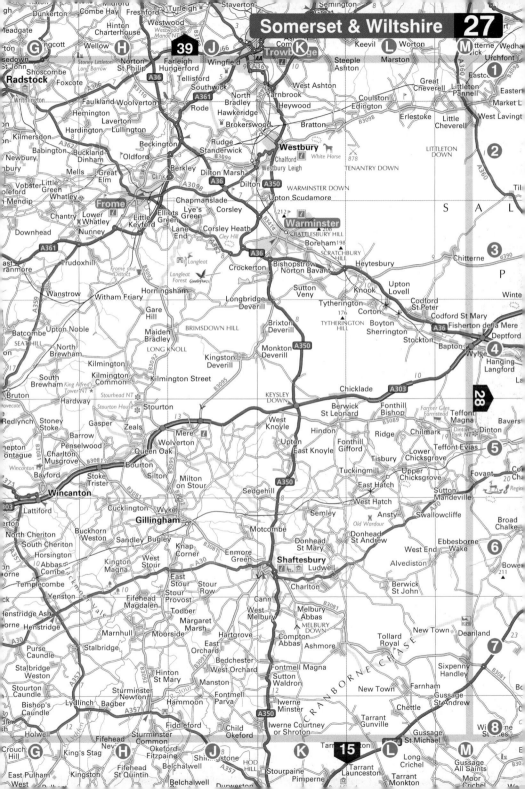

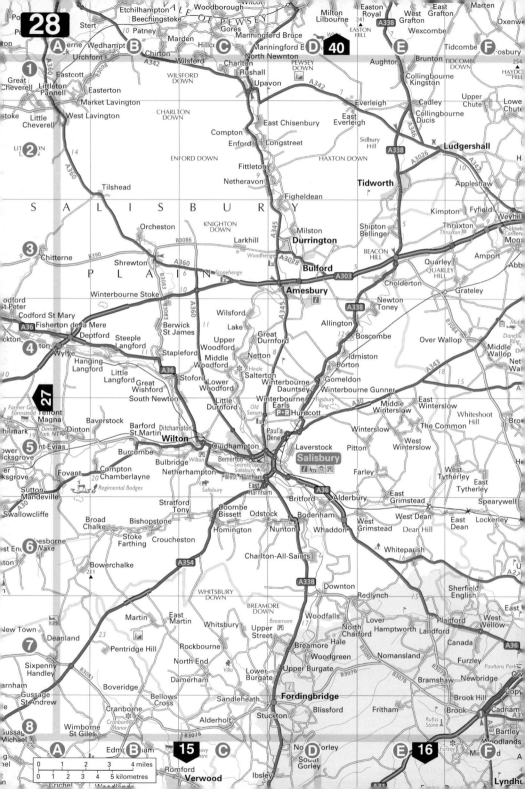

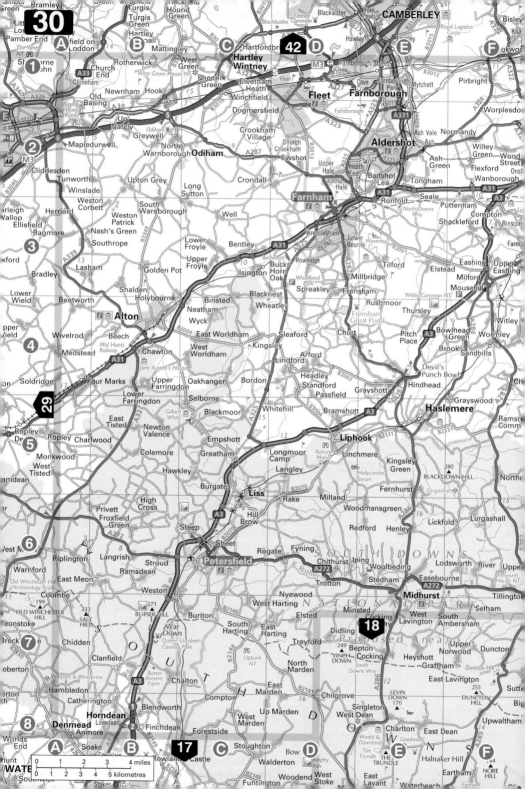

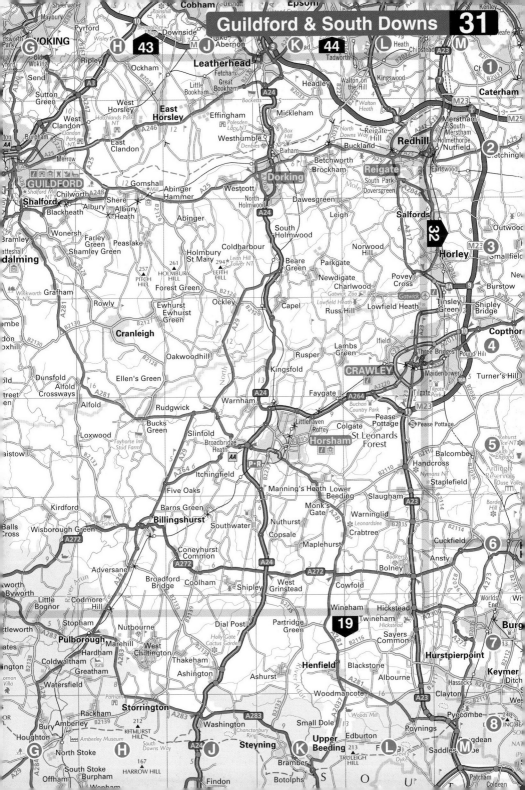

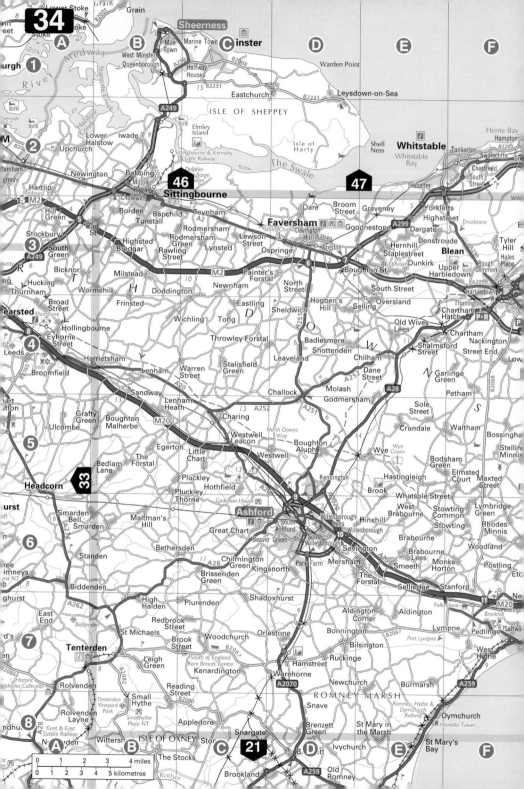

G H J K L M

① ② ③ ④ ⑤ ⑥ ⑦ ⑧

Foreness Point

MARGATE

Westgate on-Sea Westbrook Cliftonville Kingsgate
Minnis Bay Northdown NORTH FORELAND
Birchington Garlinge Reading Street St Peter's
Herne Bay Bishopstone Reculver Salmestone Grange **Broadstairs**
Beltinge A299 St Nicholas at Wade ISLE OF THANET Lydden Westwood Dumpton Hereson
Broomfield Boyden Gate Sarre A253 Acol B2190 Monkton Manston St Lawrence Dumpton **Ramsgate**
Chislet A259 Durlock **Minster** Viking Ship 'Hugin' Pegwell
Hoath Upstreet West Stourmouth R Stour Pegwell Bay
Hersden A28 East Stourmouth St Augustine's Cross
Westbere Westmarsh A256
Stodmarsh Preston Elmstone Cop Street Richborough Prince's Sandwich Bay
Old Town Hall Wickhambreaux Hoaden Ash **Sandwich**
Littlebourne Seaton Ickham Durlock Stone Cross Royal St George's
bury Bramling Wingham Marshborough Toll
Bekesbourne Staple Goodnestone Woodnesborough Worth
Patrixbourne Ratling Chillenden Eastry Statenborough Hacklinge
Adisham Higham Park Nonington Ham Finglesham The Downs
North Downs Way Betteshanger Sholden Northbourne **Deal**
ingston Aylesham Womenswold Tilmanstone Great Mongeham Upper Deal
Barham Elvington Sutton Ripple Walmer
erringstone Barfreston Lower Eythorne East Studdal Ringwould Kingsdown
Woolage Green East Kent Railway Ashley Sutton Downs
Denton Shepherdswell West Langdon Martin
Wootton Coldred North Downs Way East Langdon
Geddinge A2 Whitfield Guston St Margaret's at Cliffe
North Elham Selsted Lydden A256 Temple Ewell West Cliffe St Margaret's Bay
Swingfield Minnis Ewell Minnis Kearsney River SOUTH FORELAND
Alkham Buckland Lighthouse South Foreland Heritage Coast
sworth Densole South Alkham Maxton Langdon Cliffs
nge Upper Standen Drellingore West Hougham NT Dunkerque Calais
Hawkinge Lower Standen Battle of Britain **DOVER** Zeebrugge
Channel Tunnel Terminal Capel le-Ferne Oostende
eene Samphire Hoe Dover-Folkestone Heritage Coast Calais
Cheriton Morehall East Wear Bay Channel Tunnel
the Sandgate **FOLKESTONE**

STRAIT OF DOVER

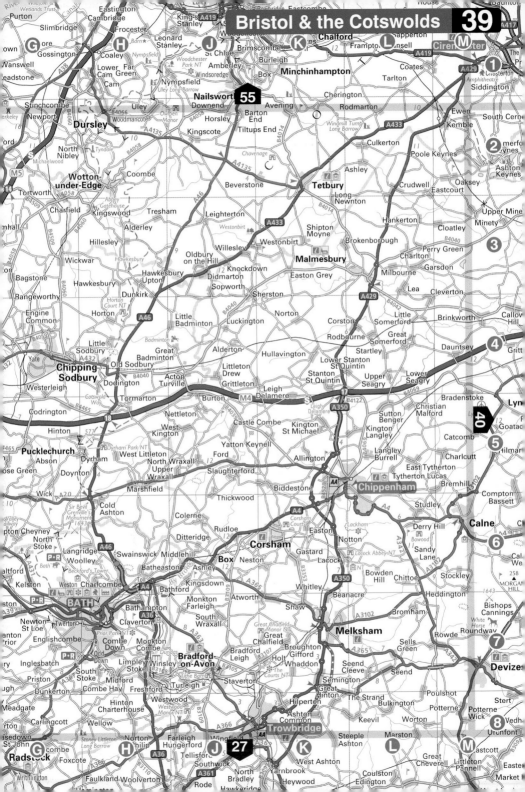

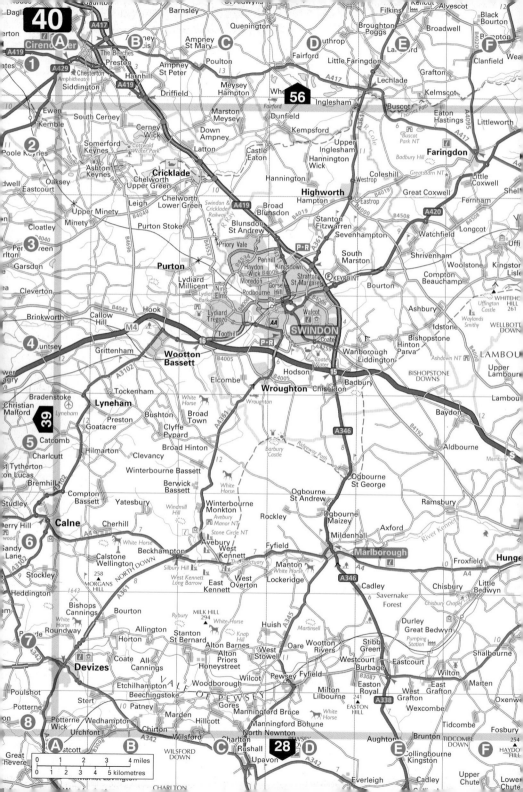

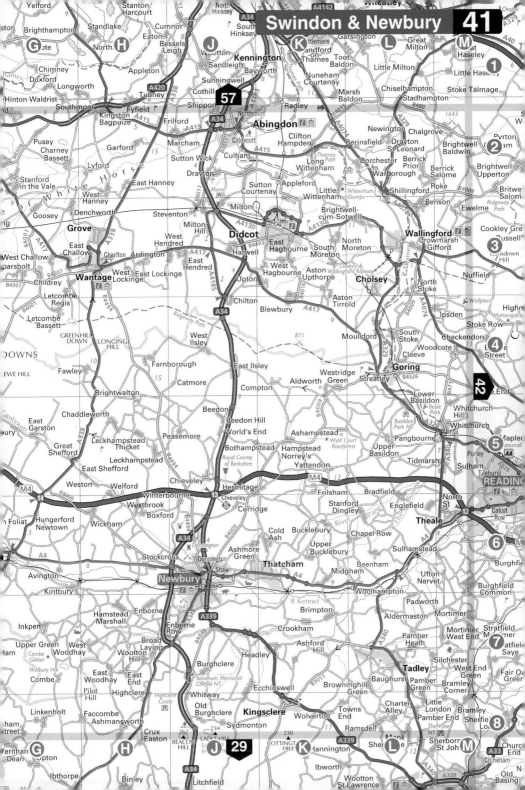

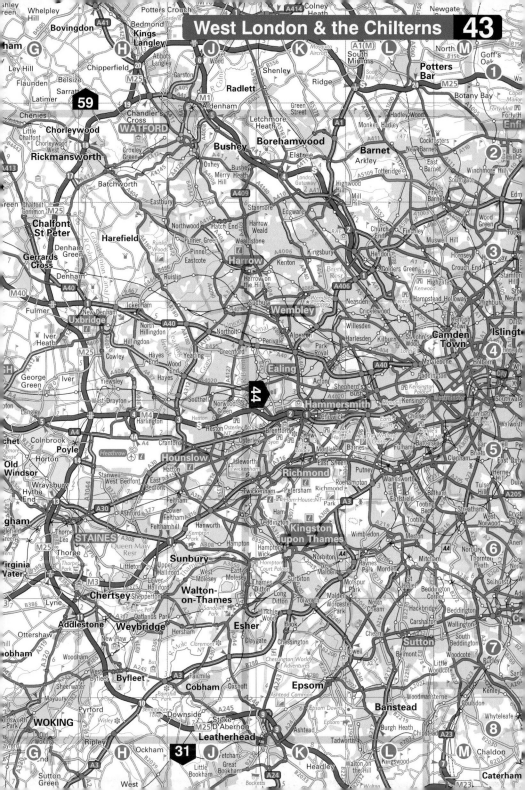

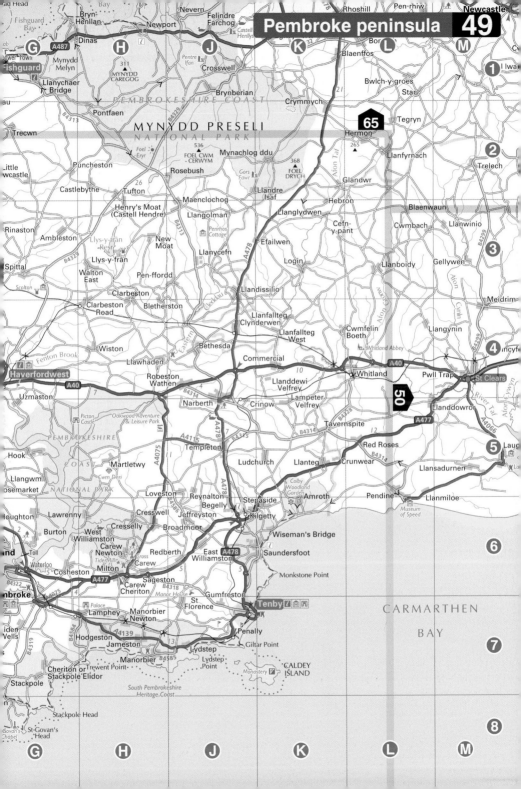

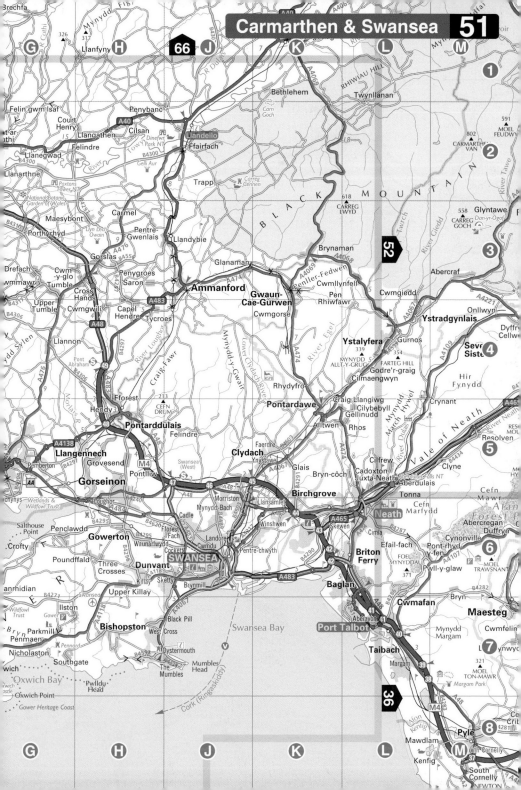

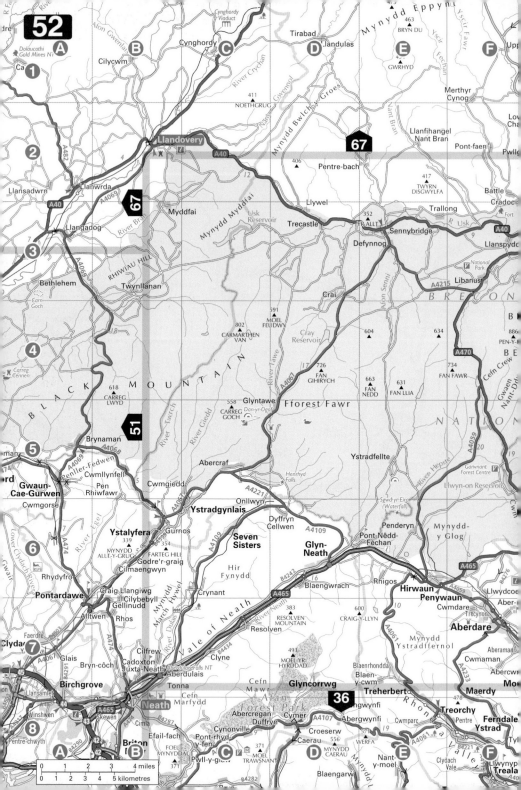

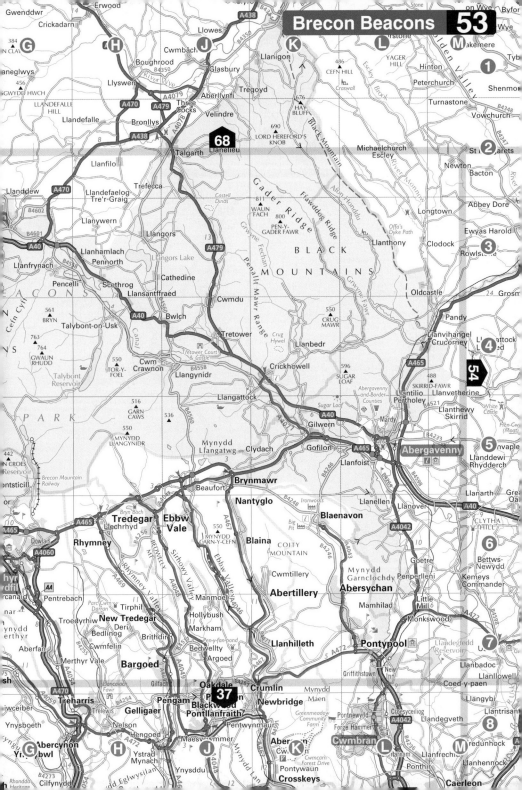

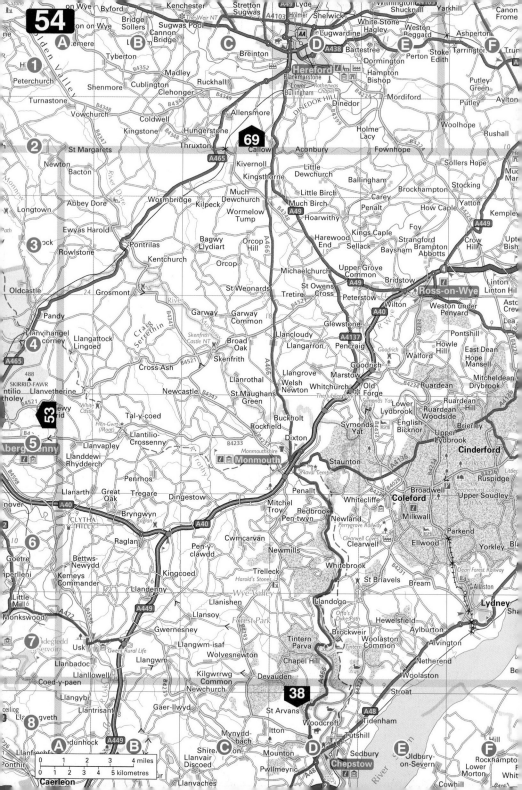

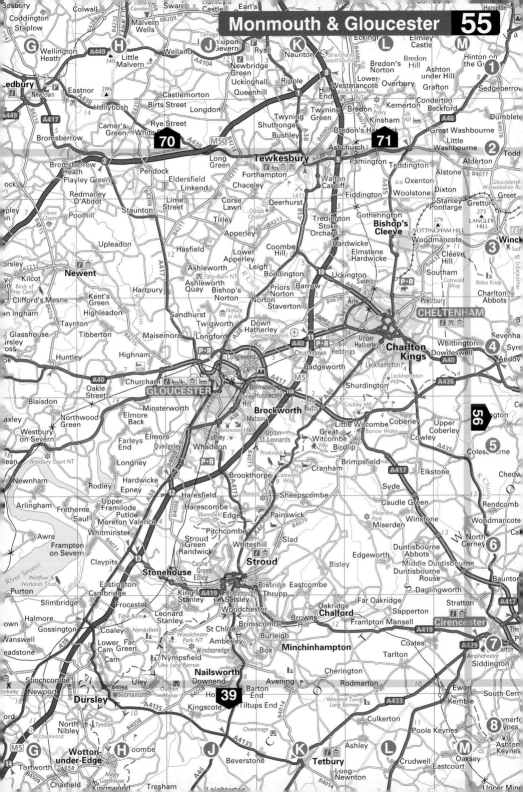

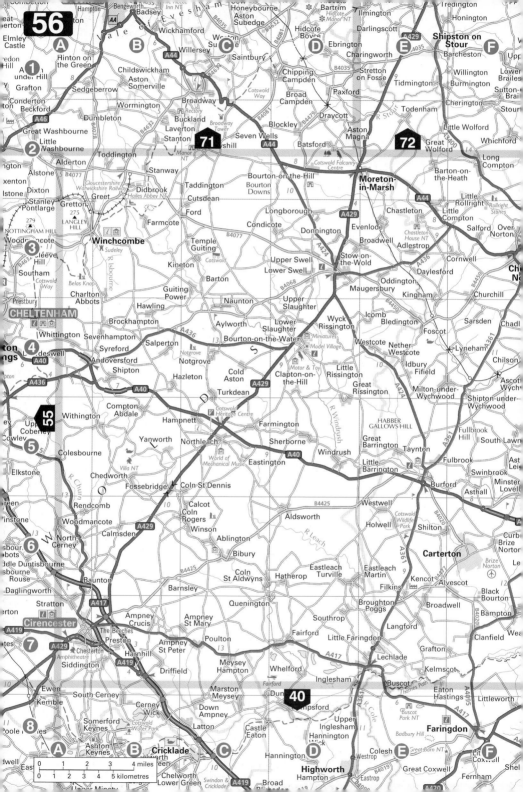

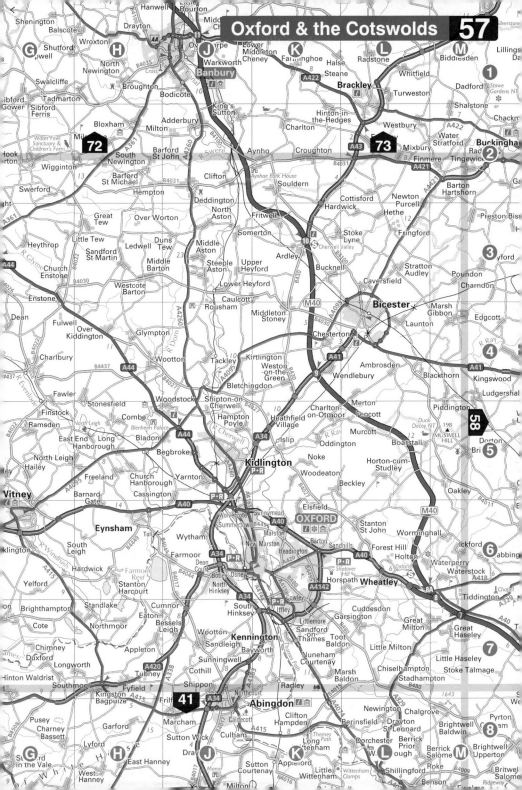

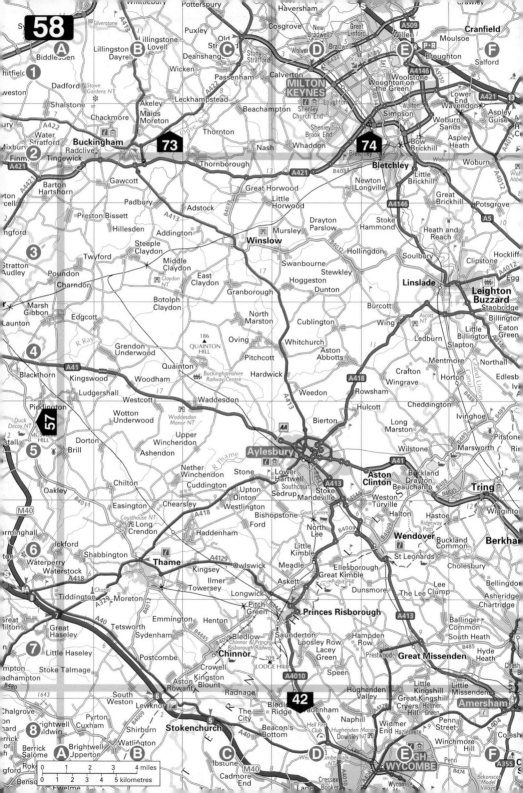

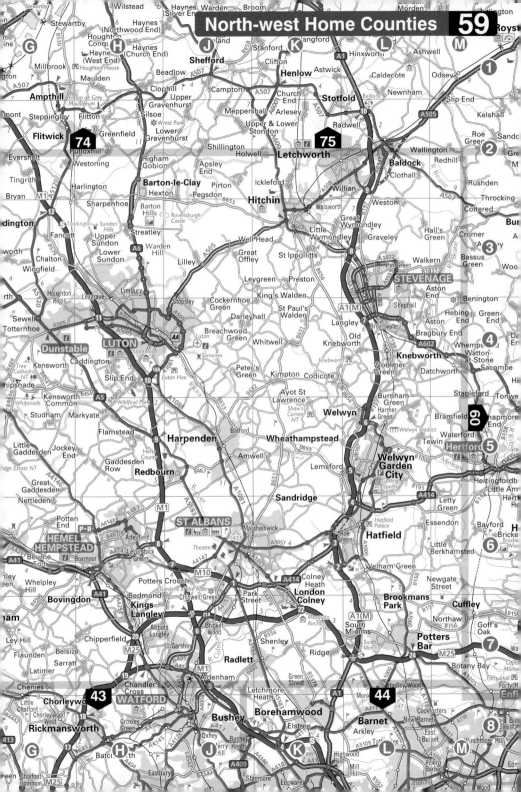

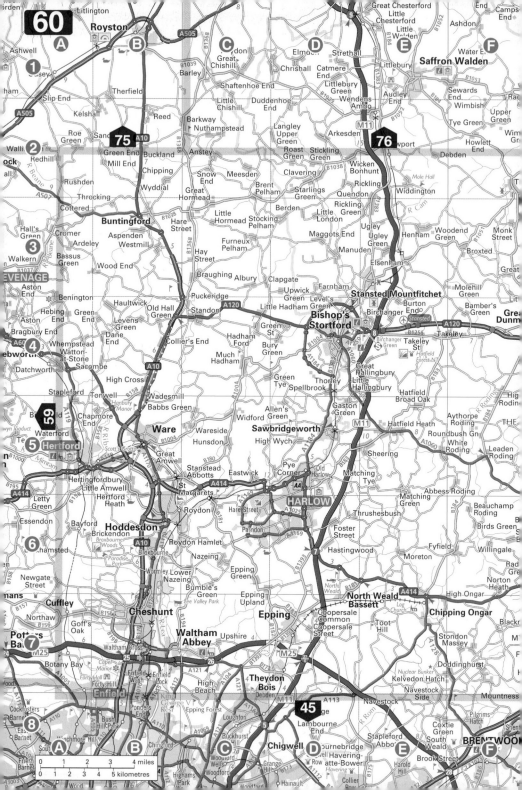

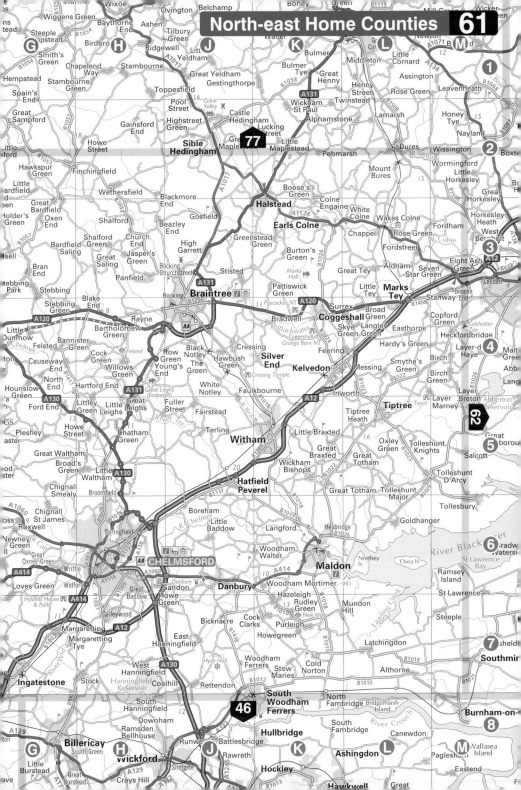

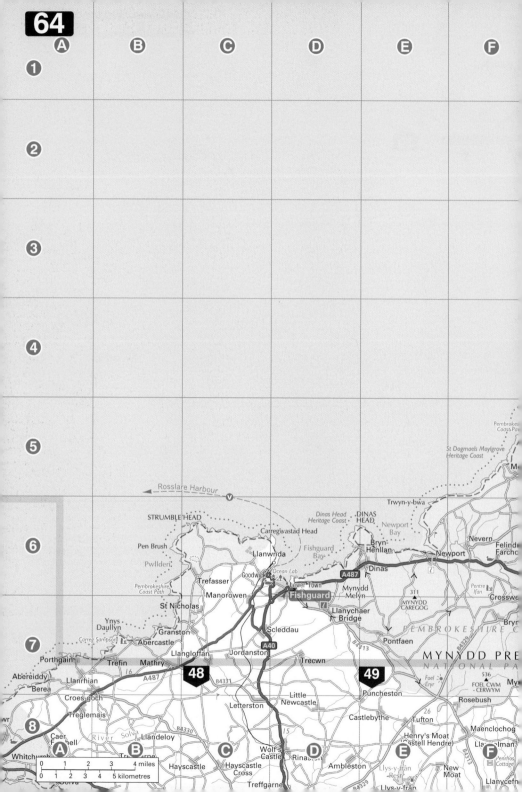

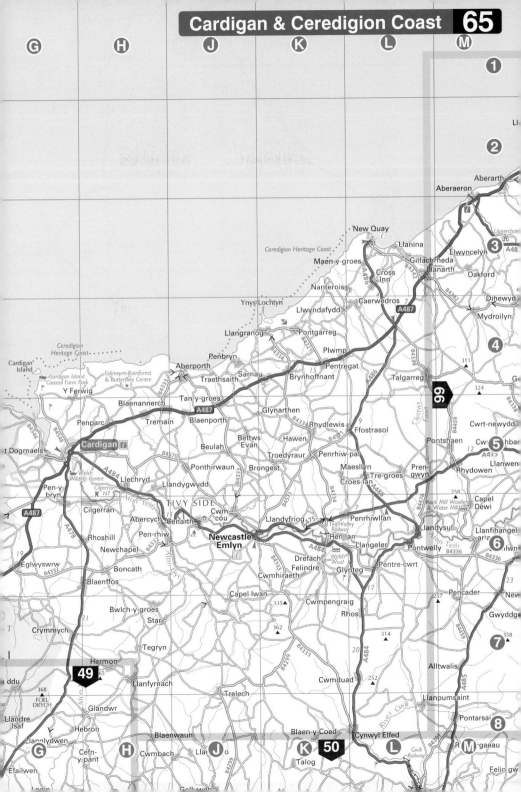

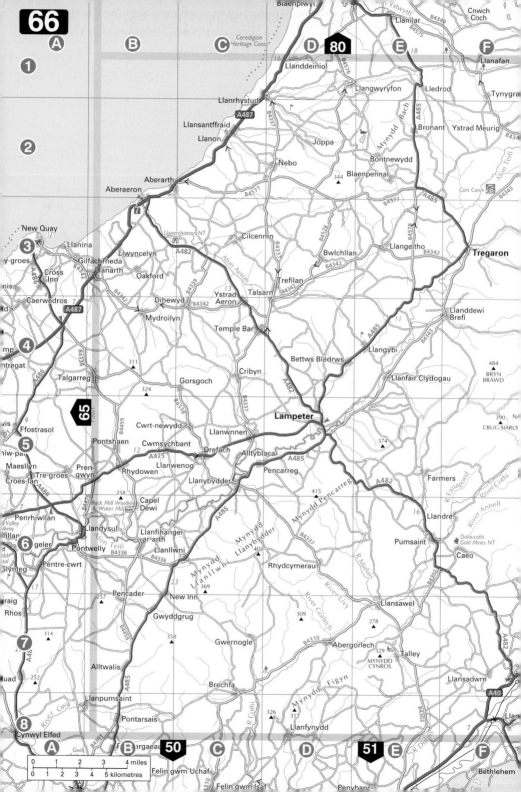

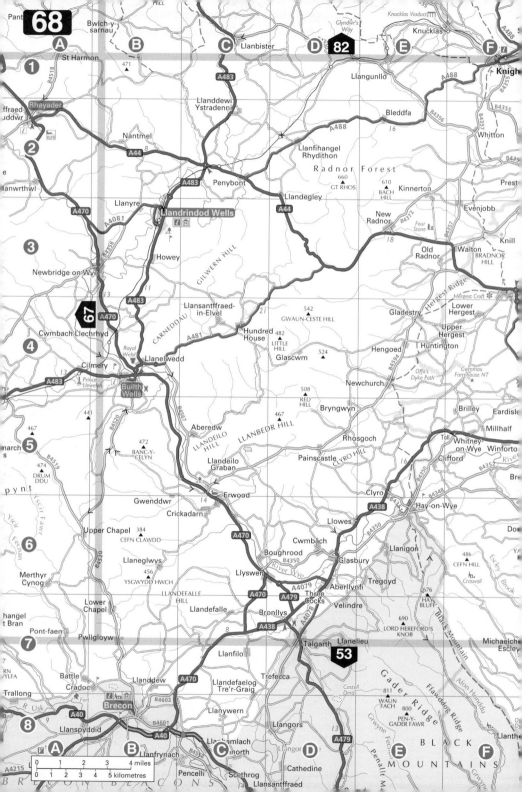

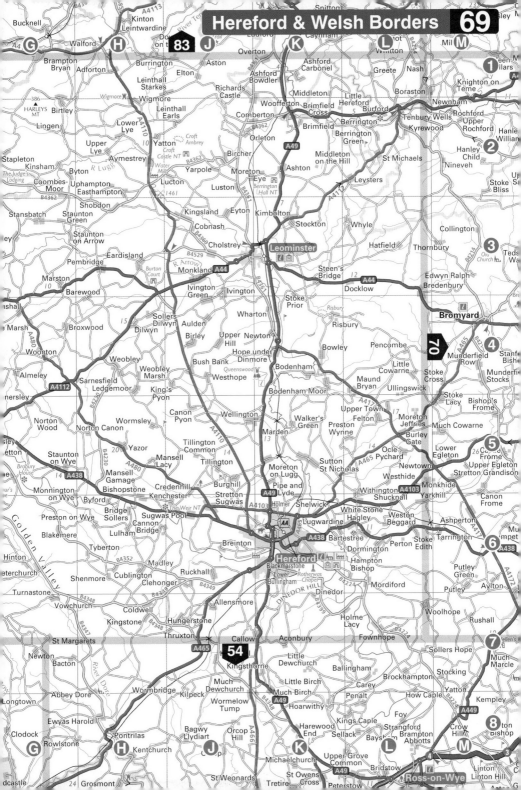

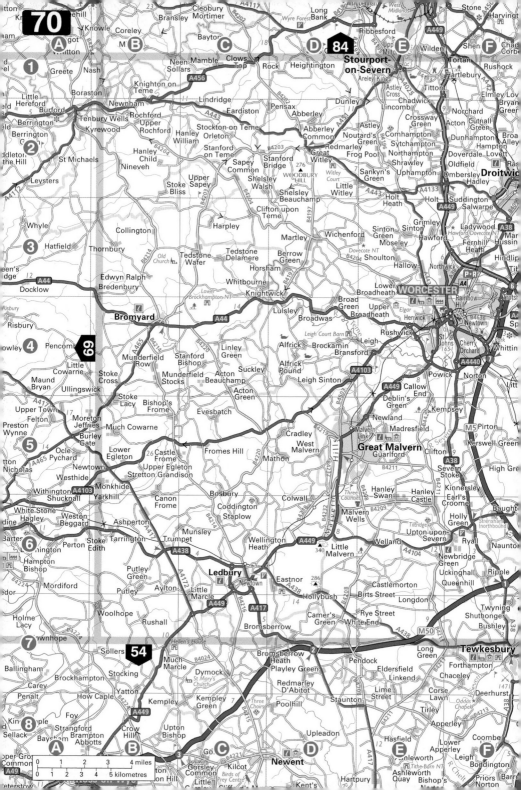

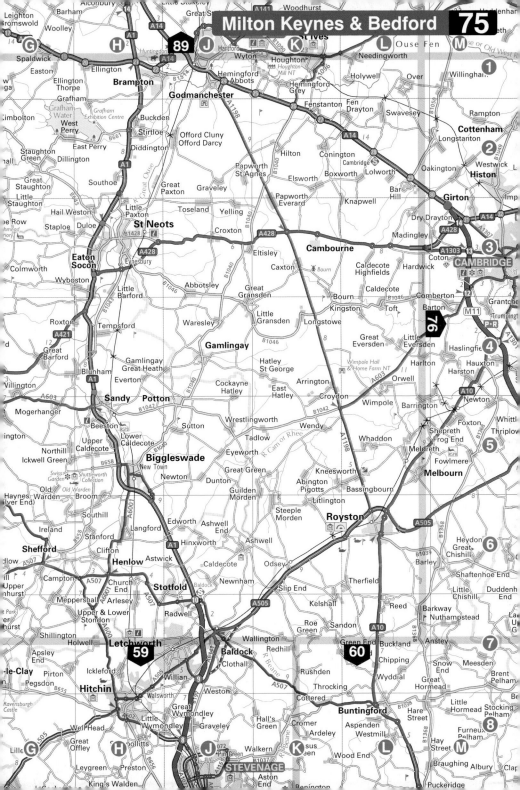

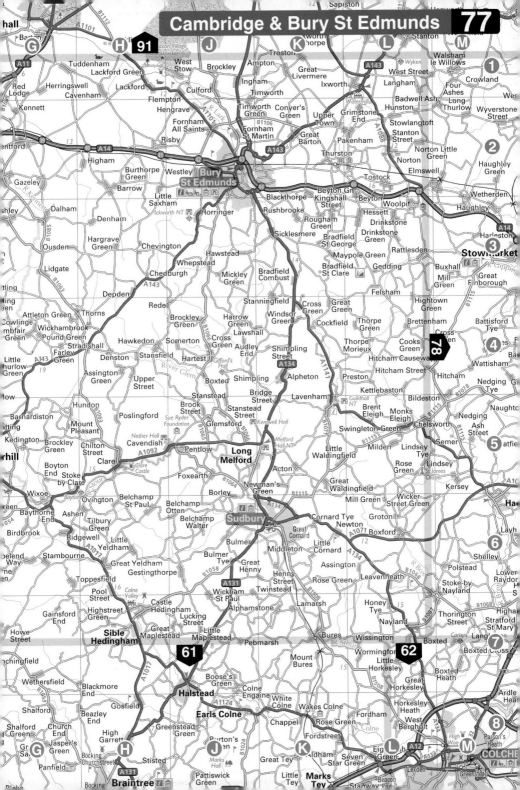

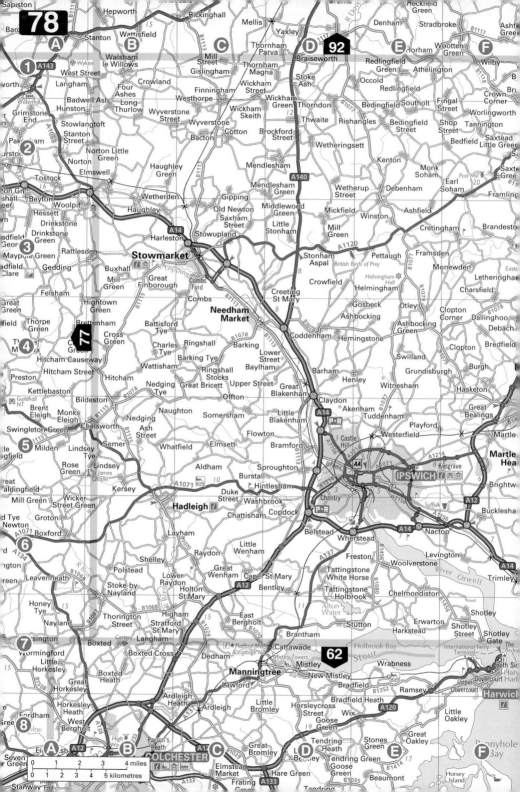

G   H   J   93   K   L   M

1
2
3
4
5
6
7
8

Cratfield
Cookley
Wennaston
Blythburgh
Huntingfield
Blackheath
Thorington
Walberswick
Walpole
Bramfield
Heveningham
Ubbeston Green
Darsham
Dunwich
Sibton
Peasenhall
Yoxford
Westleton
Badingham
Middleton
Bruisyard
Middleton Moor
Minsmere RSPB
Bruisyard Street
Rendham
Theberton
Eastbridge
Cransford
Kelsale
Shawsgate
Carlton
Leiston
Sizewell Visitor Centre
Swefling
Saxmundham
North Green
Knodishall
Leiston
Great Glemham
Benhall Street
Benhall Green
Sternfield
Coldfair Green
Aldringham
Thorpe Ness
Stratford St Andrew
Friday Street
Friston
Thorpeness
Hacheston
Farnham
Snape
Easton
Marlesford
Snape Street
The Maltings
Aldeburgh
Little Glemham
Iken
Blaxhall
High Street
Aldeburgh Bay
Campsea Ash
Tunstall
Ufford
Chillesford
Sudbourne
Eyke
Bromeswell
Butley
Orford
Orford Ness
bridge
Capel St Andrew
Sutton
Boyton
Orfordness-Havergate RSPB
Suffolk Heritage Coast
Shottisham
Hollesley
North Weir Point
Hemley
Hollesley Bay
Alderton
Bawdsey
Falkenham
Old Felixstowe
Felixstowe
Landguard Fort
Landguard Point
Esbjerg Hamburg
Hoek, Holland

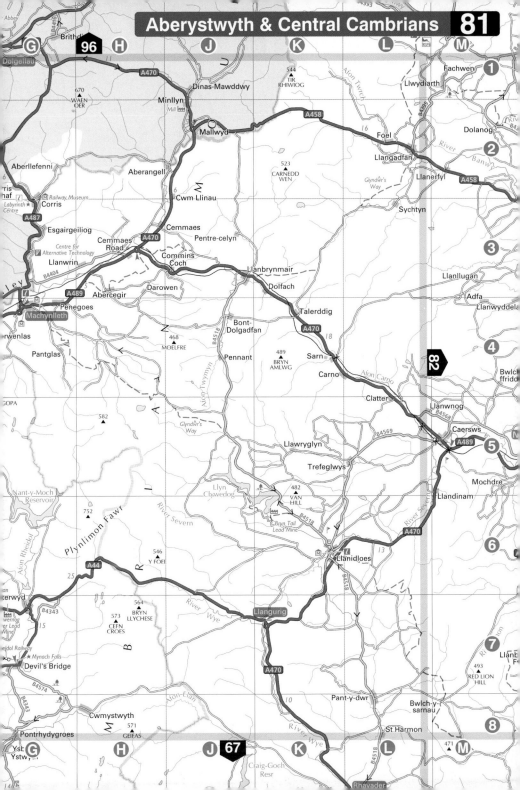

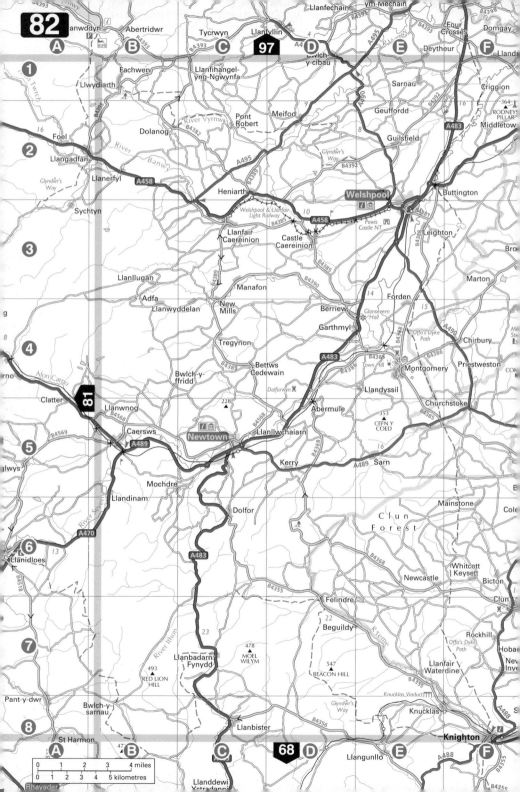

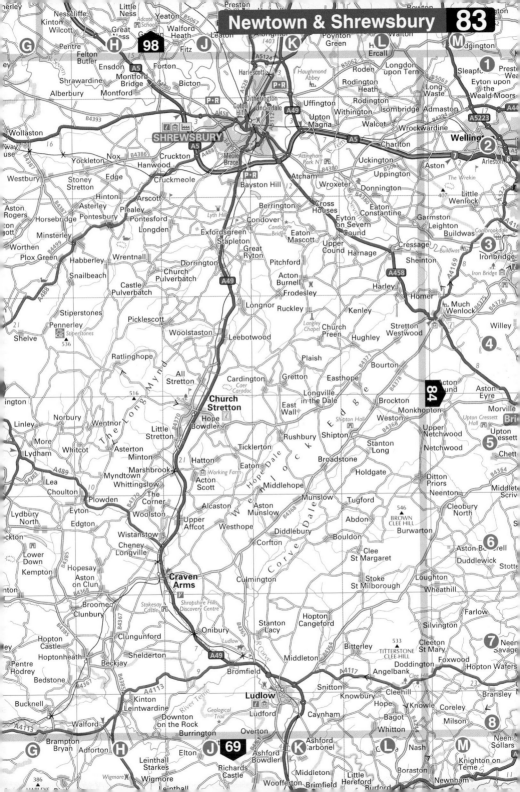

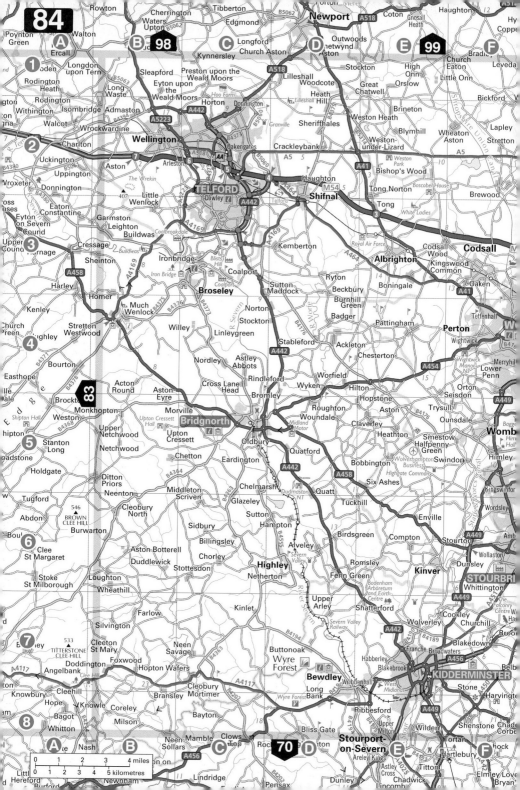

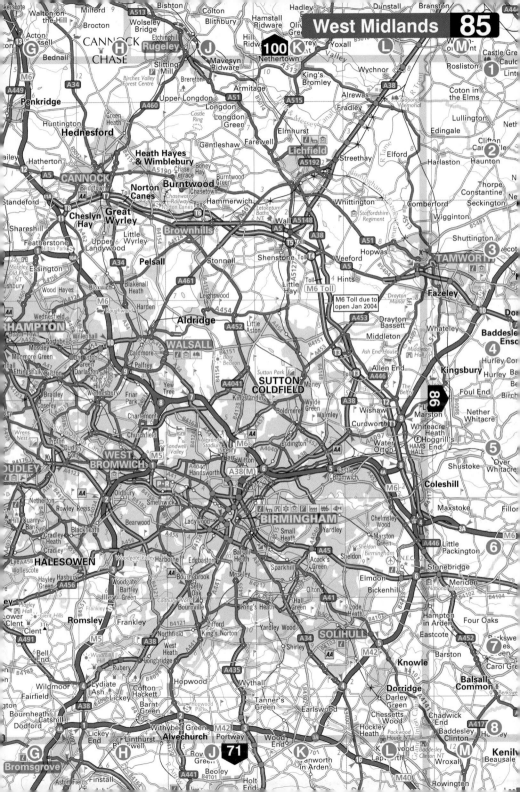

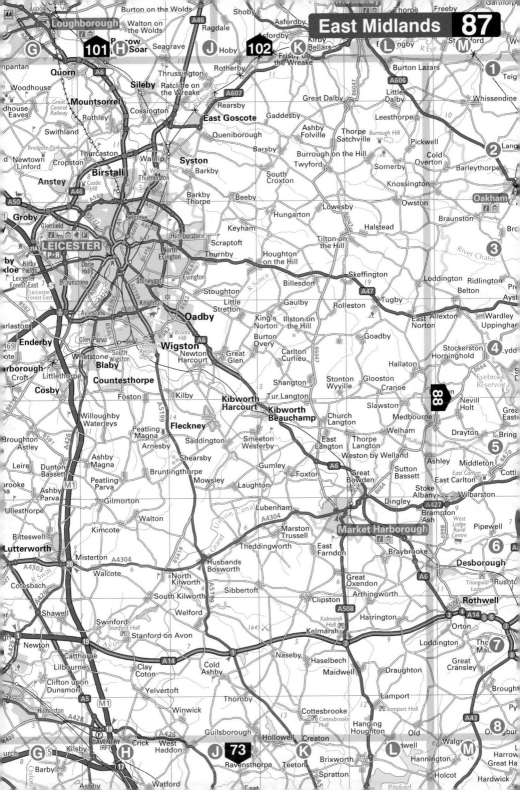

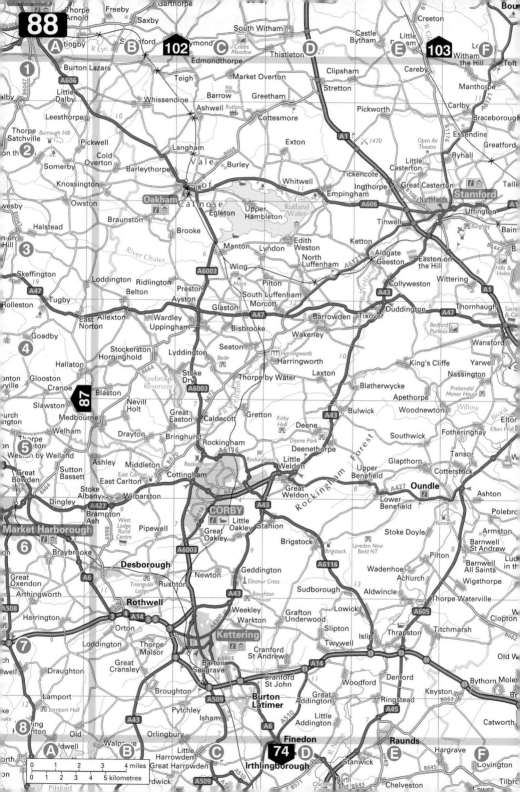

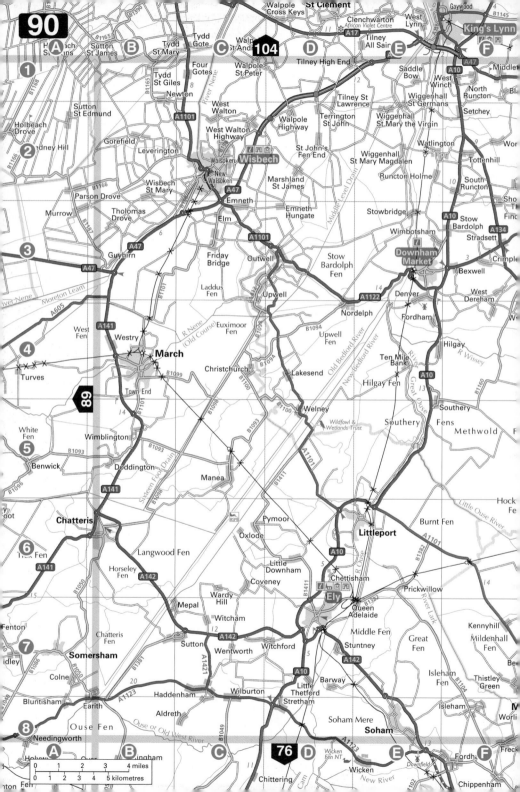

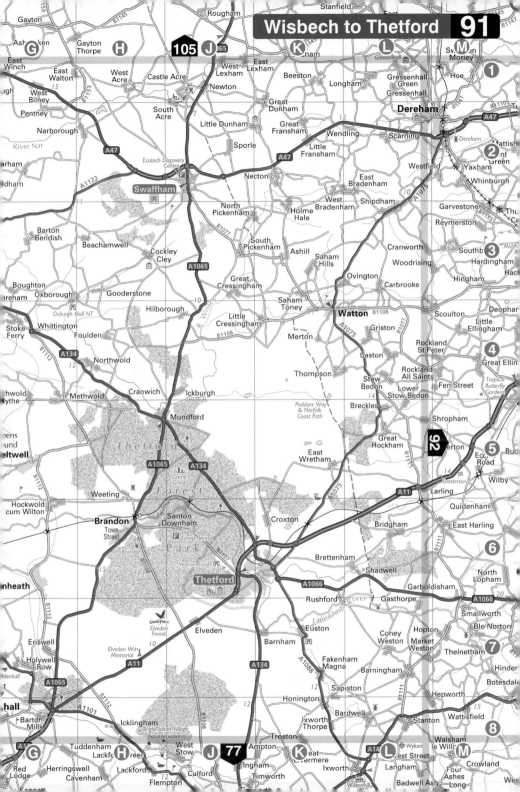

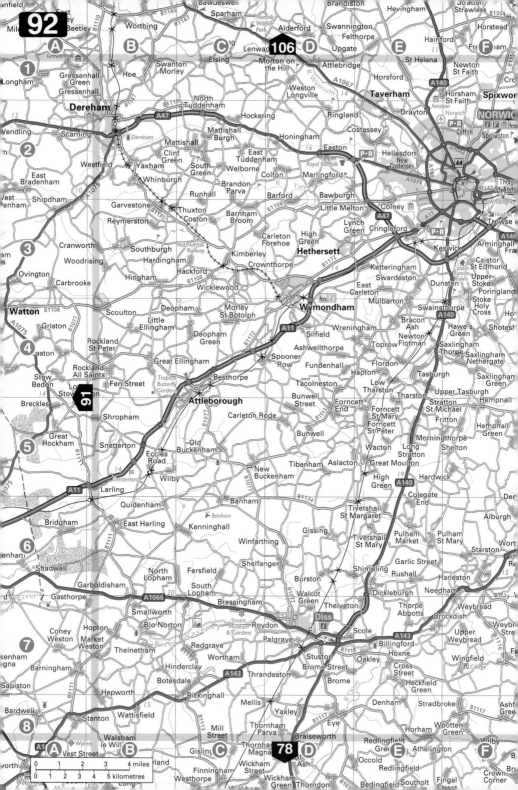

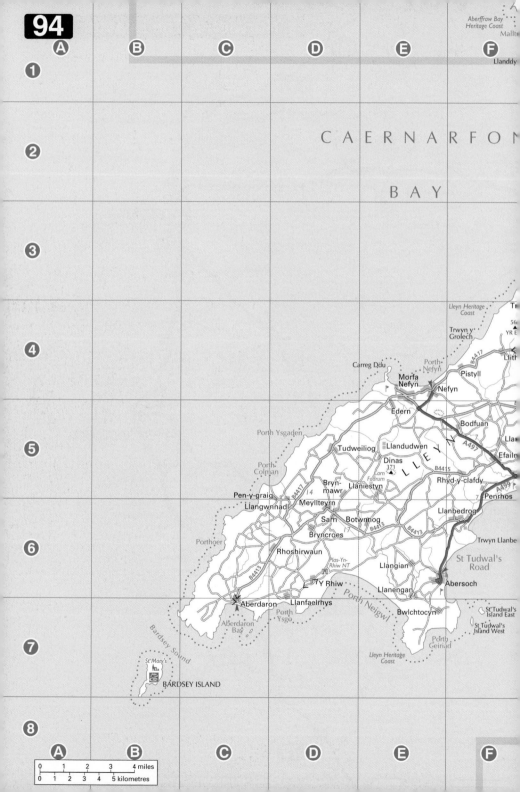

A   B   C   D   E   F

1

Aberffraw Bay
Heritage Coast
Mallt

Llanddy

2   C A E R N A R F O N

B A Y

3

Lleyn Heritage
Coast   T

4   56
YR E

Trwyn y
Grolech

Porth
Nefyn   Llitl

Carreg Ddu   Morfa
Nefyn   Pistyll

Edern   Nefyn

Bodfuan

Porth Ysgaden   Ll
Efailn

5   Tudweiliog   Llandudwen
L L E Y N

*Porth
Colman*   Dinas   371
Carn
Fadrum   B4415   Rhyd-y-clafdy

Bryn-
mawr   Llaniestyn

Pen-y-graig   14   Penrhos

Llangwnnadl   Meyllteyrn   7

Sarn   Botwnnog   Llanbedrog

Bryncroes

Porthoer   Trwyn Llanbe

6   Rhoshirwaun

*Plas-Yn-
Rhiw NT*   Llangian   St Tudwal's
Road

Y Rhiw   Llanengan   Abersoch

Aberdaron   Llanfaelrhys   Bwlchtocyn   St Tudwal's
Island East

Bardsey Sound   *Porth
Ysgo*   *Porth Neigwl*   St Tudwal's
Island West

7   *Aberdaron
Bay*   *Porth
Geiriad*

St Mary's   *Lleyn Heritage
Coast*

BARDSEY ISLAND

8

A   B   C   D   E   F

0   1   2   3   4 miles
0   1   2   3   4   5 kilometres

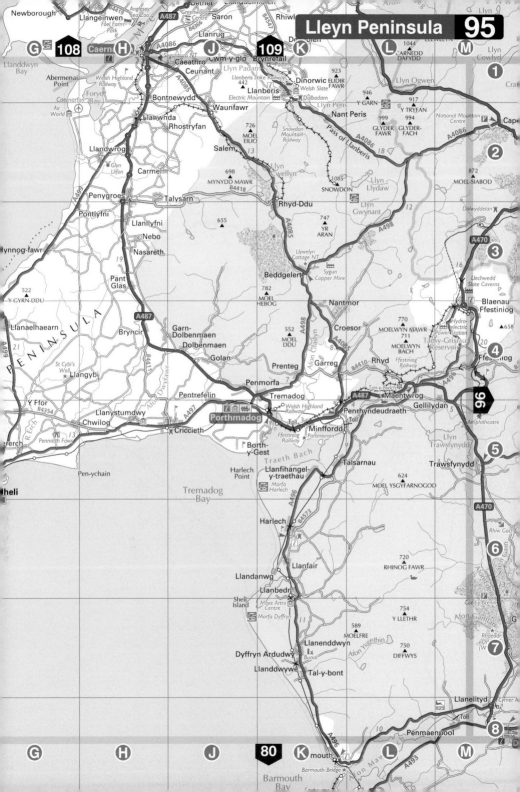

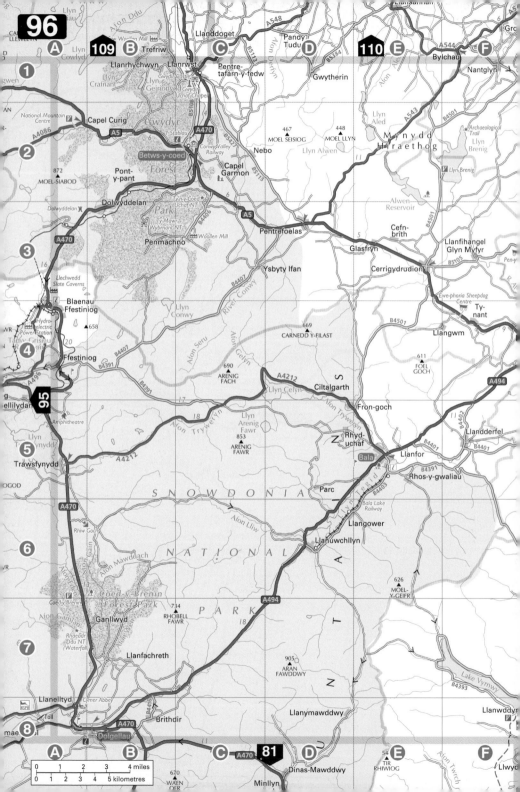

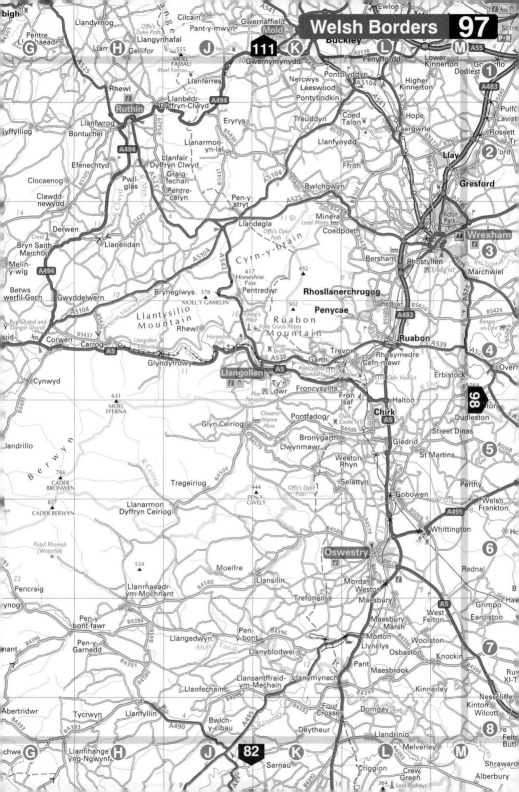

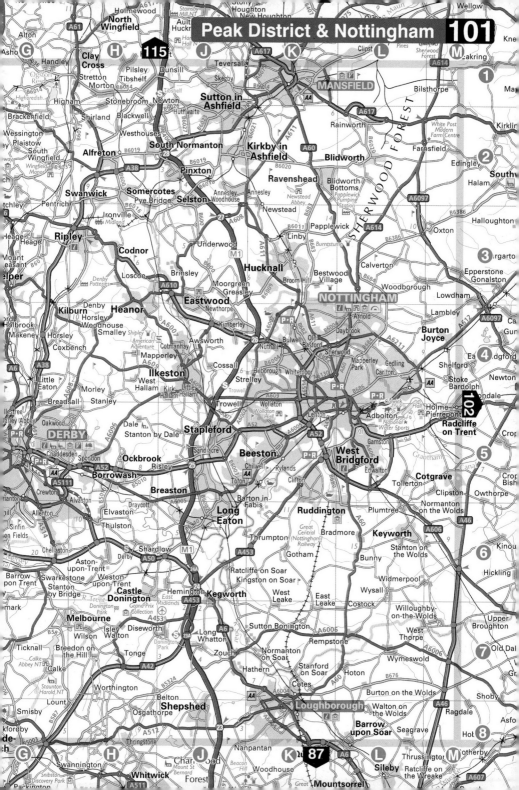

G   H   J   K   L   M

① ② ③ ④ ⑤ ⑥ ⑦ ⑧

ingham
Mundesley
Stow Mill
Paston
Knapton
Bacton
Edingthorpe
Walcott
Edingthorpe Green
Witton
Ridlington
Happisburgh
Whimpwell Green
Meeting House Hill
Happisburgh Common
Hempstead
Honing
Lessingham
Ingham Corner
Sea Palling
Briggate
East Ruston
Ingham
Waxham
Worstead
Stalham
Calthorpe Street
Dilham
Hickling
Smallburgh
Wood Street
Sutton
Hickling Green
Horsey
Tunstead
Neatishead
Catfield
Hickling Broad
Horsey Windpump NT
Irstead
Barton Broad
Potter Heigham
Hoveton
Ludham
Martham
Winterton-on-Sea
Upper Street
Bastwick
Hemsby
Hemsby Hole
Woodbastwick
Horning
er Street
Repps
Hemsby
Ormesby
Scratby
California
Thurne
Clippesby
Burgh St Margaret Ormesby St Michael
St Margaret
Salhouse
Ranworth
Pilson
Broadland Conservation Centre

93

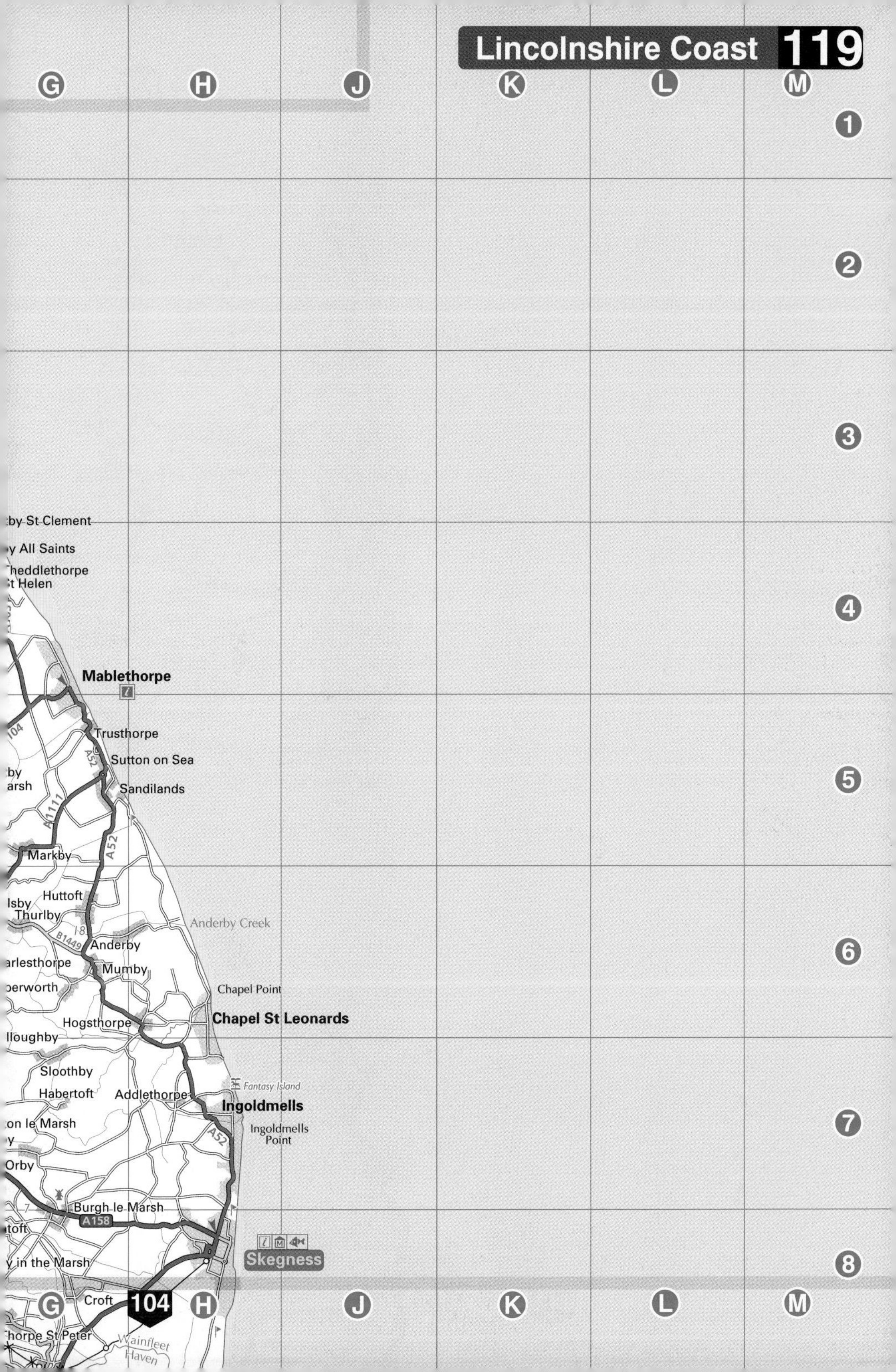

G H J K L M

1

2

3

by St Clement

y All Saints

heddlethorpe
t Helen

4

Mablethorpe

104 Trusthorpe

by Sutton on Sea
arsh Sandilands

5

Markby

Huttoft

Isby
Thurlby Anderby Creek

arlesthorpe Anderby

berworth Mumby

Chapel Point

Hogsthorpe **Chapel St Leonards**

lloughby

Sloothby

Habertoft Addlethorpe

on le Marsh **Ingoldmells**

Orby Ingoldmells
Point

Burgh le Marsh

A158
toft

y in the Marsh **Skegness**

6

7

8

G **104** H J K L M

Croft

horpe St Peter

Wainfleet
Haven

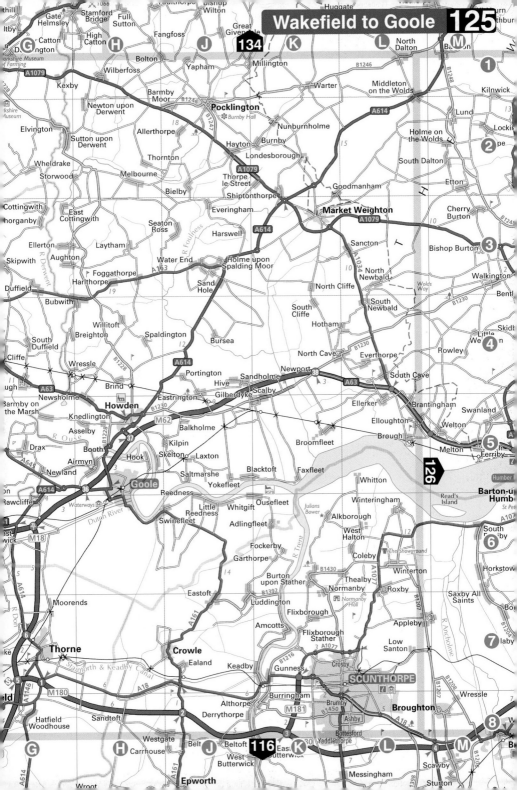

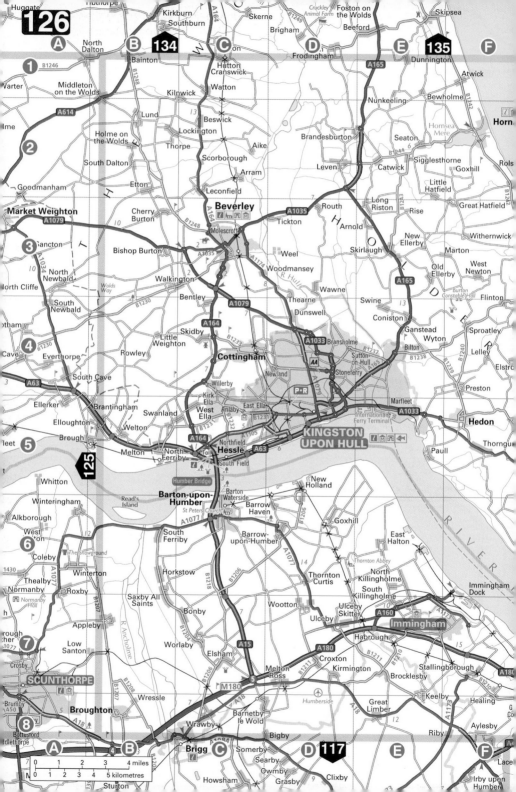

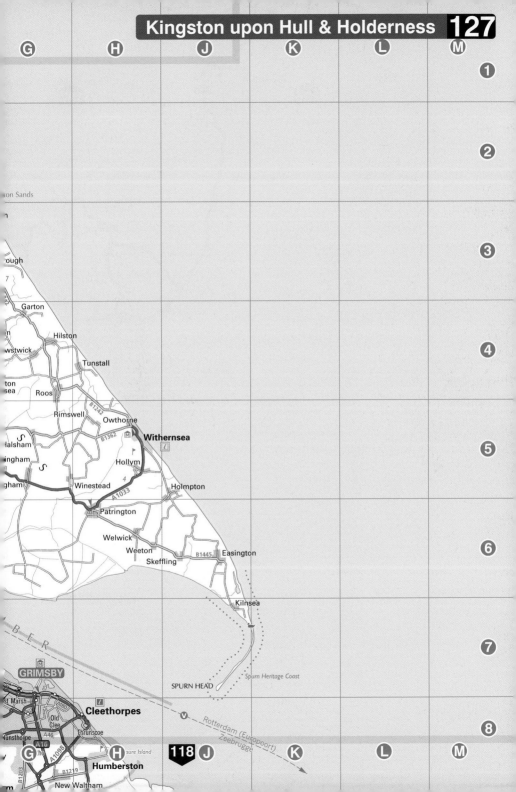

G H J K L M

1
2
3
4
5
6
7
8

on Sands

ough

Garton

Hilston

wstwick

Tunstall

ton

Roos

sea

Rimswell

Owthorne

B1242

B1362

Withernsea

alsham

Hollym

ingham

S

gham

Winestead

A1033

4

Holmpton

Patrington

Welwick

Weeton

B1445

Easington

Skeffling

Kilnsea

Spurn Heritage Coast

BER

GRIMSBY

SPURN HEAD

st Marsh

Cleethorpes

Old Clee

A46

Thrunscoe

V

Rotterdam (Europoort)
Zeebrugge

nsthorpe

A16

A1098

118 J

Humberston

B1219

New Waltham

sure Island

G H J K L M

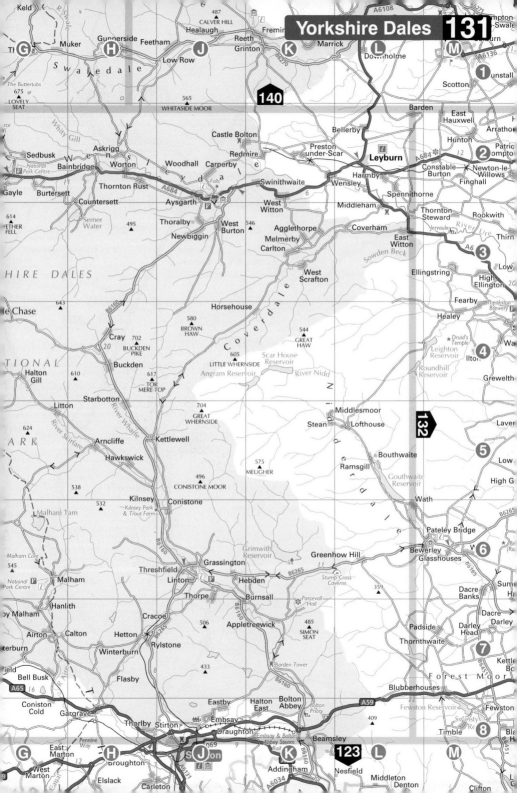

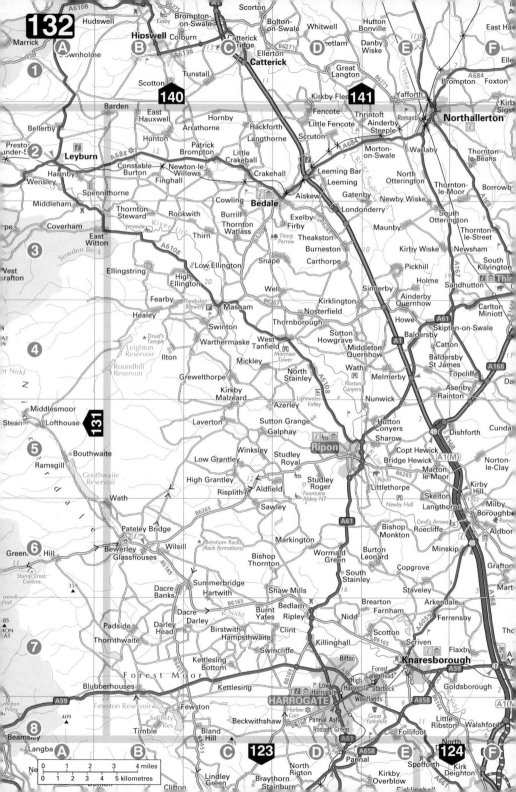

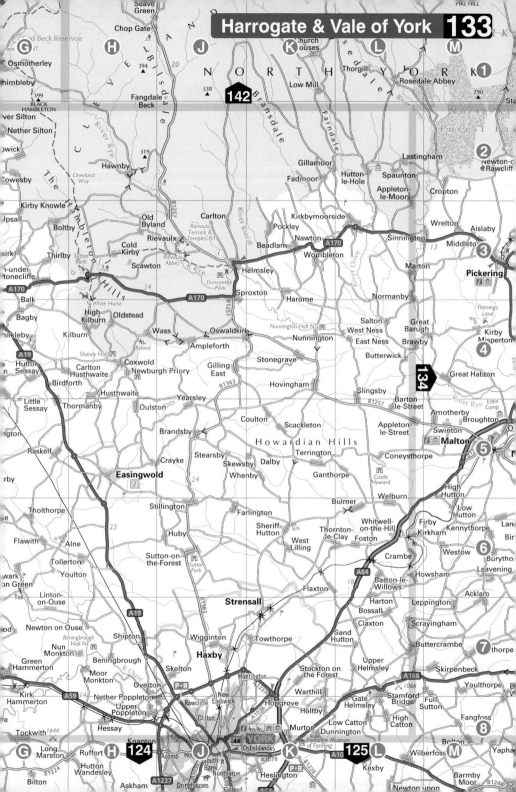

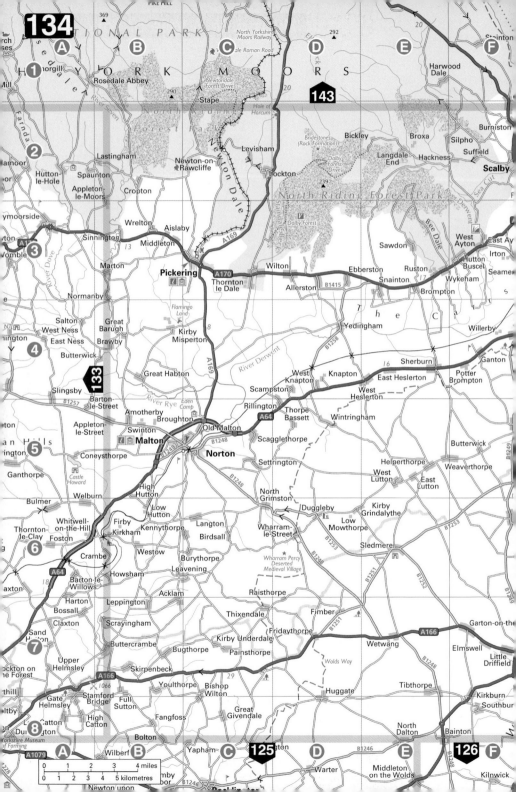

G H J K L M

1
2
3
4
5
6
7
8

ighton
yke

er Point

nd Way

Scarborough
★ Hatherleigh
Deep Sea
Trawler
P·R
Oliver's Mount

A165

field
Osgodby
Cayton
Bay

The
Wyke

B1261

yton
Lebberston
Gristhorpe
A1039
Filey Brigg

R·Hertford
olkton
Muston
A1039
Filey

on
7

Hunmanby

Fordon
Reighton

Speeton

Wold
Newton
Burton
Fleming
B1229
RSPB
Flamborough Head Heritage Coast
Thornwick
Bay

Buckton
Bempton
North Landing
Selwicks
Bay
FLAMBOROUGH
HEAD

Grindale
A165
B1229
B1259

Sewerby
B1255
Flamborough

B1253
★ Bondville
Miniature Village

Rudston
Monolith
Boynton
Bridlington
BRIDLINGTON
BAY

Bessingby
Hilderthorpe

Haisthorpe
Carnaby

Thornholme

Kilham
Burton Agnes
Norman
Manor House
A165

n Parva
Harpham
Fraisthorpe

A614
Lowthorpe

Nafferton
Gransmoor

Great Kelk
Lissett
Barmston

Wansford
Gembling
B1242

Cruckley
Animal Farm
Ulrome

Skerne
B1249
Foston on
the Wolds
Skipsea

Brigham
Beeford

North
Frodingham
H
A165
126
J
Atwick

G H J K L M

Nunkeeling
Bewholme
B1242

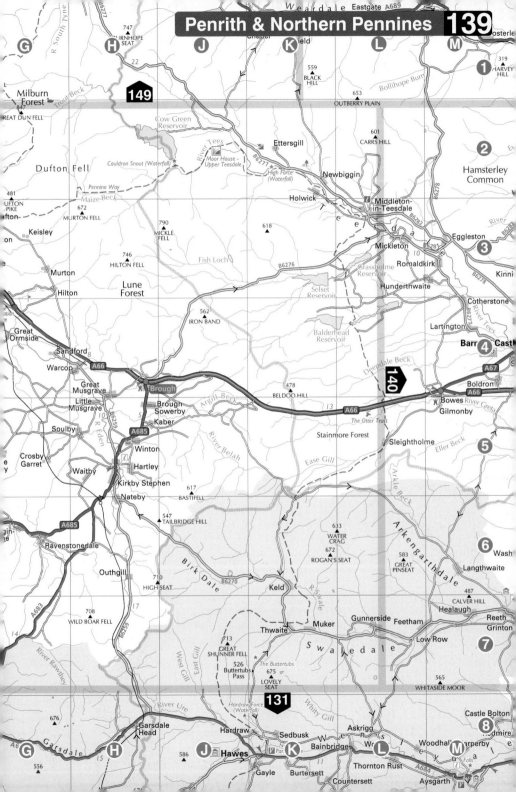

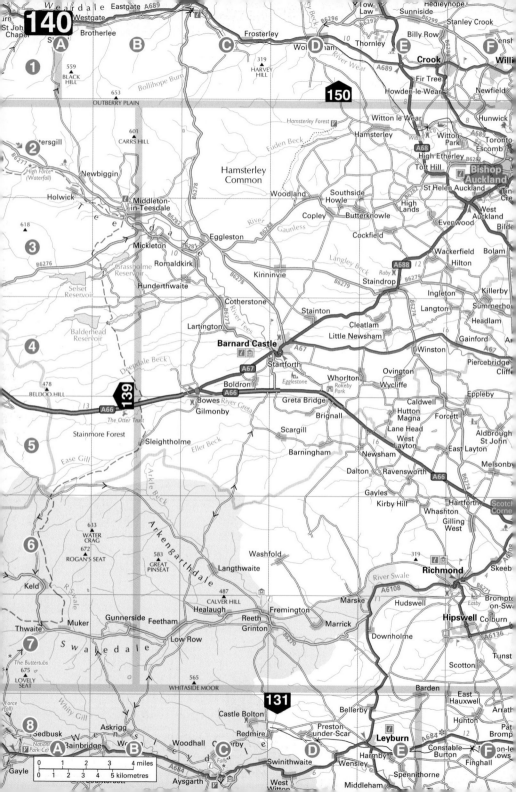

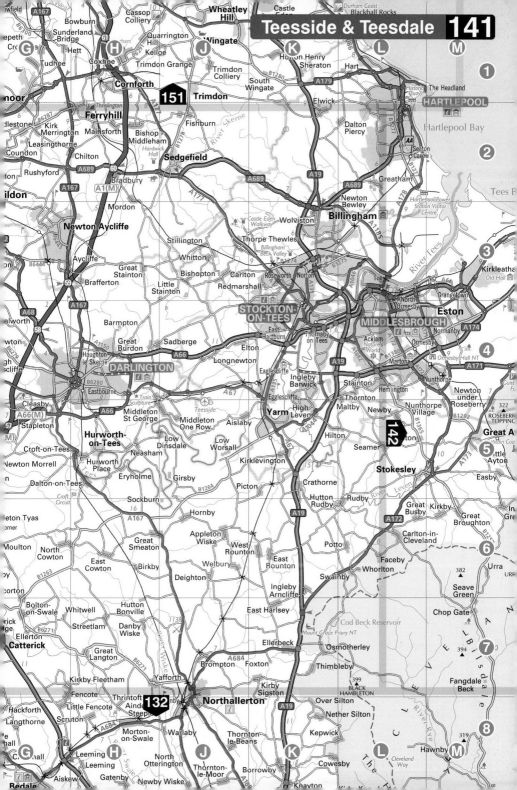

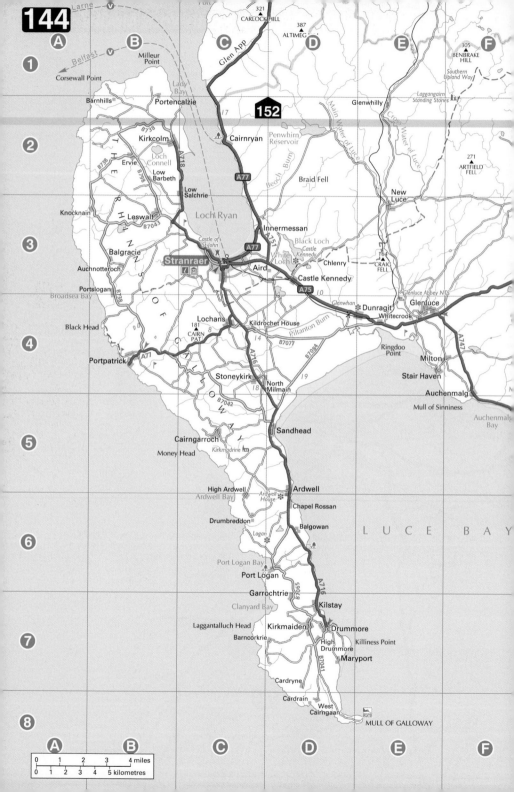

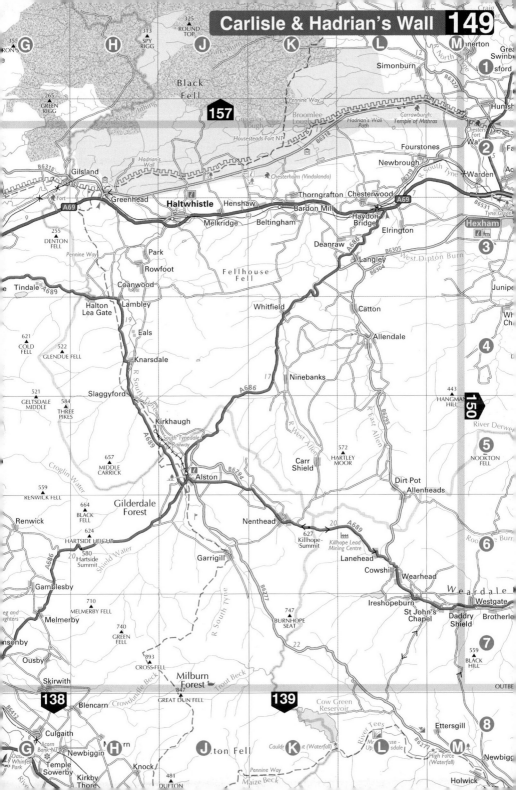

G **H** SPY RIGG **J** ROUND TOP **K** **L** **M**

1

Craig

R North Tyne

Simonburn

B6320

sford

Great Swinbu

nerton

12

Black Fell

265 GREEN RIGG

355 RON'S

157

Greenlee Lough

Broomlee Lough

Pennine Way

Hadrian's Wall Path

Housesteads Fort NT

Carrawburgh: Temple of Mithras

Humsh

Hadrian's Wall

B6318

Chesters Fort

Wa

2

Fa

Fourstones

Newbrough

Chesterholm (Vindolanda)

R South Tyne

Warden

R North Tyne

B6531

Gilsland

Fort

B6318

Greenhead

A69

Haltwhistle

Henshaw

Thorngrafton

Chesterwood

A69

Hexham

Bardon Mill

Haydon Bridge

Elrington

3

255 DENTON FELL

9

Park

Rowfoot

Melkridge

Beltingham

Tyne Green

Tyne

Pennine Way

Deanraw

Langley

West Dipton Burn

B6305

B6204

Tindale

A689

Coanwood

Lambley

Fellhouse Fell

Whitfield

Catton

Allendale

Juniper

4

Halton Lea Gate

19

Eals

Knarsdale

Ninebanks

R East Allen

443 HANGMAN HILL

150

621 COLD FELL

522 GLENDUE FELL

R South Tyne

R West Allen

B6395

River Derwer

521 GELTSDALE MIDDLE

584 THREE PIKES

Slaggyford

Kirkhaugh

South Tynedale Railway

A686

Carr Shield

572 HARTLEY MOOR

5

NOOKTON FELL

Croglin Water

657 MIDDLE CARRICK

A689

Alston

B6294

Dirt Pot

Allenheads

Roo
Burr

6

559 RENWICK FELL

664 BLACK FELL

Gilderdale Forest

Nenthead

20

A689

Renwick

624 HARTSIDE HEIGHT

Killhope Summit

627

Killhope Lead Mining Centre

Lanehead

Cowshill

Wearhead

W e a r d a l e

Westgate

7

Gamblesby

580 Hartside Summit

20

A686

Shield Water

Garrigill

B6277

Ireshopeburn

St John's Chapel

Daddry Shield

Brotherle

710 MELMERBY FELL

Melmerby

eg and ghters

740 GREEN FELL

747 BURNHOPE SEAT

R South Tyne

559 BLACK HILL

OUTBE

nsonby

Ousby

893 CROSS FELL

Milburn Forest

Trout Beck

22

Cow Green Reservoir

Skirwith

138

847 GREAT DUN FELL

139

Ettersgill

8

B6412

Blencarn

Crowdundle Beck

River Tees

High Force (Waterfall)

Newbig

G Acorn Bank NT **H** rn **J** ton Fell **K** t (Waterfall) **L** use **M**

Das
Whinfell Park

Newbiggin

Cauldr

Mi
Up sdale

B6277

Culgaith

Temple Sowerby

Kirkby Thore

Knock

481 DUFTON

Pennine Way

Maize Beck

Holwick

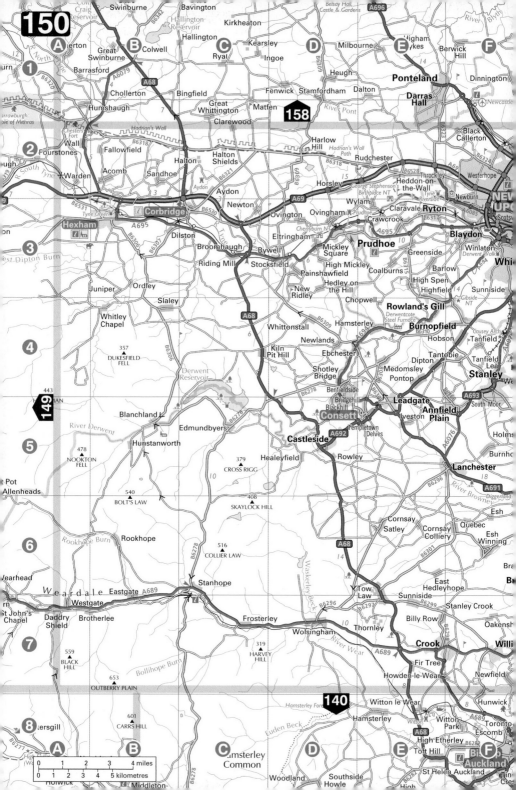

G H J K L M

1

2

3

4

5

6

7

8

New Hartley
Seaton Sluice
mlington
B1326
St Mary's L'se
A192
A193
A190
Seaton
A1149
Heaton Haval
A189
A191
Earsdon
Monkseaton
A1148
Whitley Bay
Dudley
Wide Open
B1322
Killingworth
A1056
Shiremoor
Cullercoats
Tynemouth **159**

Stavanger Haugesund
Bergen
Kristiansand Göteborg

Forest Hall
Rising Sun
AA
North Shields
Longbenton
Willington Quay
Int. Ferry
Tynemouth
South Shields
SOUTH SHIELDS
Westoe
Wallsend
Heaton
Tyne Tunnel
A183
Harton
Jarrow
Marsden
Marsden Bay
Hebburn
Monkton
Souter Lighthouse NT
Felling
Wardley
Cleadon
Souter Point
West Boldon
B1299
Whitburn
GATESHEAD
A184
East Boldon
A184
Whitburn Bay
Low Fell
A1(M)
Wrekenton
A19
Hylton
Southwick
Seaburn
Team Valley
Springwell
Usworth
Castletown
Roker
the North
Wildfowl & Wetlands Trust
South Hylton
Monkwearmouth
Birtley
65
WASHINGTON
Grindon
SUNDERLAND
Pelton
Ouston
64
Washington
High Newport
Hendon
A693
Fatfield
Penshaw
New Silksworth
Tunstall
Grangetown
Shiney Row
Herrington
Silksworth
Ryhope
Chester-le-Street
Burnmoor
Houghton le Spring
Seaham
Great Lumley
Hetton-le-Hole
Parkside
West Rainton
East Rainton
Dalton-le-Dale
Kimblesworth
Murton
A182
AA
Pity Me
Low Moorsley
South Hetton
Hawthorn
Framwellgate Moor
Pittington
Hallgarth
A19
Easington Colliery
Durham
Carrville
Haswell
Easington
Little Thorpe
Broom
Sherburn
Ludworth
Peterlee
Croxdale
Sherburn Hill
Shadforth
Thornley
Horden
Shincliffe
Wheatley Hill
Shotton
Castle Eden
Blackhall Colliery
Bowburn
Cassop Colliery
Blackhall Rocks
Durham Coast
Hett
Quarrington Hill
Wingate
Hesleden
Tudhoe
Kelloe
Hutton Henry
Coxhoe
Trimdon Grange
Sheraton
Hart
Cornforth
Trimdon Colliery
South Wingate
The Headland
Trimdon
Elwick
HARTLEPOOL
Ferryhill
141
Mainsforth
Dalton Piercy
142
Kirk Merrington
Bishop Middleham
Seaton Carew
Chilton
Hardwick Hall
Sedgefield
Greatham
Bradbury
A1(M)
Newton Bewley
Hartlepool Power Station Visitor

G H J K L M

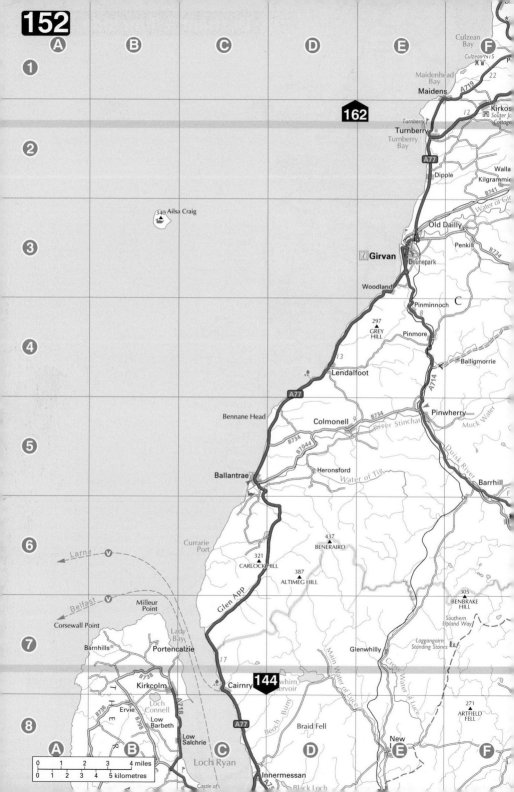

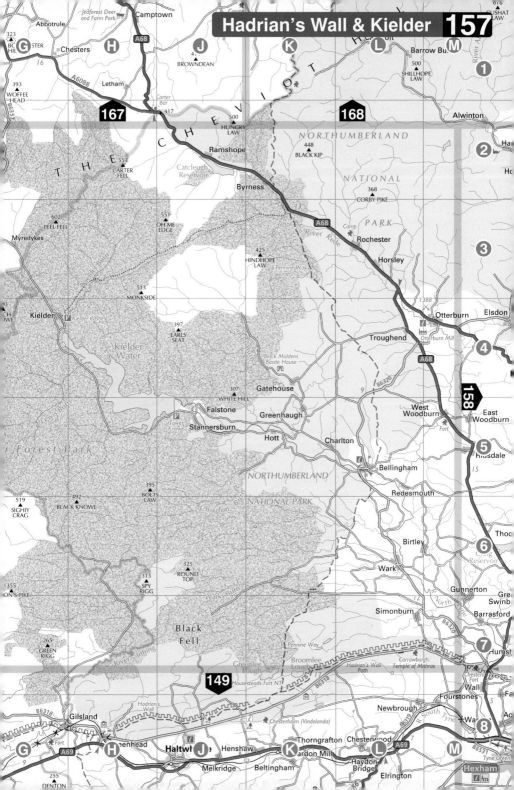

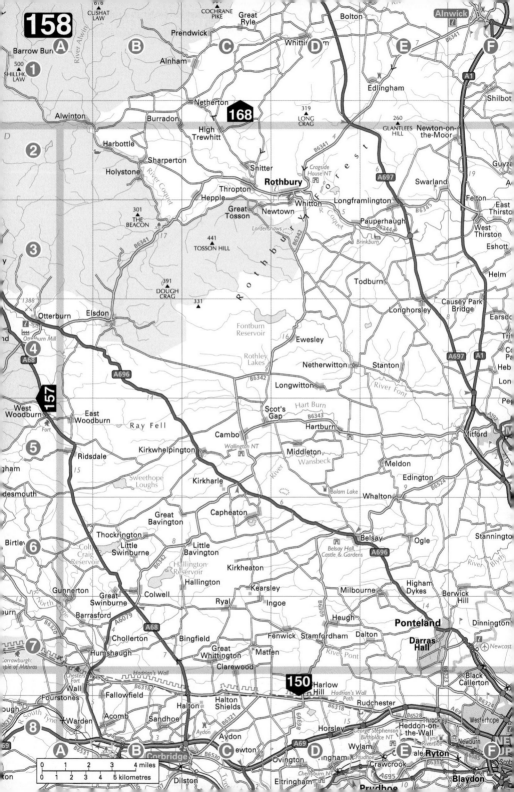

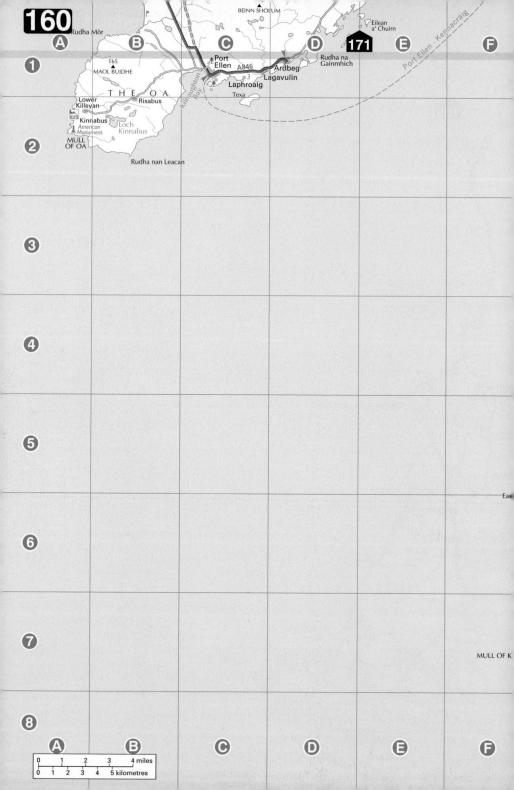

Rudha Mòr

171

Eilean
a' Chuirn

Port Ellen Kennacraig

A
B
C
D
E
F

1

165
MAOL BUIDHE

Port
Ellen

A846

Ardbeg

Rudha na
Gainmhich

T H E   O A

3
Lagavulin

Kilnaughton Bay

Laphroaig

Lower
Killeyan

Risabus

Texa

Kinnabus

American
Monument

Loch
Kinnabus

MULL
OF OA

2

Rudha nan Leacan

BEINN SHOLUM

3

4

5

Ea

6

7

MULL OF K

8

A   B   C   D   E   F

0   1   2   3   4 miles
0 1 2 3 4 5 kilometres

GIGHA

Ardminish
Achamore

Rhunahaorine
Point

CRUACH MHIC
GOUGAIN

Rhunahaorine

264
CNOC A'
SAMHLA

Cour

Catacol

G

V

H

Tayinloan

J

172

K

L

M

North Arra

1

Glen Catacol

Cara

Sound of Gigha

38

Grogport
Barmollack

Pirnmill

Penrioch

Loch
Tanna

Glen Iorsa

Muasdale

A83

354
CRUACH
NAN GABHAR

39

Carradale Water

Whitefarland

715
BEINN
BHARRAIN

2

Glenacardoch
Point

Belloch

Barr Water

Carradale

Imachar

Balliekine

Glenbarr

454
BEINN AN TUIRC

B842

B879

Dippen

Carradale House

Carradale
Point

Machrie
Bay

Torsa Water

ARRA

162

Auchagallon
Stone Circle

Machrie

3

11

MacAlister Clan

319

Cleongart

408
BORD
MOR

Saddell

Carradale
Bay

Tormore

Machrie Moor
Stone Circles

B8

Bellochantuy Bay

Bellochantuy

396
SGREADAN
HILL

Saddell
Bay

Ugadale

KILBRANNAN SOUND

Moss Farm Road
Stone Circle

Balmichael

Balmichael

BEINN

Tangy Loch

Glen Lussa

Torbeg

Shiskine

Kilkenzie

Peninver

Ardnacross
Bay

B842

Drumadoon
Bay

Blackwaterfoot

Kilpatrick

4

A83

Kilmichael

Brown Head

Kilpatrick Dun

Machrihanish
Bay

Campbeltown
P

Campbeltown

Torr a' Chaisteal Fort

Corriecravie

Sliddery

Machrihanish

B842

Campbeltown
Loch

Island Davarr

A841

5

Lagg

16

G

Drumlemble

6

B843

Kilkerran

Kildalloig

352
BEINN GHUILEAN

Achinhoan

385
THE
STATE

446
CNOC
MOY

Dalsmeran

Glen Kerran

Conie Glen

10

Ru Stafnish

6

A LICE

Strone Glen

Glen Breakeyre

B842

Cattadale

Polliwilline Bay

Carskey

Southend

Macharioch

7

Dunaverty

Carskey Bay

Sanda Sound

Sheep Island

Borgadalemore Point

Sanda Island

8

G

H

J

K

L

M

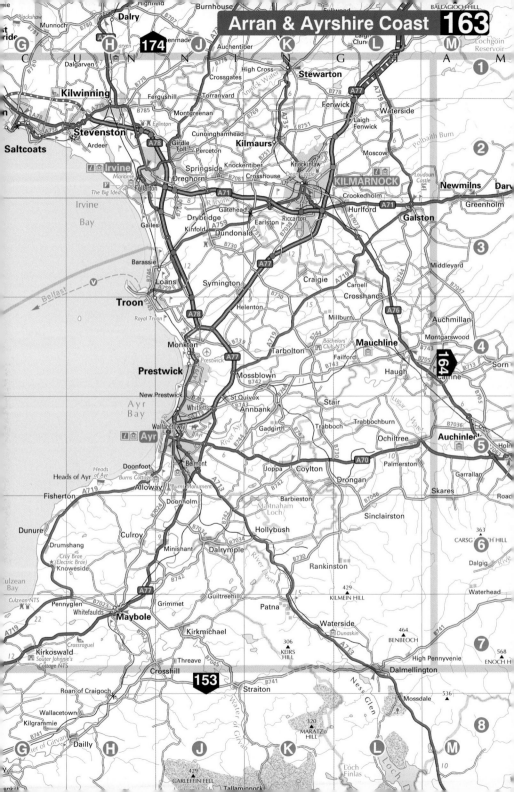

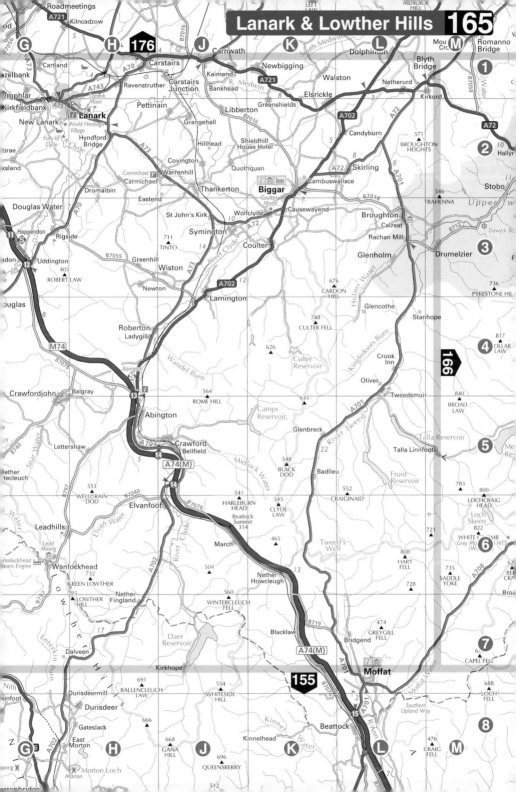

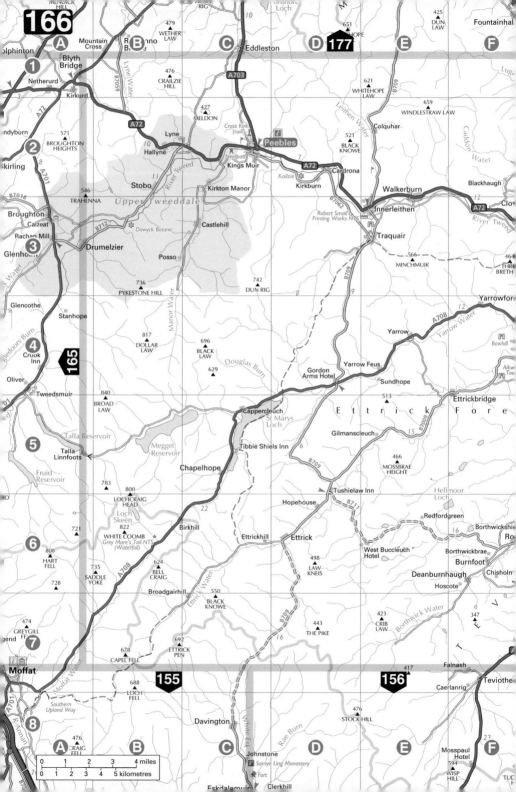

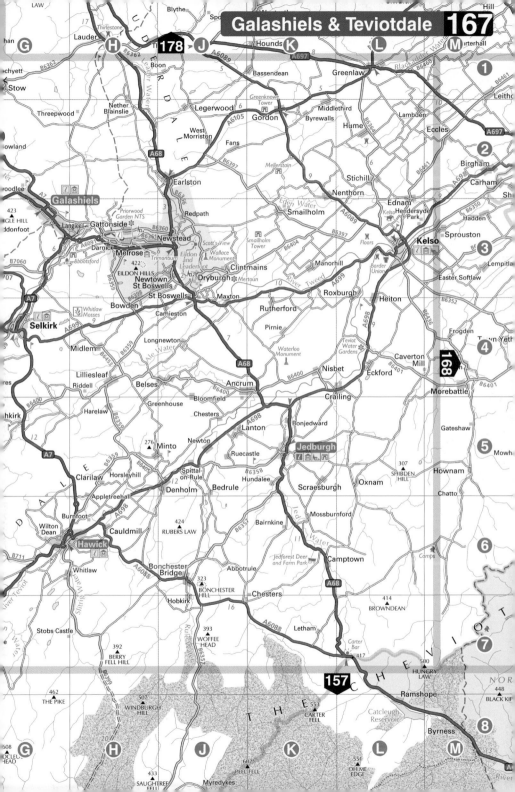

G H J K L M

1
2
3
4
5
6
7
8

CAUSEWAY FLOODED AT HIGH TIDE

HOLY ISLAND
Holy Island
Lindisfarne NT
Lindisfarne Priory
Castle Point
Guile Point

ck

FARNE ISLANDS
Staple Sound
Inner Sound
North Northumberland Heritage Coast

Budle Bay
Bamburgh
B1342
B1340
Belford
B6349

B6348

Lucker
B1341

Warenford
A1
Newstead
Ellingham
Preston
Preston Pele Tower
Brunton
Christon Bank
Embleton
Embleton Bay
Dunstanburgh NT

Seahouses
North Sunderland

Beadnell
Swinhoe
Beadnell Bay
Chathill
Tughall
Newton-by-the-Sea

267
CATERAN HILL
Bewick
Ditchburn
Eglingham
B6346
Beanley
am
tle

North Charlton
South Charlton
Falloden
B6347

Rock
Rennington
B1340
Stamford
Howick Hall
Dunstan
Craster

Howick
Cullernose Point

B6341
B6341
B6346
River Aln
Bolton
Alnwick

Denwick
Longhoughton
Boulmer
Seaton Point

Lesbury
Alnmouth
Alnmouth Bay

Edlingham
A1
A1068
Shilbottle

260
GLANTLEES HILL
Newton-on-the-Moor
Warkworth Castle & Heritage
Warkworth

159
Amble
Coquet Island

A697
Swarland
Guyzance
Togston
Gloster Hill
Hauxley
Radcliffe

Acklington
Felton
East Thirston
South Broomhill
Broomhill

amlington
B63
Pauperhaugh
West Thirston
Red Row
Drudge Bay
Brinkburn

G H J K L M

Dubh

I S

Nave Island
Ardnave
Point
Go

Ton Mhòr
Kilnave
Eilean Mòr
Sanaigmore
Loch
Gruinart
Rudha Lamanais
Loch
Gòrr
Lecht Gruinart
RSPB
Saligo Bay
B8018
B8017
Gruinart
Gleann Mòr
Loch
Gorm
Coul Point
Sunderland
B8018
Machir
Bay
Kilchoman
A847
Bruichladdich
Loch
Indaal
Kilchiaran Bay
Bowmore
R H I N N S
15
M
River
231
Port
Charlotte
BEINN TART A'MHILL
O F
Lossit Bay
Duich R
I S L A Y
Nereabolls
Rudha na
Faing
A847
Portnahaven
Laggan
Port Wemyss
Orsay
Bay
RHINNS
POINT
Rudha Mòr

165
MAOL B
THE
Lower
Ris

0   1   2   3   4 miles
0   1   2   3   4   5 kilometres

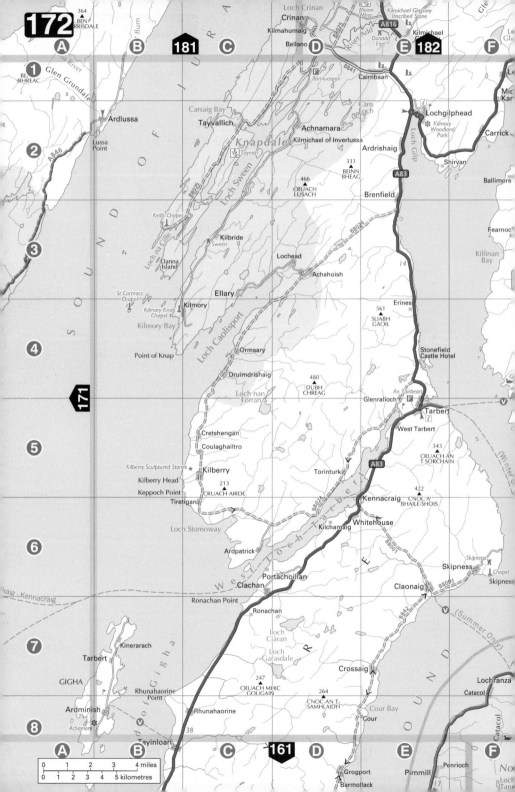

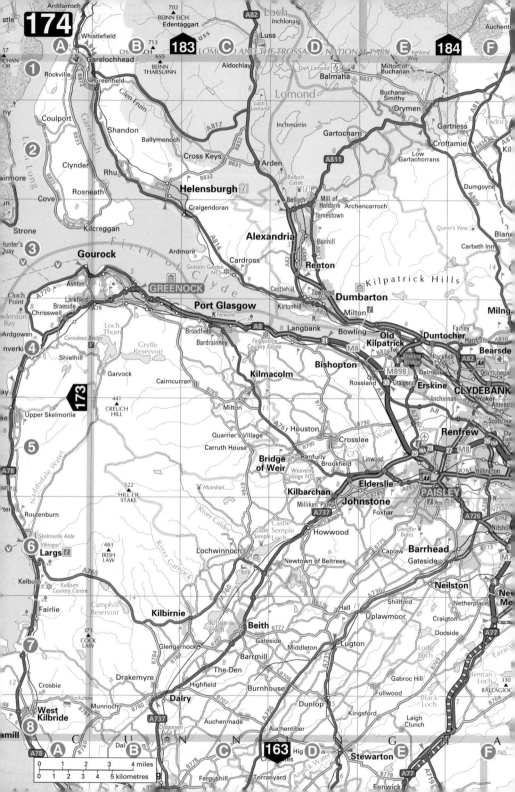

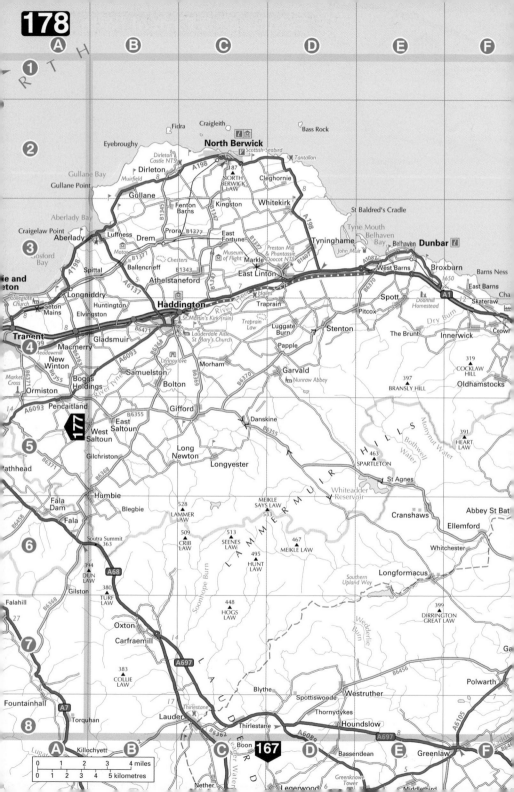

G **H** **J** **K** **L** **M**

1 **2** **3** **4** **5** **6** **7** **8**

Reed Point
Cove
Pease Bay
Siccar Point
Cockburnspath
Fast Castle Head
ST ABB'S HEAD
A1107
196 BROWN RIG
Coldingham Loch
St Abbs
Southern Upland Way
Butterdean
Grantshouse
Coldingham
Coldingham Bay
A1107
22
Eyemouth
Houndwood
B6438
Heugh Head
Cairncross
262 HORSELEY HILL
A1
Reston
Ayton
Burnmouth
B6438
Auchencrow
Marygold
Lintlaw
Lamberton
B6437
B6355
Marshall Meadows Bay
Preston
Chirnside
Cumledge
B6355
Edrom
Foulden
North Northumberland Heritage Coast
Chirnsidebridge
Edington
Whiteadder Water
1333
Broadhaugh
Allanton
Hutton
A6105
Berwick-upon-Tweed
Manderston
Tithe Barn
Duns
Crumstane
A6105
Paxton
Town Ramparts
Barracks
Blackadder
B6460
B6461
Tweedmouth
Whitsome
Hilton
Paxton
Spittal
Nisbet Hill
Sinclair's Hill
Horndean
Horncliffe
Huds Head
Netherhall
A6112
Murton
Scremerston
Ladykirk
Thornton
A1
Swinton
Norham
Cheswick
CAUSEWAY FLOODED AT HIGH TIDE
Leitholm
Simprim
Upsettlington
River Tweed
Ancroft
Haggerston

168

B6461
B6470
A698
B6525

ULVA

Ⓐ Ⓑ Ⓒ Bac Mòr or Dutchmans Cap Ⓓ **189** Ⓔ Ⓕ

Reag Little Colonsay Inch Kenneth

❶ Staffa Inchkenneth Chapel (ruin)

Fingal's Cave *Loch na Keal*
Isle of Mull

❷ 491 ▲
CREACH BHEINN

★ Fossil Tree

❸ IONA Rudha nan Cearc Lo

Abbey Kintra
Baile Mòr
Macleans Cross Fionnphort A849

Aridhglas Loch na Lathaich

St Columba Bunessan Loch Assapol CR
Exhibition
Centre ROSS OF MULL

Soa Island Uisken

❹ Erraid Ardchiavaig Ru
Bra

Rudha
Ardalanish

❺ Torran Rocks

❻

Eilean
Dubh

❼ Kiloran Bay Balnahard Rudh

COLONSAY Kiloran

Kilchattan B8085

Scalasaig

B8085 Machrins B8085

Ⓐ Ⓑ Ⓒ Ⓓ **171** Garvard Ⓔ Ⓕ

❽ Oronsay Rudha
Bàn

0 1 2 3 4 miles
0 1 2 3 4 5 kilometres Dubh Eilean

G   H   **190**   J   K   L   **M**   1

ISLE

OF

MULL

Eorsa

Macquarie Mausoleum

BEINN NAN LUS

BEINN MHEADHC

Craignure

Mull & West Highland Narrow Gauge Railway

Rudha an Ridire

Kilche

BEINN A' CHAIG

B8035

DUN DA GHAOITHE

766

Torosay Castle

Duart Castle

Duart Bay

Duart Point

Duart

1

966
BEN MORE

704
CRUACHAN DEARG

Lochdonhead

Lochdon

Gorten

Loch Don

Grass Point

247
CARN BAN

KERRE

2

Aird of Kinloch

A849

A849

17

Strathcoil

698
BEN CREACH

Loch Spelve

717
BEN BUIE

Croggan

Rudha Seanach

Pennycross

Pennyghael

Loch-Fuaran

Lochbuie

Loch Uisg

337
MAOL BAN

Barrnacarry Bay

3

503
BEINN NA CROISE

Leidle Water

376
BEINN CHREAGACH

Carsaig

Loch Buie

377
DRUIM FADA

Rudha Dubh

F   I   R   T   H

Insh Island

Clachan-Seil

SEIL

Clachan

B844

Malcolm's Point

Ellanbeich

Easdale

Balvicar

4

Easdale

Colonsay–Oban

O   F

Cuan Ferry Village

Cullipool House

Torsay Island

Degnish

182

Garbh Eileach

LUING

Loch Melf

Arduai

5

Eilean Dubh Mòr

GARVELLACHS
Monastery & Beehive Cells

Eileach an Naoimh

LUNGA

Scarba, Lunga

Toberonochy

SHUNA

L   O   R   N   E

Arduaine Garden NTS

Craobh Haven

Craigd

SCARBA

and the Garvellachs

Shuna Sound

Shuna Point

448
CRUACH SCARBA

Ardf

6

Gulf of Corryvreckan

Aird

En N

En

Glengarrisdale Bay

295
CRUACH NA SEILCHEIG

Craignish Point

Island Macaskin

Craignish Point

Aird

Clockav

7

Glendebadel Bay

J   U   R   A

364
BEN GARRISDALE

Lealt Burn

Loch Crinan

Crinan

Kilmahumaig

Bellanoch

8

Corpach Bay

G   H   **171**   466
BEIN BHREAC   J   Glen Grundale   K   L   **172**   M   Barnluasgan

Lussa River

Glen Grundale

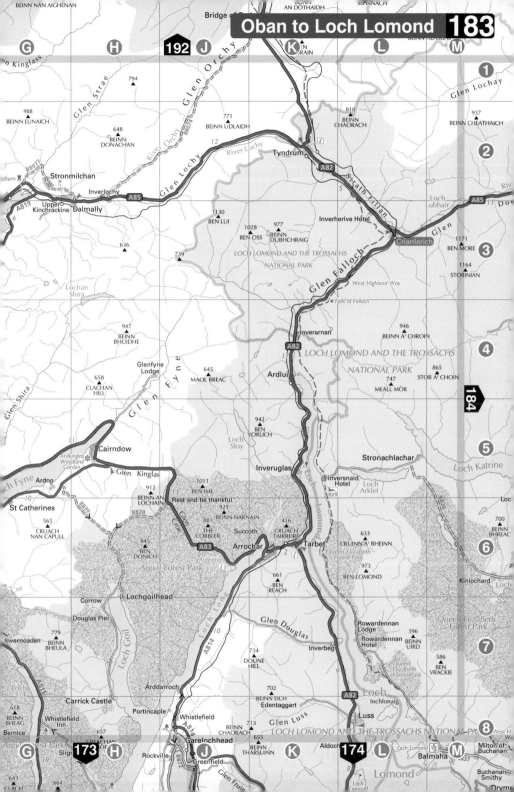

Arna
Grishipoll
Clabhach
Hogh Bay   Ballyhaugh
                  Totronald
Feall   Arileod   Acha
Bay   Uig
                        Friesla
Calgary Point   Crossapol   Bay
              Bay   Rudha
Gunna   Fasachd

Rudha Port   Clachan   Caoles   Rudha Dubh
Bhiosd   Mor   Balephetrish   B8069
              Loch   Bay
Haugh   Bhasapoll   B8069
Bay   Ballevullin   Cornoigmore   Kenovay   Ruaig
                                      Gott
Kilkenneth   Tiree   Bay
           B8066
Middleton   Moss   Heylipoll   B8065   Scarinish
Barrapoll   Crossapoll   TIREE
           Loch a   B8065
           Phuill   B8067   Balemartine
Rinn   Mannel
Thorbhais
           Balephuil   Hynish
           Bay

Hynish Bay

G H **198** J **Eilean nan Each** **MUCK** K L M

1

393

Port Mor

2

Ru Dr

Ockle Point

Sanna Point **Kilmory** **Ockle**
Sanna Bay **Branau** 3
Sanna Bay Portuairk Achnaha 436
Ardnamurchan Point **MEALL NAN CON** ARDNAMU
Achosnich
Loch Mudle

Bagh a Chaisteil and Loch Baghasdail
(Castlebay and Lochboisdale) 342 **Kilchoan**
BEINN NA SEILG Ormsaigmore Mingary 527 4
BEN HIANT
Ardslignish

Eilean Mòr Ardmore Point **190** Auliston Point Oro

Rudha Mòr Rudha Sgor-innis
Bousd Sorisdale Sorne Point Glengorm Castle Tobermory Calve Island 5 Drim

COLL Coll – Oban Quinish Point 292 'S AIRDE BEINN

Eilean Ornsay Caliach Point Dervaig Achnadrish Lodge Sou

Calgary 5 444 6
Calgary Bay 6 SPEINNE MOR
Treshnish Point Ensay 342 Loch Frisa 10
CARN MÒR
ISLE OF MULL
Rudh' a' Chaoil Burg Glen Aros Aros

Fladda Fanmore 390 Glenaros House
CNOC AN DÀ CHINN
Lunga Ballygown Eas Fors (Waterfall) 333 Killiechronan 7
BEINN NAN CARN
TRESHNISH ISLES Gometra 19 Gruline 2
ULVA Oskamull Macquarie Mausoleum
Bac Mòr or Dutchmans Cap Eorsa
Bac Beag Little Colonsay Loch na Keal, 591 8
Isle of Mull BEINN A' Gh

G H **180** J Staf K Inch neth L M
Fingal's Cave Inchkenn apel (ruin) Balnahard

966 704

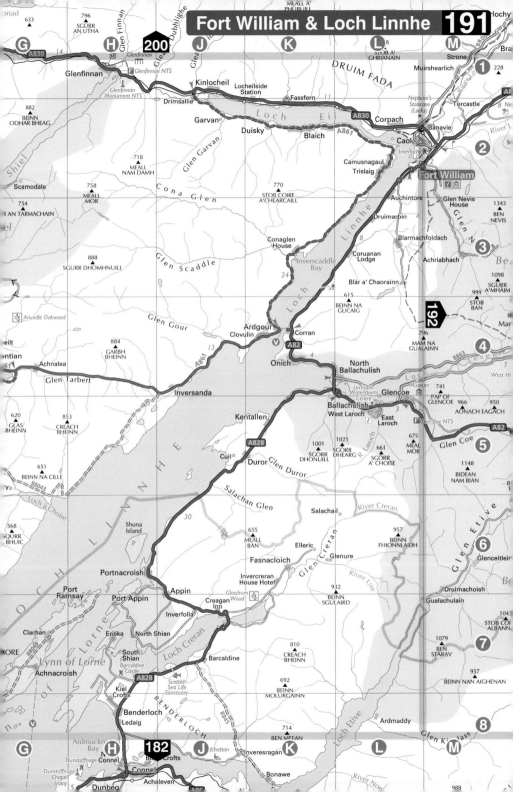

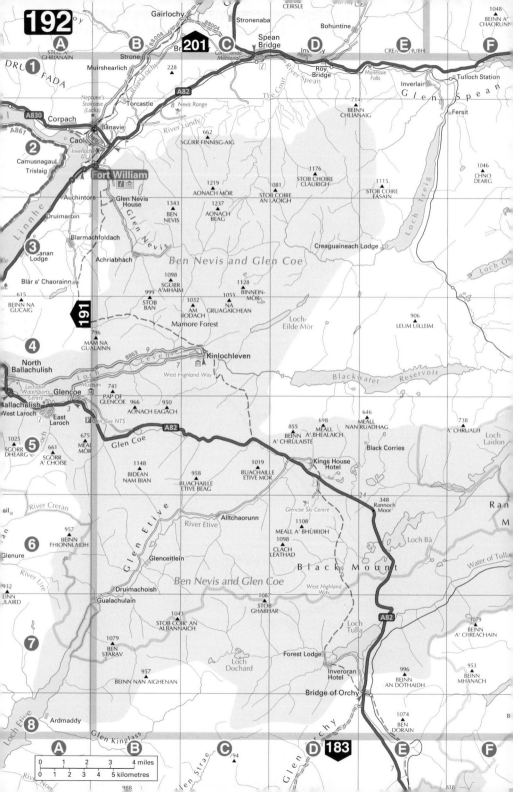

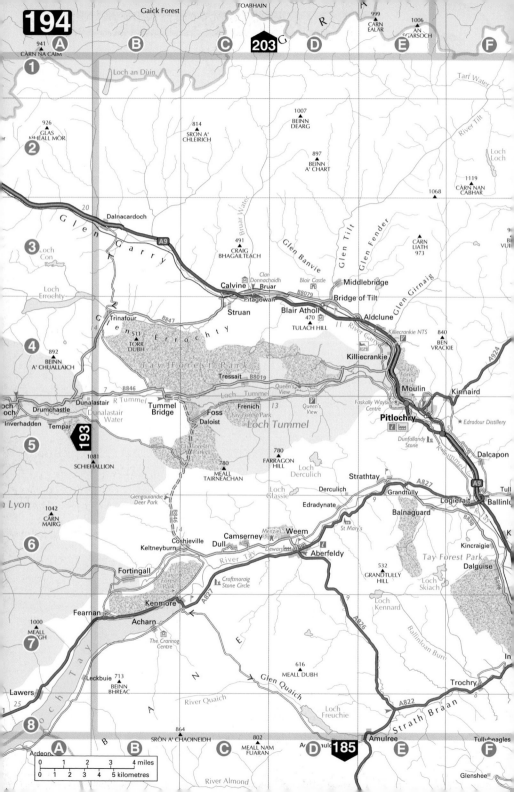

204

832 **EASTERBALLOCH** 1

996 **BROAD CAIRN**

Spittal of LOCHNAGAR

Loch 1045

Glen Ey

919 CARN G

204 H

Glen Clunie Lodge J

K

L

M

89 BE TIRR

2

831 LAIR OF ALDARARIE

Glen Doll

1018 **CARN AN TUIRC**

Glenshee Ski Area

932 670 **THE CAIRNWELL**

34

1067 **GLAS MAOL**

928 **MAYAR**

946 **DRIESH**

Clova

1050 **GLAS TULAICHEAN**

Glen Lochsie

805 **BEN GULABIN**

861 **CARN AIT**

River Isla

649 **CAIRN OF BAMS**

Glen Clo

3

867 **MEALL A' CHOIRE BHUIDHE**

Spittal of Glenshee

807 **MONAMEANOCH**

603 **CAIRN DAUNIE**

Runtaleave

508

Cormuir

Pitcarity

4 Glenca

Gleann Fearnach

792 **MEALL UAINE**

Glen Shee

700 **DUCHRAY HILL**

740 **BADENDUN HILL**

Presnerb

Glen Damff

Glen Finlet

Glen Prosen

B951

Folda

Backwater Reservoir

196

Straloch

2

Clackavoid

744 **MOUNT BLAIR**

Bridge of Brewlands

Glenisla

Balintore

Dykel

Enochdhu

Balvarran

River Ardle

Blacklunans

550 **MEALL MOR**

Bellaty

Dykends

Braes of Coul

B951

5 Kingold

Kirkmichael

B950

Milton

Forest of Alyth

Scruschloch

River Isla

Lintrathen Reservoir

Bridgend of Lintrathen

Kinnor

Westmuir

13

Strath Ardle

561 **CRAIG NAM MIAL**

479

Ballintuim

A924

A93

Netherton

Alyth Burn

Dykehead

425 **BALDUFF HILL**

Bridge of Craigisla

Kirkton of Airlie

Littleton

Craigton of Airlie

Roundyhill

6

Loch Ordie

Loch Benachally

Bridge of Cally

Gauldswell

Bamff

294 **HILL OF ALYTH**

Airlie

M

509 **EUCHARY HILL**

River Ericht

Ruthven

Alyth

New Alyth

B952

Ruthven House

Balkeerie Kirkinch

Eassie and Nevay

Glam

Charlest

Butterstone

A923

Achalader

Lornty

Westfields of Rattray

A926

Leitfie

Balhary

Kinloch

Meigle Longleys

Sculptured Stone Museum

Eassie

7

Dean Water

Concraigie

Clunie

Craigie

Kinloch

Blairgowrie

Rattray

Rosemount

A94

Newbigging

Ardler

Newtyle

Nether Handwick

CRAIGO

Little Dunkeld

Loch of the Lowes

Birnam

Spittalfield

B947

Lethendy

Muirton of Ardblair

A923

A93

A984

Kinloch

Meigle

B954

Caputh

Delvine

Meikleour

Coupar Angus

Kettins

Leys

Bonnyton

Kirkton of Auchterhouse

8

Gellyburn

Kinclaven

Meikleour & Beech Hedge

Keithick

Woodside

Campmuir

Lu

Auchterhouse

Muirhead

Birkhill

Meikle Obney

Murthly

Muir of Thorn

A984

Cargill

Balholmie

Burrelton

Strelitz

Sidlaw Hills

Fowlis

Dronley

M

G ikfoot

Airntully

H owhill

J

186

K

L

A923

Waterloo

Farkhill

Macbeth Experience

Redstone

Wolfhill

Saucher

A9

G H **206** J K L M

① ② ③ ④ ⑤ ⑥ ⑦ ⑧

LEACHIE HILL
Tannachie
Goosecruives
y Mill
Drumlithie
Temple of Fiddes
Glenbervie
Mondynes
GOYLE HILL 465
Bervie Water
Crawton
Trelong Bay
Catterline
Kinneff
Todhead Point
454 Cairn O'Mount
FINELLA HILL 414
Auchenblae
B966
Fordoun
Pittarrow
Redmyre
B967
Arbuthnott
Inverbervie
A92
Bervie Bay
Gourdon
Mains of Haulkerton
Laurencekirk
B9120
Redford
Benholm
Sauchieburn
thermuir
ogmuir
B974
Dykelands
Johnshaven
cairn
B912O
Marykirk
North Esk
A90
Hospital
Logie Pert
Graigo
Bush
Milton Ness
Lochside
Logie
Morphie
St Cyrus
Hillside
A92
Dun
House of Dun NTS
9 A935
onian
ay
Montrose
Montrose Basin
Barnhead
Maryton
Scurdie Ness
Ferryden
Craig
A934
Usan
Westerton
Boddin Point
Braehead
Lunan
Lunan Bay
Inverkeilor
Red Head
ater
13
hapelton
Cauldcots
A92
Marywell
geans
Auchmithie
Carlingheugh Bay
The Deil's Head
Arbroath

Tarsket Bay

Talisker

Glen Eynort

Gr

447
BEINN
BHREAC

Loch Eynort

434
AN CRUACHIN
Glenbrittle House

Bualintur

Loch Brittle

Rudh' an Dùnain

C U

CANNA

210
CÀRN A' GHAILL

A'Chill

Garrisdale Point

Canna
Harbour

Sanday

Rudha
Shamhnan Insir

Sound of Canna

302
MULLACH
MÒR

A Bhrideanach

570
ORVAL

Kinl

Oigh-sgeir

RÙM

810
ASKIVAL

763
SGÙRR NAN
GILLEAN

The Small Isles

Rudha nam
Meirleach

Soun

Rudha

Eilean
nan Each

M

0 1 2 3 4 miles
0 1 2 3 4 5 kilometres

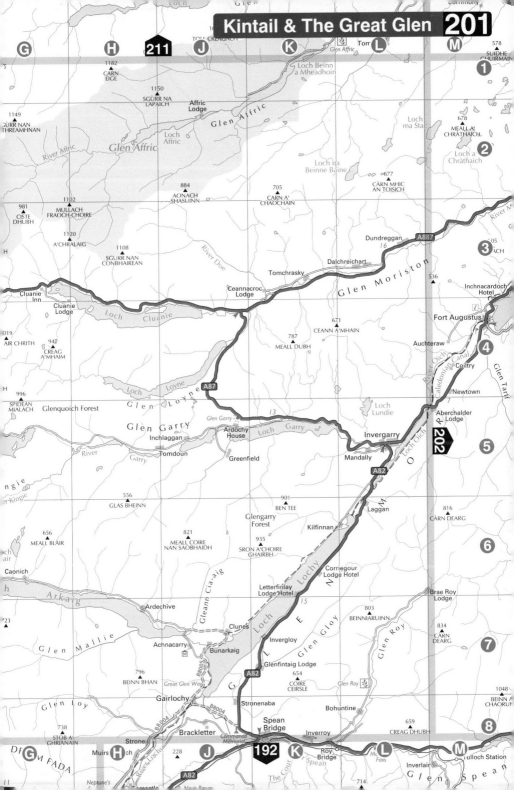

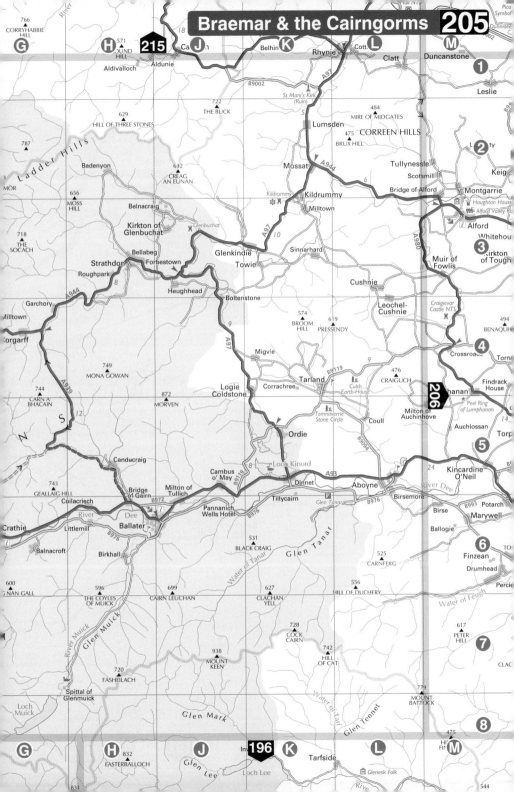

G

CORRYHABBIE HILL 766

H OUND HILL 571

215

Ca J

Belhin

K

Rhynie

Cott L

Clatt

M Duncanstone

1

Aldivalloch

Aldunie

B9002

A97

Leslie

B9002

St Mary's Kirk (Ruin)

5

Lumsden

MIRE OF MIDGATES 484

THE BUCK 722

HILL OF THREE STONES 629

787

BRUX HILL 475

CORREEN HILLS

L ty

2

Ladder Hills

Badenyon 596

CREAG AN EUNAN 632

Mossat

A944

Tullynessle

Scotsmill

Bridge of Alford

6

Keig

Montgarrie

Haughton House

Alford Valley R

MOSS HILL 656

Belnacraig

Kildrummy

Kildrummy

Milltown

Alford

3

MÒR

THE SOCACH 718

Kirkton of Glenbuchat

Glenbuchat

Glenkindie

Towie

Sinnarhard

Whitehou

Kirkton of Tough

Bellabeg

Forbestown

Cushnie

Muir of Fowlis

Strathdon

Roughpark

Heughhead

Boltenstone

Leochel-Cushnie

Craigievar Castle NTS

BENAQUH 494

Garchory

A944

8

574 BROOM HILL

619 PRESSENDY

Crossroads

Torna

4

Milltown

orgarff

A939

9

A97

Migvie

9

476 CRAIGUCH

hanan

Findrack House

744 CARN 'A' BHACAIN

749 MONA GOWAN

Logie Coldstone

Corrachree

Tarland

B9119

Culsh Earth-House

206

Peel Ring of Lumphanan

S 12

872 MORVEN

Tomnaverie Stone Circle

Coull

Milton of Auchinhove

Auchlossan

Torp

N S

Candacraig

B9094

Ordie

5

743 GEALLAIG HILL

Cambus o' May

B9119

Loch Kinord

A93

24

Kincardine O'Neil

B

Bridge of Gairn

Milton of Tullich

Dinnet

Aboyne

River Dee

Birsemore

B993

Potarch

Coilacriech

B972

River

Dee

Ballater

Pannanich Wells Hotel

Tillycairn

B976

Glen Tanar

B976

Birse

Ballogie

Marywell

Crathie

Littlemill

B976

Balnacroft

Birkhall

BLACK CRAIG 531

Water of Tanar

Glen Tanar

CARNFERG 525

6

Finzean

Drumhead

Percie

600 NAN GALL

596 THE COYLES OF MUICK

699 CAIRN LEUCHAN

627 CLACHAN YELL

HILL OF DUCHERY 556

Water of Feugh

Glen Muick

River Muick

728 COCK CAIRN

617 PETER HILL

7

720 FASHEILACH

938 MOUNT KEEN

742 HILL OF CAT

CLAC

Spittal of Glenmuick

779 MOUNT BATTOCK

475

8

Loch Muick

Glen Mark

Glen Tennet

H

Water of Tarf

HI FIN M

831

G

H EASTERBALLOCH 832

J Glen Lee

In **196**

K Tarfside

L

Loch Lee

Glenesk Folk

Rive

544

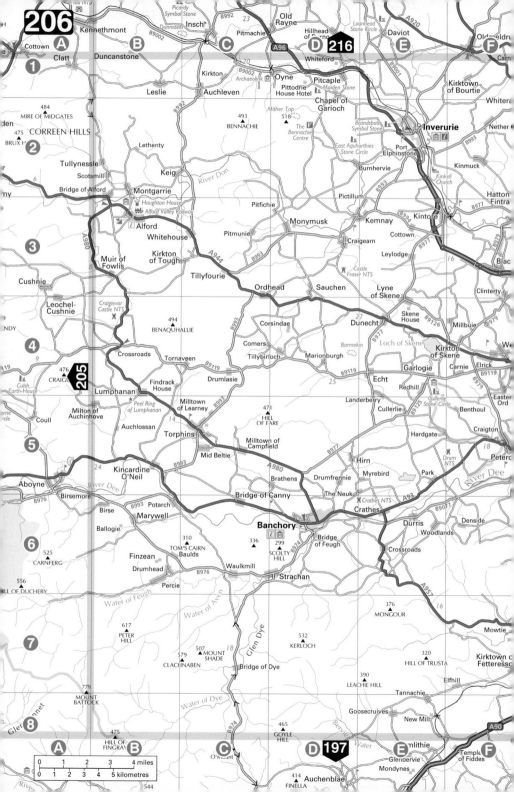

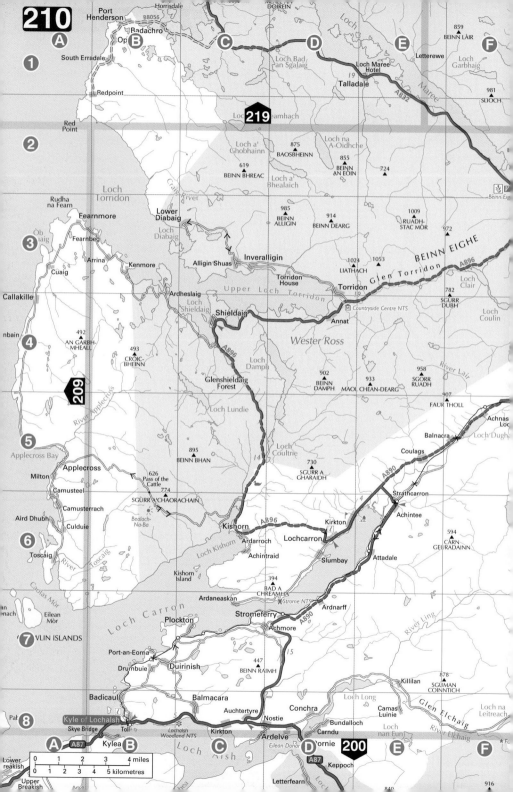

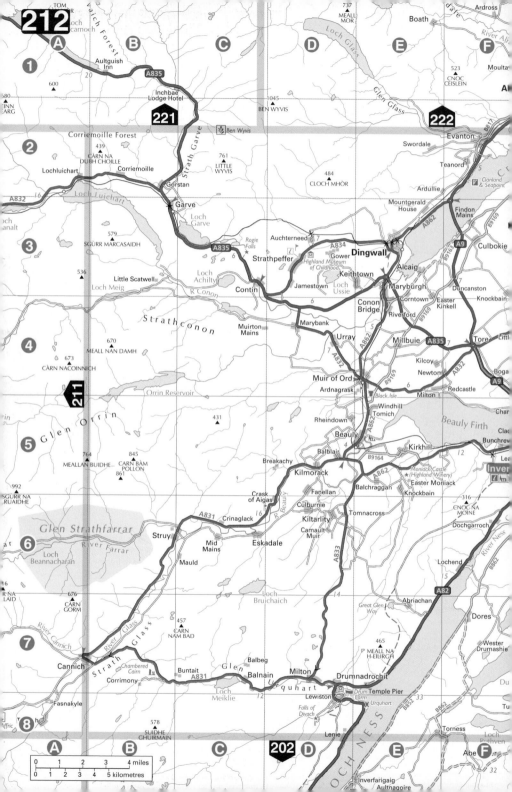

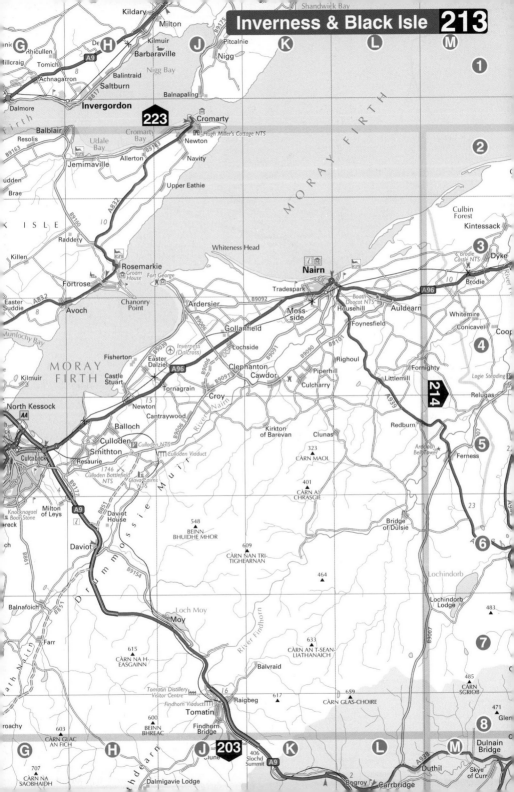

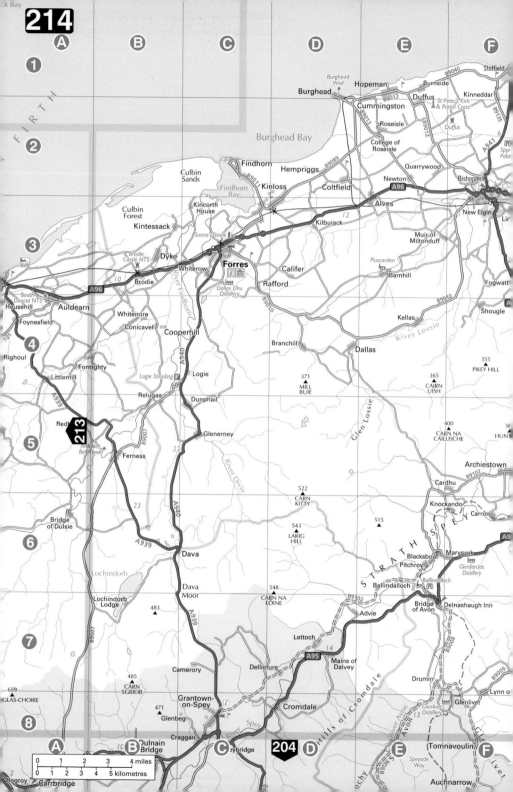

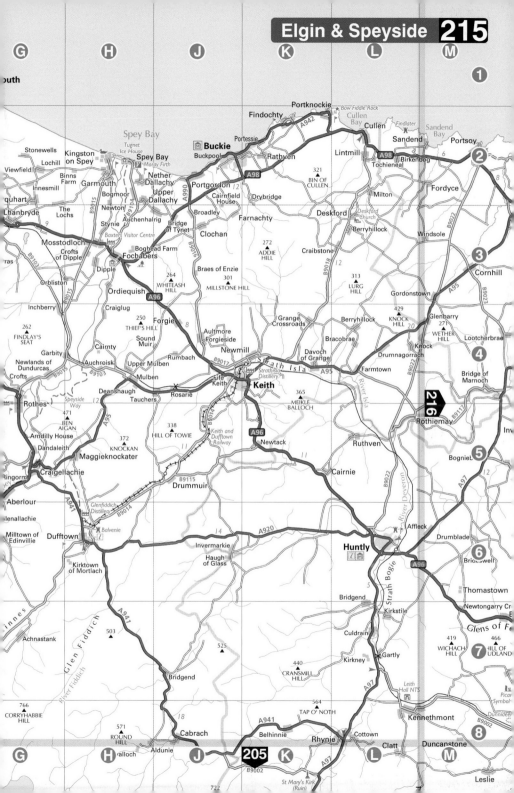

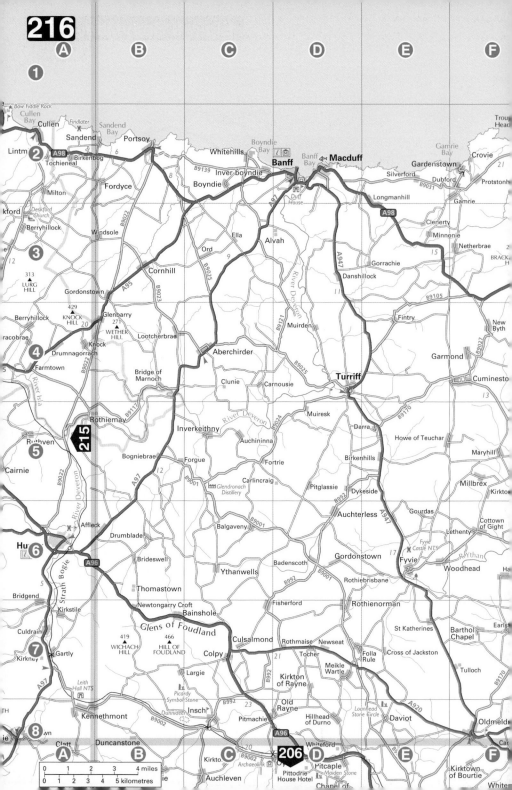

G   H   J   K   L   M

1
2
3
4
5
6
7
8

Rosehearty
Pittulie
Peathill
Craigiefield
Percyhorner
Aberdour
Bay
Coburby
B9031
Boyndlie
Mid Ardlaw
10
Lighthouse
Sandhaven
Kinnaird
Head
Kirktown
Fraserburgh
Fraserburgh
Bay
Maggie's
Hoosie
Cairnbulg
Inverallochy
Whitelinks Bay
St Combs
B9033
A90
Memsie
A98
Memsie
Cairn
Rathen
Crofts
of Savoch
Newburgh
Lonmay
A981
12
Loch of
Strathbeg
Rattray Head
B9093
sligo
234
WAUGHTON
HILL
Strichen
5
A952
12
Crimond
Blackhill
18
nykelly
New
Leeds
B9093
Leys
Denhead
Backfolds
Kirktown
St Fergus
A950
A981
Fetterangus
4
Deer
Abbey
Dunshillock
Rora
River Ugie
A90
Maud
B9106
Aden
Mintlaw
Longside
Inverugie
Buchanhaven
Peterhead
Deer
B9029
B9029
Old
Deer
Inverquhomery
A950
9
A948
Blackhill of
Clackriach
Stuartfield
Drymuir
Bulwark
Millbreck
Nether
Kinmundy
Hillhead
of Cocklaw
Peterhead
Bay
Burnhaven
Knaven
Nethermuir
Little
Dens
Stirling
Buchan
Ness
Boddam
B9030
Kinnadie
Clola
Blackhill
Lendrum
Terrace
Auchnagatt
12
Inkhorn
Kinknockie
Blackhill
Longhaven
A948
Coldwells
A952
A90
Auchiries
Bullers
of Buchan
North Haven
Arthrath
Muirtack
14
Hatton
Slains
Cruden Bay
B9005
Ythanbank
Birness
Bogbrae
Chapel
Hill
Bay of
Cruden
Auchedly
Whinnyfold
A975
The Skares
Altar Tomb of
William Forbes
Kinharrachie
Artrochie
Ythsie
Esslemont
Ellon
P·R
Kirkton of
Logie Buchan
Kirktown of Slains
Collieston
A920
10
Pitmedden
Logierieve
32
Forvie
ddon NTS
Housieside
B9000
G   H   J   K   L   M

207

Udny Station
A90
Newburgh
Pettymuk
Foveran

G   H   J   K   L   M

1

Polbain

Leornabhagh (Stornoway)

Tanera
Beg
Tanera
Mòr
Badentarbat
Bay
Horse
Island

Glas-leac Beag

2

Eilean Dubh
Leac

Priest
Island
Cailleach Head
Scoraig

3

Rudha Beag
Stattic Point
Badluachrach
A832
Badcau

GRUINARD
ISLAND

Greenstone
Point
Mellon
Udrigle
Laide
Gruinard
Bay
Gruinard

4

Foura
Cove
Mellon
Charles
Ormiscaig
Aultbea
Gruinard River
347
CREAG-
MHEAL BEAG

220

Rudha Reidh

296
AN
CUAIDH
ISLE
OF EWE
Loch
Fada
681
BEINN A'
CHAISGEIN BEAG

5

Melvaig
Aultgrishin
Loch Ewe
Inverasdale
Little Gruinard River
Gruinard River
Loch
Se

293
CNOC
BREAC
Naast
250
MEALL NA MEINE
Wester Ross
BEIN

North Erradale
B8021
Inverewe
Garden NTS
13
Fionn
Loch

6

Big Sand
Poolewe
Londubh
791
BEINN
AIRIDH CHARR
Dubh
Loch

Strath
A832
Smithstown
Auchtercairn
Heritage
Museum
Longa
Island
Loch
Gairloch
Lonemore
Gairloch
421
MEALL AN
DOIREIN
859
BEINN LÀIR

7

Port
Henderson
Eilean
Horrisdale
Charlestown
Letterewe
Loch
Garbhaig
B8056
Badachro
Opinan
Loch Bad
an Sgalaig
Loch Maree
Hotel
981
SLIOCH
Loch
Maree

South Erradale
Talladale
19
A832
Maree

Redpoint
Loch Ghaineamhach

Red
Point
Loch
Ghobhainn
210
875
BAOSBHEINN
Loch na
A-Oidhche
855
BEINN
AN EOIN
724

8
Beinn Eighe

Loch
Torridon
Rudha
na Fearn
Fearnn
Lower
Diabaig
619
BEINN BHREAC
Loch a'
Bhealaich
B.
ALLIGIN
914
BEINN DEARG
1009
RUADH-
STAC MÒR
972

Òb
Chuaig
Fearnbeg
Loch
Diabaig
Craig River
N EIGHE

G   H   J   K   L   M

A · B · C · D · E · F

1
2
3
4
5
6
7
8

Isle Ristol
Polbain
STAC POLLAIDH
Glas-leac Mòr
SUMMER ISLES
Achiltibuie
769
CUL BEAG

Tanera
Beg
Badentarbat
Bay
uglass
Loch
urgainn

Steòrnabhagh (Stornoway)
Tanera
Mòr
Horse
Island
Horse
Sound
Achduart
COIGACH
652
BEN MORE
COIGACH
18

Glas-leac Beag
Eilean Dubh
Culn
224
Strathcanaird

Priest
Island
V
Strath Kanaird

Greenstone
Point
Cailleach Head
Leac Dhonn
Isle
Martin
Ardmair
A835

Rudha Beag
Scoraig
Annat
Bay
Morefield

Mellon
Udrigle
Stattic Point
Rhireavach
635
BEINN GHOBHLACH
Ullapool
Loc
Ach

GRUINARD
ISLAND
Badluachrach
Little Loch Broom
A835
BE
EILID

Gruinard
Bay
Badcaul
Badrallach

Mellon
Charles
Ormiscaig
A832
Badcaul
Ardessie
Camusnagaul
Ardindrean
Letters

Aultbea
Gruinard
764
SAIL
MHOR
32
Dundonnell

ISL
OF EWE
4
Loch
Fada
347
CREAG
MHEAL BEAG
Gruinard River
Lochan
Gaineamhaich
507
CARN
BHIORAIN
Inverb

Loch Ewe
Inverasdale
219
681
BEINN A'
CHAISGEIN BEAG
Loch na
Sealga
1062
AN TEALLACH
Au
BRE

Inverewe
Garden NTS
13
250
MEALL NA MEINE
906
BEINN DEARG MHOR

5
Poolewe
Londubh
Wester Ross
601
MEALL AN
T-SITHE
999
A' CHAILLEACH

32
Dubh
Loch
Loch a'
Bhraoin

cairn
421
MEALL AN
DOIREIN
791
BEINN
AIRIDH CHARR
974
SGURRBAN
1019
MULLACH COIRE
MHIC FHEARCHAIR

lestown
6
Loch
859
BEINN LAIR
Lochan
Fada

Loch-Bad-
an Sgalaig
19
Loch Maree
Hotel
Letterewe
Loch
Garbhaig
Cabvie
Lodge

Talladale
A832
981
SLIOCH
711
BEINN NAN RAMH

7
Loch Chuineamhach
Maree
Kinlochewe
Forest

Loch a'
Ghobhainn
875
BAOSBHEINN
Loch na
A-Oidhche
210
680
BEINN A' MHUINIDH
Kinlochewe

619
BEINN BHREAC
Loch a'
Bhealaich
855
BEINN
AN EOIN
724
933
FIONN
BHEIN

8
Beinn Eighe
Kinlochewe

A · B · C · D · E · F

0   1   2   3   4 miles
0 1 2 3 4 5 kilometres

914
1009
RUADH-
STAC MOR
972
Glen Doch
A832
10
N EIGHE

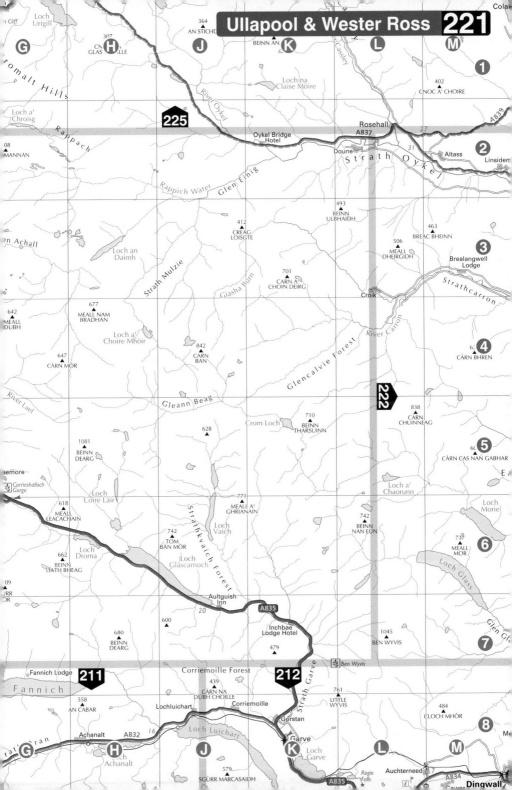

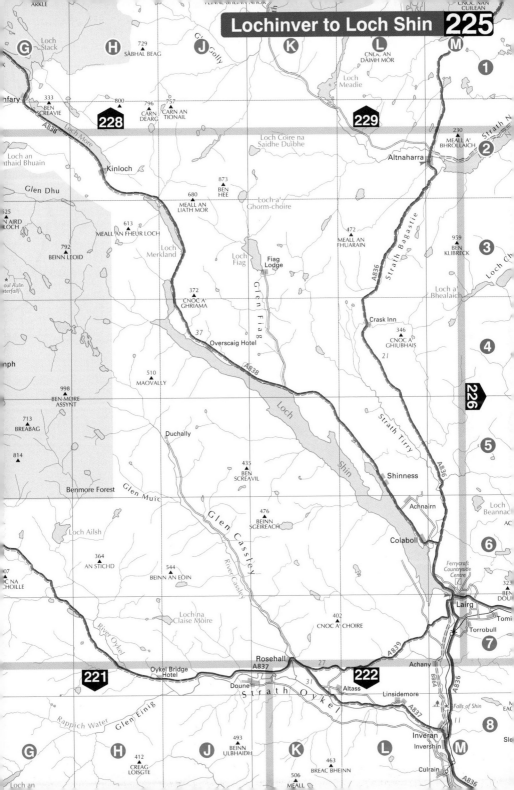

G   H   J   K   L   M

1
2

Whiten Head

Clean Hoan

408
▲ BEN HUTIG

Strathan

Talmine

Melness
Midtown

Rabbit Islands

Eilean Nan Ròn

Skerray

Achtoty

Torrisdale

Scullomie

Coldbackie

Tongue Bay

Kyle of Tongue

A838

230
BEN NABOLL

262
▲ DRUIM NAN CLIAR

Tongue

310
▲ MEALL LEATHAD NA CRAOIBHE

Neave Island

Torrisdale Bay

Farr Bay

Bettyhill

Farr

Borgie

13

River Borgie

A836

Skelpick

Ardmore Point

Kirtomy Point

Farr Point

Farr

Armad **3**
Kirtomy
Swordly

Loch Meadie

228
N I BÒ **4**

230

Loch Hope

Kinloch

Loch na Seilg

927
▲ BEN HOPE

598
▲ MEALLAN LIATH

Kyle of Tongue

318
▲ CNOC CRAGGIE

17

A836

763
▲ BEN LOYAL

Loch Craggie

527
▲ BEINN STUMANADH

Strath Naver

Skelpick Burn

12

B871

Loch Mòr na Caorach **5**

Loch nan C

213
▲ CNOC MALPELLY

Loch Strathy

335
▲ MEALL BAD NA CUAICHE **6**

Strath More

656
▲ CNOC AN DAIMH MÒR

Loch Meadie

557
▲ CNOC NAN CUILEAN

Loch Loyal

Loyal Lodge

Loch an Deerie

Loch Syre

Syre

River Naver

345
▲ CNOC NAM TRI-CHLACH

294
▲ POLE HILL

259
▲ BEINN ROSAIL

404
▲ BEINN MHADADH

B871

16 **7**

BEN

225

Loch Coire na idhe Duibhe

230
▲ MEALL A' BHROLLAICH

Altnaharra

Strath Naver

Loch Naver

12

270
▲ BEADAIG

B873

226

River

Loch Truders

Loch Rimsdale

Loch nan Clar

Loch Badanloch

Loch an Altán Fheàrna **8**

Loch a' n-cheire

472
▲ MEALL AN FHUARAIN

Bagastie

959
▲ BEN KLIBRECK

Oire Forest

694

434

G   H   J   K   L   M

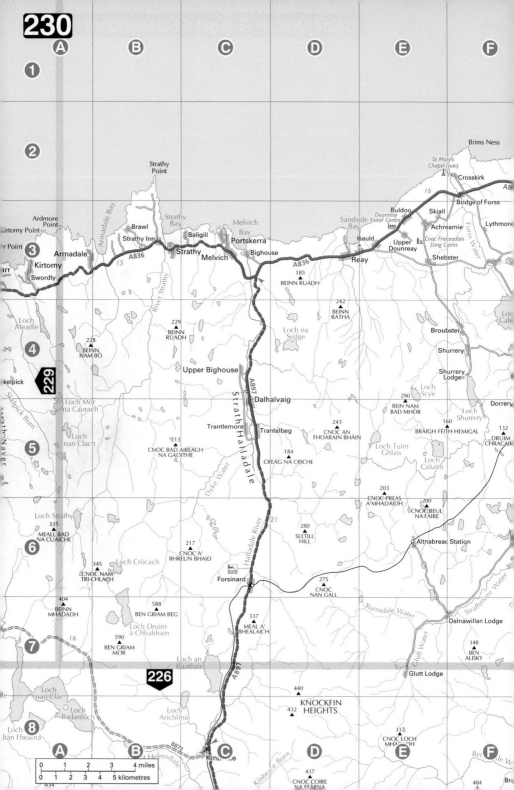

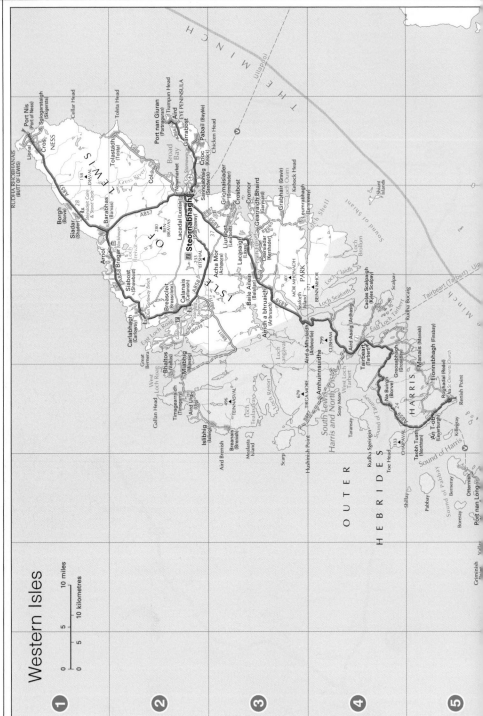

Western Isles

10 miles

0   5   10 kilometres

0   5

RONA

RAASAY

SCALPAY

EIGG

MUCK

ISLE OF SKYE

Uig

RUM

CANNA

Loch nam Madadh - Uig
(Lochmaddy)

Weaver's Point

THE HEBRIDES

Oban

Oban

Loch nam Madadh
(Lochmaddy)

Loch Euphoirt (Locheport)

BEINN NA FAOGHLA
(BENBECULA)

Ronay

Wiay

Rudha Halligro

UIBHIST A DEAS
(SOUTH UIST)

Rudha Bolum

Rudha Eyenort

Carinis
(Carinish)

Gramsdal
(Gramsdale)

Rudha nam Faoileann

Ceann a Bhaigh
(Bayhead)

Clachan nam Luib
(Clachan na Luib)

Rudha Port
Scolpaig

Baile a Mhanaich
(Balivanich)

Lionacleit

Creag Ghoraidh
(Creagorry)

Iochdar

Groigearraidh
(Grogarry)

Stadhlaigearraidh (Stilligarry)

Tobha Mor
(Howmore)

Staoinebrig
(Stoneybridge)

Rudha Ardvule

South Uist
Machair

Dalabrog
(Daliburgh)

Loch Baghasdail
(Lochboisdale)

Loch Bhaghasdail
(Loch Boisdale)

Staley

HECLA

BEINN MHOR

STULAVAL

201
RONEVAL

Ludag

Rubha Ban

ERISKAY

Rudha Hallagro

Benbecula

Heisker or
Monach Islands

Sound of Kirkibost Island

Rudha Port
Scolpaig

North Uist

Sound of Monach

Homish Point

Out Lock of the Minch

Quidnis

Benbecula

Sound of Barra

Bagh a' Chaisteil (Castlebay)
Bagh a Chaistail
(Castlebay)

Fiaray

Scurrival
Point

Eolaigearraidh

Borgh
(Barra)

Tangasdale

Vatersay

Bhatarsaigh

BARRAIGH
(BARRA)

HEAVAL
1264

Eoligarry

Gighay

Hellisay

Bruernish
Point

Fuiay

Muldoanich

Sandray

Pabbay

Mingulay

Berneray

A865

A888

A868

A867

Loch nam Madadh
(Lochmaddy)

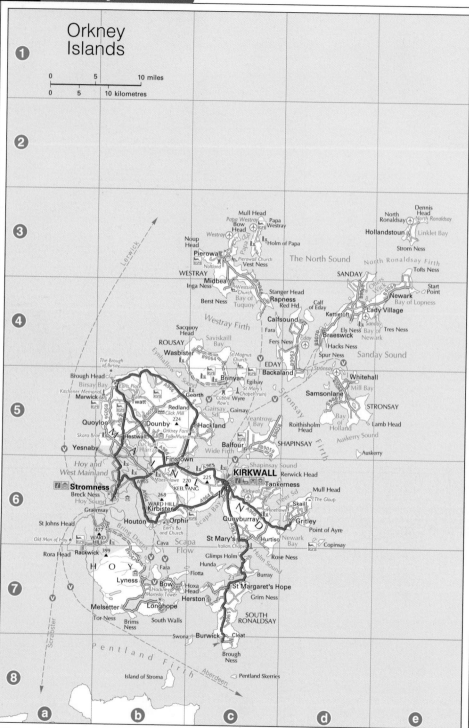

Orkney
Islands

0   5   10 miles
0   5   10 kilometres

Mull Head
Papa Westray
Bow Head
Papa Westray
Noup Head
Westray
Holm of Papa
Pierowall
Pierowall Church
WESTRAY
Vest Ness
Notland
Midbea
Inga Ness
Westside Church
Bay of Tuquoy
Berst Ness
Stanger Head
Rapness
Red Hd.
Calf of Eday

North Ronaldsay
North Ronaldsay
Dennis Head
Hollandstoun
Linklet Bay
Strom Ness
The North Sound
North Ronaldsay Firth
SANDAY
Tofts Ness
Newark
Bay of Lopness
Start Point
Lady Village

Calfsound
Fara
Fers Ness
Kettletoft
Els Ness
Bay of Newark
Tres Ness
Braeswick
Hacks Ness
Spur Ness
Sanday Sound

Westray Firth
Sacquoy Head
Saviskaill Bay
St Magnus Church
ROUSAY
Wasbister
B9064
EDAY
Backaland
Stronsay

The Brough of Birsay
Brough Head
Birsay Bay
Kitchener Memorial
Marwick
Earls Palace
A966
Twatt
Redland
Click Mill
224
Georth
Egilsay
St Mary's Chapel (ruin)
Cubbie Row's
Gairsay
Sd.
Gairsay
Whitehall
Mill Bay
Samsonlane
STRONSAY
Lamb Head

Quoyloo
Skara Brae
Dounby
Hackland
Orkney Farm Folk Museum
Yesnaby
Hestwall
Loch of Harray
Balfour
Wide Firth
SHAPINSAY
B9059
Veantrow Bay
Roithisholm Head
Bay of Holland
Auskerry Sound
Auskerry

M A I N L A N D
Finstown
Maeshowe
220
Stromness
Breck Ness
Hoy Sound
Graemsay
KEELYANG
KIRKWALL
Tankerness
Renwick Head
Shapinsay Sound
Mull Head
The Gloup
Minehow
Skaill
Gritley
Point of Ayre

Hoy and West Mainland
A965
225
A964
A960
Deer Sd.

St Johns Head
Old Man of Hoy
Rora Head
Rackwick
477 WARD HILL
399
H O Y
Lyness

WARD HILL
268
Kirbister
Houton
Orphir
Earl's Bu and Church
Cava
Scapa Flow
Bring Deeps
Quoyburray
St Mary's
Italian Chapel
Hurtiso
Newark Bay
Rose Ness
Copinsay

Graemsay
Fara
Flotta
Glimps Holm
Hunda
Burray
Holm Sound
Bow
Hackness
Martello Tower
Hoxa Head
Herston
St Margaret's Hope
Grim Ness
Melsetter
Tor Ness
Longhope
South Walls
Brims Ness
SOUTH RONALDSAY
A961
Swona
Burwick
Cleat
Brough Ness

Island of Stroma
Pentland Firth
Pentland Skerries

Scrabster
Aberdeen
Lerwick

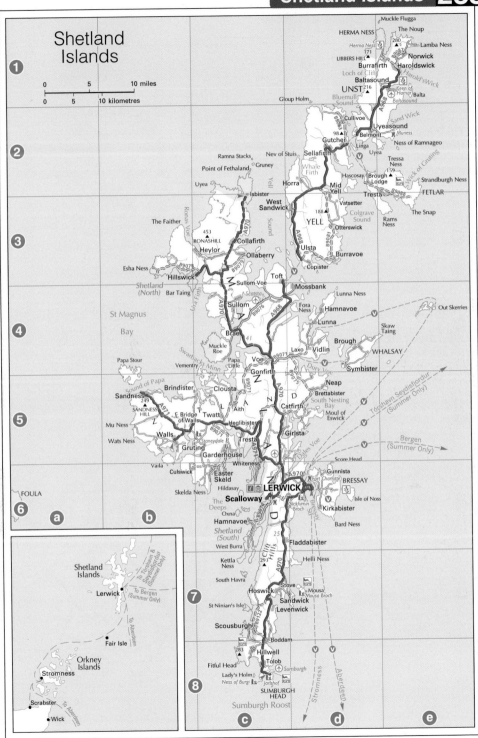

Shetland Islands

0   5   10 miles
0   5   10 kilometres

Muckle Flugga
HERMA NESS   The Noup
Herma Ness   280   Lamba Ness
LIBBERS HILL   171   Norwick
Burrafirth   Haroldswick
Loch of Cliff   Harold's Wick
Baltasound
UNST   216   Balta
Bluemull   Keen of   Baltasound
Gloup Holm   Sound   Hamar

Cullivoe
98   Belmont   Muness
Gutcher   Uyeasound
Nev of Stuis   Linga   Ness of Ramnageo
Ramna Stacks   Gruney   Sellafirth   Uyea
Point of Fethaland   Whale   Tressa
Firth   Hascosay   Brough   Ness
Uyea   Horra   Lodge   159   Strandburgh Ness
Mid   Tresta   FETLAR
Isbister   Yell   B9088
West   Vatsetter   The Snap
Sandwick   188   Colgrave   Rams
The Faither   YELL   Sound   Ness
453   Collafirth   Otterswick
RONASHILL   Sound   Ulsta   Out Skerries
Heylor   Ollaberry   Burravoe
Esha Ness   B9078   Toft   Copister
Hillswick   Sullom Voe   Mossbank   Lunna Ness
Shetland   Bar Taing   Scotsta   Lunna
(North)   Sullom   Fora   Hamnavoe
St Magnus   Ness   Lunna
Muckle   Brae   41   Laxo   Brough   Skaw
Bay   Roe   Papa   Vidlin   Taing
Papa Stour   Vementry   Little   Voe   B9071   WHALSAY
Brindister   Clousta   Gonfirth   Neap
Sandness   Aith   Brettabister   Symbister
SANDNESS   E Bridge   Twatt   South Nesting   Moul of   Tórshavn Seydisfjördur
HILL   of Walls   Heglibister   Bay   Eswick   (Summer Only)
Mu Ness   Walls   Tresta   Catfirth
Wats Ness   Gruting   Girlsta   Bergen
Vaila   Garderhouse   (Summer Only)
Culswick   Whiteness   Score Head
FOULA   Easter   Hildasay   Gunnista   BRESSAY
Skeld   LERWICK   Fort Charlotte   Isle of Noss
Skelda Ness   Scalloway   Clickimin   Kirkabister
The   Oxna   Broch   Bard Ness
Deeps   Hamnavoe
Shetland   West Burra   Fladdabister
(South)   Kettla   Helli Ness
Ness   Cliff   A970
South Havra   Hills   291   Stove
Hoswick   Mousa
St Ninian's Isle   Sandwick   Mousa Broch
Levenwick
Scousburgh
Boddam
283   Hillwell   Aberdeen
Fitful Head   Tolob   Stromness
Lady's Holm   Sumburgh
Ness of Burgi   Jarlshof
SUMBURGH
HEAD
Sumburgh Roost

Shetland
Islands
Lerwick
To Torshavn &
Seydisfjördur
(Summer Only)
To Bergen
(Summer Only)
To Aberdeen
Orkney
Islands
Stromness
Scrabster
Wick
Fair Isle

a   b   c   d   e

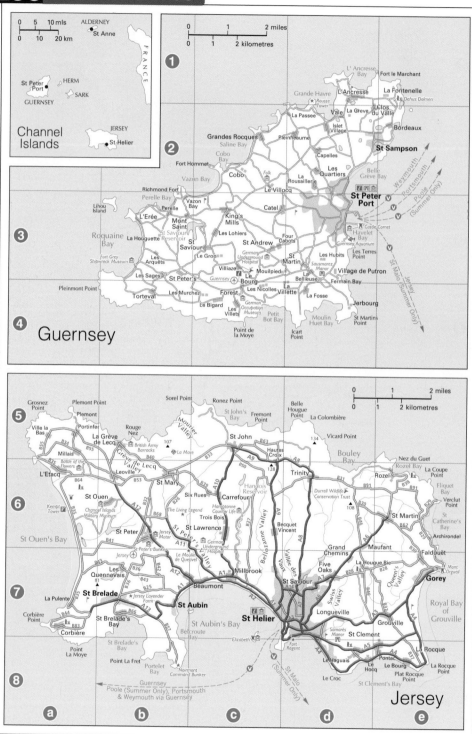

Channel Islands

ALDERNEY
St Anne

St Peter Port
HERM
SARK
GUERNSEY

JERSEY
St Helier

FRANCE

Guernsey

L'Ancresse Bay
Fort le Marchant
Grande Havre
L'Ancresse
La Fontenelle
Rousse Tower
Vale
La Greve
Clos du Valle
Le Dehus Dolmen
Bordeaux
La Passee
Islet Village
Grandes Rocques
Pleinheaume
St Sampson
Saline Bay
Capelles
Cobo Bay
Les Quartiers
Belle Greve Bay
Fort Hommet
Folk
La Rousaillerie
Vazon Bay
Cobo
Le Villocq
Weymouth
Portsmouth
Poole (Summer Only)
Richmond Fort
St Peter Port
Perelle Bay
Vazon Bay
Catel
Castle Cornet
Perelle
King's Mills
Havelet Bay
Lihou Island
L'Erée
Mont Saint
Four Cabots
Guernsey Aquarium
Roquaine Bay
St Saviour Reservoir
St Andrew
Les Hubits
Les Terres Point
Fort Grey Shipwreck Museum
La Houguette
St Saviour
Le Gron
German Underground Hospital
St Martin
Sausmarez Manor
Les Arquets
Villiaze
Moulipied
Le Bourg
Bellieuse
Village de Putron
Les Sages
St Peter's
Guernsey
Bellieuse
Fermain Bay
Pleinmont Point
Les Murchez
Forest
Les Nicolles
La Villette
La Fosse
Torteval
Le Bigard
German Occupation Museum
Jerbourg
Les Villets
Petit Bot Bay
St Martins Point
Point de la Moye
Icart Point
Moulin Huet Bay
Jersey (St Malo Summer Only)
St Malo (Summer Only)

Jersey

Grosnez Point
Plemont Point
Sorel Point
Ronez Point
Belle Hougue Point
La Colombière
Plemont
St John's Bay
Fremont Point
Ville la Bas
Portinfer
Mourier Valley
St John
Bouley Bay
Rouge Nez
107
La Mare
Hautes Croix
Vicard Point
Nez du Guet
La Grève de Lecq
British Army Barracks
134
Rozel Bay
La Coupe Point
Millais
Battle of the Flowers
Leoville
B33
A9
Trinity
Rozel
Fliquet Bay
L'Etacq
Grève de Lecq Valley
St Mary
128
B91
Verclut Point
Kempt Tower
Six Rues
Hamptonne Country Life
Durrell Wildlife Conservation Trust
St Catherine's Bay
St Ouen
Channel Islands Military Museum
Carrefour
108
St Martin
Archirondel
The Living Legend
Trois Bois
St Ouen's Bay
St Peter
Jersey Motor
St Lawrence
German Underground Hospital
Grand Chemins
Maufant
Faldouet
St Peter's Bunker
Le Moulin de Quetivel
La Hougue Bie
Mont Orgueil
Les Quennevais
Jersey Lavender Farm
Millbrook
Five Oaks
Queen's Valley
Gorey
La Pulente
St Brelade
Beaumont
St Saviour
Longueville
Royal Bay of Grouville
Corbière Point
St Brelade's Bay
St Aubin
St Helier
Swiss Valley
Grouville
Corbière
St Aubin's Bay
Samarès Manor
St Clement
La Rocque
Point La Moye
St Brelade's Bay
Bellecroute Bay
Elizabeth
Fort Regent
Le Hocq
La Rocque Point
Portelet Bay
Normont Command Bunker
St Clement's Bay
Le Bourg
Pontac
Les Haguais
Le Croc
Plat Rocque Point
Guernsey Poole (Summer Only), Portsmouth & Weymouth via Guernsey
St Malo (Summer Only)

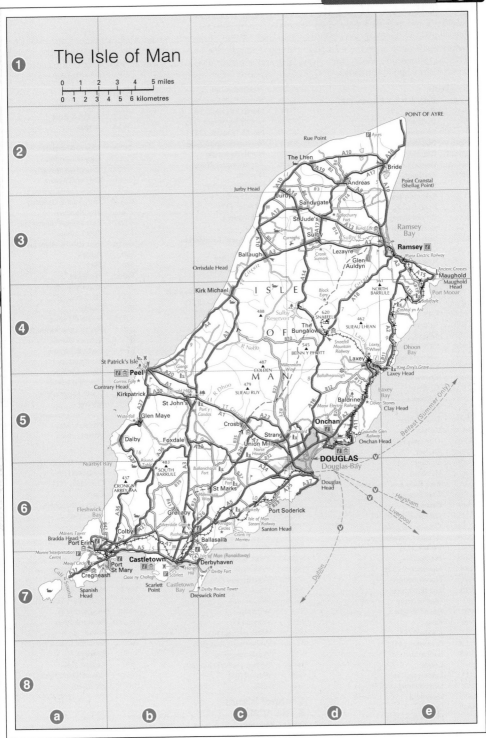

The Isle of Man

0 1 2 3 4 5 miles
0 1 2 3 4 5 6 kilometres

Index to place names

This index lists places appearing in the main-map section of the atlas in alphabetical order. The reference before each name gives the atlas page number and grid reference of the square in which the place appears. The map shows counties, unitary authorities and administrative areas, together with a list of the abbreviated name forms used in the index. 100 places of interest are indexed in red. Airports are indexed in blue.

England

BaNES	Bath & N E Somerset (18)
Barns	Barnsley (19)
Beds	Bedfordshire
Birm	Birmingham
Bl w D	Blackburn with Darwen (20)
Bmouth	Bournemouth
Bolton	Bolton (21)
Bpool	Blackpool
Brad	Bradford (22)
Br & H	Brighton and Hove (23)
Br For	Bracknell Forest (24)
Bristl	City of Bristol
Bucks	Buckinghamshire
Bury	Bury (25)
C Derb	City of Derby
C KuH	City of Kingston upon Hull
C Leic	City of Leicester
C Nott	City of Nottingham
C Pete	City of Peterborough
C Plym	City of Plymouth
C Port	City of Portsmouth
C Sotn	City of Southampton
C Stke	City of Stoke
Calder	Calderdale (26)
Cambs	Cambridgeshire
Ches	Cheshire
Cnwll	Cornwall
Covtry	Coventry
Cumb	Cumbria
Darltn	Darlington (27)
Derbys	Derbyshire
Devon	Devon
Donc	Doncaster (28)
Dorset	Dorset
Dudley	Dudley (29)
Dur	Durham
E R Yk	East Riding of Yorkshire
E Susx	East Sussex
Essex	Essex
Gatesd	Gateshead (30)
Gloucs	Gloucestershire
Gt Lon	Greater London
Halton	Halton (31)
Hants	Hampshire
Hartpl	Hartlepool (32)
Herefs	Herefordshire
Herts	Hertfordshire
IoS	Isles of Scilly
IoW	Isle of Wight
Kent	Kent
Kirk	Kirklees (33)
Knows	Knowsley (34)
Lancs	Lancashire
Leeds	Leeds
Leics	Leicestershire
Lincs	Lincolnshire
Lpool	Liverpool
Luton	Luton
M Keyn	Milton Keynes
Manch	Manchester
Medway	Medway

Middsb	Middlesbrough
NE Lin	North East Lincolnshire
N Linc	North Lincolnshire
N Som	North Somerset (35)
N Tyne	North Tyneside (36)
N u Ty	Newcastle upon Tyne
N York	North Yorkshire
Nhants	Northamptonshire
Norfk	Norfolk
Notts	Nottinghamshire
Nthumb	Northumberland
Oldham	Oldham (37)
Oxon	Oxfordshire
Poole	Poole
R & Cl	Redcar and Cleveland
Readg	Reading
Rochdl	Rochdale (38)
Rothm	Rotherham (39)
Rutlnd	Rutland
S Glos	South Gloucestershire (40)
S on T	Stockton-on-Tees (41)
S Tyne	South Tyneside (42)
Salfd	Salford (43)
Sandw	Sandwell (44)
Sefton	Sefton (45)
Sheff	Sheffield
Shrops	Shropshire
Slough	Slough (46)
Solhll	Solihull (47)
Somset	Somerset
St Hel	St Helens (48)
Staffs	Staffordshire
Sthend	Southend-on-Sea
Stockp	Stockport (49)
Suffk	Suffolk
Sundld	Sunderland
Surrey	Surrey
Swindn	Swindon
Tamesd	Tameside (50)
Thurr	Thurrock (51)
Torbay	Torbay
Traffd	Trafford (52)
W & M	Windsor & Maidenhead (53)
W Berk	West Berkshire
W Susx	West Sussex
Wakefd	Wakefield (54)
Warrtn	Warrington (55)
Warwks	Warwickshire
Wigan	Wigan (56)
Wilts	Wiltshire
Wirral	Wirral (57)
Wokham	Wokingham (58)
Wolves	Wolverhampton (59)
Worcs	Worcestershire
Wrekin	Telford and Wrekin (60)
Wsall	Walsall (61)
York	York

Channel Islands & Isle of Man

Guern	Guernsey
Jersey	Jersey
IoM	Isle of Man

Scotland

Abers	Aberdeenshire
Ag & B	Argyll & Bute
Angus	Angus
Border	Borders
C Aber	City of Aberdeen
C Dund	City of Dundee
C Edin	City of Edinburgh
C Glas	City of Glasgow
Clacks	Clackmannanshire (1)
D & G	Dumfries & Galloway
E Ayrs	East Ayrshire
E Duns	East Dunbartonshire (2)
E Loth	East Lothian
E Rens	East Renfrewshire (3)
Falk	Falkirk
Fife	Fife
Highld	Highland
Inver	Inverclyde (4)
Mdloth	Midlothian (5)
Moray	Moray
N Ayrs	North Ayrshire
N Lans	North Lanarkshire (6)
Ork	Orkney Islands
P & K	Perth & Kinross
Rens	Renfrewshire (7)
S Ayrs	South Ayrshire
Shet	Shetland Islands
S Lans	South Lanarkshire
Stirlg	Stirling
W Duns	West Dunbartonshire (8)
W Isls	Western Isles
W Loth	West Lothian

Wales

Blae G	Blaenau Gwent (9)
Brdgnd	Bridgend (10)
Caerph	Caerphilly (11)
Cardif	Cardiff
Carmth	Carmarthenshire
Cerdgn	Ceredigion
Conwy	Conwy
Denbgs	Denbighshire
Flints	Flintshire
Gwynd	Gwynedd
IoA	Isle of Anglesey
Mons	Monmouthshire
Myr Td	Merthyr Tydfil (12)
Neath	Neath Port Talbot (13)
Newpt	Newport (14)
Pembks	Pembrokeshire
Powys	Powys
Rhondd	Rhondda Cynon Taff (15)
Swans	Swansea
Torfn	Torfaen (16)
V Glam	Vale of Glamorgan (17)
Wrexhm	Wrexham

ORKNEY ISLANDS

SHETLAND ISLANDS

WESTERN

ISLES

HIGHLAND

MORAY

Aberdeen

ABERDEENSHIRE

ANGUS

PERTH & KINROSS

Dundee

ARGYLL & BUTE

STIRLING

FIFE

1

8 2 FALK

4 W

7 3 LOTH

6

E LOTH

Edinburgh

5

NORTH AYRSHIRE

S LANS

E AYRS

BORDERS

S AYRS

DUMFRIES & GALLOWAY

NORTHUMBERLAND

Newcastle upon Tyne

30

36

42

Sunderland

CUMBRIA

DURHAM

32

R & CL

27 41

Middlesbrough

IoM

NORTH YORKSHIRE

Blackpool

LANCASHIRE

22

York

EAST RIDING OF YORKSHIRE

Leeds

Kingston upon Hull

26

54

20

N LINCS

N E LINCS

45 21 25 38

33

19

28

56 37

IoA

34 48 43 50

Manchester

39

57 55 52 49

Sheffield

Liverpool

31

CONWY

FLINTS

CHESHIRE

DERBYS

NOTTS

LINCOLNSHIRE

DENBGS

Stoke-on-Trent

WREXHAM

Derby

Nottingham

GWYNEDD

STAFFS

LEICS

RUTLAND

Peterborough

NORFOLK

60

SHROPSHIRE

59 61

Leicester

29 44

Birmingham

47

Coventry

NHANTS

CAMBS

POWYS

WORCS

WARWKS

Milton Keynes

SUFFOLK

CERDGN

HEREFS

BEDS

Luton

ESSEX

PEMBKS

CARMTH

12 9

MONS

16

GLOUCS

OXON

BUCKS

HERTS

Southend-on-Sea

13

11

Swansea

15

14

BERKS

GREATER LONDON

51

10

Cardiff

40

Swindon

Reading

53 46

MEDWAY

17

Bristol

35

18

W BERKS

58 24

SURREY

KENT

WILTSHIRE

HAMPSHIRE

W SUSX

E SUSX

23

SOMERSET

DORSET

Southampton

Portsmouth

DEVON

Bournemouth

Poole

IoW

Guernsey

CHANNEL ISLANDS

CORNWALL

Plymouth

Torbay

Jersey

IoS

A

198 D4 **A'Chill** Highld
102 B7 **Ab Kettleby** Leics
27 G6 **Abbas Combe** Somset
70 D2 **Abberley** Worcs
70 D2 **Abberley Common** Worcs
62 B4 **Abberton** Essex
71 H4 **Abberton** Worcs
60 F5 **Abbess Roding** Essex
54 B3 **Abbey Dore** Herefs
99 L2 **Abbey Green** Staffs
178 F6 **Abbey St Bathans** Border
147 L5 **Abbey Town** Cumb
121 J6 **Abbey Village** Lancs
45 J4 **Abbey Wood** Gt Lon
114 F5 **Abbeydale** Sheff
130 B8 **Abbeystead** Lancs
71 J4 **Abbot's Salford** Warwks
167 J6 **Abbotrule** Border
9 K3 **Abbots Bickington** Devon
100 B7 **Abbots Bromley** Staffs
186 B5 **Abbots Deuglie** P & K
59 H7 **Abbots Langley** Herts
38 D5 **Abbots Leigh** N Som
71 H4 **Abbots Morton** Worcs
89 J7 **Abbots Ripton** Cambs
29 J5 **Abbots Worthy** Hants
14 B5 **Abbotsbury** Dorset
22 F6 **Abbotsham** Devon
7 K3 **Abbotskerswell** Devon
75 J3 **Abbotsley** Cambs
15 J3 **Abbott Street** Dorset
29 G3 **Abbotts Ann** Hants
83 L6 **Abdon** Shrops
52 F7 **Aber-nant** Rhondd
66 B3 **Aberaeron** Cerdgn
52 F7 **Aberaman** Rhondd
81 J2 **Aberangell** Gwynd
202 F1 **Aberarder** Highld
186 B4 **Aberargie** P & K
66 B2 **Aberarth** Cerdgn
51 L7 **Aberavon** Neath
185 J3 **Abercairny** P & K
53 G7 **Abercanaid** Myr Td
37 K2 **Abercarn** Caerph
64 B7 **Abercastle** Pembks
81 H3 **Abercegir** Powys
202 B5 **Aberchalder Lodge** Highld
216 C4 **Aberchirder** Abers
52 C5 **Abercraf** Powys
36 D2 **Abercregan** Neath
52 F7 **Abercwmboi** Rhondd
65 H6 **Abercych** Pembks
37 G2 **Abercynon** Rhondd
185 M4 **Aberdalgie** P & K
52 F7 **Aberdare** Rhondd
94 C7 **Aberdaron** Gwynd
207 H4 **Aberdeen** C Aber
207 G3 **Aberdeen Airport** C Aber
177 G2 **Aberdour** Fife
52 B7 **Aberdulais** Neath
80 E4 **Aberdyfi** Gwynd
68 C5 **Aberedw** Powys
48 D2 **Abereiddy** Pembks
95 G5 **Abererch** Gwynd
53 G7 **Aberfan** Myr Td
194 D6 **Aberfeldy** P & K
108 D7 **Aberffraw** IOA

124 C3 **Aberford** Leeds
184 C7 **Aberfoyle** Stirlg
53 L5 **Abergavenny** Mons
110 C6 **Abergele** Conwy
66 D7 **Abergorlech** Carmth
67 J4 **Abergwesyn** Powys
50 F2 **Abergwili** Carmth
36 D2 **Abergwynfi** Neath
109 J6 **Abergwyngregyn** Gwynd
80 F3 **Abergynolwyn** Gwynd
36 D4 **Aberkenfig** Brdgnd
178 B3 **Aberlady** E Loth
196 E5 **Aberlemno** Angus
81 G2 **Aberllefenni** Powys
68 D6 **Aberllynfi** Powys
215 G5 **Aberlour** Moray
82 D5 **Abermule** Powys
50 D2 **Abernant** Carmth
186 C4 **Abernethy** P & K
186 D2 **Abernyte** P & K
65 J4 **Aberporth** Cerdgn
94 E6 **Abersoch** Gwynd
53 K7 **Abersychan** Torfn
36 F5 **Aberthin** V Glam
53 K7 **Abertillery** Blae G
37 H3 **Abertridwr** Caerph
97 G8 **Abertridwr** Powys
185 K4 **Aberuthven** P & K
80 D6 **Aberystwyth** Cerdgn
41 J2 **Abingdon** Oxon
31 J3 **Abinger** Surrey
31 H2 **Abinger Hammer** Surrey
73 L3 **Abington** Nhants
165 H5 **Abington** S Lans
75 K5 **Abington Pigotts** Cambs
56 C6 **Ablington** Gloucs
114 D5 **Abney** Derbys
205 L5 **Aboyne** Abers
112 E2 **Abram** Wigan
212 E7 **Abriachan** Highld
45 J2 **Abridge** Essex
39 G5 **Abson** S Glos
73 J5 **Abthorpe** Nhants
118 F5 **Aby** Lincs
124 E2 **Acaster Malbis** York
124 E3 **Acaster Selby** N York
121 L5 **Accrington** Lancs
188 F5 **Acha** Ag & B
232 f3 **Acha Mor** W Isls
172 D3 **Achahoish** Ag & B
195 H7 **Achalader** P & K
182 D1 **Achaleven** Ag & B
211 K3 **Achanalt** Highld
222 E6 **Achandunie** Highld
222 D2 **Achany** Highld
190 D3 **Acharacle** Highld
190 E6 **Acharn** Highld
194 B7 **Acharn** P & K
231 H6 **Achavanich** Highld
224 C7 **Achduart** Highld
228 D7 **Achfary** Highld
224 C6 **Achiltibuie** Highld
161 J6 **Achinhoan** Ag & B
210 E6 **Achintee** Highld
210 C6 **Achintraid** Highld
224 C4 **Achmelvich** Highld
210 D7 **Achmore** Highld
232 f3 **Achmore** W Isls
224 C3 **Achnacarnin** Highld
201 J7 **Achnacarry** Highld
199 J4 **Achnacloich** Highld
202 C2 **Achnaconeran** Highld
191 G7 **Achnacroish** Ag & B
189 L6 **Achnadrish Lodge** Ag & B
185 J1 **Achnafauld** P & K
222 F7 **Achnagarron** Highld
189 L3 **Achnaha** Highld

224 B5 **Achnahaird** Highld
225 L6 **Achnairn** Highld
191 G4 **Achnalea** Highld
172 D2 **Achnamara** Ag & B
211 J3 **Achnasheen** Highld
210 F5 **Achnashellach Lodge** Highld
215 G7 **Achnastank** Moray
189 K3 **Achosnich** Highld
190 E6 **Achranich** Highld
230 E3 **Achreamie** Highld
192 B3 **Achriabhach** Highld
228 C5 **Achriesgill** Highld
229 K3 **Achtoty** Highld
88 E6 **Achurch** Nhants
222 F3 **Achvaich** Highld
231 L5 **Ackergill** Highld
141 L4 **Acklam** Middsb
134 B7 **Acklam** N York
84 D4 **Ackleton** Shrops
159 G2 **Acklington** Nthumb
124 C6 **Ackton** Wakefd
124 C7 **Ackworth Moor Top** Wakefd
93 J2 **Acle** Norfk
85 K6 **Acock's Green** Birm
35 J2 **Acol** Kent
150 B2 **Acomb** Nthumb
124 E1 **Acomb** York
54 D2 **Aconbury** Herefs
98 F2 **Acton** Ches
44 D4 **Acton** Gt Lon
99 J4 **Acton** Staffs
77 K5 **Acton** Suffk
70 E2 **Acton** Worcs
70 C4 **Acton Beauchamp** Herefs
112 E6 **Acton Bridge** Ches
83 K3 **Acton Burnell** Shrops
70 C4 **Acton Green** Herefs
97 M3 **Acton Park** Wrexhm
84 B4 **Acton Round** Shrops
83 J5 **Acton Scott** Shrops
99 L8 **Acton Trussell** Staffs
39 J4 **Acton Turville** S Glos
99 H6 **Adbaston** Staffs
26 E7 **Adber** Dorset
101 L5 **Adbolton** Notts
72 F7 **Adderbury** Oxon
98 F4 **Adderley** Shrops
176 D5 **Addiewell** W Loth
123 G1 **Addingham** Brad
58 C3 **Addington** Bucks
33 H2 **Addington** Gt Lon
45 G6 **Addiscombe** Gt Lon
43 H7 **Addlestone** Surrey
119 H7 **Addlethorpe** Lincs
59 H6 **Adeyfield** Herts
82 B4 **Adfa** Powys
69 H1 **Adforton** Herefs
35 G4 **Adisham** Kent
56 E3 **Adlestrop** Gloucs
125 K6 **Adlingfleet** E R Yk
121 J7 **Adlington** Lancs
100 B7 **Admaston** Staffs
84 B2 **Admaston** Wrekin
71 L5 **Admington** Warwks
25 L5 **Adsborough** Somset
25 J4 **Adscombe** Somset
58 C3 **Adstock** Bucks
31 H6 **Adversane** W Susx
214 D7 **Advie** Highld
124 E8 **Adwick Le Street** Donc
115 J2 **Adwick upon Dearne** Donc
155 H4 **Ae** D & G
155 H5 **Ae Bridgend** D & G
36 D2 **Afan Forest Park** Neath
216 B6 **Affleck** Abers
14 F4 **Affpuddle** Dorset
201 J2 **Affric Lodge** Highld

110 F6 **Afon-wen** Flints
131 K3 **Agglethorpe** N York
111 L4 **Aigburth** Lpool
126 C2 **Aike** E R Yk
148 E5 **Aiketgate** Cumb
148 B4 **Aikton** Cumb
89 G4 **Ailsworth** C Pete
132 E4 **Ainderby Quernhow** N York
132 E2 **Ainderby Steeple** N York
62 D4 **Aingers Green** Essex
120 D7 **Ainsdale** Sefton
148 F5 **Ainstable** Cumb
142 E5 **Ainthorpe** N York
176 F5 **Ainville** W Loth
181 M7 **Aird** Ag & B
144 D3 **Aird** D & G
232 g2 **Aird** W Isls
232 e3 **Aird a Mhulaidh** W Isls
232 e4 **Aird Asaig** W Isls
209 L6 **Aird Dhubh** Highld
181 H2 **Aird of Kinloch** Ag & B
199 J5 **Aird of Sleat** Highld
232 d2 **Aird Uig** W Isls
182 E2 **Airdeny** Ag & B
175 K5 **Airdrie** N Lans
175 K5 **Airdriehill** N Lans
182 E2 **Airds Bay** Ag & B
154 B7 **Airds of Kells** D & G
232 e3 **Airidh a bhruaich** W Isls
146 D4 **Airieland** D & G
195 L6 **Airlie** Angus
125 H5 **Airmyn** E R Yk
186 A1 **Airntully** P & K
199 L4 **Airor** Highld
176 B2 **Airth** Falk
131 G7 **Airton** N York
116 E3 **Aisby** Lincs
103 G5 **Aisby** Lincs
7 G4 **Aish** Devon
7 J4 **Aish** Devon
25 J4 **Aisholt** Somset
132 D2 **Aiskew** N York
143 H5 **Aislaby** N York
134 B3 **Aislaby** N York
141 J5 **Aislaby** S on T
116 F5 **Aisthorpe** Lincs
235 c5 **Aith** Shet
168 E4 **Akeld** Nthumb
73 K6 **Akeley** Bucks
78 D5 **Akenham** Suffk
6 B2 **Albaston** Devon
83 G1 **Alberbury** Shrops
19 H3 **Albourne** W Susx
98 C8 **Albrighton** Shrops
84 E3 **Albrighton** Shrops
92 F6 **Alburgh** Norfk
60 C3 **Albury** Herts
31 H2 **Albury** Surrey
31 H3 **Albury Heath** Surrey
212 E3 **Alcaig** Highld
83 J6 **Alcaston** Shrops
71 K3 **Alcester** Warwks
20 B5 **Alciston** E Susx
89 H7 **Alconbury** Cambs
89 H7 **Alconbury Weston** Cambs
132 F6 **Aldborough** N York
106 E5 **Aldborough** Norfk
40 E5 **Aldbourne** Wilts
127 G3 **Aldbrough** E R Yk
140 F5 **Aldbrough St John** N York
58 F5 **Aldbury** Herts
129 K7 **Aldcliffe** Lancs
194 E4 **Aldclune** P & K
79 K3 **Aldeburgh** Suffk
93 J5 **Aldeby** Norfk
43 J2 **Aldenham** Herts

28 D6	**Alderbury** Wilts
106 D8	**Alderford** Norfk
28 C8	**Alderholt** Dorset
39 H3	**Alderley** Gloucs
113 J5	**Alderley Edge** Ches
41 L7	**Aldermaston** W Berk
72 B5	**Alderminster** Warwks
30 E2	**Aldershot** Hants
55 M2	**Alderton** Gloucs
73 K5	**Alderton** Nhants
79 H6	**Alderton** Suffk
39 J4	**Alderton** Wilts
100 F2	**Alderwasley** Derbys
132 D5	**Aldfield** N York
98 B1	**Aldford** Ches
88 E3	**Aldgate** Rutlnd
61 L3	**Aldham** Essex
78 C5	**Aldham** Suffk
18 C5	**Aldingbourne** W Susx
129 G5	**Aldingham** Cumb
34 E7	**Aldington** Kent
71 J5	**Aldington** Worcs
34 E7	**Aldington Corner** Kent
205 H1	**Aldivalloch** Moray
174 C1	**Aldochlay** Ag & B
90 C8	**Aldreth** Cambs
85 J4	**Aldridge** Wsall
79 J3	**Aldringham** Suffk
56 D6	**Aldsworth** Gloucs
215 H8	**Aldunie** Moray
100 E2	**Aldwark** Derbys
133 G6	**Aldwark** N York
18 C6	**Aldwick** W Susx
88 E6	**Aldwincle** Nhants
41 K4	**Aldworth** W Berk
174 D3	**Alexandria** W Duns
25 J4	**Aley** Somset
12 E3	**Alfington** Devon
31 H5	**Alfold** Surrey
31 H4	**Alfold Crossways** Surrey
206 B3	**Alford** Abers
118 F6	**Alford** Lincs
26 E5	**Alford** Somset
101 H2	**Alfreton** Derbys
70 D4	**Alfrick** Worcs
70 D4	**Alfrick Pound** Worcs
20 B5	**Alfriston** E Susx
103 M5	**Algarkirk** Lincs
26 F4	**Alhampton** Somset
125 K6	**Alkborough** N Linc
35 H6	**Alkham** Kent
100 D5	**Alkmonton** Derbys
40 B7	**All Cannings** Wilts
93 H6	**All Saints South Elmham** Suffk
83 J4	**All Stretton** Shrops
7 J5	**Allaleigh** Devon
204 D6	**Allanaquoich** Abers
175 L6	**Allanbank** N Lans
179 H7	**Allanton** Border
175 L6	**Allanton** N Lans
175 K7	**Allanton** S Lans
54 F6	**Allaston** Gloucs
29 J7	**Allbrook** Hants
85 L4	**Allen End** Warwks
60 D5	**Allen's Green** Herts
149 L4	**Allendale** Nthumb
149 L6	**Allenheads** Nthumb
69 J7	**Allensmore** Herefs
101 G6	**Allenton** C Derb
24 B6	**Aller** Devon
26 B5	**Aller** Somset
147 J6	**Allerby** Cumb
12 D4	**Allercombe** Devon
24 D3	**Allerford** Somset
134 D3	**Allerston** N York
125 J2	**Allerthorpe** E R Yk
123 G4	**Allerton** Brad
213 H2	**Allerton** Highld
111 L4	**Allerton** Lpool
124 C5	**Allerton Bywater** Leeds
132 F7	**Allerton Mauleverer** N York
86 C7	**Allesley** Covtry
101 G5	**Allestree** C Derb
88 B4	**Allexton** Leics
113 L7	**Allgreave** Ches
46 D4	**Allhallows** Medway
210 C3	**Alligin Shuas** Highld
13 L4	**Allington** Dorset
102 E4	**Allington** Lincs
39 K5	**Allington** Wilts
40 B7	**Allington** Wilts
28 D4	**Allington** Wilts
129 J4	**Allithwaite** Cumb
185 J8	**Alloa** Clacks
147 J6	**Allonby** Cumb
163 J5	**Alloway** S Ayrs
26 B8	**Allowenshay** Somset
192 C6	**Alltchaorunn** Highld
66 B7	**Alltwalis** Carmth
51 K5	**Alltwen** Neath
66 C5	**Alltyblaca** Cerdgn
26 F8	**Allweston** Dorset
69 G4	**Almeley** Herefs
124 E8	**Almholme** Donc
99 G5	**Almington** Staffs
185 M3	**Almondbank** P & K
123 H7	**Almondbury** Kirk
38 E4	**Almondsbury** S Glos
133 G6	**Alne** N York
222 E7	**Alness** Highld
168 E7	**Alnham** Nthumb
169 J7	**Alnmouth** Nthumb
169 J6	**Alnwick** Nthumb
44 D4	**Alperton** Gt Lon
77 K7	**Alphamstone** Essex
77 K4	**Alpheton** Suffk
11 L6	**Alphington** Devon
114 E8	**Alport** Derbys
98 E1	**Alpraham** Ches
62 C4	**Alresford** Essex
85 L1	**Alrewas** Staffs
99 H2	**Alsager** Ches
100 D2	**Alsop en le Dale** Derbys
149 J5	**Alston** Cumb
13 H2	**Alston** Devon
26 B2	**Alston Sutton** Somset
55 M2	**Alstone** Gloucs
100 C2	**Alstonefield** Staffs
23 L6	**Alswear** Devon
224 B6	**Altandhu** Highld
9 G8	**Altarnun** Cnwll
222 C2	**Altass** Highld
190 D8	**Altcreich** Ag & B
173 H4	**Altgaltraig** Ag & B
61 L7	**Althorne** Essex
125 K8	**Althorpe** N Linc
230 E6	**Altnabreac Station** Highld
182 B2	**Altnacraig** Ag & B
225 M2	**Altnaharra** Highld
115 G8	**Alton** Derbys
30 B4	**Alton** Hants
100 B4	**Alton** Staffs
40 C7	**Alton Barnes** Wilts
14 D3	**Alton Pancras** Dorset
40 C7	**Alton Priors** Wilts
100 B4	**Alton Towers** Staffs
113 H4	**Altrincham** Traffd
184 B6	**Altskeith Hotel** Stirlg
185 J7	**Alva** Clacks
216 D3	**Alvah** Abers
112 D6	**Alvanley** Ches
101 H5	**Alvaston** C Derb
85 J8	**Alvechurch** Worcs
86 B3	**Alvecote** Warwks
27 L6	**Alvediston** Wilts
84 D6	**Alveley** Shrops
23 H6	**Alverdiscott** Devon
17 H3	**Alverstoke** Hants
17 H5	**Alverstone** IOW
123 L6	**Alverthorpe** Wakefd
102 C4	**Alverton** Notts
214 E3	**Alves** Moray
56 F6	**Alvescot** Oxon
38 F3	**Alveston** Gloucs
72 B3	**Alveston** Warwks
118 E4	**Alvingham** Lincs
54 E7	**Alvington** Gloucs
89 G4	**Alwalton** Cambs
168 D7	**Alwinton** Nthumb
123 K3	**Alwoodley** Leeds
195 K6	**Alyth** P & K
101 G3	**Ambergate** Derbys
55 J7	**Amberley** Gloucs
18 D3	**Amberley** W Susx
159 G2	**Amble** Nthumb
84 F6	**Amblecote** Dudley
123 G5	**Ambler Thorn** Brad
137 K6	**Ambleside** Cumb
49 G3	**Ambleston** Pembks
57 L4	**Ambrosden** Oxon
125 K7	**Amcotts** N Linc
42 F2	**Amersham** Bucks
28 D3	**Amesbury** Wilts
232 d4	**Amhuinnsuidhe** W Isls
155 H5	**Amisfield Town** D & G
108 F3	**Amlwch** IOA
51 J3	**Ammanford** Carmth
134 B5	**Amotherby** N York
29 H6	**Ampfield** Hants
133 J4	**Ampleforth** N York
56 B7	**Ampney Crucis** Gloucs
56 C7	**Ampney St Mary** Gloucs
56 B7	**Ampney St Peter** Gloucs
28 F3	**Amport** Hants
74 F6	**Ampthill** Beds
77 J1	**Ampton** Suffk
49 K6	**Amroth** Pembks
185 J1	**Amulree** P & K
59 K5	**Amwell** Herts
232 d5	**An t-Ob** W Isls
191 G4	**Anaheilt** Highld
103 G4	**Ancaster** Lincs
168 E1	**Ancroft** Nthumb
167 K4	**Ancrum** Border
119 G6	**Anderby** Lincs
29 G3	**Andover** Hants
56 A4	**Andoversford** Gloucs
237 d2	**Andreas** IOM
45 G6	**Anerley** Gt Lon
111 K3	**Anfield** Lpool
3 G4	**Angarrack** Cnwll
83 L7	**Angelbank** Shrops
25 J7	**Angersleigh** Somset
48 E6	**Angle** Pembks
108 E5	**Anglesey** IOA
18 E5	**Angmering** W Susx
124 D2	**Angram** N York
223 H6	**Ankerville** Highld
126 C5	**Anlaby** E R Yk
105 H6	**Anmer** Norfk
17 J1	**Anmore** Hants
29 G3	**Anna Valley** Hants
147 L2	**Annan** D & G
210 D4	**Annat** Highld
175 J4	**Annathill** N Lans
163 K5	**Annbank** S Ayrs
71 L4	**Anne Hathaway's Cottage** Warwks
101 J2	**Annesley** Notts
101 J2	**Annesley Woodhouse** Notts
150 F5	**Annfield Plain** Dur
174 F5	**Anniesland** C Glas
120 D5	**Ansdell** Lancs
26 F5	**Ansford** Somset
86 C5	**Ansley** Warwks
100 E7	**Anslow** Staffs
100 D7	**Anslow Gate** Staffs
60 C2	**Anstey** Herts
87 G2	**Anstey** Leics
187 J6	**Anstruther** Fife
19 J2	**Ansty** W Susx
86 E6	**Ansty** Warwks
27 L6	**Ansty** Wilts
147 L4	**Anthorn** Cumb
106 F5	**Antingham** Norfk
103 M3	**Anton's Gowt** Lincs
6 B5	**Antony** Cnwll
112 F5	**Antrobus** Ches
103 J3	**Anwick** Lincs
145 M4	**Anwoth** D & G
32 D2	**Aperfield** Gt Lon
88 E4	**Apethorpe** Nhants
117 J6	**Apley** Lincs
115 G5	**Apperknowle** Derbys
55 K3	**Apperley** Gloucs
191 J6	**Appin** Ag & B
126 B7	**Appleby** N Linc
86 C2	**Appleby Magna** Leics
86 C2	**Appleby Parva** Leics
139 G3	**Appleby-in-Westmorland** Cumb
209 L5	**Applecross** Highld
23 G5	**Appledore** Devon
25 G8	**Appledore** Devon
34 C8	**Appledore** Kent
41 K2	**Appleford** Oxon
155 J5	**Applegarth Town** D & G
28 F2	**Appleshaw** Hants
112 D4	**Appleton** Halton
57 H7	**Appleton** Oxon
124 E3	**Appleton Roebuck** N York
112 F5	**Appleton Thorn** Warrtn
141 J6	**Appleton Wiske** N York
133 L3	**Appleton-le-Moors** N York
134 B5	**Appleton-le-Street** N York
167 H6	**Appletreehall** Border
131 K7	**Appletreewick** N York
25 G6	**Appley** Somset
121 G8	**Appley Bridge** Lancs
17 G5	**Apse Heath** IOW
59 J2	**Apsley End** Beds
18 A5	**Apuldram** W Susx
223 H6	**Arabella** Highld
196 F7	**Arbirlot** Angus
223 J5	**Arboll** Highld
42 C6	**Arborfield** Wokham
42 C6	**Arborfield Cross** Wokham
197 G7	**Arbroath** Angus
197 K2	**Arbuthnott** Abers
50 F5	**Archddu** Carmth
141 G4	**Archdeacon Newton** Darltn
174 D3	**Archencarroch** W Duns
214 F5	**Archiestown** Moray
236 e6	**Archirondel** Jersey
99 H1	**Arclid Green** Ches
182 F3	**Ardanaiseig Hotel** Ag & B
210 C7	**Ardaneaskan** Highld
210 C6	**Ardarroch** Highld
160 D1	**Ardbeg** Ag & B
173 J5	**Ardbeg** Ag & B
173 K2	**Ardbeg** Ag & B
220 F4	**Ardcharnich** Highld

180 E4 **Ardchiavaig** Ag & B
182 D5 **Ardchonnel** Ag & B
184 D5 **Ardchullarie More** Stirlg
183 J7 **Arddarroch** Ag & B
201 H7 **Ardechive** Highld
163 H2 **Ardeer** N Ayrs
60 A3 **Ardeley** Herts
210 D8 **Ardelve** Highld
174 C2 **Arden** Ag & B
71 K4 **Ardens Grafton** Warwks
182 B3 **Ardentallen** Ag & B
173 L2 **Ardentinny** Ag & B
173 H4 **Ardentraive** Ag & B
184 E1 **Ardeonaig Hotel** Stirlg
213 J4 **Ardersier** Highld
220 D4 **Ardessie** Highld
182 A6 **Ardfern** Ag & B
222 D4 **Ardgay** Highld
191 K4 **Ardgour** Highld
173 L4 **Ardgowan** Inver
173 K4 **Ardhallow** Ag & B
232 e4 **Ardhasig** W Isls
210 B3 **Ardheslaig** Highld
220 F4 **Ardindrean** Highld
32 C7 **Ardingly** W Susx
41 H4 **Ardington** Oxon
173 G5 **Ardlamont** Ag & B
62 C3 **Ardleigh** Essex
62 C2 **Ardleigh Heath** Essex
195 L7 **Ardler** P & K
57 K3 **Ardley** Oxon
183 K4 **Ardlui** Ag & B
172 B2 **Ardlussa** Ag & B
191 L8 **Ardmaddy** Ag & B
220 E2 **Ardmair** Highld
173 J5 **Ardmaleish** Ag & B
172 B8 **Ardminish** Ag & B
190 E3 **Ardmolich** Highld
174 C3 **Ardmore** Ag & B
222 F4 **Ardmore** Highld
173 K3 **Ardnadam** Ag & B
212 E4 **Ardnagrask** Highld
210 D7 **Ardnarff** Highld
190 F4 **Ardnastang** Highld
183 G5 **Ardno** Ag & B
201 J5 **Ardochy House** Highld
172 C6 **Ardpatrick** Ag & B
172 E2 **Ardrishaig** Ag & B
222 E6 **Ardross** Highld
163 G2 **Ardrossan** N Ayrs
123 K5 **Ardsley East** Leeds
190 B4 **Ardslignish** Highld
171 J7 **Ardtalla** Ag & B
190 C3 **Ardtoe** Highld
182 A5 **Arduaine** Ag & B
212 E2 **Ardullie** Highld
199 K5 **Ardvasar** Highld
184 D3 **Ardvorlich** P & K
232 e3 **Ardvourlie** W Isls
144 D5 **Ardwell** D & G
113 J3 **Ardwick** Manch
70 E1 **Areley Kings** Worcs
190 D3 **Arevegaig** Highld
30 D4 **Arford** Hants
53 J7 **Argoed** Caerph
183 J6 **Argyll Forest Park** Ag & B
232 e3 **Aribruach** W Isls
180 D3 **Aridhglas** Ag & B
188 F5 **Arileod** Ag & B
189 G5 **Arinagour** Ag & B
182 C3 **Ariogan** Ag & B
199 K7 **Arisaig** Highld
199 L7 **Arisaig House** Highld
132 F7 **Arkendale** N York
76 C7 **Arkesden** Essex
130 B5 **Arkholme** Lancs
156 C4 **Arkleton** D & G

44 E2 **Arkley** Gt Lon
115 L1 **Arksey** Donc
115 H7 **Arkwright Town** Derbys
55 L4 **Arle** Gloucs
136 E4 **Arlecdon** Cumb
75 H7 **Arlesey** Beds
84 B2 **Arleston** Wrekin
112 F5 **Arley** Ches
86 C5 **Arley** Warwks
55 G6 **Arlingham** Gloucs
23 K4 **Arlington** Devon
20 B4 **Arlington** E Susx
230 A3 **Armadale** Highld
199 K5 **Armadale** Highld
176 C5 **Armadale** W Loth
137 G2 **Armaside** Cumb
148 E5 **Armathwaite** Cumb
92 F3 **Arminghall** Norfk
85 J1 **Armitage** Staffs
123 K4 **Armley** Leeds
88 F6 **Armston** Nhants
115 L1 **Armthorpe** Donc
188 F4 **Arnabost** Ag & B
131 H5 **Arncliffe** N York
187 H6 **Arncroach** Fife
215 G5 **Arndilly House** Moray
15 H5 **Arne** Dorset
87 H5 **Arnesby** Leics
186 B5 **Arngask** P & K
200 C3 **Arnisdale** Highld
209 J5 **Arnish** Highld
177 K6 **Arniston** Mdloth
232 f1 **Arnol** W Isls
126 E3 **Arnold** E R Yk
101 L4 **Arnold** Notts
184 D7 **Arnprior** Stirlg
129 K4 **Arnside** Cumb
190 B7 **Aros** Ag & B
129 G4 **Arrad Foot** Cumb
126 C2 **Arram** E R Yk
162 B3 **Arran** N Ayrs
132 C2 **Arrathorne** N York
17 G5 **Arreton** IOW
210 B3 **Arrina** Highld
75 K4 **Arrington** Cambs
183 K6 **Arrochar** Ag & B
71 J3 **Arrow** Warwks
83 J2 **Arscott** Shrops
212 F4 **Artafallie** Highld
123 K2 **Arthington** Leeds
87 L7 **Arthingworth** Nhants
217 H6 **Arthrath** Abers
217 J7 **Artrochie** Abers
18 D4 **Arundel** W Susx
136 E3 **Asby** Cumb
173 J5 **Ascog** Ag & B
42 F6 **Ascot** W & M
56 F4 **Ascott-under-Wychwood** Oxon
132 F4 **Asenby** N York
102 B8 **Asfordby** Leics
102 B8 **Asfordby Hill** Leics
103 J4 **Asgarby** Lincs
118 D7 **Asgarby** Lincs
45 L6 **Ash** Kent
35 H3 **Ash** Kent
26 C7 **Ash** Somset
30 E2 **Ash** Surrey
30 E2 **Ash Green** Surrey
86 D6 **Ash Green** Warwks
98 E4 **Ash Magna** Shrops
24 C6 **Ash Mill** Devon
98 E5 **Ash Parva** Shrops
25 J5 **Ash Priors** Somset
78 B5 **Ash Street** Suffk
12 C1 **Ash Thomas** Devon
30 E2 **Ash Vale** Surrey
41 K5 **Ashampstead** W Berk
78 E4 **Ashbocking** Suffk

78 E4 **Ashbocking Green** Suffk
100 D3 **Ashbourne** Derbys
25 G6 **Ashbrittle** Somset
7 H2 **Ashburton** Devon
10 D5 **Ashbury** Devon
40 E4 **Ashbury** Oxon
125 L8 **Ashby** N Linc
118 F7 **Ashby by Partney** Lincs
118 C2 **Ashby cum Fenby** NE Lin
103 H2 **Ashby de la Launde** Lincs
87 K2 **Ashby Folville** Leics
87 H5 **Ashby Magna** Leics
87 G5 **Ashby Parva** Leics
118 D7 **Ashby Puerorum** Lincs
73 H2 **Ashby St Ledgers** Nhants
93 G3 **Ashby St Mary** Norfk
86 D1 **Ashby-de-la-Zouch** Leics
55 L2 **Ashchurch** Gloucs
11 L8 **Ashcombe** Devon
37 M7 **Ashcombe** N Som
26 C4 **Ashcott** Somset
76 E6 **Ashdon** Essex
29 K2 **Ashe** Hants
62 A7 **Asheldham** Essex
77 H6 **Ashen** Essex
58 B5 **Ashendon** Bucks
58 F6 **Asheridge** Bucks
185 G6 **Ashfield** Stirlg
78 E3 **Ashfield** Suffk
92 F8 **Ashfield Green** Suffk
23 H4 **Ashford** Devon
7 G4 **Ashford** Devon
34 D6 **Ashford** Kent
43 H6 **Ashford** Surrey
69 K1 **Ashford Bowdler** Shrops
69 K1 **Ashford Carbonel** Shrops
41 K7 **Ashford Hill** Hants
114 D7 **Ashford in the Water** Derbys
175 K7 **Ashgill** S Lans
12 E1 **Ashill** Devon
91 K3 **Ashill** Norfk
25 L7 **Ashill** Somset
46 E2 **Ashingdon** Essex
159 G5 **Ashington** Nthumb
26 E6 **Ashington** Somset
18 F3 **Ashington** W Susx
167 G5 **Ashkirk** Border
55 J3 **Ashleworth** Gloucs
55 J3 **Ashleworth Quay** Gloucs
77 G3 **Ashley** Cambs
113 H5 **Ashley** Ches
10 F3 **Ashley** Devon
39 L2 **Ashley** Gloucs
29 G5 **Ashley** Hants
16 B4 **Ashley** Hants
35 J5 **Ashley** Kent
87 L5 **Ashley** Nhants
99 H5 **Ashley** Staffs
39 J6 **Ashley** Wilts
58 F6 **Ashley Green** Bucks
41 H8 **Ashmansworth** Hants
22 E7 **Ashmansworthy** Devon
27 K7 **Ashmore** Dorset
41 J6 **Ashmore Green** W Berk
72 C3 **Ashorne** Warwks
115 G8 **Ashover** Derbys
72 C1 **Ashow** Warwks
70 B6 **Ashperton** Herefs
7 J4 **Ashprington** Devon

10 F3 **Ashreigney** Devon
44 D8 **Ashtead** Surrey
112 D7 **Ashton** Ches
3 G5 **Ashton** Cnwll
11 K7 **Ashton** Devon
69 K2 **Ashton** Herefs
173 L3 **Ashton** Inver
73 L5 **Ashton** Nhants
88 F5 **Ashton** Nhants
39 K8 **Ashton Common** Wilts
40 B2 **Ashton Keynes** Wilts
71 H6 **Ashton under Hill** Worcs
112 E2 **Ashton-in-Makerfield** Wigan
113 L2 **Ashton-under-Lyne** Tamesd
16 D1 **Ashurst** Hants
32 F5 **Ashurst** Kent
19 G3 **Ashurst** W Susx
32 D5 **Ashurstwood** W Susx
9 K5 **Ashwater** Devon
75 J6 **Ashwell** Herts
88 C2 **Ashwell** Rutlnd
75 J6 **Ashwell End** Herts
92 D4 **Ashwellthorpe** Norfk
26 F2 **Ashwick** Somset
105 H8 **Ashwicken** Norfk
128 F4 **Askam in Furness** Cumb
124 E7 **Askern** Donc
14 A4 **Askerswell** Dorset
58 D6 **Askett** Bucks
138 D3 **Askham** Cumb
116 C6 **Askham** Notts
124 E2 **Askham Bryan** York
124 E2 **Askham Richard** York
172 F1 **Asknish** Ag & B
131 H2 **Askrigg** N York
123 H2 **Askwith** N York
103 H6 **Aslackby** Lincs
92 D5 **Aslacton** Norfk
102 C4 **Aslockton** Notts
147 K6 **Aspatria** Cumb
60 B3 **Aspenden** Herts
74 D7 **Aspley Guise** Beds
74 D7 **Aspley Heath** Beds
121 J8 **Aspull** Wigan
125 H5 **Asselby** E R Yk
77 L6 **Assington** Suffk
77 H4 **Assington Green** Suffk
99 J1 **Astbury** Ches
73 J4 **Astcote** Nhants
118 C5 **Asterby** Lincs
83 H3 **Asterley** Shrops
83 H5 **Asterton** Shrops
56 F5 **Asthall** Oxon
56 F5 **Asthall Leigh** Oxon
223 G3 **Astle** Highld
98 D8 **Astley** Shrops
86 C5 **Astley** Warwks
113 G2 **Astley** Wigan
70 D2 **Astley** Worcs
84 C4 **Astley Abbots** Shrops
121 K7 **Astley Bridge** Bolton
70 E1 **Astley Cross** Worcs
112 E5 **Aston** Ches
98 E3 **Aston** Ches
114 D5 **Aston** Derbys
111 J7 **Aston** Flints
69 J1 **Aston** Herefs
59 L4 **Aston** Herts
57 G7 **Aston** Oxon
115 J4 **Aston** Rothm
98 D6 **Aston** Shrops
84 E5 **Aston** Shrops
99 H4 **Aston** Staffs
99 K7 **Aston** Staffs
99 K6 **Aston** Staffs

42 C4	**Aston** Wokham	
84 B2	**Aston** Wrekin	
58 D4	**Aston Abbotts** Bucks	
84 B6	**Aston Botterell** Shrops	
71 K3	**Aston Cantlow** Warwks	
58 E5	**Aston Clinton** Bucks	
54 F4	**Aston Crews** Herefs	
59 L3	**Aston End** Herts	
71 G1	**Aston Fields** Worcs	
86 F5	**Aston Flamville** Leics	
55 G4	**Aston Ingham** Herefs	
72 F4	**Aston le Walls** Nhants	
71 L7	**Aston Magna** Gloucs	
83 K6	**Aston Munslow** Shrops	
83 H6	**Aston on Clun** Shrops	
83 G3	**Aston Pigott** Shrops	
83 G3	**Aston Rogers** Shrops	
58 B7	**Aston Rowant** Oxon	
71 J6	**Aston Somerville** Worcs	
71 K6	**Aston Subedge** Gloucs	
41 K3	**Aston Tirrold** Oxon	
41 K3	**Aston Upthorpe** Oxon	
84 B5	**Aston-Eyre** Shrops	
101 H6	**Aston-upon-Trent** Derbys	
75 J6	**Astwick** Beds	
74 D5	**Astwood** M Keyn	
71 G2	**Astwood** Worcs	
71 J3	**Astwood Bank** Worcs	
103 H4	**Aswarby** Lincs	
118 E7	**Aswardby** Lincs	
83 K2	**Atcham** Shrops	
14 E4	**Athelhampton** Dorset	
78 E1	**Athelington** Suffk	
25 M5	**Athelney** Somset	
178 C3	**Athelstaneford** E Loth	
23 J6	**Atherington** Devon	
86 C4	**Atherstone** Warwks	
72 B4	**Atherstone on Stour** Warwks	
113 G2	**Atherton** Wigan	
100 E3	**Atlow** Derbys	
210 E6	**Attadale** Highld	
117 G3	**Atterby** Lincs	
115 G4	**Attercliffe** Sheff	
86 D4	**Atterton** Leics	
92 C4	**Attleborough** Norfk	
86 D5	**Attleborough** Warwks	
92 D1	**Attlebridge** Norfk	
77 G4	**Attleton Green** Suffk	
126 F1	**Atwick** E R Yk	
39 J7	**Atworth** Wilts	
116 F8	**Aubourn** Lincs	
217 G7	**Auchedly** Abers	
197 H1	**Auchenblae** Abers	
175 L2	**Auchenbowie** Stirlg	
146 D5	**Auchencairn** D & G	
155 G5	**Auchencairn** D & G	
162 D4	**Auchencairn** N Ayrs	
179 H6	**Auchencrow** Border	
177 H6	**Auchendinny** Mdloth	
176 D7	**Auchengray** S Lans	
215 J3	**Auchenhalrig** Moray	
164 F2	**Auchenheath** S Lans	
154 E3	**Auchenhessnane** D & G	
173 G4	**Auchenlochan** Ag & B	
174 C8	**Auchenmade** N Ayrs	
144 F4	**Auchenmalg** D & G	
174 C8	**Auchentiber** N Ayrs	
184 C8	**Auchentroig** Stirlg	
221 G5	**Auchindrean** Highld	
216 C5	**Auchininna** Abers	
164 B5	**Auchinleck** E Ayrs	
175 H4	**Auchinloch** N Lans	
175 J3	**Auchinstarry** N Lans	
191 L2	**Auchintore** Highld	
217 K6	**Auchiries** Abers	
207 G6	**Auchlee** Abers	
206 C1	**Auchleven** Abers	
164 F2	**Auchlochan** S Lans	
206 B5	**Auchlossan** Abers	
184 B2	**Auchlyne** Stirlg	
164 A4	**Auchmillan** E Ayrs	
197 G7	**Auchmithie** Angus	
186 C6	**Auchmuirbridge** Fife	
196 D4	**Auchnacree** Angus	
217 H4	**Auchnagatt** Abers	
204 F2	**Auchnarrow** Moray	
144 B3	**Auchnotteroch** D & G	
215 H4	**Auchroisk** Moray	
185 K5	**Auchterarder** P & K	
202 R4	**Auchteraw** Highld	
203 L2	**Auchterblair** Highld	
219 J6	**Auchtercairn** Highld	
186 C7	**Auchterderran** Fife	
196 B8	**Auchterhouse** Angus	
216 D6	**Auchterless** Abers	
186 D5	**Auchtermuchty** Fife	
212 D3	**Auchterneed** Highld	
177 H1	**Auchtertool** Fife	
210 C8	**Auchtertyre** Highld	
184 C4	**Auchtubh** Stirlg	
231 L3	**Auckengill** Highld	
115 M2	**Auckley** Donc	
113 K3	**Audenshaw** Tamesd	
98 F4	**Audlem** Ches	
99 J3	**Audley** Staffs	
76 D6	**Audley End** Essex	
76 D6	**Audley End** Essex	
77 J4	**Audley End** Suffk	
148 A7	**Aughertree** Cumb	
125 G3	**Aughton** E R Yk	
111 L1	**Aughton** Lancs	
129 L6	**Aughton** Lancs	
115 J4	**Aughton** Rothm	
28 E1	**Aughton** Wilts	
112 B1	**Aughton Park** Lancs	
213 L4	**Auldearn** Highld	
69 J4	**Aulden** Herefs	
154 F5	**Auldgirth** D & G	
175 H7	**Auldhouse** S Lans	
200 E2	**Ault a' chruinn** Highld	
115 J7	**Ault Hucknall** Derbys	
219 K4	**Aultbea** Highld	
219 H4	**Aultgrishin** Highld	
221 J7	**Aultguish Inn** Highld	
215 J4	**Aultmore** Moray	
202 E2	**Aultnagoire** Highld	
222 F5	**Aultnamain Inn** Highld	
103 H5	**Aunsby** Lincs	
38 E3	**Aust** S Glos	
116 A3	**Austerfield** Donc	
86 C3	**Austrey** Warwks	
130 E5	**Austwick** N York	
118 E5	**Authorpe** Lincs	
40 C6	**Avebury** Wilts	
45 L4	**Aveley** Thurr	
39 K2	**Avening** Gloucs	
102 C2	**Averham** Notts	
7 G6	**Aveton Gifford** Devon	
203 L3	**Aviemore** Highld	
41 G6	**Avington** W Berk	
213 G4	**Avoch** Highld	
15 L3	**Avon** Dorset	
72 E4	**Avon Dassett** Warwks	
176 B4	**Avonbridge** Falk	
38 D5	**Avonmouth** Bristl	
7 G4	**Avonwick** Devon	
28 F6	**Awbridge** Hants	
12 E3	**Awliscombe** Devon	
55 G6	**Awre** Gloucs	
101 J4	**Awsworth** Notts	
26 B1	**Axbridge** Somset	
29 L3	**Axford** Hants	
40 E6	**Axford** Wilts	
13 H3	**Axminster** Devon	
13 G4	**Axmouth** Devon	
141 G3	**Aycliffe** Dur	
150 C2	**Aydon** Nthumb	
54 E7	**Aylburton** Gloucs	
12 D4	**Aylesbeare** Devon	
58 D5	**Aylesbury** Bucks	
126 F8	**Aylesby** NE Lin	
33 J2	**Aylesford** Kent	
35 H4	**Aylesham** Kent	
87 H4	**Aylestone** C Leic	
106 E4	**Aylmerton** Norfk	
106 E6	**Aylsham** Norfk	
70 B6	**Aylton** Gloucs	
56 C4	**Aylworth** Gloucs	
69 H2	**Aymestrey** Herefs	
57 K2	**Aynho** Nhants	
59 K5	**Ayot St Lawrence** Herts	
163 J5	**Ayr** S Ayrs	
131 J2	**Aysgarth** N York	
25 G7	**Ayshford** Devon	
129 J3	**Ayside** Cumb	
88 C4	**Ayston** Rutlnd	
60 F5	**Aythorpe Roding** Essex	
179 J6	**Ayton** Border	
132 C5	**Azerley** N York	

B

7 L3	**Babbacombe** Torbay	
60 C5	**Babbs Green** Herts	
26 E5	**Babcary** Somset	
27 G2	**Babington** Somset	
76 D4	**Babraham** Cambs	
116 B5	**Babworth** Notts	
199 K7	**Back of Keppoch** Highld	
234 d4	**Backaland** Ork	
217 J4	**Backfolds** Abers	
111 L6	**Backford** Ches	
223 H2	**Backies** Highld	
231 H5	**Backlass** Highld	
38 C6	**Backwell** N Som	
106 D5	**Baconsthorpe** Norfk	
54 A2	**Bacton** Herefs	
107 H5	**Bacton** Norfk	
78 C2	**Bacton** Suffk	
122 C6	**Bacup** Lancs	
219 J6	**Badachro** Highld	
40 D4	**Badbury** Swindn	
73 H3	**Badby** Nhants	
228 B7	**Badcall** Highld	
228 C4	**Badcall** Highld	
220 D3	**Badcaul** Highld	
86 B8	**Baddesley Clinton** Warwks	
86 C4	**Baddesley Ensor** Warwks	
224 D4	**Baddidarrach** Highld	
176 F7	**Baddinsgill** Border	
216 D6	**Badenscoth** Abers	
205 H2	**Badenyon** Abers	
84 D4	**Badger** Shrops	
55 K4	**Badgeworth** Gloucs	
26 B2	**Badgworth** Somset	
210 B8	**Badicaul** Highld	
79 G2	**Badingham** Suffk	
34 D4	**Badlesmere** Kent	
165 K5	**Badlieu** Border	
231 J5	**Badlipster** Highld	
220 C3	**Badluachrach** Highld	
223 G3	**Badninish** Highld	
220 D3	**Badrallach** Highld	
71 J5	**Badsey** Worcs	
30 E2	**Badshot Lea** Surrey	
124 C7	**Badsworth** Wakefd	
78 B2	**Badwell Ash** Suffk	
118 E6	**Bag Enderby** Lincs	
27 H8	**Bagber** Dorset	
133 G4	**Bagby** N York	
233 b9	**Bagh a Chaisteil** W Isls	
233 b9	**Bagh a Tuath** W Isls	
111 H6	**Bagillt** Flints	
86 D8	**Baginton** Warwks	
51 L6	**Baglan** Neath	
98 B6	**Bagley** Shrops	
26 C3	**Bagley** Somset	
30 A3	**Bagmore** Hants	
99 L3	**Bagnall** Staffs	
83 L8	**Bagot** Shrops	
42 E7	**Bagshot** Surrey	
39 G3	**Bagstone** S Glos	
86 F2	**Bagworth** Leics	
54 C3	**Bagwy Llydiart** Herefs	
123 H3	**Baildon** Brad	
123 H3	**Baildon Green** Brad	
233 b6	**Baile a Mhanaich** W Isls	
232 f3	**Baile Ailein** W Isls	
180 D3	**Baile Mor** Ag & B	
175 J3	**Baillieston** C Glas	
131 H2	**Bainbridge** N York	
216 B7	**Bainshole** Abers	
89 C3	**Bainton** C Pete	
126 B1	**Bainton** E R Yk	
186 F6	**Baintown** Fife	
167 K6	**Bairnkine** Border	
114 E7	**Bakewell** Derbys	
96 E5	**Bala** Gwynd	
232 f3	**Balallan** W Isls	
212 C7	**Balbeg** Highld	
186 C2	**Balbeggie** P & K	
212 D5	**Balblair** Highld	
213 G2	**Balblair** Highld	
115 K2	**Balby** Donc	
146 E5	**Balcary** D & G	
212 E5	**Balchraggan** Highld	
228 B4	**Balchreick** Highld	
32 B6	**Balcombe** W Susx	
187 K5	**Balcomie Links** Fife	
132 E4	**Baldersby** N York	
132 E4	**Baldersby St James** N York	
121 J4	**Balderstone** Lancs	
102 D3	**Balderton** Notts	
187 G5	**Baldinnie** Fife	
185 L4	**Baldinnies** P & K	
75 J7	**Baldock** Herts	
122 C6	**Baldovie** C Dund	
237 d5	**Baldrine** IOM	
20 F3	**Baldslow** E Susx	
106 B5	**Bale** Norfk	
186 D2	**Baledgarno** P & K	
188 C7	**Balemartine** Ag & B	
177 G5	**Balerno** C Edin	
186 D6	**Balfarg** Fife	
196 E3	**Balfield** Angus	
234 c5	**Balfour** Ork	
174 F1	**Balfron** Stirlg	
216 C6	**Balgaveny** Abers	
196 E6	**Balgavies** Angus	
185 L8	**Balgonar** Fife	
144 D6	**Balgowan** D & G	
202 F6	**Balgowan** Highld	
218 B7	**Balgown** Highld	
144 B3	**Balgracie** D & G	
196 C8	**Balgray** Angus	
165 H5	**Balgray** S Lans	
44 F5	**Balham** Gt Lon	
195 L6	**Balhary** P & K	
186 B1	**Balholmie** P & K	
230 C3	**Baligill** Highld	
195 L5	**Balintore** Angus	

223 J6 **Balintore** Highld
223 G7 **Balintraid** Highld
233 b6 **Balivanich** W Isls
133 G4 **Balk** N York
196 B7 **Balkeerie** Angus
125 J5 **Balkholme** E R Yk
191 L5 **Ballachulish** Highld
173 H6 **Ballanlay** Ag & B
152 C5 **Ballantrae** S Ayrs
237 b6 **Ballasalla** IOM
205 A6 **Ballater** Abers
237 c3 **Ballaugh** IOM
223 G6 **Ballchraggan** Highld
178 B3 **Ballencrieff** E Loth
188 B6 **Ballevullin** Ag & B
100 D2 **Ballidon** Derbys
161 L2 **Balliekine** N Ayrs
182 F7 **Balliemore** Ag & B
152 F4 **Balligmorrie** S Ayrs
172 F2 **Ballimore** Ag & B
184 C4 **Ballimore** Stirlg
214 E6 **Ballindalloch** Moray
186 D2 **Ballindean** P & K
58 E7 **Ballinger Common** Bucks
54 E2 **Ballingham** Herefs
186 C7 **Ballingry** Fife
194 F6 **Ballinluig** P & K
196 C5 **Ballinshoe** Angus
195 H5 **Ballintuim** P & K
213 H5 **Balloch** Highld
175 K4 **Balloch** N Lans
185 H4 **Balloch** P & K
153 G3 **Balloch** S Ayrs
174 D3 **Balloch** W Duns
206 B6 **Ballogie** Abers
31 G6 **Balls Cross** W Susx
32 E6 **Balls Green** E Susx
189 K7 **Ballygown** Ag & B
171 G5 **Ballygrant** Ag & B
188 F5 **Ballyhaugh** Ag & B
174 B2 **Ballymenoch** Ag & B
210 C8 **Balmacara** Highld
154 B6 **Balmaclellan** D & G
146 C6 **Balmae** D & G
174 D1 **Balmaha** Stirlg
186 E5 **Balmalcolm** Fife
146 B5 **Balmangan** D & G
207 H2 **Balmedie** Abers
186 F3 **Balmerino** Fife
162 B3 **Balmichael** N Ayrs
205 G6 **Balmoral Castle Grounds** Abers
175 G4 **Balmore** E Duns
223 J5 **Balmuchy** Highld
196 F6 **Balmuir** Angus
177 G2 **Balmule** Fife
187 G4 **Balmullo** Fife
226 E6 **Balnacoil Lodge** Highld
210 F5 **Balnacra** Highld
205 G6 **Balnacroft** Abers
213 G7 **Balnafoich** Highld
194 E6 **Balnaguard** P & K
180 F1 **Balnahard** Ag & B
180 F7 **Balnahard** Ag & B
212 C7 **Balnain** Highld
228 F2 **Balnakeil** Highld
223 H7 **Balnapaling** Highld
185 L1 **Balquharn** P & K
184 C3 **Balquhidder** Stirlg
86 B7 **Balsall Common** Solhll
85 J6 **Balsall Heath** Birm
72 E6 **Balscote** Oxon
76 E4 **Balsham** Cambs
235 e1 **Baltasound** Shet
235 e1 **Baltasound Airport** Shet
145 J3 **Baltersan** D & G
26 D4 **Baltonsborough** Somset
195 G4 **Balvarran** P & K

181 M4 **Balvicar** Ag & B
200 C3 **Balvraid** Highld
213 K7 **Balvraid** Highld
121 H5 **Bamber Bridge** Lancs
60 F4 **Bamber's Green** Essex
169 H3 **Bamburgh** Nthumb
169 H3 **Bamburgh Castle** Nthumb
195 K6 **Bamff** P & K
114 E5 **Bamford** Derbys
138 D4 **Bampton** Cumb
24 E6 **Bampton** Devon
56 F7 **Bampton** Oxon
138 D4 **Bampton Grange** Cumb
191 L2 **Banavie** Highld
72 F6 **Banbury** Oxon
50 F3 **Bancffosfelen** Carmth
206 D6 **Banchory** Abers
207 G5 **Banchory-Devenick** Abers
50 E3 **Bancycapel** Carmth
50 D2 **Bancyfelin** Carmth
186 C2 **Bandirran** P & K
216 D2 **Banff** Abers
109 H6 **Bangor** Gwynd
98 B4 **Bangor-is-y-coed** Wrexhm
9 G5 **Bangors** Cnwll
92 C6 **Banham** Norfk
16 C2 **Bank** Hants
147 H2 **Bankend** D & G
185 M1 **Bankfoot** P & K
164 C6 **Bankglen** E Ayrs
207 G4 **Bankhead** C Aber
165 J1 **Bankhead** S Lans
175 K3 **Banknock** Falk
120 E6 **Banks** Lancs
155 L5 **Bankshill** D & G
106 F6 **Banningham** Norfk
61 H4 **Bannister Green** Essex
175 L1 **Bannockburn** Stirlg
44 E7 **Banstead** Surrey
6 F6 **Bantham** Devon
175 K3 **Banton** N Lans
38 B8 **Banwell** N Som
34 C3 **Bapchild** Kent
27 M4 **Bapton** Wilts
75 L2 **Bar Hill** Cambs
232 f1 **Barabhas** W Isls
163 J3 **Barassie** S Ayrs
223 G6 **Barbaraville** Highld
163 K5 **Barbieston** S Ayrs
130 C3 **Barbon** Cumb
23 L2 **Barbrook** Devon
73 G1 **Barby** Nhants
191 J7 **Barcaldine** Ag & B
72 C6 **Barcheston** Warwks
19 L3 **Barcombe** E Susx
19 L3 **Barcombe Cross** E Susx
131 L2 **Barden** N York
33 G4 **Barden Park** Kent
61 G2 **Bardfield End Green** Essex
61 G3 **Bardfield Saling** Essex
117 J7 **Bardney** Lincs
86 F2 **Bardon** Leics
149 K3 **Bardon Mill** Nthumb
175 G4 **Bardowie** E Duns
174 C4 **Bardrainney** Inver
129 G5 **Bardsea** Cumb
124 B2 **Bardsey** Leeds
91 L8 **Bardwell** Suffk
129 K6 **Bare** Lancs
69 H4 **Barewood** Herefs
145 G2 **Barfad** D & G
92 D3 **Barford** Norfk

72 C3 **Barford** Warwks
57 H2 **Barford St John** Oxon
28 B5 **Barford St Martin** Wilts
57 H2 **Barford St Michael** Oxon
35 H5 **Barfrestone** Kent
175 J5 **Bargeddie** N Lans
53 J7 **Bargoed** Caerph
153 H6 **Bargrennan** D & G
89 G7 **Barham** Cambs
35 G5 **Barham** Kent
78 D4 **Barham** Suffk
88 F2 **Barholm** Lincs
87 J2 **Barkby** Leics
87 J2 **Barkby Thorpe** Leics
102 C5 **Barkestone-le-Vale** Leics
42 C6 **Barkham** Wokham
45 H3 **Barking** Gt Lon
78 C4 **Barking** Suffk
78 C4 **Barking Tye** Suffk
45 H3 **Barkingside** Gt Lon
122 F6 **Barkisland** Calder
3 J2 **Barkla Shop** Cnwll
102 F4 **Barkston** Lincs
124 D4 **Barkston Ash** N York
75 L7 **Barkway** Herts
175 H5 **Barlanark** C Glas
99 K5 **Barlaston** Staffs
18 C3 **Barlavington** W Susx
115 J6 **Barlborough** Derbys
124 F4 **Barlby** N York
86 E3 **Barlestone** Leics
76 B6 **Barley** Herts
122 B3 **Barley** Lancs
88 B2 **Barleythorpe** Rutlnd
46 F3 **Barling** Essex
117 H6 **Barlings** Lincs
146 E4 **Barlochan** D & G
115 G6 **Barlow** Derbys
150 E3 **Barlow** Gatesd
124 F5 **Barlow** N York
125 J2 **Barmby Moor** E R Yk
125 G5 **Barmby on the Marsh** E R Yk
161 K1 **Barmollack** Ag & B
80 E1 **Barmouth** Gwynd
141 H4 **Barmpton** Darltn
135 J7 **Barmston** E R Yk
182 E8 **Barnacarry** Ag & B
88 F3 **Barnack** C Pete
140 D4 **Barnard Castle** Dur
57 H6 **Barnard Gate** Oxon
77 G5 **Barnardiston** Suffk
146 E4 **Barnbarroch** D & G
115 J2 **Barnburgh** Donc
93 K5 **Barnby** Suffk
124 F8 **Barnby Dun** Donc
102 E3 **Barnby in the Willows** Notts
116 A5 **Barnby Moor** Notts
144 D7 **Barncorkrie** D & G
44 E5 **Barnes** Gt Lon
33 H4 **Barnes Street** Kent
44 E2 **Barnet** Gt Lon
126 C8 **Barnetby le Wold** N Linc
106 B6 **Barney** Norfk
91 K7 **Barnham** Suffk
18 C5 **Barnham** W Susx
92 C3 **Barnham Broom** Norfk
197 G6 **Barnhead** Angus
187 H2 **Barnhill** C Dund
214 E3 **Barnhill** Moray
152 B7 **Barnhills** D & G
140 D5 **Barningham** Dur
91 L7 **Barningham** Suffk
118 C2 **Barnoldby le Beck** NE Lin
122 C2 **Barnoldswick** Lancs

31 J6 **Barns Green** W Susx
115 G1 **Barnsley** Barns
56 B6 **Barnsley** Gloucs
23 J5 **Barnstaple** Devon
61 G4 **Barnston** Essex
111 J5 **Barnston** Wirral
102 B5 **Barnstone** Notts
85 H8 **Barnt Green** Worcs
177 G4 **Barnton** C Edin
112 F6 **Barnton** Ches
88 F6 **Barnwell All Saints** Nhants
88 F6 **Barnwell St Andrew** Nhants
55 K4 **Barnwood** Gloucs
153 G4 **Barr** S Ayrs
233 b9 **Barra Airport** W Isls
145 H5 **Barrachan** D & G
188 B7 **Barrapoll** Ag & B
158 A7 **Barrasford** Nthumb
174 H4 **Barrhead** E Rens
152 F5 **Barrhill** S Ayrs
76 B5 **Barrington** Cambs
26 B7 **Barrington** Somset
3 H4 **Barripper** Cnwll
174 C7 **Barrmill** N Ayrs
182 B3 **Barrnacarry Bay** Ag & B
231 J2 **Barrock** Highld
55 K3 **Barrow** Gloucs
121 L3 **Barrow** Lancs
88 C1 **Barrow** Rutlnd
27 G5 **Barrow** Somset
77 H2 **Barrow** Suffk
168 C7 **Barrow Burn** Nthumb
38 D6 **Barrow Gurney** N Som
126 D6 **Barrow Haven** N Linc
128 E5 **Barrow Island** Cumb
101 L8 **Barrow upon Soar** Leics
101 G6 **Barrow upon Trent** Derbys
128 E5 **Barrow-in-Furness** Cumb
126 D6 **Barrow-upon-Humber** N Linc
102 E5 **Barrowby** Lincs
88 D4 **Barrowden** Rutlnd
122 C3 **Barrowford** Lancs
187 J1 **Barry** Angus
37 H6 **Barry** V Glam
87 K2 **Barsby** Leics
93 H5 **Barsham** Suffk
86 B7 **Barston** Solhll
69 L6 **Bartestree** Herefs
216 F7 **Barthol Chapel** Abers
61 H4 **Bartholomew Green** Essex
99 H3 **Barthomley** Ches
28 F8 **Bartley** Hants
85 H6 **Bartley Green** Birm
76 E5 **Bartlow** Cambs
76 B4 **Barton** Cambs
98 C2 **Barton** Ches
56 C3 **Barton** Gloucs
120 E8 **Barton** Lancs
121 G3 **Barton** Lancs
141 G5 **Barton** N York
57 K6 **Barton** Oxon
7 K3 **Barton** Torbay
91 G3 **Barton Bendish** Norfk
39 J2 **Barton End** Gloucs
57 M2 **Barton Hartshorn** Bucks
101 K6 **Barton in Fabis** Notts
86 E3 **Barton in the Beans** Leics
91 G8 **Barton Mills** Suffk

88 C7 **Barton Seagrave**
Nhants
26 D5 **Barton St David**
Somset
29 H3 **Barton Stacey** Hants
23 L4 **Barton Town** Devon
126 C6 **Barton Waterside**
N Linc
59 H2 **Barton-le-Clay** Beds
133 L5 **Barton-le-Street**
N York
133 L6 **Barton-le-Willows**
N York
16 B4 **Barton-on-Sea** Hants
56 E2 **Barton-on-the-**
Heath Warwks
100 D8 **Barton-under-**
Needwood Staffs
126 C6 **Barton-upon-**
Humber N Linc
232 f1 **Barvas** W Isls
90 D7 **Barway** Cambs
86 F4 **Barwell** Leics
10 E4 **Barwick** Devon
26 E8 **Barwick** Somset
124 B3 **Barwick in Elmet**
Leeds
98 B7 **Baschurch** Shrops
72 E2 **Bascote** Warwks
121 K2 **Bashall Eaves** Lancs
46 B3 **Basildon** Essex
29 M2 **Basingstoke** Hants
114 E6 **Baslow** Derbys
25 M3 **Bason Bridge**
Somset
37 L3 **Bassaleg** Newpt
167 K1 **Bassendean** Border
137 H2 **Bassenthwaite** Cumb
29 H7 **Bassett** C Sotn
75 K5 **Bassingbourn** Cambs
102 E1 **Bassingham** Lincs
102 F6 **Bassingthorpe** Lincs
60 A3 **Bassus Green** Herts
89 G2 **Baston** Lincs
107 J8 **Bastwick** Norfk
43 H2 **Batchworth** Herts
14 C2 **Batcombe** Dorset
27 G4 **Batcombe** Somset
59 J5 **Batford** Herts
39 H7 **Bath** BaNES
62 F2 **Bath Side** Essex
39 H6 **Bathampton** BaNES
25 G6 **Bathealton** Somset
39 H6 **Batheaston** BaNES
39 H6 **Bathford** BaNES
176 D5 **Bathgate** W Loth
102 C2 **Bathley** Notts
5 L2 **Bathpool** Cnwll
25 K6 **Bathpool** Somset
176 C5 **Bathville** W Loth
26 E2 **Bathway** Somset
123 J5 **Batley** Kirk
71 L7 **Batsford** Gloucs
142 D5 **Battersby** N York
44 F5 **Battersea** Gt Lon
78 B4 **Battisford Tye** Suffk
20 F3 **Battle** E Susx
52 F2 **Battle** Powys
103 L2 **Battle of Britain**
Memorial Flight
Lincs
196 D5 **Battledykes** Angus
46 C2 **Battlesbridge** Essex
24 E6 **Battleton** Somset
70 F6 **Baughton** Worcs
41 J7 **Baughurst** Hants
206 B6 **Baulds** Abers
40 F3 **Baulking** Oxon
117 L6 **Baumber** Lincs
56 A6 **Baunton** Gloucs
28 B5 **Baverstock** Wilts
92 D2 **Bawburgh** Norfk
106 C7 **Bawdeswell** Norfk

25 M4 **Bawdrip** Somset
79 H6 **Bawdsey** Suffk
115 M3 **Bawtry** Donc
122 B5 **Baxenden** Lancs
86 C4 **Baxterley** Warwks
208 D4 **Bay** Highld
232 g2 **Bayble** W Isls
29 K6 **Baybridge** Hants
129 G5 **Baycliff** Cumb
40 F5 **Baydon** Wilts
60 A6 **Bayford** Herts
27 G5 **Bayford** Somset
233 b6 **Bayhead** W Isls
78 D4 **Baylham** Suffk
54 E3 **Baysham** Herefs
83 J2 **Bayston Hill** Shrops
77 G6 **Baythorne End**
Essex
84 C8 **Bayton** Worcs
57 J7 **Bayworth** Oxon
73 L6 **Beachampton** Bucks
91 H3 **Beachamwell** Norfk
20 C6 **Beachy Head** E Susx
12 F2 **Beacon** Devon
62 A3 **Beacon End** Essex
42 C2 **Beacon's Bottom**
Bucks
42 F3 **Beaconsfield** Bucks
133 K3 **Beadlam** N York
75 G6 **Beadlow** Beds
169 J4 **Beadnell** Nthumb
10 E2 **Beaford** Devon
124 E5 **Beal** N York
169 G2 **Beal** Nthumb
6 A1 **Bealsmill** Cnwll
13 L3 **Beaminster** Dorset
150 F4 **Beamish** Dur
131 K8 **Beamsley** N York
39 K7 **Beanacre** Wilts
169 G5 **Beanley** Nthumb
10 D7 **Beardon** Devon
12 C3 **Beare** Devon
31 K3 **Beare Green** Surrey
71 L3 **Bearley** Warwks
151 G6 **Bearpark** Dur
174 F4 **Bearsden** E Duns
33 K3 **Bearsted** Kent
99 G5 **Bearstone** Shrops
85 H6 **Bearwood** Birm
15 K3 **Bearwood** Poole
155 J2 **Beattock** D & G
60 F6 **Beauchamp Roding**
Essex
53 J5 **Beaufort** Blae G
16 E3 **Beaulieu** Hants
16 E2 **Beaulieu House**
Hants
212 E5 **Beauly** Highld
109 H6 **Beaumaris** IOA
148 C3 **Beaumont** Cumb
62 E3 **Beaumont** Essex
236 c7 **Beaumont** Jersey
72 B1 **Beausale** Warwks
29 L6 **Beauworth** Hants
34 D6 **Beaver Green** Kent
10 C5 **Beaworthy** Devon
61 H3 **Beazley End** Essex
111 K5 **Bebington** Wirral
93 J5 **Beccles** Suffk
120 F6 **Becconsall** Lancs
91 G7 **Beck Row** Suffk
128 F3 **Beck Side** Cumb
84 D3 **Beckbury** Shrops
45 G6 **Beckenham** Gt Lon
117 J5 **Beckering** Lincs
136 E6 **Beckermet** Cumb
147 J5 **Beckfoot** Cumb
71 H7 **Beckford** Worcs
40 C6 **Beckhampton** Wilts
102 C2 **Beckingham** Lincs
116 C4 **Beckingham** Notts
27 J2 **Beckington** Somset
83 H7 **Beckjay** Shrops

21 G2 **Beckley** E Susx
57 K5 **Beckley** Oxon
45 H4 **Beckton** Gt Lon
132 D8 **Beckwithshaw**
N York
45 J3 **Becontree** Gt Lon
236 c6 **Becquet Vincent**
Jersey
132 D2 **Bedale** N York
27 J7 **Bedchester** Dorset
37 G4 **Beddau** Rhondd
95 K3 **Beddgelert** Gwynd
19 L4 **Beddingham** E Susx
44 F6 **Beddington** Gt Lon
44 F6 **Beddington Corner**
Gt Lon
78 F2 **Bedfield** Suffk
74 F5 **Bedford** Beds
17 K2 **Bedhampton** Hants
78 E2 **Bedingfield** Suffk
78 E2 **Bedingfield Street**
Suffk
132 D7 **Bedlam** N York
34 B5 **Bedlam Lane** Kent
159 G5 **Bedlington** Nthumb
53 H7 **Bedlinog** Myr Td
38 E6 **Bedminster** Bristl
38 E6 **Bedminster Down**
Bristl
59 J7 **Bedmond** Herts
99 L8 **Bednall** Staffs
167 J5 **Bedrule** Border
83 G7 **Bedstone** Shrops
37 J3 **Bedwas** Caerph
53 J7 **Bedwellty** Caerph
86 D6 **Bedworth** Warwks
87 J2 **Beeby** Leics
30 B4 **Beech** Hants
99 J5 **Beech** Staffs
42 B7 **Beech Hill** W Berk
40 C8 **Beechingstoke** Wilts
41 J5 **Beedon** W Berk
41 J5 **Beedon Hill** W Berk
135 H8 **Beeford** E R Yk
114 E7 **Beeley** Derbys
117 K2 **Beelsby** NE Lin
41 L6 **Beenham** W Berk
13 G5 **Beer** Devon
26 B5 **Beer** Somset
14 B1 **Beer Hackett** Dorset
25 L7 **Beercrocombe**
Somset
7 J7 **Beesands** Devon
118 F5 **Beesby** Lincs
7 J7 **Beeson** Devon
75 H5 **Beeston** Beds
98 D2 **Beeston** Ches
123 K4 **Beeston** Leeds
91 K1 **Beeston** Norfk
101 K5 **Beeston** Notts
106 E4 **Beeston Regis** Norfk
146 F2 **Beeswing** D & G
129 K4 **Beetham** Cumb
25 L8 **Beetham** Somset
106 A8 **Beetley** Norfk
57 J5 **Begbroke** Oxon
49 J6 **Begelly** Pembks
82 D7 **Beguildy** Powys
93 H2 **Beighton** Norfk
115 H5 **Beighton** Sheff
100 F3 **Beighton Hill** Derbys
186 B5 **Bein Inn** P & K
174 C7 **Beith** N Ayrs
35 G4 **Bekesbourne** Kent
107 G8 **Belaugh** Norfk
85 G7 **Belbroughton** Worcs
14 E1 **Belchalwell** Dorset
14 F1 **Belchalwell Street**
Dorset
77 J6 **Belchamp Otten**
Essex
77 H6 **Belchamp St Paul**
Essex

77 J6 **Belchamp Walter**
Essex
118 D6 **Belchford** Lincs
169 G3 **Belford** Nthumb
87 H3 **Belgrave** C Leic
178 E3 **Belhaven** E Loth
207 H2 **Belhelvie** Abers
215 K8 **Belhinnie** Abers
131 G7 **Bell Busk** N York
85 G7 **Bell End** Worcs
98 D4 **Bell o' th' Hill** Ches
205 H3 **Bellabeg** Abers
182 A8 **Bellanoch** Ag & B
195 K4 **Bellaty** Angus
148 C4 **Belle Vue** Cumb
123 L6 **Belle Vue** Wakefd
118 E5 **Belleau** Lincs
131 L2 **Bellerby** N York
164 F3 **Bellfield** S Lans
165 J5 **Bellfield** S Lans
58 F6 **Bellingdon** Bucks
157 L5 **Bellingham** Nthumb
161 H2 **Belloch** Ag & B
161 H3 **Bellochantuy** Ag & B
33 G6 **Bells Yew Green**
E Susx
175 J6 **Bellshill** N Lans
175 L6 **Bellside** N Lans
176 E5 **Bellsquarry** W Loth
38 E7 **Belluton** BaNES
121 K7 **Belmont** Bl w D
44 E7 **Belmont** Gt Lon
163 J5 **Belmont** S Ayrs
235 d2 **Belmont** Shet
205 J3 **Belnacraig** Abers
101 G3 **Belper** Derbys
101 G3 **Belper Lane End**
Derbys
158 D6 **Belsay** Nthumb
167 J4 **Belses** Border
7 H4 **Belsford** Devon
59 G7 **Belsize** Herts
78 D6 **Belstead** Suffk
10 F6 **Belstone** Devon
121 L5 **Belthorn** Lancs
47 K6 **Beltinge** Kent
149 K3 **Beltingham** Nthumb
116 D1 **Beltoft** N Linc
101 H7 **Belton** Leics
102 F4 **Belton** Lincs
116 C1 **Belton** N Linc
93 K3 **Belton** Norfk
88 B3 **Belton** Rutlnd
45 J4 **Belvedere** Gt Lon
102 D5 **Belvoir** Leics
102 D5 **Belvoir Castle** Leics
17 J5 **Bembridge** IOW
28 C5 **Bemerton** Wilts
135 J5 **Bempton** E R Yk
192 B3 **Ben Nevis** Highld
123 H2 **Ben Rhydding** Brad
93 K6 **Benacre** Suffk
233 c6 **Benbecula Airport**
W Isls
154 C3 **Benbuie** D & G
191 H8 **Benderloch** Ag & B
33 K6 **Benenden** Kent
150 D4 **Benfieldside** Dur
71 J3 **Bengeworth** Worcs
79 H3 **Benhall Green** Suffk
79 H3 **Benhall Street** Suffk
197 K3 **Benholm** Abers
133 H7 **Beningbrough**
N York
59 M4 **Benington** Herts
104 C3 **Benington** Lincs
109 G5 **Benllech** IOA
173 K2 **Benmore** Ag & B
9 H6 **Bennacott** Cnwll
162 C5 **Bennan** N Ayrs
117 K5 **Benniworth** Lincs
33 J4 **Benover** Kent
41 L3 **Benson** Oxon

206 F5 **Benthoul** C Aber
115 K1 **Bentley** Donc
126 C4 **Bentley** E R Yk
30 C3 **Bentley** Hants
78 D6 **Bentley** Suffk
86 C4 **Bentley** Warwks
23 K4 **Benton** Devon
156 B4 **Bentpath** D & G
24 B5 **Bentwichen** Devon
30 A4 **Bentworth** Hants
186 E2 **Benvie** Angus
14 A2 **Benville** Dorset
89 L5 **Benwick** Cambs
71 J1 **Beoley** Worcs
199 L6 **Beoraidbeg** Highld
18 B3 **Bepton** W Susx
60 D3 **Berden** Essex
6 C3 **Bere Alston** Devon
6 C3 **Bere Ferrers** Devon
14 F4 **Bere Regis** Dorset
48 D2 **Berea** Pembks
93 G4 **Bergh Apton** Norfk
41 L2 **Berinsfield** Oxon
55 G7 **Berkeley** Gloucs
59 G6 **Berkhamsted** Herts
27 J2 **Berkley** Somset
86 B7 **Berkswell** Solhll
45 G4 **Bermondsey** Gt Lon
200 C2 **Bernera** Highld
183 G8 **Bernice** Ag & B
208 F4 **Bernisdale** Highld
41 L2 **Berrick Prior** Oxon
41 L2 **Berrick Salome** Oxon
227 K4 **Berriedale** Highld
137 L2 **Berrier** Cumb
82 D4 **Berriew** Powys
83 K3 **Berrington** Shrops
69 L2 **Berrington** Worcs
69 L2 **Berrington Green** Worcs
25 L2 **Berrow** Somset
70 D3 **Berrow Green** Worcs
7 J4 **Berry Pomeroy** Devon
215 L4 **Berryhillock** Moray
215 L3 **Berryhillock** Moray
23 J3 **Berrynarbor** Devon
97 L3 **Bersham** Wrexhm
20 B5 **Berwick** E Susx
40 C5 **Berwick Bassett** Wilts
158 F6 **Berwick Hill** Nthumb
28 B4 **Berwick St James** Wilts
27 L6 **Berwick St John** Wilts
27 L5 **Berwick St Leonard** Wilts
179 K7 **Berwick-upon-Tweed** Nthumb
102 D7 **Bescaby** Leics
120 E7 **Bescar** Lancs
71 G5 **Besford** Worcs
115 L2 **Bessacarr** Donc
57 J7 **Bessels Leigh** Oxon
135 J6 **Bessingby** E R Yk
106 E5 **Bessingham** Norfk
92 C4 **Besthorpe** Norfk
116 D8 **Besthorpe** Notts
101 K3 **Bestwood Village** Notts
126 C2 **Beswick** E R Yk
31 K2 **Betchworth** Surrey
62 C3 **Beth Chatto Garden** Essex
109 G7 **Bethel** Gwynd
108 E7 **Bethel** IOA
34 C6 **Bethersden** Kent
109 J7 **Bethesda** Gwynd
49 J4 **Bethesda** Pembks
51 K1 **Bethlehem** Carmth
45 G4 **Bethnal Green** Gt Lon
99 H3 **Betley** Staffs

45 L5 **Betsham** Kent
35 J4 **Betteshanger** Kent
13 K3 **Bettiscombe** Dorset
98 C5 **Bettisfield** Wrexhm
37 L3 **Bettws** Newpt
66 D4 **Bettws Bledrws** Cerdgn
82 C4 **Bettws Cedewain** Powys
65 J5 **Bettws Evan** Cerdgn
54 A6 **Bettws-Newydd** Mons
229 L3 **Bettyhill** Highld
36 D3 **Betws** Brdgnd
97 G3 **Betws Gwerfil Goch** Denbgs
96 C2 **Betws-y-coed** Conwy
110 C6 **Betws-yn-Rhos** Conwy
65 J5 **Beulah** Cerdgn
67 K4 **Beulah** Powys
116 B6 **Bevercotes** Notts
126 C3 **Beverley** E R Yk
39 K2 **Beverstone** Gloucs
156 F7 **Bewcastle** Cumb
84 D7 **Bewdley** Worcs
132 B6 **Bewerley** N York
126 E1 **Bewholme** E R Yk
20 E4 **Bexhill** E Susx
45 J5 **Bexley** Gt Lon
45 J5 **Bexleyheath** Gt Lon
90 F3 **Bexwell** Norfk
77 L2 **Beyton** Suffk
77 L2 **Beyton Green** Suffk
232 d2 **Bhaltos** W Isls
233 b10 **Bhatarsaigh** W Isls
56 C6 **Bibury** Gloucs
57 L4 **Bicester** Oxon
85 L6 **Bickenhill** Solhll
103 L5 **Bicker** Lincs
112 C2 **Bickerstaffe** Lancs
124 C1 **Bickerton** N York
84 F2 **Bickford** Staffs
23 H5 **Bickington** Devon
7 J2 **Bickington** Devon
12 B2 **Bickleigh** Devon
6 D4 **Bickleigh** Devon
45 H6 **Bickley** Gt Lon
134 E2 **Bickley** N York
98 D3 **Bickley Moss** Ches
61 J7 **Bicknacre** Essex
25 H4 **Bicknoller** Somset
33 L2 **Bicknor** Kent
83 J1 **Bicton** Shrops
82 F6 **Bicton** Shrops
32 F5 **Bidborough** Kent
33 L5 **Biddenden** Kent
74 E4 **Biddenham** Beds
39 K5 **Biddestone** Wilts
26 B2 **Biddisham** Somset
73 J6 **Biddlesden** Bucks
99 K2 **Biddulph** Staffs
99 K2 **Biddulph Moor** Staffs
23 G6 **Bideford** Devon
71 K4 **Bidford-on-Avon** Warwks
125 J2 **Bielby** E R Yk
207 G5 **Bieldside** C Aber
17 G6 **Bierley** IOW
58 D5 **Bierton** Bucks
145 H6 **Big Balcraig** D & G
154 B3 **Big Carlae** D & G
53 K6 **Big Pit Blaenavon** Torfn
219 H5 **Big Sand** Highld
6 F6 **Bigbury** Devon
6 F6 **Bigbury-on-Sea** Devon
117 H1 **Bigby** Lincs
165 K2 **Biggar** S Lans
100 E3 **Biggin** Derbys
100 D2 **Biggin** Derbys
124 E4 **Biggin** N York

32 D2 **Biggin Hill** Gt Lon
45 H7 **Biggin Hill Airport** Gt Lon
75 H5 **Biggleswade** Beds
156 B6 **Bigholms** D & G
230 C3 **Bighouse** Highld
29 L4 **Bighton** Hants
148 A4 **Biglands** Cumb
18 D3 **Bignor** W Susx
136 D5 **Bigrigg** Cumb
101 K4 **Bilborough** C Nott
25 G3 **Bilbrook** Somset
124 E2 **Bilbrough** N York
231 K5 **Bilbster** Highld
140 F3 **Bildershaw** Dur
78 B5 **Bildeston** Suffk
46 B2 **Billericay** Essex
87 K3 **Billesdon** Leics
71 K3 **Billesley** Warwks
103 J5 **Billingborough** Lincs
112 D2 **Billinge** St Hel
106 B7 **Billingford** Norfk
92 E7 **Billingford** Norfk
141 K3 **Billingham** S on T
103 J2 **Billinghay** Lincs
115 H1 **Billingley** Barns
31 H6 **Billingshurst** W Susx
84 C6 **Billingsley** Shrops
58 F4 **Billington** Beds
121 L4 **Billington** Lancs
93 J2 **Billockby** Norfk
150 E7 **Billy Row** Dur
121 G3 **Bilsborrow** Lancs
119 G6 **Bilsby** Lincs
18 D5 **Bilsham** W Susx
34 D7 **Bilsington** Kent
101 M1 **Bilsthorpe** Notts
177 H5 **Bilston** Mdloth
85 G4 **Bilston** Wolves
86 D3 **Bilstone** Leics
126 E4 **Bilton** E R Yk
124 D1 **Bilton** N York
132 D7 **Bilton** N York
86 F8 **Bilton** Warwks
117 K3 **Binbrook** Lincs
14 D5 **Bincombe** Dorset
26 E2 **Binegar** Somset
42 D6 **Binfield** Br For
42 C5 **Binfield Heath** Oxon
158 B7 **Bingfield** Nthumb
102 B4 **Bingham** Notts
14 E3 **Bingham's Melcombe** Dorset
123 G3 **Bingley** Brad
106 B5 **Binham** Norfk
86 E7 **Binley** Covtry
29 H2 **Binley** Hants
15 G5 **Binnegar** Dorset
176 B4 **Binniehill** Falk
215 H2 **Binns Farm** Moray
30 F3 **Binscombe** Surrey
17 H4 **Binstead** IOW
30 C3 **Binsted** Hants
18 D4 **Binsted** W Susx
71 K4 **Binton** Warwks
106 B7 **Bintree** Norfk
61 M4 **Birch** Essex
100 C6 **Birch Cross** Staffs
61 M4 **Birch Green** Essex
114 A4 **Birch Vale** Derbys
25 K8 **Birch Wood** Somset
105 J2 **Bircham Newton** Norfk
105 J6 **Bircham Tofts** Norfk
60 E4 **Birchanger** Essex
69 J2 **Bircher** Herefs
37 J4 **Birchgrove** Cardif
32 D7 **Birchgrove** E Susx
51 K5 **Birchgrove** Swans
35 J2 **Birchington** Kent
86 C5 **Birchley Heath** Warwks
100 E1 **Birchover** Derbys

112 F4 **Birchwood** Warrtn
115 M3 **Bircotes** Notts
77 G6 **Birdbrook** Essex
133 G4 **Birdforth** N York
17 M3 **Birdham** W Susx
72 E2 **Birdingbury** Warwks
55 L5 **Birdlip** Gloucs
123 J8 **Birds Edge** Kirk
60 F6 **Birds Green** Essex
134 C6 **Birdsall** N York
84 D6 **Birdsgreen** Shrops
13 K3 **Birdsmoorgate** Dorset
115 G2 **Birdwell** Barns
168 B2 **Birgham** Border
223 G3 **Birichin** Highld
141 H6 **Birkby** N York
120 D7 **Birkdale** Sefton
215 L2 **Birkenbog** Abers
111 K4 **Birkenhead** Wirral
216 E5 **Birkenhills** Abers
123 J5 **Birkenshaw** Kirk
205 H6 **Birkhall** Abers
186 F1 **Birkhill** Angus
166 B6 **Birkhill** D & G
124 E5 **Birkin** N York
69 J4 **Birley** Herefs
115 G3 **Birley Carr** Sheff
46 B7 **Birling** Kent
71 G5 **Birlingham** Worcs
85 J6 **Birmingham** Birm
85 L6 **Birmingham Airport** Solhll
195 M2 **Birnam** P & K
217 J7 **Birness** Abers
206 B6 **Birse** Abers
205 L5 **Birsemore** Abers
123 J5 **Birstall** Kirk
87 H2 **Birstall** Leics
132 C7 **Birstwith** N York
151 G4 **Birtley** Gatesd
69 G2 **Birtley** Herefs
157 L6 **Birtley** Nthumb
70 D7 **Birts Street** Worcs
88 C4 **Bisbrooke** Rutlnd
118 C5 **Biscathorpe** Lincs
24 B6 **Bish Mill** Devon
42 D4 **Bisham** W & M
71 H4 **Bishampton** Worcs
140 F2 **Bishop Auckland** Dur
126 B3 **Bishop Burton** E R Yk
141 H2 **Bishop Middleham** Dur
132 E6 **Bishop Monkton** N York
117 G3 **Bishop Norton** Lincs
38 E7 **Bishop Sutton** BaNES
132 D6 **Bishop Thornton** N York
134 C7 **Bishop Wilton** E R Yk
83 G5 **Bishop's Castle** Shrops
27 G8 **Bishop's Caundle** Dorset
55 L3 **Bishop's Cleeve** Gloucs
70 B5 **Bishop's Frome** Herefs
61 G4 **Bishop's Green** Essex
72 E3 **Bishop's Itchington** Warwks
55 J3 **Bishop's Norton** Gloucs
24 B6 **Bishop's Nympton** Devon
99 H6 **Bishop's Offley** Staffs
60 D4 **Bishop's Stortford** Herts
29 L5 **Bishop's Sutton** Hants
72 C3 **Bishop's Tachbrook** Warwks

23 J5 **Bishop's Tawton** Devon
29 K7 **Bishop's Waltham** Hants
84 E2 **Bishop's Wood** Staffs
117 G4 **Bishopbridge** Lincs
175 G4 **Bishopbriggs** E Duns
214 F2 **Bishopmill** Moray
40 B7 **Bishops Cannings** Wilts
25 J6 **Bishops Hull** Somset
25 J5 **Bishops Lydeard** Somset
35 G4 **Bishopsbourne** Kent
7 K2 **Bishopsteignton** Devon
29 J7 **Bishopstoke** Hants
51 H7 **Bishopston** Swans
58 D6 **Bishopstone** Bucks
19 M5 **Bishopstone** E Susx
69 H5 **Bishopstone** Herefs
47 K6 **Bishopstone** Kent
40 E4 **Bishopstone** Swindn
28 B6 **Bishopstone** Wilts
27 K3 **Bishopstrow** Wilts
25 K8 **Bishopswood** Somset
38 E6 **Bishopsworth** Bristl
124 F2 **Bishopthorpe** York
141 J3 **Bishopton** Darltn
174 E4 **Bishopton** Rens
38 B3 **Bishton** Newpt
100 A7 **Bishton** Staffs
55 K6 **Bisley** Gloucs
42 F8 **Bisley** Surrey
3 K3 **Bissoe** Cnwll
15 L3 **Bisterne** Hants
103 G6 **Bitchfield** Lincs
23 J3 **Bittadon** Devon
6 F4 **Bittaford** Devon
83 L7 **Bitterley** Shrops
29 J8 **Bitterne** C Sotn
87 G6 **Bitteswell** Leics
39 G6 **Bitton** S Glos
42 B4 **Bix** Oxon
87 H4 **Blaby** Leics
56 F6 **Black Bourton** Oxon
150 F2 **Black Callerton** N u Ty
192 E5 **Black Corries** Highld
182 D1 **Black Crofts** Ag & B
11 J3 **Black Dog** Devon
61 J4 **Black Notley** Essex
51 J7 **Black Pill** Swans
93 K6 **Black Street** Suffk
10 C4 **Black Torrington** Devon
179 H7 **Blackadder** Border
7 J5 **Blackawton** Devon
12 E1 **Blackborough** Devon
90 F1 **Blackborough End** Norfk
20 B2 **Blackboys** E Susx
101 G3 **Blackbrook** Derbys
99 H5 **Blackbrook** Staffs
206 F3 **Blackburn** Abers
121 K5 **Blackburn** Bl w D
176 D5 **Blackburn** W Loth
164 C7 **Blackcraig** E Ayrs
207 H3 **Blackdog** Abers
13 K2 **Blackdown** Dorset
115 G2 **Blacker Hill** Barns
45 J5 **Blackfen** Gt Lon
16 E3 **Blackfield** Hants
185 J5 **Blackford** P & K
26 B2 **Blackford** Somset
26 F6 **Blackford** Somset
101 G8 **Blackfordby** Leics
177 G4 **Blackhall** C Edin
151 K6 **Blackhall Colliery** Dur
166 F2 **Blackhaugh** Border
45 G5 **Blackheath** Gt Lon

85 H6 **Blackheath** Sandw
93 J8 **Blackheath** Suffk
31 G3 **Blackheath** Surrey
217 J6 **Blackhill** Abers
217 K3 **Blackhill** Abers
217 K5 **Blackhill** Abers
150 D5 **Blackhill** Dur
217 H5 **Blackhill of Clackriach** Abers
12 C4 **Blackhorse** Devon
165 K7 **Blacklaw** D & G
113 J2 **Blackley** Manch
195 J4 **Blacklunans** P & K
69 K6 **Blackmarstone** Herefs
36 E3 **Blackmill** Brdgnd
30 C5 **Blackmoor** Hants
38 C7 **Blackmoor** N Som
123 G7 **Blackmoorfoot** Kirk
60 F7 **Blackmore** Essex
61 H2 **Blackmore End** Essex
176 E3 **Blackness** Falk
30 D3 **Blacknest** Hants
122 C3 **Blacko** Lancs
120 D4 **Blackpool** Bpool
7 K6 **Blackpool** Devon
120 D4 **Blackpool Airport** Lancs
176 B5 **Blackridge** W Loth
121 J7 **Blackrod** Bolton
214 E6 **Blacksboat** Moray
147 J2 **Blackshaw** D & G
122 E5 **Blackshaw Head** Calder
121 K6 **Blacksnape** Bl w D
19 H3 **Blackstone** W Susx
57 L4 **Blackthorn** Oxon
77 K2 **Blackthorpe** Suffk
125 J5 **Blacktoft** E R Yk
207 G4 **Blacktop** C Aber
100 E3 **Blackwall** Derbys
3 J3 **Blackwater** Cnwll
42 D7 **Blackwater** Hants
17 G5 **Blackwater** IOW
25 K7 **Blackwater** Somset
162 A4 **Blackwaterfoot** N Ayrs
148 D4 **Blackwell** Cumb
114 C6 **Blackwell** Derbys
101 H2 **Blackwell** Derbys
72 B5 **Blackwell** Warwks
71 H1 **Blackwell** Worcs
37 J2 **Blackwood** Caerph
154 F5 **Blackwood** D & G
164 F1 **Blackwood** S Lans
111 L7 **Blacon** Ches
145 J4 **Bladnoch** D & G
57 J5 **Bladon** Oxon
50 D1 **Blaen-y-Coed** Carmth
52 E7 **Blaen-y-cwm** Rhondd
65 H5 **Blaenannerch** Cerdgn
96 A4 **Blaenau Ffestiniog** Gwynd
53 K6 **Blaenavon** Torfn
65 H6 **Blaenffos** Pembks
36 D2 **Blaengarw** Brdgnd
52 D6 **Blaengwrach** Neath
36 D2 **Blaengwynfi** Neath
66 E2 **Blaenpennal** Cerdgn
80 D7 **Blaenplwyf** Cerdgn
65 J3 **Blaenporth** Cerdgn
52 E7 **Blaenrhondda** Rhondd
50 B4 **Blaenwaun** Carmth
38 D8 **Blagdon** N Som
25 K7 **Blagdon** Somset
7 K4 **Blagdon** Torbay
25 K7 **Blagdon Hill** Somset
191 K2 **Blaich** Highld
190 D3 **Blain** Highld

53 J6 **Blaina** Blae G
194 D4 **Blair Atholl** P & K
184 F7 **Blair Drummond** Stirlg
173 G4 **Blair's Ferry** Ag & B
195 J7 **Blairgowrie** P & K
185 K7 **Blairingone** P & K
185 H7 **Blairlogie** Stirlg
173 L2 **Blairmore** Ag & B
228 C4 **Blairmore** Highld
204 F3 **Blairnamarrow** Moray
55 G5 **Blaisdon** Gloucs
61 H4 **Blake End** Essex
84 E7 **Blakebrook** Worcs
84 F7 **Blakedown** Worcs
112 D7 **Blakemere** Ches
69 G6 **Blakemere** Herefs
85 H3 **Blakenall Heath** Wsall
54 F6 **Blakeney** Gloucs
106 B4 **Blakeney** Norfk
99 G3 **Blakenhall** Ches
85 G4 **Blakenhall** Wolves
73 J4 **Blakesley** Nhants
150 B5 **Blanchland** Nthumb
132 C8 **Bland Hill** N York
15 G2 **Blandford Forum** Dorset
15 G2 **Blandford St Mary** Dorset
174 F3 **Blanefield** Stirlg
103 H1 **Blankney** Lincs
175 J6 **Blantyre** S Lans
191 L3 **Blar a' Chaorainn** Highld
202 F6 **Blargie** Highld
191 L3 **Blarmachfoldach** Highld
88 B4 **Blaston** Leics
88 D4 **Blatherwycke** Nhants
129 G2 **Blawith** Cumb
154 B5 **Blawquhairn** D & G
79 H3 **Blaxhall** Suffk
116 A2 **Blaxton** Donc
150 F3 **Blaydon** Gatesd
26 C3 **Bleadney** Somset
37 M8 **Bleadon** N Som
34 F3 **Blean** Kent
102 B3 **Bleasby** Notts
121 H2 **Bleasdale** Lancs
187 G4 **Blebocraigs** Fife
68 E2 **Bleddfa** Powys
56 E4 **Bledington** Gloucs
58 C7 **Bledlow** Bucks
42 D2 **Bledlow Ridge** Bucks
178 B6 **Blegbie** E Loth
138 F2 **Blencarn** Cumb
147 L5 **Blencogo** Cumb
30 B8 **Blendworth** Hants
147 L6 **Blennerhasset** Cumb
57 J4 **Bletchingdon** Oxon
32 B3 **Bletchingley** Surrey
58 E2 **Bletchley** M Keyn
98 F5 **Bletchley** Shrops
49 H4 **Bletherston** Pembks
74 E3 **Bletsoe** Beds
41 K4 **Blewbury** Oxon
106 E6 **Blickling** Norfk
101 L2 **Blidworth** Notts
101 L2 **Blidworth Bottoms** Notts
147 K7 **Blindcrake** Cumb
32 C4 **Blindley Heath** Surrey
5 H2 **Blisland** Cnwll
84 D8 **Bliss Gate** Worcs
28 D8 **Blissford** Hants
73 K4 **Blisworth** Nhants
100 B8 **Blithbury** Staffs
92 B7 **Blo Norton** Norfk
71 L7 **Blockley** Gloucs
93 G2 **Blofield** Norfk

167 J4 **Bloomfield** Border
99 G5 **Blore** Staffs
100 C3 **Blore** Staffs
72 E7 **Bloxham** Oxon
103 H2 **Bloxholm** Lincs
85 H3 **Bloxwich** Wsall
15 G4 **Bloxworth** Dorset
132 B7 **Blubberhouses** N York
24 F3 **Blue Anchor** Somset
46 C7 **Blue Bell Hill** Kent
114 C5 **Blue John Cavern** Derbys
111 J2 **Blundellsands** Sefton
93 L4 **Blundeston** Suffk
75 H4 **Blunham** Beds
40 C3 **Blunsdon St Andrew** Swindn
84 F8 **Bluntington** Worcs
89 L8 **Bluntisham** Cambs
116 F3 **Blyborough** Lincs
93 J7 **Blyford** Suffk
84 E2 **Blymhill** Staffs
115 L4 **Blyth** Notts
159 H5 **Blyth** Nthumb
165 M1 **Blyth Bridge** Border
93 J7 **Blythburgh** Suffk
178 D7 **Blythe** Border
116 D3 **Blyton** Lincs
176 D3 **Bo'ness** Falk
187 J5 **Boarhills** Fife
17 H2 **Boarhunt** Hants
57 L5 **Boarstall** Bucks
203 L2 **Boat of Garten** Highld
222 D6 **Boath** Highld
46 E6 **Bobbing** Kent
84 E5 **Bobbington** Staffs
61 J4 **Bocking** Essex
61 J3 **Bocking Churchstreet** Essex
217 L6 **Boddam** Abers
235 c7 **Boddam** Shet
55 K3 **Boddington** Gloucs
108 D5 **Bodedern** IOA
110 D6 **Bodelwyddan** Denbgs
69 K4 **Bodenham** Herefs
28 D6 **Bodenham** Wilts
69 K4 **Bodenham Moor** Herefs
108 E4 **Bodewryd** IOA
110 F7 **Bodfari** Denbgs
108 F6 **Bodffordd** IOA
94 F5 **Bodfuan** Gwynd
106 D4 **Bodham** Norfk
33 K7 **Bodiam** E Susx
33 K7 **Bodiam Castle** E Susx
72 F6 **Bodicote** Oxon
5 H5 **Bodinnick** Cnwll
20 D3 **Bodle Street Green** E Susx
5 G3 **Bodmin** Cnwll
5 J1 **Bodmin Moor** Cnwll
109 M6 **Bodnant Garden** Conwy
34 E5 **Bodsham Green** Kent
5 G4 **Bodwen** Cnwll
212 F4 **Bogallan** Highld
217 J7 **Bogbrae** Abers
177 L4 **Boggs Holdings** E Loth
177 H5 **Boghall** Mdloth
176 D5 **Boghall** W Loth
164 F2 **Boghead** S Lans
215 H3 **Boghead Farm** Moray
215 H2 **Bogmoor** Moray
197 G3 **Bogmuir** Abers
216 B5 **Bogniebrae** Abers
18 C6 **Bognor Regis** W Susx

203 L2 **Bogroy** Highld
154 B6 **Bogue** D & G
3 L5 **Bohortha** Cnwll
201 L8 **Bohuntine** Highld
140 F3 **Bolam** Dur
7 G7 **Bolberry** Devon
85 K5 **Boldmere** Birm
16 C3 **Boldre** Hants
140 C4 **Boldron** Dur
116 C4 **Bole** Notts
100 F2 **Bolehill** Derbys
24 E7 **Bolham** Devon
25 J8 **Bolham Water** Devon
3 K1 **Bolingey** Cnwll
113 L6 **Bollington** Ches
31 L6 **Bolney** W Susx
74 F3 **Bolnhurst** Beds
197 G6 **Bolshan** Angus
115 J7 **Bolsover** Derbys
114 F3 **Bolsterstone** Sheff
133 G3 **Boltby** N York
205 J3 **Boltenstone** Abers
121 L8 **Bolton** Bolton
138 F3 **Bolton** Cumb
178 B4 **Bolton** E Loth
125 J1 **Bolton** E R Yk
169 G6 **Bolton** Nthumb
131 K8 **Bolton Abbey** N York
122 B1 **Bolton by Bowland** Lancs
129 K6 **Bolton le Sands** Lancs
147 M6 **Bolton Low Houses** Cumb
124 E3 **Bolton Percy** N York
115 J2 **Bolton Upon Dearne** Barns
141 G7 **Bolton-on-Swale** N York
148 E2 **Boltonfellend** Cumb
147 M6 **Boltongate** Cumb
5 J1 **Bolventor** Cnwll
98 C8 **Bomere Heath** Shrops
222 E3 **Bonar Bridge** Highld
182 E2 **Bonawe** Ag & B
126 C7 **Bonby** N Linc
65 H6 **Boncath** Pembks
167 J6 **Bonchester Bridge** Border
10 F4 **Bondleigh** Devon
121 G2 **Bonds** Lancs
85 J2 **Boney Hay** Staffs
174 D3 **Bonhill** W Duns
84 E3 **Boningale** Shrops
167 K5 **Bonjedward** Border
175 L6 **Bonkle** N Lans
196 F7 **Bonnington** Angus
34 E7 **Bonnington** Kent
186 F6 **Bonnybank** Fife
175 L3 **Bonnybridge** Falk
217 G4 **Bonnykelly** Abers
177 J5 **Bonnyrigg** Mdloth
196 B8 **Bonnyton** Angus
100 F2 **Bonsall** Derbys
155 M7 **Bonshaw Tower** D & G
81 J4 **Bont-Dolgadfan** Powys
66 E2 **Bontnewydd** Cerdgn
95 H1 **Bontnewydd** Gwynd
97 G2 **Bontuchel** Denbgs
37 G5 **Bonvilston** V Glam
23 H4 **Boode** Devon
7 K5 **Boohay** Devon
42 D3 **Booker** Bucks
98 E7 **Booley** Shrops
167 J1 **Boon** Border
142 E4 **Boosbeck** R & Cl
61 K2 **Boose's Green** Essex
137 G6 **Boot** Cumb
122 F5 **Booth** Calder

125 H5 **Booth** E R Yk
103 G2 **Boothby Graffoe** Lincs
102 F6 **Boothby Pagnell** Lincs
113 G2 **Boothstown** Salfd
128 D2 **Bootle** Cumb
111 K3 **Bootle** Sefton
70 B1 **Boraston** Shrops
236 e2 **Bordeaux** Guern
34 B3 **Borden** Kent
157 G5 **Border Forest Park**
30 D4 **Bordon** Hants
61 J6 **Boreham** Essex
27 K3 **Boreham** Wilts
20 D4 **Boreham Street** E Susx
44 D2 **Borehamwood** Herts
155 L4 **Boreland** D & G
208 C4 **Boreraig** Highld
232 f1 **Borgh** W Isls
233 b9 **Borgh** W Isls
229 K4 **Borgie** Highld
146 B5 **Borgue** D & G
227 K4 **Borgue** Highld
77 J6 **Borley** Essex
218 B7 **Borneskitaig** Highld
146 A5 **Borness** D & G
33 G2 **Borough Green** Kent
132 F6 **Boroughbridge** N York
101 H5 **Borrowash** Derbys
132 F2 **Borrowby** N York
176 D3 **Borrowstoun** Falk
46 B6 **Borstal** Medway
80 E5 **Borth** Cerdgn
95 K5 **Borth-y-Gest** Gwynd
166 F6 **Borthwickbrae** Border
166 F6 **Borthwickshiels** Border
209 G5 **Borve** Highld
232 f1 **Borve** W Isls
233 b9 **Borve** W Isls
232 d4 **Borve** W Isls
129 L5 **Borwick** Lancs
70 C5 **Bosbury** Herefs
8 E6 **Boscastle** Cnwll
15 L4 **Boscombe** Bmouth
28 D4 **Boscombe** Wilts
17 L2 **Bosham** W Susx
49 G8 **Bosherston** Pembks
113 K7 **Bosley** Ches
4 D4 **Bosoughan** Cnwll
133 L7 **Bossall** N York
8 E6 **Bossiney** Cnwll
34 F5 **Bossingham** Kent
24 D2 **Bossington** Somset
112 F7 **Bostock Green** Ches
104 B4 **Boston** Lincs
124 C2 **Boston Spa** Leeds
4 F7 **Boswinger** Cnwll
2 C5 **Botallack** Cnwll
187 H4 **Botanic Gardens** Fife
59 M7 **Botany Bay** Gt Lon
92 C7 **Botesdale** Suffk
159 G5 **Bothal** Nthumb
41 J5 **Bothampstead** W Berk
116 A6 **Bothamsall** Notts
147 L6 **Bothel** Cumb
13 L4 **Bothenhampton** Dorset
175 J6 **Bothwell** S Lans
59 G7 **Botley** Bucks
29 K8 **Botley** Hants
57 J6 **Botley** Oxon
58 B3 **Botolph Claydon** Bucks
19 G4 **Botolphs** W Susx
102 D5 **Bottesford** Leics
116 E1 **Bottesford** N Linc

76 D3 **Bottisham** Cambs
186 F3 **Bottomcraig** Fife
122 D6 **Bottoms** Calder
6 B4 **Botusfleming** Cnwll
94 E6 **Botwnnog** Gwynd
32 E4 **Bough Beech** Kent
68 C6 **Boughrood** Powys
73 L2 **Boughton** Nhants
91 G3 **Boughton** Norfk
116 B7 **Boughton** Notts
34 D5 **Boughton Aluph** Kent
33 K3 **Boughton Green** Kent
34 B5 **Boughton Malherbe** Kent
33 K3 **Boughton Monchelsea** Kent
34 E3 **Boughton Street** Kent
83 K6 **Bouldon** Shrops
169 K6 **Boulmer** Nthumb
116 F7 **Boultham** Lincs
75 K3 **Bourn** Cambs
103 H7 **Bourne** Lincs
74 D5 **Bourne End** Beds
42 E3 **Bourne End** Bucks
59 G6 **Bourne End** Herts
45 J2 **Bournebridge** Essex
85 J6 **Bournebrook** Birm
15 K4 **Bournemouth** Bmouth
15 L3 **Bournemouth Airport** Dorset
46 E3 **Bournes Green** Sthend
85 G8 **Bournheath** Worcs
85 J7 **Bournville** Birm
27 H5 **Bourton** Dorset
40 E3 **Bourton** Oxon
83 L4 **Bourton** Shrops
40 B7 **Bourton** Wilts
72 E1 **Bourton on Dunsmore** Warwks
56 D2 **Bourton-on-the-Hill** Gloucs
56 D4 **Bourton-on-the-Water** Gloucs
189 G4 **Bousd** Ag & B
129 H3 **Bouth** Cumb
131 L5 **Bouthwaite** N York
184 C2 **Bovain** Stirlg
28 B7 **Boveridge** Dorset
7 J1 **Bovey Tracey** Devon
59 G7 **Bovingdon** Herts
14 F5 **Bovington Tank Museum** Dorset
11 G4 **Bow** Devon
45 G4 **Bow** Gt Lon
234 b7 **Bow** Ork
74 C7 **Bow Brickhill** M Keyn
186 E5 **Bow of Fife** Fife
80 E6 **Bow Street** Cerdgn
55 J6 **Bowbridge** Gloucs
151 H7 **Bowburn** Dur
16 F5 **Bowcombe** IOW
12 E4 **Bowd** Devon
167 H4 **Bowden** Border
39 L6 **Bowden Hill** Wilts
113 H4 **Bowdon** Traffd
231 J3 **Bower** Highld
124 B5 **Bower's Row** Leeds
28 A6 **Bowerchalke** Wilts
231 J3 **Bowermadden** Highld
99 J5 **Bowers** Staffs
46 C3 **Bowers Gifford** Essex
176 F1 **Bowershall** Fife
140 C4 **Bowes** Dur
121 G2 **Bowgreave** Lancs
147 H2 **Bowhouse** D & G
167 G2 **Bowland** Border

69 K4 **Bowley** Herefs
30 E4 **Bowlhead Green** Surrey
123 H4 **Bowling** Brad
174 E4 **Bowling** W Duns
137 J7 **Bowmanstead** Cumb
170 F6 **Bowmore** Ag & B
147 L3 **Bowness-on-Solway** Cumb
137 L7 **Bowness-on-Windermere** Cumb
196 E6 **Bowriefauld** Angus
168 E2 **Bowsden** Nthumb
55 K7 **Box** Gloucs
39 J6 **Box** Wilts
77 L6 **Boxford** Suffk
41 H6 **Boxford** W Berk
18 B4 **Boxgrove** W Susx
33 K2 **Boxley** Kent
59 H6 **Boxmoor** Herts
62 B2 **Boxted** Essex
77 J4 **Boxted** Suffk
62 B2 **Boxted Cross** Essex
62 B2 **Boxted Heath** Essex
75 L2 **Boxworth** Cambs
47 L6 **Boyden Gate** Kent
100 D5 **Boylestone** Derbys
216 C2 **Boyndie** Abers
217 G2 **Boyndlie** Abers
135 H6 **Boynton** E R Yk
197 G6 **Boysack** Angus
9 J6 **Boyton** Cnwll
79 H5 **Boyton** Suffk
27 L4 **Boyton** Wilts
61 G6 **Boyton Cross** Essex
77 G5 **Boyton End** Suffk
74 C3 **Bozeat** Nhants
34 E6 **Brabourne** Kent
34 E6 **Brabourne Lees** Kent
231 K2 **Brabstermire** Highld
208 E6 **Bracadale** Highld
88 F2 **Braceborough** Lincs
117 G7 **Bracebridge Heath** Lincs
116 F7 **Bracebridge Low Fields** Lincs
103 G5 **Braceby** Lincs
122 C2 **Bracewell** Lancs
101 G2 **Brackenfield** Derbys
175 K5 **Brackenhirst** N Lans
201 J8 **Brackletter** Highld
73 H6 **Brackley** Nhants
42 E6 **Bracknell** Br For
185 H5 **Braco** P & K
215 L4 **Bracobrae** Moray
92 E4 **Bracon Ash** Norfk
199 L6 **Braco** Highld
199 L6 **Bracorina** Highld
100 D3 **Bradbourne** Derbys
141 H2 **Bradbury** Dur
73 J5 **Bradden** Nhants
42 D2 **Bradenham** Bucks
39 M4 **Bradenstoke** Wilts
12 D1 **Bradfield** Devon
62 D2 **Bradfield** Essex
106 F5 **Bradfield** Norfk
114 F3 **Bradfield** Sheff
41 L6 **Bradfield** W Berk
77 K3 **Bradfield Combust** Suffk
99 G2 **Bradfield Green** Ches
62 D3 **Bradfield Heath** Essex
77 K3 **Bradfield St Clare** Suffk
77 K3 **Bradfield St George** Suffk
123 H4 **Bradford** Brad
9 L4 **Bradford** Devon
26 E8 **Bradford Abbas** Dorset

39 J7	**Bradford Leigh** Wilts
14 C4	**Bradford Peverell** Dorset
39 J7	**Bradford-on-Avon** Wilts
25 J6	**Bradford-on-Tone** Somset
23 J4	**Bradiford** Devon
17 H5	**Brading** IOW
100 E4	**Bradley** Derbys
29 M3	**Bradley** Hants
118 C1	**Bradley** NE Lin
99 K8	**Bradley** Staffs
85 G4	**Bradley** Wolves
71 H3	**Bradley** Worcs
71 H3	**Bradley Green** Worcs
100 B4	**Bradley in the Moors** Staffs
38 E4	**Bradley Stoke** S Glos
101 L6	**Bradmore** Notts
12 C2	**Bradninch** Devon
100 A2	**Bradnop** Staffs
13 L4	**Bradpole** Dorset
123 G4	**Bradshaw** Calder
9 K8	**Bradstone** Devon
113 H8	**Bradwall Green** Ches
114 D5	**Bradwell** Derbys
61 K4	**Bradwell** Essex
74 B6	**Bradwell** M Keyn
93 K3	**Bradwell** Norfk
62 B6	**Bradwell Waterside** Essex
62 B6	**Bradwell-on-Sea** Essex
9 J3	**Bradworthy** Devon
213 G2	**Brae** Highld
235 C4	**Brae** Shet
201 L6	**Brae Roy Lodge** Highld
175 K3	**Braeface** Falk
197 H5	**Braehead** Angus
145 J4	**Braehead** D & G
176 C7	**Braehead** S Lans
204 E6	**Braemar** Abers
227 J3	**Braemore** Highld
221 G5	**Braemore** Highld
195 L5	**Braes of Coul** Angus
215 J3	**Braes of Enzie** Moray
173 L4	**Braeside** Inver
234 d4	**Braeswick** Ork
182 D6	**Braevallich** Ag & B
141 H3	**Brafferton** Darltn
132 F5	**Brafferton** N York
74 B3	**Brafield-on-the-Green** Nhants
232 f2	**Bragar** W Isls
59 L4	**Bragbury End** Herts
175 L8	**Braidwood** S Lans
100 E4	**Brailsford** Derbys
61 J4	**Braintree** Essex
78 D1	**Braiseworth** Suffk
29 G6	**Braishfield** Hants
137 H3	**Braithwaite** Cumb
115 K3	**Braithwell** Donc
19 G4	**Bramber** W Susx
86 E5	**Bramcote** Warwks
29 L5	**Bramdean** Hants
93 G3	**Bramerton** Norfk
59 M5	**Bramfield** Herts
93 H8	**Bramfield** Suffk
78 D5	**Bramford** Suffk
113 K5	**Bramhall** Stockp
124 C2	**Bramham** Leeds
123 K2	**Bramhope** Leeds
41 M8	**Bramley** Hants
123 K4	**Bramley** Leeds
115 J3	**Bramley** Rothm
31 G3	**Bramley** Surrey
41 M8	**Bramley Corner** Hants
35 G4	**Bramling** Kent
11 L5	**Brampford Speke** Devon
75 J1	**Brampton** Cambs
148 F3	**Brampton** Cumb
138 F3	**Brampton** Cumb
116 D5	**Brampton** Lincs
106 F7	**Brampton** Norfk
115 H2	**Brampton** Rothm
93 J6	**Brampton** Suffk
54 E3	**Brampton Abbotts** Herefs
87 L6	**Brampton Ash** Nhants
83 G8	**Brampton Bryan** Herefs
115 J4	**Brampton-en-le-Morthen** Rothm
100 B6	**Bramshall** Staffs
28 F7	**Bramshaw** Hants
30 D5	**Bramshott** Hants
26 B5	**Bramwell** Somset
61 G3	**Bran End** Essex
190 B3	**Branault** Highld
105 J4	**Brancaster** Norfk
105 J4	**Brancaster Staithe** Norfk
150 F7	**Brancepeth** Dur
214 D4	**Branchill** Moray
214 F1	**Branderburgh** Moray
126 E2	**Brandesburton** E R Yk
78 F3	**Brandeston** Suffk
106 D7	**Brandiston** Norfk
151 G6	**Brandon** Dur
102 E3	**Brandon** Lincs
91 H6	**Brandon** Suffk
86 E7	**Brandon** Warwks
92 C2	**Brandon Parva** Norfk
133 J5	**Brandsby** N York
117 G3	**Brandy Wharf** Lincs
15 K4	**Branksome** Poole
15 K4	**Branksome Park** Poole
29 H3	**Bransbury** Hants
116 E5	**Bransby** Lincs
12 F5	**Branscombe** Devon
70 E4	**Bransford** Worcs
16 A3	**Bransgore** Hants
126 D4	**Bransholme** C KuH
84 B7	**Bransley** Shrops
102 D6	**Branston** Leics
117 G7	**Branston** Lincs
100 E7	**Branston** Staffs
117 H7	**Branston Booths** Lincs
17 G5	**Branstone** IOW
102 E2	**Brant Broughton** Lincs
78 D7	**Brantham** Suffk
136 E3	**Branthwaite** Cumb
148 B7	**Branthwaite** Cumb
125 L5	**Brantingham** E R Yk
115 M2	**Branton** Donc
168 F6	**Branton** Nthumb
132 F6	**Branton Green** N York
168 D2	**Branxton** Nthumb
100 E2	**Brassington** Derbys
32 E3	**Brasted** Kent
32 E3	**Brasted Chart** Kent
206 D5	**Brathens** Abers
119 G8	**Bratoft** Lincs
116 F5	**Brattleby** Lincs
27 K2	**Bratton** Wilts
10 C6	**Bratton Clovelly** Devon
23 K4	**Bratton Fleming** Devon
26 G5	**Bratton Seymour** Somset
60 C3	**Braughing** Herts
73 G2	**Braunston** Nhants
88 B3	**Braunston** Rutlnd
87 G3	**Braunstone** Leics
23 H4	**Braunton** Devon
134 B4	**Brawby** N York
230 B3	**Brawl** Highld
42 E4	**Bray** W & M
5 M2	**Bray Shop** Cnwll
87 L6	**Braybrooke** Nhants
23 L4	**Brayford** Devon
123 K2	**Braythorn** N York
124 F4	**Brayton** N York
42 E4	**Braywick** W & M
59 J4	**Breachwood Green** Herts
101 G5	**Breadsall** Derbys
55 G7	**Breadstone** Gloucs
3 G5	**Breage** Cnwll
212 D5	**Breakachy** Highld
222 C3	**Brealangwell Lodge** Highld
54 E6	**Bream** Gloucs
28 D7	**Breamore** Hants
25 L1	**Brean** Somset
232 d3	**Breanais** W Isls
132 E7	**Brearton** N York
232 e2	**Breascleit** W Isls
232 e2	**Breasclete** W Isls
101 J5	**Breaston** Derbys
66 C7	**Brechfa** Carmth
196 F4	**Brechin** Angus
91 L5	**Breckles** Norfk
154 E4	**Breckonside** D & G
53 G3	**Brecon** Powys
52 F3	**Brecon Beacons National Park**
113 L3	**Bredbury** Stockp
21 G3	**Brede** E Susx
69 L3	**Bredenbury** Herefs
78 F4	**Bredfield** Suffk
34 B3	**Bredgar** Kent
46 D7	**Bredhurst** Kent
71 G6	**Bredon** Worcs
71 G7	**Bredon's Hardwick** Worcs
71 G6	**Bredon's Norton** Worcs
69 G5	**Bredwardine** Herefs
101 H7	**Breedon on the Hill** Leics
176 C6	**Breich** W Loth
121 L8	**Breightmet** Bolton
125 G4	**Breighton** E R Yk
69 J6	**Breinton** Herefs
39 L5	**Bremhill** Wilts
33 H5	**Brenchley** Kent
24 B2	**Brendon** Devon
172 E2	**Brenfield** Ag & B
232 d3	**Brenish** W Isls
77 L5	**Brent Eleigh** Suffk
25 M2	**Brent Knoll** Somset
7 G4	**Brent Mill** Devon
60 C2	**Brent Pelham** Herts
44 D5	**Brentford** Gt Lon
102 C8	**Brentingby** Leics
45 L2	**Brentwood** Essex
21 K1	**Brenzett** Kent
34 D8	**Brenzett Green** Kent
85 J1	**Brereton** Staffs
113 H8	**Brereton Green** Ches
92 C7	**Bressingham** Norfk
100 F7	**Bretby** Derbys
86 E7	**Bretford** Warwks
71 K5	**Bretforton** Worcs
121 G6	**Bretherton** Lancs
235 d5	**Brettabister** Shet
91 L6	**Brettenham** Norfk
77 L4	**Brettenham** Suffk
111 K8	**Bretton** Flints
84 F2	**Brewood** Staffs
14 F4	**Briantspuddle** Dorset
114 F5	**Brick Houses** Sheff
60 A6	**Brickendon** Herts
59 J7	**Bricket Wood** Herts
71 H6	**Bricklehampton** Worcs
237 e2	**Bride** IOM
147 K7	**Bridekirk** Cumb
10 D6	**Bridestowe** Devon
216 B6	**Brideswell** Abers
11 J7	**Bridford** Devon
3 H3	**Bridge** Cnwll
35 G4	**Bridge** Kent
132 E5	**Bridge Hewick** N York
206 B2	**Bridge of Alford** Abers
185 G7	**Bridge of Allan** Stirlg
214 E7	**Bridge of Avon** Moray
204 E2	**Bridge of Avon** Moray
193 J6	**Bridge of Balgie** P & K
195 J4	**Bridge of Brewlands** Angus
204 D2	**Bridge of Brown** Highld
195 J6	**Bridge of Cally** P & K
206 C6	**Bridge of Canny** Abers
195 K5	**Bridge of Craigisla** Angus
146 C3	**Bridge of Dee** D & G
207 H4	**Bridge of Don** C Aber
213 L6	**Bridge of Dulsie** Highld
206 C7	**Bridge of Dye** Abers
186 B4	**Bridge of Earn** P & K
193 H5	**Bridge of Ericht** P & K
206 D6	**Bridge of Feugh** Abers
230 F2	**Bridge of Forss** Highld
205 H6	**Bridge of Gairn** Abers
193 H5	**Bridge of Gaur** P & K
216 B4	**Bridge of Marnoch** Abers
192 E7	**Bridge of Orchy** Ag & B
194 D4	**Bridge of Tilt** P & K
215 J3	**Bridge of Tynet** Moray
235 b5	**Bridge of Walls** Shet
174 D5	**Bridge of Weir** Rens
69 H6	**Bridge Sollers** Herefs
77 K5	**Bridge Street** Suffk
112 C7	**Bridge Trafford** Ches
26 E6	**Bridgehampton** Somset
150 D5	**Bridgehill** Dur
17 H2	**Bridgemary** Hants
215 L7	**Bridgend** Abers
171 G6	**Bridgend** Ag & B
196 E3	**Bridgend** Angus
36 E4	**Bridgend** Brdgnd
165 L7	**Bridgend** D & G
6 E6	**Bridgend** Devon
186 F5	**Bridgend** Fife
215 J7	**Bridgend** Moray
186 B3	**Bridgend** P & K
176 E3	**Bridgend** W Loth
195 L5	**Bridgend of Lintrathen** Angus
9 H4	**Bridgerule** Devon
24 E5	**Bridgetown** Somset
91 L6	**Bridgham** Norfk
84 C5	**Bridgnorth** Shrops
85 H2	**Bridgtown** Staffs
25 L4	**Bridgwater** Somset
135 J6	**Bridlington** E R Yk
13 L4	**Bridport** Dorset
54 E3	**Bridstow** Herefs

122 C3	**Brierfield** Lancs
124 C7	**Brierley** Barns
54 F5	**Brierley** Gloucs
85 G6	**Brierley Hill** Dudley
184 C6	**Brig o'Turk** Stirlg
117 G1	**Brigg** N Linc
107 G6	**Briggate** Norfk
143 H5	**Briggswath** N York
136 F2	**Brigham** Cumb
135 G8	**Brigham** E R Yk
123 H6	**Brighouse** Calder
16 E5	**Brighstone** IOW
57 G7	**Brighthampton** Oxon
10 E5	**Brightley** Devon
20 D2	**Brightling** E Susx
62 C4	**Brightlingsea** Essex
19 J3	**Brighton** Br & H
111 J2	**Brighton le Sands** Sefton
176 C3	**Brightons** Falk
41 H5	**Brightwalton** W Berk
78 F5	**Brightwell** Suffk
41 M2	**Brightwell Baldwin** Oxon
42 A2	**Brightwell Upperton** Oxon
41 L3	**Brightwell-cum-Sotwell** Oxon
140 D5	**Brignall** Dur
118 C2	**Brigsley** NE Lin
129 K2	**Brigsteer** Cumb
88 D6	**Brigstock** Nhants
58 A5	**Brill** Bucks
3 J5	**Brill** Cnwll
68 F5	**Brilley** Herefs
69 K2	**Brimfield** Herefs
69 K2	**Brimfield Cross** Herefs
115 H6	**Brimington** Derbys
7 J1	**Brimley** Devon
55 L5	**Brimpsfield** Gloucs
41 K7	**Brimpton** W Berk
55 K7	**Brimscombe** Gloucs
111 J5	**Brimstage** Wirral
114 G4	**Brincliffe** Sheff
125 H4	**Brind** E R Yk
235 C5	**Brindister** Shet
121 J5	**Brindle** Lancs
84 E2	**Brineton** Staffs
88 B5	**Bringhurst** Leics
88 F7	**Brington** Cambs
106 C5	**Briningham** Norfk
118 E6	**Brinkhill** Lincs
76 F4	**Brinkley** Cambs
86 E7	**Brinklow** Warwks
40 A4	**Brinkworth** Wilts
121 J6	**Brinscall** Lancs
101 J3	**Brinsley** Notts
115 H4	**Brinsworth** Rothm
106 C5	**Brinton** Norfk
234 c5	**Brinyan** Ork
105 M7	**Brisley** Norfk
38 F6	**Brislington** Bristl
34 C6	**Brissenden Green** Kent
38 E5	**Bristol** Bristl
38 D7	**Bristol Airport** N Som
38 E5	**Bristol Zoo** Bristl
106 C6	**Briston** Norfk
28 D5	**Britford** Wilts
53 J7	**Brithdir** Caerph
96 B8	**Brithdir** Gwynd
33 J2	**British Legion Village** Kent
51 L6	**Briton Ferry** Neath
42 A2	**Britwell Salome** Oxon
7 L5	**Brixham** Torbay
6 E5	**Brixton** Devon
44 F5	**Brixton** Gt Lon
27 K4	**Brixton Deverill** Wilts
73 L1	**Brixworth** Nhants
56 F6	**Brize Norton** Oxon
56 F6	**Brize Norton Airport** Oxon
70 F2	**Broad Alley** Worcs
40 D3	**Broad Blunsdon** Swindn
71 L6	**Broad Campden** Gloucs
123 G6	**Broad Carr** Calder
28 B6	**Broad Chalke** Wilts
61 L4	**Broad Green** Essex
70 D4	**Broad Green** Worcs
48 E5	**Broad Haven** Pembks
40 C5	**Broad Hinton** Wilts
41 H7	**Broad Laying** Hants
71 K5	**Broad Marston** Worcs
21 G2	**Broad Oak** E Susx
20 C2	**Broad Oak** E Susx
54 C4	**Broad Oak** Herefs
35 G3	**Broad Oak** Kent
112 D3	**Broad Oak** St Hel
21 H3	**Broad Street** E Susx
33 L2	**Broad Street** Kent
40 C5	**Broad Town** Wilts
61 H5	**Broad's Green** Essex
113 M3	**Broadbottom** Tamesd
17 M2	**Broadbridge** W Susx
31 J5	**Broadbridge Heath** W Susx
12 C3	**Broadclyst** Devon
174 C4	**Broadfield** Inver
199 K2	**Broadford** Highld
31 H6	**Broadford Bridge** W Susx
166 C7	**Broadgairhill** Border
179 H7	**Broadhaugh** Border
113 H4	**Broadheath** Traffd
12 E2	**Broadhembury** Devon
7 J3	**Broadhempston** Devon
21 G2	**Broadland Row** E Susx
215 J3	**Broadley** Moray
14 D5	**Broadmayne** Dorset
49 J6	**Broadmoor** Pembks
13 K3	**Broadoak** Dorset
35 K2	**Broadstairs** Kent
15 J4	**Broadstone** Poole
83 K5	**Broadstone** Shrops
70 D4	**Broadwas** Worcs
59 L4	**Broadwater** Herts
18 F5	**Broadwater** W Susx
84 E7	**Broadwaters** Worcs
48 E5	**Broadway** Pembks
25 L7	**Broadway** Somset
71 K6	**Broadway** Worcs
56 D3	**Broadwell** Gloucs
56 E6	**Broadwell** Oxon
72 F2	**Broadwell** Warwks
13 K2	**Broadwindsor** Dorset
10 F4	**Broadwood Kelly** Devon
9 K6	**Broadwoodwidger** Devon
209 J5	**Brochel** Highld
70 D4	**Brockamin** Worcs
29 L7	**Brockbridge** Hants
92 E7	**Brockdish** Norfk
16 C3	**Brockenhurst** Hants
164 F2	**Brocketsbrae** S Lans
78 D2	**Brockford Street** Suffk
73 J2	**Brockhall** Nhants
31 K2	**Brockham** Surrey
56 B4	**Brockhampton** Gloucs
17 K2	**Brockhampton** Hants
54 E2	**Brockhampton** Herefs
123 H7	**Brockholes** Kirk
126 E7	**Brocklesby** Lincs
38 C6	**Brockley** N Som
77 J1	**Brockley** Suffk
77 G5	**Brockley Green** Suffk
77 J4	**Brockley Green** Suffk
83 G3	**Brockton** Shrops
83 G6	**Brockton** Shrops
83 L5	**Brockton** Shrops
99 J6	**Brockton** Staffs
54 D7	**Brockweir** Gloucs
55 K5	**Brockworth** Gloucs
99 L8	**Brocton** Staffs
162 C1	**Brodick** N Ayrs
214 B3	**Brodie** Moray
115 J1	**Brodsworth** Donc
218 C7	**Brogaig** Highld
113 K6	**Broken Cross** Ches
39 K3	**Brokenborough** Wilts
27 J2	**Brokerswood** Wilts
111 K5	**Bromborough** Wirral
92 D7	**Brome** Suffk
92 D7	**Brome Street** Suffk
79 G4	**Bromeswell** Suffk
147 L5	**Bromfield** Cumb
83 J7	**Bromfield** Shrops
74 E4	**Bromham** Beds
39 L7	**Bromham** Wilts
45 H6	**Bromley** Gt Lon
84 D4	**Bromley** Shrops
46 C6	**Brompton** Medway
141 J7	**Brompton** N York
134 E3	**Brompton** N York
25 G5	**Brompton Ralph** Somset
24 E1	**Brompton Regis** Somset
140 F7	**Brompton-on-Swale** N York
70 D7	**Bromsberrow** Gloucs
55 G2	**Bromsberrow Heath** Gloucs
71 G1	**Bromsgrove** Worcs
70 B4	**Bromyard** Herefs
66 E2	**Bronant** Cerdgn
65 K5	**Brongest** Cerdgn
98 C4	**Bronington** Wrexhm
68 D7	**Bronllys** Powys
50 E2	**Bronwydd** Carmth
97 K5	**Bronygarth** Shrops
28 F8	**Brook** Hants
16 E5	**Brook** IOW
34 E6	**Brook** Kent
30 F4	**Brook** Surrey
28 F8	**Brook Hill** Hants
45 L2	**Brook Street** Essex
34 C7	**Brook Street** Kent
77 J5	**Brook Street** Suffk
93 G4	**Brooke** Norfk
88 B3	**Brooke** Rutlnd
117 K3	**Brookenby** Lincs
174 D5	**Brookfield** Rens
26 F5	**Brookhampton** Somset
129 L6	**Brookhouse** Lancs
115 K4	**Brookhouse** Rothm
99 J1	**Brookhouse Green** Ches
114 B4	**Brookhouses** Derbys
21 K1	**Brookland** Kent
113 H4	**Brooklands** Traffd
59 L7	**Brookmans Park** Herts
55 J5	**Brookthorpe** Gloucs
42 F8	**Brookwood** Surrey
75 H6	**Broom** Beds
151 G6	**Broom** Dur
115 H3	**Broom** Rothm
71 K4	**Broom** Warwks
115 H2	**Broom Hill** Barns
101 K3	**Broom Hill** Notts
34 D3	**Broom Street** Kent
93 H5	**Broome** Norfk
83 H7	**Broome** Shrops
84 F7	**Broome** Worcs
113 G4	**Broomedge** Warrtn
61 H5	**Broomfield** Essex
33 L3	**Broomfield** Kent
47 K6	**Broomfield** Kent
25 K5	**Broomfield** Somset
125 K5	**Broomfleet** E R Yk
150 C3	**Broomhaugh** Nthumb
159 G2	**Broomhill** Nthumb
226 F7	**Brora** Highld
84 C3	**Broseley** Shrops
150 A7	**Brotherlee** Dur
124 D5	**Brotherton** N York
142 E4	**Brotton** R & Cl
230 F4	**Broubster** Highld
139 H4	**Brough** Cumb
125 L5	**Brough** E R Yk
231 J2	**Brough** Highld
102 D2	**Brough** Notts
235 d4	**Brough** Shet
235 d2	**Brough Lodge** Shet
139 H5	**Brough Sowerby** Cumb
98 E4	**Broughall** Shrops
165 L3	**Broughton** Border
89 K7	**Broughton** Cambs
111 K8	**Broughton** Flints
28 F5	**Broughton** Hants
121 G4	**Broughton** Lancs
74 C6	**Broughton** M Keyn
126 B8	**Broughton** N Linc
122 D1	**Broughton** N York
134 B5	**Broughton** N York
88 B7	**Broughton** Nhants
72 E6	**Broughton** Oxon
113 J2	**Broughton** Salfd
99 H5	**Broughton** Staffs
36 E6	**Broughton** V Glam
87 G5	**Broughton Astley** Leics
39 K7	**Broughton Gifford** Wilts
71 G3	**Broughton Green** Worcs
71 G4	**Broughton Hackett** Worcs
145 J6	**Broughton Mains** D & G
128 F2	**Broughton Mills** Cumb
147 J7	**Broughton Moor** Cumb
56 E7	**Broughton Poggs** Oxon
128 F3	**Broughton-in-Furness** Cumb
187 H2	**Broughty Ferry** C Dund
29 L4	**Brown Candover** Hants
99 K2	**Brown Edge** Staffs
217 G6	**Brownhill** Abers
187 H4	**Brownhills** Fife
85 J3	**Brownhills** Wsall
41 L7	**Browninghill Green** Hants
55 K7	**Browns Hill** Gloucs
7 G5	**Brownston** Devon
134 E2	**Broxa** N York
60 B6	**Broxbourne** Herts
178 E3	**Broxburn** E Loth
176 E4	**Broxburn** W Loth
60 F3	**Broxted** Essex
69 G4	**Broxwood** Herefs
231 K7	**Bruan** Highld
194 C3	**Bruar** P & K
223 K4	**Brucefield** Highld
173 J6	**Bruchag** Ag & B

170 E6 **Bruichladdich** Ag & B	31 K2 **Buckland** Surrey	212 C7 **Buntait** Highld	105 K4 **Burnham Overy** Norfk
79 G2 **Bruisyard** Suffk	22 F7 **Buckland Brewer** Devon	60 B3 **Buntingford** Herts	105 K4 **Burnham Overy Staithe** Norfk
79 G2 **Bruisyard Street** Suffk	58 F6 **Buckland Common** Bucks	92 D5 **Bunwell** Norfk	105 K4 **Burnham Thorpe** Norfk
125 K8 **Brumby** N Linc	27 H2 **Buckland Dinham** Somset	92 D5 **Bunwell Street** Norfk	46 F2 **Burnham-on-Crouch** Essex
100 C1 **Brund** Staffs	10 C3 **Buckland Filleigh** Devon	86 F5 **Burbage** Leics	25 L2 **Burnham-on-Sea** Somset
93 G2 **Brundall** Norfk	7 G2 **Buckland in the Moor** Devon	40 E7 **Burbage** Wilts	217 L5 **Burnhaven** Abers
78 F1 **Brundish** Suffk	6 D3 **Buckland Monachorum** Devon	42 D4 **Burchett's Green** W & M	154 E3 **Burnhead** D & G
78 F1 **Brundish Street** Suffk	14 D2 **Buckland Newton** Dorset	28 B5 **Burcombe** Wilts	206 D2 **Burnhervie** Abers
122 F2 **Brunthwaite** Brad	14 C6 **Buckland Ripers** Dorset	58 E4 **Burcott** Bucks	84 E4 **Burnhill Green** Staffs
87 H5 **Bruntingthorpe** Leics	25 L8 **Buckland St Mary** Somset	77 K7 **Bures** Essex	150 F5 **Burnhope** Dur
186 E3 **Brunton** Fife	7 H6 **Buckland-Tout-Saints** Devon	56 E5 **Burford** Oxon	174 D7 **Burnhouse** N Ayrs
169 J4 **Brunton** Nthumb	41 K6 **Bucklebury** W Berk	69 L2 **Burford** Shrops	134 F2 **Burniston** N York
28 E1 **Brunton** Wilts	16 E3 **Bucklers Hard** Hants	189 J7 **Burg** Ag & B	122 C4 **Burnley** Lancs
24 E6 **Brushford** Somset	78 F6 **Bucklesham** Suffk	30 C5 **Burgates** Hants	151 H5 **Burnmoor** Dur
11 G4 **Brushford Barton** Devon	111 J8 **Buckley** Flints	19 J2 **Burgess Hill** W Susx	179 K6 **Burnmouth** Border
27 G4 **Bruton** Somset	113 G5 **Bucklow Hill** Ches	78 F4 **Burgh** Suffk	150 F4 **Burnopfield** Dur
70 F2 **Bryan's Green** Worcs	102 E7 **Buckminster** Leics	148 B3 **Burgh by Sands** Cumb	131 J7 **Burnsall** N York
15 G2 **Bryanston** Dorset	99 K3 **Bucknall** C Stke	93 K3 **Burgh Castle** Norfk	196 E6 **Burnside** Angus
155 L7 **Brydekirk** D & G	117 K7 **Bucknall** Lincs	44 E7 **Burgh Heath** Surrey	196 C4 **Burnside** Angus
26 D7 **Brympton** Somset	57 K3 **Bucknell** Oxon	119 G7 **Burgh le Marsh** Lincs	186 B5 **Burnside** Fife
36 C3 **Bryn** Neath	83 G8 **Bucknell** Shrops	106 F7 **Burgh next Aylsham** Norfk	214 E1 **Burnside** Moray
112 E2 **Bryn Gates** Wigan	215 J2 **Buckpool** Moray	117 L4 **Burgh on Bain** Lincs	176 E3 **Burnside** W Loth
97 G3 **Bryn Saith Marchog** Denbgs	31 H5 **Bucks Green** W Susx	93 J2 **Burgh St Margaret** Norfk	187 G1 **Burnside of Duntrune** Angus
51 L5 **Bryn-coch** Neath	30 D3 **Bucks Horn Oak** Hants	93 K5 **Burgh St Peter** Norfk	132 C7 **Burnt Yates** N York
64 E6 **Bryn-Henllan** Pembks	207 G4 **Bucksburn** C Aber	41 J7 **Burghclere** Hants	177 H2 **Burntisland** Fife
94 D5 **Bryn-mawr** Gwynd	135 J5 **Buckton** E R Yk	214 D1 **Burghead** Moray	85 J2 **Burntwood** Staffs
110 B6 **Bryn-y-Maen** Conwy	169 G2 **Buckton** Nthumb	42 A6 **Burghfield** W Berk	85 J2 **Burntwood Green** Staffs
51 K3 **Brynaman** Carmth	89 G7 **Buckworth** Cambs	42 A6 **Burghfield Common** W Berk	25 J7 **Burnworthy** Somset
64 F7 **Brynberian** Pembks	115 L7 **Budby** Notts	69 J5 **Burghill** Herefs	31 G2 **Burpham** Surrey
95 H4 **Bryncir** Gwynd	9 H5 **Budd's Titson** Cnwll	124 E7 **Burghwallis** Donc	18 E4 **Burpham** W Susx
94 D6 **Bryncroes** Gwynd	187 H2 **Buddon** Angus	46 B7 **Burham** Kent	168 E7 **Burradon** Nthumb
80 E3 **Bryncrug** Gwynd	9 G4 **Bude** Cnwll	30 C7 **Buriton** Hants	235 e1 **Burrafirth** Shet
97 H3 **Bryneglwys** Denbgs	5 M4 **Budge's Shop** Cnwll	98 E2 **Burland** Ches	235 d3 **Burravoe** Shet
111 G6 **Brynford** Flints	12 D6 **Budleigh Salterton** Devon	4 F2 **Burlawn** Cnwll	138 F4 **Burrells** Cumb
108 D6 **Bryngwran** IOA	3 K5 **Budock Water** Cnwll	55 K7 **Burleigh** Gloucs	195 K8 **Burrelton** P & K
54 B6 **Bryngwyn** Mons	99 G4 **Buerton** Ches	25 G7 **Burlescombe** Devon	13 H2 **Burridge** Devon
68 D5 **Bryngwyn** Powys	73 J3 **Bugbrooke** Nhants	14 E4 **Burleston** Dorset	17 G1 **Burridge** Hants
65 K4 **Brynhoffnant** Cerdgn	4 F4 **Bugle** Cnwll	16 B2 **Burley** Hants	132 C3 **Burrill** N York
53 J5 **Brynmawr** Blae G	27 H6 **Bugley** Dorset	88 C2 **Burley** Rutlnd	125 K8 **Burringham** N Linc
36 D4 **Brynmenyn** Brdgnd	134 B7 **Bugthorpe** E R Yk	69 L5 **Burley Gate** Herefs	10 F2 **Burrington** Devon
51 J6 **Brynmill** Swans	84 B3 **Buildwas** Shrops	123 H2 **Burley in Wharfedale** Brad	69 J1 **Burrington** Herefs
36 F4 **Brynna** Rhondd	68 B4 **Builth Wells** Powys	16 B2 **Burley Street** Hants	38 C8 **Burrington** N Som
109 H8 **Brynrefail** Gwynd	28 C5 **Bulbridge** Wilts	123 H2 **Burley Wood Head** Brad	76 F4 **Burrough Green** Cambs
37 G4 **Brynsadler** Rhondd	230 E3 **Buldoo** Highld	98 E4 **Burleydam** Ches	87 L2 **Burrough on the Hill** Leics
108 F7 **Brynsiencyn** IOA	28 D3 **Bulford** Wilts	93 H2 **Burlingham Green** Norfk	130 C4 **Burrow** Lancs
198 F2 **Bualintur** Highld	98 D2 **Bulkeley** Ches	98 C7 **Burlton** Shrops	24 E3 **Burrow** Somset
86 D8 **Bubbenhall** Warwks	86 E6 **Bulkington** Warwks	34 E7 **Burmarsh** Kent	26 A5 **Burrow Bridge** Somset
125 H4 **Bubwith** E R Yk	39 L8 **Bulkington** Wilts	72 C6 **Burmington** Warwks	42 F7 **Burrowhill** Surrey
174 E1 **Buchanan Smithy** Stirlg	9 K3 **Bulkworthy** Devon	124 F5 **Burn** N York	50 F7 **Burry Green** Swans
217 L5 **Buchanhaven** Abers	42 E6 **Bullbrook** Br For	184 F6 **Burn of Cambus** Stirlg	50 F5 **Burry Port** Carmth
185 J2 **Buchanty** P & K	29 J3 **Bullington** Hants	113 K3 **Burnage** Manch	120 F7 **Burscough** Lancs
184 F6 **Buchany** Stirlg	117 H6 **Bullington** Lincs	100 F6 **Burnaston** Derbys	120 F7 **Burscough Bridge** Lancs
184 C8 **Buchlyvie** Stirlg	77 J6 **Bulmer** Essex	176 B6 **Burnbrae** N Lans	125 J4 **Bursea** E R Yk
22 E6 **Buck's Cross** Devon	133 L6 **Bulmer** N York	125 K2 **Burnby** E R Yk	16 F1 **Burseldon** Hants
22 E6 **Buck's Mills** Devon	77 J6 **Bulmer Tye** Essex	138 D7 **Burneside** Cumb	99 K3 **Burslem** C Stke
148 C5 **Buckabank** Cumb	45 M2 **Bulphan** Thurr	132 D3 **Burneston** N York	78 D5 **Burstall** Suffk
75 H2 **Buckden** Cambs	217 H5 **Bulwark** Abers	38 F7 **Burnett** BaNES	13 K2 **Burstock** Dorset
131 H4 **Buckden** N York	101 K4 **Bulwell** C Nott	166 F6 **Burnfoot** Border	92 D6 **Burston** Norfk
93 H3 **Buckenham** Norfk	88 D5 **Bulwick** Nhants	167 H6 **Burnfoot** Border	32 B5 **Burstow** Surrey
12 E3 **Buckerell** Devon	60 C6 **Bumble's Green** Essex	155 G4 **Burnfoot** D & G	126 F5 **Burstwick** E R Yk
7 H3 **Buckfast** Devon	199 K7 **Bunacaimb** Highld	156 C4 **Burnfoot** D & G	131 G2 **Burtersett** N York
7 H3 **Buckfastleigh** Devon	201 J7 **Bunarkaig** Highld	156 C3 **Burnfoot** D & G	148 F3 **Burtholme** Cumb
186 F7 **Buckhaven** Fife	98 E2 **Bunbury** Ches	185 K6 **Burnfoot** P & K	77 H2 **Burthorpe Green** Suffk
54 D5 **Buckholt** Mons	212 F5 **Bunchrew** Highld	42 F4 **Burnham** Bucks	103 L5 **Burtoft** Lincs
27 H6 **Buckhorn Weston** Dorset	210 D8 **Bundalloch** Highld	105 J4 **Burnham Deepdale** Norfk	111 K6 **Burton** Ches
45 H2 **Buckhurst Hill** Essex	180 E3 **Bunessan** Ag & B	59 L5 **Burnham Green** Herts	112 D8 **Burton** Ches
215 J2 **Buckie** Moray	93 G5 **Bungay** Suffk	105 K4 **Burnham Market** Norfk	15 M4 **Burton** Dorset
73 K7 **Buckingham** Bucks	171 H4 **Bunnahabhain** Ag & B	105 K4 **Burnham Norton** Norfk	116 F6 **Burton** Lincs
58 E5 **Buckland** Bucks	101 L6 **Bunny** Notts		49 G6 **Burton** Pembks
7 G6 **Buckland** Devon			25 J3 **Burton** Somset
71 J7 **Buckland** Gloucs			39 J4 **Burton** Wilts
75 L7 **Buckland** Herts			
35 J6 **Buckland** Kent			
41 G2 **Buckland** Oxon			

135 H6 **Burton Agnes** E R Yk
13 L4 **Burton Bradstock** Dorset
103 G7 **Burton Coggles** Lincs
126 F4 **Burton Constable Hall** E R Yk
60 E4 **Burton End** Essex
135 G5 **Burton Fleming** E R Yk
86 E5 **Burton Hastings** Warwks
130 C5 **Burton in Lonsdale** N York
101 M4 **Burton Joyce** Notts
88 C8 **Burton Latimer** Nhants
87 L1 **Burton Lazars** Leics
132 E6 **Burton Leonard** N York
101 L7 **Burton on the Wolds** Leics
87 J4 **Burton Overy** Leics
103 J4 **Burton Pedwardine** Lincs
127 G4 **Burton Pidsea** E R Yk
124 D5 **Burton Salmon** N York
125 K6 **Burton upon Stather** N Linc
100 E7 **Burton upon Trent** Staffs
61 K3 **Burton's Green** Essex
129 L4 **Burton-in-Kendal** Cumb
112 E3 **Burtonwood** Warrtn
98 D2 **Burwardsley** Ches
84 B6 **Burwarton** Shrops
33 H7 **Burwash** E Susx
20 D2 **Burwash Common** E Susx
20 D2 **Burwash Weald** E Susx
76 E2 **Burwell** Cambs
118 E5 **Burwell** Lincs
108 E3 **Burwen** IOA
234 c8 **Burwick** Ork
122 B7 **Bury** Bury
89 K6 **Bury** Cambs
24 E6 **Bury** Somset
18 D3 **Bury** W Susx
60 D4 **Bury Green** Herts
77 J2 **Bury St Edmunds** Suffk
134 C6 **Burythorpe** N York
175 G6 **Busby** E Rens
40 E2 **Buscot** Wilts
197 J4 **Bush** Abers
69 J4 **Bush Bank** Herefs
45 G2 **Bush Hill Park** Gt Lon
85 G3 **Bushbury** Wolves
43 J2 **Bushey** Herts
43 J2 **Bushey Heath** Herts
70 F7 **Bushley** Worcs
40 B5 **Bushton** Wilts
26 A4 **Bussex** Somset
38 D7 **Butcombe** N Som
26 D5 **Butleigh** Somset
26 D4 **Butleigh Wootton** Somset
72 D4 **Butlers Marston** Warwks
79 H4 **Butley** Suffk
133 L7 **Buttercrambe** N York
179 G5 **Butterdean** Border
140 E3 **Butterknowle** Dur
12 C2 **Butterleigh** Devon
137 G4 **Buttermere** Cumb
123 H5 **Buttershaw** Brad
195 G7 **Butterstone** P & K
99 J4 **Butterton** Staffs
100 B2 **Butterton** Staffs
104 C4 **Butterwick** Lincs

133 L4 **Butterwick** N York
134 F5 **Butterwick** N York
82 E2 **Buttington** Powys
84 D7 **Buttonoak** Shrops
78 B3 **Buxhall** Suffk
20 A2 **Buxted** E Susx
114 B6 **Buxton** Derbys
106 F7 **Buxton** Norfk
106 E7 **Buxton Heath** Norfk
53 J4 **Bwlch** Powys
97 J8 **Bwlch-y-cibau** Powys
82 B4 **Bwlch-y-ffridd** Powys
65 H7 **Bwlch-y-groes** Pembks
82 B8 **Bwlch-y-sarnau** Powys
97 K2 **Bwlchgwyn** Wrexhm
66 D3 **Bwlchllan** Cerdgn
94 E7 **Bwlchtocyn** Gwynd
150 F7 **Byers Green** Dur
73 G4 **Byfield** Nhants
43 H7 **Byfleet** Surrey
69 H6 **Byford** Herefs
151 G3 **Byker** N u Ty
110 D8 **Bylchau** Conwy
113 G7 **Byley** Ches
167 K2 **Byrewalls** Border
157 K2 **Byrness** Nthumb
12 D4 **Bystock** Devon
88 F7 **Bythorn** Cambs
69 G2 **Byton** Herefs
150 D3 **Bywell** Nthumb
31 G7 **Byworth** W Susx

C

117 J2 **Cabourne** Lincs
171 J5 **Cabrach** Ag & B
215 J8 **Cabrach** Moray
121 G2 **Cabus** Lancs
220 F7 **Cabvie Lodge** Highld
11 L4 **Cadbury** Devon
175 G4 **Cadder** E Duns
59 H4 **Caddington** Beds
167 G3 **Caddonfoot** Border
20 C2 **Cade Street** E Susx
115 K2 **Cadeby** Donc
86 E3 **Cadeby** Leics
11 L4 **Cadeleigh** Devon
3 J7 **Cadgwith** Cnwll
186 D6 **Cadham** Fife
113 G3 **Cadishead** Salfd
51 J6 **Cadle** Swans
121 G4 **Cadley** Lancs
40 E6 **Cadley** Wilts
28 E2 **Cadley** Wilts
42 C3 **Cadmore End** Bucks
28 F8 **Cadnam** Hants
117 G2 **Cadney** N Linc
37 H6 **Cadoxton** V Glam
51 L5 **Cadoxton Juxta-Neath** Neath
95 J1 **Caeathro** Gwynd
117 G4 **Caenby** Lincs
66 F6 **Caeo** Carmth
48 D3 **Caer Farchell** Pembks
36 D2 **Caerau** Brdgnd
37 H5 **Caerau** Cardif
108 D5 **Caergeiliog** IOA
97 L2 **Caergwrle** Flints
156 D2 **Caerlanrig** Border
37 M3 **Caerleon** Newpt
108 F8 **Caernarfon** Gwynd
95 G2 **Caernarfon Airport** Gwynd
108 F8 **Caernarfon Castle** Gwynd
37 J3 **Caerphilly** Caerph

82 B5 **Caersws** Powys
65 L4 **Caerwedros** Cerdgn
38 C3 **Caerwent** Mons
110 F6 **Caerwys** Flints
233 c6 **Cairinis** W Isls
172 E1 **Cairnbaan** Ag & B
217 J2 **Cairnbulg** Abers
179 J5 **Cairncross** Border
174 C4 **Cairncurran** Inver
183 H5 **Cairndow** Ag & B
176 E2 **Cairneyhill** Fife
215 J3 **Cairnfield House** Moray
144 C5 **Cairngarroch** D & G
204 B5 **Cairngorm Mountains** Highld
207 G6 **Cairngrassie** Abers
215 K5 **Cairnie** Abers
217 G6 **Cairnorrie** Abers
144 C2 **Cairnryan** D & G
215 H4 **Cairnty** Moray
93 L2 **Caister-on-Sea** Norfk
117 J2 **Caistor** Lincs
92 F3 **Caistor St Edmund** Norfk
232 e2 **Calanais** W Isls
16 E5 **Calbourne** IOW
111 G6 **Calcot** Flints
56 C6 **Calcot** Gloucs
42 A6 **Calcot Row** W Berk
215 G2 **Calcots** Moray
148 B6 **Caldbeck** Cumb
89 G5 **Caldecote** Cambs
75 L3 **Caldecote** Cambs
75 J6 **Caldecote** Herts
75 L3 **Caldecote Highfields** Cambs
74 E2 **Caldecott** Nhants
41 J2 **Caldecott** Oxon
88 C5 **Caldecott** Rutlnd
136 E6 **Calder Bridge** Cumb
123 L6 **Calder Grove** Wakefd
121 G2 **Calder Vale** Lancs
175 K5 **Calderbank** N Lans
175 L5 **Caldercruix** N Lans
164 D2 **Caldermill** S Lans
175 H7 **Calderwood** S Lans
38 C3 **Caldicot** Mons
85 H4 **Caldmore** W Mids
140 E5 **Caldwell** N York
234 d4 **Calfsound** Ork
189 J6 **Calgary** Ag & B
214 D3 **Califer** Moray
176 B3 **California** Falk
93 K1 **California** Norfk
101 G7 **Calke** Derbys
209 L4 **Callakille** Highld
184 D5 **Callander** Stirlg
232 e2 **Callanish** W Isls
3 K2 **Callestick** Cnwll
199 K5 **Calligarry** Highld
6 A3 **Callington** Cnwll
69 J7 **Callow** Herefs
70 E4 **Callow End** Worcs
40 B4 **Callow Hill** Wilts
29 G7 **Calmore** Hants
56 B6 **Calmsden** Gloucs
39 M6 **Calne** Wilts
16 F3 **Calshot** Hants
6 C3 **Calstock** Cnwll
40 B6 **Calstone Wellington** Wilts
106 E6 **Calthorpe** Norfk
107 J7 **Calthorpe Street** Norfk
148 E6 **Calthwaite** Cumb
131 G7 **Calton** N York
100 C3 **Calton** Staffs
98 E2 **Calveley** Ches
114 E6 **Calver** Derbys
98 E5 **Calverhall** Shrops
11 L3 **Calverleigh** Devon
73 L6 **Calverton** M Keyn

101 L3 **Calverton** Notts
194 C3 **Calvine** P & K
147 K4 **Calvo** Cumb
165 L3 **Calzeat** Border
55 H7 **Cam** Gloucs
210 E8 **Camas Luinie** Highld
190 F4 **Camasachoirce** Highld
190 F4 **Camasine** Highld
209 H6 **Camastianavaig** Highld
212 D6 **Camault Muir** Highld
21 J2 **Camber** E Susx
42 E7 **Camberley** Surrey
44 F5 **Camberwell** Gt Lon
124 F5 **Camblesforth** N York
158 C5 **Cambo** Nthumb
3 H4 **Camborne** Cnwll
75 K3 **Cambourne** Cambs
76 C3 **Cambridge** Cambs
55 H7 **Cambridge** Gloucs
76 C3 **Cambridge Airport** Cambs
3 H3 **Cambrose** Cnwll
185 H8 **Cambus** Clacks
205 J5 **Cambus o' May** Abers
223 G3 **Cambusavie Platform** Highld
185 G8 **Cambusbarron** Stirlg
185 G8 **Cambuskenneth** Stirlg
175 H6 **Cambuslang** S Lans
165 K2 **Cambuswallace** S Lans
44 F4 **Camden Town** Gt Lon
38 E8 **Cameley** BaNES
8 E7 **Camelford** Cnwll
176 B3 **Camelon** Falk
70 D7 **Camer's Green** Worcs
214 C7 **Camerory** Highld
39 G8 **Camerton** BaNES
136 E2 **Camerton** Cumb
193 J5 **Camghouran** P & K
167 J4 **Camieston** Border
207 G6 **Cammachmore** Abers
116 F5 **Cammeringham** Lincs
223 G4 **Camore** Highld
161 J5 **Campbeltown** Ag & B
161 H5 **Campbeltown Airport** Ag & B
154 F4 **Cample** D & G
195 K8 **Campmuir** Angus
176 E5 **Camps** W Loth
76 E6 **Camps End** Cambs
124 E7 **Campsall** Donc
79 G4 **Campsea Ash** Suffk
75 G6 **Campton** Beds
167 K6 **Camptown** Border
48 F4 **Camrose** Pembks
194 E6 **Camserney** P & K
220 D4 **Camusnagaul** Highld
191 L2 **Camusnagaul** Highld
209 L6 **Camusteel** Highld
209 L6 **Camusterrach** Highld
28 F7 **Canada** Hants
205 H5 **Candacraig** Abers
118 F7 **Candlesby** Lincs
165 L2 **Candyburn** Border
42 B4 **Cane End** Oxon
46 E2 **Canewdon** Essex
15 K5 **Canford Cliffs** Poole
15 J4 **Canford Heath** Poole
15 J3 **Canford Magna** Poole
231 L2 **Canisbay** Highld
86 C7 **Canley** Covtry
27 K7 **Cann** Dorset
211 L7 **Cannich** Highld
45 H4 **Canning Town** Gt Lon

25 K4 **Cannington** Somset
85 H2 **Cannock** Staffs
99 M8 **Cannock Chase** Staffs
69 H6 **Cannon Bridge** Herefs
70 B5 **Canon Frome** Herefs
69 J5 **Canon Pyon** Herefs
156 C6 **Canonbie** D & G
73 H4 **Canons Ashby** Nhants
2 F4 **Canonstown** Cnwll
34 F3 **Canterbury** Kent
34 F3 **Canterbury Cathedral** Kent
93 H3 **Cantley** Norfk
37 J5 **Canton** Cardif
213 J5 **Cantraywood** Highld
130 C5 **Cantsfield** Lancs
46 D4 **Canvey Island** Essex
117 G2 **Canwick** Lincs
9 G6 **Canworthy Water** Cnwll
191 L2 **Caol** Highld
232 e4 **Caolas Scalpaigh** W Isls
188 D6 **Caoles** Ag & B
201 G6 **Caonich** Highld
33 H4 **Capel** Kent
31 K4 **Capel** Surrey
80 E7 **Capel Bangor** Cerdgn
108 F5 **Capel Coch** IOA
96 A2 **Capel Curig** Conwy
50 F2 **Capel Dewi** Carmth
66 B6 **Capel Dewi** Cerdgn
96 C2 **Capel Garmon** Conwy
51 H4 **Capel Hendre** Carmth
65 J7 **Capel Iwan** Carmth
35 H6 **Capel le Ferne** Kent
108 E6 **Capel Mawr** IOA
80 E7 **Capel Seion** Cerdgn
79 H5 **Capel St Andrew** Suffk
78 C6 **Capel St Mary** Suffk
80 E7 **Capel-Dewi** Cerdgn
236 d2 **Capelles** Guern
109 L6 **Capelulo** Conwy
111 K6 **Capenhurst** Ches
158 C6 **Capheaton** Nthumb
174 E6 **Caplaw** E Rens
166 C5 **Cappercleuch** Border
7 J5 **Capton** Devon
195 H7 **Caputh** P & K
102 B4 **Car Colston** Notts
174 F3 **Carbeth Inn** Stirlg
2 B4 **Carbis Bay** Cnwll
208 F7 **Carbost** Highld
208 F5 **Carbost** Highld
115 G4 **Carbrook** Sheff
91 L3 **Carbrooke** Norfk
124 E8 **Carcroft** Donc
186 C7 **Cardenden** Fife
214 F5 **Cardhu** Moray
37 J5 **Cardiff** Cardif
37 G6 **Cardiff Airport** V Glam
65 G5 **Cardigan** Cerdgn
74 F5 **Cardington** Beds
83 K4 **Cardington** Shrops
5 H3 **Cardinham** Cnwll
144 D8 **Cardrain** D & G
166 D2 **Cardrona** Border
174 C3 **Cardross** Ag & B
144 D7 **Cardryne** D & G
147 L3 **Cardurnock** Cumb
88 E1 **Careby** Lincs
196 E4 **Careston** Angus
49 H6 **Carew** Pembks
49 H6 **Carew Cheriton** Pembks
49 H6 **Carew Newton** Pembks
54 E2 **Carey** Herefs
175 K6 **Carfin** N Lans

178 B7 **Carfraemill** Border
93 H2 **Cargate Green** Norfk
155 G7 **Cargen** D & G
155 G6 **Cargenbridge** D & G
195 J8 **Cargill** P & K
148 C3 **Cargo** Cumb
6 C4 **Cargreen** Cnwll
168 B2 **Carham** Nthumb
24 F3 **Carhampton** Somset
3 J3 **Carharrack** Cnwll
193 K5 **Carie** P & K
233 c6 **Carinish** W Isls
16 F5 **Carisbrooke** IOW
129 H4 **Cark** Cumb
6 B4 **Carkeel** Cnwll
232 e2 **Carlabhagh** W Isls
140 F4 **Carlbury** Darltn
88 F2 **Carlby** Lincs
168 C6 **Carlcroft** Nthumb
3 G5 **Carleen** Cnwll
122 E1 **Carleton** N York
92 C3 **Carleton Forehoe** Norfk
92 D5 **Carleton Rode** Norfk
93 H3 **Carleton St Peter** Norfk
216 D5 **Carlincraig** Abers
39 G8 **Carlingcott** BaNES
148 D4 **Carlisle** Cumb
148 E3 **Carlisle Airport** Cumb
177 G6 **Carlops** Border
232 e2 **Carloway** W Isls
124 B7 **Carlton** Barns
74 D4 **Carlton** Beds
76 F4 **Carlton** Cambs
123 L5 **Carlton** Leeds
86 E3 **Carlton** Leics
131 K3 **Carlton** N York
133 J3 **Carlton** N York
124 F5 **Carlton** N York
101 L4 **Carlton** Notts
141 J3 **Carlton** S on T
79 H2 **Carlton** Suffk
93 K5 **Carlton Colville** Suffk
87 K4 **Carlton Curlieu** Leics
76 F4 **Carlton Green** Cambs
133 G4 **Carlton Husthwaite** N York
115 L5 **Carlton in Lindrick** Notts
132 F4 **Carlton Miniott** N York
102 F4 **Carlton Scroop** Lincs
142 B6 **Carlton-in-Cleveland** N York
102 E2 **Carlton-le-Moorland** Lincs
116 D8 **Carlton-on-Trent** Notts
175 L7 **Carluke** S Lans
164 F4 **Carmacoup** S Lans
50 E2 **Carmarthen** Carmth
51 H3 **Carmel** Carmth
111 G6 **Carmel** Flints
95 H2 **Carmel** Gwynd
165 H2 **Carmichael** S Lans
175 G6 **Carmunnock** C Glas
175 H6 **Carmyle** C Glas
196 E7 **Carmyllie** Angus
3 H3 **Carn Brea** Cnwll
200 B2 **Carn-gorm** Highld
135 H6 **Carnaby** E R Yk
187 J6 **Carnbee** Fife
185 L6 **Carnbo** P & K
216 F8 **Carnbrogie** Abers
210 D8 **Carndu** Highld
164 D1 **Carnduff** S Lans
163 L3 **Carnell** E Ayrs
129 K5 **Carnforth** Lancs
3 G4 **Carnhell Green** Cnwll
206 F4 **Carnie** Abers
3 J4 **Carnkie** Cnwll

3 H4 **Carnkie** Cnwll
81 K4 **Carno** Powys
200 D6 **Carnoch** Highld
176 E1 **Carnock** Fife
4 C7 **Carnon Downs** Cnwll
216 C4 **Carnousie** Abers
187 J1 **Carnoustie** Angus
165 J1 **Carnwath** S Lans
86 C7 **Carol Green** Solhll
131 J2 **Carperby** N York
123 L5 **Carr Gate** Wakefd
149 K5 **Carr Shield** Nthumb
161 K2 **Carradale** Ag & B
203 L2 **Carrbridge** Highld
236 C6 **Carrefour** Jersey
108 E4 **Carreglefn** IOA
116 C1 **Carrhouse** N Linc
172 F2 **Carrick** Ag & B
183 H8 **Carrick Castle** Ag & B
176 D3 **Carriden** Falk
177 J6 **Carrington** Mdloth
113 H3 **Carrington** Traffd
97 H4 **Carrog** Denbgs
176 B2 **Carron** Falk
214 F6 **Carron** Moray
175 K2 **Carron Bridge** Stirlg
154 F3 **Carronbridge** D & G
176 B2 **Carronshore** Falk
174 C5 **Carruth House** Inver
155 J7 **Carrutherstown** D & G
151 H6 **Carrville** Dur
181 H3 **Carsaig** Ag & B
196 D5 **Carse Gray** Angus
145 G2 **Carseriggan** D & G
147 H3 **Carsethorn** D & G
44 F6 **Carshalton** Gt Lon
100 E2 **Carsington** Derbys
161 H7 **Carskey** Ag & B
145 K4 **Carsluith** D & G
153 L4 **Carsphairn** D & G
165 H1 **Carstairs** S Lans
165 J1 **Carstairs Junction** S Lans
56 F6 **Carterton** Oxon
4 F5 **Carthew** Cnwll
132 D3 **Carthorpe** N York
165 G1 **Cartland** S Lans
129 H4 **Cartmel** Cumb
50 F4 **Carway** Carmth
55 J6 **Cashe's Green** Gloucs
57 J5 **Cassington** Oxon
151 J7 **Cassop Colliery** Dur
130 C4 **Casterton** Lancs
91 J1 **Castle Acre** Norfk
74 C3 **Castle Ashby** Nhants
131 J2 **Castle Bolton** N York
85 K5 **Castle Bromwich** Solhll
103 G8 **Castle Bytham** Lincs
82 D3 **Castle Caereinion** Powys
76 F6 **Castle Camps** Cambs
148 F4 **Castle Carrock** Cumb
26 F5 **Castle Cary** Somset
39 J5 **Castle Combe** Wilts
101 H6 **Castle Donington** Leics
146 D3 **Castle Douglas** D & G
40 C2 **Castle Eaton** Swindn
151 K7 **Castle Eden** Dur
70 C5 **Castle Frome** Herefs
100 F8 **Castle Gresley** Derbys
77 H7 **Castle Hedingham** Essex
78 D5 **Castle Hill** Suffk
144 D3 **Castle Kennedy** D & G
182 E7 **Castle Lachlan** Ag & B
156 A4 **Castle O'er** D & G
83 H3 **Castle Pulverbatch** Shrops

105 G7 **Castle Rising** Norfk
213 H4 **Castle Stuart** Highld
233 b9 **Castlebay** W Isls
49 H2 **Castlebythe** Pembks
175 K3 **Castlecary** Falk
124 C5 **Castleford** Wakefd
166 C3 **Castlehill** Border
231 H2 **Castlehill** Highld
174 D3 **Castlehill** W Duns
48 F7 **Castlemartin** Pembks
175 G6 **Castlemilk** C Glas
70 E6 **Castlemorton** Worcs
137 J3 **Castlerigg** Cumb
150 D5 **Castleside** Dur
74 B5 **Castlethorpe** M Keyn
156 E4 **Castleton** Border
114 D5 **Castleton** Derbys
142 E5 **Castleton** N York
37 K4 **Castleton** Newpt
122 D7 **Castleton** Rochdl
231 H3 **Castletown** Highld
237 b7 **Castletown** IOM
151 J4 **Castletown** Sundld
123 K2 **Castley** N York
91 L4 **Caston** Norfk
89 G4 **Castor** C Pete
172 F7 **Catacol** N Ayrs
115 H4 **Catcliffe** Rothm
40 A5 **Catcomb** Wilts
26 B4 **Catcott** Somset
26 B3 **Catcott Burtle** Somset
236 c3 **Catel** Guern
32 C3 **Caterham** Surrey
107 H7 **Catfield** Norfk
235 C5 **Catfirth** Shet
45 G5 **Catford** Gt Lon
121 G4 **Catforth** Lancs
175 G6 **Cathcart** C Glas
53 H3 **Cathedine** Powys
30 B8 **Catherington** Hants
13 J4 **Catherston Leweston** Dorset
17 G2 **Catisfield** Hants
202 F6 **Catlodge** Highld
76 C6 **Catmere End** Essex
41 J4 **Catmore** W Berk
129 L6 **Caton** Lancs
129 L6 **Caton Green** Lancs
164 B4 **Catrine** E Ayrs
20 E3 **Catsfield** E Susx
26 D6 **Catsgore** Somset
85 G8 **Catshill** Worcs
161 H7 **Cattadale** Ag & B
133 G8 **Cattal** N York
62 D2 **Cattawade** Suffk
121 G3 **Catterall** Lancs
141 G7 **Catterick** N York
141 G7 **Catterick Bridge** N York
148 E7 **Catterlen** Cumb
197 L2 **Catterline** Abers
124 D2 **Catterton** N York
31 G3 **Catteshall** Surrey
87 G7 **Catthorpe** Leics
14 B3 **Cattistock** Dorset
149 L4 **Catton** Cumb
132 E4 **Catton** N York
92 F2 **Catton** Norfk
126 E2 **Catwick** E R Yk
88 F8 **Catworth** Cambs
55 L6 **Caudle Green** Gloucs
57 K3 **Caulcott** Oxon
197 G6 **Cauldcots** Angus
184 E8 **Cauldhame** Stirlg
167 H6 **Cauldmill** Border
100 B3 **Cauldon** Staffs
86 B1 **Cauldwell** Derbys
147 G4 **Caulkerbush** D & G
156 D6 **Caulside** D & G
27 G8 **Caundle Marsh** Dorset
102 C1 **Caunton** Notts

145 J3	**Causeway End** D & G
61 G4	**Causeway End** Essex
165 K3	**Causewayend** S Lans
185 G7	**Causewayhead** Stirlg
158 F3	**Causey Park Bridge** Nthumb
207 H2	**Causeyend** Abers
77 J5	**Cavendish** Suffk
77 H1	**Cavenham** Suffk
57 L3	**Caversfield** Oxon
42 B5	**Caversham** Readg
99 L4	**Caverswall** Staffs
167 L4	**Caverton Mill** Border
213 K4	**Cawdor** Highld
124 E3	**Cawood** N York
6 C5	**Cawsand** Cnwll
106 D7	**Cawston** Norfk
123 K8	**Cawthorne** Barns
75 K3	**Caxton** Cambs
83 K8	**Caynham** Shrops
102 F3	**Caythorpe** Lincs
102 B4	**Caythorpe** Notts
135 G3	**Cayton** N York
233 b6	**Ceann a Bhaigh** W Isls
201 K3	**Ceannacroc Lodge** Highld
232 f3	**Cearsiadar** W Isls
37 L3	**Cefn** Newpt
36 D4	**Cefn Cribwr** Brdgnd
96 E3	**Cefn-brith** Conwy
97 L4	**Cefn-mawr** Wrexhm
49 K3	**Cefn-y-pant** Carmth
67 J5	**Cefngorwydd** Powys
187 J6	**Cellardyke** Fife
99 L3	**Cellarhead** Staffs
108 E3	**Cemaes** IOA
81 H3	**Cemmaes** Powys
81 H3	**Cemmaes Road** Powys
65 J6	**Cenarth** Cerdgn
186 F5	**Ceres** Fife
14 C3	**Cerne Abbas** Dorset
40 B2	**Cerney Wick** Gloucs
108 E6	**Cerrigceinwen** IOA
96 E3	**Cerrigydrudion** Conwy
95 J1	**Ceunant** Gwynd
55 J2	**Chaceley** Gloucs
3 K3	**Chacewater** Cnwll
73 K7	**Chackmore** Bucks
72 F5	**Chacombe** Nhants
71 H5	**Chadbury** Worcs
113 K1	**Chadderton** Oldham
101 G5	**Chaddesden** C Derb
84 F8	**Chaddesley Corbett** Worcs
6 C1	**Chaddlehanger** Devon
41 H5	**Chaddleworth** W Berk
57 G4	**Chadlington** Oxon
72 D4	**Chadshunt** Warwks
102 C7	**Chadwell** Leics
45 J3	**Chadwell Heath** Gt Lon
45 M4	**Chadwell St Mary** Thurr
70 E2	**Chadwick** Worcs
86 B8	**Chadwick End** Solhll
13 J1	**Chaffcombe** Somset
11 G7	**Chagford** Devon
19 K2	**Chailey** E Susx
33 J4	**Chainhurst** Kent
32 B3	**Chaldon** Surrey
16 F6	**Chale** IOW
16 F6	**Chale Green** IOW
43 G3	**Chalfont Common** Bucks
43 G2	**Chalfont St Giles** Bucks
43 G3	**Chalfont St Peter** Bucks
55 K7	**Chalford** Gloucs
27 K2	**Chalford** Wilts
41 M2	**Chalgrove** Oxon
46 A5	**Chalk** Kent
34 B2	**Chalkwell** Kent
23 L3	**Challacombe** Devon
145 H2	**Challoch** D & G
34 D5	**Challock** Kent
59 G3	**Chalton** Beds
30 B7	**Chalton** Hants
42 F4	**Chalvey** Slough
20 B4	**Chalvington** E Susx
43 H2	**Chandler's Cross** Herts
29 H7	**Chandler's Ford** Hants
27 G3	**Chantry** Somset
78 D5	**Chantry** Suffk
186 D8	**Chapel** Fife
123 L3	**Chapel Allerton** Leeds
26 B2	**Chapel Allerton** Somset
4 F2	**Chapel Amble** Cnwll
73 K2	**Chapel Brampton** Nhants
99 J5	**Chapel Chorlton** Staffs
72 F3	**Chapel Green** Warwks
124 E5	**Chapel Haddlesey** N York
217 K7	**Chapel Hill** Abers
103 K2	**Chapel Hill** Lincs
54 D7	**Chapel Hill** Mons
123 L2	**Chapel Hill** N York
82 F7	**Chapel Lawn** Shrops
130 E4	**Chapel le Dale** N York
25 H5	**Chapel Leigh** Somset
206 D1	**Chapel of Garioch** Abers
144 D6	**Chapel Rossan** D & G
41 L6	**Chapel Row** W Berk
119 H6	**Chapel St Leonards** Lincs
137 K6	**Chapel Stile** Cumb
114 B5	**Chapel-en-le-Frith** Derbys
77 G6	**Chapelend Way** Essex
175 K5	**Chapelhall** N Lans
166 C5	**Chapelhope** Border
156 B7	**Chapelknowe** D & G
197 G6	**Chapelton** Angus
23 J6	**Chapelton** Devon
175 J8	**Chapelton** S Lans
121 L7	**Chapeltown** Bl w D
204 F2	**Chapeltown** Moray
115 G3	**Chapeltown** Sheff
9 J6	**Chapmans Well** Devon
27 J2	**Chapmanslade** Wilts
60 B5	**Chapmore End** Herts
61 L3	**Chappel** Essex
13 H2	**Chard** Somset
13 J2	**Chard Junction** Somset
13 H1	**Chardleigh Green** Somset
13 H2	**Chardstock** Devon
39 G3	**Charfield** S Glos
34 C5	**Charing** Kent
71 L6	**Charingworth** Gloucs
57 G4	**Charlbury** Oxon
39 H6	**Charlcombe** BaNES
39 M5	**Charlcutt** Wilts
72 C3	**Charlecote** Warwks
85 H5	**Charlemont** W Mids
23 L5	**Charles** Devon
78 B4	**Charles Tye** Suffk
196 C7	**Charleston** Angus
123 H3	**Charlestown** Brad
207 H5	**Charlestown** C Aber
122 E5	**Charlestown** Calder
5 G5	**Charlestown** Cnwll
176 E2	**Charlestown** Fife
219 J6	**Charlestown** Highld
213 G5	**Charlestown** Highld
113 J2	**Charlestown** Salfd
114 A3	**Charlesworth** Derbys
25 K4	**Charlinch** Somset
186 E5	**Charlottetown** Fife
45 H4	**Charlton** Gt Lon
73 G7	**Charlton** Nhants
157 K5	**Charlton** Nthumb
41 H3	**Charlton** Oxon
25 L6	**Charlton** Somset
27 G2	**Charlton** Somset
18 B3	**Charlton** W Susx
27 K6	**Charlton** Wilts
39 L3	**Charlton** Wilts
28 C1	**Charlton** Wilts
71 H5	**Charlton** Worcs
83 L2	**Charlton** Wrekin
56 B3	**Charlton Abbots** Gloucs
26 D5	**Charlton Adam** Somset
26 F6	**Charlton Horethorne** Somset
55 L4	**Charlton Kings** Gloucs
26 D5	**Charlton Mackrell** Somset
15 G2	**Charlton Marshall** Dorset
27 G5	**Charlton Musgrove** Somset
15 G2	**Charlton on the Hill** Dorset
28 D6	**Charlton-all-Saints** Wilts
57 K5	**Charlton-on-Otmoor** Oxon
30 A5	**Charlwood** Hants
31 L3	**Charlwood** Surrey
14 D4	**Charminster** Dorset
13 J4	**Charmouth** Dorset
58 A3	**Charndon** Bucks
41 G2	**Charney Bassett** Oxon
121 H7	**Charnock Richard** Lancs
78 F3	**Charsfield** Suffk
33 K4	**Chart Sutton** Kent
41 L8	**Charter Alley** Hants
179 G8	**Charterhall** Border
26 D1	**Charterhouse** Somset
175 K1	**Chartershall** Stirlg
34 E4	**Chartham** Kent
34 E4	**Chartham Hatch** Kent
58 F7	**Chartridge** Bucks
42 C5	**Charvil** Wokham
73 G4	**Charwelton** Nhants
85 J2	**Chase Terrace** Staffs
85 J2	**Chasetown** Staffs
56 E3	**Chastleton** Oxon
9 J4	**Chasty** Devon
122 B2	**Chatburn** Lancs
99 H5	**Chatcull** Staffs
46 C6	**Chatham** Medway
61 H5	**Chatham Green** Essex
169 J4	**Chathill** Nthumb
114 E7	**Chatsworth House** Derbys
46 C5	**Chattenden** Medway
90 B6	**Chatteris** Cambs
122 B6	**Chatterton** Lancs
78 C6	**Chattisham** Suffk
168 B5	**Chatto** Border
168 B5	**Chatton** Nthumb
11 G3	**Chawleigh** Devon
30 B4	**Chawton** Hants
100 A4	**Cheadle** Staffs
113 K4	**Cheadle** Stockp
113 K4	**Cheadle Hulme** Stockp
44 E7	**Cheam** Gt Lon
58 B6	**Chearsley** Bucks
99 J6	**Chebsey** Staffs
42 A4	**Checkendon** Oxon
99 G4	**Checkley** Ches
100 B5	**Checkley** Staffs
77 H3	**Chedburgh** Suffk
26 C2	**Cheddar** Somset
58 F4	**Cheddington** Bucks
99 L3	**Cheddleton** Staffs
25 K6	**Cheddon Fitzpaine** Somset
93 H4	**Chedgrave** Norfk
13 L2	**Chedington** Dorset
93 H7	**Chediston** Suffk
56 B5	**Chedworth** Gloucs
25 M4	**Chedzoy** Somset
113 J2	**Cheetham Hill** Manch
11 H3	**Cheldon** Devon
113 J6	**Chelford** Ches
101 G6	**Chellaston** C Derb
74 D4	**Chellington** Beds
84 C5	**Chelmarsh** Shrops
78 E6	**Chelmondiston** Suffk
114 C7	**Chelmorton** Derbys
61 H6	**Chelmsford** Essex
85 L6	**Chelmsley Wood** Solhll
44 F4	**Chelsea** Gt Lon
45 J7	**Chelsfield** Gt Lon
77 L5	**Chelsworth** Suffk
55 L4	**Cheltenham** Gloucs
74 E1	**Chelveston** Nhants
38 C6	**Chelvey** N Som
38 F7	**Chelwood** BaNES
32 D6	**Chelwood Gate** E Susx
40 C2	**Chelworth Lower Green** Wilts
40 B2	**Chelworth Upper Green** Wilts
83 H6	**Cheney Longville** Shrops
43 G2	**Chenies** Bucks
38 D2	**Chepstow** Mons
40 B6	**Cherhill** Wilts
55 K7	**Cherington** Gloucs
72 C6	**Cherington** Warwks
29 L5	**Cheriton** Hants
35 G7	**Cheriton** Kent
50 F6	**Cheriton** Swans
11 H6	**Cheriton Bishop** Devon
11 K4	**Cheriton Fitzpaine** Devon
49 G7	**Cheriton or Stackpole Elidor** Pembks
98 F8	**Cherrington** Wrekin
126 B3	**Cherry Burton** E R Yk
76 C3	**Cherry Hinton** Cambs
70 F4	**Cherry Orchard** Worcs
117 G6	**Cherry Willingham** Lincs
43 H6	**Chertsey** Surrey
14 E3	**Cheselbourne** Dorset
58 F7	**Chesham** Bucks
122 B7	**Chesham** Bury
58 F7	**Chesham Bois** Bucks
60 B7	**Cheshunt** Herts
14 B6	**Chesil Beach** Dorset
85 H3	**Cheslyn Hay** Staffs
85 L8	**Chessetts Wood** Warwks
44 D7	**Chessington** Surrey

44 D7 Chessington World
  of Adventures Gt Lon
112 B7 Chester Ches
112 B7 Chester Cathedral
  Ches
151 G5 Chester Moor Dur
112 B7 Chester Zoo Ches
151 G5 Chester-le-Street Dur
26 F3 Chesterblade Somset
115 G7 Chesterfield Derbys
177 K5 Chesterhill Mdloth
167 J5 Chesters Border
167 K7 Chesters Border
89 G4 Chesterton Cambs
76 C3 Chesterton Cambs
56 A7 Chesterton Gloucs
57 K4 Chesterton Oxon
84 D4 Chesterton Shrops
72 D3 Chesterton Green
  Warwks
149 L3 Chesterwood
  Nthumb
47 J6 Chestfield Kent
7 G4 Cheston Devon
99 G6 Cheswardine Shrops
168 F1 Cheswick Nthumb
14 B2 Chetnole Dorset
90 D6 Chettisham Cambs
27 L8 Chettle Dorset
84 B5 Chetton Shrops
99 G7 Chetwynd Wrekin
99 H8 Chetwynd Aston
  Wrekin
76 F3 Cheveley Cambs
32 K2 Chevening Kent
77 H3 Chevington Suffk
168 A7 Cheviot Hills
24 F7 Chevithorne Devon
38 E7 Chew Magna BaNES
38 E7 Chew Stoke BaNES
38 F6 Chewton Keynsham
  BaNES
26 E2 Chewton Mendip
  Somset
74 C5 Chicheley M Keyn
18 B5 Chichester W Susx
14 C6 Chickerell Dorset
27 K4 Chicklade Wilts
30 A7 Chidden Hants
30 F4 Chiddingfold Surrey
20 B3 Chiddingly E Susx
32 E4 Chiddingstone Kent
32 F4 Chiddingstone
  Causeway Kent
13 K4 Chideock Dorset
17 L2 Chidham W Susx
123 K6 Chidswell Kirk
41 J5 Chieveley W Berk
61 G5 Chignall Smealy
  Essex
61 G6 Chignall St James
  Essex
45 H2 Chigwell Essex
45 J2 Chigwell Row Essex
29 H4 Chilbolton Hants
29 J5 Chilcomb Hants
13 M4 Chilcombe Dorset
26 F2 Chilcompton Somset
86 C2 Chilcote Leics
27 J8 Child Okeford Dorset
98 F7 Child's Ercall Shrops
111 K6 Childer Thornton
  Ches
41 G3 Childrey Oxon
71 J6 Childswickham
  Worcs
112 B4 Childwall Lpool
14 B3 Chilfrome Dorset
18 A3 Chilgrove W Susx
34 E4 Chilham Kent
10 C8 Chillaton Devon
35 H4 Chillenden Kent
16 F5 Chillerton IOW

79 H4 Chillesford Suffk
168 F4 Chillingham Nthumb
7 J7 Chillington Devon
13 K1 Chillington Somset
27 L5 Chilmark Wilts
34 C6 Chilmington Green
  Kent
56 F4 Chilson Oxon
6 B2 Chilsworthy Cnwll
9 J4 Chilsworthy Devon
42 C2 Chiltern Hills
26 D7 Chilthorne Domer
  Somset
58 B5 Chilton Bucks
141 H2 Chilton Dur
41 J4 Chilton Oxon
29 L4 Chilton Candover
  Hants
26 E6 Chilton Cantelo
  Somset
40 F6 Chilton Foliat Wilts
26 B4 Chilton Polden
  Somset
77 H5 Chilton Street Suffk
25 L4 Chilton Trinity
  Somset
101 K5 Chilwell Notts
29 H7 Chilworth Hants
31 G3 Chilworth Surrey
57 G7 Chimney Oxon
30 A1 Chineham Hants
45 G2 Chingford Gt Lon
114 B5 Chinley Derbys
58 C7 Chinnor Oxon
99 G6 Chipnall Shrops
76 F1 Chippenham Cambs
39 L5 Chippenham Wilts
59 H7 Chipperfield Herts
60 B2 Chipping Herts
121 J2 Chipping Lancs
71 L6 Chipping Campden
  Gloucs
56 F3 Chipping Norton
  Oxon
60 E7 Chipping Ongar
  Essex
39 G4 Chipping Sodbury
  S Glos
72 F5 Chipping Warden
  Nhants
25 G6 Chipstable Somset
32 E3 Chipstead Kent
32 B2 Chipstead Surrey
82 F4 Chirbury Shrops
97 L5 Chirk Wrexhm
179 H6 Chirnside Border
179 H7 Chirnsidebridge
  Border
40 B8 Chirton Wilts
40 F6 Chisbury Wilts
26 C8 Chiselborough
  Somset
40 D4 Chiseldon Swindn
57 L7 Chiselhampton Oxon
166 F6 Chisholme Border
45 H6 Chislehurst Gt Lon
47 L6 Chislet Kent
122 F5 Chisley Calder
59 J6 Chiswell Green Herts
44 E4 Chiswick Gt Lon
113 M3 Chisworth Derbys
30 D6 Chithurst W Susx
76 C1 Chittering Cambs
27 M3 Chitterne Wilts
23 K7 Chittlehamholt
  Devon
23 K6 Chittlehampton
  Devon
10 F3 Chittlehampton
  Devon
39 L6 Chittoe Wilts
7 H7 Chivelstone Devon
23 H4 Chivenor Devon

144 D3 Chlenry D & G
42 F7 Chobham Surrey
28 E3 Cholderton Wilts
58 F6 Cholesbury Bucks
158 B7 Chollerton Nthumb
41 L3 Cholsey Oxon
69 J3 Cholstrey Herefs
142 C7 Chop Gate N York
159 G5 Choppington
  Nthumb
150 E4 Chopwell Gatesd
98 E3 Chorley Ches
121 H6 Chorley Lancs
84 C6 Chorley Shrops
43 H2 Chorleywood Herts
43 G2 Chorleywood West
  Herts
99 G3 Chorlton Ches
98 C3 Chorlton Lane Ches
113 J3 Chorlton-cum-
  Hardy Manch
83 H5 Choulton Shrops
76 C6 Chrishall Essex
173 L4 Chrisswell Inver
90 C4 Christchurch Cambs
15 M4 Christchurch Dorset
37 M3 Christchurch Mons
39 L5 Christian Malford
  Wilts
112 C7 Christleton Ches
38 B8 Christon N Som
169 J5 Christon Bank
  Nthumb
11 J7 Christow Devon
11 K8 Chudleigh Devon
7 J1 Chudleigh Knighton
  Devon
11 G3 Chulmleigh Devon
121 L5 Church Lancs
99 H8 Church Aston Wrekin
73 K2 Church Brampton
  Nhants
100 D5 Church Broughton
  Derbys
30 D2 Church Crookham
  Hants
99 J8 Church Eaton Staffs
75 H6 Church End Beds
61 H3 Church End Essex
44 E3 Church End Gt Lon
30 A1 Church End Hants
57 G3 Church Enstone
  Oxon
124 D3 Church Fenton
  N York
12 F3 Church Green Devon
57 H5 Church Hanborough
  Oxon
112 F7 Church Hill Ches
142 E7 Church Houses
  N York
15 H6 Church Knowle
  Dorset
87 K5 Church Langton Leics
86 F7 Church Lawford
  Warwks
99 J2 Church Lawton Ches
100 A5 Church Leigh Staffs
71 H4 Church Lench Worcs
100 D4 Church Mayfield
  Staffs
98 F1 Church Minshull
  Ches
18 B6 Church Norton
  W Susx
83 K4 Church Preen Shrops
83 H3 Church Pulverbatch
  Shrops
73 J3 Church Stowe
  Nhants
46 B5 Church Street Kent
83 J5 Church Stretton
  Shrops

37 G3 Church Village
  Rhondd
115 K7 Church Warsop
  Notts
55 H4 Churcham Gloucs
55 K4 Churchdown Gloucs
47 G2 Churchend Essex
85 H5 Churchfield Birm
13 H3 Churchill Devon
38 C7 Churchill N Som
56 F3 Churchill Oxon
84 F7 Churchill Worcs
71 G4 Churchill Worcs
25 K8 Churchinford
  Somset
87 G7 Churchover Warwks
25 J8 Churchstanton
  Somset
82 F5 Churchstoke Powys
7 G6 Churchstow Devon
114 E8 Churchtown Derbys
121 G2 Churchtown Lancs
7 K5 Churston Ferrers
  Torbay
30 D4 Churt Surrey
98 B2 Churton Ches
123 K5 Churwell Leeds
95 G5 Chwilog Gwynd
2 E5 Chyandour Cnwll
2 E4 Chysauster Cnwll
111 G7 Cilcain Flints
66 C3 Cilcennin Cerdgn
52 B7 Cilfrew Neath
37 G3 Cilfynydd Rhondd
65 H6 Cilgerran Pembks
51 L4 Cilmaengwyn Neath
67 L4 Cilmery Powys
51 H2 Cilsan Carmth
96 D4 Ciltalgarth Gwynd
51 L5 Cilybebyll Neath
67 G6 Cilycwm Carmth
36 B2 Cimla Neath
54 F5 Cinderford Gloucs
42 F4 Cippenham Slough
56 A7 Cirencester Gloucs
45 G4 City Gt Lon
45 H4 City Airport Gt Lon
188 F5 Clabhach Ag & B
173 J3 Clachaig Ag & B
182 A4 Clachan Ag & B
191 G7 Clachan Ag & B
172 C6 Clachan Ag & B
209 H6 Clachan Highld
188 C6 Clachan Mor Ag & B
233 c6 Clachan na Luib
  W Isls
175 G3 Clachan of Campsie
  E Duns
233 c6 Clachan-a-Luib W Isls
181 M4 Clachan-Seil Ag & B
153 H6 Clachaneasy D & G
213 G5 Clachnaharry Highld
224 C3 Clachtoll Highld
195 J4 Clackavoid P & K
185 J8 Clackmannan Clacks
214 F3 Clackmarras Moray
62 E5 Clacton-on-Sea Essex
182 F3 Cladich Ag & B
71 J3 Cladswell Worcs
190 E6 Claggan Highld
208 C4 Claigan Highld
30 B7 Clanfield Hants
56 F7 Clanfield Oxon
28 F2 Clanville Hants
26 F5 Clanville Somset
172 E6 Claonaig Ag & B
60 C3 Clapgate Herts
74 F4 Clapham Beds
44 F5 Clapham Gt Lon
130 E5 Clapham N York
18 F4 Clapham W Susx
13 K2 Clapton Somset

26 F2 **Clapton** Somset
38 C5 **Clapton-in-Gordano** N Som
56 D4 **Clapton-on-the-Hill** Gloucs
150 E3 **Claravale** Gatesd
49 H3 **Clarbeston** Pembks
49 H4 **Clarbeston Road** Pembks
116 B5 **Clarborough** Notts
77 H5 **Clare** Suffk
146 D2 **Clarebrand** D & G
147 J2 **Clarencefield** D & G
150 C2 **Clarewood** Nthumb
167 H5 **Clarilaw** Border
175 G6 **Clarkston** E Rens
224 C3 **Clashmore** Highld
223 G4 **Clashmore** Highld
224 C3 **Clashnessie** Highld
204 F2 **Clashnoir** Moray
185 K4 **Clathy** P & K
185 L3 **Clathymore** P & K
205 L1 **Clatt** Abers
81 L5 **Clatter** Powys
25 G5 **Clatworthy** Somset
121 G3 **Claughton** Lancs
130 B6 **Claughton** Lancs
111 J4 **Claughton** Wirral
71 L2 **Claverdon** Warwks
38 C6 **Claverham** N Som
60 D2 **Clavering** Essex
84 E5 **Claverley** Shrops
39 H7 **Claverton** BaNES
37 G5 **Clawdd-coch** V Glam
97 G3 **Clawdd-newydd** Denbgs
9 J5 **Clawton** Devon
117 J3 **Claxby** Lincs
133 L7 **Claxton** N York
93 H3 **Claxton** Norfk
87 H7 **Clay Coton** Nhants
115 H8 **Clay Cross** Derbys
86 F5 **Claybrooke Magna** Leics
72 F4 **Claydon** Oxon
78 D5 **Claydon** Suffk
156 D6 **Claygate** D & G
33 J4 **Claygate** Kent
44 D7 **Claygate** Surrey
45 H3 **Clayhall** Gt Lon
24 F6 **Clayhanger** Devon
25 J7 **Clayhidon** Devon
21 G2 **Clayhill** E Susx
231 H4 **Clayock** Highld
55 H6 **Claypits** Gloucs
102 D3 **Claypole** Lincs
123 G4 **Clayton** Brad
124 C8 **Clayton** Donc
19 J3 **Clayton** W Susx
123 K7 **Clayton West** Kirk
121 L4 **Clayton-le-Moors** Lancs
121 H6 **Clayton-le-Woods** Lancs
116 B4 **Clayworth** Notts
199 G2 **Cleadale** Highld
151 J3 **Cleadon** S Tyne
6 D3 **Clearbrook** Devon
54 E6 **Clearwell** Gloucs
141 G5 **Cleasby** N York
234 C8 **Cleat** Ork
140 E4 **Cleatlam** Dur
136 D4 **Cleator** Cumb
136 E4 **Cleator Moor** Cumb
123 J5 **Cleckheaton** Kirk
83 L6 **Clee St Margaret** Shrops
83 L7 **Cleehill** Shrops
175 K6 **Cleekhimin** N Lans
127 H8 **Cleethorpes** NE Lin
84 B7 **Cleeton St Mary** Shrops
38 C7 **Cleeve** N Som

41 L4 **Cleeve** Oxon
55 M3 **Cleeve Hill** Gloucs
71 J5 **Cleeve Prior** Worcs
178 D2 **Cleghornie** E Loth
69 J6 **Clehonger** Herefs
186 A7 **Cleish** P & K
175 L6 **Cleland** N Lans
182 C2 **Clenamacrie** Ag & B
104 F7 **Clenchwarton** Norfk
216 E3 **Clenerty** Abers
85 G7 **Clent** Worcs
84 C7 **Cleobury Mortimer** Shrops
84 B6 **Cleobury North** Shrops
161 H3 **Cleongart** Ag & B
213 J4 **Clephanton** Highld
156 A3 **Clerkhill** D & G
154 E3 **Cleuch-head** D & G
40 B5 **Clevancy** Wilts
38 B6 **Clevedon** N Som
120 D2 **Cleveleys** Lancs
39 L4 **Cleverton** Wilts
26 C2 **Clewer** Somset
106 C4 **Cley next the Sea** Norfk
138 E3 **Cliburn** Cumb
29 M2 **Cliddesden** Hants
21 H3 **Cliff End** E Susx
46 C5 **Cliffe** Medway
140 F4 **Cliffe** N York
125 G4 **Cliffe** N York
46 C5 **Cliffe Woods** Medway
68 E5 **Clifford** Herefs
124 C2 **Clifford** Leeds
71 L4 **Clifford Chambers** Warwks
55 G4 **Clifford's Mesne** Gloucs
75 H6 **Clifton** Beds
38 E5 **Clifton** Bristl
101 K5 **Clifton** C Nott
123 H6 **Clifton** Calder
138 D2 **Clifton** Cumb
100 D4 **Clifton** Derbys
115 K3 **Clifton** Donc
120 F4 **Clifton** Lancs
123 J2 **Clifton** N York
57 J2 **Clifton** Oxon
70 F5 **Clifton** Worcs
133 J8 **Clifton** York
86 B2 **Clifton Campville** Staffs
41 K2 **Clifton Hampden** Oxon
74 C4 **Clifton Reynes** M Keyn
87 G7 **Clifton upon Dunsmore** Warwks
70 C3 **Clifton upon Teme** Worcs
35 K1 **Cliftonville** Kent
18 D5 **Climping** W Susx
27 H2 **Clink** Somset
132 D7 **Clint** N York
92 B2 **Clint Green** Norfk
206 F3 **Clinterty** C Aber
167 J3 **Clintmains** Border
93 J2 **Clippesby** Norfk
88 D1 **Clipsham** Rutlnd
87 K7 **Clipston** Nhants
101 M5 **Clipston** Notts
58 F3 **Clipstone** Beds
115 L8 **Clipstone** Notts
121 L3 **Clitheroe** Lancs
98 D7 **Clive** Shrops
117 J2 **Clixby** Lincs
39 M3 **Cloatley** Wilts
97 G2 **Clocaenog** Denbgs
215 J3 **Clochan** Moray
196 D5 **Clochtow** Angus
53 L3 **Clodock** Herefs
217 J5 **Clola** Abers

74 F6 **Clophill** Beds
88 F7 **Clopton** Nhants
78 D4 **Clopton** Suffk
78 F4 **Clopton Corner** Suffk
236 d2 **Clos du Valle** Guern
154 F4 **Closeburn** D & G
154 F3 **Closeburnmill** D & G
14 B1 **Closworth** Somset
59 L2 **Clothall** Herts
112 D8 **Clotton** Ches
122 F6 **Clough Foot** Calder
123 G6 **Clough Head** Calder
143 K7 **Cloughton** N York
235 c5 **Clousta** Shet
196 B2 **Clova** Angus
22 E6 **Clovelly** Devon
167 G3 **Clovenfords** Border
191 K4 **Clovulin** Highld
122 C5 **Clow Bridge** Lancs
115 J6 **Clowne** Derbys
70 C1 **Clows Top** Worcs
201 G3 **Cluanie Inn** Highld
201 G3 **Cluanie Lodge** Highld
145 H4 **Clugston** D & G
82 F7 **Clun** Shrops
213 K5 **Clunas** Highld
83 G7 **Clunbury** Shrops
203 J1 **Clune** Highld
201 J7 **Clunes** Highld
83 H7 **Clungunford** Shrops
216 C4 **Clunie** Abers
195 H7 **Clunie** P & K
83 G7 **Clunton** Shrops
186 D7 **Cluny** Fife
38 F8 **Clutton** BaNES
98 C2 **Clutton** Ches
38 F8 **Clutton Hill** BaNES
53 K5 **Clydach** Mons
51 K5 **Clydach** Swans
36 F2 **Clydach Vale** Rhondd
174 F4 **Clydebank** W Duns
40 B5 **Clyffe Pypard** Wilts
174 A2 **Clynder** Ag & B
49 J4 **Clynderwen** Carmth
52 C7 **Clyne** Neath
95 G3 **Clynnog-fawr** Gwynd
68 E5 **Clyro** Powys
12 C4 **Clyst Honiton** Devon
12 D3 **Clyst Hydon** Devon
12 C5 **Clyst St George** Devon
12 D3 **Clyst St Lawrence** Devon
12 C4 **Clyst St Mary** Devon
232 g2 **Cnoc** W Isls
80 F8 **Cnwch Coch** Cerdgn
5 L1 **Coad's Green** Cnwll
164 F3 **Coalburn** S Lans
150 E3 **Coalburns** Gatesd
55 H7 **Coaley** Gloucs
61 J7 **Coalhill** Essex
38 F4 **Coalpit Heath** S Glos
84 C3 **Coalport** Wrekin
185 J7 **Coalsnaughton** Clacks
186 E7 **Coaltown of Balgonie** Fife
186 E7 **Coaltown of Wemyss** Fife
86 E2 **Coalville** Leics
149 H3 **Coanwood** Nthumb
26 C2 **Coat** Somset
175 J5 **Coatbridge** N Lans
175 K5 **Coatdyke** N Lans
40 D4 **Coate** Swindn
40 B7 **Coate** Wilts
89 K4 **Coates** Cambs
55 L7 **Coates** Gloucs
116 E5 **Coates** Lincs
18 D3 **Coates** W Susx
23 K6 **Cobbaton** Devon
55 L5 **Coberley** Gloucs
46 A6 **Cobham** Kent

43 J7 **Cobham** Surrey
69 J3 **Cobnash** Herefs
236 C2 **Cobo** Guern
217 H2 **Coburby** Abers
205 G4 **Cock Bridge** Abers
61 K7 **Cock Clarks** Essex
61 H4 **Cock Green** Essex
21 K2 **Cock Marling** E Susx
75 J5 **Cockayne Hatley** Beds
179 G4 **Cockburnspath** Border
177 L4 **Cockenzie and Port Seton** E Loth
120 F1 **Cockerham** Lancs
136 F2 **Cockermouth** Cumb
59 J4 **Cockernhoe Green** Herts
51 J6 **Cockett** Swans
140 E3 **Cockfield** Dur
77 K4 **Cockfield** Suffk
44 F2 **Cockfosters** Gt Lon
18 B3 **Cocking** W Susx
18 B2 **Cocking Causeway** W Susx
7 K3 **Cockington** Torbay
26 C2 **Cocklake** Somset
158 F4 **Cockle Park** Nthumb
91 H3 **Cockley Cley** Norfk
42 D4 **Cockpole Green** Wokham
98 B6 **Cockshutt** Shrops
106 B4 **Cockthorpe** Norfk
12 C6 **Cockwood** Devon
114 B5 **Cockyard** Derbys
78 D4 **Coddenham** Suffk
70 C6 **Coddington** Herefs
102 D2 **Coddington** Notts
27 L4 **Codford St Mary** Wilts
27 L4 **Codford St Peter** Wilts
59 K4 **Codicote** Herts
31 H7 **Codmore Hill** W Susx
101 H3 **Codnor** Derbys
39 G5 **Codrington** S Glos
84 F3 **Codsall** Staffs
84 F3 **Codsall Wood** Staffs
97 L2 **Coed Talon** Flints
53 M7 **Coed-y-paen** Mons
108 F5 **Coedana** IOA
97 L3 **Coedpoeth** Wrexhm
7 K3 **Coffinswell** Devon
12 C6 **Cofton** Devon
85 H7 **Cofton Hackett** Worcs
37 J6 **Cogan** V Glam
74 B3 **Cogenhoe** Nhants
61 K4 **Coggeshall** Essex
203 H2 **Coignafearn** Highld
205 H6 **Coilacriech** Abers
184 D6 **Coilantogle** Stirlg
208 E6 **Coillore** Highld
202 B8 **Coilty** Highld
36 E4 **Coity** Brdgnd
232 g2 **Col** W Isls
225 L6 **Colaboll** Highld
4 D4 **Colan** Cnwll
12 D5 **Colaton Raleigh** Devon
208 C5 **Colbost** Highld
140 F7 **Colburn** N York
138 F3 **Colby** Cumb
237 b6 **Colby** IOM
106 F6 **Colby** Norfk
62 B3 **Colchester** Essex
41 K6 **Cold Ash** W Berk
87 J7 **Cold Ashby** Nhants
39 H6 **Cold Ashton** S Glos
56 C4 **Cold Aston** Gloucs
74 D4 **Cold Brayfield** M Keyn
117 G5 **Cold Hanworth** Lincs

73 J4 **Cold Higham** Nhants
133 H3 **Cold Kirby** N York
61 K7 **Cold Norton** Essex
88 B2 **Cold Overton** Leics
229 J4 **Coldbackie** Highld
19 J4 **Coldean** Br & H
7 J2 **Coldeast** Devon
122 E5 **Colden** Calder
29 J6 **Colden Common** Hants
79 J3 **Coldfair Green** Suffk
31 J3 **Coldharbour** Surrey
179 J5 **Coldingham** Border
99 J6 **Coldmeece** Staffs
35 H5 **Coldred** Kent
11 G4 **Coldridge** Devon
168 C2 **Coldstream** Border
18 D3 **Coldwaltham** W Susx
69 H7 **Coldwell** Herefs
217 H6 **Coldwells** Abers
26 F5 **Cole** Somset
83 G6 **Colebatch** Shrops
12 C2 **Colebrook** Devon
11 H5 **Colebrooke** Devon
102 F1 **Coleby** Lincs
125 L6 **Coleby** N Linc
11 H5 **Coleford** Devon
54 E6 **Coleford** Gloucs
27 G2 **Coleford** Somset
25 H5 **Coleford Water** Somset
92 E6 **Colegate End** Norfk
15 J3 **Colehill** Dorset
32 D6 **Coleman's Hatch** E Susx
98 B6 **Colemere** Shrops
30 B5 **Colemore** Hants
186 B2 **Colenden** P & K
39 J6 **Colerne** Wilts
56 A5 **Colesbourne** Gloucs
42 F2 **Coleshill** Bucks
40 E2 **Coleshill** Oxon
85 L5 **Coleshill** Warwks
26 E1 **Coley** BaNES
31 L5 **Colgate** W Susx
187 H6 **Colinsburgh** Fife
177 H5 **Colinton** C Edin
173 H4 **Colintraive** Ag & B
105 L7 **Colkirk** Norfk
186 C2 **Collace** P & K
235 c3 **Collafirth** Shet
7 G7 **Collaton** Devon
7 K4 **Collaton St Mary** Torbay
214 E2 **College of Roseisle** Moray
42 D7 **College Town** Br For
186 E5 **Collessie** Fife
45 J2 **Collier Row** Gt Lon
33 J4 **Collier Street** Kent
60 B4 **Collier's End** Herts
217 K8 **Collieston** Abers
155 H6 **Collin** D & G
28 E2 **Collingbourne Ducis** Wilts
28 E1 **Collingbourne Kingston** Wilts
124 B2 **Collingham** Leeds
102 D1 **Collingham** Notts
70 B3 **Collington** Herefs
73 L4 **Collingtree** Nhants
112 E3 **Collins Green** Warrtn
196 F7 **Colliston** Angus
12 E2 **Colliton** Devon
88 E3 **Collyweston** Nhants
152 D5 **Colmonell** S Ayrs
75 G3 **Colmworth** Beds
56 B6 **Coln Rogers** Gloucs
56 C6 **Coln St Aldwyns** Gloucs
56 B5 **Coln St Dennis** Gloucs
43 G5 **Colnbrook** Slough

89 L7 **Colne** Cambs
122 D3 **Colne** Lancs
61 K3 **Colne Engaine** Essex
92 E3 **Colney** Norfk
59 K6 **Colney Heath** Herts
216 C7 **Colpy** Abers
166 E2 **Colquhar** Border
102 F7 **Colsterworth** Lincs
102 B5 **Colston Bassett** Notts
33 H4 **Colt's Hill** Kent
214 D2 **Coltfield** Moray
106 F8 **Coltishall** Norfk
129 G3 **Colton** Cumb
124 B4 **Colton** Leeds
124 E2 **Colton** N York
92 D2 **Colton** Norfk
100 B7 **Colton** Staffs
146 E4 **Colvend** D & G
70 D6 **Colwall** Herefs
158 B6 **Colwell** Nthumb
100 A7 **Colwich** Staffs
36 E5 **Colwinston** V Glam
18 C5 **Colworth** W Susx
110 B5 **Colwyn Bay** Conwy
13 G4 **Colyford** Devon
13 G4 **Colyton** Devon
57 H5 **Combe** Oxon
41 G7 **Combe** W Berk
39 H7 **Combe Down** BaNES
7 J3 **Combe Fishacre** Devon
25 J5 **Combe Florey** Somset
39 G7 **Combe Hay** BaNES
23 J3 **Combe Martin** Devon
12 F3 **Combe Raleigh** Devon
13 H1 **Combe St Nicholas** Somset
7 K2 **Combeinteignhead** Devon
112 F6 **Comberbach** Ches
85 L3 **Comberford** Staffs
75 L4 **Comberton** Cambs
69 K2 **Comberton** Herefs
72 C4 **Combrook** Warwks
114 B4 **Combs** Derbys
78 C3 **Combs** Suffk
78 C3 **Combs Ford** Suffk
25 K3 **Combwich** Somset
206 D4 **Comers** Abers
70 E2 **Comhampton** Worcs
49 K4 **Commercial** Pembks
81 J3 **Commins Coch** Powys
5 K2 **Common Moor** Cnwll
142 E5 **Commondale** N York
113 L4 **Compstall** Stockp
146 B4 **Compstonend** D & G
7 K3 **Compton** Devon
29 J6 **Compton** Hants
84 E6 **Compton** Staffs
30 F3 **Compton** Surrey
41 K4 **Compton** W Berk
30 C7 **Compton** W Susx
28 C2 **Compton** Wilts
27 K7 **Compton Abbas** Dorset
56 B5 **Compton Abdale** Gloucs
40 B6 **Compton Bassett** Wilts
40 F3 **Compton Beauchamp** Oxon
26 B1 **Compton Bishop** Somset
28 B5 **Compton Chamberlayne** Wilts
38 F7 **Compton Dando** BaNES
26 C5 **Compton Dundon** Somset

26 B7 **Compton Durville** Somset
38 E4 **Compton Greenfield** S Glos
38 D8 **Compton Martin** BaNES
26 F6 **Compton Pauncefoot** Somset
14 B4 **Compton Valence** Dorset
176 D1 **Comrie** Fife
185 G3 **Comrie** P & K
191 K3 **Conaglen House** Highld
210 D8 **Conchra** Highld
195 H7 **Concraigie** P & K
71 G6 **Conderton** Worcs
56 D3 **Condicote** Gloucs
175 K4 **Condorrat** N Lans
83 J3 **Condover** Shrops
55 J4 **Coney Hill** Gloucs
91 L7 **Coney Weston** Suffk
31 J6 **Coneyhurst Common** W Susx
133 L5 **Coneysthorpe** N York
5 L1 **Congdon's Shop** Cnwll
86 D3 **Congerstone** Leics
105 H7 **Congham** Norfk
113 J8 **Congleton** Ches
38 C7 **Congresbury** N Som
147 H2 **Conheath** D & G
214 B4 **Conicavel** Moray
103 L2 **Coningsby** Lincs
89 H6 **Conington** Cambs
75 K2 **Conington** Cambs
115 K2 **Conisbrough** Donc
118 E3 **Conisholme** Lincs
137 J7 **Coniston** Cumb
126 E4 **Coniston** E R Yk
131 G8 **Coniston Cold** N York
131 J6 **Conistone** N York
111 J7 **Connah's Quay** Flints
182 C1 **Connel** Ag & B
164 C6 **Connel Park** E Ayrs
3 G4 **Connor Downs** Cnwll
212 E4 **Conon Bridge** Highld
122 E2 **Cononley** N York
99 M3 **Consall** Staffs
150 E5 **Consett** Dur
132 B2 **Constable Burton** N York
3 J5 **Constantine** Cnwll
4 D2 **Constantine Bay** Cnwll
212 C3 **Contin** Highld
109 L6 **Conwy** Conwy
77 K2 **Conyer's Green** Suffk
20 E4 **Cooden** E Susx
62 E4 **Cook's Green** Essex
9 K4 **Cookbury** Devon
42 E4 **Cookham** W & M
42 E4 **Cookham Dean** W & M
42 E4 **Cookham Rise** W & M
71 J3 **Cookhill** Warwks
93 H7 **Cookley** Suffk
84 E7 **Cookley** Worcs
42 B3 **Cookley Green** Oxon
207 G6 **Cookney** Abers
77 L4 **Cooks Green** Suffk
61 G6 **Cooksmill Green** Essex
31 J6 **Coolham** W Susx
46 C5 **Cooling** Medway
7 L2 **Coombe** Devon
12 E4 **Coombe** Devon
39 H2 **Coombe** Gloucs
30 A7 **Coombe** Hants
28 C6 **Coombe Bissett** Wilts
7 K2 **Coombe Cellars** Devon

25 G5 **Coombe End** Somset
55 K3 **Coombe Hill** Gloucs
14 F5 **Coombe Keynes** Dorset
7 L3 **Coombe Pafford** Torbay
69 G2 **Coombes-Moor** Herefs
214 B4 **Cooperhill** Moray
60 D7 **Coopersale Common** Essex
60 D7 **Coopersale Street** Essex
35 J3 **Cop Street** Kent
78 D6 **Copdock** Suffk
61 L4 **Copford Green** Essex
132 E6 **Copgrove** N York
235 d3 **Copister** Shet
75 G5 **Cople** Beds
140 D3 **Copley** Dur
124 E2 **Copmanthorpe** York
99 J6 **Copmere End** Staffs
120 F3 **Copp** Lancs
9 G5 **Coppathorne** Cnwll
99 K8 **Coppenhall** Staffs
2 F4 **Copperhouse** Cnwll
89 H7 **Coppingford** Cambs
11 H4 **Copplestone** Devon
121 H7 **Coppull** Lancs
31 K6 **Copsale** W Susx
121 K4 **Copster Green** Lancs
86 F5 **Copston Magna** Warwks
132 E5 **Copt Hewick** N York
86 F2 **Copt Oak** Leics
32 B5 **Copthorne** W Susx
28 F8 **Copythorne** Hants
45 K3 **Corbets Tey** Gt Lon
236 a7 **Corbiere** Jersey
150 C3 **Corbridge** Nthumb
88 C5 **Corby** Nhants
103 G7 **Corby Glen** Lincs
162 D4 **Cordon** N Ayrs
84 B8 **Coreley** Shrops
25 K7 **Corfe** Somset
15 H6 **Corfe Castle** Dorset
15 J3 **Corfe Mullen** Dorset
83 J6 **Corfton** Shrops
205 G4 **Corgarff** Abers
29 L7 **Corhampton** Hants
86 C6 **Corley** Warwks
86 C6 **Corley Ash** Warwks
86 C6 **Corley Moor** Warwks
195 L3 **Cormuir** Angus
77 K6 **Cornard Tye** Suffk
151 H7 **Cornforth** Dur
216 B3 **Cornhill** Abers
168 C2 **Cornhill-on-Tweed** Nthumb
122 D5 **Cornholme** Calder
188 C6 **Cornoigmore** Ag & B
150 E6 **Cornsay** Dur
150 F6 **Cornsay Colliery** Dur
212 E3 **Corntown** Highld
36 E5 **Corntown** V Glam
56 F3 **Cornwell** Oxon
6 E4 **Cornwood** Devon
7 J5 **Cornworthy** Devon
191 L2 **Corpach** Highld
106 D6 **Corpusty** Norfk
205 K4 **Corrachree** Abers
200 C4 **Corran** Highld
191 K4 **Corran** Highld
155 L5 **Corrie** D & G
162 C2 **Corrie** N Ayrs
162 B5 **Corriecravie** N Ayrs
162 D3 **Corriegills** N Ayrs
201 K6 **Corriegour Lodge Hotel** Highld
212 B2 **Corriemoillie** Highld
212 B7 **Corrimony** Highld
116 E4 **Corringham** Lincs
46 B4 **Corringham** Thurr
81 G2 **Corris** Gwynd

81 G2 **Corris Uchaf** Gwynd
183 H7 **Corrow** Ag & B
199 K1 **Corry** Highld
10 F5 **Corscombe** Devon
13 M2 **Corscombe** Dorset
55 J2 **Corse Lawn** Gloucs
39 K6 **Corsham** Wilts
206 D4 **Corsindae** Abers
27 J3 **Corsley** Wilts
27 J3 **Corsley Heath** Wilts
154 D6 **Corsock** D & G
39 G7 **Corston** BaNES
39 L4 **Corston** Wilts
177 G4 **Corstorphine** C Edin
196 C4 **Cortachy** Angus
93 L4 **Corton** Suffk
27 L4 **Corton** Wilts
26 F6 **Corton Denham**
Somset
191 L3 **Coruanan Lodge**
Highld
97 G4 **Corwen** Denbgs
10 C7 **Coryton** Devon
46 C4 **Coryton** Thurr
87 G4 **Cosby** Leics
85 G5 **Coseley** Dudley
73 L6 **Cosgrove** Nhants
17 J2 **Cosham** C Port
49 G6 **Cosheston** Pembks
194 C6 **Coshieville** P & K
101 J4 **Cossall** Notts
87 H2 **Cossington** Leics
26 A4 **Cossington** Somset
92 E2 **Costessey** Norfk
101 L7 **Costock** Notts
102 D7 **Coston** Leics
92 C3 **Coston** Norfk
57 G2 **Cote** Oxon
112 E7 **Cotebrook** Ches
148 E5 **Cotehill** Cumb
101 K7 **Cotes** Leics
87 G6 **Cotesbach** Leics
101 M5 **Cotgrave** Notts
207 G3 **Cothal** Abers
102 C3 **Cotham** Notts
140 C4 **Cotherstone** Dur
57 J7 **Cothill** Oxon
13 G3 **Cotleigh** Devon
101 J4 **Cotmanhay** Derbys
76 B3 **Coton** Cambs
73 J1 **Coton** Nhants
99 J7 **Coton** Staffs
99 K7 **Coton Clanford** Staffs
83 J2 **Coton Hill** Shrops
86 B1 **Coton in the Elms**
Derbys
55 M6 **Cotswolds**
7 H4 **Cott** Devon
121 G4 **Cottam** Lancs
116 D5 **Cottam** Notts
76 C2 **Cottenham** Cambs
60 A3 **Cottered** Herts
88 F5 **Cotterstock** Nhants
87 K8 **Cottesbrooke**
Nhants
88 C2 **Cottesmore** Rutlnd
126 C4 **Cottingham** E R Yk
88 B5 **Cottingham** Nhants
123 G3 **Cottingley** Brad
57 L2 **Cottisford** Oxon
78 C2 **Cotton** Suffk
215 L8 **Cottown** Abers
206 E3 **Cottown** Abers
216 F6 **Cottown of Gight**
Abers
6 C3 **Cotts** Devon
71 J3 **Coughton** Warwks
172 C5 **Coulaghailtro** Ag & B
210 E5 **Coulags** Highld
205 L5 **Coull** Abers
173 L2 **Coulport** Ag & B
32 B2 **Coulsdon** Gt Lon
27 L2 **Coulston** Wilts

165 K3 **Coulter** S Lans
133 K5 **Coulton** N York
186 F3 **Coultra** Fife
83 L3 **Cound** Shrops
141 G2 **Coundon** Dur
131 H2 **Countersett** N York
12 B4 **Countess Wear**
Devon
87 H4 **Countesthorpe** Leics
24 B2 **Countisbury** Devon
195 K7 **Coupar Angus** P & K
168 D3 **Coupland** Nthumb
172 D8 **Cour** Ag & B
155 J4 **Courance** D & G
51 H2 **Court Henry** Carmth
199 L6 **Courteachan** Highld
73 L4 **Courteenhall** Nhants
47 G2 **Courtsend** Essex
25 J5 **Courtway** Somset
177 K5 **Cousland** Mdloth
33 H6 **Cousley Wood** E Susx
173 L2 **Cove** Ag & B
179 G4 **Cove** Border
24 E7 **Cove** Devon
30 E1 **Cove** Hants
219 J3 **Cove** Highld
207 H5 **Cove Bay** C Aber
93 L6 **Covehithe** Suffk
85 G3 **Coven** Staffs
90 C6 **Coveney** Cambs
118 D3 **Covenham St**
Bartholomew Lincs
118 D3 **Covenham St Mary**
Lincs
86 D7 **Coventry** Covtry
86 D8 **Coventry Airport**
Warwks
3 K7 **Coverack** Cnwll
3 H5 **Coverack Bridges**
Cnwll
131 L3 **Coverham** N York
74 F1 **Covington** Cambs
165 J2 **Covington** S Lans
71 K5 **Cow Honeybourne**
Worcs
130 C4 **Cowan Bridge** Lancs
20 C3 **Cowbeech** E Susx
103 L8 **Cowbit** Lincs
36 F5 **Cowbridge** V Glam
32 E5 **Cowden** Kent
177 G1 **Cowdenbeath** Fife
100 F3 **Cowers Lane** Derbys
16 F3 **Cowes** IOW
133 G2 **Cowesby** N York
31 K6 **Cowfold** W Susx
38 E3 **Cowhill** S Glos
175 L1 **Cowie** Stirlg
11 K5 **Cowley** Devon
55 L5 **Cowley** Gloucs
43 H4 **Cowley** Gt Lon
57 K7 **Cowley** Oxon
121 H6 **Cowling** Lancs
122 E2 **Cowling** N York
132 C3 **Cowling** N York
77 G4 **Cowlinge** Suffk
159 H5 **Cowpen** Nthumb
17 K1 **Cowplain** Hants
149 L6 **Cowshill** Dur
38 C7 **Cowslip Green**
N Som
132 F8 **Cowthorpe** N York
98 F4 **Coxbank** Ches
101 G4 **Coxbench** Derbys
8 F5 **Coxford** Cnwll
105 K6 **Coxford** Norfk
33 J3 **Coxheath** Kent
151 H7 **Coxhoe** Dur
26 D3 **Coxley** Somset
26 D3 **Coxley Wick** Somset
45 K2 **Coxtie Green** Essex
133 H4 **Coxwold** N York
36 E4 **Coychurch** Brdgnd
163 K5 **Coylton** S Ayrs

203 L3 **Coylumbridge** Highld
36 D4 **Coytrahen** Brdgnd
71 J2 **Crabbs Cross** Worcs
31 K6 **Crabtree** W Susx
138 F3 **Crackenthorpe**
Cumb
8 F5 **Crackington Haven**
Cnwll
84 D2 **Crackleybank** Shrops
131 J7 **Cracoe** N York
25 G8 **Craddock** Devon
85 G6 **Cradley** Dudley
70 D5 **Cradley** Herefs
85 G6 **Cradley Heath** Sandw
52 F2 **Cradoc** Powys
6 B5 **Crafthole** Cnwll
58 E4 **Crafton** Bucks
122 E5 **Cragg Vale** Calder
204 C1 **Craggan** Highld
150 F5 **Craghead** Dur
52 D3 **Crai** Powys
215 L3 **Craibstone** Moray
196 E6 **Craichie** Angus
197 H5 **Craig** Angus
211 G4 **Craig** Highld
51 K4 **Craig Llangiwg** Neath
164 C6 **Craigbank** E Ayrs
177 H7 **Craigburn** Border
156 C5 **Craigcleuch** D & G
216 F7 **Craigdam** Abers
182 B6 **Craigdhu** Ag & B
206 D3 **Craigearn** Abers
215 G5 **Craigellachie** Moray
186 B3 **Craigend** P & K
174 E4 **Craigend** Rens
174 C3 **Craigendoran** Ag & B
145 G3 **Craighlaw** D & G
171 K5 **Craighouse** Ag & B
195 H7 **Craigie** P & K
163 K3 **Craigie** S Ayrs
217 H2 **Craigiefold** Abers
146 D4 **Craigley** D & G
177 H4 **Craiglockhart** C Edin
215 H4 **Craiglug** Moray
177 J4 **Craigmillar** C Edin
154 D5 **Craigneston** D & G
175 K5 **Craigneuk** N Lans
175 K6 **Craigneuk** N Lans
190 E8 **Craignure** Ag & B
197 H4 **Craigo** Angus
186 F5 **Craigrothie** Fife
184 B4 **Craigruie** Stirlg
196 E8 **Craigton** Angus
206 F5 **Craigton** C Aber
174 F7 **Craigton** E Rens
196 B6 **Craigton of Airlie**
Angus
187 K5 **Crail** Fife
167 L4 **Crailing** Border
116 C2 **Craiselound** N Linc
132 C2 **Crakehall** N York
133 L6 **Crambe** N York
159 G6 **Cramlington** Nthumb
177 G3 **Cramond** C Edin
177 G4 **Cramond Bridge**
C Edin
113 H7 **Cranage** Ches
99 J5 **Cranberry** Staffs
28 B8 **Cranborne** Dorset
33 K6 **Cranbrook** Kent
74 D6 **Cranfield** Beds
43 J5 **Cranford** Gt Lon
88 D7 **Cranford St Andrew**
Nhants
88 D7 **Cranford St John**
Nhants
55 K5 **Cranham** Gloucs
112 D2 **Crank** St Hel
31 H4 **Cranleigh** Surrey
26 F3 **Cranmore** Somset
87 L4 **Cranoe** Leics
79 G2 **Cransford** Suffk
178 E6 **Cranshaws** Border

4 C4 **Crantock** Cnwll
103 G3 **Cranwell** Lincs
91 H4 **Cranwich** Norfk
92 B3 **Cranworth** Norfk
182 A6 **Craobh Haven**
Ag & B
182 E7 **Crarae** Ag & B
225 L4 **Crask Inn** Highld
212 D6 **Crask of Aigas**
Highld
169 K5 **Craster** Nthumb
93 G7 **Cratfield** Suffk
206 E6 **Crathes** Abers
206 D6 **Crathes Castle** Abers
205 G6 **Crathie** Abers
202 E6 **Crathie** Highld
141 K5 **Crathorne** N York
83 H6 **Craven Arms** Shrops
150 E3 **Crawcrook** Gatesd
165 J5 **Crawford** S Lans
165 G5 **Crawfordjohn** S Lans
164 F6 **Crawick** D & G
29 H4 **Crawley** Hants
57 G5 **Crawley** Oxon
31 L4 **Crawley** W Susx
32 C5 **Crawley Down**
W Susx
122 B5 **Crawshawbooth**
Lancs
197 L1 **Crawton** Abers
131 H4 **Cray** N York
45 K5 **Crayford** Gt Lon
133 H5 **Crayke** N York
46 B2 **Crays Hill** Essex
24 F8 **Craze Lowman**
Devon
24 C7 **Creacombe** Devon
233 C7 **Creag Ghoraidh**
W Isls
191 J7 **Creagan Inn** Ag & B
233 C7 **Creagorry** W Isls
192 E3 **Creaguaineach**
Lodge Highld
73 K1 **Creaton** Nhants
155 M7 **Creca** D & G
69 J5 **Credenhill** Herefs
11 J5 **Crediton** Devon
153 H6 **Creebank** D & G
145 J2 **Creebridge** D & G
25 L6 **Creech Heathfield**
Somset
25 L6 **Creech St Michael**
Somset
4 E6 **Creed** Cnwll
45 J4 **Creekmouth** Gt Lon
78 D3 **Creeting St Mary**
Suffk
103 G8 **Creeton** Lincs
145 K3 **Creetown** D & G
237 a7 **Cregneash** IOM
186 E3 **Creich** Fife
37 G6 **Creigiau** Cardif
6 C5 **Cremyll** Cnwll
83 L3 **Cressage** Shrops
114 D6 **Cressbrook** Derbys
49 H6 **Cresselly** Pembks
42 D3 **Cressex** Bucks
61 J4 **Cressing** Essex
159 H4 **Cresswell** Nthumb
49 H6 **Cresswell** Pembks
99 L5 **Cresswell** Staffs
115 K6 **Cresswell** Derbys
78 F3 **Cretingham** Suffk
172 C5 **Cretshengan** Ag & B
83 G1 **Crew Green** Powys
98 B2 **Crewe** Ches
99 G2 **Crewe** Ches
99 G2 **Crewe Green** Ches
13 K1 **Crewkerne** Somset
101 G5 **Crewton** C Derb
183 L3 **Crianlarich** Stirlg
66 C4 **Cribyn** Cerdgn
95 J5 **Criccieth** Gwynd

101 G2 **Crich** Derbys
177 K6 **Crichton** Mdloth
87 H8 **Crick** Nhants
68 C6 **Crickadarn** Powys
13 J2 **Cricket St Thomas** Somset
53 K4 **Crickhowell** Powys
40 C2 **Cricklade** Wilts
44 E3 **Cricklewood** Gt Lon
124 D6 **Cridling Stubbs** N York
185 H3 **Crieff** P & K
82 F1 **Criggion** Powys
123 L7 **Crigglestone** Wakefd
217 K3 **Crimond** Abers
90 F3 **Crimplesham** Norfk
72 B5 **Crimscote** Warwks
212 C6 **Crinaglack** Highld
182 A8 **Crinan** Ag & B
175 L6 **Crindledyke** N Lans
92 E3 **Cringleford** Norfk
49 J5 **Crinow** Pembks
213 G8 **Croachy** Highld
154 F6 **Crochmore House** D & G
45 J6 **Crockenhill** Kent
42 B3 **Crocker End** Oxon
11 H6 **Crockernwell** Devon
27 K3 **Crockerton** Wilts
154 E7 **Crocketford** D & G
32 D3 **Crockham Hill** Kent
48 D2 **Croes-goch** Pembks
65 L5 **Croes-lan** Cerdgn
36 D2 **Croeserw** Neath
95 L4 **Croesor** Gwynd
50 E3 **Croesyceiliog** Carmth
37 L2 **Croesyceiliog** Torfn
87 G4 **Croft** Leics
104 E1 **Croft** Lincs
112 F3 **Croft** Warrtn
141 H5 **Croft-on-Tees** N York
174 E2 **Croftamie** Stirlg
124 B6 **Crofton** Wakefd
146 C2 **Crofts** D & G
215 G4 **Crofts** Moray
215 H3 **Crofts of Dipple** Moray
217 K3 **Crofts of Savoch** Abers
51 G6 **Crofty** Swans
181 L3 **Croggan** Ag & B
148 F5 **Croglin** Cumb
222 B3 **Croik** Highld
223 H7 **Cromarty** Highld
176 E2 **Crombie** Fife
214 D8 **Cromdale** Highld
59 M3 **Cromer** Herts
106 F4 **Cromer** Norfk
100 F2 **Cromford** Derbys
39 G3 **Cromhall** S Glos
232 f3 **Cromor** W Isls
102 D1 **Cromwell** Notts
164 C5 **Cronberry** E Ayrs
30 C2 **Crondall** Hants
112 C4 **Cronton** Knows
138 C7 **Crook** Cumb
150 E7 **Crook** Dur
165 L4 **Crook Inn** Border
185 L7 **Crook of Devon** P & K
148 E3 **Crooked Holme** Cumb
163 L3 **Crookedholm** E Ayrs
114 F4 **Crookes** Sheff
168 D2 **Crookham** Nthumb
41 K7 **Crookham** W Berk
30 C2 **Crookham Village** Hants
129 L3 **Crooklands** Cumb
72 F5 **Cropredy** Oxon
87 G2 **Cropston** Leics
115 H5 **Cropthorne** Worcs
134 B2 **Cropton** N York

102 B5 **Cropwell Bishop** Notts
102 B5 **Cropwell Butler** Notts
232 g1 **Cros** W Isls
173 L7 **Crosbie** N Ayrs
232 f3 **Crosbost** W Isls
147 J2 **Crosby** Cumb
237 c5 **Crosby** IOM
125 K7 **Crosby** N Linc
111 J2 **Crosby** Sefton
139 G5 **Crosby Garret** Cumb
138 F4 **Crosby Ravensworth** Cumb
26 E3 **Croscombe** Somset
26 B1 **Cross** Somset
54 B4 **Cross Ash** Mons
123 G3 **Cross Flatts** Brad
124 B4 **Cross Gates** Leeds
123 L4 **Cross Green** Leeds
77 J4 **Cross Green** Suffk
77 K4 **Cross Green** Suffk
78 B4 **Cross Green** Suffk
51 H3 **Cross Hands** Carmth
83 K3 **Cross Houses** Shrops
20 B2 **Cross in Hand** E Susx
65 L3 **Cross Inn** Cerdgn
174 C2 **Cross Keys** Ag & B
17 G4 **Cross Lane** IOW
84 C4 **Cross Lane Head** Shrops
100 F4 **Cross o' th' hands** Derbys
216 E7 **Cross of Jackston** Abers
92 E7 **Cross Street** Suffk
113 H5 **Cross Town** Ches
33 K4 **Cross-at-Hand** Kent
172 E7 **Crossaig** Ag & B
188 C7 **Crossapoll** Ag & B
147 J6 **Crosscanonby** Cumb
106 F5 **Crossdale Street** Norfk
176 E2 **Crossford** Fife
175 L8 **Crossford** S Lans
177 K5 **Crossgatehall** E Loth
163 J1 **Crossgates** E Ayrs
176 F1 **Crossgates** Fife
129 L6 **Crossgill** Lancs
163 L4 **Crosshands** E Ayrs
186 C7 **Crosshill** Fife
163 J7 **Crosshill** S Ayrs
163 K2 **Crosshouse** E Ayrs
37 K3 **Crosskeys** Caerph
230 F2 **Crosskirk** Highld
129 H2 **Crosslands** Cumb
174 D3 **Crosslee** Rens
146 C2 **Crossmichael** D & G
206 B4 **Crossroads** Abers
206 E6 **Crossroads** Abers
196 E5 **Crosston** Angus
70 E2 **Crossway Green** Worcs
14 E5 **Crossways** Dorset
64 F6 **Crosswell** Pembks
121 G6 **Croston** Lancs
92 F1 **Crostwick** Norfk
44 F3 **Crouch End** Gt Lon
14 D1 **Crouch Hill** Dorset
28 B6 **Croucheston** Wilts
73 G7 **Croughton** Nhants
216 F2 **Crovie** Abers
114 D2 **Crow Edge** Barns
54 F3 **Crow Hill** Herefs
3 H4 **Crowan** Cnwll
32 F6 **Crowborough** E Susx
25 H4 **Crowcombe** Somset
114 C7 **Crowdecote** Derbys
58 C7 **Crowell** Oxon
78 D3 **Crowfield** Suffk
178 F4 **Crowhill** E Loth
20 F3 **Crowhurst** E Susx

32 D4 **Crowhurst** Surrey
89 J2 **Crowland** Lincs
78 B1 **Crowland** Suffk
2 F5 **Crowlas** Cnwll
125 J7 **Crowle** N Linc
71 G4 **Crowle** Worcs
71 G3 **Crowle Green** Worcs
41 L3 **Crowmarsh Gifford** Oxon
78 F1 **Crown Corner** Suffk
6 C4 **Crownhill** C Plym
92 C3 **Crownthorpe** Norfk
3 H5 **Crowntown** Cnwll
2 D5 **Crows-an-Wra** Cnwll
42 D7 **Crowthorne** Wokham
112 E6 **Crowton** Ches
151 G7 **Croxdale** Dur
100 B5 **Croxden** Staffs
43 H2 **Croxley Green** Herts
75 J3 **Croxton** Cambs
126 D7 **Croxton** N Linc
106 B6 **Croxton** Norfk
91 K6 **Croxton** Norfk
99 H6 **Croxton** Staffs
102 D6 **Croxton Kerrial** Leics
213 J4 **Croy** Highld
175 J3 **Croy** N Lans
23 G4 **Croyde** Devon
75 K5 **Croydon** Cambs
44 F6 **Croydon** Gt Lon
203 G7 **Crubenmore** Highld
83 H2 **Cruckmeole** Shrops
83 H2 **Cruckton** Shrops
217 K6 **Cruden Bay** Abers
98 F8 **Crudgington** Wrekin
39 L2 **Crudwell** Wilts
37 K2 **Crumlin** Caerph
5 K5 **Crumplehorn** Cnwll
113 J2 **Crumpsall** Manch
34 E5 **Crundale** Kent
49 K5 **Crunwear** Pembks
29 H1 **Crux Easton** Hants
50 F3 **Crwbin** Carmth
42 E2 **Cryers Hill** Bucks
65 G7 **Crymmych** Pembks
52 C6 **Crynant** Neath
45 G5 **Crystal Palace** Gt Lon
209 L3 **Cuaig** Highld
181 L4 **Cuan Ferry Village** Ag & B
72 D2 **Cubbington** Warwks
4 C4 **Cubert** Cnwll
58 D4 **Cublington** Bucks
69 H6 **Cublington** Herefs
32 B7 **Cuckfield** W Susx
27 H6 **Cucklington** Somset
115 K7 **Cuckney** Notts
57 L7 **Cuddesdon** Oxon
58 C5 **Cuddington** Bucks
112 E7 **Cuddington** Ches
98 C3 **Cuddington Heath** Ches
32 D2 **Cudham** Gt Lon
10 D8 **Cudliptown** Devon
15 K3 **Cudnell** Bmouth
124 B8 **Cudworth** Barns
13 J1 **Cudworth** Somset
59 M7 **Cuffley** Herts
191 J5 **Cuil** Highld
199 G2 **Cuillin Hills** Highld
212 F3 **Culbokie** Highld
212 D6 **Culburnie** Highld
213 G5 **Culcabock** Highld
213 K4 **Culcharry** Highld
112 F3 **Culcheth** Warrtn
215 L7 **Culdrain** Abers
209 L6 **Culduie** Highld
77 J1 **Culford** Suffk
138 E2 **Culgaith** Cumb
41 J2 **Culham** Oxon
224 C2 **Culkein** Highld
224 D2 **Culkein Drumbeg** Highld

39 L2 **Culkerton** Gloucs
215 L2 **Cullen** Moray
159 J7 **Cullercoats** N Tyne
206 E5 **Cullerlie** Abers
213 G2 **Cullicudden** Highld
123 G3 **Cullingworth** Brad
181 L5 **Cullipool House** Ag & B
235 d2 **Cullivoe** Shet
213 H5 **Culloden** Highld
12 C2 **Cullompton** Devon
25 H7 **Culm Davy** Devon
83 J6 **Culmington** Shrops
25 H8 **Culmstock** Devon
224 C7 **Culnacraig** Highld
146 D5 **Culnaightrie** D & G
209 H2 **Culnaknock** Highld
222 D3 **Culrain** Highld
176 D2 **Culross** Fife
163 H6 **Culroy** S Ayrs
216 C7 **Culsalmond** Abers
145 K5 **Culscadden** D & G
145 G5 **Culshabbin** D & G
235 b6 **Culswick** Shet
207 H1 **Cultercullen** Abers
207 G5 **Cults** C Aber
45 M7 **Culverstone Green** Kent
103 G4 **Culverthorpe** Lincs
73 G5 **Culworth** Nhants
163 G7 **Culzean Castle** S Ayrs
175 K4 **Cumbernauld** N Lans
175 K3 **Cumbernauld Village** N Lans
119 G6 **Cumberworth** Lincs
216 F4 **Cuminestown** Abers
179 G6 **Cumledge** Border
148 D4 **Cummersdale** Cumb
147 K2 **Cummertrees** D & G
214 E1 **Cummingston** Moray
164 B5 **Cumnock** E Ayrs
57 J7 **Cumnor** Oxon
148 F5 **Cumrew** Cumb
155 J5 **Cumrew** Cumb
148 D4 **Cumwhinton** Cumb
148 E4 **Cumwhitton** Cumb
132 F5 **Cundall** N York
163 J2 **Cunninghamhead** N Ayrs
186 F4 **Cupar** Fife
186 E6 **Cupar Muir** Fife
114 E6 **Curbar** Derbys
17 G1 **Curbridge** Hants
57 G6 **Curbridge** Oxon
29 K8 **Curdridge** Hants
85 L5 **Curdworth** Warwks
25 L7 **Curland** Somset
41 J6 **Curridge** W Berk
177 G5 **Currie** C Edin
25 L6 **Curry Mallet** Somset
26 B6 **Curry Rivel** Somset
33 J5 **Curtisden Green** Kent
7 H5 **Curtisknowle** Devon
3 H6 **Cury** Cnwll
205 L3 **Cushnie** Abers
145 J7 **Cutcloy** D & G
24 E4 **Cutcombe** Somset
223 G4 **Cuthill** Highld
70 F2 **Cutnall Green** Worcs
56 C3 **Cutsdean** Gloucs
115 G6 **Cutthorpe** Derbys
42 A2 **Cuxham** Oxon
46 B6 **Cuxton** Medway
117 K2 **Cuxwold** Lincs
110 E6 **Cwm** Denbgs
53 H4 **Cwm Crawnon** Powys
81 J2 **Cwm Llinau** Powys
65 J6 **Cwm-cou** Cerdgn
51 H3 **Cwm-y-glo** Carmth

109 H8 **Cwm-y-glo** Gwynd
36 B3 **Cwmafan** Neath
52 F7 **Cwmaman** Rhondd
50 B1 **Cwmbach** Carmth
68 D6 **Cwmbach** Powys
52 F7 **Cwmbach** Rhondd
68 B4 **Cwmbach Llechrhyd** Powys
37 L2 **Cwmbran** Torfn
37 K2 **Cwmcarn** Caerph
54 C6 **Cwmcarvan** Mons
52 F7 **Cwmdare** Rhondd
53 J4 **Cwmdu** Powys
51 J6 **Cwmdu** Swans
65 L7 **Cwmduad** Carmth
36 D3 **Cwmfelin** Brdgnd
53 H7 **Cwmfelin** Myr Td
49 K4 **Cwmfelin Boeth** Carmth
37 J3 **Cwmfelinfach** Caerph
50 E3 **Cwmffrwd** Carmth
52 C5 **Cwmgiedd** Powys
51 K4 **Cwmgorse** Carmth
51 H4 **Cwmgwili** Carmth
65 K6 **Cwmhiraeth** Carmth
51 L3 **Cwmllynfell** Neath
51 G3 **Cwmmawr** Carmth
36 E2 **Cwmparc** Rhondd
65 K6 **Cwmpengraig** Carmth
66 B5 **Cwmsychbant** Cerdgn
53 K6 **Cwmtillery** Blae G
81 H8 **Cwmystwyth** Cerdgn
66 C5 **Cwrt-newydd** Cerdgn
36 D2 **Cymer** Neath
36 G3 **Cymmer** Rhondd
67 H6 **Cynghordy** Carmth
36 C2 **Cynonville** Neath
97 G4 **Cynwyd** Denbgs
65 L8 **Cynwyl Elfed** Carmth

D

7 K3 **Daccombe** Devon
138 C2 **Dacre** Cumb
132 B7 **Dacre** N York
132 B6 **Dacre Banks** N York
149 M7 **Daddry Shield** Dur
73 J6 **Dadford** Bucks
86 E4 **Dadlington** Leics
45 J3 **Dagenham** Gt Lon
55 M6 **Daglingworth** Gloucs
59 G5 **Dagnall** Bucks
152 F2 **Dailly** S Ayrs
187 G4 **Dairsie** Fife
233 D8 **Dalabrog** W Isls
182 D5 **Dalavich** Ag & B
146 E3 **Dalbeattie** D & G
237 D5 **Dalby** IOM
133 K5 **Dalby** N York
194 F5 **Dalcapon** P & K
226 F7 **Dalchalm** Highld
201 L3 **Dalchreichart** Highld
184 F4 **Dalchruin** P & K
185 L2 **Dalcrue** P & K
12 D5 **Dalditch** Devon
101 H5 **Dale** Derbys
48 D6 **Dale** Pembks
163 H1 **Dalgarven** N Ayrs
177 G2 **Dalgety Bay** Fife
164 B6 **Dalgig** E Ayrs
185 G3 **Dalginross** P & K
194 F6 **Dalguise** P & K
230 C5 **Dalhalvaig** Highld
77 G3 **Dalham** Suffk
233 b8 **Daliburgh** W Isls
177 K5 **Dalkeith** Mdloth
214 D4 **Dallas** Moray

78 F4 **Dallinghoo** Suffk
20 D2 **Dallington** E Susx
73 K3 **Dallington** Nhants
183 H3 **Dalmally** Ag & B
184 C7 **Dalmary** Stirlg
153 K2 **Dalmellington** E Ayrs
176 F3 **Dalmeny** C Edin
203 H2 **Dalmigavie** Highld
203 H2 **Dalmigavie Lodge** Highld
222 F7 **Dalmore** Highld
174 E4 **Dalmuir** W Duns
190 E3 **Dalnabreck** Highld
194 B3 **Dalnacardoch** P & K
203 K2 **Dalnahaitnach** Highld
193 K2 **Dalnaspidal** P & K
230 F7 **Dalnawillan Lodge** Highld
194 C5 **Daloist** P & K
186 A6 **Dalqueich** P & K
153 G3 **Dalquhairn** S Ayrs
226 D6 **Dalreavoch Lodge** Highld
174 B7 **Dalry** N Ayrs
163 J6 **Dalrymple** E Ayrs
175 L7 **Dalserf** S Lans
161 G6 **Dalsmeran** Ag & B
148 C5 **Dalston** Cumb
45 G3 **Dalston** Gt Lon
155 C5 **Dalswinton** D & G
155 K7 **Dalton** D & G
140 E5 **Dalton** N York
132 F4 **Dalton** N York
158 E7 **Dalton** Nthumb
141 L2 **Dalton Piercy** Hartpl
128 F5 **Dalton-in-Furness** Cumb
151 K4 **Dalton-le-Dale** Dur
141 H5 **Dalton-on-Tees** N York
165 G7 **Dalveen** D & G
184 D3 **Dalveich** Stirlg
202 F7 **Dalwhinnie** Highld
13 G3 **Dalwood** Devon
28 C7 **Damerham** Hants
93 J2 **Damgate** Norfk
61 J6 **Danbury** Essex
142 F5 **Danby** N York
141 H7 **Danby Wiske** N York
215 G5 **Dandaleith** Moray
177 J5 **Danderhall** Mdloth
60 B4 **Dane End** Herts
87 H3 **Dane Hills** C Leic
34 E4 **Dane Street** Kent
113 L7 **Danebridge** Ches
32 D7 **Danehill** E Susx
216 D3 **Danshillock** Abers
178 C5 **Danskine** E Loth
45 K5 **Darenth** Kent
112 E5 **Daresbury** Halton
115 H1 **Darfield** Barns
34 E3 **Dargate** Kent
5 K3 **Darite** Cnwll
85 H4 **Darlaston** Wsall
85 H4 **Darlaston Green** Wsall
132 C7 **Darley** N York
101 G5 **Darley Abbey** C Derb
100 E1 **Darley Bridge** Derbys
114 F8 **Darley Dale** Derbys
85 L8 **Darley Green** Solhll
132 B7 **Darley Head** N York
59 J4 **Darleyhall** Herts
72 B6 **Darlingscott** Warwks
141 H4 **Darlington** Darltn
116 C6 **Darlton** Notts
167 H3 **Darnick** Border
81 H3 **Darowen** Powys
216 E5 **Darra** Abers
9 G2 **Darracott** Devon
23 G4 **Darracott** Devon
158 E7 **Darras Hall** Nthumb

124 D6 **Darrington** Wakefd
79 J1 **Darsham** Suffk
26 E3 **Darshill** Somset
45 K5 **Dartford** Kent
7 H4 **Dartington** Devon
11 G8 **Dartmoor National Park** Devon
7 K5 **Dartmouth** Devon
123 L7 **Darton** Barns
164 B2 **Darvel** E Ayrs
121 K6 **Darwen** Bl w D
43 G5 **Datchet** W & M
59 L4 **Datchworth** Herts
121 K8 **Daubhill** Bolton
39 M4 **Dauntsey** Wilts
214 C6 **Dava** Highld
112 F7 **Davenham** Ches
73 H3 **Daventry** Nhants
177 H3 **Davidson's Mains** C Edin
8 F7 **Davidstow** Cnwll
155 M2 **Davington** D & G
34 D3 **Davington Hill** Kent
216 E8 **Daviot** Abers
213 H6 **Daviot** Highld
213 H6 **Daviot House** Highld
215 K4 **Davoch of Grange** Moray
31 K3 **Dawesgreen** Surrey
84 C2 **Dawley** Wrekin
12 B6 **Dawlish** Devon
12 C6 **Dawlish Warren** Devon
110 B8 **Dawn** Conwy
101 L4 **Daybrook** Notts
56 E3 **Daylesford** Gloucs
35 K4 **Deal** Kent
136 E3 **Dean** Cumb
23 L2 **Dean** Devon
7 H3 **Dean** Devon
29 H5 **Dean** Hants
29 K7 **Dean** Hants
57 G4 **Dean** Oxon
26 F3 **Dean** Somset
45 L6 **Dean Bottom** Kent
57 J6 **Dean Court** Oxon
7 H3 **Dean Prior** Devon
166 F6 **Deanburnhaugh** Border
7 G3 **Deancombe** Devon
121 K8 **Deane** Bolton
29 K2 **Deane** Hants
122 F7 **Deanhead** Kirk
27 M7 **Deanland** Dorset
149 L3 **Deanraw** Nthumb
176 D5 **Deans** W Loth
136 F2 **Deanscales** Cumb
73 L6 **Deanshanger** Nhants
215 H4 **Deanshaugh** Moray
184 F6 **Deanston** Stirlg
147 J7 **Dearham** Cumb
78 F4 **Debach** Suffk
60 E2 **Debden** Essex
45 H2 **Debden** Essex
78 E2 **Debenham** Suffk
70 E5 **Deblin's Green** Worcs
176 E4 **Dechmont** W Loth
176 D4 **Dechmont Road** W Loth
57 J2 **Deddington** Oxon
62 C2 **Dedham** Essex
42 F5 **Dedworth** W & M
88 D5 **Deene** Nhants
88 D5 **Deenethorpe** Nhants
114 F3 **Deepcar** Sheff
89 G2 **Deeping Gate** C Pete
89 H2 **Deeping St James** Lincs
89 J1 **Deeping St Nicholas** Lincs
55 K3 **Deerhurst** Gloucs
71 G5 **Defford** Worcs
52 E3 **Defynnog** Powys

109 L5 **Deganwy** Conwy
182 A5 **Degnish** Ag & B
141 J6 **Deighton** N York
124 F2 **Deighton** York
109 H8 **Deiniolen** Gwynd
8 E7 **Delabole** Cnwll
112 E7 **Delamere** Ches
207 H2 **Delfrigs** Abers
18 A5 **Dell Quay** W Susx
214 D7 **Delliefure** Highld
214 E7 **Delnashaugh Inn** Moray
223 G6 **Delny** Highld
150 E5 **Delves** Dur
195 H7 **Delvine** P & K
103 H5 **Dembleby** Lincs
186 D4 **Den of Lindores** Fife
115 J2 **Denaby** Donc
110 E7 **Denbigh** Denbgs
186 F4 **Denbrae** Fife
7 J3 **Denbury** Devon
101 H4 **Denby** Derbys
123 J8 **Denby Dale** Kirk
41 G3 **Denchworth** Oxon
128 F5 **Dendron** Cumb
185 K4 **Denfield** P & K
88 E7 **Denford** Nhants
62 B7 **Dengie** Essex
43 H3 **Denham** Bucks
77 H3 **Denham** Suffk
92 E8 **Denham** Suffk
43 H3 **Denham Green** Bucks
217 J4 **Denhead** Abers
187 G5 **Denhead** Fife
186 F2 **Denhead of Gray** C Dund
167 J5 **Denholm** Border
123 G4 **Denholme** Brad
30 A8 **Denmead** Hants
207 H3 **Denmore** C Aber
79 G2 **Dennington** Suffk
175 L2 **Denny** Falk
175 L3 **Dennyloanhead** Falk
206 F6 **Denside** Abers
35 G6 **Densole** Kent
77 H4 **Denston** Suffk
100 C4 **Denstone** Staffs
34 E3 **Denstroude** Kent
130 D3 **Dent** Cumb
89 G6 **Denton** Cambs
140 F4 **Denton** Darltn
19 L5 **Denton** E Susx
35 G5 **Denton** Kent
102 E6 **Denton** Lincs
123 H2 **Denton** N York
74 B3 **Denton** Nhants
93 G5 **Denton** Norfk
113 L3 **Denton** Tamesd
90 E3 **Denver** Norfk
169 J6 **Denwick** Nthumb
92 C4 **Deopham** Norfk
92 C4 **Deopham Green** Norfk
77 H3 **Depden** Suffk
28 A4 **Deptford** Gt Lon
28 A4 **Deptford** Wilts
101 G5 **Derby** C Derb
23 J5 **Derby** Devon
237 b7 **Derbyhaven** IOM
194 D5 **Derculich** P & K
92 B2 **Dereham** Norfk
53 H7 **Deri** Caerph
35 G5 **Derringstone** Kent
99 K7 **Derrington** Staffs
39 L6 **Derry Hill** Wilts
125 J8 **Derrythorpe** N Linc
105 H6 **Dersingham** Norfk
189 K6 **Dervaig** Ag & B
97 G3 **Derwen** Denbgs
80 F4 **Derwenlas** Powys
137 J3 **Derwent Water** Cumb
88 B6 **Desborough** Nhants

86 F3	**Desford** Leics	
215 L3	**Deskford** Moray	
33 K2	**Detling** Kent	
54 C7	**Devauden** Mons	
81 G7	**Devil's Bridge** Cerdgn	
40 A7	**Devizes** Wilts	
6 C5	**Devonport** C Plym	
185 J7	**Devonside** Clacks	
4 C7	**Devoran** Cnwll	
177 K5	**Dewarton** Mdloth	
14 E3	**Dewlish** Dorset	
123 K6	**Dewsbury** Kirk	
97 K8	**Deytheur** Powys	
121 L4	**Dial Hall** Lancs	
18 F2	**Dial Post** W Susx	
16 E2	**Dibden** Hants	
16 E2	**Dibden Purlieu** Hants	
92 E6	**Dickleburgh** Norfk	
56 B2	**Didbrook** Gloucs	
41 K3	**Didcot** Oxon	
41 K3	**Didcot Railway Centre** Oxon	
75 H2	**Diddington** Cambs	
83 K6	**Diddlebury** Shrops	
18 A3	**Didling** W Susx	
39 J3	**Didmarton** Gloucs	
113 J3	**Didsbury** Manch	
103 H2	**Digby** Lincs	
218 C7	**Digg** Highld	
122 F8	**Diggle** Oldham	
112 C1	**Digmoor** Lancs	
66 C4	**Dihewyd** Cerdgn	
107 G7	**Dilham** Norfk	
99 L4	**Dilhorne** Staffs	
75 G2	**Dillington** Cambs	
150 B3	**Dilston** Nthumb	
27 K2	**Dilton** Wilts	
27 J2	**Dilton Marsh** Wilts	
69 H4	**Dilwyn** Herefs	
94 E5	**Dinas** Gwynd	
64 E6	**Dinas** Pembks	
37 J6	**Dinas Powys** V Glam	
81 J1	**Dinas-Mawddwy** Gwynd	
26 E3	**Dinder** Somset	
69 K6	**Dinedor** Herefs	
54 C6	**Dingestow** Mons	
111 K4	**Dingle** Lpool	
87 L6	**Dingley** Nhants	
212 E3	**Dingwall** Highld	
205 K5	**Dinnet** Abers	
158 F7	**Dinnington** N u Ty	
115 K4	**Dinnington** Rothm	
26 B8	**Dinnington** Somset	
95 K1	**Dinorwic** Gwynd	
58 C5	**Dinton** Bucks	
28 A5	**Dinton** Wilts	
155 K4	**Dinwoodie** D & G	
9 J2	**Dinworthy** Devon	
25 J6	**Dipford** Somset	
161 K2	**Dippen** Ag & B	
162 D5	**Dippen** N Ayrs	
10 C7	**Dippertown** Devon	
215 H3	**Dipple** Moray	
152 E2	**Dipple** S Ayrs	
7 G4	**Diptford** Devon	
150 E4	**Dipton** Dur	
178 B2	**Dirleton** E Loth	
149 L5	**Dirt Pot** Nthumb	
101 J7	**Diseworth** Leics	
132 F5	**Dishforth** N York	
113 L5	**Disley** Ches	
92 D7	**Diss** Norfk	
136 D3	**Distington** Cumb	
28 C5	**Ditchampton** Wilts	
169 H5	**Ditchburn** Nthumb	
26 F4	**Ditcheat** Somset	
93 G5	**Ditchingham** Norfk	
19 J3	**Ditchling** E Susx	
83 K2	**Ditherington** Shrops	
39 J6	**Ditteridge** Wilts	
7 K5	**Dittisham** Devon	
112 D4	**Ditton** Halton	

33 J2	**Ditton** Kent	
76 F3	**Ditton Green** Cambs	
83 L5	**Ditton Priors** Shrops	
55 M2	**Dixton** Gloucs	
54 D5	**Dixton** Mons	
113 M1	**Dobcross** Oldham	
5 K3	**Dobwalls** Cnwll	
11 H7	**Doccombe** Devon	
212 F6	**Dochgarroch** Highld	
130 B5	**Docker** Lancs	
105 J5	**Docking** Norfk	
69 L3	**Docklow** Herefs	
137 L3	**Dockray** Cumb	
100 A5	**Dod's Leigh** Staffs	
98 E4	**Dodd's Green** Ches	
60 F7	**Doddinghurst** Essex	
90 B5	**Doddington** Cambs	
34 C4	**Doddington** Kent	
116 E7	**Doddington** Lincs	
168 E3	**Doddington** Nthumb	
84 B7	**Doddington** Shrops	
11 K7	**Doddiscombsleigh** Devon	
73 H3	**Dodford** Nhants	
85 G8	**Dodford** Worcs	
39 H4	**Dodington** S Glos	
25 J4	**Dodington** Somset	
98 A1	**Doddleston** Ches	
174 F7	**Dodside** E Rens	
114 F1	**Dodworth** Barns	
103 K2	**Dogdyke** Lincs	
30 C2	**Dogmersfield** Hants	
82 B2	**Dolanog** Powys	
95 J4	**Dolbenmaen** Gwynd	
81 K3	**Dolfach** Powys	
82 C6	**Dolfor** Powys	
109 L7	**Dolgarrog** Conwy	
96 B8	**Dolgellau** Gwynd	
226 F7	**Doll** Highld	
185 K7	**Dollar** Clacks	
185 K7	**Dollarfield** Clacks	
111 H6	**Dolphin** Flints	
129 L8	**Dolphinholme** Lancs	
176 F8	**Dolphinton** S Lans	
10 E3	**Dolton** Devon	
110 B6	**Dolwen** Conwy	
96 B3	**Dolwyddelan** Conwy	
97 L8	**Domgay** Powys	
115 L2	**Doncaster** Donc	
27 K6	**Donhead St Andrew** Wilts	
27 K6	**Donhead St Mary** Wilts	
177 G2	**Donibristle** Fife	
25 G3	**Doniford** Somset	
103 K5	**Donington** Lincs	
118 C5	**Donington on Bain** Lincs	
86 C2	**Donisthorpe** Leics	
56 D3	**Donnington** Gloucs	
83 L2	**Donnington** Shrops	
41 J6	**Donnington** W Berk	
18 B5	**Donnington** W Susx	
84 C2	**Donnington** Wrekin	
25 M8	**Donyatt** Somset	
163 H5	**Doonfoot** S Ayrs	
163 J6	**Doonholm** S Ayrs	
204 D3	**Dorback Lodge** Highld	
14 D4	**Dorchester** Dorset	
41 L2	**Dorchester** Oxon	
86 C4	**Dordon** Warwks	
114 F5	**Dore** Sheff	
212 F7	**Dores** Highld	
31 K2	**Dorking** Surrey	
32 D5	**Dormans Land** Surrey	
71 H3	**Dormington** Herefs	
71 H3	**Dormston** Worcs	
42 F5	**Dorney** Bucks	
200 D1	**Dornie** Highld	
223 H4	**Dornoch** Highld	
147 M2	**Dornock** D & G	
230 F5	**Dorrery** Highld	

85 L8	**Dorridge** Solhll	
103 H2	**Dorrington** Lincs	
83 J3	**Dorrington** Shrops	
99 G4	**Dorrington** Shrops	
71 K4	**Dorsington** Warwks	
69 G6	**Dorstone** Herefs	
58 B5	**Dorton** Bucks	
237 d6	**Douglas** IOM	
165 G4	**Douglas** S Lans	
187 G2	**Douglas and Angus** C Dund	
165 G3	**Douglas Castle** S Lans	
183 H7	**Douglas Pier** Ag & B	
165 G3	**Douglas Water** S Lans	
164 F3	**Douglas West** S Lans	
196 C6	**Douglastown** Angus	
26 F3	**Doulting** Somset	
234 b5	**Dounby** Ork	
221 L2	**Doune** Highld	
184 F6	**Doune** Stirlg	
152 E3	**Dounepark** S Ayrs	
222 D4	**Dounie** Highld	
6 D3	**Dousland** Devon	
114 B6	**Dove Holes** Derbys	
147 J7	**Dovenby** Cumb	
35 J6	**Dover** Kent	
35 J6	**Dover Castle** Kent	
62 F2	**Dovercourt** Essex	
70 F2	**Doverdale** Worcs	
100 C5	**Doveridge** Derbys	
31 L2	**Doversgreen** Surrey	
194 F6	**Dowally** P & K	
55 M4	**Dowdeswell** Gloucs	
53 G6	**Dowlais** Myr Td	
10 E3	**Dowland** Devon	
26 A8	**Dowlish Wake** Somset	
40 C2	**Down Ampney** Gloucs	
55 K4	**Down Hatherley** Gloucs	
11 H4	**Down St Mary** Devon	
6 D5	**Down Thomas** Devon	
5 L5	**Downderry** Cnwll	
45 H7	**Downe** Gt Lon	
39 J2	**Downend** Gloucs	
38 F5	**Downend** S Glos	
186 F2	**Downfield** C Dund	
5 L2	**Downgate** Cnwll	
6 A2	**Downgate** Cnwll	
46 B2	**Downham** Essex	
45 H5	**Downham** Gt Lon	
122 B2	**Downham** Lancs	
90 E3	**Downham Market** Norfk	
26 E6	**Downhead** Somset	
27 G3	**Downhead** Somset	
186 A2	**Downhill** P & K	
140 E7	**Downholme** N York	
207 H6	**Downies** Abers	
42 D2	**Downley** Bucks	
43 J8	**Downside** Surrey	
16 C4	**Downton** Hants	
28 D6	**Downton** Wilts	
83 H8	**Downton on the Rock** Herefs	
103 J6	**Dowsby** Lincs	
39 G5	**Doynton** S Glos	
37 K3	**Draethen** Caerph	
164 F1	**Draffan** S Lans	
116 B4	**Drakeholes** Notts	
174 B7	**Drakemyre** N Ayrs	
71 G5	**Drakes Broughton** Worcs	
48 B5	**Draughton** N York	
87 L7	**Draughton** Nhants	
125 G5	**Drax** N York	
72 F1	**Draycote** Warwks	
101 H6	**Draycott** Derbys	
71 L7	**Draycott** Gloucs	
26 C2	**Draycott** Somset	
100 D6	**Draycott in the Clay** Staffs	

99 M4	**Draycott in the Moors** Staffs	
17 J2	**Drayton** C Port	
88 B5	**Drayton** Leics	
92 E2	**Drayton** Norfk	
72 E6	**Drayton** Oxon	
41 J2	**Drayton** Oxon	
26 B6	**Drayton** Somset	
85 G7	**Drayton** Worcs	
85 L4	**Drayton Bassett** Staffs	
58 E5	**Drayton Beauchamp** Bucks	
85 L4	**Drayton Manor Park** Staffs	
58 D3	**Drayton Parslow** Bucks	
41 L2	**Drayton St Leonard** Oxon	
48 F5	**Dreen Hill** Pembks	
65 K6	**Drefach** Carmth	
51 G3	**Drefach** Carmth	
66 C5	**Drefach** Cerdgn	
163 J2	**Dreghorn** N Ayrs	
35 H6	**Drellingore** Kent	
178 B3	**Drem** E Loth	
11 H6	**Drewsteignton** Devon	
118 E6	**Driby** Lincs	
134 F7	**Driffield** E R Yk	
56 B7	**Driffield** Gloucs	
2 D5	**Drift** Cnwll	
136 E7	**Drigg** Cumb	
123 J5	**Drighlington** Leeds	
190 B5	**Drimnin** Highld	
13 K2	**Drimpton** Dorset	
191 J1	**Drimsallie** Highld	
124 E2	**Dringhouses** York	
77 L3	**Drinkstone** Suffk	
77 L3	**Drinkstone Green** Suffk	
100 A6	**Drointon** Staffs	
70 F2	**Droitwich** Worcs	
186 B4	**Dron** P & K	
115 G5	**Dronfield** Derbys	
163 K5	**Drongan** S Ayrs	
186 E1	**Dronley** Angus	
14 E2	**Droop** Dorset	
29 L7	**Droxford** Hants	
113 K2	**Droylsden** Tamesd	
97 G4	**Druid** Denbgs	
48 E4	**Druidston** Pembks	
192 B6	**Druimachoish** Highld	
191 L3	**Druimarbin** Highld	
172 C4	**Druimdrishaig** Ag & B	
199 L7	**Druimindarroch** Highld	
172 F3	**Drum** Ag & B	
185 L7	**Drum** P & K	
165 H2	**Drumalbin** S Lans	
224 D3	**Drumbeg** Highld	
216 B6	**Drumblade** Abers	
144 C6	**Drumbreddon** D & G	
210 B7	**Drumbuie** Highld	
148 A3	**Drumburgh** Cumb	
146 F4	**Drumburn** D & G	
174 F4	**Drumchapel** C Glas	
193 L5	**Drumchastle** P & K	
164 C2	**Drumclog** S Lans	
187 G6	**Drumeldrie** Fife	
165 M3	**Drumelzier** Border	
199 L3	**Drumfearn** Highld	
206 D5	**Drumfrennie** Abers	
203 J5	**Drumguish** Highld	
206 B6	**Drumhead** Abers	
214 E7	**Drumin** Moray	
153 L3	**Drumjohn** D & G	
153 G6	**Drumlamford** S Ayrs	
206 C4	**Drumlasie** Abers	
148 A5	**Drumleaning** Cumb	
161 H5	**Drumlemble** Ag & B	
197 J1	**Drumlithie** Abers	

145 H6 **Drummoddie** D & G
144 D7 **Drummore** D & G
215 J5 **Drummuir** Moray
212 D7 **Drumnadrochit** Highld
215 L4 **Drumnagorrach** Moray
154 F6 **Drumpark** D & G
224 E7 **Drumrunie Lodge** Highld
163 G6 **Drumshang** S Ayrs
209 G5 **Drumuie** Highld
204 B2 **Drumuillie** Highld
184 E6 **Drumvaich** Stirlg
186 B5 **Drunzie** P & K
102 D3 **Dry Doddington** Lincs
75 L3 **Dry Drayton** Cambs
138 F4 **Drybeck** Cumb
215 K2 **Drybridge** Moray
163 J3 **Drybridge** N Ayrs
54 F4 **Drybrook** Gloucs
167 J3 **Dryburgh** Border
3 G5 **Drym** Cnwll
174 E2 **Drymen** Stirlg
217 G5 **Drymuir** Abers
208 F7 **Drynoch** Highld
216 F2 **Dubford** Abers
225 J5 **Duchally** Highld
57 G6 **Ducklington** Oxon
76 C7 **Duddenhoe End** Essex
177 J4 **Duddingston** C Edin
88 E4 **Duddington** Nhants
25 K7 **Duddlestone** Somset
84 B6 **Duddlewick** Shrops
168 D2 **Duddo** Nthumb
112 D8 **Duddon** Ches
97 M5 **Dudleston** Shrops
85 G5 **Dudley** Dudley
159 G7 **Dudley** N Tyne
85 G5 **Dudley Port** Sandw
15 K3 **Dudsbury** Dorset
101 G4 **Duffield** Derbys
36 C2 **Duffryn** Neath
215 H6 **Dufftown** Moray
214 E2 **Duffus** Moray
139 G3 **Dufton** Cumb
134 D6 **Duggleby** N York
210 B7 **Duirinish** Highld
199 L3 **Duisdalemore** Highld
191 K2 **Duisky** Highld
78 C6 **Duke Street** Suffk
113 L2 **Dukinfield** Tamesd
26 E3 **Dulcote** Somset
12 D2 **Dulford** Devon
194 C6 **Dull** P & K
175 K3 **Dullatur** N Lans
76 F3 **Dullingham** Cambs
76 F3 **Dullingham Ley** Cambs
204 B1 **Dulnain Bridge** Highld
75 H3 **Duloe** Beds
5 K4 **Duloe** Cnwll
24 E5 **Dulverton** Somset
45 G5 **Dulwich** Gt Lon
174 D4 **Dumbarton** W Duns
71 H7 **Dumbleton** Gloucs
155 G6 **Dumfries** D & G
174 F2 **Dumgoyne** Stirlg
29 L3 **Dummer** Hants
35 K2 **Dumpton** Kent
197 G4 **Dun** Angus
193 L5 **Dunalastair** P & K
173 K4 **Dunan** Ag & B
209 J8 **Dunan** Highld
193 G5 **Dunan** P & K
161 H7 **Dunaverty** Ag & B
25 L3 **Dunball** Somset
178 E3 **Dunbar** E Loth
227 L3 **Dunbeath** Highld
182 C2 **Dunbeg** Ag & B

185 G6 **Dunblane** Stirlg
186 E4 **Dunbog** Fife
212 F3 **Duncanston** Highld
216 B8 **Duncanstone** Abers
11 K7 **Dunchideock** Devon
72 F1 **Dunchurch** Warwks
155 G5 **Duncow** D & G
186 B5 **Duncrievie** P & K
18 C3 **Duncton** W Susx
186 F2 **Dundee** D & G
186 F2 **Dundee Airport** C Dund
26 C5 **Dundon** Somset
163 J3 **Dundonald** S Ayrs
220 E4 **Dundonnell** Highld
147 L5 **Dundraw** Cumb
201 L3 **Dundreggan** Highld
146 D5 **Dundrennan** D & G
38 E6 **Dundry** N Som
206 E4 **Dunecht** Abers
176 F2 **Dunfermline** Fife
40 C2 **Dunfield** Gloucs
164 D3 **Dungavel** S Lans
21 L3 **Dungeness** Kent
116 D6 **Dunham** Notts
113 H4 **Dunham Town** Traffd
113 G4 **Dunham Woodhouses** Traffd
112 C6 **Dunham-on-the-Hill** Ches
70 F2 **Dunhampton** Worcs
117 G5 **Dunholme** Lincs
187 J5 **Dunino** Fife
175 L2 **Dunipace** Falk
33 G3 **Dunk's Green** Kent
195 G7 **Dunkeld** P & K
39 G8 **Dunkerton** BaNES
12 E2 **Dunkeswell** Devon
123 L2 **Dunkeswick** N York
34 E3 **Dunkirk** Kent
39 H4 **Dunkirk** S Glos
196 F3 **Dunlappie** Angus
70 E2 **Dunley** Worcs
174 D8 **Dunlop** E Ayrs
202 F2 **Dunmaglass** Highld
176 B1 **Dunmore** Falk
231 J2 **Dunnet** Highld
196 E6 **Dunnichen** Angus
185 L4 **Dunning** P & K
126 E1 **Dunnington** E R Yk
71 J4 **Dunnington** Warwks
133 K8 **Dunnington** York
122 B5 **Dunnockshaw** Lancs
173 K3 **Dunoon** Ag & B
214 C5 **Dunphail** Moray
144 E4 **Dunragit** D & G
179 G7 **Duns** Border
57 J3 **Duns Tew** Oxon
103 J6 **Dunsby** Lincs
154 F5 **Dunscore** D & G
124 F8 **Dunscroft** Donc
142 D4 **Dunsdale** R & Cl
42 C5 **Dunsden Green** Oxon
9 J3 **Dunsdon** Devon
31 G4 **Dunsfold** Surrey
11 J6 **Dunsford** Devon
186 D5 **Dunshalt** Fife
217 J5 **Dunshillock** Abers
101 J1 **Dunsill** Notts
143 H5 **Dunsley** N York
84 F6 **Dunsley** Staffs
58 E6 **Dunsmore** Bucks
121 K1 **Dunsop Bridge** Lancs
59 G4 **Dunstable** Beds
100 D7 **Dunstall** Staffs
169 K5 **Dunstan** Nthumb
24 F3 **Dunster** Somset
151 G3 **Dunston** Gatesd
117 H8 **Dunston** Lincs
92 F3 **Dunston** Norfk
99 L8 **Dunston** Staffs
6 E5 **Dunstone** Devon
7 G2 **Dunstone** Devon

126 D4 **Dunswell** E R Yk
176 E8 **Dunsyre** S Lans
6 B1 **Dunterton** Devon
55 L6 **Duntisbourne Abbots** Gloucs
55 M6 **Duntisbourne Rouse** Gloucs
14 D2 **Duntish** Dorset
174 E4 **Duntocher** W Duns
75 J5 **Dunton** Beds
58 D3 **Dunton** Bucks
105 L6 **Dunton** Norfk
87 G5 **Dunton Bassett** Leics
32 F2 **Dunton Green** Kent
218 C6 **Duntulm** Highld
163 G6 **Dunure** S Ayrs
51 H6 **Dunvant** Swans
208 D5 **Dunvegan** Highld
79 K1 **Dunwich** Suffk
3 K5 **Durgan** Cnwll
151 G6 **Durham** Dur
151 G6 **Durham Cathedral** Dur
154 F2 **Durisdeer** D & G
154 F2 **Durisdeermill** D & G
25 L4 **Durleigh** Somset
29 K7 **Durley** Hants
40 E7 **Durley** Wilts
29 K7 **Durley Street** Hants
35 H3 **Durlock** Kent
35 J2 **Durlock** Kent
196 C6 **Durmgley** Angus
228 F3 **Durness** Highld
191 K5 **Duror** Highld
182 D5 **Durran** Ag & B
18 F5 **Durrington** W Susx
28 D3 **Durrington** Wilts
206 E6 **Durris** Abers
39 H2 **Dursley** Gloucs
55 G4 **Dursley Cross** Gloucs
25 L5 **Durston** Somset
15 G2 **Durweston** Dorset
73 K3 **Duston** Nhants
203 L1 **Duthil** Highld
112 E5 **Dutton** Ches
76 C5 **Duxford** Cambs
57 G7 **Duxford** Oxon
76 C5 **Duxford Aircraft Museum** Cambs
109 L6 **Dwygyfylchi** Conwy
108 F7 **Dwyran** IOA
207 G3 **Dyce** C Aber
95 K7 **Dyffryn Ardudwy** Gwynd
52 D6 **Dyffryn Cellwen** Neath
103 J7 **Dyke** Lincs
214 B3 **Dyke** Moray
195 K5 **Dykehead** Angus
196 C4 **Dykehead** Angus
176 B6 **Dykehead** N Lans
184 D7 **Dykehead** Stirlg
197 H3 **Dykelands** Abers
195 K5 **Dykends** Angus
216 D5 **Dykeside** Abers
34 E8 **Dymchurch** Kent
55 G2 **Dymock** Gloucs
39 H5 **Dyrham** S Glos
186 E8 **Dysart** Fife
110 E5 **Dyserth** Denbgs

125 J7 **Ealand** N Linc
44 D4 **Ealing** Gt Lon
149 H4 **Eals** Nthumb
138 D2 **Eamont Bridge** Cumb
122 D2 **Earby** Lancs
84 C5 **Eardington** Shrops
69 H3 **Eardisland** Herefs
68 F5 **Eardisley** Herefs
98 A7 **Eardiston** Shrops
70 C2 **Eardiston** Worcs
89 L8 **Earith** Cambs
86 F4 **Earl Shilton** Leics
78 F2 **Earl Soham** Suffk
114 C7 **Earl Sterndale** Derbys
70 F6 **Earl's Croome** Worcs
112 E3 **Earlestown** St Hel
42 C6 **Earley** Wokham
208 F3 **Earlish** Highld
74 C2 **Earls Barton** Nhants
61 K3 **Earls Colne** Essex
71 G3 **Earls Common** Worcs
86 D7 **Earlsdon** Covtry
187 H7 **Earlsferry** Fife
44 E5 **Earlsfield** Gt Lon
216 F7 **Earlsford** Abers
123 K6 **Earlsheaton** Kirk
167 J2 **Earlston** Border
163 K3 **Earlston** E Ayrs
32 B4 **Earlswood** Surrey
85 K8 **Earlswood** Warwks
17 M3 **Earnley** W Susx
159 H7 **Earsdon** N Tyne
158 F4 **Earsdon** Nthumb
93 G5 **Earsham** Norfk
18 C4 **Eartham** W Susx
142 C5 **Easby** N York
181 L4 **Easdale** Ag & B
30 E6 **Easebourne** W Susx
86 F7 **Easenhall** Warwks
30 F3 **Eashing** Surrey
58 B6 **Easington** Bucks
151 K6 **Easington** Dur
127 J6 **Easington** E R Yk
142 F4 **Easington** R & Cl
151 K6 **Easington Colliery** Dur
133 H5 **Easingwold** N York
196 B7 **Eassie and Nevay** Angus
37 G6 **East Aberthaw** V Glam
7 H6 **East Allington** Devon
24 D6 **East Anstey** Devon
17 H5 **East Ashey** IOW
17 M2 **East Ashling** W Susx
134 F3 **East Ayton** N York
117 K5 **East Barkwith** Lincs
33 J3 **East Barming** Kent
143 G5 **East Barnby** N York
44 F2 **East Barnet** Gt Lon
178 F3 **East Barns** E Loth
105 L5 **East Barsham** Norfk
106 E4 **East Beckham** Norfk
43 H5 **East Bedfont** Gt Lon
78 C7 **East Bergholt** Suffk
106 A8 **East Bilney** Norfk
20 A5 **East Blatchington** E Susx
151 J3 **East Boldon** S Tyne
16 D3 **East Boldre** Hants
91 L2 **East Bradenham** Norfk
25 M2 **East Brent** Somset
102 B4 **East Bridgford** Notts
23 L5 **East Buckland** Devon
12 D5 **East Budleigh** Devon
116 D1 **East Butterwick** N Linc
176 E5 **East Calder** W Loth
92 E3 **East Carleton** Norfk
123 J2 **East Carlton** Leeds
88 B5 **East Carlton** Nhants

14 E5	East Chaldon (Chaldon Herring) Dorset	
41 G3	East Challow Oxon	
7 H7	East Charleton Devon	
14 A2	East Chelborough Dorset	
19 K3	East Chiltington E Susx	
26 C8	East Chinnock Somset	
28 C2	East Chisenbury Wilts	
31 H2	East Clandon Surrey	
58 C3	East Claydon Bucks	
26 D8	East Coker Somset	
25 J5	East Combe Somset	
26 E3	East Compton Somset	
7 J5	East Cornworthy Devon	
125 G3	East Cottingwith E R Yk	
16 F4	East Cowes IOW	
125 G6	East Cowick E R Yk	
141 H6	East Cowton N York	
27 G3	East Cranmore Somset	
15 H6	East Creech Dorset	
20 B6	East Dean E Susx	
54 F4	East Dean Gloucs	
28 F6	East Dean Hants	
18 B3	East Dean W Susx	
23 J3	East Down Devon	
116 C6	East Drayton Notts	
45 G5	East Dulwich Gt Lon	
38 E7	East Dundry N Som	
126 C5	East Ella C KuH	
41 H7	East End Hants	
16 D3	East End Hants	
33 L6	East End Kent	
57 H5	East End Oxon	
26 F3	East End Somset	
28 D2	East Everleigh Wilts	
33 J3	East Farleigh Kent	
87 K6	East Farndon Nhants	
116 D2	East Ferry Lincs	
178 C3	East Fortune E Loth	
41 G5	East Garston W Berk	
87 J2	East Goscote Leics	
40 E7	East Grafton Wilts	
28 E5	East Grimstead Wilts	
32 D5	East Grinstead W Susx	
21 J2	East Guldeford E Susx	
73 J2	East Haddon Nhants	
41 K3	East Hagbourne Oxon	
126 E6	East Halton N Linc	
45 H4	East Ham Gt Lon	
41 H2	East Hanney Oxon	
61 J7	East Hanningfield Essex	
124 C6	East Hardwick Wakefd	
92 B6	East Harling Norfk	
141 K7	East Harlsey N York	
28 C5	East Harnham Wilts	
26 E1	East Harptree BaNES	
141 K4	East Hartburn S on T	
30 D7	East Harting W Susx	
27 L5	East Hatch Wilts	
75 K4	East Hatley Cambs	
132 B2	East Hauxwell N York	
187 J1	East Haven Angus	
103 K4	East Heckington Lincs	
150 E6	East Hedleyhope Dur	
227 H5	East Helmsdale Highld	

41 J3	East Hendred Oxon	
134 E4	East Heslerton N York	
20 B3	East Hoathly E Susx	
15 G5	East Holme Dorset	
26 E3	East Horrington Somset	
31 H2	East Horsley Surrey	
15 K4	East Howe Bmouth	
25 M3	East Huntspill Somset	
41 J4	East Ilsley W Berk	
118 E8	East Keal Lincs	
40 C6	East Kennett Wilts	
124 B2	East Keswick Leeds	
175 H7	East Kilbride S Lans	
118 D8	East Kirkby Lincs	
14 F5	East Knighton Dorset	
27 K5	East Knoyle Wilts	
26 B7	East Lambrook Somset	
35 J5	East Langdon Kent	
87 K5	East Langton Leics	
191 L5	East Laroch Highld	
18 B4	East Lavant W Susx	
18 C3	East Lavington W Susx	
140 E5	East Layton N York	
101 K7	East Leake Notts	
11 G4	East Leigh Devon	
7 H4	East Leigh Devon	
105 K8	East Lexham Norfk	
178 D3	East Linton E Loth	
41 H3	East Lockinge Oxon	
116 C2	East Lound N Linc	
15 G6	East Lulworth Dorset	
134 E5	East Lutton N York	
26 E5	East Lydford Somset	
33 J2	East Malling Kent	
30 D8	East Marden W Susx	
116 C6	East Markham Notts	
28 B7	East Martin Hants	
122 D1	East Marton N York	
30 B6	East Meon Hants	
62 C5	East Mersea Essex	
101 J7	East Midlands Airport Leics	
43 J6	East Molesey Surrey	
15 G4	East Morden Dorset	
123 G3	East Morton Brad	
154 F3	East Morton D & G	
133 L4	East Ness N York	
87 L4	East Norton Leics	
7 J2	East Ogwell Devon	
27 J7	East Orchard Dorset	
33 H4	East Peckham Kent	
49 G6	East Pennar Pembks	
26 E4	East Pennard Somset	
75 G2	East Perry Cambs	
7 H7	East Portlemouth Devon	
7 H8	East Prawle Devon	
18 E5	East Preston W Susx	
14 D1	East Pulham Dorset	
9 K2	East Putford Devon	
25 H3	East Quantoxhead Somset	
151 H5	East Rainton Sundld	
118 C2	East Ravendale NE Lin	
105 L7	East Raynham Norfk	
124 B2	East Rigton Leeds	
141 K6	East Rounton N York	
105 K6	East Rudham Norfk	
106 E4	East Runton Norfk	
107 H6	East Ruston Norfk	
178 B5	East Saltoun E Loth	
44 D5	East Sheen Gt Lon	
41 H5	East Shefford W Berk	
116 C3	East Stockwith Lincs	
15 G5	East Stoke Dorset	
102 C3	East Stoke Notts	

27 J6	East Stour Dorset	
35 H3	East Stourmouth Kent	
23 K6	East Stowford Devon	
29 K4	East Stratton Hants	
35 J5	East Studdal Kent	
5 J3	East Taphouse Cnwll	
158 F3	East Thirston Nthumb	
46 B5	East Tilbury Thurr	
30 B5	East Tisted Hants	
117 J5	East Torrington Lincs	
92 C2	East Tuddenham Norfk	
28 F5	East Tytherley Hants	
39 L5	East Tytherton Wilts	
11 J4	East Village Devon	
83 K5	East Wall Shrops	
91 G1	East Walton Norfk	
26 D2	East Water Somset	
10 F6	East Week Devon	
28 F7	East Wellow Hants	
186 E7	East Wemyss Fife	
176 C5	East Whitburn W Loth	
45 J5	East Wickham Gt Lon	
49 J6	East Williamston Pembks	
91 G1	East Winch Norfk	
28 E5	East Winterslow Wilts	
17 L3	East Wittering W Susx	
131 L3	East Witton N York	
158 A5	East Woodburn Nthumb	
41 H7	East Woodhay Hants	
30 C4	East Worldham Hants	
91 K5	East Wretham Norfk	
9 H2	East Youlstone Devon	
23 G6	East-the-Water Devon	
141 H4	Eastbourne Darltn	
20 C5	Eastbourne E Susx	
79 J2	Eastbridge Suffk	
122 F2	Eastburn Brad	
43 J2	Eastbury Herts	
41 G5	Eastbury W Berk	
131 J8	Eastby N York	
47 G5	Eastchurch Kent	
55 K6	Eastcombe Gloucs	
43 J3	Eastcote Gt Lon	
73 K4	Eastcote Nhants	
85 L7	Eastcote Solhll	
28 A1	Eastcott Wilts	
39 L2	Eastcourt Wilts	
40 E7	Eastcourt Wilts	
46 F2	Eastend Essex	
165 J2	Eastend S Lans	
205 G6	Easter Balmoral Abers	
38 E4	Easter Compton S Glos	
213 H4	Easter Dalziel Highld	
177 H5	Easter Howgate Mdloth	
212 E4	Easter Kinkell Highld	
212 E5	Easter Moniack Highld	
206 E4	Easter Ord Abers	
187 J6	Easter Pitkierie Fife	
235 C6	Easter Skeld Shet	
168 A3	Easter Softlaw Border	
213 G4	Easter Suddie Highld	
18 C5	Eastergate W Susx	
175 J5	Easterhouse C Glas	
86 C7	Eastern Green Covtry	
28 A1	Easterton Wilts	
176 B5	Eastfield N Lans	
135 G3	Eastfield N York	

150 B7	Eastgate Dur	
106 D7	Eastgate Norfk	
42 E6	Easthampstead Br For	
69 K4	Easthampton Herefs	
83 L4	Easthope Shrops	
61 L4	Easthorpe Essex	
11 H3	Eastington Devon	
56 C5	Eastington Gloucs	
55 H6	Eastington Gloucs	
154 E7	Eastlands D & G	
56 D6	Eastleach Martin Gloucs	
56 D6	Eastleach Turville Gloucs	
23 H5	Eastleigh Devon	
29 J7	Eastleigh Hants	
34 C4	Eastling Kent	
17 J3	Eastney C Port	
70 D6	Eastnor Herefs	
125 J7	Eastoft N Linc	
75 G1	Easton Cambs	
148 B3	Easton Cumb	
11 G6	Easton Devon	
14 D7	Easton Dorset	
29 K5	Easton Hants	
102 F6	Easton Lincs	
92 D2	Easton Norfk	
26 D3	Easton Somset	
79 G3	Easton Suffk	
39 K6	Easton Wilts	
39 K3	Easton Grey Wilts	
74 C3	Easton Maudit Nhants	
88 E3	Easton on the Hill Nhants	
40 D7	Easton Royal Wilts	
38 D5	Easton-in-Gordano N Som	
89 K4	Eastrea Cambs	
147 M2	Eastriggs D & G	
125 J4	Eastrington E R Yk	
40 D2	Eastrop Swindn	
35 J4	Eastry Kent	
38 E5	Eastville Bristl	
104 C2	Eastville Lincs	
102 C6	Eastwell Leics	
60 C5	Eastwick Herts	
122 E5	Eastwood Calder	
101 J3	Eastwood Notts	
46 D3	Eastwood Sthend	
72 E2	Eathorpe Warwks	
112 E8	Eaton Ches	
113 K7	Eaton Ches	
102 D6	Eaton Leics	
92 E3	Eaton Norfk	
116 B6	Eaton Notts	
57 H7	Eaton Oxon	
83 K5	Eaton Shrops	
58 F4	Eaton Bray Beds	
83 L3	Eaton Constantine Shrops	
58 F4	Eaton Green Beds	
56 E7	Eaton Hastings Oxon	
83 K3	Eaton Mascott Shrops	
75 H3	Eaton Socon Cambs	
98 F7	Eaton upon Tern Shrops	
134 D3	Ebberston N York	
27 M6	Ebbesborne Wake Wilts	
53 J6	Ebbw Vale Blae G	
150 D4	Ebchester Dur	
12 C5	Ebford Devon	
55 J6	Ebley Gloucs	
98 C3	Ebnal Ches	
71 L6	Ebrington Gloucs	
41 J8	Ecchinswell Hants	
178 F5	Ecclaw Border	
155 L7	Ecclefechan D & G	
168 A2	Eccles Border	
46 B7	Eccles Kent	

113 H2 **Eccles** Salfd
92 B5 **Eccles Road** Norfk
114 F5 **Ecclesall** Sheff
115 G3 **Ecclesfield** Sheff
99 J6 **Eccleshall** Staffs
123 H4 **Eccleshill** Brad
176 E4 **Ecclesmachan** W Loth
112 B8 **Eccleston** Ches
121 G6 **Eccleston** Lancs
112 C3 **Eccleston** St Hel
206 E4 **Echt** Abers
167 L4 **Eckford** Border
115 H5 **Eckington** Derbys
71 G6 **Eckington** Worcs
74 B2 **Ecton** Nhants
114 C4 **Edale** Derbys
234 d4 **Eday Airport** Ork
19 H4 **Edburton** W Susx
222 F4 **Edderton** Highld
177 H8 **Eddleston** Border
175 J7 **Eddlewood** S Lans
45 G6 **Eden Park** Gt Lon
32 D4 **Edenbridge** Kent
122 B6 **Edenfield** Lancs
138 E2 **Edenhall** Cumb
103 H7 **Edenham** Lincs
114 E7 **Edensor** Derbys
183 K8 **Edentaggart** Ag & B
115 L1 **Edenthorpe** Donc
94 E5 **Edern** Gwynd
85 J6 **Edgbaston** Birm
58 B4 **Edgcott** Bucks
24 D4 **Edgcott** Somset
55 J6 **Edge** Gloucs
83 H2 **Edge** Shrops
106 C5 **Edgefield** Norfk
106 D5 **Edgefield Green** Norfk
123 H6 **Edgerton** Kirk
55 L6 **Edgeworth** Gloucs
99 G8 **Edgmond** Wrekin
83 H6 **Edgton** Shrops
44 D2 **Edgware** Gt Lon
121 L6 **Edgworth** Bl w D
208 E4 **Edinbane** Highld
177 H4 **Edinburgh** C Edin
176 F4 **Edinburgh Airport** C Edin
177 H4 **Edinburgh Castle** C Edin
177 G4 **Edinburgh Zoo** C Edin
86 B2 **Edingale** Staffs
146 E3 **Edingham** D & G
102 A2 **Edingley** Notts
107 G6 **Edingthorpe** Norfk
107 G6 **Edingthorpe Green** Norfk
179 J7 **Edington** Border
158 E5 **Edington** Nthumb
26 B4 **Edington** Somset
27 L2 **Edington** Wilts
26 B3 **Edington Burtle** Somset
26 A2 **Edingworth** Somset
88 D3 **Edith Weston** Rutlnd
25 M2 **Edithmead** Somset
58 F4 **Edlesborough** Bucks
169 G7 **Edlingham** Nthumb
118 C7 **Edlington** Lincs
15 K1 **Edmondsham** Dorset
151 G5 **Edmondsley** Dur
102 E8 **Edmondthorpe** Leics
45 G2 **Edmonton** Gt Lon
150 C5 **Edmundbyers** Dur
167 L2 **Ednam** Border
194 D6 **Edradynate** P & K
179 H7 **Edrom** Border
98 D6 **Edstaston** Shrops
71 L3 **Edstone** Warwks
101 L5 **Edwalton** Notts
115 L7 **Edwinstowe** Notts

75 J6 **Edworth** Beds
70 B3 **Edwyn Ralph** Herefs
196 F3 **Edzell** Angus
197 G3 **Edzell Woods** Angus
37 G4 **Efail Isaf** Rhondd
36 B2 **Efail-fach** Neath
94 F5 **Efailnewydd** Gwynd
49 K3 **Efailwen** Carmth
97 H2 **Efenechtyd** Denbgs
156 B4 **Effgill** D & G
31 J2 **Effingham** Surrey
11 K5 **Efford** Devon
121 K7 **Egerton** Bolton
34 B5 **Egerton** Kent
6 C4 **Eggbuckland** C Plym
11 G3 **Eggesford** Devon
73 G3 **Eggington** Beds
100 E6 **Egginton** Derbys
141 K4 **Egglescliffe** S on T
140 C3 **Eggleston** Dur
43 G6 **Egham** Surrey
88 C3 **Egleton** Rutlnd
169 G5 **Eglingham** Nthumb
4 F2 **Egloshayle** Cnwll
9 H7 **Egloskerry** Cnwll
98 C4 **Eglwys Cross** Wrexhm
109 M7 **Eglwysbach** Conwy
65 G6 **Eglwyswrw** Pembks
116 B7 **Egmanton** Notts
136 D5 **Egremont** Cumb
111 K3 **Egremont** Wirral
143 G6 **Egton** N York
143 G6 **Egton Bridge** N York
61 M3 **Eight Ash Green** Essex
200 C2 **Eilanreach** Highld
67 K2 **Eilan Village** Powys
38 E3 **Elberton** S Glos
6 D5 **Elburton** C Plym
40 C4 **Elcombe** Swindn
55 H2 **Eldersfield** Worcs
174 E5 **Elderslie** Rens
141 G2 **Eldon** Dur
206 F7 **Elfhill** Abers
85 L2 **Elford** Staffs
214 F2 **Elgin** Moray
199 H3 **Elgol** Highld
35 G6 **Elham** Kent
187 H7 **Elie** Fife
108 D4 **Elim** IOA
29 G8 **Eling** Hants
116 B6 **Elkesley** Notts
55 L5 **Elkstone** Gloucs
216 C3 **Ella** Abers
7 L3 **Ellacombe** Torbay
181 L4 **Ellanbeich** Ag & B
123 G6 **Elland** Calder
172 C3 **Ellary** Ag & B
100 C4 **Ellastone** Staffs
129 K7 **Ellel** Lancs
178 F6 **Ellemford** Border
31 H4 **Ellen's Green** Surrey
99 J7 **Ellenhall** Staffs
141 K7 **Ellerbeck** N York
143 G4 **Ellerby** N York
98 F7 **Ellerdine Heath** Wrekin
191 K6 **Elleric** Ag & B
125 L5 **Ellerker** E R Yk
125 G3 **Ellerton** E R Yk
141 G7 **Ellerton** N York
58 D6 **Ellesborough** Bucks
98 B5 **Ellesmere** Shrops
111 L6 **Ellesmere Port** Ches
93 H5 **Ellingham** Norfk
169 H4 **Ellingham** Nthumb
132 B3 **Ellingstring** N York
75 H1 **Ellington** Cambs
159 G4 **Ellington** Nthumb
27 J3 **Elliots Green** Somset
29 M3 **Ellisfield** Hants
209 H2 **Ellishader** Highld

86 E2 **Ellistown** Leics
217 H7 **Ellon** Abers
148 D7 **Ellonby** Cumb
126 B5 **Elloughton** E R Yk
54 E6 **Ellwood** Gloucs
90 C3 **Elm** Cambs
45 K3 **Elm Park** Gt Lon
70 F2 **Elmbridge** Worcs
76 C6 **Elmdon** Essex
85 L6 **Elmdon** Solhll
45 G6 **Elmers End** Gt Lon
86 F4 **Elmesthorpe** Leics
85 K2 **Elmhurst** Staffs
71 H6 **Elmley Castle** Worcs
70 F1 **Elmley Lovett** Worcs
55 H5 **Elmore** Gloucs
55 H5 **Elmore Back** Gloucs
78 C5 **Elmsett** Suffk
62 C3 **Elmstead Market** Essex
34 F5 **Elmsted Court** Kent
35 H3 **Elmstone** Kent
55 K3 **Elmstone Hardwicke** Gloucs
134 F7 **Elmswell** E R Yk
78 B2 **Elmswell** Suffk
115 J6 **Elmton** Derbys
224 F6 **Elphin** Highld
177 K4 **Elphinstone** E Loth
206 F4 **Elrick** Abers
145 G5 **Elrig** D & G
149 L5 **Elrington** Nthumb
158 B4 **Elsdon** Nthumb
60 E3 **Elsenham** Essex
57 K6 **Elsfield** Oxon
126 C7 **Elsham** N Linc
207 H7 **Elsick House** Abers
92 C1 **Elsing** Norfk
122 D2 **Elslack** N York
17 H3 **Elson** Hants
165 K2 **Elsrickle** S Lans
30 D7 **Elstead** Surrey
30 D7 **Elsted** W Susx
103 H7 **Elsthorpe** Lincs
102 C3 **Elston** Notts
11 G2 **Elstone** Devon
74 F7 **Elstow** Beds
44 D2 **Elstree** Herts
126 F4 **Elstronwick** E R Yk
120 F3 **Elswick** Lancs
151 G3 **Elswick** N u Ty
75 K2 **Elsworth** Cambs
137 K6 **Elterwater** Cumb
45 H5 **Eltham** Gt Lon
75 J3 **Eltisley** Cambs
88 F5 **Elton** Cambs
112 C6 **Elton** Ches
100 E1 **Elton** Derbys
69 J1 **Elton** Herefs
102 C5 **Elton** Notts
141 J4 **Elton** S on T
150 D3 **Eltringham** Nthumb
165 J6 **Elvanfoot** S Lans
101 H6 **Elvaston** Derbys
91 J7 **Elveden** Suffk
30 D1 **Elvetham Heath** Hants
178 A4 **Elvington** E Loth
35 H5 **Elvington** Kent
125 G2 **Elvington** York
141 K2 **Elwick** Hartpl
99 H1 **Elworth** Ches
25 G4 **Elworthy** Somset
90 D7 **Ely** Cambs
37 H5 **Ely** Cardif
74 C5 **Emberton** M Keyn
169 J3 **Embleton** Nthumb
223 H3 **Embo** Highld
223 H3 **Embo Street** Highld
26 E2 **Emborough** Somset
131 J8 **Embsay** N York
16 C2 **Emery Down** Hants
123 K7 **Emley** Kirk

58 C7 **Emmington** Oxon
90 C3 **Emneth** Cambs
90 D3 **Emneth Hungate** Norfk
88 D2 **Empingham** Rutlnd
30 C5 **Empshott** Hants
17 L2 **Emsworth** Hants
41 H7 **Enborne** W Berk
41 H7 **Enborne Row** W Berk
87 G4 **Enderby** Leics
129 L3 **Endmoor** Cumb
99 L2 **Endon** Staffs
99 L2 **Endon Bank** Staffs
60 B7 **Enfield** Gt Lon
60 B7 **Enfield Lock** Gt Lon
60 B7 **Enfield Wash** Gt Lon
28 C2 **Enford** Wilts
39 G4 **Engine Common** S Glos
41 L6 **Englefield** W Berk
43 G6 **Englefield Green** Surrey
54 E5 **English Bicknor** Gloucs
98 C6 **English Frankton** Shrops
39 G7 **Englishcombe** BaNES
29 G2 **Enham-Alamein** Hants
25 K4 **Enmore** Somset
27 J6 **Enmore Green** Dorset
136 E4 **Ennerdale Bridge** Cumb
195 G4 **Enochdhu** P & K
189 J6 **Ensay** Ag & B
15 K3 **Ensbury** Bmouth
83 H1 **Ensdon** Shrops
23 J6 **Ensis** Devon
57 G3 **Enstone** Oxon
154 E2 **Enterkinfoot** D & G
84 E6 **Enville** Staffs
233 b9 **Eolaigearraidh** W Isls
55 H5 **Epney** Gloucs
101 M3 **Epperstone** Notts
60 D7 **Epping** Essex
60 C6 **Epping Green** Essex
60 C6 **Epping Upland** Essex
140 F5 **Eppleby** N York
44 E7 **Epsom** Surrey
72 D6 **Epwell** Oxon
116 C2 **Epworth** N Linc
97 M4 **Erbistock** Wrexhm
85 K5 **Erdington** Birm
32 F6 **Eridge Green** E Susx
172 E4 **Erines** Ag & B
191 H7 **Eriska** Ag & B
91 G7 **Eriswell** Suffk
45 K4 **Erith** Gt Lon
27 L2 **Erlestoke** Wilts
6 F5 **Ermington** Devon
106 E6 **Erpingham** Norfk
202 E2 **Errogie** Highld
186 D3 **Errol** P & K
174 E4 **Erskine** Rens
144 B2 **Ervie** D & G
78 F7 **Erwarton** Suffk
68 C6 **Erwood** Powys
141 H5 **Eryholme** N York
97 J2 **Eryrys** Denbgs
140 F2 **Escomb** Dur
124 F2 **Escrick** York
81 G3 **Esgairgeiliog** Powys
150 F6 **Esh** Dur
150 F6 **Esh Winning** Dur
43 J7 **Esher** Surrey
158 F3 **Eshott** Nthumb
212 C6 **Eskadale** Highld
177 J5 **Eskbank** Mdloth
137 G6 **Eskdale Green** Cumb
156 A3 **Eskdalemuir** D & G
120 E3 **Esprick** Lancs

88 F2 **Essendine** Rutlnd
59 L6 **Essendon** Herts
213 G6 **Essich** Highld
85 G3 **Essington** Staffs
217 H7 **Esslemont** Abers
142 C4 **Eston** R & Cl
168 D2 **Etal** Nthumb
40 B7 **Etchilhampton** Wilts
33 J7 **Etchingham** E Susx
34 F6 **Etchinghill** Kent
100 B8 **Etchinghill** Staffs
42 F5 **Eton** W & M
42 F5 **Eton Wick** W & M
99 K3 **Etruria** C Stke
203 G6 **Etteridge** Highld
139 K2 **Ettersgill** Dur
99 G1 **Ettiley Heath** Ches
85 G4 **Ettingshall** Wolves
72 C5 **Ettington** Warwks
89 G3 **Etton** C Pete
126 B2 **Etton** E R Yk
166 D6 **Ettrick** Border
166 F4 **Ettrickbridge** Border
166 C6 **Ettrickhill** Border
100 F6 **Etwall** Derbys
91 K7 **Euston** Suffk
121 H6 **Euxton** Lancs
212 F2 **Evanton** Highld
103 H3 **Evedon** Lincs
223 G4 **Evelix** Highld
68 F3 **Evenjobb** Powys
73 H7 **Evenley** Oxon
56 E3 **Evenlode** Gloucs
140 E3 **Evenwood** Dur
26 F4 **Evercreech** Somset
125 J3 **Everingham** E R Yk
28 D2 **Everleigh** Wilts
59 G2 **Eversholt** Beds
14 B2 **Evershot** Dorset
42 C7 **Eversley** Hants
42 C7 **Eversley Cross** Hants
125 L4 **Everthorpe** E R Yk
75 H4 **Everton** Beds
16 C4 **Everton** Hants
111 K3 **Everton** Lpool
116 B4 **Everton** Notts
156 C6 **Evertown** D & G
70 C5 **Evesbatch** Herefs
71 J5 **Evesham** Worcs
87 J3 **Evington** C Leic
114 F3 **Ewden Village** Sheff
44 E7 **Ewell** Surrey
35 H6 **Ewell Minnis** Kent
41 M3 **Ewelme** Oxon
40 A2 **Ewen** Gloucs
36 D5 **Ewenny** V Glam
103 J3 **Ewerby** Lincs
158 D4 **Ewesley** Nthumb
31 H4 **Ewhurst** Surrey
20 F2 **Ewhurst Green** E Susx
31 H4 **Ewhurst Green** Surrey
111 J7 **Ewloe** Flints
10 C6 **Eworthy** Devon
30 D2 **Ewshot** Hants
54 B3 **Ewyas Harold** Herefs
10 E4 **Exbourne** Devon
16 E3 **Exbury** Hants
24 E6 **Exebridge** Somset
132 D3 **Exelby** N York
11 L6 **Exeter** Devon
12 C4 **Exeter Airport** Devon
24 D4 **Exford** Somset
83 J3 **Exfordsgreen** Shrops
71 K4 **Exhall** Warwks
86 D6 **Exhall** Warwks
42 A4 **Exlade Street** Oxon
12 B5 **Exminster** Devon
24 D4 **Exmoor National Park**
12 C6 **Exmouth** Devon
76 E2 **Exning** Suffk

35 G5 **Exted** Kent
12 C5 **Exton** Devon
29 L7 **Exton** Hants
88 D2 **Exton** Rutlnd
24 E5 **Exton** Somset
11 K6 **Exwick** Devon
114 E6 **Eyam** Derbys
73 G4 **Eydon** Nhants
89 J3 **Eye** C Pete
69 J2 **Eye** Herefs
92 D8 **Eye** Suffk
179 K5 **Eyemouth** Border
75 J5 **Eyeworth** Beds
33 L3 **Eyhorne Street** Kent
79 G4 **Eyke** Suffk
75 H3 **Eynesbury** Cambs
45 K6 **Eynsford** Kent
57 H6 **Eynsham** Oxon
13 L4 **Eype** Dorset
208 F4 **Eyre** Highld
35 H5 **Eythorne** Kent
69 J3 **Eyton** Herefs
98 C7 **Eyton** Shrops
83 G6 **Eyton** Shrops
83 L3 **Eyton on Severn** Shrops
84 B1 **Eyton upon the Weald Moors** Wrekin

F

41 H8 **Faccombe** Hants
141 L6 **Faceby** N York
82 B1 **Fachwen** Powys
98 E3 **Faddiley** Ches
133 K2 **Fadmoor** N York
51 K5 **Faerdre** Swans
174 F4 **Faifley** W Duns
38 D6 **Failand** N Som
163 L4 **Failford** S Ayrs
113 K2 **Failsworth** Oldham
29 J7 **Fair Oak** Hants
42 A7 **Fair Oak Green** Hants
80 E2 **Fairbourne** Gwynd
124 D5 **Fairburn** N York
114 B6 **Fairfield** Derbys
85 G7 **Fairfield** Worcs
56 D7 **Fairford** Gloucs
146 F4 **Fairgirth** D & G
120 D5 **Fairhaven** Lancs
173 L7 **Fairlie** N Ayrs
21 G4 **Fairlight** E Susx
12 E3 **Fairmile** Devon
43 J7 **Fairmile** Surrey
167 G3 **Fairnilee** Border
99 H6 **Fairoak** Staffs
45 L7 **Fairseat** Kent
61 J5 **Fairstead** Essex
32 E7 **Fairwarp** E Susx
37 H5 **Fairwater** Cardif
22 F6 **Fairy Cross** Devon
105 L6 **Fakenham** Norfk
91 K7 **Fakenham Magna** Suffk
177 L6 **Fala** Mdloth
177 L6 **Fala Dam** Mdloth
177 L7 **Falahill** Border
117 H5 **Faldingworth** Lincs
236 e7 **Faldouet** Jersey
39 G2 **Falfield** S Glos
79 G6 **Falkenham** Suffk
176 B3 **Falkirk** Falk
186 D6 **Falkland** Fife
185 H8 **Fallin** Stirlg
169 J3 **Falloden** Nthumb
113 J3 **Fallowfield** Manch
150 B2 **Fallowfield** Nthumb
182 E5 **Falls of Blarghour** Ag & B
19 K4 **Falmer** E Susx
3 K5 **Falmouth** Cnwll

156 D2 **Falnash** Border
134 F2 **Falsgrave** N York
157 J5 **Falstone** Nthumb
228 B5 **Fanagmore** Highld
59 G3 **Fancott** Beds
212 D5 **Fanellan** Highld
142 C7 **Fangdale Beck** N York
134 B8 **Fangfoss** E R Yk
189 K7 **Fanmore** Ag & B
211 K2 **Fannich Lodge** Highld
167 J2 **Fans** Border
74 C7 **Far Bletchley** M Keyn
73 L3 **Far Cotton** Nhants
137 J7 **Far End** Cumb
55 H7 **Far Green** Gloucs
112 D2 **Far Moor** Wigan
55 L7 **Far Oakridge** Gloucs
137 K7 **Far Sawrey** Cumb
118 C6 **Far Thorpe** Lincs
89 H5 **Farcet** Cambs
17 H2 **Fareham** Hants
85 J2 **Farewell** Staffs
40 F2 **Faringdon** Oxon
121 H5 **Farington** Lancs
185 L1 **Farkhill** P & K
148 F3 **Farlam** Cumb
38 D6 **Farleigh** N Som
32 C2 **Farleigh** Surrey
39 J8 **Farleigh Hungerford** Somset
29 L3 **Farleigh Wallop** Hants
119 G6 **Farlesthorpe** Lincs
129 L4 **Farleton** Cumb
130 B6 **Farleton** Lancs
100 B4 **Farley** Staffs
28 E5 **Farley** Wilts
77 G4 **Farley Green** Suffk
31 H3 **Farley Green** Surrey
42 C7 **Farley Hill** Wokham
55 H5 **Farleys End** Gloucs
17 J2 **Farlington** C Port
133 J6 **Farlington** N York
84 B7 **Farlow** Shrops
38 F7 **Farmborough** BaNES
56 B3 **Farmcote** Gloucs
66 E5 **Farmers** Carmth
56 C5 **Farmington** Gloucs
57 J6 **Farmoor** Oxon
215 L4 **Farmtown** Moray
215 J3 **Farnachty** Moray
45 H7 **Farnborough** Gt Lon
30 E2 **Farnborough** Hants
41 H4 **Farnborough** W Berk
72 E5 **Farnborough** Warwks
30 E1 **Farnborough Park** Hants
30 E1 **Farnborough Street** Hants
31 G3 **Farncombe** Surrey
74 D2 **Farndish** Beds
98 B2 **Farndon** Ches
102 C3 **Farndon** Notts
169 K2 **Farne Islands** Nthumb
197 G5 **Farnell** Angus
27 L7 **Farnham** Dorset
60 D3 **Farnham** Essex
132 E7 **Farnham** N York
79 H3 **Farnham** Suffk
30 D3 **Farnham** Surrey
42 F4 **Farnham Common** Bucks
42 F4 **Farnham Royal** Bucks
45 K6 **Farningham** Kent
123 J2 **Farnley** Leeds
123 K4 **Farnley** Leeds
123 H7 **Farnley Tyas** Kirk
101 M2 **Farnsfield** Notts

113 G1 **Farnworth** Bolton
112 D4 **Farnworth** Halton
229 L3 **Farr** Highld
213 G7 **Farr** Highld
203 K5 **Farr** Highld
202 E2 **Farraline** Highld
12 C4 **Farringdon** Devon
26 F1 **Farrington Gurney** BaNES
73 G6 **Farthinghoe** Nhants
73 H4 **Farthingstone** Nhants
123 H6 **Fartown** Kirk
123 J4 **Fartown** Leeds
12 F4 **Farway Street** Devon
191 K6 **Fasnacloich** Ag & B
211 L8 **Fasnakyle** Highld
191 K2 **Fassfern** Highld
151 H4 **Fatfield** Sundld
176 C6 **Fauldhouse** W Loth
61 J5 **Faulkbourne** Essex
27 H1 **Faulkland** Somset
98 E6 **Fauls** Shrops
34 D3 **Faversham** Kent
132 F5 **Fawdington** N York
151 G2 **Fawdon** N u Ty
168 F6 **Fawdon** Nthumb
45 L6 **Fawkham Green** Kent
57 G4 **Fawler** Oxon
42 C3 **Fawley** Bucks
16 F2 **Fawley** Hants
41 H4 **Fawley** W Berk
125 K5 **Faxfleet** E R Yk
31 K5 **Faygate** W Susx
111 K3 **Fazakerley** Lpool
85 L3 **Fazeley** Staffs
132 B4 **Fearby** N York
223 H5 **Fearn** Highld
194 B7 **Fearnan** P & K
210 B3 **Fearnbeg** Highld
209 L3 **Fearnmore** Highld
172 F3 **Fearnoch** Ag & B
85 G3 **Featherstone** Staffs
124 C6 **Featherstone** Wakefd
71 H3 **Feckenham** Worcs
61 L4 **Feering** Essex
140 C7 **Feetham** N York
32 C5 **Felbridge** Surrey
106 E5 **Felbrigg** Norfk
32 C5 **Felcourt** Surrey
51 G2 **Felin gwm Isaf** Carmth
51 G1 **Felin gwm Uchaf** Carmth
51 G2 **Felindre** Carmth
65 K6 **Felindre** Carmth
82 D7 **Felindre** Powys
51 J5 **Felindre** Swans
64 F6 **Felindre Farchog** Pembks
133 G3 **Felixkirk** N York
79 G7 **Felixstowe** Suffk
151 G5 **Felling** Gatesd
74 E3 **Felmersham** Beds
106 F6 **Felmingham** Norfk
18 C5 **Felpham** W Susx
77 L3 **Felsham** Suffk
61 G4 **Felsted** Essex
43 J5 **Feltham** Gt Lon
43 H6 **Felthamhill** Gt Lon
106 E8 **Felthorpe** Norfk
69 L5 **Felton** Herefs
38 D7 **Felton** N Som
158 F3 **Felton** Nthumb
98 B8 **Felton Butler** Shrops
91 G5 **Feltwell** Norfk
76 C3 **Fen Ditton** Cambs
75 L2 **Fen Drayton** Cambs
92 B4 **Fen Street** Norfk
122 C3 **Fence** Lancs
115 H4 **Fence** Rothm

132 D2 **Fencote** N York
57 L5 **Fencott** Oxon
104 D1 **Fendike Corner** Lincs
121 J5 **Feniscowles** Bl w D
12 E3 **Feniton** Devon
84 D6 **Fenn Green** Shrops
46 D5 **Fenn Street** Medway
100 D3 **Fenny Bentley** Derbys
12 E3 **Fenny Bridges** Devon
72 E4 **Fenny Compton** Warwks
86 D4 **Fenny Drayton** Leics
75 K2 **Fenstanton** Cambs
99 K4 **Fenton** C Stke
89 K7 **Fenton** Cambs
148 E4 **Fenton** Cumb
116 D6 **Fenton** Lincs
102 E3 **Fenton** Lincs
116 C5 **Fenton** Notts
168 E3 **Fenton** Nthumb
178 B3 **Fenton Barns** E Loth
124 F7 **Fenwick** Donc
163 L2 **Fenwick** E Ayrs
169 G2 **Fenwick** Nthumb
158 D7 **Fenwick** Nthumb
4 C7 **Feock** Cnwll
171 H4 **Feolin Ferry** Ag & B
163 J2 **Fergushill** N Ayrs
208 B4 **Feriniquarrie** Highld
196 D4 **Fern** Angus
36 F2 **Ferndale** Rhondd
15 K3 **Ferndown** Dorset
214 B5 **Ferness** Moray
40 F3 **Fernham** Oxon
70 F3 **Fernhill Heath** Worcs
30 E5 **Fernhurst** W Susx
186 E4 **Fernie** Fife
175 K7 **Ferniegair** S Lans
208 F7 **Fernilea** Highld
114 A5 **Fernilee** Derbys
132 E7 **Ferrensby** N York
199 K4 **Ferrindonald** Highld
18 F5 **Ferring** W Susx
223 G4 **Ferry Point** Highld
197 H5 **Ferryden** Angus
141 H2 **Ferryhill** Dur
50 D4 **Ferryside** Carmth
223 G4 **Ferrytown** Highld
92 C6 **Fersfield** Norfk
192 F2 **Fersit** Highld
203 K4 **Feshiebridge** Highld
31 J1 **Fetcham** Surrey
217 J4 **Fetterangus** Abers
197 G2 **Fettercairn** Abers
132 B8 **Fewston** N York
67 G2 **Ffair Rhos** Cerdgn
51 J2 **Ffairfach** Carmth
96 A4 **Ffestiniog** Gwynd
95 L4 **Ffestiniog Railway** Gwynd
51 H5 **Fforest** Carmth
51 J6 **Fforest Fach** Swans
65 L5 **Ffostrasol** Cerdgn
97 L2 **Ffrith** Flints
111 G5 **Ffynnongroyw** Flints
225 K3 **Fiag Lodge** Highld
32 C2 **Fickleshole** Surrey
55 L2 **Fiddington** Gloucs
25 K4 **Fiddington** Somset
27 J8 **Fiddleford** Dorset
4 C5 **Fiddlers Green** Cnwll
100 A5 **Field** Staffs
129 J3 **Field Broughton** Cumb
106 B5 **Field Dalling** Norfk
86 F2 **Field Head** Leics
215 J4 **Fife Keith** Moray
27 H6 **Fifehead Magdalen** Dorset

14 E1 **Fifehead Neville** Dorset
14 E1 **Fifehead St Quintin** Dorset
56 E4 **Fifield** Oxon
42 E5 **Fifield** W & M
28 D3 **Figheldean** Wilts
93 K2 **Filby** Norfk
135 H4 **Filey** N York
74 C5 **Filgrave** M Keyn
56 E6 **Filkins** Oxon
23 L5 **Filleigh** Devon
11 H3 **Filleigh** Devon
116 F4 **Fillingham** Lincs
86 C6 **Fillongley** Warwks
38 E5 **Filton** S Glos
134 D7 **Fimber** E R Yk
196 D5 **Finavon** Angus
91 G3 **Fincham** Norfk
42 D7 **Finchampstead** Wokham
182 C6 **Fincharn** Ag & B
30 C8 **Finchdean** Hants
61 G2 **Finchingfield** Essex
44 F2 **Finchley** Ct Lon
100 F6 **Findern** Derbys
214 C2 **Findhorn** Moray
213 J8 **Findhorn Bridge** Highld
185 L4 **Findo Gask** P & K
215 K2 **Findochty** Moray
207 H6 **Findon** Abers
18 F4 **Findon** W Susx
212 F4 **Findon Mains** Highld
206 B4 **Findrack House** Abers
74 D1 **Finedon** Nhants
78 F1 **Fingal Street** Suffk
186 C4 **Fingask** P & K
42 C3 **Fingest** Bucks
132 B2 **Finghall** N York
164 E6 **Fingland** D & G
35 J4 **Finglesham** Kent
62 B4 **Fingringhoe** Essex
184 C1 **Finlarig** Stirlg
57 M2 **Finmere** Oxon
193 H5 **Finnart** P & K
78 C1 **Finningham** Suffk
116 A2 **Finningley** Donc
232 d5 **Finsbay** W Isls
71 H1 **Finstall** Worcs
129 H2 **Finsthwaite** Cumb
57 G5 **Finstock** Oxon
234 b6 **Finstown** Ork
216 E4 **Fintry** Abers
175 H2 **Fintry** Stirlg
206 B6 **Finzean** Abers
180 D3 **Fionnphort** Ag & B
232 d5 **Fionnsbhagh** W Isls
150 E7 **Fir Tree** Dur
130 C2 **Firbank** Cumb
115 K4 **Firbeck** Rothm
132 D3 **Firby** N York
134 B6 **Firby** N York
118 F8 **Firsby** Lincs
17 G4 **Fishbourne** IOW
18 A5 **Fishbourne** W Susx
18 A5 **Fishbourne Roman Palace** W Susx
141 J2 **Fishburn** Dur
185 J7 **Fishcross** Clacks
29 J7 **Fisher's Pond** Hants
216 C7 **Fisherford** Abers
177 K4 **Fisherrow** E Loth
213 H4 **Fisherton** Highld
163 H6 **Fisherton** S Ayrs
27 M4 **Fisherton de la Mere** Wilts
64 D6 **Fishguard** Pembks
125 G7 **Fishlake** Donc
190 D7 **Fishnish Pier** Ag & B
38 F5 **Fishponds** Bristl
104 B4 **Fishtoft** Lincs

104 A3 **Fishtoft Drove** Lincs
208 E7 **Fiskavaig** Highld
117 H6 **Fiskerton** Lincs
102 C3 **Fiskerton** Notts
28 D7 **Fittleton** Wilts
18 D2 **Fittleworth** W Susx
98 C8 **Fitz** Shrops
25 H5 **Fitzhead** Somset
124 C7 **Fitzwilliam** Wakefd
19 M2 **Five Ash Down** E Susx
32 F7 **Five Ashes** E Susx
33 H4 **Five Oak Green** Kent
236 d7 **Five Oaks** Jersey
31 H5 **Five Oaks** W Susx
26 A6 **Fivehead** Somset
9 G8 **Fivelanes** Cnwll
42 E3 **Flackwell Heath** Bucks
71 H5 **Fladbury** Worcs
235 C6 **Fladdabister** Shet
114 C7 **Flagg** Derbys
135 K5 **Flamborough** E R Yk
135 K5 **Flamborough Head** E R Yk
134 B4 **Flamingo Land Theme Park** N York
59 H5 **Flamstead** Herts
18 C5 **Flansham** W Susx
123 L6 **Flanshaw** Wakefd
131 H7 **Flasby** N York
114 A7 **Flash** Staffs
208 E4 **Flashader** Highld
59 G7 **Flaunden** Herts
102 C4 **Flawborough** Notts
133 G6 **Flawith** N York
38 D6 **Flax Bourton** N Som
132 F7 **Flaxby** N York
55 G5 **Flaxley** Gloucs
25 H4 **Flaxpool** Somset
133 K6 **Flaxton** N York
87 J5 **Fleckney** Leics
73 G2 **Flecknoe** Warwks
116 D6 **Fledborough** Notts
14 C6 **Fleet** Dorset
30 D2 **Fleet** Hants
104 C7 **Fleet** Lincs
104 C7 **Fleet Hargate** Lincs
120 D2 **Fleetwood** Lancs
36 F6 **Flemingston** V Glam
175 H6 **Flemington** S Lans
77 J1 **Flempton** Suffk
147 L6 **Fletchertown** Cumb
19 L2 **Fletching** E Susx
9 G4 **Flexbury** Cnwll
30 F2 **Flexford** Surrey
147 H7 **Flimby** Cumb
33 J6 **Flimwell** E Susx
111 H6 **Flint** Flints
102 C4 **Flintham** Notts
126 F4 **Flinton** E R Yk
105 H6 **Flitcham** Norfk
74 F7 **Flitton** Beds
74 F7 **Flitwick** Beds
125 K7 **Flixborough** N Linc
125 K7 **Flixborough Stather** N Linc
135 G4 **Flixton** N York
93 G6 **Flixton** Suffk
113 H3 **Flixton** Traffd
123 J7 **Flockton** Kirk
123 K7 **Flockton Green** Kirk
218 C6 **Flodigarry** Highld
129 H4 **Flookburgh** Cumb
92 E4 **Flordon** Norfk
73 J3 **Flore** Nhants
78 C5 **Flowton** Suffk
3 L4 **Flushing** Cnwll
12 E4 **Fluxton** Devon
71 H4 **Flyford Flavell** Worcs
46 B4 **Fobbing** Thurr
215 H3 **Fochabers** Moray

125 K6 **Fockerby** N Linc
26 E5 **Foddington** Somset
81 L2 **Foel** Powys
125 H3 **Foggathorpe** E R Yk
179 G8 **Fogo** Border
214 F3 **Fogwatt** Moray
228 B5 **Foindle** Highld
195 J4 **Folda** Angus
100 B5 **Fole** Staffs
86 D6 **Foleshill** Covtry
26 F8 **Folke** Dorset
35 H7 **Folkestone** Kent
103 H5 **Folkingham** Lincs
20 B5 **Folkington** E Susx
89 G5 **Folksworth** Cambs
135 G4 **Folkton** N York
216 D7 **Folla Rule** Abers
132 E8 **Follifoot** N York
10 E5 **Folly Gate** Devon
27 L5 **Fonthill Bishop** Wilts
27 L5 **Fonthill Gifford** Wilts
27 K7 **Fontmell Magna** Dorset
27 J8 **Fontmell Parva** Dorset
18 C4 **Fontwell** W Susx
114 D6 **Foolow** Derbys
205 H3 **Forbestown** Abers
140 F5 **Forcett** N York
182 C6 **Ford** Ag & B
58 C6 **Ford** Bucks
115 H5 **Ford** Derbys
22 F6 **Ford** Devon
7 J7 **Ford** Devon
56 C3 **Ford** Gloucs
168 E2 **Ford** Nthumb
25 H5 **Ford** Somset
100 B2 **Ford** Staffs
18 D5 **Ford** W Susx
39 J5 **Ford** Wilts
61 G5 **Ford End** Essex
25 J7 **Ford Street** Somset
32 F5 **Fordcombe** Kent
177 G2 **Fordell** Fife
82 E4 **Forden** Powys
7 H3 **Forder Green** Devon
76 F1 **Fordham** Cambs
61 L3 **Fordham** Essex
90 E4 **Fordham** Norfk
28 D8 **Fordingbridge** Hants
135 G4 **Fordon** E R Yk
197 J2 **Fordoun** Abers
61 L3 **Fordstreet** Essex
35 G3 **Fordwich** Kent
216 B2 **Fordyce** Abers
99 L7 **Forebridge** Staffs
101 G7 **Foremark** Derbys
236 c4 **Forest** Guern
122 B1 **Forest Becks** Lancs
113 L6 **Forest Chapel** Ches
54 F5 **Forest of Dean** Gloucs
45 H3 **Forest Gate** Gt Lon
31 J3 **Forest Green** Surrey
151 G2 **Forest Hall** N Tyne
45 G5 **Forest Hill** Gt Lon
57 L6 **Forest Hill** Oxon
132 E7 **Forest Lane Head** N York
192 D7 **Forest Lodge** Ag & B
185 K8 **Forest Mill** Clacks
32 D6 **Forest Row** E Susx
30 C8 **Forestside** W Susx
196 D6 **Forfar** Angus
186 A4 **Forgandenny** P & K
37 L2 **Forge Hammer** Torfn
215 J4 **Forgie** Moray
215 J4 **Forgieside** Moray
216 B5 **Forgue** Abers
111 J1 **Formby** Sefton
92 D5 **Forncett End** Norfk
92 E5 **Forncett St Mary** Norfk

92 E5 **Forncett St Peter** Norfk
77 J2 **Fornham All Saints** Suffk
77 J2 **Fornham St Martin** Suffk
213 L4 **Fornighty** Highld
214 C3 **Forres** Moray
99 L4 **Forsbrook** Staffs
227 M2 **Forse** Highld
227 M2 **Forse House** Highld
230 C6 **Forsinard** Highld
202 B4 **Fort Augustus** Highld
236 c2 **Fort Hommet** Guern
236 d1 **Fort le Marchant** Guern
191 L2 **Fort William** Highld
185 L4 **Forteviot** P & K
176 C7 **Forth** S Lans
55 K2 **Forthampton** Gloucs
194 B6 **Fortingall** P & K
29 H3 **Forton** Hants
121 G1 **Forton** Lancs
83 H1 **Forton** Shrops
13 J2 **Forton** Somset
99 H7 **Forton** Staffs
216 C5 **Fortrie** Abers
213 H3 **Fortrose** Highld
14 D7 **Fortuneswell** Dorset
60 B7 **Forty Hill** Gt Lon
40 F8 **Fosbury** Wilts
56 E4 **Foscot** Oxon
104 A5 **Fosdyke** Lincs
194 C5 **Foss** P & K
56 B5 **Fossebridge** Gloucs
60 D6 **Foster Street** Essex
100 D6 **Foston** Derbys
87 H4 **Foston** Leics
102 E4 **Foston** Lincs
133 L6 **Foston** N York
135 H7 **Foston on the Wolds** E R Yk
118 D3 **Fotherby** Lincs
88 F5 **Fotheringhay** Nhants
86 B4 **Foul End** Warwks
179 J7 **Foulden** Border
91 H4 **Foulden** Norfk
122 D3 **Foulridge** Lancs
106 B7 **Foulsham** Norfk
177 L8 **Fountainhall** Border
78 B1 **Four Ashes** Suffk
236 c3 **Four Cabots** Guern
97 K8 **Four Crosses** Powys
32 E4 **Four Elms** Kent
25 K4 **Four Forks** Somset
90 C1 **Four Gotes** Cambs
3 J4 **Four Lanes** Cnwll
30 A4 **Four Marks** Hants
108 C5 **Four Mile Bridge** IOA
86 B7 **Four Oaks** Solhll
50 F4 **Four Roads** Carmth
33 K7 **Four Throws** Kent
223 H3 **Fourpenny** Highld
149 M2 **Fourstones** Nthumb
28 A5 **Fovant** Wilts
207 H2 **Foveran** Abers
5 H5 **Fowey** Cnwll
33 J4 **Fowlhall** Kent
186 E2 **Fowlis** Angus
185 J3 **Fowlis Wester** P & K
76 B5 **Fowlmere** Cambs
69 L7 **Fownhope** Herefs
174 E6 **Foxbar** Rens
27 G1 **Foxcote** Somset
237 b5 **Foxdale** IOM
77 J5 **Foxearth** Essex
128 F3 **Foxfield** Cumb
4 F5 **Foxhole** Cnwll
134 F5 **Foxholes** N York
106 C7 **Foxley** Norfk
100 B3 **Foxt** Staffs
76 B5 **Foxton** Cambs

87 K5 **Foxton** Leics
141 K7 **Foxton** N York
84 B7 **Foxwood** Shrops
54 E3 **Foy** Herefs
202 D2 **Foyers** Highld
213 L4 **Foynesfield** Highld
4 E4 **Fraddon** Cnwll
85 L2 **Fradley** Staffs
99 M6 **Fradswell** Staffs
135 J7 **Fraisthorpe** E R Yk
20 A2 **Framfield** E Susx
92 F3 **Framingham Earl** Norfk
92 F3 **Framingham Pigot** Norfk
79 G2 **Framlingham** Suffk
14 C4 **Frampton** Dorset
104 B5 **Frampton** Lincs
38 F4 **Frampton Cotterell** S Glos
55 L7 **Frampton Mansell** Gloucs
55 H6 **Frampton on Severn** Gloucs
78 E3 **Framsden** Suffk
151 G6 **Framwellgate Moor** Dur
121 J3 **Frances Green** Lancs
84 E7 **Franche** Worcs
111 H4 **Frankby** Wirral
85 H7 **Frankley** Worcs
72 E1 **Frankton** Warwks
33 G6 **Frant** E Susx
217 J2 **Fraserburgh** Abers
62 C4 **Frating** Essex
62 C4 **Frating Green** Essex
17 J3 **Fratton** C Port
6 B5 **Freathy** Cnwll
76 F1 **Freckenham** Suffk
120 F5 **Freckleton** Lancs
102 D7 **Freeby** Leics
29 J2 **Freefolk** Hants
57 H5 **Freeland** Oxon
93 J3 **Freethorpe** Norfk
93 J3 **Freethorpe Common** Norfk
104 B4 **Freiston** Lincs
23 H5 **Fremington** Devon
140 D7 **Fremington** N York
38 F5 **Frenchay** S Glos
194 C5 **Frenich** P & K
30 D3 **Frensham** Surrey
120 C8 **Freshfield** Sefton
39 H7 **Freshford** Wilts
16 D5 **Freshwater** IOW
92 F7 **Fressingfield** Suffk
78 E6 **Freston** Suffk
231 L3 **Freswick** Highld
55 G6 **Fretherne** Gloucs
106 F8 **Frettenham** Norfk
186 E6 **Freuchie** Fife
49 G5 **Freystrop** Pembks
85 H4 **Friar Park** W Mids
90 C3 **Friday Bridge** Cambs
79 H3 **Friday Street** Suffk
134 D7 **Fridaythorpe** E R Yk
44 F2 **Friern Barnet** Gt Lon
188 F5 **Friesland Bay** Ag & B
117 H5 **Friesthorpe** Lincs
102 F3 **Frieston** Lincs
42 D3 **Frieth** Bucks
41 H2 **Frilford** Oxon
41 K5 **Frilsham** W Berk
42 E8 **Frimley** Surrey
46 C6 **Frindsbury** Medway
105 H5 **Fring** Norfk
57 L3 **Fringford** Oxon
34 B4 **Frinsted** Kent
62 F4 **Frinton-on-Sea** Essex
196 F6 **Friockheim** Angus
102 B8 **Frisby on the Wreake** Leics
104 D2 **Friskney** Lincs

20 B6 **Friston** E Susx
79 J3 **Friston** Suffk
101 G3 **Fritchley** Derbys
28 E8 **Fritham** Hants
23 G7 **Frithelstock** Devon
23 G7 **Frithelstock Stone** Devon
104 A3 **Frithville** Lincs
33 K5 **Frittenden** Kent
7 J6 **Frittiscombe** Devon
93 K4 **Fritton** Norfk
92 F5 **Fritton** Norfk
57 K3 **Fritwell** Oxon
123 H4 **Frizinghall** Brad
136 E4 **Frizington** Cumb
55 H7 **Frocester** Gloucs
83 K3 **Frodesley** Shrops
112 D6 **Frodsham** Ches
76 B5 **Frog End** Cambs
70 E2 **Frog Pool** Worcs
168 B4 **Frogden** Border
114 E6 **Froggatt** Derbys
100 A3 **Froghall** Staffs
7 H7 **Frogmore** Devon
89 H2 **Frognall** Lincs
6 A3 **Frogwell** Cnwll
87 G5 **Frolesworth** Leics
27 H2 **Frome** Somset
14 B2 **Frome St Quintin** Dorset
70 C5 **Fromes Hill** Herefs
97 L4 **Fron Isaf** Wrexhm
96 D5 **Fron-goch** Gwynd
97 K4 **Froncysyllte** Denbgs
150 C7 **Frosterley** Dur
40 F6 **Froxfield** Wilts
30 B6 **Froxfield Green** Hants
29 H7 **Fryern Hill** Hants
61 G7 **Fryerning** Essex
190 C6 **Fuinary** Highld
102 F3 **Fulbeck** Lincs
76 D4 **Fulbourn** Cambs
56 E5 **Fulbrook** Oxon
29 J5 **Fulflood** Hants
25 K5 **Fulford** Somset
99 L5 **Fulford** Staffs
124 F2 **Fulford** York
44 E5 **Fulham** Gt Lon
19 H4 **Fulking** W Susx
134 B7 **Full Sutton** E R Yk
163 H2 **Fullarton** N Ayrs
61 H5 **Fuller Street** Essex
29 G4 **Fullerton** Hants
118 D6 **Fulletby** Lincs
72 C5 **Fullready** Warwks
174 E7 **Fullwood** E Ayrs
43 G4 **Fulmer** Bucks
106 B6 **Fulmodeston** Norfk
117 H5 **Fulnetby** Lincs
103 L7 **Fulney** Lincs
118 D3 **Fulstow** Lincs
57 G4 **Fulwell** Oxon
151 J3 **Fulwell** Sundld
121 H4 **Fulwood** Lancs
114 F4 **Fulwood** Sheff
92 D4 **Fundenhall** Norfk
17 L2 **Funtington** W Susx
184 F3 **Funtullich** P & K
13 H2 **Furley** Devon
182 E7 **Furnace** Ag & B
51 G5 **Furnace** Carmth
114 A5 **Furness Vale** Derbys
60 C3 **Furneux Pelham** Herts
28 F7 **Furzley** Hants
60 F6 **Fyfett** Essex
28 F3 **Fyfield** Hants
57 H7 **Fyfield** Oxon
40 C6 **Fyfield** Wilts

40 D7 **Fyfield** Wilts
143 J6 **Fylingthorpe** N York
30 D6 **Fyning** W Susx
216 E6 **Fyvie** Abers

G

174 E7 **Gabroc Hill** E Ayrs
87 K2 **Gaddesby** Leics
59 H5 **Gaddesden Row** Herts
163 K5 **Gadgirth** S Ayrs
38 C2 **Gaer-llwyd** Mons
108 F7 **Gaerwen** IOA
163 H3 **Gailes** N Ayrs
85 G2 **Gailey** Staffs
140 F4 **Gainford** Dur
116 D4 **Gainsborough** Lincs
77 G7 **Gainsford End** Essex
219 J6 **Gairloch** Highld
201 J8 **Gairlochy** Highld
186 B7 **Gairneybridge** P & K
123 H3 **Gaisby** Brad
148 C5 **Gaitsgill** Cumb
167 G3 **Galashiels** Border
129 K7 **Galgate** Lancs
26 F5 **Galhampton** Somset
182 B3 **Gallanach** Ag & B
186 E8 **Gallatown** Fife
61 H7 **Galleywood** Essex
202 E7 **Gallovie** Highld
153 J5 **Galloway Forest Park**
196 D7 **Gallowfauld** Angus
186 B1 **Gallowhill** P & K
200 C2 **Galltair** Highld
7 G7 **Galmpton** Devon
7 K5 **Galmpton** Torbay
132 C5 **Galphay** N York
163 L3 **Galston** E Ayrs
14 E5 **Galton** Dorset
149 G6 **Gamblesby** Cumb
75 J4 **Gamlingay** Cambs
75 J4 **Gamlingay Great Heath** Beds
216 F2 **Gamrie** Abers
116 B6 **Gamston** Notts
101 L5 **Gamston** Notts
182 B2 **Ganavan Bay** Ag & B
96 B7 **Ganllwyd** Gwynd
196 F3 **Gannachy** Angus
126 E4 **Ganstead** E R Yk
133 L5 **Ganthorpe** N York
134 F4 **Ganton** N York
215 H4 **Garbity** Moray
92 B7 **Garboldisham** Norfk
205 G4 **Garchory** Abers
114 E2 **Garden Village** Sheff
42 D6 **Gardeners Green** Wokham
216 F2 **Gardenstown** Abers
235 c5 **Garderhouse** Shet
27 H4 **Gare Hill** Somset
173 L1 **Garelochhead** Ag & B
41 H2 **Garford** Oxon
124 B4 **Garforth** Leeds
131 H8 **Gargrave** N York
184 F8 **Gargunnock** Stirlg
92 E6 **Garlic Street** Norfk
145 K5 **Garlieston** D & G
35 J2 **Garlinge** Kent
34 F4 **Garlinge Green** Kent
206 E4 **Garlogie** Abers
216 F4 **Garmond** Abers
215 H2 **Garmouth** Moray
83 L3 **Garmston** Shrops
95 J4 **Garn-Dolbenmaen** Gwynd
175 J5 **Garnkirk** N Lans
232 g2 **Garrabost** W Isls

164 B5 **Garrallan** E Ayrs
3 J6 **Garras** Cnwll
95 K4 **Garreg** Gwynd
149 J6 **Garrigill** Cumb
153 M6 **Garroch** D & G
144 D7 **Garrochtrie** D & G
173 J7 **Garrochty** Ag & B
209 H2 **Garros** Highld
130 E2 **Garsdale Head** Cumb
39 L3 **Garsdon** Wilts
99 L5 **Garshall Green** Staffs
57 L7 **Garsington** Oxon
121 G2 **Garstang** Lancs
59 J7 **Garston** Herts
112 B5 **Garston** Lpool
171 G6 **Gartachossan** Ag & B
175 J5 **Gartcosh** N Lans
97 K4 **Garth** Denbgs
67 K5 **Garth** Powys
80 E6 **Garth Penrhyncoch** Cerdgn
138 D7 **Garth Row** Cumb
175 H6 **Garthamlock** C Glas
82 E4 **Garthmyl** Powys
102 D7 **Garthorpe** Leics
125 K6 **Garthorpe** N Linc
215 L7 **Gartly** Abers
184 C7 **Gartmore** Stirlg
175 K5 **Gartness** N Lans
174 F2 **Gartness** Stirlg
174 D2 **Gartocharn** W Duns
127 G4 **Garton** E R Yk
134 F7 **Garton-on-the-Wolds** E R Yk
227 H5 **Gartymore** Highld
178 D4 **Garvald** E Loth
191 J2 **Garvan** Highld
171 G1 **Garvard** Ag & B
212 B3 **Garve** Highld
92 B3 **Garvestone** Norfk
174 B4 **Garvock** Inver
54 C4 **Garway** Herefs
54 C4 **Garway Common** Herefs
232 f3 **Garyvard** W Isls
27 H5 **Gasper** Wilts
39 K6 **Gastard** Wilts
91 L7 **Gasthorpe** Norfk
60 D5 **Gaston Green** Essex
16 F5 **Gatcombe** IOW
116 D5 **Gate Burton** Lincs
133 L7 **Gate Helmsley** N York
124 E5 **Gateforth** N York
163 K3 **Gatehead** E Ayrs
157 K4 **Gatehouse** Nthumb
145 M4 **Gatehouse of Fleet** D & G
106 A7 **Gateley** Norfk
132 E3 **Gatenby** N York
168 B5 **Gateshaw** Border
151 G3 **Gateshead** Gatesd
196 D7 **Gateside** Angus
174 E6 **Gateside** E Rens
186 C5 **Gateside** Fife
174 C7 **Gateside** N Ayrs
154 F2 **Gateslack** D & G
113 J4 **Gatley** Stockp
167 H3 **Gattonside** Border
32 B5 **Gatwick Airport** W Susx
87 K4 **Gaulby** Leics
186 F3 **Gauldry** Fife
195 K6 **Gauldswell** P & K
117 K6 **Gautby** Lincs
179 G7 **Gavinton** Border
58 B2 **Gawcott** Bucks
113 K7 **Gawsworth** Ches
130 D3 **Gawthrop** Cumb
129 G3 **Gawthwaite** Cumb
72 D4 **Gaydon** Warwks
74 B5 **Gayhurst** M Keyn
131 G2 **Gayle** N York
140 E5 **Gayles** N York

73 K4 **Gayton** Nhants
105 H8 **Gayton** Norfk
99 M6 **Gayton** Staffs
118 F5 **Gayton le Marsh** Lincs
105 H8 **Gayton Thorpe** Norfk
105 G7 **Gaywood** Norfk
77 G2 **Gazeley** Suffk
232 f3 **Gearraidh Bhaird** W Isls
208 D3 **Geary** Highld
77 L3 **Gedding** Suffk
35 H5 **Geddinge** Kent
88 C6 **Geddington** Nhants
101 L4 **Gedling** Notts
104 C7 **Gedney** Lincs
104 C7 **Gedney Broadgate** Lincs
104 D6 **Gedney Drove End** Lincs
104 C7 **Gedney Dyke** Lincs
89 L2 **Gedney Hill** Lincs
88 E3 **Geeston** Rutlnd
93 H5 **Geldeston** Norfk
110 F8 **Gellifor** Denbgs
37 H2 **Gelligaer** Caerph
95 M4 **Gellilydan** Gwynd
51 K5 **Gellinudd** Neath
195 H8 **Gellyburn** P & K
50 C2 **Gellywen** Carmth
146 D3 **Gelston** D & G
102 E4 **Gelston** Lincs
135 H7 **Gembling** E R Yk
85 J2 **Gentleshaw** Staffs
43 G4 **George Green** Bucks
23 L6 **George Nympton** Devon
156 B4 **Georgefield** D & G
23 G4 **Georgeham** Devon
234 b5 **Georth** Ork
10 C6 **Germansweek** Devon
4 D8 **Gerrans** Cnwll
43 G3 **Gerrards Cross** Bucks
142 E5 **Gerrick** R & Cl
77 J6 **Gestingthorpe** Essex
82 E2 **Geuffordd** Powys
45 K3 **Gidea Park** Gt Lon
175 G6 **Giffnock** E Rens
178 C5 **Gifford** E Loth
186 E5 **Giffordtown** Fife
130 F6 **Giggleswick** N York
125 K5 **Gilberdyke** E R Yk
178 B5 **Gilchriston** E Loth
147 K7 **Gilcrux** Cumb
123 K5 **Gildersome** Leeds
115 K4 **Gildingwells** Rothm
151 H6 **Gilesgate Moor** Dur
36 F6 **Gileston** V Glam
53 J7 **Gilfach** Caerph
36 F3 **Gilfach Goch** Brdgnd
65 L3 **Gilfachrheda** Cerdgn
136 E3 **Gilgarran** Cumb
133 K2 **Gillamoor** N York
208 D3 **Gillen** Highld
155 L4 **Gillesbie** D & G
133 J4 **Gilling East** N York
140 F6 **Gilling West** N York
27 J6 **Gillingham** Dorset
46 C6 **Gillingham** Medway
93 J5 **Gillingham** Norfk
231 J4 **Gillock** Highld
231 K2 **Gills** Highld
166 E5 **Gilmanscleuch** Border
177 J5 **Gilmerton** C Edin
185 J3 **Gilmerton** P & K
140 C5 **Gilmonby** Dur
87 H6 **Gilmorton** Leics
149 G2 **Gilsland** Nthumb
177 L6 **Gilston** Mdloth
53 K5 **Gilwern** Mons
107 G5 **Gimingham** Norfk

78 C2 **Gipping** Suffk
103 M3 **Gipsey Bridge** Lincs
163 J2 **Girdle Toll** N Ayrs
235 C5 **Girista** Shet
141 J5 **Girsby** N York
146 A4 **Girthon** D & G
76 B3 **Girton** Cambs
116 D7 **Girton** Notts
152 E3 **Girvan** S Ayrs
122 C2 **Gisburn** Lancs
93 K5 **Gisleham** Suffk
78 C1 **Gislingham** Suffk
92 D6 **Gissing** Norfk
12 E3 **Gittisham** Devon
68 E4 **Gladestry** Powys
177 M4 **Gladsmuir** E Loth
51 K5 **Glais** Swans
143 G6 **Glaisdale** N York
196 C6 **Glamis** Angus
111 G5 **Glan-y-don** Flints
51 J3 **Glanaman** Carmth
106 C4 **Glandford** Norfk
49 K2 **Glandwr** Pembks
80 F4 **Glandyfi** Cerdgn
36 D3 **Glanllynfi** Brdgnd
169 G6 **Glanton** Nthumb
14 D2 **Glanvilles Wootton** Dorset
88 E5 **Glapthorn** Nhants
115 J7 **Glapwell** Derbys
68 D6 **Glasbury** Powys
68 D4 **Glascwm** Powys
96 E3 **Glasfryn** Conwy
175 G5 **Glasgow** C Glas
174 E5 **Glasgow Airport** Rens
175 G5 **Glasgow Science Centre** C Glas
109 H7 **Glasinfryn** Gwynd
199 L6 **Glasnacardoch Bay** Highld
199 H3 **Glasnakille** Highld
145 J7 **Glasserton** D & G
175 J8 **Glassford** S Lans
55 G4 **Glasshouse** Gloucs
132 B6 **Glasshouses** N York
148 A3 **Glasson** Cumb
129 K7 **Glasson** Lancs
149 G7 **Glassonby** Cumb
196 F6 **Glasterlaw** Angus
88 C4 **Glaston** Rutlnd
26 D4 **Glastonbury** Somset
89 H6 **Glatton** Cambs
113 G3 **Glazebrook** Warrtn
112 F3 **Glazebury** Warrtn
84 C5 **Glazeley** Shrops
128 F5 **Gleaston** Cumb
202 D2 **Glebe** Highld
123 L3 **Gledhow** Leeds
146 B5 **Gledpark** D & G
97 L5 **Gledrid** Shrops
77 J5 **Glemsford** Suffk
237 d3 **Glen Auldyn** IOM
204 E8 **Glen Clunie Lodge** Abers
237 b5 **Glen Maye** IOM
192 B3 **Glen Nevis House** Highld
87 H4 **Glen Parva** Leics
153 J6 **Glen Trool Lodge** D & G
215 G6 **Glenallachie** Highld
199 K6 **Glenancross** Highld
190 B7 **Glenaros House** Ag & B
161 H3 **Glenbarr** Ag & B
216 B4 **Glenbarry** Abers
190 C4 **Glenbeg** Highld
214 C8 **Glenbeg** Highld
197 J1 **Glenbervie** Abers
175 J5 **Glenboig** N Lans
190 C4 **Glenborrodale** Highld
183 G7 **Glenbranter** Ag & B

165 K5 **Glenbreck** Border
198 F2 **Glenbrittle House** Highld
164 E4 **Glenbuck** E Ayrs
196 B4 **Glencally** Angus
147 H2 **Glencaple** D & G
211 G4 **Glencarron Lodge** Highld
186 C3 **Glencarse** P & K
192 B6 **Glenceitlein** Highld
191 L5 **Glencoe** Highld
165 L4 **Glencothe** Border
186 C7 **Glencraig** Fife
154 D4 **Glencrosh** D & G
208 B4 **Glendale** Highld
173 G2 **Glendaruel** Ag & B
185 K6 **Glendevon** P & K
202 C4 **Glendoe Lodge** Highld
186 C3 **Glendoick** P & K
186 D4 **Glenduckie** Fife
185 J5 **Gleneagles** P & K
185 J5 **Gleneagles Hotel** P & K
170 F7 **Glenegedale** Ag & B
200 C2 **Glenelg** Highld
214 C5 **Glenerney** Moray
186 B5 **Glenfarg** P & K
203 K6 **Glenfeshie Lodge** Highld
87 G3 **Glenfield** Leics
191 H1 **Glenfinnan** Highld
201 K7 **Glenfintaig Lodge** Highld
186 C4 **Glenfoot** P & K
183 H4 **Glenfyne Lodge** Ag & B
174 C7 **Glengarnock** N Ayrs
231 G3 **Glengolly** Highld
189 K5 **Glengorm Castle** Ag & B
209 G5 **Glengrasco** Highld
165 L3 **Glenholm** Border
154 A5 **Glenhoul** D & G
195 K4 **Glenisla** Angus
173 K3 **Glenkin** Ag & B
205 K3 **Glenkindie** Abers
214 F8 **Glenlivet** Moray
146 C3 **Glenlochar** D & G
186 C6 **Glenlomond** P & K
144 E4 **Glenluce** D & G
173 J2 **Glenmassen** Ag & B
175 K5 **Glenmavis** N Lans
209 G6 **Glenmore** Highld
204 B4 **Glenmore Lodge** Highld
196 C4 **Glenquiech** Angus
172 E5 **Glenralloch** Ag & B
137 L4 **Glenridding** Cumb
186 D7 **Glenrothes** Fife
185 K1 **Glenshee** P & K
202 E6 **Glenshera Lodge** Highld
173 J3 **Glenstriven** Ag & B
117 G4 **Glentham** Lincs
203 J6 **Glentromie Lodge** Highld
153 H6 **Glentrool Village** D & G
203 G6 **Glentruim House** Highld
116 F4 **Glentworth** Lincs
190 D2 **Glenuig** Highld
191 K6 **Glenure** Ag & B
209 G6 **Glenvarragill** Highld
152 E7 **Glenwhilly** D & G
164 F4 **Glespin** S Lans
54 E4 **Glewstone** Herefs
89 H3 **Glinton** C Pete
87 L4 **Glooston** Leics
114 B3 **Glossop** Derbys
159 G2 **Gloster Hill** Nthumb
55 J4 **Gloucester** Gloucs

55 K4 Gloucestershire
    Airport Gloucs
122 F2 Glusburn N York
227 H2 Glutt Lodge Highld
4 E3 Gluvian Cnwll
57 H4 Glympton Oxon
97 J5 Glyn Ceiriog Wrexhm
52 D6 Glyn-Neath Neath
65 K5 Glynarthen Cerdgn
52 D7 Glyncorrwg Neath
19 L4 Glynde E Susx
97 J4 Glyndyfrdwy Denbgs
52 D5 Glyntawe Powys
65 K6 Glynteg Carmth
99 J7 Gnosall Staffs
99 J7 Gnosall Heath Staffs
87 L4 Goadby Leics
102 C7 Goadby Marwood
    Leics
40 A5 Goatacre Wilts
182 E7 Goatfield Ag & B
26 F7 Goathill Dorset
143 H6 Goathland N York
25 K5 Goathurst Somset
97 L5 Gobowen Shrops
30 F3 Godalming Surrey
33 L6 Goddard's Green
    Kent
75 J1 Godmanchester
    Cambs
14 C3 Godmanstone
    Dorset
34 E5 Godmersham Kent
26 C3 Godney Somset
3 G5 Godolphin Cross
    Cnwll
51 L4 Godre'r-graig Neath
17 G6 Godshill IOW
32 C3 Godstone Surrey
53 L6 Goetre Mons
60 B7 Goff's Oak Herts
53 K5 Gofilon Mons
177 G4 Gogar C Edin
80 F7 Goginan Cerdgn
95 J4 Golan Gwynd
5 H5 Golant Cnwll
5 M2 Golberdon Cnwll
112 E3 Golborne Wigan
123 G7 Golcar Kirk
38 A4 Goldcliff Newpt
33 H4 Golden Green Kent
30 B3 Golden Pot Hants
44 E3 Golders Green Gt Lon
61 L6 Goldhanger Essex
74 F4 Goldington Beds
143 H4 Goldsborough
    N York
132 F7 Goldsborough
    N York
2 F5 Goldsithney Cnwll
43 G8 Goldsworth Park
    Surrey
115 J2 Goldthorpe Barns
22 F6 Goldworthy Devon
213 J4 Gollanfield Highld
223 H2 Golspie Highld
28 D4 Gomeldon Wilts
31 H2 Gomshall Surrey
102 B3 Gonalston Notts
235 c4 Gonfirth Shet
60 F5 Good Easter Essex
91 H3 Gooderstone Norfk
23 J5 Goodleigh Devon
125 K2 Goodmanham E R Yk
45 J3 Goodmayes Gt Lon
34 D3 Goodnestone Kent
35 H4 Goodnestone Kent
54 E4 Goodrich Herefs
54 E4 Goodrich Castle
    Herefs
7 K4 Goodrington Torbay
122 B5 Goodshaw Fold
    Lancs

64 C6 Goodwick Pembks
29 G3 Goodworth
    Clatford Hants
125 H5 Goole E R Yk
71 H4 Goom's Hill Worcs
3 J2 Goonbell Cnwll
3 K1 Goonhavern Cnwll
3 J2 Goonvrea Cnwll
62 D3 Goose Green Essex
62 D3 Goose Green Essex
38 F5 Goose Green S Glos
206 E8 Goosecruives Abers
11 G6 Gooseford Devon
41 G3 Goosey Oxon
121 H3 Goosnargh Lancs
113 H7 Goostrey Ches
167 K2 Gordon Border
166 D4 Gordon Arms Hotel
    Border
216 B3 Gordonstown Abers
216 D6 Gordonstown Abers
177 K6 Gorebridge Mdloth
90 B2 Gorefield Cambs
40 C8 Gores Wilts
236 e7 Gorey Jersey
41 L4 Goring Oxon
18 F5 Goring-by-Sea
    W Susx
93 L3 Gorleston on Sea
    Norfk
216 E3 Gorrachie Abers
4 F7 Gorran Cnwll
4 F7 Gorran Haven Cnwll
40 D3 Gorse Hill Swindn
111 G6 Gorsedd Flints
51 H5 Gorseinon Swans
66 C4 Gorsgoch Cerdgn
51 H3 Gorslas Carmth
55 G3 Gorsley Gloucs
54 F3 Gorsley Common
    Herefs
212 B2 Gorstan Highld
98 A1 Gorstello Ches
100 C6 Gorsty Hill Staffs
181 L2 Gorten Ag & B
202 E2 Gorthleck Highld
113 K3 Gorton Manch
78 D4 Gosbeck Suffk
103 L6 Gosberton Lincs
61 J3 Gosfield Essex
136 E6 Gosforth Cumb
151 G2 Gosforth N u Ty
84 F5 Gospel End Staffs
17 H3 Gosport Hants
55 H7 Gossington Gloucs
101 K6 Gotham Notts
55 L3 Gotherington Gloucs
25 K5 Gotton Devon
33 J5 Goudhurst Kent
118 C5 Goulceby Lincs
216 E6 Gourdas Abers
186 F2 Gourdie Angus
197 J3 Gourdon Abers
173 L3 Gourock Inver
174 F5 Govan C Glas
7 H6 Goveton Devon
124 F6 Gowdall E R Yk
212 D3 Gower Highld
51 G7 Gower Swans
51 H6 Gowerton Swans
176 E1 Gowkhall Fife
126 F2 Goxhill E R Yk
126 D6 Goxhill N Linc
232 f3 Grabhair W Isls
18 C3 Graffham W Susx
75 H2 Grafham Cambs
31 G3 Grafham Surrey
132 F6 Grafton N York
56 F7 Grafton Oxon
98 B8 Grafton Shrops
71 H6 Grafton Worcs
71 G4 Grafton Flyford
    Worcs

73 L5 Grafton Regis
    Nhants
88 D7 Grafton Underwood
    Nhants
34 B5 Grafty Green Kent
109 M6 Graig Conwy
97 J2 Graig-fechan Denbgs
46 E5 Grain Medway
118 C2 Grainsby Lincs
118 E3 Grainthorpe Lincs
4 E6 Grampound Cnwll
4 E5 Grampound Road
    Cnwll
233 c6 Gramsdal W Isls
233 c6 Gramsdale W Isls
58 C3 Granborough Bucks
102 C5 Granby Notts
236 d7 Grand Chemins
    Jersey
101 H7 Grand Prix Collection
    Donington Leics
72 F2 Grandborough
    Warwks
236 c2 Grandes Rocques
    Guern
194 E5 Grandtully P & K
137 H4 Grange Cumb
46 D6 Grange Medway
186 D3 Grange P & K
215 K4 Grange Crossroads
    Moray
214 C3 Grange Hall Moray
45 H2 Grange Hill Gt Lon
123 J7 Grange Moor Kirk
186 D4 Grange of Lindores
    Fife
151 G4 Grange Villa Dur
129 J4 Grange-over-Sands
    Cumb
165 J2 Grangehall S Lans
100 E2 Grangemill Derbys
176 C3 Grangemouth Falk
176 D3 Grangepans Falk
142 C3 Grangetown R & Cl
151 K4 Grangetown Sundld
135 H7 Gransmoor E R Yk
64 C7 Granston Pembks
76 B4 Grantchester Cambs
102 E5 Grantham Lincs
177 H3 Granton C Edin
214 C8 Grantown-on-Spey
    Highld
179 G5 Grantshouse Border
117 H1 Grasby Lincs
137 K5 Grasmere Cumb
113 L1 Grasscroft Oldham
111 L4 Grassendale Lpool
131 J6 Grassington N York
115 H7 Grassmoor Derbys
116 C7 Grassthorpe Notts
28 F3 Grateley Hants
75 J2 Graveley Cambs
59 L3 Graveley Herts
34 E3 Graveney Kent
46 A5 Gravesend Kent
232 f3 Gravir W Isls
116 F3 Grayingham Lincs
138 E7 Grayrigg Cumb
45 L4 Grays Thurr
30 E4 Grayshott Hants
30 F4 Grayswood Surrey
115 H3 Greasbrough Rothm
111 H4 Greasby Wirral
101 J3 Greasley Notts
76 D5 Great Abington
    Cambs
88 D7 Great Addington
    Nhants
71 K3 Great Alne Warwks
111 K1 Great Altcar Lancs
60 B5 Great Amwell Herts
138 F5 Great Asby Cumb
142 C5 Great Ayton N York

61 H6 Great Baddow Essex
39 J4 Great Badminton
    S Glos
61 G2 Great Bardfield
    Essex
75 G4 Great Barford Beds
85 J4 Great Barr Sandw
56 E5 Great Barrington
    Gloucs
112 C7 Great Barrow Ches
77 K2 Great Barton Suffk
134 B4 Great Barugh N York
158 C6 Great Bavington
    Nthumb
78 F5 Great Bealings Suffk
40 F7 Great Bedwyn Wilts
62 D4 Great Bentley Essex
74 B3 Great Billing Nhants
105 J6 Great Bircham Norfk
78 D4 Great Blakenham
    Suffk
138 C2 Great Blencow Cumb
98 F7 Great Bolas Wrekin
31 J1 Great Bookham
    Surrey
2 D4 Great Bosullow Cnwll
72 F5 Great Bourton Oxon
87 L5 Great Bowden Leics
76 F4 Great Bradley Suffk
61 K5 Great Braxted Essex
78 C4 Great Bricett Suffk
58 E3 Great Brickhill Bucks
99 K6 Great Bridgeford
    Staffs
73 J2 Great Brington
    Nhants
62 C3 Great Bromley Essex
136 E2 Great Broughton
    Cumb
142 C6 Great Broughton
    N York
112 F6 Great Budworth
    Ches
141 H4 Great Burdon Darltn
46 B2 Great Burstead Essex
142 B6 Great Busby N York
118 E4 Great Carlton Lincs
88 E2 Great Casterton
    Rutlnd
39 K7 Great Chalfield Wilts
34 C6 Great Chart Kent
84 E1 Great Chatwell Staffs
76 D6 Great Chesterford
    Essex
27 M1 Great Cheverell Wilts
76 B6 Great Chishill Cambs
62 E5 Great Clacton Essex
136 E2 Great Clifton Cumb
126 F8 Great Coates NE Lin
71 G6 Great Comberton
    Worcs
148 E4 Great Corby Cumb
77 K6 Great Cornard Suffk
126 F3 Great Cowden E R Yk
40 F2 Great Coxwell Oxon
88 B7 Great Cransley
    Nhants
91 J3 Great Cressingham
    Norfk
137 J3 Great Crosthwaite
    Cumb
100 D5 Great Cubley Derbys
87 L2 Great Dalby Leics
74 C2 Great Doddington
    Nhants
91 K1 Great Dunham Norfk
61 G4 Great Dunmow
    Essex
28 C4 Great Durnford Wilts
60 F3 Great Easton Essex
88 B5 Great Easton Leics
120 F3 Great Eccleston
    Lancs

92 B4 Great Ellingham Norfk
27 H2 Great Elm Somset
7 H4 Great Englebourne Devon
73 H3 Great Everdon Nhants
75 L4 Great Eversden Cambs
78 B3 Great Finborough Suffk
91 K2 Great Fransham Norfk
59 G5 Great Gaddesden Herts
89 G6 Great Gidding Cambs
134 C8 Great Givendale E R Yk
79 H3 Great Glemham Suffk
87 J4 Great Glen Leics
102 E5 Great Gonerby Lincs
75 J4 Great Gransden Cambs
75 K5 Great Green Cambs
77 K4 Great Green Suffk
134 B4 Great Habton N York
103 J4 Great Hale Lincs
60 E4 Great Hallingbury Essex
74 C1 Great Harrowden Nhants
121 L4 Great Harwood Lancs
57 M7 Great Haseley Oxon
126 F3 Great Hatfield E R Yk
99 M7 Great Haywood Staffs
124 F6 Great Heck N York
77 K6 Great Henny Essex
39 K8 Great Hinton Wilts
91 L5 Great Hockham Norfk
62 E4 Great Holland Essex
62 B2 Great Horkesley Essex
60 C3 Great Hormead Herts
123 H4 Great Horton Brad
58 C2 Great Horwood Bucks
115 H1 Great Houghton Barns
73 L3 Great Houghton Nhants
114 D6 Great Hucklow Derbys
135 H7 Great Kelk E R Yk
58 D6 Great Kimble Bucks
42 E2 Great Kingshill Bucks
137 J6 Great Langdale Cumb
141 H7 Great Langton N York
61 H4 Great Leighs Essex
126 E8 Great Limber Lincs
74 C6 Great Linford M Keyn
77 K1 Great Livermere Suffk
114 D6 Great Longstone Derbys
151 H5 Great Lumley Dur
70 D5 Great Malvern Worcs
77 J7 Great Maplestead Essex
120 D4 Great Marton Bpool
105 J7 Great Massingham Norfk
57 L7 Great Milton Oxon
58 E7 Great Missenden Bucks
121 K3 Great Mitton Lancs
35 K4 Great Mongeham Kent

92 E5 Great Moulton Norfk
139 H4 Great Musgrave Cumb
98 B8 Great Ness Shrops
54 B6 Great Oak Mons
62 E3 Great Oakley Essex
88 C6 Great Oakley Nhants
59 J3 Great Offley Herts
139 G4 Great Ormside Cumb
148 B4 Great Orton Cumb
133 G6 Great Ouseburn N York
87 K6 Great Oxendon Nhants
61 G6 Great Oxney Green Essex
75 H2 Great Paxton Cambs
120 E4 Great Plumpton Lancs
93 G2 Great Plumstead Norfk
102 F6 Great Ponton Lincs
124 B5 Great Preston Leeds
89 J7 Great Raveley Cambs
56 D5 Great Rissington Gloucs
56 F2 Great Rollright Oxon
106 A6 Great Ryburgh Norfk
168 F6 Great Ryle Nthumb
83 J3 Great Ryton Shrops
61 H3 Great Saling Essex
148 F7 Great Salkeld Cumb
76 F7 Great Sampford Essex
111 K7 Great Saughall Ches
41 G5 Great Shefford W Berk
76 C4 Great Shelford Cambs
141 H6 Great Smeaton N York
105 M5 Great Snoring Norfk
39 L4 Great Somerford Wilts
99 G6 Great Soudley Shrops
141 H3 Great Stainton Darltn
46 E2 Great Stambridge Essex
75 G2 Great Staughton Cambs
118 F8 Great Steeping Lincs
38 F4 Great Stoke S Glos
138 D3 Great Strickland Cumb
89 J8 Great Stukeley Cambs
117 K6 Great Sturton Lincs
158 B6 Great Swinburne Nthumb
57 H3 Great Tew Oxon
61 L3 Great Tey Essex
23 H7 Great Torrington Devon
158 C3 Great Tosson Nthumb
61 K5 Great Totham Essex
61 L5 Great Totham Essex
129 G5 Great Urswick Cumb
46 F3 Great Wakering Essex
77 K5 Great Waldingfield Suffk
105 M5 Great Walsingham Norfk
61 H5 Great Waltham Essex
45 L2 Great Warley Essex
71 H7 Great Washbourne Gloucs
11 G7 Great Weeke Devon
88 D5 Great Weldon Nhants
78 C6 Great Wenham Suffk

158 C7 Great Whittington Nthumb
62 A5 Great Wigborough Essex
76 D3 Great Wilbraham Cambs
28 B4 Great Wishford Wilts
55 K5 Great Witcombe Gloucs
70 D2 Great Witley Worcs
72 B7 Great Wolford Warwks
77 G5 Great Wratting Essex
59 K3 Great Wymondley Herts
85 H3 Great Wyrley Staffs
93 L3 Great Yarmouth Norfk
77 H6 Great Yeldham Essex
88 F2 Greatford Lincs
100 B4 Greatgate Staffs
30 C5 Greatham Hants
141 L2 Greatham Hartpl
18 E3 Greatham W Susx
21 L2 Greatstone-on-Sea Kent
73 G6 Greatworth Nhants
60 B4 Green End Herts
60 B2 Green End Herts
133 G7 Green Hammerton N York
85 H2 Green Heath Staffs
26 E2 Green Ore Somset
138 C6 Green Quarter Cumb
60 D4 Green Street Herts
59 K7 Green Street Herts
45 L6 Green Street Green Kent
60 C4 Green Tye Herts
176 C6 Greenburn W Loth
173 M1 Greenfield Ag & B
74 F7 Greenfield Beds
111 H6 Greenfield Flints
201 J5 Greenfield Highld
113 M2 Greenfield Oldham
43 J4 Greenford Gt Lon
175 K4 Greengairs N Lans
123 J3 Greengates Brad
120 E4 Greenhalgh Lancs
25 G7 Greenham Somset
157 K5 Greenhaugh Nthumb
155 J6 Greenhill D & G
175 L3 Greenhill Falk
47 K6 Greenhill Kent
165 H3 Greenhill S Lans
45 L5 Greenhithe Kent
164 B3 Greenholm E Ayrs
167 H5 Greenhouse Border
131 L6 Greenhow Hill N York
231 J3 Greenland Highld
115 H4 Greenland Sheff
167 L1 Greenlaw Border
155 H6 Greenlea D & G
185 H6 Greenloaning P & K
122 B7 Greenmount Bury
174 B3 Greenock Inver
129 G3 Greenodd Cumb
73 J4 Greens Norton Nhants
165 K2 Greenshields S Lans
150 E3 Greenside Gatesd
123 H7 Greenside Kirk
62 B3 Greenstead Essex
61 K3 Greenstead Green Essex
25 L6 Greenway Somset
45 G4 Greenwich Gt Lon
56 B3 Greet Gloucs
69 L2 Greete Shrops
118 D7 Greetham Lincs
88 D2 Greetham Rutlnd
123 G6 Greetland Calder

26 B4 Greinton Somset
237 b6 Grenaby IOM
74 C3 Grendon Nhants
86 C4 Grendon Warwks
58 B4 Grendon Underwood Bucks
115 G3 Grenoside Sheff
232 e4 Greosabhagh W Isls
97 M2 Gresford Wrexhm
106 E5 Gresham Norfk
208 E4 Greshornish House Hotel Highld
91 L1 Gressenhall Norfk
91 L1 Gressenhall Green Norfk
130 B5 Gressingham Lancs
140 D5 Greta Bridge Dur
148 B2 Gretna D & G
148 B2 Gretna Green D & G
56 A2 Gretton Gloucs
88 C5 Gretton Nhants
83 K4 Gretton Shrops
132 C4 Grewelthorpe N York
155 J4 Greyrigg D & G
42 B4 Greys Green Oxon
136 E2 Greysouthen Cumb
138 B2 Greystoke Cumb
196 E7 Greystone Angus
30 B2 Greywell Hants
86 D5 Griff Warwks
53 L7 Griffithstown Torfn
121 J7 Grimeford Village Lancs
115 G4 Grimesthorpe Sheff
124 C8 Grimethorpe Barns
70 E3 Grimley Worcs
163 H7 Grimmet S Ayrs
118 E4 Grimoldby Lincs
98 A7 Grimpo Shrops
121 H4 Grimsargh Lancs
127 G7 Grimsby NE Lin
73 J4 Grimscote Nhants
9 H4 Grimscott Cnwll
232 f3 Grimshader W Isls
103 H7 Grimsthorpe Lincs
102 B7 Grimston Leics
105 H7 Grimston Norfk
14 C4 Grimston Dorset
77 L2 Grimstone End Suffk
135 H5 Grindale E R Yk
114 E6 Grindleford Derbys
121 L2 Grindleton Lancs
98 D4 Grindley Brook Shrops
114 D6 Grindlow Derbys
100 B4 Grindon Staffs
151 J4 Grindon Sundld
116 C4 Gringley on the Hill Notts
148 C4 Grinsdale Cumb
98 D7 Grinshill Shrops
140 D7 Grinton N York
232 f3 Griomaisiader W Isls
233 c6 Griomsaigh W Isls
188 F4 Grishipoll Ag & B
135 H3 Gristhorpe N York
91 L4 Griston Norfk
234 d6 Gritley Ork
40 B4 Grittenham Wilts
39 K4 Grittleton Wilts
128 F3 Grizebeck Cumb
137 K7 Grizedale Cumb
87 G3 Groby Leics
110 D8 Groes Conwy
37 G4 Groes-faen Rhondd
37 H3 Groes-Wen Caerph
233 b7 Grogarry W Isls
161 K1 Grogport Ag & B
233 b7 Groigearraidh W Isls
110 F5 Gronant Flints
32 F5 Groombridge E Susx
232 e4 Grosebay W Isls

54 B3 **Grosmont** Mons
143 H6 **Grosmont** N York
77 L6 **Groton** Suffk
236 e7 **Grouville** Jersey
116 C5 **Grove** Notts
41 H3 **Grove** Oxon
33 K3 **Grove Green** Kent
45 H5 **Grove Park** Gt Lon
51 H5 **Grovesend** Swans
219 L4 **Gruinard** Highld
170 F5 **Gruinart** Ag & B
208 F8 **Grula** Highld
190 B7 **Gruline** Ag & B
78 F4 **Grundisburgh** Suffk
235 c5 **Gruting** Shet
192 B7 **Gualachulain** Highld
187 G4 **Guardbridge** Fife
70 E5 **Guarlford** Worcs
194 F6 **Guay** P & K
236 c3 **Guernsey Airport** Guern
21 G3 **Guestling Green** E Susx
21 G3 **Guestling Thorn** E Susx
106 C6 **Guestwick** Norfk
121 K5 **Guide** Bl w D
159 G5 **Guide Post** Nthumb
75 K5 **Guilden Morden** Cambs
112 C7 **Guilden Sutton** Ches
31 G2 **Guildford** Surrey
186 B2 **Guildtown** P & K
87 J8 **Guilsborough** Nhants
82 E2 **Guilsfield** Powys
163 J7 **Guiltreehill** S Ayrs
23 J4 **Guineaford** Devon
142 D4 **Guisborough** R & Cl
123 J3 **Guiseley** Leeds
106 B7 **Guist** Norfk
56 C3 **Guiting Power** Gloucs
178 B2 **Gullane** E Loth
2 E5 **Gulval** Cnwll
6 C2 **Gulworthy** Devon
49 J7 **Gumfreston** Pembks
87 K5 **Gumley** Leics
20 C3 **Gun Hill** E Susx
102 E7 **Gunby** Lincs
118 F7 **Gunby** Lincs
29 L5 **Gundleton** Hants
23 K5 **Gunn** Devon
139 L7 **Gunnerside** N York
158 A7 **Gunnerton** Nthumb
125 K7 **Gunness** N Linc
6 C2 **Gunnislake** Cnwll
235 d6 **Gunnista** Shet
116 D3 **Gunthorpe** N Linc
106 B5 **Gunthorpe** Norfk
102 B4 **Gunthorpe** Notts
3 H6 **Gunwalloe** Cnwll
16 F4 **Gurnard** IOW
26 F2 **Gurney Slade** Somset
52 B6 **Gurnos** Powys
15 J1 **Gussage All Saints** Dorset
27 L8 **Gussage St Andrew** Dorset
15 J1 **Gussage St Michael** Dorset
35 J5 **Guston** Kent
235 d2 **Gutcher** Shet
196 F6 **Guthrie** Angus
90 B3 **Guyhirn** Cambs
158 F2 **Guyzance** Nthumb
110 F5 **Gwaenysgor** Flints
108 E6 **Gwalchmai** IOA
51 K3 **Gwaun-Cae-Gurwen** Carmth
3 J6 **Gweek** Cnwll
68 B6 **Gwenddwr** Powys
3 J4 **Gwennap** Cnwll
111 H7 **Gwernaffield** Flints

54 B7 **Gwernesney** Mons
66 C7 **Gwernogle** Carmth
111 H8 **Gwernymynydd** Flints
110 F5 **Gwespyr** Flints
3 G4 **Gwinear** Cnwll
3 G3 **Gwithian** Cnwll
97 G3 **Gwyddelwern** Denbgs
66 B7 **Gwyddgrug** Carmth
96 D1 **Gwytherin** Conwy

H

83 H3 **Habberley** Shrops
84 E7 **Habberley** Worcs
122 B4 **Habergham** Lancs
119 G7 **Habertoft** Lincs
126 E7 **Habrough** NE Lin
103 J7 **Hacconby** Lincs
103 G5 **Haceby** Lincs
79 G3 **Hacheston** Suffk
44 F6 **Hackbridge** Gt Lon
115 H5 **Hackenthorpe** Sheff
92 C3 **Hackford** Norfk
132 C2 **Hackforth** N York
234 c5 **Hackland** Ork
74 B4 **Hackleton** Nhants
35 J4 **Hacklinge** Kent
134 F2 **Hackness** N York
45 G3 **Hackney** Gt Lon
117 G5 **Hackthorn** Lincs
138 D3 **Hackthorpe** Cumb
168 B3 **Hadden** Border
58 C6 **Haddenham** Bucks
90 C7 **Haddenham** Cambs
178 B4 **Haddington** E Loth
116 E8 **Haddington** Lincs
93 J4 **Haddiscoe** Norfk
216 F6 **Haddo** Abers
89 G5 **Haddon** Cambs
114 A3 **Hadfield** Derbys
60 C4 **Hadham Ford** Herts
46 D3 **Hadleigh** Essex
78 B6 **Hadleigh** Suffk
70 F2 **Hadley** Worcs
100 C7 **Hadley End** Staffs
44 E1 **Hadley Wood** Gt Lon
33 H3 **Hadlow** Kent
20 B2 **Hadlow Down** E Susx
98 D7 **Hadnall** Shrops
76 D5 **Hadstock** Essex
71 G3 **Hadzor** Worcs
168 F2 **Haffenden** Nthumb
175 K3 **Haggs** Falk
69 L6 **Hagley** Herefs
85 G7 **Hagley** Worcs
118 D7 **Hagworthingham** Lincs
75 H3 **Hail Weston** Cambs
136 E5 **Haile** Cumb
57 G5 **Hailey** Oxon
20 C4 **Hailsham** E Susx
45 J2 **Hainault** Gt Lon
106 F8 **Hainford** Norfk
117 K5 **Hainton** Lincs
135 H6 **Haisthorpe** E R Yk
48 F6 **Hakin** Pembks
102 B2 **Halam** Notts
176 F1 **Halbeath** Fife
24 F8 **Halberton** Devon
231 J4 **Halcro** Highld
129 K4 **Hale** Cumb
112 C5 **Hale** Halton
28 D7 **Hale** Hants
30 D2 **Hale** Surrey
113 H4 **Hale** Traffd
20 B3 **Hale Green** E Susx
33 H4 **Hale Street** Kent
93 H4 **Hales** Norfk
99 G5 **Hales** Staffs

34 F3 **Hales Place** Kent
85 G6 **Halesowen** Dudley
93 H7 **Halesworth** Suffk
112 C4 **Halewood** Knows
7 J2 **Halford** Devon
72 C5 **Halford** Warwks
84 E5 **Halfpenny Green** Staffs
83 G2 **Halfway House** Shrops
46 F5 **Halfway Houses** Kent
123 G5 **Halifax** Calder
231 G4 **Halkirk** Highld
111 H7 **Halkyn** Flints
174 D7 **Hall** E Rens
137 H7 **Hall Dunnerdale** Cumb
176 B3 **Hall Glen** Falk
85 K7 **Hall Green** Birm
59 L3 **Hall's Green** Herts
20 A3 **Halland** E Susx
87 L4 **Hallaton** Leics
38 F8 **Hallatrow** BaNES
149 G3 **Hallbankgate** Cumb
38 D4 **Hallen** S Glos
151 H6 **Hallgarth** Dur
208 D3 **Hallin** Highld
46 B7 **Halling** Medway
118 D4 **Hallington** Lincs
158 C6 **Hallington** Nthumb
121 K7 **Halliwell** Bolton
102 B3 **Halloughton** Notts
70 E3 **Hallow** Worcs
7 J7 **Hallsands** Devon
166 B2 **Hallyne** Border
55 G7 **Halmore** Gloucs
18 B4 **Halnaker** W Susx
120 E7 **Halsall** Lancs
73 H6 **Halse** Nhants
25 H5 **Halse** Somset
2 E4 **Halsetown** Cnwll
127 G5 **Halsham** E R Yk
61 K2 **Halstead** Essex
45 J7 **Halstead** Kent
87 L3 **Halstead** Leics
14 A2 **Halstock** Dorset
25 H4 **Halsway** Somset
118 C8 **Haltham** Lincs
58 E6 **Halton** Bucks
129 K6 **Halton** Lancs
123 L4 **Halton** Leeds
150 C2 **Halton** Nthumb
97 L4 **Halton** Wrexhm
131 K8 **Halton East** N York
131 G4 **Halton Gill** N York
118 F7 **Halton Holegate** Lincs
149 H4 **Halton Lea Gate** Nthumb
150 C2 **Halton Shields** Nthumb
130 F8 **Halton West** N York
149 J3 **Haltwhistle** Nthumb
93 J3 **Halvergate** Norfk
7 H5 **Halwell** Devon
10 C5 **Halwill** Devon
10 C5 **Halwill Junction** Devon
13 G3 **Ham** Devon
55 G7 **Ham** Gloucs
44 D5 **Ham** Gt Lon
35 J4 **Ham** Kent
25 L6 **Ham** Somset
41 G7 **Ham** Wilts
71 H2 **Ham Green** Worcs
26 D4 **Ham Street** Somset
16 F2 **Hamble-le-Rice** Hants
42 C3 **Hambleden** Bucks
29 M7 **Hambledon** Hants
30 F4 **Hambledon** Surrey
120 E3 **Hambleton** Lancs

124 E4 **Hambleton** N York
26 B6 **Hambridge** Somset
17 L2 **Hambrook** W Susx
118 D7 **Hameringham** Lincs
89 G7 **Hamerton** Cambs
175 J7 **Hamilton** S Lans
14 B2 **Hamlet** Dorset
44 E4 **Hammersmith** Gt Lon
85 J3 **Hammerwich** Staffs
27 J8 **Hammoon** Dorset
235 c6 **Hamnavoe** Shet
235 d4 **Hamnavoe** Shet
20 C5 **Hampden Park** E Susx
58 D7 **Hampden Row** Bucks
56 C5 **Hampnett** Gloucs
124 D7 **Hampole** Donc
15 K3 **Hampreston** Dorset
44 E3 **Hampstead** Gt Lon
41 K5 **Hampstead Norrey's** W Berk
132 C7 **Hampsthwaite** N York
43 J6 **Hampton** Gt Lon
47 K6 **Hampton** Kent
84 D6 **Hampton** Shrops
40 D3 **Hampton** Swindn
71 H5 **Hampton** Worcs
69 L6 **Hampton Bishop** Herefs
44 D6 **Hampton Court Palace & Gardens** Gt Lon
98 D3 **Hampton Heath** Ches
86 B7 **Hampton in Arden** Solhll
70 F2 **Hampton Lovett** Worcs
72 B3 **Hampton Lucy** Warwks
72 C2 **Hampton Magna** Warwks
57 J5 **Hampton Poyle** Oxon
44 D6 **Hampton Wick** Gt Lon
28 E7 **Hamptworth** Wilts
19 L3 **Hamsey** E Susx
100 C8 **Hamstall Ridware** Staffs
41 H7 **Hamstead Marshall** W Berk
150 E4 **Hamsterley** Dur
140 E2 **Hamsterley** Dur
34 D7 **Hamstreet** Kent
15 J4 **Hamworthy** Poole
100 D6 **Hanbury** Staffs
71 G2 **Hanbury** Worcs
99 J4 **Hanchurch** Staffs
12 D4 **Hand and Pen** Devon
112 B7 **Handbridge** Ches
31 L5 **Handcross** W Susx
113 J5 **Handforth** Ches
98 C2 **Handley** Ches
101 G1 **Handley** Derbys
85 J5 **Handsworth** Birm
115 H4 **Handsworth** Sheff
87 L8 **Hanging Houghton** Nhants
28 B4 **Hanging Langford** Wilts
19 H4 **Hangleton** Br & H
38 F6 **Hanham** S Glos
98 F4 **Hankelow** Ches
39 L3 **Hankerton** Wilts
99 K3 **Hanley** C Stke
70 E6 **Hanley Castle** Worcs
70 B2 **Hanley Child** Worcs
70 E6 **Hanley Swan** Worcs
70 C2 **Hanley William** Worcs
131 G7 **Hanlith** N York
98 C4 **Hanmer** Wrexhm

23 J5	**Hannaford** Devon
29 K1	**Hannington** Hants
74 B1	**Hannington** Nhants
40 D2	**Hannington** Swindn
40 D2	**Hannington Wick** Swindn
74 B5	**Hanslope** M Keyn
103 H7	**Hanthorpe** Lincs
44 D4	**Hanwell** Gt Lon
72 E4	**Hanwell** Oxon
83 J2	**Hanwood** Shrops
43 J6	**Hanworth** Gt Lon
106 C5	**Hanworth** Norfk
165 G3	**Happendon** S Lans
107 H6	**Happisburgh** Norfk
107 H6	**Happisburgh Common** Norfk
112 C6	**Hapsford** Ches
122 B4	**Hapton** Lancs
92 E4	**Hapton** Norfk
7 H4	**Harberton** Devon
7 H5	**Harbertonford** Devon
34 F3	**Harbledown** Kent
85 H6	**Harborne** Birm
86 F7	**Harborough Magna** Warwks
158 B2	**Harbottle** Nthumb
7 G4	**Harbourneford** Devon
72 D3	**Harbury** Warwks
102 C6	**Harby** Leics
116 E7	**Harby** Notts
11 K8	**Harcombe** Devon
12 F4	**Harcombe** Devon
13 J4	**Harcombe Bottom** Devon
123 G3	**Harden** Brad
85 H4	**Harden** Wsall
206 E5	**Hardgate** Abers
146 E2	**Hardgate** D & G
174 F4	**Hardgate** W Duns
18 E3	**Hardham** W Susx
92 C3	**Hardingham** Norfk
73 L3	**Hardingstone** Nhants
27 H2	**Hardington** Somset
13 M1	**Hardington Mandeville** Somset
13 M1	**Hardington Marsh** Somset
26 D8	**Hardington Moor** Somset
22 C7	**Hardisworthy** Devon
16 E2	**Hardley** Hants
93 H4	**Hardley Street** Norfk
131 G2	**Hardraw** N York
115 H8	**Hardstoft** Derbys
17 H3	**Hardway** Hants
27 G5	**Hardway** Somset
58 D4	**Hardwick** Bucks
75 L3	**Hardwick** Cambs
74 B1	**Hardwick** Nhants
92 F5	**Hardwick** Norfk
57 G6	**Hardwick** Oxon
57 L3	**Hardwick** Oxon
55 H5	**Hardwicke** Gloucs
55 K3	**Hardwicke** Gloucs
61 M4	**Hardy's Green** Essex
123 G4	**Hare Croft** Brad
62 D3	**Hare Green** Essex
42 D5	**Hare Hatch** Wokham
60 C6	**Hare Street** Essex
60 C3	**Hare Street** Herts
118 D7	**Hareby** Lincs
43 H3	**Harefield** Gt Lon
100 D5	**Harehill** Derbys
123 L4	**Harehills** Leeds
167 H5	**Harelaw** Border
156 D6	**Harelaw** D & G
55 J6	**Harescombe** Gloucs
55 J6	**Haresfield** Gloucs
29 J5	**Harestock** Hants
123 L2	**Harewood** Leeds
54 D3	**Harewood End** Herefs
6 F4	**Harford** Devon
98 C1	**Hargrave** Ches
74 F1	**Hargrave** Nhants
77 H3	**Hargrave Green** Suffk
78 E7	**Harkstead** Suffk
86 B2	**Harlaston** Staffs
102 E6	**Harlaxton** Lincs
122 C4	**Harle Syke** Lancs
95 K6	**Harlech** Gwynd
83 K1	**Harlescott** Shrops
44 E4	**Harlesden** Gt Lon
115 J6	**Harlesthorpe** Derbys
7 J6	**Harleston** Devon
92 F6	**Harleston** Norfk
78 B3	**Harleston** Suffk
73 K2	**Harlestone** Nhants
115 G2	**Harley** Rothm
83 L3	**Harley** Shrops
59 G2	**Harlington** Beds
115 J2	**Harlington** Donc
43 H5	**Harlington** Gt Lon
208 D6	**Harlosh** Highld
60 D6	**Harlow** Essex
150 D2	**Harlow Hill** Nthumb
125 H3	**Harlthorpe** E R Yk
76 B4	**Harlton** Cambs
4 D2	**Harlyn** Cnwll
15 J6	**Harman's Cross** Dorset
131 L2	**Harmby** N York
59 L5	**Harmer Green** Herts
98 C7	**Harmer Hill** Shrops
116 F8	**Harmston** Lincs
83 L3	**Harnage** Shrops
56 B7	**Harnhill** Gloucs
45 K2	**Harold Hill** Gt Lon
45 K3	**Harold Wood** Gt Lon
48 E4	**Haroldston West** Pembks
235 e1	**Haroldswick** Shet
133 K3	**Harome** N York
59 J5	**Harpenden** Herts
12 E4	**Harpford** Devon
135 H7	**Harpham** E R Yk
105 J7	**Harpley** Norfk
70 C3	**Harpley** Worcs
73 K3	**Harpole** Nhants
231 G4	**Harpsdale** Highld
116 F4	**Harpswell** Lincs
113 K2	**Harpurhey** Manch
148 D4	**Harraby** Cumb
23 J6	**Harracott** Devon
199 K2	**Harrapool** Highld
185 K2	**Harrietfield** P & K
33 L3	**Harrietsham** Kent
44 F3	**Harringay** Gt Lon
136 D3	**Harrington** Cumb
118 E6	**Harrington** Lincs
87 L7	**Harrington** Nhants
88 D4	**Harringworth** Nhants
132 D8	**Harrogate** N York
74 D3	**Harrold** Beds
44 D3	**Harrow** Gt Lon
77 J4	**Harrow Green** Suffk
44 D3	**Harrow on the Hill** Gt Lon
44 D2	**Harrow Weald** Gt Lon
6 B2	**Harrowbarrow** Cnwll
76 B4	**Harston** Cambs
102 D6	**Harston** Leics
125 J3	**Harswell** E R Yk
151 L7	**Hart** Hartpl
158 D5	**Hartburn** Nthumb
77 J4	**Hartest** Suffk
32 E6	**Hartfield** E Susx
89 J8	**Hartford** Cambs
112 F6	**Hartford** Ches
61 G4	**Hartford End** Essex
42 C8	**Hartfordbridge** Hants
140 F6	**Hartforth** N York
27 J7	**Hartgrove** Dorset
98 D2	**Harthill** Ches
176 B5	**Harthill** N Lans
115 J5	**Harthill** Rothm
100 C1	**Hartington** Derbys
22 D6	**Hartland** Devon
22 C6	**Hartland Quay** Devon
70 E1	**Hartlebury** Worcs
151 L7	**Hartlepool** Hartpl
139 H5	**Hartley** Cumb
45 L6	**Hartley** Kent
33 K6	**Hartley** Kent
42 B8	**Hartley Wespall** Hants
30 C1	**Hartley Wintney** Hants
46 D7	**Hartlip** Kent
133 L6	**Harton** N York
151 J2	**Harton** S Tyne
55 J3	**Hartpury** Gloucs
123 J6	**Hartshead** Kirk
99 J4	**Hartshill** C Stke
86 D5	**Hartshill** Warwks
100 F7	**Hartshorne** Derbys
168 E6	**Hartside** Nthumb
73 L4	**Hartwell** Nhants
132 C6	**Hartwith** N York
175 L6	**Hartwood** N Lans
166 F4	**Hartwoodmyres** Border
46 A7	**Harvel** Kent
84 F8	**Harvington** Worcs
71 J5	**Harvington** Worcs
116 B3	**Harwell** Notts
41 J3	**Harwell** Oxon
62 F2	**Harwich** Essex
143 K7	**Harwood Dale** N York
115 L3	**Harworth** Notts
85 G6	**Hasbury** Dudley
31 G4	**Hascombe** Surrey
87 K7	**Haselbech** Nhants
13 L1	**Haselbury Plucknett** Somset
72 B2	**Haseley** Warwks
71 K3	**Haselor** Warwks
55 J3	**Hasfield** Gloucs
120 E8	**Haskayne** Lancs
78 F4	**Hasketon** Suffk
30 E5	**Haslemere** Surrey
122 B6	**Haslingden** Lancs
76 B4	**Haslingfield** Cambs
99 G2	**Haslington** Ches
93 H3	**Hassingham** Norfk
19 J3	**Hassocks** W Susx
114 E6	**Hassop** Derbys
231 K5	**Haster** Highld
34 E5	**Hastingleigh** Kent
21 G4	**Hastings** E Susx
60 D6	**Hastingwood** Essex
58 F6	**Hastoe** Herts
151 J6	**Haswell** Dur
151 J6	**Haswell Plough** Dur
25 L7	**Hatch Beauchamp** Somset
43 J3	**Hatch End** Gt Lon
112 D6	**Hatchmere** Ches
117 K2	**Hatcliffe** NE Lin
125 G8	**Hatfield** Donc
69 L3	**Hatfield** Herefs
59 L6	**Hatfield** Herts
60 E5	**Hatfield Broad Oak** Essex
60 E5	**Hatfield Heath** Essex
61 J5	**Hatfield Peverel** Essex
125 G8	**Hatfield Woodhouse** Donc
41 G6	**Hatford** Oxon
29 G2	**Hatherden** Hants
10 D4	**Hatherleigh** Devon
101 J7	**Hathern** Leics
56 D6	**Hatherop** Gloucs
114 E5	**Hathersage** Derbys
114 E5	**Hathersage Booths** Derbys
99 G3	**Hatherton** Ches
85 G2	**Hatherton** Staffs
75 K4	**Hatley St George** Cambs
6 B4	**Hatt** Cnwll
113 M3	**Hattersley** Tamesd
217 K6	**Hatton** Abers
196 D7	**Hatton** Angus
100 E6	**Hatton** Derbys
43 J5	**Hatton** Gt Lon
117 K6	**Hatton** Lincs
83 J5	**Hatton** Shrops
112 E5	**Hatton** Warrtn
72 B2	**Hatton** Warwks
206 F3	**Hatton of Fintray** Abers
163 L4	**Haugh** E Ayrs
215 J6	**Haugh of Glass** Moray
146 E2	**Haugh of Urr** D & G
118 D5	**Haugham** Lincs
175 G3	**Haughhead Inn** E Duns
78 B3	**Haughley** Suffk
78 B2	**Haughley Green** Suffk
98 B6	**Haughton** Shrops
84 D2	**Haughton** Shrops
99 K7	**Haughton** Staffs
141 H4	**Haughton le Skerne** Darltn
98 E2	**Haughton Moss** Ches
60 B4	**Haultwick** Herts
86 B2	**Haunton** Staffs
236 c6	**Hautes Croix** Jersey
159 G2	**Hauxley** Nthumb
76 B4	**Hauxton** Cambs
17 K2	**Havant** Hants
17 G4	**Havenstreet** IOW
124 B7	**Havercroft** Wakefd
48 F4	**Haverfordwest** Pembks
76 F5	**Haverhill** Suffk
128 E4	**Haverigg** Cumb
45 K2	**Havering-atte-Bower** Essex
74 B6	**Haversham** M Keyn
129 H3	**Haverthwaite** Cumb
38 C7	**Havyat** N Som
111 J7	**Hawarden** Flints
61 J4	**Hawbush Green** Essex
92 F4	**Hawe's Green** Norfk
65 K5	**Hawen** Cerdgn
131 G2	**Hawes** N York
70 E3	**Hawford** Worcs
167 G6	**Hawick** Border
13 J3	**Hawkchurch** Devon
77 H4	**Hawkedon** Suffk
27 K2	**Hawkeridge** Wilts
39 H3	**Hawkesbury** S Glos
39 H3	**Hawkesbury Upton** S Glos
33 K6	**Hawkhurst** Kent
35 G6	**Hawkinge** Kent
30 C5	**Hawkley** Hants
24 D5	**Hawkridge** Somset
137 K7	**Hawkshead** Cumb
137 K7	**Hawkshead Hill** Cumb
165 G2	**Hawksland** S Lans
61 G2	**Hawkspur Green** Essex
98 E6	**Hawkstone** Shrops
131 H5	**Hawkswick** N York
123 H3	**Hawksworth** Leeds

102 C4 **Hawksworth** Notts
46 E2 **Hawkwell** Essex
42 E8 **Hawley** Hants
56 B4 **Hawling** Gloucs
133 H2 **Hawnby** N York
122 F3 **Haworth** Brad
77 J3 **Hawstead** Suffk
151 K5 **Hawthorn** Dur
103 K2 **Hawthorn Hill** Lincs
102 C3 **Hawton** Notts
133 J7 **Haxby** York
116 C2 **Haxey** N Linc
60 C3 **Hay Street** Herts
68 E6 **Hay-on-Wye** Powys
112 E3 **Haydock** St Hel
149 L3 **Haydon Bridge** Nthumb
40 C3 **Haydon Wick** Swindn
43 J4 **Hayes** Gt Lon
45 H6 **Hayes** Gt Lon
43 H4 **Hayes End** Gt Lon
182 F3 **Hayfield** Ag & B
114 B4 **Hayfield** Derbys
196 E7 **Hayhillock** Angus
2 F4 **Hayle** Cnwll
85 G6 **Hayley Green** Dudley
17 K3 **Hayling Island** Hants
24 E7 **Hayne** Devon
11 H7 **Hayne** Devon
74 F6 **Haynes (Church End)** Beds
75 G6 **Haynes (Northwood End)** Beds
75 G6 **Haynes (Silver End)** Beds
74 F6 **Haynes (West End)** Beds
48 F3 **Hayscastle** Pembks
48 F3 **Hayscastle Cross** Pembks
147 K6 **Hayton** Cumb
148 E4 **Hayton** Cumb
125 J2 **Hayton** E R Yk
116 B5 **Hayton** Notts
7 H1 **Haytor Vale** Devon
9 K3 **Haytown** Devon
19 J2 **Haywards Heath** W Susx
124 E7 **Haywood** Donc
113 L4 **Hazel Grove** Stockp
165 G1 **Hazelbank** S Lans
14 E2 **Hazelbury Bryan** Dorset
61 K7 **Hazeleigh** Essex
186 E3 **Hazelton Walls** Fife
101 G4 **Hazelwood** Derbys
42 E2 **Hazlemere** Bucks
159 G7 **Hazlerigg** N u Ty
56 B4 **Hazleton** Gloucs
105 G5 **Heacham** Norfk
29 J5 **Headbourne Worthy** Hants
33 L4 **Headcorn** Kent
123 K4 **Headingley** Leeds
57 K6 **Headington** Oxon
140 F4 **Headlam** Dur
176 B6 **Headlesscross** N Lans
41 K7 **Headley** Hants
30 D4 **Headley** Hants
31 K1 **Headley** Surrey
116 C6 **Headon** Notts
175 J8 **Heads** S Lans
148 E4 **Heads Nook** Cumb
101 G3 **Heage** Derbys
140 C7 **Healaugh** N York
124 D2 **Healaugh** N York
113 J4 **Heald Green** Stockp
25 K7 **Heale** Somset
26 B6 **Heale** Somset
132 B4 **Healey** N York
150 D5 **Healeyfield** Dur
126 F7 **Healing** NE Lin
2 E5 **Heamoor** Cnwll

101 H3 **Heanor** Derbys
23 H4 **Heanton Punchardon** Devon
116 E4 **Heapham** Lincs
24 B5 **Heasley Mill** Devon
199 K2 **Heast** Highld
115 J7 **Heath** Derbys
123 L6 **Heath** Wakefd
58 F3 **Heath and Reach** Beds
30 D2 **Heath End** Surrey
71 J1 **Heath Green** Worcs
155 H6 **Heath Hall** D & G
85 H2 **Heath Hayes & Wimblebury** Staffs
84 D2 **Heath Hill** Shrops
85 G4 **Heath Town** Wolves
100 D1 **Heathcote** Derbys
86 E2 **Heather** Leics
20 C2 **Heathfield** E Susx
25 J6 **Heathfield** Somset
43 H5 **Heathrow Airport** Gt Lon
84 E5 **Heathton** Shrops
100 B6 **Heatley** Staffs
113 G4 **Heatley** Warrtn
123 H4 **Heaton** Brad
151 G2 **Heaton** N u Ty
113 L8 **Heaton** Staffs
120 E7 **Heaton's Bridge** Lancs
33 G2 **Heaverham** Kent
12 B4 **Heavitree** Devon
151 H3 **Hebburn** S Tyne
131 J6 **Hebden** N York
122 E5 **Hebden Bridge** Calder
60 A4 **Hebing End** Herts
49 K3 **Hebron** Carmth
158 F4 **Hebron** Nthumb
42 B7 **Heckfield** Hants
92 E7 **Heckfield Green** Suffk
61 M4 **Heckfordbridge** Essex
103 J4 **Heckington** Lincs
123 J5 **Heckmondwike** Kirk
39 M6 **Heddington** Wilts
150 E2 **Heddon-on-the-Wall** Nthumb
93 G5 **Hedenham** Norfk
29 J8 **Hedge End** Hants
42 F3 **Hedgerley** Bucks
25 L5 **Hedging** Somset
150 D3 **Hedley on the Hill** Nthumb
85 H2 **Hednesford** Staffs
126 F5 **Hedon** E R Yk
42 E3 **Hedsor** Bucks
235 C5 **Heglibister** Shet
141 G3 **Heighington** Darltn
117 G7 **Heighington** Lincs
70 D1 **Heightington** Worcs
167 L4 **Heiton** Border
23 H3 **Hele** Devon
12 C2 **Hele** Devon
25 J6 **Hele** Somset
174 B2 **Helensburgh** Ag & B
163 J4 **Helenton** S Ayrs
3 K6 **Helford** Cnwll
3 K5 **Helford Passage** Cnwll
105 K7 **Helhoughton** Norfk
76 F6 **Helions Bumpstead** Essex
5 G2 **Helland** Cnwll
9 H6 **Hellescott** Cnwll
92 E2 **Hellesdon** Norfk
73 G3 **Hellidon** Nhants
131 G7 **Hellifield** N York
20 C4 **Hellingly** E Susx
158 E3 **Helm** Nthumb
73 H5 **Helmdon** Nhants

123 G7 **Helme** Kirk
78 E3 **Helmingham** Suffk
227 H5 **Helmsdale** Highld
122 B6 **Helmshore** Lancs
133 J3 **Helmsley** N York
133 G5 **Helperby** N York
134 E5 **Helperthorpe** N York
103 J4 **Helpringham** Lincs
89 G3 **Helpston** C Pete
112 C6 **Helsby** Ches
3 H5 **Helston** Cnwll
8 E8 **Helstone** Cnwll
138 D3 **Helton** Cumb
93 H2 **Hemblington** Norfk
59 H6 **Hemel Hempstead** Herts
6 E4 **Hemerdon** Devon
125 G4 **Hemingbrough** N York
118 C6 **Hemingby** Lincs
75 K1 **Hemingford Abbots** Cambs
75 K1 **Hemingford Grey** Cambs
78 D4 **Hemingstone** Suffk
101 J6 **Hemington** Leics
88 F6 **Hemington** Nhants
27 G2 **Hemington** Somset
79 G6 **Hemley** Suffk
142 B4 **Hemlington** Middsb
92 F5 **Hempnall** Norfk
92 F5 **Hempnall Green** Norfk
214 D2 **Hempriggs** Moray
76 F6 **Hempstead** Essex
106 D5 **Hempstead** Norfk
107 J6 **Hempstead** Norfk
105 L6 **Hempton** Norfk
57 H2 **Hempton** Oxon
107 K8 **Hemsby** Norfk
116 F4 **Hemswell** Lincs
116 F4 **Hemswell Cliff** Lincs
124 C7 **Hemsworth** Wakefd
25 H8 **Hemyock** Devon
167 L3 **Hendersyde Park** Border
44 E3 **Hendon** Gt Lon
151 K4 **Hendon** Sundld
51 H5 **Hendy** Carmth
19 G3 **Henfield** W Susx
37 J2 **Hengoed** Caerph
68 E4 **Hengoed** Powys
77 J2 **Hengrave** Suffk
60 E3 **Henham** Essex
46 A6 **Henhurst** Kent
82 C2 **Heniarth** Powys
25 L6 **Henlade** Somset
14 D2 **Henley** Dorset
26 B5 **Henley** Somset
78 E4 **Henley** Suffk
30 E6 **Henley** W Susx
20 E3 **Henley's Down** E Susx
71 L2 **Henley-in-Arden** Warwks
42 C4 **Henley-on-Thames** Oxon
65 K6 **Henllan** Cerdgn
110 E7 **Henllan** Denbgs
37 K3 **Henllys** Torfn
75 H6 **Henlow** Beds
11 J8 **Hennock** Devon
77 K6 **Henny Street** Essex
49 H3 **Henry's Moat (Castell Hendre)** Pembks
109 L6 **Henryd** Conwy
124 F5 **Hensall** N York
149 K3 **Henshaw** Nthumb
136 D4 **Hensingham** Cumb
93 K6 **Henstead** Suffk
29 J6 **Hensting** Hants
27 G7 **Henstridge** Somset

27 G7 **Henstridge Ash** Somset
58 C7 **Henton** Oxon
26 C3 **Henton** Somset
70 E4 **Henwick** Worcs
5 L2 **Henwood** Cnwll
36 E4 **Heol-y-Cyw** Brdgnd
158 C2 **Hepple** Nthumb
158 F5 **Hepscott** Nthumb
122 E5 **Heptonstall** Calder
114 D1 **Hepworth** Kirk
92 B8 **Hepworth** Suffk
48 E6 **Herbrandston** Pembks
69 K6 **Hereford** Herefs
35 K2 **Hereson** Kent
218 B7 **Heribusta** Highld
177 L7 **Heriot** Border
177 G4 **Hermiston** C Edin
156 E3 **Hermitage** Border
14 C2 **Hermitage** Dorset
41 J5 **Hermitage** W Berk
49 L2 **Hermon** Pembks
47 K6 **Herne** Kent
47 K6 **Herne Bay** Kent
44 F5 **Herne Hill** Gt Lon
33 H3 **Herne Pound** Kent
23 J6 **Herner** Devon
34 E3 **Hernhill** Kent
5 K4 **Herodsfoot** Cnwll
152 D5 **Heronsford** S Ayrs
30 A3 **Herriard** Hants
93 K4 **Herringfleet** Suffk
77 G1 **Herringswell** Suffk
115 J3 **Herringthorpe** Rothm
151 H4 **Herrington** Sundld
35 G3 **Hersden** Kent
43 J7 **Hersham** Surrey
20 D3 **Herstmonceux** E Susx
234 C7 **Herston** Ork
60 B5 **Hertford** Herts
60 B5 **Hertford Heath** Herts
60 A5 **Hertingfordbury** Herts
148 C7 **Hesket Newmarket** Cumb
120 F5 **Hesketh Bank** Lancs
121 J3 **Hesketh Lane** Lancs
151 K7 **Hesleden** Dur
124 F1 **Heslington** York
133 H8 **Hessay** York
5 L4 **Hessenford** Cnwll
77 L3 **Hessett** Suffk
126 C5 **Hessle** E R Yk
124 C6 **Hessle** Wakefd
43 J5 **Heston** Gt Lon
234 b5 **Hestwall** Ork
111 J5 **Heswall** Wirral
57 L3 **Hethe** Oxon
92 D3 **Hethersett** Norfk
148 E2 **Hethersgill** Cumb
168 D4 **Hethpool** Nthumb
151 J2 **Hett** Dur
131 H7 **Hetton** N York
151 J5 **Hetton-le-Hole** Sundld
158 D7 **Heugh** Nthumb
179 H6 **Heugh Head** Border
205 J3 **Heughhead** Abers
93 G8 **Heveningham** Suffk
32 E4 **Hever** Kent
129 K3 **Heversham** Cumb
106 E7 **Hevingham** Norfk
4 F6 **Hewas Water** Cnwll
54 E7 **Hewelsfield** Gloucs
13 K2 **Hewish** Somset
13 J2 **Hewood** Dorset
150 B3 **Hexham** Nthumb
45 K6 **Hextable** Kent
115 K2 **Hexthorpe** Donc
59 J2 **Hexton** Herts
9 K8 **Hexworthy** Cnwll

6 F2 **Hexworthy** Devon
61 K6 **Heybridge** Essex
61 G7 **Heybridge** Essex
6 D6 **Heybrook Bay** Devon
76 B6 **Heydon** Cambs
106 D6 **Heydon** Norfk
103 G5 **Heydour** Lincs
188 C7 **Heylipoll** Ag & B
235 C3 **Heylor** Shet
129 J7 **Heysham** Lancs
18 B3 **Heyshott** W Susx
27 L3 **Heytesbury** Wilts
57 G3 **Heythrop** Oxon
122 C7 **Heywood** Rochdl
27 K2 **Heywood** Wilts
116 F2 **Hibaldstow** N Linc
115 J1 **Hickleton** Donc
107 J7 **Hickling** Norfk
102 B6 **Hickling** Notts
107 J7 **Hickling Green** Norfk
31 L7 **Hickstead** W Susx
71 L6 **Hidcote Bartrim** Gloucs
71 L6 **Hidcote Boyce** Gloucs
124 C6 **High Ackworth** Wakefd
144 C6 **High Ardwell** D & G
154 F5 **High Auldgirth** D & G
148 F6 **High Bankhill** Cumb
60 C7 **High Beach** Essex
130 C5 **High Bentham** N York
23 J7 **High Bickington** Devon
130 B4 **High Biggins** Cumb
175 J6 **High Blantyre** S Lans
175 L3 **High Bonnybridge** Falk
23 L5 **High Bray** Devon
33 G5 **High Brooms** Kent
130 C4 **High Casterton** Cumb
133 L8 **High Catton** E R Yk
141 G4 **High Coniscliffe** Darltn
148 E3 **High Crosby** Cumb
163 K1 **High Cross** E Ayrs
30 B6 **High Cross** Hants
60 B4 **High Cross** Herts
71 L2 **High Cross** Warwks
144 D7 **High Drummore** D & G
60 F5 **High Easter** Essex
132 B3 **High Ellington** N York
98 E8 **High Ercall** Wrekin
140 F2 **High Etherley** Dur
61 J3 **High Garrett** Essex
132 C5 **High Grantley** N York
92 D3 **High Green** Norfk
92 E5 **High Green** Norfk
115 G3 **High Green** Sheff
70 F5 **High Green** Worcs
34 B7 **High Halden** Kent
46 C5 **High Halstow** Medway
26 B5 **High Ham** Somset
132 D7 **High Harrogate** N York
98 E7 **High Hatton** Shrops
143 J5 **High Hawsker** N York
148 E6 **High Hesket** Cumb
123 K8 **High Hoyland** Barns
32 E7 **High Hurstwood** E Susx
134 B5 **High Hutton** N York
147 M7 **High Ireby** Cumb
133 H4 **High Kilburn** N York
140 E3 **High Lands** Dur
113 L4 **High Lane** Stockp
3 G4 **High Lanes** Cnwll
113 G5 **High Legh** Ches
141 K5 **High Leven** S on T
38 F8 **High Littleton** BaNES
137 G3 **High Lorton** Cumb

116 D7 **High Marnham** Notts
115 K2 **High Melton** Donc
150 D3 **High Mickley** Nthumb
151 J4 **High Newport** Sundld
129 J3 **High Newton** Cumb
129 G2 **High Nibthwaite** Cumb
99 H7 **High Offley** Staffs
60 E7 **High Ongar** Essex
84 E1 **High Onn** Staffs
62 C4 **High Park Corner** Essex
163 L7 **High Pennyvenie** E Ayrs
60 F4 **High Roding** Essex
18 F4 **High Salvington** W Susx
150 E3 **High Spen** Gatesd
4 F5 **High Street** Cnwll
79 J4 **High Street** Suffk
118 C7 **High Toynton** Lincs
158 C2 **High Trewhitt** Nthumb
151 G4 **High Urpeth** Dur
176 D2 **High Valleyfield** Fife
137 K7 **High Wray** Cumb
60 D5 **High Wych** Herts
42 E2 **High Wycombe** Bucks
114 F1 **Higham** Barns
101 H2 **Higham** Derbys
33 G4 **Higham** Kent
46 B5 **Higham** Kent
122 B3 **Higham** Lancs
77 H2 **Higham** Suffk
78 B7 **Higham** Suffk
158 E6 **Higham Dykes** Nthumb
74 D2 **Higham Ferrers** Nhants
59 J2 **Higham Gobion** Beds
45 G3 **Higham Hill** Gt Lon
86 E4 **Higham on the Hill** Leics
10 C4 **Highampton** Devon
45 H2 **Highams Park** Gt Lon
25 L3 **Highbridge** Somset
32 C7 **Highbrook** W Susx
123 J7 **Highburton** Kirk
44 F3 **Highbury** Gt Lon
27 G2 **Highbury** Somset
41 H8 **Highclere** Hants
16 B4 **Highcliffe** Dorset
14 E2 **Higher Ansty** Dorset
121 G4 **Higher Bartle** Lancs
14 D4 **Higher Bockhampton** Dorset
7 L5 **Higher Brixham** Torbay
13 K1 **Higher Chillington** Somset
7 L3 **Higher Gabwell** Devon
129 J7 **Higher Heysham** Lancs
113 G3 **Higher Irlam** Salfd
97 L1 **Higher Kinnerton** Flints
23 J4 **Higher Muddiford** Devon
121 G5 **Higher Penwortham** Lancs
4 C6 **Higher Town** Cnwll
4 F4 **Higher Town** Cnwll
2 b1 **Higher Town** IOS
121 H5 **Higher Walton** Lancs
112 E4 **Higher Walton** Warrtn
13 H2 **Higher Wambrook** Somset

14 D4 **Higher Waterston** Dorset
121 J6 **Higher Wheelton** Lancs
112 F5 **Higher Whitley** Ches
14 B3 **Higher Wraxhall** Dorset
98 C4 **Higher Wych** Ches
150 E3 **Highfield** Gatesd
174 C7 **Highfield** N Ayrs
44 F3 **Highgate** Gt Lon
203 J4 **Highland Wildlife Park** Highld
115 H5 **Highlane** Derbys
55 H4 **Highleadon** Gloucs
18 A6 **Highleigh** W Susx
84 D6 **Highley** Shrops
42 B4 **Highmoor** Oxon
42 B4 **Highmoor Cross** Oxon
55 H4 **Highnam** Gloucs
34 B3 **Highsted** Kent
34 E3 **Highstreet** Kent
77 H7 **Highstreet Green** Essex
31 G4 **Highstreet Green** Surrey
155 H6 **Hightae** D & G
111 J2 **Hightown** Sefton
77 L4 **Hightown Green** Suffk
7 J2 **Highweek** Devon
44 E2 **Highwood Hill** Gt Lon
40 D2 **Highworth** Swindn
91 J4 **Hilborough** Norfk
33 G4 **Hilden Park** Kent
32 F4 **Hildenborough** Kent
76 D5 **Hildersham** Cambs
99 L5 **Hilderstone** Staffs
135 J6 **Hilderthorpe** E R Yk
14 C2 **Hilfield** Dorset
90 E4 **Hilgay** Norfk
38 F2 **Hill** S Glos
72 F2 **Hill** Warwks
30 C6 **Hill Brow** Hants
99 H5 **Hill Chorlton** Staffs
25 H6 **Hill Common** Somset
104 B3 **Hill Dyke** Lincs
185 L7 **Hill End** Fife
70 F6 **Hill End** Gloucs
46 D7 **Hill Green** Kent
17 G2 **Hill Head** Hants
176 F1 **Hill of Beath** Fife
223 H5 **Hill of Fearn** Highld
100 B8 **Hill Ridware** Staffs
123 H6 **Hill Side** Kirk
186 F5 **Hill of Tarvit Mansion House** Fife
123 L7 **Hill Top** Wakefd
124 D5 **Hillam** N York
15 J3 **Hillbutts** Dorset
100 F3 **Hillclifflane** Derbys
40 C8 **Hillcott** Wilts
176 F2 **Hillend** Fife
177 H5 **Hillend** Mdloth
175 L5 **Hillend** N Lans
58 B3 **Hillesden** Bucks
39 H3 **Hillesley** Gloucs
25 J6 **Hillfarrance** Somset
165 J2 **Hillhead** S Lans
217 K5 **Hillhead of Cocklaw** Abers
216 D8 **Hillhead of Durno** Abers
231 H3 **Hilliclay** Highld
43 H4 **Hillingdon** Gt Lon
174 F5 **Hillington** C Glas
105 H7 **Hillington** Norfk
87 G8 **Hillmorton** Warwks
146 D3 **Hillowton** D & G
115 J7 **Hills Town** Derbys
207 H5 **Hillside** Abers
197 H4 **Hillside** Angus

29 G7 **Hillstreet** Hants
235 C3 **Hillswick** Shet
10 D8 **Hilltown** Devon
177 J4 **Hilltown** E Loth
235 C8 **Hillwell** Shet
40 A5 **Hilmarton** Wilts
39 K8 **Hilperton** Wilts
17 J2 **Hilsea** C Port
127 G4 **Hilston** E R Yk
179 H7 **Hilton** Border
75 K2 **Hilton** Cambs
139 G3 **Hilton** Cumb
100 E6 **Hilton** Derbys
14 E2 **Hilton** Dorset
140 F3 **Hilton** Dur
223 J6 **Hilton** Highld
141 K5 **Hilton** S on T
84 D4 **Hilton** Shrops
71 G3 **Himbleton** Worcs
84 F5 **Himley** Staffs
129 L3 **Hincaster** Cumb
44 D6 **Hinchley Wood** Surrey
86 E5 **Hinckley** Leics
92 B7 **Hinderclay** Suffk
143 G4 **Hinderwell** N York
30 E4 **Hindhead** Surrey
112 F1 **Hindley** Wigan
70 F3 **Hindlip** Worcs
106 C6 **Hindolveston** Norfk
27 K5 **Hindon** Wilts
106 B5 **Hindringham** Norfk
92 B3 **Hingham** Norfk
99 G7 **Hinstock** Shrops
78 C5 **Hintlesham** Suffk
69 G6 **Hinton** Herefs
39 G5 **Hinton** S Glos
83 H2 **Hinton** Shrops
29 L6 **Hinton Ampner** Hants
26 E1 **Hinton Blewett** BaNES
39 H8 **Hinton Charterhouse** BaNES
15 J2 **Hinton Martell** Dorset
71 H6 **Hinton on the Green** Worcs
40 E4 **Hinton Parva** Swindn
26 B8 **Hinton St George** Somset
27 H7 **Hinton St Mary** Dorset
57 G7 **Hinton Waldrist** Oxon
73 H6 **Hinton-in-the-Hedges** Nhants
85 L3 **Hints** Staffs
74 D3 **Hinwick** Beds
34 D6 **Hinxhill** Kent
76 C5 **Hinxton** Cambs
75 J6 **Hinxworth** Herts
123 H5 **Hipperholme** Calder
140 F7 **Hipswell** N York
206 D5 **Hirn** Abers
97 G7 **Hirnant** Powys
159 G5 **Hirst** Nthumb
124 F5 **Hirst Courtney** N York
52 E6 **Hirwaun** Rhondd
23 J6 **Hiscott** Devon
76 B2 **Histon** Cambs
78 B4 **Hitcham** Suffk
78 B4 **Hitcham Causeway** Suffk
78 B4 **Hitcham Street** Suffk
59 K3 **Hitchin** Herts
45 H5 **Hither Green** Gt Lon
11 H5 **Hittisleigh** Devon
125 J4 **Hive** E R Yk
100 A7 **Hixon** Staffs
35 H5 **Hoaden** Kent
100 C7 **Hoar Cross** Staffs

54 D3 Hoarwithy Herefs
47 K7 Hoath Kent
82 F7 Hobarris Shrops
167 J7 Hobkirk Border
150 F4 Hobson Dur
102 A8 Hoby Leics
92 C2 Hockering Norfk
102 B2 Hockerton Notts
46 D2 Hockley Essex
85 L8 Hockley Heath Solhll
58 F3 Hockliffe Beds
91 G6 Hockwold cum Wilton Norfk
25 G7 Hockworthy Devon
60 B6 Hoddesdon Herts
121 L6 Hoddlesden Bl w D
155 L7 Hoddom Cross D & G
155 K7 Hoddom Mains D & G
49 H7 Hodgeston Pembks
98 E6 Hodnet Shrops
45 L7 Hodsall Street Kent
115 L4 Hodsock Notts
40 D4 Hodson Swindn
115 K6 Hodthorpe Derbys
92 B1 Hoe Norfk
34 D4 Hogben's Hill Kent
58 D3 Hoggeston Bucks
86 B5 Hoggrill's End Warwks
121 J5 Hoghton Lancs
100 E3 Hognaston Derbys
119 H6 Hogsthorpe Lincs
104 B7 Holbeach Lincs
89 K2 Holbeach Drove Lincs
104 C6 Holbeach Hurn Lincs
104 B8 Holbeach St Johns Lincs
104 B6 Holbeach St Mark's Lincs
104 C6 Holbeach St Matthew Lincs
115 K6 Holbeck Notts
71 H3 Holberrow Green Worcs
6 F5 Holbeton Devon
44 F4 Holborn Gt Lon
101 G4 Holbrook Derbys
78 E6 Holbrook Suffk
16 E2 Holbury Hants
12 B7 Holcombe Devon
26 F2 Holcombe Somset
25 G7 Holcombe Rogus Devon
73 L1 Holcot Nhants
122 B1 Holden Lancs
73 K2 Holdenby Nhants
61 G3 Holder's Green Essex
83 L5 Holdgate Shrops
103 H3 Holdingham Lincs
13 J2 Holditch Dorset
10 B4 Hole Devon
25 J3 Holford Somset
124 E1 Holgate York
129 H4 Holker Cumb
105 L4 Holkham Norfk
105 L4 Holkham Hall Norfk
9 K4 Hollacombe Devon
103 L3 Holland Fen Lincs
62 E5 Holland-on-Sea Essex
234 e3 Hollandstoun Ork
148 A2 Hollee D & G
79 H5 Hollesley Suffk
7 K4 Hollicombe Torbay
33 L3 Hollingbourne Kent
19 J4 Hollingbury Br & H
58 E3 Hollingdon Bucks
100 E5 Hollington Derbys
100 B5 Hollington Staffs
114 A3 Hollingworth Tamesd
113 G4 Hollins Green Warrtn
114 B7 Hollinsclough Staffs

10 F3 Hollocombe Devon
100 F2 Holloway Derbys
44 F3 Holloway Gt Lon
73 K1 Hollowell Nhants
112 C7 Hollowmoor Heath Ches
156 C6 Hollows D & G
70 F6 Holly Green Worcs
53 J7 Hollybush Caerph
163 K6 Hollybush E Ayrs
70 D6 Hollybush Herefs
127 H5 Hollym E R Yk
114 C1 Holmbridge Kirk
31 J3 Holmbury St Mary Surrey
5 G5 Holmbush Cnwll
99 K7 Holmcroft Staffs
89 H6 Holme Cambs
129 L4 Holme Cumb
114 C1 Holme Kirk
132 E3 Holme N York
102 D2 Holme Notts
122 C5 Holme Chapel Lancs
124 E3 Holme Green N York
91 K3 Holme Hale Norfk
69 L7 Holme Lacy Herefs
69 G4 Holme Marsh Herefs
105 H4 Holme next the Sea Norfk
126 B2 Holme on the Wolds E R Yk
101 L5 Holme Pierrepont Notts
147 J5 Holme St Cuthbert Cumb
125 J3 Holme upon Spalding Moor E R Yk
69 K6 Holmer Herefs
42 E2 Holmer Green Bucks
113 H7 Holmes Chapel Ches
114 F6 Holmesfield Derbys
120 F6 Holmeswood Lancs
32 B3 Holmethorpe Surrey
115 H7 Holmewood Derbys
123 H8 Holmfirth Kirk
164 B5 Holmhead E Ayrs
127 J5 Holmpton E R Yk
136 E7 Holmrook Cumb
150 F5 Holmside Dur
7 G3 Holne Devon
14 C1 Holnest Dorset
24 E3 Holnicote Somset
9 J4 Holsworthy Devon
9 K3 Holsworthy Beacon Devon
15 J2 Holt Dorset
106 C5 Holt Norfk
39 K7 Holt Wilts
70 E3 Holt Worcs
98 B2 Holt Wrexhm
71 J1 Holt End Worcs
70 E2 Holt Heath Worcs
133 K8 Holtby York
57 L6 Holton Oxon
27 G6 Holton Somset
93 J7 Holton Suffk
117 J5 Holton cum Beckering Lincs
118 C2 Holton le Clay Lincs
117 H3 Holton le Moor Lincs
78 C6 Holton St Mary Suffk
14 D1 Holwell Dorset
59 K2 Holwell Herts
102 B7 Holwell Leics
56 E6 Holwell Oxon
139 K2 Holwick Dur
169 H2 Holy Island Nthumb
30 B4 Holybourne Hants
108 C5 Holyhead IOA
115 G7 Holymoorside Derbys
42 E5 Holyport W & M
158 B2 Holystone Nthumb

175 K6 Holytown N Lans
75 L1 Holywell Cambs
4 B4 Holywell Cnwll
14 B2 Holywell Dorset
111 G6 Holywell Flints
123 G6 Holywell Green Calder
25 H7 Holywell Lake Somset
91 G7 Holywell Row Suffk
155 G6 Holywood D & G
155 G6 Holywood Village D & G
84 B3 Homer Shrops
111 K2 Homer Green Sefton
93 G6 Homersfield Suffk
28 C6 Homington Wilts
77 L7 Honey Tye Suffk
71 K5 Honeybourne Worcs
10 F4 Honeychurch Devon
40 C7 Honeystreet Wilts
86 B8 Honiley Warwks
107 G6 Honing Norfk
92 D2 Honingham Norfk
102 F4 Honington Lincs
91 K8 Honington Suffk
72 C6 Honington Warwks
12 F3 Honiton Devon
123 H7 Honley Kirk
113 G5 Hoo Green Ches
46 C5 Hoo St Werburgh Medway
6 D5 Hooe C Plym
20 E4 Hooe E Susx
120 D3 Hoohill Bpool
125 H5 Hook E R Yk
30 B1 Hook Hants
45 L6 Hook Kent
49 G5 Hook Pembks
44 D7 Hook Surrey
40 B4 Hook Wilts
33 H6 Hook Green Kent
57 G2 Hook Norton Oxon
14 A3 Hooke Dorset
11 K5 Hookway Devon
115 K3 Hooton Levitt Rothm
124 D7 Hooton Pagnell Donc
115 J3 Hooton Roberts Rothm
114 D5 Hope Derbys
7 G7 Hope Devon
97 L2 Hope Flints
83 L8 Hope Shrops
100 C2 Hope Staffs
83 J5 Hope Bowdler Shrops
54 F4 Hope Mansell Herefs
69 K4 Hope under Dinmore Herefs
166 D6 Hopehouse Border
214 E4 Hopeman Moray
83 H6 Hopesay Shrops
133 K8 Hopgrove York
132 F7 Hopperton N York
84 D5 Hopstone Shrops
100 E2 Hopton Derbys
99 L7 Hopton Staffs
92 B7 Hopton Suffk
83 K7 Hopton Cangeford Shrops
83 G7 Hopton Castle Shrops
93 L4 Hopton on Sea Norfk
84 B7 Hopton Wafers Shrops
83 H7 Hoptonheath Shrops
85 L3 Hopwas Staffs
85 J7 Hopwood Worcs
20 C3 Horam E Susx
103 J5 Horbling Lincs
123 K6 Horbury Wakefd
151 K6 Horden Dur

16 C4 Hordle Hants
98 B6 Hordley Shrops
38 E5 Horfield Bristl
92 E8 Horham Suffk
62 B3 Horkesley Heath Essex
126 B6 Horkstow N Linc
72 E5 Horley Oxon
32 B5 Horley Surrey
26 E5 Hornblotton Green Somset
130 B5 Hornby Lancs
141 J6 Hornby N York
132 C2 Hornby N York
118 C7 Horncastle Lincs
45 K3 Hornchurch Gt Lon
179 J7 Horncliffe Nthumb
179 J8 Horndean Border
30 B8 Horndean Hants
10 D8 Horndon Devon
46 A4 Horndon on the Hill Thurr
32 C4 Horne Surrey
24 D3 Horner Somset
107 H8 Horning Norfk
88 B4 Horninghold Leics
100 E7 Horninglow Staffs
76 C3 Horningsea Cambs
27 J3 Horningsham Wilts
105 M7 Horningtoft Norfk
22 F6 Horns Cross Devon
126 F2 Hornsea E R Yk
44 F3 Hornsey Gt Lon
72 E5 Hornton Oxon
235 d2 Horra Shet
6 D2 Horrabridge Devon
7 H2 Horridge Devon
77 J3 Horringer Suffk
121 L2 Horrocksford Lancs
6 B2 Horsebridge Devon
20 C4 Horsebridge E Susx
29 G5 Horsebridge Hants
83 G3 Horsebridge Shrops
76 E5 Horseheath Cambs
131 K4 Horsehouse N York
43 G8 Horsell Surrey
98 C4 Horseman's Green Wrexhm
107 K7 Horsey Norfk
25 L4 Horsey Somset
92 E1 Horsford Norfk
123 J3 Horsforth Leeds
31 K5 Horsham W Susx
70 D3 Horsham Worcs
92 E1 Horsham St Faith Norfk
117 K7 Horsington Lincs
27 G6 Horsington Somset
101 G4 Horsley Derbys
39 J2 Horsley Gloucs
157 L3 Horsley Nthumb
150 D2 Horsley Nthumb
101 H4 Horsley Woodhouse Derbys
62 D3 Horsleycross Street Essex
167 H5 Horsleyhill Border
33 J5 Horsmonden Kent
57 L6 Horspath Oxon
106 F8 Horstead Norfk
32 C7 Horsted Keynes W Susx
58 F4 Horton Bucks
15 J2 Horton Dorset
122 C1 Horton Lancs
74 B4 Horton Nhants
39 H4 Horton S Glos
25 L7 Horton Somset
99 L2 Horton Staffs
50 F7 Horton Swans
43 G5 Horton W & M
40 B7 Horton Wilts
84 C1 Horton Wrekin

98 C3 **Horton Green** Ches
130 F5 **Horton in Ribblesdale** N York
45 K6 **Horton Kirby** Kent
57 L5 **Horton-cum-Studley** Oxon
121 J7 **Horwich** Bolton
23 H6 **Horwood** Devon
166 F6 **Hoscote** Border
102 B6 **Hose** Leics
185 H3 **Hosh** P & K
235 C7 **Hoswick** Shet
125 L4 **Hotham** E R Yk
34 C5 **Hothfield** Kent
101 L7 **Hoton** Leics
157 K5 **Hott** Nthumb
99 G3 **Hough** Ches
112 C4 **Hough Green** Halton
102 F3 **Hough-on-the-Hill** Lincs
102 E4 **Hougham** Lincs
75 K1 **Houghton** Cambs
29 G5 **Houghton** Hants
49 G6 **Houghton** Pembks
18 D4 **Houghton** W Susx
74 F6 **Houghton Conquest** Beds
21 H2 **Houghton Green** E Susx
151 H5 **Houghton le Spring** Sundld
87 J3 **Houghton on the Hill** Leics
59 G4 **Houghton Regis** Beds
105 L5 **Houghton St Giles** Norfk
42 B8 **Hound Green** Hants
178 D8 **Houndslow** Border
179 H5 **Houndwood** Border
43 J5 **Hounslow** Gt Lon
61 G4 **Hounslow Green** Essex
213 L4 **Househill** Highld
123 J6 **Houses Hill** Kirk
149 K2 **Housesteads Roman Fort** Nthumb
207 G1 **Housieside** Abers
174 D5 **Houston** Rens
227 K2 **Houstry** Highld
234 b6 **Houton** Ork
19 J5 **Hove** Br & H
102 B3 **Hoveringham** Notts
107 G8 **Hoveton** Norfk
133 K4 **Hovingham** N York
54 E3 **How Caple** Herefs
148 E4 **How Mill** Cumb
125 H5 **Howden** E R Yk
150 E7 **Howden-le-Wear** Dur
231 K3 **Howe** Highld
132 E4 **Howe** N York
92 F4 **Howe** Norfk
61 J7 **Howe Green** Essex
216 E5 **Howe of Teuchar** Abers
61 H5 **Howe Street** Essex
77 G7 **Howe Street** Essex
61 K7 **Howegreen** Essex
103 J4 **Howell** Lincs
147 L2 **Howes** D & G
68 B3 **Howey** Powys
177 H6 **Howgate** Mdloth
169 K5 **Howick** Nthumb
140 D3 **Howle** Dur
99 G7 **Howle** Wrekin
54 E4 **Howle Hill** Herefs
76 E7 **Howlett End** Essex
13 H1 **Howley** Somset
233 b7 **Howmore** W Isls
168 B5 **Hownam** Border
117 H2 **Howsham** N Linc
133 L6 **Howsham** N York
168 D3 **Howtel** Nthumb
174 D6 **Howwood** Rens

92 E7 **Hoxne** Suffk
111 H4 **Hoylake** Wirral
115 G2 **Hoyland Nether** Barns
114 E1 **Hoyland Swaine** Barns
48 E6 **Hubberston** Pembks
123 K2 **Huby** N York
133 J6 **Huby** N York
55 K4 **Hucclecote** Gloucs
33 L2 **Hucking** Kent
101 K3 **Hucknall** Notts
123 H7 **Huddersfield** Kirk
71 G3 **Huddington** Worcs
140 E7 **Hudswell** N York
134 D7 **Huggate** E R Yk
2 b2 **Hugh Town** IOS
42 E2 **Hughenden Valley** Bucks
83 L4 **Hughley** Shrops
10 D3 **Huish** Devon
40 C7 **Huish** Wilts
25 G5 **Huish Champflower** Somset
26 B6 **Huish Episcopi** Somset
58 D5 **Hulcott** Bucks
12 C5 **Hulham** Devon
100 E3 **Hulland** Derbys
100 E3 **Hulland Ward** Derbys
39 K4 **Hullavington** Wilts
46 D2 **Hullbridge** Essex
113 J3 **Hulme** Manch
99 L4 **Hulme** Staffs
112 E4 **Hulme** Warrtn
100 C2 **Hulme End** Staffs
113 J7 **Hulme Walfield** Ches
93 K6 **Hulver Street** Suffk
16 E5 **Hulverstone** IOW
126 D7 **Humberside Airport** N Linc
118 D1 **Humberston** NE Lin
87 J3 **Humberstone** C Leic
178 B4 **Humbie** E Loth
126 F4 **Humbleton** E R Yk
103 G6 **Humby** Lincs
167 L2 **Hume** Border
158 A7 **Humshaugh** Nthumb
231 M2 **Huna** Highld
87 G4 **Huncote** Leics
167 K5 **Hundalee** Border
140 C3 **Hunderthwaite** Dur
118 E7 **Hundleby** Lincs
49 G7 **Hundleton** Pembks
77 G5 **Hundon** Suffk
120 F6 **Hundred End** Lancs
68 C4 **Hundred House** Powys
87 K3 **Hungarton** Leics
25 G4 **Hungerford** Somset
41 G6 **Hungerford** W Berk
41 G6 **Hungerford Newtown** W Berk
69 J7 **Hungerstone** Herefs
135 H4 **Hunmanby** N York
72 D2 **Hunningham** Warwks
60 C5 **Hunsdon** Herts
132 F8 **Hunsingore** N York
123 L4 **Hunslet** Leeds
149 G7 **Hunsonby** Cumb
105 G4 **Hunstanton** Norfk
150 B5 **Hunstanworth** Dur
99 G4 **Hunsterson** Ches
77 L2 **Hunston** Suffk
18 B5 **Hunston** W Susx
38 F7 **Hunstrete** BaNES
123 J5 **Hunsworth** Kirk
173 K3 **Hunter's Quay** Ag & B
25 M6 **Huntham** Somset
196 D3 **Hunthill Lodge** Angus
75 J1 **Huntingdon** Cambs

93 G8 **Huntingfield** Suffk
112 B8 **Huntington** Ches
178 B4 **Huntington** E Loth
68 E4 **Huntington** Herefs
85 H2 **Huntington** Staffs
133 J7 **Huntington** York
55 G4 **Huntley** Gloucs
215 L6 **Huntly** Abers
29 J4 **Hunton** Hants
33 J4 **Hunton** Kent
132 B2 **Hunton** N York
24 E3 **Huntscott** Somset
24 F7 **Huntsham** Devon
23 H6 **Huntshaw** Devon
25 L3 **Huntspill** Somset
25 K5 **Huntstile** Somset
25 L4 **Huntworth** Somset
140 F2 **Hunwick** Dur
106 C5 **Hunworth** Norfk
28 D5 **Hurdcott** Wilts
113 L6 **Hurdsfield** Ches
42 D4 **Hurley** W & M
86 B4 **Hurley** Warwks
86 B4 **Hurley Common** Warwks
163 L3 **Hurlford** E Ayrs
15 L3 **Hurn** Dorset
29 H6 **Hursley** Hants
42 C5 **Hurst** Wokham
33 J7 **Hurst Green** E Susx
62 C5 **Hurst Green** Essex
121 K3 **Hurst Green** Lancs
32 D3 **Hurst Green** Surrey
29 H3 **Hurstbourne Priors** Hants
29 G2 **Hurstbourne Tarrant** Hants
19 J3 **Hurstpierpoint** W Susx
122 C4 **Hurstwood** Lancs
234 c6 **Hurtiso** Ork
141 H5 **Hurworth Place** Darltn
141 H5 **Hurworth-on-Tees** Darltn
87 J6 **Husbands Bosworth** Leics
74 D7 **Husborne Crawley** Beds
133 H4 **Husthwaite** N York
101 J2 **Huthwaite** Notts
119 G6 **Huttoft** Lincs
179 J7 **Hutton** Border
134 F8 **Hutton** E R Yk
45 M2 **Hutton** Essex
121 G5 **Hutton** Lancs
37 M8 **Hutton** N Som
141 H7 **Hutton Bonville** N York
134 F3 **Hutton Buscel** N York
132 E5 **Hutton Conyers** N York
126 C1 **Hutton Cranswick** E R Yk
148 D7 **Hutton End** Cumb
151 K7 **Hutton Henry** Dur
142 D4 **Hutton Lowcross** R & Cl
140 E5 **Hutton Magna** Dur
148 C7 **Hutton Roof** Cumb
130 B4 **Hutton Roof** Cumb
141 K6 **Hutton Rudby** N York
133 G4 **Hutton Sessay** N York
124 D1 **Hutton Wandesley** N York
133 L2 **Hutton-le-Hole** N York
12 B3 **Huxham** Devon
98 D1 **Huxley** Ches
112 C4 **Huyton** Knows
128 D2 **Hycemoor** Cumb
113 L3 **Hyde** Tamesd

58 F7 **Hyde Heath** Bucks
99 K8 **Hyde Lea** Staffs
165 H2 **Hyndford Bridge** S Lans
188 C8 **Hynish** Ag & B
82 F5 **Hyssington** Powys
16 E2 **Hythe** Hants
34 F7 **Hythe** Kent
43 G6 **Hythe End** W & M

I

14 E2 **Ibberton** Dorset
100 E2 **Ible** Derbys
15 L1 **Ibsley** Hants
86 E2 **Ibstock** Leics
42 C2 **Ibstone** Bucks
29 G2 **Ibthorpe** Hants
143 H5 **Iburndale** N York
29 K1 **Ibworth** Hants
91 J4 **Ickburgh** Norfk
43 H3 **Ickenham** Gt Lon
57 M6 **Ickford** Bucks
35 G3 **Ickham** Kent
59 K2 **Ickleford** Herts
21 H3 **Icklesham** E Susx
76 C5 **Ickleton** Cambs
91 H8 **Icklingham** Suffk
122 E2 **Ickornshaw** N York
75 G5 **Ickwell Green** Beds
77 J3 **Ickworth** Suffolk
56 E4 **Icomb** Gloucs
56 E4 **Idbury** Oxon
10 E3 **Iddesleigh** Devon
11 K6 **Ide** Devon
32 E3 **Ide Hill** Kent
7 K1 **Ideford** Devon
21 H2 **Iden** E Susx
33 J5 **Iden Green** Kent
33 K6 **Iden Green** Kent
123 H3 **Idle** Brad
4 C6 **Idless** Cnwll
72 C5 **Idlicote** Warwks
28 D1 **Idmiston** Wilts
100 F3 **Idridgehay** Derbys
208 F2 **Idrigill** Highld
40 E4 **Idstone** Oxon
57 K7 **Iffley** Oxon
31 L4 **Ifield** W Susx
15 L4 **Iford** Bmouth
19 L4 **Iford** E Susx
38 C3 **Ifton** Mons
98 E5 **Ightfield** Shrops
33 G2 **Ightham** Kent
79 J4 **Iken** Suffk
100 C3 **Ilam** Staffs
26 D6 **Ilchester** Somset
168 F5 **Ilderton** Nthumb
45 H3 **Ilford** Gt Lon
26 A7 **Ilford** Somset
23 H2 **Ilfracombe** Devon
101 J4 **Ilkeston** Derbys
93 H6 **Ilketshall St Andrew** Suffk
93 H6 **Ilketshall St Margaret** Suffk
123 G2 **Ilkley** Brad
5 L1 **Illand** Cnwll
85 H7 **Illey** Dudley
3 H3 **Illogan** Cnwll
87 K4 **Illston on the Hill** Leics
58 C6 **Ilmer** Bucks
72 B5 **Ilmington** Warwks
26 A8 **Ilminster** Somset
7 H2 **Ilsington** Devon
51 H7 **Ilston** Swans
132 B4 **Ilton** N York
25 M7 **Ilton** Somset
161 L2 **Imachar** N Ayrs
126 F7 **Immingham** NE Lin

126 F7 **Immingham Dock** NE Lin
76 C2 **Impington** Cambs
112 C6 **Ince** Ches
111 K2 **Ince Blundell** Sefton
112 E1 **Ince-in-Makerfield** Wigan
221 K7 **Inchbae Lodge Hotel** Highld
196 F4 **Inchbare** Angus
215 G4 **Inchberry** Moray
174 E5 **Inchinnan** Rens
201 J5 **Inchlaggan** Highld
186 D3 **Inchmichael** P & K
202 B3 **Inchnacardoch Hotel** Highld
224 F4 **Inchnadamph** Highld
186 D2 **Inchture** P & K
211 K6 **Inchvuilt** Highld
186 C4 **Inchyra** P & K
4 E4 **Indian Queens** Cnwll
61 G7 **Ingatestone** Essex
114 E1 **Ingbirchworth** Barns
99 L7 **Ingestre** Staffs
116 F5 **Ingham** Lincs
107 H7 **Ingham** Norfk
77 J1 **Ingham** Suffk
107 H6 **Ingham Corner** Norfk
101 G6 **Ingleby** Derbys
141 K6 **Ingleby Arncliffe** N York
141 K4 **Ingleby Barwick** S on T
142 C6 **Ingleby Greenhow** N York
10 E4 **Ingleigh Green** Devon
39 E7 **Inglesbatch** BaNES
56 D7 **Inglesham** Swindn
147 G2 **Ingleston** D & G
140 F3 **Ingleton** Dur
130 D5 **Ingleton** N York
121 H3 **Inglewhite** Lancs
158 C7 **Ingoe** Nthumb
121 G4 **Ingol** Lancs
105 G6 **Ingoldisthorpe** Norfk
119 H7 **Ingoldmells** Lincs
103 G6 **Ingoldsby** Lincs
168 F6 **Ingram** Nthumb
45 M2 **Ingrave** Essex
122 F3 **Ingrow** Brad
38 E3 **Ingst** S Glos
88 E2 **Ingthorpe** Lincs
106 E6 **Ingworth** Norfk
71 H3 **Inkberrow** Worcs
217 H6 **Inkhorn** Abers
41 G7 **Inkpen** W Berk
231 J2 **Inkstack** Highld
173 K4 **Innellan** Ag & B
166 E3 **Innerleithen** Border
186 F7 **Innerleven** Fife
144 C3 **Innermessan** D & G
178 F4 **Innerwick** E Loth
215 G2 **Innesmill** Moray
216 C8 **Insch** Abers
203 J5 **Insh** Highld
120 F3 **Inskip** Lancs
23 G5 **Instow** Devon
115 H5 **Intake** Sheff
204 F6 **Inver** Abers
223 J5 **Inver** Highld
194 F7 **Inver** P & K
216 C2 **Inver-boyndie** Abers
190 F1 **Inverailort** Highld
210 C3 **Inveralligin** Highld
217 K2 **Inverallochy** Abers
222 D2 **Inveran** Highld
182 F5 **Inveraray** Ag & B
209 J7 **Inverarish** Highld
196 D7 **Inverarity** Angus
183 K4 **Inverarnan** Stirlg
219 J4 **Inverasdale** Highld
176 C3 **Inveravon** Falk

182 E2 **Inverawe** Ag & B
183 K7 **Inverbeg** Ag & B
197 K2 **Inverbervie** Abers
220 F5 **Inverbroom** Highld
191 K6 **Invercreran House Hotel** Ag & B
203 L3 **Inverdruie** Highld
177 K4 **Inveresk** E Loth
182 E1 **Inveresragan** Ag & B
219 K5 **Inverewe Garden** Highld
204 D7 **Inverey** Abers
202 D2 **Inverfarigaig** Highld
191 J7 **Inverfolla** Ag & B
201 L5 **Invergarry** Highld
184 F2 **Invergeldie** P & K
201 K7 **Invergloy** Highld
222 F7 **Invergordon** Highld
186 F2 **Invergowrie** P & K
200 B4 **Inverguseran** Highld
193 L5 **Inverhadden** P & K
183 L3 **Inverherive Hotel** Stirlg
200 B5 **Inverie** Highld
182 E4 **Inverinan** Ag & B
200 E2 **Inverinate** Highld
197 G6 **Inverkeilor** Angus
176 F2 **Inverkeithing** Fife
216 C5 **Inverkeithny** Abers
173 L4 **Inverkip** Inver
224 C4 **Inverkirkaig** Highld
220 F4 **Inverlael** Highld
192 E1 **Inverliever** Highld
182 C6 **Inverliever Lodge** Ag & B
183 H2 **Inverlochy** Ag & B
196 D1 **Invermark** Angus
215 J6 **Invermarkie** Abers
202 C3 **Invermoriston** Highld
213 G5 **Inverness** Highld
213 J4 **Inverness Dalcross Airport** Highld
183 G7 **Invernoaden** Ag & B
192 D7 **Inveroran Hotel** Ag & B
196 C5 **Inverquharity** Angus
217 J5 **Inverquhomery** Abers
201 K8 **Inverroy** Highld
191 J4 **Inversanda** Highld
200 E2 **Invershiel** Highld
222 D3 **Invershin** Highld
231 J8 **Invershore** Highld
183 K5 **Inversnaid Hotel** Stirlg
217 L5 **Inverugie** Abers
183 K5 **Inveruglas** Ag & B
203 J5 **Inveruglass** Highld
206 E2 **Inverurie** Abers
10 E5 **Inwardleigh** Devon
61 L4 **Inworth** Essex
233 b7 **Iochdar** W Isls
180 C3 **Iona** Ag & B
30 D6 **Iping** W Susx
7 J3 **Ipplepen** Devon
41 M4 **Ipsden** Oxon
100 A3 **Ipstones** Staffs
78 E5 **Ipswich** Suffk
111 J5 **Irby** Wirral
118 F8 **Irby in the Marsh** Lincs
117 K1 **Irby upon Humber** NE Lin
74 D2 **Irchester** Nhants
147 M7 **Ireby** Cumb
130 C4 **Ireby** Lancs
75 G6 **Ireland** Beds
128 F4 **Ireleth** Cumb
149 L7 **Ireshopeburn** Dur
100 F3 **Ireton Wood** Derbys
113 G3 **Irlam** Salfd
103 G7 **Irnham** Lincs
39 G4 **Iron Acton** S Glos

84 C3 **Iron Bridge Museum** Wrekin
84 C3 **Ironbridge** Wrekin
154 B6 **Ironmacannie** D & G
101 H3 **Ironville** Derbys
107 H7 **Irstead** Norfk
148 E3 **Irthington** Cumb
74 D1 **Irthlingborough** Nhants
134 F3 **Irton** N York
163 H2 **Irvine** N Ayrs
230 E3 **Isauld** Highld
235 C2 **Isbister** Shet
19 L3 **Isfield** E Susx
88 C8 **Isham** Nhants
30 C3 **Isington** Hants
170 F7 **Islay Airport** Ag & B
26 A7 **Isle Abbotts** Somset
26 A7 **Isle Brewers** Somset
45 G4 **Isle of Dogs** Gt Lon
237 b7 **Isle of Man Ronaldsway Airport** IOM
15 J5 **Isle of Purbeck** Dorset
46 F6 **Isle of Sheppey** Kent
145 K7 **Isle of Whithorn** D & G
17 G5 **Isle of Wight** IOW
90 F8 **Isleham** Cambs
199 L3 **Isleornsay** Highld
2 b2 **Isles of Scilly St Mary's Airport** IOS
155 G7 **Islesteps** D & G
236 d2 **Islet Village** Guern
44 D5 **Isleworth** Gt Lon
101 H7 **Isley Walton** Leics
232 d3 **Islibhig** W Isls
44 F3 **Islington** Gt Lon
88 E7 **Islip** Nhants
57 K5 **Islip** Oxon
232 d3 **Islivig** W Isls
83 L2 **Isombridge** Wrekin
29 K5 **Itchen Abbas** Hants
29 K5 **Itchen Stoke** Hants
31 J5 **Itchingfield** W Susx
106 D6 **Itteringham** Norfk
11 G5 **Itton** Devon
38 C2 **Itton** Mons
148 D6 **Ivegill** Cumb
43 G4 **Iver** Bucks
43 G4 **Iver Heath** Bucks
150 E5 **Iveston** Dur
58 F5 **Ivinghoe** Bucks
58 F4 **Ivinghoe Aston** Bucks
69 J3 **Ivington** Herefs
69 J4 **Ivington Green** Herefs
33 G3 **Ivy Hatch** Kent
6 F5 **Ivybridge** Devon
21 K1 **Ivychurch** Kent
46 E6 **Iwade** Kent
27 K8 **Iwerne Courtney or Shroton** Dorset
27 K8 **Iwerne Minster** Dorset
77 L1 **Ixworth** Suffk
91 K8 **Ixworth Thorpe** Suffk

J

12 C4 **Jack-in-the-Green** Devon
175 L2 **Jackton** S Lans
9 G5 **Jacobstow** Cnwll
10 E4 **Jacobstowe** Devon
49 H7 **Jameston** Pembks
212 D3 **Jamestown** Highld
174 D3 **Jamestown** W Duns

231 L5 **Janets-town** Highld
227 L3 **Janetstown** Highld
155 J5 **Jardine Hall** D & G
151 H3 **Jarrow** S Tyne
61 H3 **Jasper's Green** Essex
175 L4 **Jawcraig** Falk
62 D5 **Jaywick** Essex
167 K5 **Jedburgh** Border
49 J6 **Jeffreyston** Pembks
213 H2 **Jemimaville** Highld
236 d4 **Jerbourg** Guern
236 b7 **Jersey Airport** Jersey
151 G2 **Jesmond** N u Ty
20 B5 **Jevington** E Susx
59 H5 **Jockey End** Herts
112 B5 **John Lennon Airport** Lpool
231 L2 **John o' Groats** Highld
148 D7 **Johnby** Cumb
197 J3 **Johnshaven** Abers
48 F5 **Johnston** Pembks
155 M3 **Johnstone** D & G
174 D5 **Johnstone** Rens
155 J4 **Johnstonebridge** D & G
50 E2 **Johnstown** Carmth
97 L4 **Johnstown** Wrexhm
177 J4 **Joppa** C Edin
66 D2 **Joppa** Cerdgn
163 K5 **Joppa** S Ayrs
64 C7 **Jordanston** Pembks
45 K5 **Joyden's Wood** Kent
150 B3 **Juniper** Nthumb
177 G5 **Juniper Green** C Edin
237 C2 **Jurby** IOM

K

139 H5 **Kaber** Cumb
165 J1 **Kaimend** S Lans
173 G4 **Kames** Ag & B
164 D4 **Kames** E Ayrs
4 C7 **Kea** Cnwll
125 K7 **Keadby** N Linc
104 B1 **Keal Cotes** Lincs
113 H1 **Kearsley** Bolton
158 C6 **Kearsley** Nthumb
35 H6 **Kearsney** Kent
130 B4 **Kearstwick** Cumb
77 G5 **Kedington** Suffk
100 F4 **Kedleston** Derbys
126 E8 **Keelby** Lincs
99 J4 **Keele** Staffs
123 G4 **Keelham** Brad
48 F4 **Keeston** Pembks
39 L8 **Keevil** Wilts
101 J7 **Kegworth** Leics
3 G3 **Kehelland** Cnwll
206 B2 **Keig** Abers
122 F3 **Keighley** Brad
185 J8 **Keilarsbrae** Clacks
185 K3 **Keillour** P & K
204 E6 **Keiloch** Abers
171 K5 **Keils** Ag & B
26 D5 **Keinton Mandeville** Somset
154 E4 **Keir Mill** D & G
139 G3 **Keisley** Cumb
231 L4 **Keiss** Highld
215 J4 **Keith** Moray
195 K8 **Keithick** P & K
196 F4 **Keithock** Angus
212 E3 **Keithtown** Highld
122 D2 **Kelbrook** Lancs
173 L6 **Kelburn** N Ayrs
103 G4 **Kelby** Lincs
139 K6 **Keld** N York
124 F3 **Kelfield** N York
102 C2 **Kelham** Notts
147 K2 **Kelhead** D & G

120 E5 **Kellamergh** Lancs
187 G1 **Kellas** Angus
214 E4 **Kellas** Moray
7 J7 **Kellaton** Devon
106 C4 **Kelling** Norfk
124 E5 **Kellington** N York
151 J7 **Kelloe** Dur
164 E6 **Kelloholm** D & G
9 K8 **Kelly** Devon
87 K7 **Kelmarsh** Nhants
56 E7 **Kelmscot** Oxon
79 H2 **Kelsale** Suffk
112 D7 **Kelsall** Ches
75 K7 **Kelshall** Herts
147 L5 **Kelsick** Cumb
167 L3 **Kelso** Border
115 G8 **Kelstedge** Derbys
118 C4 **Kelstern** Lincs
39 G6 **Kelston** BaNES
194 B6 **Keltneyburn** P & K
155 H7 **Kelton** D & G
186 B8 **Kelty** Fife
61 K4 **Kelvedon** Essex
60 F7 **Kelvedon Hatch**
        Essex
2 C5 **Kelynack** Cnwll
187 G4 **Kemback** Fife
84 D3 **Kemberton** Shrops
39 M2 **Kemble** Gloucs
71 G6 **Kemerton** Worcs
53 M6 **Kemeys**
        Commander Mons
206 E3 **Kemnay** Abers
19 J5 **Kemp Town** Br & H
54 F3 **Kempley** Gloucs
55 G3 **Kempley Green**
        Gloucs
70 F5 **Kempsey** Worcs
40 D2 **Kempsford** Gloucs
29 L2 **Kempshott** Hants
74 F5 **Kempston** Beds
83 G6 **Kempton** Shrops
32 F2 **Kemsing** Kent
34 C7 **Kenardington** Kent
69 J6 **Kenchester** Herefs
56 E6 **Kencot** Oxon
129 L2 **Kendal** Cumb
36 C4 **Kenfig** Brdgnd
72 C1 **Kenilworth** Warwks
32 B2 **Kenley** Gt Lon
83 L4 **Kenley** Shrops
210 B3 **Kenmore** Highld
194 B7 **Kenmore** P & K
11 L7 **Kenn** Devon
38 B6 **Kenn** N Som
172 D5 **Kennacraig** Ag & B
11 J4 **Kennerleigh** Devon
111 L2 **Kennessee Green**
        Sefton
176 C1 **Kennett** Clacks
215 L8 **Kennethmont** Abers
77 G2 **Kennett** Cambs
11 L7 **Kennford** Devon
92 C6 **Kenninghall** Norfk
34 D5 **Kennington** Kent
57 K7 **Kennington** Oxon
186 F6 **Kennoway** Fife
25 L7 **Kenny** Somset
90 F7 **Kennyhill** Suffk
134 C6 **Kennythorpe** N York
188 C6 **Kenovay** Ag & B
208 F4 **Kensaleyre** Highld
44 E4 **Kensington** Gt Lon
59 G4 **Kensworth** Beds
59 G4 **Kensworth**
        Common Beds
55 H4 **Kent's Green** Gloucs
28 F6 **Kent's Oak** Hants
191 K5 **Kentallen** Highld
54 B3 **Kentchurch** Herefs
77 G2 **Kentford** Suffk
12 D2 **Kentisbeare** Devon
23 K3 **Kentisbury** Devon

44 F3 **Kentish Town** Gt Lon
138 C6 **Kentmere** Cumb
12 B5 **Kenton** Devon
44 D3 **Kenton** Gt Lon
150 F2 **Kenton** N u Ty
78 E2 **Kenton** Suffk
190 D3 **Kentra** Highld
4 C6 **Kenwyn** Cnwll
228 F3 **Keoldale** Highld
200 D1 **Keppoch** Highld
133 G2 **Kepwick** N York
86 D6 **Keresley** Covtry
2 D5 **Kerris** Cnwll
82 D5 **Kerry** Powys
173 J6 **Kerrycroy** Ag & B
116 B8 **Kersall** Notts
12 D5 **Kersbrook** Devon
78 B5 **Kersey** Suffk
232 f3 **Kershader** W Isls
12 D2 **Kerswell** Devon
70 F5 **Kerswell Green**
        Worcs
78 F5 **Kesgrave** Suffk
93 L6 **Kessingland** Suffk
4 F6 **Kestle** Cnwll
4 D4 **Kestle Mill** Cnwll
45 H7 **Keston** Gt Lon
137 J3 **Keswick** Cumb
92 E3 **Keswick** Norfk
118 E6 **Kesby** Lincs
88 C7 **Kettering** Nhants
92 E3 **Ketteringham** Norfk
195 K8 **Kettins** Angus
77 L4 **Kettlebaston** Suffk
186 E6 **Kettlebridge** Fife
78 F3 **Kettleburgh** Suffk
155 K6 **Kettleholm** D & G
113 M5 **Kettleshulme** Ches
132 C7 **Kettlesing** N York
132 C7 **Kettlesing Bottom**
        N York
106 A6 **Kettlestone** Norfk
116 D6 **Kettlethorpe** Lincs
234 d4 **Kettletoft** Ork
131 H5 **Kettlewell** N York
88 E3 **Ketton** Rutlnd
44 D5 **Kew** Gt Lon
44 D5 **Kew Gardens** Gt Lon
37 M7 **Kewstoke** N Som
116 E4 **Kexby** Lincs
125 G1 **Kexby** York
113 K8 **Key Green** Ches
87 J3 **Keyham** Leics
16 C4 **Keyhaven** Hants
127 G5 **Keyingham** E R Yk
19 J3 **Keymer** W Susx
38 F6 **Keynsham** BaNES
74 F3 **Keysoe** Beds
74 F3 **Keysoe Row** Beds
88 F7 **Keyston** Cambs
101 L6 **Keyworth** Notts
151 G4 **Kibblesworth** Gatesd
87 K5 **Kibworth**
        Beauchamp Leics
87 K5 **Kibworth Harcourt**
        Leics
45 H5 **Kidbrooke** Gt Lon
84 E7 **Kidderminster** Worcs
57 L5 **Kidlington** Oxon
42 B5 **Kidmore End** Oxon
145 J7 **Kidsdale** D & G
99 J2 **Kidsgrove** Staffs
50 E4 **Kidwelly** Carmth
191 H8 **Kiel Crofts** Ag & B
157 G4 **Kielder** Nthumb
171 H5 **Kiells** Ag & B
174 D5 **Kilbarchan** Rens
199 K4 **Kilbeg** Highld
172 C5 **Kilberry** Ag & B
174 C7 **Kilbirnie** N Ayrs
182 B3 **Kilbride** Ag & B
172 C3 **Kilbride** Ag & B
173 H5 **Kilbride** Ag & B

214 D3 **Kilbuiack** Moray
101 G4 **Kilburn** Derbys
44 E4 **Kilburn** Gt Lon
133 H4 **Kilburn** N York
87 J4 **Kilby** Leics
172 D6 **Kilchamaig** Ag & B
180 E7 **Kilchattan** Ag & B
173 J7 **Kilchattan** Ag & B
191 G8 **Kilcheran** Ag & B
189 L4 **Kilchoan** Highld
170 D5 **Kilchoman** Ag & B
182 E3 **Kilchrenan** Ag & B
187 H6 **Kilconquhar** Fife
55 G3 **Kilcot** Gloucs
212 E4 **Kilcoy** Highld
173 L3 **Kilcreggan** Ag & B
142 D5 **Kildale** N York
161 J5 **Kildalloig** Ag & B
223 G6 **Kildary** Highld
173 G5 **Kildavaig** Ag & B
173 H5 **Kildavanan** Ag & B
227 G4 **Kildonan** Highld
162 D5 **Kildonan** N Ayrs
226 F4 **Kildonan Lodge**
        Highld
199 G7 **Kildonnan** Highld
144 C4 **Kildrochet House**
        D & G
205 K2 **Kildrummy** Abers
122 F2 **Kildwick** N York
172 F3 **Kilfinan** Ag & B
201 K6 **Kilfinnan** Highld
49 J6 **Kilgetty** Pembks
152 F2 **Kilgrammie** S Ayrs
38 C2 **Kilgwrrwg Common**
        Mons
135 G6 **Kilham** E R Yk
188 B7 **Kilkenneth** Ag & B
161 H4 **Kilkenzie** Ag & B
161 J5 **Kilkerran** Ag & B
9 H3 **Kilkhampton** Cnwll
115 J5 **Killamarsh** Derbys
51 H6 **Killay** Swans
174 F2 **Killearn** Stirlg
213 G3 **Killen** Highld
140 F3 **Killerby** Darltn
12 C3 **Killerton** Devon
193 J5 **Killichonan** P & K
190 B7 **Killiechronan** Ag & B
194 E4 **Killiecrankie** P & K
210 E7 **Killilan** Highld
184 C2 **Killin** Stirlg
132 D7 **Killinghall** N York
130 C2 **Killington** Cumb
159 G7 **Killingworth** N Tyne
167 G1 **Killochyett** Border
174 C4 **Kilmacolm** Inver
184 D5 **Kilmahog** Stirlg
182 A8 **Kilmahumaig** Ag & B
218 C6 **Kilmaluag** Highld
186 F3 **Kilmany** Fife
163 K2 **Kilmarnock** E Ayrs
182 B7 **Kilmartin** Ag & B
163 K2 **Kilmaurs** E Ayrs
182 B5 **Kilmelford** Ag & B
27 G2 **Kilmersdon** Somset
29 L6 **Kilmeston** Hants
161 H5 **Kilmichael** Ag & B
182 B8 **Kilmichael Glassary**
        Ag & B
172 D2 **Kilmichael of**
        Inverlussa Ag & B
13 H3 **Kilmington** Devon
27 H4 **Kilmington** Wilts
27 H4 **Kilmington**
        Common Wilts
27 H4 **Kilmington Street**
        Wilts
212 D5 **Kilmorack** Highld
182 C3 **Kilmore** Ag & B
199 K4 **Kilmore** Highld
172 C4 **Kilmory** Ag & B
190 B3 **Kilmory** Highld

162 B5 **Kilmory** N Ayrs
208 D5 **Kilmuir** Highld
218 B7 **Kilmuir** Highld
213 G4 **Kilmuir** Highld
223 G6 **Kilmuir** Highld
173 K3 **Kilmun** Ag & B
150 C4 **Kiln Pit Hill** Nthumb
170 F4 **Kilnave** Ag & B
176 B8 **Kilncadzow** S Lans
33 J6 **Kilndown** Kent
182 B3 **Kilninver** Ag & B
127 J7 **Kilnsea** E R Yk
131 H6 **Kilnsey** N York
126 C1 **Kilnwick** E R Yk
180 E7 **Kiloran** Ag & B
162 A4 **Kilpatrick** N Ayrs
54 C3 **Kilpeck** Herefs
125 J5 **Kilpin** E R Yk
187 J6 **Kilrenny** Fife
73 H1 **Kilsby** Nhants
186 C3 **Kilspindie** P & K
144 D7 **Kilstay** D & G
175 J3 **Kilsyth** N Lans
212 D6 **Kiltarlity** Highld
142 E4 **Kilton** R & Cl
142 E4 **Kilton Thorpe** R & Cl
218 B7 **Kilvaxter** Highld
25 H3 **Kilve** Somset
102 D4 **Kilvington** Notts
163 H2 **Kilwinning** N Ayrs
92 C3 **Kimberley** Norfk
101 J4 **Kimberley** Notts
115 H3 **Kimberworth** Rothm
151 G5 **Kimblesworth** Dur
75 G2 **Kimbolton** Cambs
69 K3 **Kimbolton** Herefs
87 H6 **Kimcote** Leics
15 H6 **Kimmeridge** Dorset
28 F3 **Kimpton** Hants
59 K4 **Kimpton** Herts
226 F3 **Kinbrace** Highld
185 G6 **Kinbuck** Stirlg
187 G4 **Kincaple** Fife
176 C2 **Kincardine** Fife
222 E4 **Kincardine** Highld
206 B5 **Kincardine O'Neil**
        Abers
195 J8 **Kinclaven** P & K
207 H5 **Kincorth** C Aber
214 C3 **Kincorth House**
        Moray
203 K4 **Kincraig** Highld
194 F6 **Kincraigie** P & K
194 F6 **Kindallachan** P & K
172 B7 **Kinerarach** Ag & B
56 C3 **Kineton** Gloucs
72 D4 **Kineton** Warwks
186 C3 **Kinfauns** P & K
163 J3 **Kinfold** S Ayrs
81 G3 **King Arthur's**
        Labyrinth Gwynd
85 K1 **King's Bromley** Staffs
88 E4 **King's Cliffe** Nhants
71 J3 **King's Coughton**
        Warwks
85 J7 **King's Heath** Birm
85 H4 **King's Hill** Wsall
104 F8 **King's Lynn** Norfk
236 c3 **King's Mills** Guern
85 J7 **King's Norton** Birm
87 K4 **King's Norton** Leics
23 L7 **King's Nympton**
        Devon
69 J4 **King's Pyon** Herefs
29 G5 **King's Somborne**
        Hants
14 D1 **King's Stag** Dorset
55 J7 **King's Stanley**
        Gloucs
72 C7 **King's Sutton** Oxon
59 K4 **King's Walden** Herts
173 J6 **Kingarth** Ag & B
207 G5 **Kingcausie** Abers

54	B6	**Kingcoed** Mons
117	H3	**Kingerby** Lincs
9	H4	**Kingford** Devon
56	E3	**Kingham** Oxon
155	G7	**Kingholm Quay** D & G
177	H2	**Kinghorn** Fife
186	D7	**Kinglassie** Fife
196	B5	**Kingoldrum** Angus
186	E2	**Kingoodie** P & K
54	E3	**Kings Caple** Herefs
33	H3	**Kings Hill** Kent
192	D5	**Kings House Hotel** Highld
59	H7	**Kings Langley** Herts
138	E3	**Kings Meaburn** Cumb
166	C2	**Kings Muir** Border
86	F7	**Kings Newnham** Warwks
89	J7	**Kings Ripton** Cambs
38	D5	**Kings Weston** Bristl
29	J5	**Kings Worthy** Hants
6	C5	**Kingsand** Cnwll
187	K5	**Kingsbarns** Fife
7	H6	**Kingsbridge** Devon
24	F4	**Kingsbridge** Somset
208	F4	**Kingsburgh** Highld
44	D3	**Kingsbury** Gt Lon
86	B4	**Kingsbury** Warwks
26	B7	**Kingsbury Episcopi** Somset
41	K8	**Kingsclere** Hants
39	J2	**Kingscote** Gloucs
23	H7	**Kingscott** Devon
162	D4	**Kingscross** N Ayrs
26	D6	**Kingsdon** Somset
35	K5	**Kingsdown** Kent
40	D3	**Kingsdown** Swindn
39	J6	**Kingsdown** Wilts
176	F1	**Kingseat** Fife
58	C6	**Kingsey** Bucks
31	K4	**Kingsfold** W Susx
206	F4	**Kingsford** C Aber
174	E8	**Kingsford** E Ayrs
35	K1	**Kingsgate** Kent
77	K3	**Kingshall Street** Suffk
23	J4	**Kingsheanton** Devon
184	C4	**Kingshouse Hotel** Stirlg
7	K3	**Kingskerswell** Devon
186	E5	**Kingskettle** Fife
69	J3	**Kingsland** Herefs
108	C5	**Kingsland** IOA
112	D6	**Kingsley** Ches
30	C4	**Kingsley** Hants
100	A3	**Kingsley** Staffs
30	E5	**Kingsley Green** W Susx
73	L3	**Kingsley Park** Nhants
196	D6	**Kingsmuir** Angus
187	J5	**Kingsmuir** Fife
34	D6	**Kingsnorth** Kent
85	J4	**Kingstanding** Birm
7	K2	**Kingsteignton** Devon
54	D2	**Kingsthorne** Herefs
73	L2	**Kingsthorpe** Nhants
75	L4	**Kingston** Cambs
6	A2	**Kingston** Cnwll
6	F6	**Kingston** Devon
14	E1	**Kingston** Dorset
15	H6	**Kingston** Dorset
178	C3	**Kingston** E Loth
16	F6	**Kingston** IOW
35	G4	**Kingston** Kent
57	H7	**Kingston Bagpuize** Oxon
58	C7	**Kingston Blount** Oxon
27	J4	**Kingston Deverill** Wilts
40	F3	**Kingston Lisle** Oxon
19	K4	**Kingston near Lewes** E Susx
101	J6	**Kingston on Soar** Notts
215	H2	**Kingston on Spey** Moray
14	B4	**Kingston Russell** Dorset
38	B6	**Kingston Seymour** N Som
25	K5	**Kingston St Mary** Somset
126	D5	**Kingston upon Hull** C KuH
44	D6	**Kingston upon Thames** Gt Lon
69	H7	**Kingstone** Herefs
26	B8	**Kingstone** Somset
100	B6	**Kingstone** Staffs
7	K5	**Kingswear** Devon
207	G4	**Kingswells** C Aber
84	F5	**Kingswinford** Dudley
58	B4	**Kingswood** Bucks
39	H3	**Kingswood** Gloucs
38	F5	**Kingswood** S Glos
25	H4	**Kingswood** Somset
31	L1	**Kingswood** Surrey
71	L1	**Kingswood** Warwks
84	E3	**Kingswood Common** Staffs
117	J6	**Kingthorpe** Lincs
68	F3	**Kington** Herefs
38	F3	**Kington** S Glos
71	H4	**Kington** Worcs
39	L5	**Kington Langley** Wilts
27	H6	**Kington Magna** Dorset
39	K3	**Kington St Michael** Wilts
203	H5	**Kingussie** Highld
26	D5	**Kingweston** Somset
217	H7	**Kinharrachie** Abers
147	G2	**Kinharvie** D & G
185	J4	**Kinkell Bridge** P & K
217	J6	**Kinknockie** Abers
177	G5	**Kinleith** C Edin
84	C7	**Kinlet** Shrops
225	H2	**Kinloch** Highld
229	H5	**Kinloch** Highld
198	F5	**Kinloch** Highld
195	J7	**Kinloch** P & K
195	L1	**Kinloch** P & K
200	E4	**Kinloch Hourn** Highld
193	L5	**Kinloch Rannoch** P & K
184	B6	**Kinlochard** Stirlg
228	C4	**Kinlochbervie** Highld
191	J1	**Kinlocheil** Highld
210	F3	**Kinlochewe** Highld
202	E7	**Kinlochlaggan** Highld
192	C4	**Kinlochleven** Highld
190	E2	**Kinlochmoidart** Highld
200	B8	**Kinlochnanuagh** Highld
214	C3	**Kinloss** Moray
110	D5	**Kinmel Bay** Conwy
206	F2	**Kinmuck** Abers
207	G2	**Kinmundy** Abers
160	B2	**Kinnabus** Ag & B
217	H5	**Kinnadie** Abers
194	F5	**Kinnaird** P & K
197	G5	**Kinnaird Castle** Angus
214	F1	**Kinneddar** Moray
197	K2	**Kinneff** Abers
155	H2	**Kinnelhead** D & G
196	F6	**Kinnell** Angus
97	M7	**Kinnerley** Shrops
69	G5	**Kinnersley** Herefs
70	F5	**Kinnersley** Worcs
68	E2	**Kinnerton** Powys
186	C6	**Kinnesswood** P & K
140	D3	**Kinninvie** Dur
196	B5	**Kinnordy** Angus
102	B6	**Kinoulton** Notts
186	B6	**Kinross** P & K
186	C2	**Kinrossie** P & K
69	G2	**Kinsham** Herefs
71	G7	**Kinsham** Worcs
124	C7	**Kinsley** Wakefd
15	K3	**Kinson** Bmouth
41	G6	**Kintbury** W Berk
214	B3	**Kintessack** Moray
200	F2	**Kintail** Highld
186	B4	**Kintillo** P & K
83	H8	**Kinton** Herefs
98	A8	**Kinton** Shrops
206	E3	**Kintore** Abers
171	H7	**Kintour** Ag & B
180	D3	**Kintra** Ag & B
182	B6	**Kintraw** Ag & B
161	J2	**Kintyre** Ag & B
203	L2	**Kinveachy** Highld
84	E6	**Kinver** Staffs
124	C4	**Kippax** Leeds
184	E7	**Kippen** Stirlg
146	E4	**Kippford or Scaur** D & G
33	H5	**Kipping's Cross** Kent
234	b6	**Kirbister** Ork
165	M1	**Kirburd** Border
93	G3	**Kirby Bedon** Norfk
102	B8	**Kirby Bellars** Leics
93	H5	**Kirby Cane** Norfk
62	E4	**Kirby Cross** Essex
87	G3	**Kirby Fields** Leics
134	D6	**Kirby Grindalythe** N York
140	E6	**Kirby Hill** N York
132	F5	**Kirby Hill** N York
133	G3	**Kirby Knowle** N York
62	F4	**Kirby le Soken** Essex
134	B4	**Kirby Misperton** N York
87	G3	**Kirby Muxloe** Leics
93	H5	**Kirby Row** Norfk
141	K7	**Kirby Sigston** N York
134	C7	**Kirby Underdale** E R Yk
132	E3	**Kirby Wiske** N York
147	G2	**Kirconnel** D & G
31	G6	**Kirdford** W Susx
231	K4	**Kirk** Highld
124	F7	**Kirk Bramwith** Donc
124	B1	**Kirk Deighton** N York
126	C5	**Kirk Ella** E R Yk
101	J4	**Kirk Hallam** Derbys
133	G7	**Kirk Hammerton** N York
100	E3	**Kirk Ireton** Derbys
100	F5	**Kirk Langley** Derbys
141	G2	**Kirk Merrington** Dur
237	C4	**Kirk Michael** IOM
175	L5	**Kirk of Shotts** N Lans
124	F8	**Kirk Sandall** Donc
124	D7	**Kirk Smeaton** N York
168	C4	**Kirk Yetholm** Border
235	d6	**Kirkabister** Shet
146	A5	**Kirkandrews** D & G
148	C4	**Kirkandrews upon Eden** Cumb
148	B4	**Kirkbampton** Cumb
147	G3	**Kirkbean** D & G
147	M4	**Kirkbride** Cumb
196	E7	**Kirkbuddo** Angus
166	D2	**Kirkburn** Border
134	F7	**Kirkburn** E R Yk
123	J7	**Kirkburton** Kirk
111	L2	**Kirkby** Knows
117	H3	**Kirkby** Lincs
142	C6	**Kirkby** N York
141	G7	**Kirkby Fleetham** N York
103	H2	**Kirkby Green** Lincs
101	J2	**Kirkby in Ashfield** Notts
103	J4	**Kirkby la Thorpe** Lincs
130	B4	**Kirkby Lonsdale** Cumb
131	G7	**Kirkby Malham** N York
86	F4	**Kirkby Mallory** Leics
132	C5	**Kirkby Malzeard** N York
118	C8	**Kirkby on Bain** Lincs
123	L2	**Kirkby Overblow** N York
139	H5	**Kirkby Stephen** Cumb
138	F3	**Kirkby Thore** Cumb
103	H6	**Kirkby Underwood** Lincs
124	D3	**Kirkby Wharf** N York
128	F3	**Kirkby-in-Furness** Cumb
133	L3	**Kirkbymoorside** N York
186	D8	**Kirkcaldy** Fife
148	F2	**Kirkcambeck** Cumb
146	B5	**Kirkchrist** D & G
144	B2	**Kirkcolm** D & G
164	E6	**Kirkconnel** D & G
146	B3	**Kirkconnell** D & G
145	G3	**Kirkcowan** D & G
146	B5	**Kirkcudbright** D & G
111	K3	**Kirkdale** Lpool
165	G2	**Kirkfieldbank** S Lans
146	F2	**Kirkgunzeon** D & G
120	F4	**Kirkham** Lancs
134	B6	**Kirkham** N York
123	K6	**Kirkhamgate** Wakefd
158	C5	**Kirkharle** Nthumb
149	H5	**Kirkhaugh** Nthumb
123	H6	**Kirkheaton** Kirk
158	C6	**Kirkheaton** Nthumb
212	E5	**Kirkhill** Highld
165	J7	**Kirkhope** S Lans
199	H2	**Kirkibost** Highld
195	L1	**Kirkinch** P & K
145	J5	**Kirkinner** D & G
175	H4	**Kirkintilloch** E Duns
136	H4	**Kirkland** Cumb
164	E6	**Kirkland** D & G
154	E4	**Kirkland** D & G
155	H4	**Kirkland** D & G
142	D3	**Kirkleatham** R & Cl
141	K5	**Kirklevington** S on T
93	L5	**Kirkley** Suffk
132	D4	**Kirklington** N York
102	B2	**Kirklington** Notts
148	D2	**Kirklinton** Cumb
176	F4	**Kirkliston** C Edin
145	K4	**Kirkmabreck** D & G
144	D7	**Kirkmaiden** D & G
195	H4	**Kirkmichael** P & K
163	J7	**Kirkmichael** S Ayrs
146	F2	**Kirkmuirhill** S Lans
168	D4	**Kirknewton** Nthumb
176	F5	**Kirknewton** W Loth
215	L7	**Kirkney** Abers
148	F6	**Kirkoswald** Cumb
163	G7	**Kirkoswald** S Ayrs
154	F4	**Kirkpatrick** D & G
237	b5	**Kirkpatrick** IOM
154	D7	**Kirkpatrick Durham** D & G
156	B7	**Kirkpatrick-Fleming** D & G
128	D4	**Kirksanton** Cumb
123	K4	**Kirkstall** Leeds
103	K1	**Kirkstead** Lincs
215	L7	**Kirkstile** Abers
156	C4	**Kirkstile** D & G
231	L2	**Kirkstyle** Highld
124	B6	**Kirkthorpe** Wakefd
206	C1	**Kirkton** Abers

216 F5 **Kirkton** Abers
155 G6 **Kirkton** D & G
186 F3 **Kirkton** Fife
210 C8 **Kirkton** Highld
210 D6 **Kirkton** Highld
185 K4 **Kirkton** P & K
166 C2 **Kirkton Manor**
　　　　Border
195 L6 **Kirkton of Airlie**
　　　　Angus
196 B8 **Kirkton of**
　　　　Auchterhouse Angus
213 K5 **Kirkton of Barevan**
　　　　Highld
186 C2 **Kirkton of Collace**
　　　　P & K
205 J3 **Kirkton of**
　　　　Glenbuchat Abers
217 J7 **Kirkton of Logie**
　　　　Buchan Abers
196 E4 **Kirkton of Menmuir**
　　　　Angus
196 E8 **Kirkton of Monikie**
　　　　Angus
216 D7 **Kirkton of Rayne**
　　　　Abers
206 F4 **Kirkton of Skene**
　　　　Abers
186 F1 **Kirkton of**
　　　　Strathmartine Angus
196 C8 **Kirkton of Tealing**
　　　　Angus
206 C3 **Kirkton of Tough**
　　　　Abers
217 J2 **Kirktown** Abers
217 K4 **Kirktown** Abers
206 F1 **Kirktown of Bourtie**
　　　　Abers
206 F7 **Kirktown of**
　　　　Fetteresso Abers
215 H6 **Kirktown of**
　　　　Mortlach Moray
217 K8 **Kirktown of Slains**
　　　　Abers
234 c6 **Kirkwall** Ork
234 c6 **Kirkwall Airport** Ork
158 C5 **Kirkwhelpington**
　　　　Nthumb
126 D7 **Kirmington** N Linc
117 K3 **Kirmond le Mire** Lincs
173 K3 **Kirn** Ag & B
196 C5 **Kirriemuir** Angus
93 G4 **Kirstead Green** Norfk
155 M7 **Kirtlebridge** D & G
77 G3 **Kirtling** Cambs
76 F4 **Kirtling Green** Suffk
57 J4 **Kirtlington** Oxon
229 M3 **Kirtomy** Highld
104 A5 **Kirton** Lincs
116 B7 **Kirton** Notts
78 F6 **Kirton** Suffk
116 F2 **Kirton in Lindsey**
　　　　N Linc
174 D4 **Kirtonhill** W Duns
145 J4 **Kirwaugh** D & G
210 C6 **Kishorn** Highld
73 K3 **Kislingbury** Nhants
25 G6 **Kittisford** Somset
207 H4 **Kittybrewster** C Aber
54 C2 **Kivernoll** Herefs
116 D5 **Knaith** Lincs
27 J6 **Knap Corner** Dorset
42 F8 **Knaphill** Surrey
25 L6 **Knapp** Somset
134 D4 **Knapton** N York
107 G5 **Knapton** Norfk
124 E1 **Knapton** York
75 K2 **Knapwell** Cambs
132 E7 **Knaresborough**
　　　　N York
149 H4 **Knarsdale** Nthumb
217 G5 **Knaven** Abers
132 F2 **Knayton** N York

59 L4 **Knebworth** Herts
125 H5 **Knedlington** E R Yk
116 B8 **Kneesall** Notts
75 L5 **Kneesworth** Cambs
102 B4 **Kneeton** Notts
50 F7 **Knelston** Swans
99 L5 **Knenhall** Staffs
72 E4 **Knightcote** Warwks
99 J7 **Knightley** Staffs
87 H4 **Knighton** C Leic
14 C1 **Knighton** Dorset
82 F8 **Knighton** Powys
25 J3 **Knighton** Somset
99 G4 **Knighton** Staffs
99 H6 **Knighton** Staffs
70 B1 **Knighton on Teme**
　　　　Worcs
70 D4 **Knightwick** Worcs
68 F3 **Knill** Herefs
102 D6 **Knipton** Leics
100 E3 **Kniveton** Derbys
138 F2 **Knock** Cumb
199 K4 **Knock** Highld
215 L4 **Knock** Moray
232 g2 **Knock** W Isls
173 L5 **Knock Castle** N Ayrs
227 K3 **Knockally** Highld
224 F6 **Knockan** Highld
214 F6 **Knockando** Moray
212 E5 **Knockbain** Highld
212 F3 **Knockbain** Highld
231 H4 **Knockdee** Highld
39 J3 **Knockdown** Wilts
153 G3 **Knockeen** S Ayrs
162 D4 **Knockenkelly** N Ayrs
163 K2 **Knockentiber** E Ayrs
32 E2 **Knockholt** Kent
32 E2 **Knockholt Pound**
　　　　Kent
97 M7 **Knockin** Shrops
163 K2 **Knockinlaw** E Ayrs
144 B3 **Knocknain** D & G
153 M5 **Knocksheen** D & G
154 D7 **Knockvennie**
　　　　Smithy D & G
79 J3 **Knodishall** Suffk
26 C6 **Knole** Somset
113 J5 **Knolls Green** Ches
98 B5 **Knolton** Wrexhm
27 L3 **Knook** Wilts
88 B2 **Knossington** Leics
120 E2 **Knott End-on-Sea**
　　　　Lancs
74 E2 **Knotting** Beds
74 E3 **Knotting Green**
　　　　Beds
124 D5 **Knottingley** Wakefd
112 B3 **Knotty Ash** Lpool
83 L7 **Knowbury** Shrops
153 G7 **Knowe** D & G
154 A4 **Knowehead** D & G
163 G6 **Knoweside** S Ayrs
42 D4 **Knowl Hill** W & M
38 E6 **Knowle** Bristl
23 H4 **Knowle** Devon
11 H5 **Knowle** Devon
12 C2 **Knowle** Devon
12 D6 **Knowle** Devon
83 L8 **Knowle** Shrops
85 L7 **Knowle** Solhll
24 E3 **Knowle** Somset
121 J3 **Knowle Green** Lancs
13 J1 **Knowle St Giles**
　　　　Somset
148 D4 **Knowlefield** Cumb
112 C3 **Knowsley** Knows
112 H7 **Knowsley Safari**
　　　　Park Knows
24 C6 **Knowstone** Devon
33 K5 **Knox Bridge** Kent
82 F8 **Knucklas** Powys
74 D2 **Knuston** Nhants
113 H5 **Knutsford** Ches

122 F6 **Krumlin** Calder
3 J7 **Kuggar** Cnwll
210 B8 **Kyle of Lochalsh**
　　　　Highld
200 B1 **Kyleakin** Highld
200 B2 **Kylerhea** Highld
232 e4 **Kyles Scalpay** W Isls
224 F2 **Kylesku** Highld
200 C6 **Kylesmorar** Highld
224 F2 **Kylestrome** Highld
84 C1 **Kynnersley** Wrekin
69 L2 **Kyrewood** Worcs

L

236 d1 **L'Ancresse** Guern
236 b3 **L'Eree** Guern
236 a6 **L'Etacq** Jersey
236 d3 **La Bellieuse** Guern
236 e1 **La Fontenelle** Guern
236 d4 **La Fosse** Guern
236 d2 **La Greve** Guern
236 b5 **La Greve de Lecq**
　　　　Jersey
236 d7 **La Hougue Bie**
　　　　Jersey
236 b3 **La Houguette** Guern
236 d2 **La Passee** Guern
236 a7 **La Pulente** Jersey
236 e8 **La Rocque** Jersey
236 d2 **La Rousaillerie** Guern
236 d4 **La Villette** Guern
232 f2 **Lacadal** W Isls
232 f3 **Lacasaigh** W Isls
117 K1 **Laceby** NE Lin
58 D7 **Lacey Green** Bucks
113 G6 **Lach Dennis** Ches
77 H1 **Lackford** Suffk
77 H1 **Lackford Green** Suffk
39 K6 **Lacock** Wilts
72 E3 **Ladbroke** Warwks
33 J4 **Laddingford** Kent
4 D5 **Ladock** Cnwll
128 E3 **Lady Hall** Cumb
234 d4 **Lady Village** Ork
186 E5 **Ladybank** Fife
165 H4 **Ladygill** S Lans
179 J8 **Ladykirk** Border
85 J6 **Ladywood** Birm
70 F3 **Ladywood** Worcs
154 F5 **Lag** D & G
190 D4 **Laga** Highld
160 C1 **Lagavulin** Ag & B
162 B5 **Lagg** N Ayrs
201 L6 **Laggan** Highld
202 F6 **Laggan** Highld
228 F4 **Laid** Highld
219 L3 **Laide** Highld
199 G7 **Laig** Highld
174 E8 **Laigh Clunch** E Ayrs
163 L2 **Laigh Fenwick** E Ayrs
164 C5 **Laigh Glenmuir**
　　　　E Ayrs
175 J7 **Laighstonehall**
　　　　S Lans
46 B3 **Laindon** Essex
225 M7 **Lairg** Highld
123 J4 **Laisterdyke** Brad
17 H5 **Lake** IOW
15 J4 **Lake** Poole
28 C4 **Lake** Wilts
137 H5 **Lake District**
　　　　National Park Cumb
91 G6 **Lakenheath** Suffk
90 D4 **Lakesend** Norfk
36 D4 **Laleston** Brdgnd
177 G2 **Lamancha** Border
77 K7 **Lamarsh** Essex
106 F7 **Lamas** Norfk
167 L2 **Lambden** Border
33 H6 **Lamberhurst** Kent

33 H6 **Lamberhurst Down**
　　　　Kent
179 K6 **Lamberton** Border
44 F4 **Lambeth** Gt Lon
77 G4 **Lambfair Green**
　　　　Suffk
101 M4 **Lambley** Notts
149 H4 **Lambley** Nthumb
40 F5 **Lambourn** W Berk
45 J2 **Lambourne End**
　　　　Essex
31 L4 **Lambs Green** W Susx
5 K3 **Lamellion** Cnwll
6 C1 **Lamerton** Devon
151 G4 **Lamesley** Gatesd
165 J3 **Lamington** S Lans
162 C3 **Lamlash** N Ayrs
148 D7 **Lamonby** Cumb
2 E6 **Lamorna** Cnwll
4 D7 **Lamorran** Cnwll
66 D5 **Lampeter** Cerdgn
49 K5 **Lampeter Velfrey**
　　　　Pembks
49 H7 **Lamphey** Pembks
136 F3 **Lamplugh** Cumb
87 L8 **Lamport** Nhants
26 F4 **Lamyatt** Somset
165 G2 **Lanark** S Lans
129 K7 **Lancaster** Lancs
150 F5 **Lanchester** Dur
19 G5 **Lancing** W Susx
2 C6 **Land's End** Cnwll
2 C5 **Land's End Airport**
　　　　Cnwll
227 L2 **Land-hallow** Highld
76 C2 **Landbeach** Cambs
23 G6 **Landcross** Devon
206 E4 **Landerberry** Abers
28 E7 **Landford** Wilts
50 F6 **Landimore** Swans
23 J5 **Landkey** Devon
23 J5 **Landkey Town** Devon
51 J6 **Landore** Swans
6 B4 **Landrake** Cnwll
7 H3 **Landscove** Devon
6 C4 **Landulph** Cnwll
4 C4 **Lane** Cnwll
42 D3 **Lane End** Bucks
27 J3 **Lane End** Wilts
128 D2 **Lane End**
　　　　Waberthwaite Cumb
100 E5 **Lane Ends** Derbys
140 E5 **Lane Head** Dur
9 G7 **Laneast** Cnwll
116 D6 **Laneham** Notts
149 L6 **Lanehead** Dur
25 K6 **Langaller** Somset
102 B5 **Langar** Notts
174 D4 **Langbank** Rens
123 G1 **Langbar** N York
130 F6 **Langcliffe** N York
134 E2 **Langdale End** N York
16 E2 **Langdown** Hants
186 E6 **Langdyke** Fife
62 B4 **Langenhoe** Essex
75 H6 **Langford** Beds
12 D2 **Langford** Devon
61 K6 **Langford** Essex
102 D2 **Langford** Notts
56 E7 **Langford** Oxon
25 H6 **Langford Budville**
　　　　Somset
78 B7 **Langham** Essex
106 B4 **Langham** Norfk
88 B2 **Langham** Rutlnd
77 L1 **Langham** Suffk
121 K4 **Langho** Lancs
156 C5 **Langholm** D & G
167 H3 **Langlee** Border
16 F3 **Langley** Hants
59 K4 **Langley** Herts
33 K3 **Langley** Kent
149 L3 **Langley** Nthumb

43 G5 **Langley** Slough
25 G5 **Langley** Somset
30 D5 **Langley** W Susx
71 L3 **Langley** Warwks
39 L5 **Langley Burrell** Wilts
61 L4 **Langley Green** Essex
25 G5 **Langley Marsh** Somset
150 F6 **Langley Park** Dur
93 H3 **Langley Street** Norfk
76 C7 **Langley Upper Green** Essex
20 D5 **Langney** E Susx
115 L4 **Langold** Notts
9 J7 **Langore** Cnwll
26 B6 **Langport** Somset
103 L3 **Langrick** Lincs
39 H6 **Langridge** BaNES
147 K5 **Langrigg** Cumb
30 B6 **Langrish** Hants
114 E2 **Langsett** Barns
185 G5 **Langside** P & K
132 C2 **Langthorne** N York
132 F6 **Langthorpe** N York
140 C6 **Langthwaite** N York
134 F6 **Langtoft** E R Yk
89 G2 **Langtoft** Lincs
140 F4 **Langton** Dur
118 C7 **Langton** Lincs
118 E7 **Langton** Lincs
134 C6 **Langton** N York
117 J6 **Langton by Wragby** Lincs
32 F5 **Langton Green** Kent
14 C6 **Langton Herring** Dorset
15 J6 **Langton Matravers** Dorset
10 C2 **Langtree** Devon
148 F7 **Langwathby** Cumb
227 K4 **Langwell House** Highld
117 H6 **Langworth** Lincs
5 H3 **Lanhydrock House & Gardens** Cnwll
5 G3 **Lanivet** Cnwll
5 H2 **Lank** Cnwll
5 G4 **Lanlivery** Cnwll
3 J4 **Lanner** Cnwll
5 J4 **Lanreath** Cnwll
5 J5 **Lansallos** Cnwll
8 E7 **Lanteglos** Cnwll
5 J5 **Lanteglos Highway** Cnwll
167 J5 **Lanton** Border
168 D3 **Lanton** Nthumb
11 H3 **Lapford** Devon
160 C1 **Laphroaig** Ag & B
84 F2 **Lapley** Staffs
71 L1 **Lapworth** Warwks
190 E6 **Larachbeg** Highld
176 B3 **Larbert** Falk
216 B7 **Largie** Abers
172 F2 **Largiemore** Ag & B
187 H5 **Largoward** Fife
173 L6 **Largs** N Ayrs
162 D5 **Largybeg** N Ayrs
162 D4 **Largymore** N Ayrs
173 L4 **Larkfield** Inver
33 J2 **Larkfield** Kent
175 K7 **Larkhall** S Lans
28 C3 **Larkhill** Wilts
92 B5 **Larling** Norfk
140 C4 **Lartington** Dur
30 A3 **Lasham** Hants
99 K2 **Lask Edge** Staffs
186 B8 **Lassodie** Fife
177 J5 **Lasswade** Mdloth
133 L2 **Lastingham** N York
61 L7 **Latchingdon** Essex
6 B2 **Latchley** Cnwll
74 C5 **Lathbury** M Keyn
227 L2 **Latheron** Highld

227 L3 **Latheronwheel** Highld
187 H5 **Lathones** Fife
59 G7 **Latimer** Bucks
38 F4 **Latteridge** S Glos
27 G6 **Lattiford** Somset
40 C2 **Latton** Wilts
178 C8 **Lauder** Border
50 C4 **Laugharne** Carmth
116 D6 **Laughterton** Lincs
20 A3 **Laughton** E Susx
87 J5 **Laughton** Leics
116 D3 **Laughton** Lincs
103 H6 **Laughton** Lincs
115 K4 **Laughton-en-le-Morthen** Rothm
9 H4 **Launcells** Cnwll
9 J7 **Launceston** Cnwll
57 L4 **Launton** Oxon
197 H3 **Laurencekirk** Abers
146 B3 **Laurieston** D & G
176 B3 **Laurieston** Falk
74 D4 **Lavendon** M Keyn
77 K5 **Lavenham** Suffk
37 J6 **Lavernock** V Glam
148 E3 **Laversdale** Cumb
28 D5 **Laverstock** Wilts
29 J2 **Laverstoke** Hants
71 J7 **Laverton** Gloucs
132 C5 **Laverton** N York
27 H2 **Laverton** Somset
98 A2 **Lavister** Wrexhm
175 L7 **Law** S Lans
175 L7 **Law Hill** S Lans
193 L1 **Lawers** P & K
62 C2 **Lawford** Essex
25 H4 **Lawford** Somset
186 A3 **Lawgrove** P & K
9 J7 **Lawhitton** Cnwll
130 E6 **Lawkland** N York
49 H6 **Lawrenny** Pembks
77 K4 **Lawshall** Suffk
232 H3 **Laxay** W Isls
232 f2 **Laxdale** W Isls
237 d4 **Laxey** IOM
93 G8 **Laxfield** Suffk
228 C6 **Laxford Bridge** Highld
235 d4 **Laxo** Shet
125 J5 **Laxton** E R Yk
88 D4 **Laxton** Nhants
116 B7 **Laxton** Notts
122 F3 **Laycock** Brad
61 M4 **Layer Breton** Essex
61 L4 **Layer Marney** Essex
62 A4 **Layer-de-la-Haye** Essex
78 B6 **Laytham** Suffk
13 K2 **Laymore** Dorset
125 H3 **Laytham** E R Yk
147 M4 **Laythes** Cumb
148 F6 **Lazonby** Cumb
236 c4 **Le Bigard** Guern
236 c4 **Le Bourg** Guern
236 e8 **Le Bourg** Jersey
236 c3 **Le Gron** Guern
236 d8 **Le Haguais** Jersey
236 d8 **Le Hocq** Jersey
236 c4 **Le Villocq** Guern
101 G2 **Lea** Derbys
54 F4 **Lea** Herefs
116 D4 **Lea** Lincs
83 G5 **Lea** Shrops
39 L3 **Lea** Wilts
86 B5 **Lea Marston** Warwks
212 F5 **Leachkin** Highld
177 H7 **Leadburn** Mdloth
60 F5 **Leaden Roding** Essex
102 F3 **Leadenham** Lincs
150 E5 **Leadgate** Dur
165 G6 **Leadhills** S Lans
56 F5 **Leafield** Oxon

59 H4 **Leagrave** Luton
104 C3 **Leake Common Side** Lincs
142 F5 **Lealholm** N York
209 H3 **Lealt** Highld
72 F2 **Leamington Hastings** Warwks
72 D2 **Leamington Spa** Warwks
20 C4 **Leap Cross** E Susx
129 K3 **Leasgill** Cumb
103 H3 **Leasingham** Lincs
141 G2 **Leasingthorne** Dur
31 K1 **Leatherhead** Surrey
123 J2 **Leathley** N York
98 C8 **Leaton** Shrops
34 D4 **Leaveland** Kent
77 L6 **Leavenheath** Suffk
134 C6 **Leavening** N York
45 H7 **Leaves Green** Gt Lon
135 G3 **Lebberston** N York
56 E7 **Lechlade** Gloucs
170 E5 **Lecht Gruinart** Ag & B
130 C4 **Leck** Lancs
193 L7 **Leckbuie** P & K
29 G4 **Leckford** Hants
73 K6 **Leckhampstead** Bucks
41 H5 **Leckhampstead** W Berk
41 H5 **Leckhampstead Thicket** W Berk
55 L4 **Leckhampton** Gloucs
220 F4 **Leckmelm** Highld
126 C2 **Leconfield** E R Yk
191 H8 **Ledaig** Ag & B
58 E4 **Ledburn** Bucks
70 C6 **Ledbury** Herefs
69 H4 **Ledgemoor** Herefs
224 F6 **Ledmore Junction** Highld
124 C4 **Ledsham** Leeds
124 C5 **Ledston** Leeds
57 H3 **Ledwell** Oxon
23 H3 **Lee** Devon
45 H5 **Lee** Gt Lon
98 D6 **Lee Brockhurst** Shrops
46 B3 **Lee Chapel** Essex
58 E6 **Lee Clump** Bucks
6 E5 **Lee Mill** Devon
17 G3 **Lee-on-the-Solent** Hants
83 J4 **Leebotwood** Shrops
128 F5 **Leece** Cumb
33 L3 **Leeds** Kent
123 K4 **Leeds** Leeds
123 J3 **Leeds Bradford Airport** Leeds
33 L3 **Leeds Castle** Kent
3 G4 **Leedstown** Cnwll
99 M2 **Leek** Staffs
72 C2 **Leek Wootton** Warwks
132 D2 **Leeming** N York
132 D2 **Leeming Bar** N York
100 E5 **Lees** Derbys
113 L2 **Lees** Oldham
100 E5 **Lees Green** Derbys
87 L2 **Leesthorpe** Leics
97 K1 **Leeswood** Flints
186 C3 **Leetown** P & K
112 F6 **Leftwich** Ches
118 E5 **Legbourne** Lincs
167 J2 **Legerwood** Border
42 F5 **Legoland** W & M
117 J4 **Legsby** Lincs
87 H3 **Leicester** C Leic
87 G3 **Leicester Forest East** Leics
14 C2 **Leigh** Dorset
55 K3 **Leigh** Gloucs

32 F4 **Leigh** Kent
31 J3 **Leigh** Surrey
112 F2 **Leigh** Wigan
40 B3 **Leigh** Wilts
70 D4 **Leigh** Worcs
46 D4 **Leigh Beck** Essex
39 K5 **Leigh Delamere** Wilts
34 B7 **Leigh Green** Kent
175 H7 **Leigh Knoweglass** S Lans
15 J3 **Leigh Park** Dorset
70 D4 **Leigh Sinton** Worcs
27 G3 **Leigh upon Mendip** Somset
38 E6 **Leigh Woods** N Som
46 D3 **Leigh-on-Sea** Sthend
85 J3 **Leighswood** W Mids
39 J3 **Leighterton** Gloucs
82 E3 **Leighton** Powys
84 B3 **Leighton** Shrops
89 G7 **Leighton Bromswold** Cambs
58 F3 **Leighton Buzzard** Beds
69 J2 **Leinthall Earls** Herefs
69 J1 **Leinthall Starkes** Herefs
83 H8 **Leintwardine** Herefs
87 G5 **Leire** Leics
79 J3 **Leiston** Suffk
195 L7 **Leitfie** P & K
177 H3 **Leith** C Edin
168 B1 **Leitholm** Border
2 F4 **Lelant** Cnwll
126 F4 **Lelley** E R Yk
168 B3 **Lempitlaw** Border
232 f3 **Lemreway** W Isls
59 L5 **Lemsford** Herts
71 J5 **Lenchwick** Worcs
152 D4 **Lendalfoot** S Ayrs
184 C6 **Lendrick** Stirlg
217 L6 **Lendrum Terrace** Abers
34 B4 **Lenham** Kent
34 B5 **Lenham Heath** Kent
202 D1 **Lenie** Highld
168 C2 **Lennel** Border
146 A5 **Lennox Plunton** D & G
175 H3 **Lennoxtown** E Duns
101 K5 **Lenton** C Nott
103 G6 **Lenton** Lincs
106 D8 **Lenwade** Norfk
175 H4 **Lenzie** E Duns
205 L4 **Leochel-Cushnie** Abers
69 K3 **Leominster** Herefs
55 J7 **Leonard Stanley** Gloucs
236 b6 **Leoville** Jersey
208 B4 **Lephin** Highld
134 B7 **Leppington** N York
123 J7 **Lepton** Kirk
5 J4 **Lerryn** Cnwll
235 d6 **Lerwick** Shet
236 b3 **Les Arquets** Guern
236 d3 **Les Hubits** Guern
236 c3 **Les Lohiers** Guern
236 c4 **Les Murchez** Guern
236 c4 **Les Nicolles** Guern
236 d2 **Les Quartiers** Guern
236 b7 **Les Quennevais** Jersey
236 b3 **Les Sages** Guern
236 c4 **Les Villets** Guern
169 J6 **Lesbury** Nthumb
206 B1 **Leslie** Abers
186 D6 **Leslie** Fife
164 F2 **Lesmahagow** S Lans
8 F6 **Lesnewth** Cnwll
107 H6 **Lessingham** Norfk
147 L5 **Lessonhall** Cumb
144 B3 **Leswalt** D & G

43 J2 **Letchmore Heath** Herts
59 L2 **Letchworth** Herts
41 G4 **Letcombe Bassett** Oxon
41 G3 **Letcombe Regis** Oxon
196 E6 **Letham** Angus
167 K7 **Letham** Border
176 B2 **Letham** Falk
186 E4 **Letham** Fife
197 G7 **Letham Grange** Angus
195 H7 **Lethendy** P & K
206 B2 **Lethenty** Abers
216 F6 **Lethenty** Abers
78 F3 **Letheringham** Suffk
106 C5 **Letheringsett** Norfk
219 L6 **Letterewe** Highld
200 D2 **Letterfearn** Highld
201 K6 **Letterfinlay Lodge Hotel** Highld
199 M7 **Lettermorar** Highld
220 F4 **Letters** Highld
165 H5 **Lettershaw** S Lans
48 F2 **Letterston** Pembks
204 C2 **Lettoch** Highld
214 D7 **Lettoch** Highld
69 G5 **Letton** Herefs
59 M5 **Letty Green** Herts
115 K4 **Letwell** Rothm
187 G3 **Leuchars** Fife
232 f3 **Leumrabhagh** W Isls
232 f3 **Leurbost** W Isls
84 F1 **Levedale** Staffs
60 D3 **Level's Green** Essex
126 D2 **Leven** E R Yk
186 F7 **Leven** Fife
129 K3 **Levens** Cumb
60 B4 **Levens Green** Herts
113 K3 **Levenshulme** Manch
235 c7 **Levenwick** Shet
232 d5 **Leverburgh** W Isls
90 C2 **Leverington** Cambs
59 H6 **Leverstock Green** Herts
104 C3 **Leverton** Lincs
78 F6 **Levington** Suffk
134 C2 **Levisham** N York
56 F6 **Lew** Oxon
9 H8 **Lewannick** Cnwll
10 C7 **Lewdown** Devon
19 L4 **Lewes** E Susx
48 F3 **Leweston** Pembks
45 G5 **Lewisham** Gt Lon
212 D8 **Lewiston** Highld
42 B2 **Lewknor** Oxon
34 C3 **Lewson Street** Kent
10 C7 **Lewtrenchard** Devon
62 A3 **Lexden** Essex
25 K4 **Lexworthy** Somset
59 G7 **Ley Hill** Bucks
33 H2 **Leybourne** Kent
131 L2 **Leyburn** N York
59 K3 **Leygreen** Herts
121 H6 **Leyland** Lancs
206 E3 **Leylodge** Abers
217 J4 **Leys** Abers
195 K8 **Leys** Angus
196 C6 **Leys of Cossans** Angus
47 G6 **Leysdown-on-Sea** Kent
196 F6 **Leysmill** Angus
69 L2 **Leysters** Herefs
45 G3 **Leyton** Gt Lon
45 H3 **Leytonstone** Gt Lon
5 M1 **Lezant** Cnwll
237 d3 **Lezayre** IOM
215 G3 **Lhanbryde** Moray
52 F3 **Libanus** Powys

165 J2 **Libberton** S Lans
177 J4 **Liberton** C Edin
85 K2 **Lichfield** Staffs
85 H7 **Lickey** Worcs
85 H8 **Lickey End** Worcs
30 F6 **Lickfold** W Susx
190 F4 **Liddesdale** Highld
40 E4 **Liddington** Swindn
77 G3 **Lidgate** Suffk
74 E6 **Lidlington** Beds
186 E2 **Liff** Angus
85 J7 **Lifford** Birm
9 K7 **Lifton** Devon
9 K7 **Liftondown** Devon
72 D4 **Lighthorne** Warwks
72 D4 **Lighthorne Heath** Warwks
42 F7 **Lightwater** Surrey
87 H7 **Lilbourne** Nhants
84 D1 **Lilleshall** Wrekin
59 J3 **Lilley** Herts
167 H4 **Lilliesleaf** Border
73 K6 **Lillingstone Dayrell** Bucks
73 K6 **Lillingstone Lovell** Bucks
26 F8 **Lillington** Dorset
15 K4 **Lilliput** Poole
25 J3 **Lilstock** Somset
59 H3 **Limbury** Luton
55 J2 **Lime Street** Worcs
175 J7 **Limekilnburn** S Lans
176 E2 **Limekilns** Fife
176 B4 **Limerigg** Falk
16 E6 **Limerstone** IOW
26 D6 **Limington** Somset
164 C4 **Limmerhaugh** E Ayrs
93 H3 **Limpenhoe** Norfk
39 H7 **Limpley Stoke** Wilts
32 D3 **Limpsfield** Surrey
32 D3 **Limpsfield Chart** Surrey
101 K3 **Linby** Notts
30 E5 **Linchmere** W Susx
155 G6 **Lincluden** D & G
116 F7 **Lincoln** Lincs
70 E2 **Lincomb** Worcs
128 F4 **Lindal in Furness** Cumb
129 J4 **Lindale** Cumb
32 C7 **Lindfield** W Susx
30 D4 **Lindford** Hants
123 G6 **Lindley** Kirk
123 J2 **Lindley Green** N York
70 C2 **Lindridge** Worcs
61 G3 **Lindsell** Essex
77 L5 **Lindsey** Suffk
78 B5 **Lindsey Tye** Suffk
142 E4 **Lingdale** R & Cl
69 G2 **Lingen** Herefs
32 C4 **Lingfield** Surrey
93 H2 **Lingwood** Norfk
218 B7 **Linicro** Highld
55 J2 **Linkend** Worcs
41 G8 **Linkenholt** Hants
5 L2 **Linkinhorne** Cnwll
177 J1 **Linktown** Fife
214 F3 **Linkwood** Moray
83 G5 **Linley** Shrops
70 C4 **Linley Green** Herefs
84 C4 **Linleygreen** Shrops
176 D3 **Linlithgow** W Loth
222 D2 **Linsidemore** Highld
58 E3 **Linslade** Beds
93 G7 **Linstead Parva** Suffk
148 D4 **Linstock** Cumb
85 H8 **Linthurst** Worcs
123 G7 **Linthwaite** Kirk
179 H6 **Lintlaw** Border
215 L2 **Lintmill** Moray
168 B4 **Linton** Border
76 E5 **Linton** Cambs
86 C1 **Linton** Derbys

54 F3 **Linton** Herefs
33 K3 **Linton** Kent
124 B2 **Linton** Leeds
131 J6 **Linton** N York
54 F3 **Linton Hill** Gloucs
133 G7 **Linton-on-Ouse** N York
117 J4 **Linwood** Lincs
174 E5 **Linwood** Rens
233 b7 **Lionacleit** W Isls
232 g1 **Lional** W Isls
30 D5 **Liphook** Hants
111 J3 **Liscard** Wirral
24 D5 **Liscombe** Somset
5 K3 **Liskeard** Cnwll
30 C5 **Liss** Hants
135 H7 **Lissett** E R Yk
117 J5 **Lissington** Lincs
37 J4 **Lisvane** Cardif
37 M3 **Liswerry** Newpt
105 L8 **Litcham** Norfk
73 J4 **Litchborough** Nhants
29 J2 **Litchfield** Hants
111 K2 **Litherland** Sefton
75 K6 **Litlington** Cambs
20 B5 **Litlington** E Susx
76 D5 **Little Abington** Cambs
88 D8 **Little Addington** Nhants
145 J5 **Little Airies** D & G
71 K3 **Little Alne** Warwks
111 J1 **Little Altcar** Sefton
60 B5 **Little Amwell** Herts
139 G5 **Little Asby** Cumb
85 K4 **Little Aston** Staffs
142 C5 **Little Ayton** N York
61 J6 **Little Baddow** Essex
39 J4 **Little Badminton** S Glos
148 A4 **Little Bampton** Cumb
61 G2 **Little Bardfield** Essex
75 H3 **Little Barford** Beds
106 D5 **Little Barningham** Norfk
56 D5 **Little Barrington** Gloucs
112 C7 **Little Barrow** Ches
158 C6 **Little Bavington** Nthumb
40 F7 **Little Bedwyn** Wilts
62 D3 **Little Bentley** Essex
59 M6 **Little Berkhamsted** Herts
74 B3 **Little Billing** Nhants
58 F4 **Little Bilington** Beds
54 D2 **Little Birch** Herefs
78 D5 **Little Blakenham** Suffk
148 E7 **Little Blencow** Cumb
31 G7 **Little Bognor** W Susx
100 F2 **Little Bolehill** Derbys
113 G4 **Little Bollington** Ches
31 J1 **Little Bookham** Surrey
72 F5 **Little Bourton** Oxon
77 G4 **Little Bradley** Suffk
61 K5 **Little Braxted** Essex
196 F4 **Little Brechin** Angus
58 E2 **Little Brickhill** M Keyn
73 J2 **Little Brington** Nhants
62 C3 **Little Bromley** Essex
112 E7 **Little Budworth** Ches
46 A2 **Little Burstead** Essex
103 G8 **Little Bytham** Lincs
118 E4 **Little Carlton** Lincs
88 E2 **Little Casterton** Rutlnd

118 E5 **Little Cawthorpe** Lincs
43 G2 **Little Chalfont** Bucks
34 C5 **Little Chart** Kent
76 D6 **Little Chesterford** Essex
27 M2 **Little Cheverell** Wilts
76 B6 **Little Chishill** Cambs
62 E4 **Little Clacton** Essex
136 E2 **Little Clifton** Cumb
71 G5 **Little Comberton** Worcs
20 E4 **Little Common** E Susx
56 E3 **Little Compton** Warwks
77 K6 **Little Cornard** Suffk
69 L4 **Little Cowarne** Herefs
40 F2 **Little Coxwell** Oxon
132 C2 **Little Crakehall** N York
91 K4 **Little Cressingham** Norfk
111 K2 **Little Crosby** Sefton
100 D5 **Little Cubley** Derbys
87 L2 **Little Dalby** Leics
217 K5 **Little Dens** Abers
54 D2 **Little Dewchurch** Herefs
76 F3 **Little Ditton** Cambs
90 D6 **Little Downham** Cambs
134 F7 **Little Driffield** E R Yk
91 K2 **Little Dunham** Norfk
195 G2 **Little Dunkeld** P & K
61 G4 **Little Dunmow** Essex
28 C5 **Little Durnford** Wilts
60 F3 **Little Easton** Essex
101 G4 **Little Eaton** Derbys
92 B4 **Little Ellingham** Norfk
73 H3 **Little Everdon** Nhants
75 L4 **Little Eversden** Cambs
56 E7 **Little Faringdon** Oxon
132 D2 **Little Fencote** N York
124 D4 **Little Fenton** N York
91 K2 **Little Fransham** Norfk
59 G5 **Little Gaddesden** Herts
79 H3 **Little Glemham** Suffk
55 G3 **Little Gorsley** Herefs
75 J4 **Little Gransden** Cambs
27 G2 **Little Green** Somset
118 D3 **Little Grimsby** Lincs
60 C4 **Little Hadham** Herts
103 J4 **Little Hale** Lincs
101 J4 **Little Hallam** Derbys
60 D4 **Little Hallingbury** Essex
74 C1 **Little Harrowden** Nhants
57 M7 **Little Haseley** Oxon
126 E2 **Little Hatfield** E R Yk
48 E5 **Little Haven** Pembks
85 K3 **Little Hay** Staffs
100 A7 **Little Haywood** Staffs
86 D6 **Little Heath** Covtry
69 L2 **Little Hereford** Herefs
62 A2 **Little Horkesley** Essex
60 C3 **Little Hormead** Herts
19 M3 **Little Horsted** E Susx
123 H4 **Little Horton** Brad
58 C2 **Little Horwood** Bucks

115	H1	Little Houghton Barns
74	B3	Little Houghton Nhants
114	D5	Little Hucklow Derbys
133	G4	Little Hutton N York
74	C2	Little Irchester Nhants
27	H3	Little Keyford Somset
58	D6	Little Kimble Bucks
72	D4	Little Kineton Warwks
58	E7	Little Kingshill Bucks
146	E3	Little Knox D & G
137	J6	Little Langdale Cumb
28	B4	Little Langford Wilts
9	K4	Little Lashbrook Devon
112	F6	Little Leigh Ches
61	H5	Little Leighs Essex
121	L8	Little Lever Bolton
74	B5	Little Linford M Keyn
26	C6	Little Load Somset
20	C2	Little London E Susx
60	D3	Little London Essex
29	G2	Little London Hants
41	L8	Little London Hants
114	D6	Little Longstone Derbys
70	D6	Little Malvern Worcs
77	J7	Little Maplestead Essex
70	C7	Little Marcle Herefs
42	E3	Little Marlow Bucks
105	J7	Little Massingham Norfk
92	E3	Little Melton Norfk
53	L7	Little Mill Mons
57	L7	Little Milton Oxon
58	F7	Little Missenden Bucks
139	H5	Little Musgrave Cumb
98	B8	Little Ness Shrops
49	G2	Little Newcastle Pembks
140	E4	Little Newsham Dur
26	C7	Little Norton Somset
62	F3	Little Oakley Essex
88	C6	Little Oakley Nhants
84	E1	Little Onn Staffs
148	C4	Little Orton Cumb
86	B6	Little Packington Warwks
75	H3	Little Paxton Cambs
4	E2	Little Petherick Cnwll
93	G2	Little Plumstead Norfk
102	F6	Little Ponton Lincs
73	H4	Little Preston Nhants
89	J7	Little Raveley Cambs
125	J6	Little Reedness E R Yk
132	F8	Little Ribston N York
56	D4	Little Rissington Gloucs
56	F3	Little Rollright Oxon
106	A6	Little Ryburgh Norfk
148	F7	Little Salkeld Cumb
76	F7	Little Sampford Essex
111	K7	Little Saughall Ches
77	H2	Little Saxham Suffk
212	B3	Little Scatwell Highld
133	G5	Little Sessay N York
76	C4	Little Shelford Cambs
11	K5	Little Silver Devon
120	E3	Little Singleton Lancs
125	G3	Little Skipwith N York

124	D6	Little Smeaton N York
106	A6	Little Snoring Norfk
39	H4	Little Sodbury S Glos
29	G5	Little Somborne Hants
39	L4	Little Somerford Wilts
99	G6	Little Soudley Shrops
141	J3	Little Stainton Darltn
112	B6	Little Stanney Ches
75	G3	Little Staughton Beds
118	F8	Little Steeping Lincs
78	D3	Little Stonham Suffk
87	J4	Little Stretton Leics
83	J5	Little Stretton Shrops
138	E4	Little Strickland Cumb
89	H7	Little Stukeley Cambs
99	J6	Little Sugnall Staffs
158	B6	Little Swinburne Nthumb
146	C4	Little Sypland D & G
57	G3	Little Tew Oxon
61	L4	Little Tey Essex
90	D7	Little Thetford Cambs
151	K6	Little Thorpe Dur
77	G4	Little Thurlow Green Suffk
45	L4	Little Thurrock Thurr
10	D2	Little Torrington Devon
121	K4	Little Town Lancs
128	F5	Little Urswick Cumb
46	F3	Little Wakering Essex
76	D6	Little Walden Essex
77	K5	Little Waldingfield Suffk
105	M5	Little Walsingham Norfk
61	H5	Little Waltham Essex
55	M2	Little Washbourne Gloucs
126	B4	Little Weighton E R Yk
88	D5	Little Weldon Nhants
78	C6	Little Wenham Suffk
84	B3	Little Wenlock Wrekin
26	F6	Little Weston Somset
17	H4	Little Whitefield IOW
76	D3	Little Wilbraham Cambs
55	K5	Little Witcombe Gloucs
70	D2	Little Witley Worcs
41	K2	Little Wittenham Oxon
72	C7	Little Wolford Warwks
44	F7	Little Woodcote Surrey
77	G5	Little Wratting Suffk
74	D2	Little Wymington Beds
59	K3	Little Wymondley Herts
85	H4	Little Wyrley Staffs
77	H6	Little Yeldham Essex
116	D5	Littleborough Notts
122	D7	Littleborough Rochdl
35	G3	Littlebourne Kent
14	B5	Littlebredy Dorset
212	F4	Littleburn Highld
76	D6	Littlebury Essex
76	C6	Littlebury Green Essex
54	F5	Littledean Gloucs
23	G6	Littleham Devon

12	D6	Littleham Devon
18	D5	Littlehampton W Susx
31	K5	Littlehaven W Susx
7	J4	Littlehempston Devon
205	H6	Littlemill Abers
213	L4	Littlemill Highld
57	K7	Littlemore Oxon
101	G5	Littleover C Derb
90	E6	Littleport Cambs
21	L2	Littlestone-on-Sea Kent
87	G4	Littlethorpe Leics
132	E5	Littlethorpe N York
196	B6	Littleton Angus
112	C7	Littleton Ches
146	B4	Littleton D & G
29	J5	Littleton Hants
26	C5	Littleton Somset
43	H6	Littleton Surrey
39	J4	Littleton Drew Wilts
27	M2	Littleton Pannell Wilts
38	E3	Littleton-on-Severn S Glos
151	H6	Littletown Dur
42	D4	Littlewick Green W & M
40	F2	Littleworth Oxon
99	L7	Littleworth Staffs
70	F4	Littleworth Worcs
61	H4	Littley Green Essex
26	E1	Litton BaNES
114	D6	Litton Derbys
131	G5	Litton N York
14	A4	Litton Cheney Dorset
232	f3	Liurbost W Isls
111	K4	Liverpool Lpool
123	J5	Liversedge Kirk
7	J2	Liverton Devon
142	F4	Liverton R & Cl
176	E5	Livingston W Loth
176	E5	Livingston Village W Loth
7	G5	Lixton Devon
111	G7	Lixwm Flints
3	J8	Lizard Cnwll
95	G4	Llanaelhaearn Gwynd
66	F1	Llanafan Cerdgn
109	G4	Llanallgo IOA
97	J6	Llanarmon Dyffryn Ceiriog Wrexhm
97	J2	Llanarmon-yn-Ial Denbgs
65	L3	Llanarth Cerdgn
54	B5	Llanarth Mons
51	G2	Llanarthne Carmth
110	F5	Llanasa Flints
80	E7	Llanbadarn Fawr Cerdgn
82	C7	Llanbadarn Fynydd Powys
54	B7	Llanbadoc Mons
38	B3	Llanbeder Newpt
95	K6	Llanbedr Gwynd
53	K4	Llanbedr Powys
97	H1	Llanbedr-Dyffryn-Clwyd Denbgs
109	L7	Llanbedr-y-Cennin Conwy
109	G5	Llanbedrgoch IOA
94	F6	Llanbedrog Gwynd
95	K1	Llanberis Gwynd
37	G6	Llanbethery V Glam
82	C8	Llanbister Powys
36	F5	Llanblethian V Glam
49	L3	Llanboidy Carmth
37	J3	Llanbradach Caerph
81	J3	Llanbrynmair Powys
37	G6	Llancadle V Glam
37	G6	Llancarfan V Glam
54	D4	Llancloudy Herefs

37	J5	Llandaff Cardif
95	K6	Llandanwg Gwynd
109	G7	Llanddaniel-fab IOA
51	G3	Llanddarog Carmth
66	D1	Llanddeiniol Cerdgn
109	H7	Llanddeiniolen Gwynd
96	F5	Llandderfel Gwynd
108	D4	Llanddeusant IOA
53	G2	Llanddew Powys
50	F7	Llanddewi Swans
66	F4	Llanddewi Brefi Cerdgn
53	M5	Llanddewi Rhydderch Mons
49	K4	Llanddewi Velfrey Pembks
68	C2	Llanddewi Ystradenni Powys
109	M8	Llanddoget Conwy
109	H5	Llanddona IOA
50	B3	Llanddowror Carmth
110	C6	Llanddulas Conwy
95	K7	Llanddwywe Gwynd
109	G5	Llanddyfnan IOA
53	H3	Llandefaelog-Trer-Graig Powys
68	C7	Llandefalle Powys
109	H6	Llandegfan IOA
97	J3	Llandegla Denbgs
68	D2	Llandegley Powys
37	M2	Llandegveth Mons
51	J2	Llandeilo Carmth
68	C5	Llandeilo Graban Powys
48	E3	Llandeloy Pembks
54	B7	Llandenny Mons
38	B3	Llandevaud Newpt
38	B3	Llandevenny Mons
82	B5	Llandinam Powys
49	J3	Llandissilio Pembks
54	D7	Llandogo Mons
36	F6	Llandough V Glam
37	J5	Llandough V Glam
67	G7	Llandovery Carmth
36	E5	Llandow V Glam
66	F6	Llandre Carmth
80	E6	Llandre Cerdgn
49	J2	Llandre Isaf Pembks
97	G5	Llandrillo Denbgs
110	B5	Llandrillo-yn-Rhos Conwy
68	B3	Llandrindod Wells Powys
97	L8	Llandrinio Powys
109	L5	Llandudno Conwy
109	M6	Llandudno Junction Conwy
94	E5	Llandudwen Gwynd
67	J6	Llandulas Powys
95	H2	Llandwrog Gwynd
51	J3	Llandybie Carmth
50	E3	Llandyfaelog Carmth
65	K6	Llandyfriog Cerdgn
109	H7	Llandygai Gwynd
65	H5	Llandygwydd Cerdgn
110	F8	Llandyrnog Denbgs
82	E4	Llandyssil Powys
65	L6	Llandysul Cerdgn
37	K4	Llanedeyrn Cardif
68	B6	Llaneglwys Powys
80	D3	Llanegryn Gwynd
51	G2	Llanegwad Carmth
108	F3	Llaneilian IOA
110	B6	Llanelian-yn-Rhos Conwy
97	H3	Llanelidan Denbgs
68	D7	Llanelieu Powys
53	L5	Llanellen Mons
51	G5	Llanelli Carmth
96	A8	Llanelltyd Gwynd
68	B4	Llanelwedd Powys
95	K7	Llanenddwyn Gwynd

94 E6 **Llanengan** Gwynd
108 E5 **Llanerchymedd** IOA
82 B2 **Llanerfyl** Powys
108 D5 **Llanfachraeth** IOA
96 B7 **Llanfachreth** Gwynd
108 D6 **Llanfaelog** IOA
94 D6 **Llanfaelrhys** Gwynd
108 D4 **Llanfaethlu** IOA
95 K6 **Llanfair** Gwynd
82 C3 **Llanfair Caereinion** Powys
66 E4 **Llanfair Clydogau** Cerdgn
97 H2 **Llanfair Dyffryn Clwyd** Denbgs
109 G6 **Llanfair P G** IOA
110 C7 **Llanfair Talhaiarn** Conwy
82 E7 **Llanfair Waterdine** Shrops
109 G7 **Llanfair-is-gaer** Gwynd
108 F7 **Llanfair-y-Cwmwd** IOA
108 C6 **Llanfair-yn-Neubwll** IOA
109 K6 **Llanfairfechan** Conwy
108 D4 **Llanfairynghornwy** IOA
49 K4 **Llanfallteg** Carmth
49 K4 **Llanfallteg West** Carmth
80 D7 **Llanfarian** Cerdgn
97 J7 **Llanfechain** Powys
108 E3 **Llanfechell** IOA
97 J1 **Llanferres** Denbgs
96 F3 **Llanfihangel Glyn Myfyr** Conwy
67 K7 **Llanfihangel Nant Bran** Powys
68 D2 **Llanfihangel Rhydithon** Powys
38 C3 **Llanfihangel Rogiet** Mons
108 D6 **Llanfihangel yn Nhowyn** IOA
66 B6 **Llanfihangel-ar-Arth** Carmth
80 F7 **Llanfihangel-y-Creuddyn** Cerdgn
95 K5 **Llanfihangel-y-traethau** Gwynd
82 C1 **Llanfihangel-yng-Ngwynfa** Powys
53 H2 **Llanfilo** Powys
53 L5 **Llanfoist** Mons
96 E5 **Llanfor** Gwynd
37 L2 **Llanfrechfa** Torfn
53 G3 **Llanfrynach** Powys
97 H2 **Llanfwrog** Denbgs
108 C5 **Llanfwrog** IOA
97 H8 **Llanfyllin** Powys
66 D8 **Llanfynydd** Carmth
97 L2 **Llanfynydd** Flints
49 L2 **Llanfyrnach** Pembks
81 L2 **Llangadfan** Powys
66 F8 **Llangadog** Powys
108 E7 **Llangadwaladr** IOA
108 F7 **Llangaffo** IOA
67 K5 **Llangammarch Wells** Powys
36 E5 **Llangan** V Glam
54 D4 **Llangarron** Herefs
51 H2 **Llangathen** Carmth
53 K4 **Llangattock** Powys
54 A4 **Llangattock Lingoed** Mons
97 J7 **Llangedwyn** Powys
108 F6 **Llangefni** IOA
36 E3 **Llangeinor** Brdgnd
108 F7 **Llangeinwen** IOA
66 E3 **Llangeitho** Cerdgn

65 L6 **Llangeler** Carmth
80 D3 **Llangelynin** Gwynd
50 F3 **Llangendeirne** Carmth
51 H5 **Llangennech** Carmth
50 E7 **Llangennith** Swans
110 B7 **Llangenny** Conwy
94 E6 **Llangian** Gwynd
64 C7 **Llangloffan** Pembks
49 K3 **Llanglydwen** Carmth
109 J5 **Llangoed** IOA
97 K4 **Llangollen** Denbgs
49 J3 **Llangolman** Pembks
53 H3 **Llangors** Powys
96 D6 **Llangower** Gwynd
65 K4 **Llangranog** Cerdgn
108 F6 **Llangristiolus** IOA
54 D4 **Llangrove** Herefs
68 E1 **Llangunllo** Powys
50 E2 **Llangunnor** Carmth
81 K7 **Llangurig** Powys
96 F4 **Llangwm** Conwy
54 B7 **Llangwm** Mons
49 G5 **Llangwm** Pembks
54 B7 **Llangwm-isaf** Mons
94 D6 **Llangwnnadl** Gwynd
66 D1 **Llangwyryfon** Cerdgn
66 E4 **Llangybi** Cerdgn
95 G4 **Llangybi** Gwynd
38 A2 **Llangybi** Mons
110 F8 **Llangynhafal** Denbgs
53 J4 **Llangynidr** Powys
50 B2 **Llangynin** Carmth
50 D3 **Llangynog** Carmth
97 G7 **Llangynog** Powys
36 D3 **Llangynwyd** Brdgnd
53 H3 **Llanhamlach** Powys
36 F4 **Llanharan** Rhondd
36 F4 **Llanharry** Rhondd
38 A2 **Llanhennock** Mons
53 K7 **Llanhilleth** Blae G
81 K6 **Llanidloes** Powys
94 E5 **Llaniestyn** Gwynd
68 E6 **Llanigon** Powys
80 E8 **Llanilar** Cerdgn
36 F4 **Llanilid** Rhondd
65 L3 **Llanina** Cerdgn
37 J4 **Llanishen** Cardif
54 C7 **Llanishen** Mons
109 J7 **Llanllechid** Gwynd
54 B7 **Llanllowell** Mons
82 B3 **Llanllugan** Powys
50 E2 **Llanllwch** Carmth
82 C5 **Llanllwchaiarn** Powys
66 C6 **Llanllwni** Carmth
95 H3 **Llanllyfni** Gwynd
50 F6 **Llanmadoc** Swans
36 F6 **Llanmaes** V Glam
38 B3 **Llanmartin** Newpt
50 B4 **Llanmiloe** Carmth
110 D7 **Llannefydd** Conwy
51 G4 **Llannon** Carmth
94 F5 **Llannor** Gwynd
66 C2 **Llanon** Cerdgn
53 L6 **Llanover** Mons
65 L8 **Llanpumsaint** Carmth
97 H7 **Llanrhaeadr-ym-Mochnant** Powys
48 D2 **Llanrhian** Pembks
50 F6 **Llanrhidian** Swans
96 B1 **Llanrhychwyn** Conwy
108 D4 **Llanrhyddlad** IOA
66 C1 **Llanrhystud** Cerdgn
54 C4 **Llanrothal** Herefs
109 G8 **Llanrug** Gwynd
37 K4 **Llanrumney** Cardif
96 C1 **Llanrwst** Conwy
50 C4 **Llansadurnen** Carmth
66 F7 **Llansadwrn** Carmth
109 H6 **Llansadwrn** IOA

50 E4 **Llansaint** Carmth
51 K6 **Llansamlet** Swans
109 M6 **Llansanffraid Glan Conwy** Conwy
110 C7 **Llansannan** Conwy
53 H4 **Llansantffraed** Powys
67 L2 **Llansantffraed-Cwmdeuddwr** Powys
68 C4 **Llansantffraed-in-Elvel** Powys
66 C2 **Llansantffraid** Cerdgn
97 K7 **Llansantffraid-ym-Mechain** Powys
66 E7 **Llansawel** Carmth
97 K6 **Llansilin** Powys
54 C7 **Llansoy** Mons
52 F3 **Llanspyddid** Powys
48 F6 **Llanstadwell** Pembks
50 D4 **Llansteffan** Carmth
37 L2 **Llantarnam** Torfn
49 K5 **Llanteg** Pembks
53 M5 **Llanthewy Skirrid** Mons
53 L3 **Llanthony** Mons
53 L5 **Llantilio Pertholey** Mons
54 B5 **Llantilio-Crossenny** Mons
38 B2 **Llantrisant** Mons
37 G4 **Llantrisant** Rhondd
37 G6 **Llantrithyd** V Glam
37 G3 **Llantwit Fardre** Rhondd
36 F6 **Llantwit Major** V Glam
96 D6 **Llanuwchllyn** Gwynd
38 B3 **Llanvaches** Newpt
38 C3 **Llanvair Discoed** Mons
54 A5 **Llanvapley** Mons
54 A5 **Llanvetherine** Mons
53 L4 **Llanvihangel Crucorney** Mons
96 F8 **Llanwddyn** Powys
66 C5 **Llanwenog** Cerdgn
38 A3 **Llanwern** Newpt
50 C1 **Llanwinio** Carmth
95 H2 **Llanwnda** Gwynd
64 C6 **Llanwnda** Pembks
55 C5 **Llanwnnen** Cerdgn
82 B5 **Llanwnog** Powys
66 F7 **Llanwrda** Carmth
81 H3 **Llanwrin** Powys
67 L2 **Llanwrthwl** Powys
67 J5 **Llanwrtyd Wells** Powys
82 C4 **Llanwyddelan** Powys
97 K7 **Llanyblodwel** Shrops
50 D3 **Llanybri** Carmth
66 C5 **Llanybydder** Carmth
49 J3 **Llanycefn** Pembks
64 D7 **Llanychaer Bridge** Pembks
96 D8 **Llanymawddwy** Gwynd
97 K7 **Llanymynech** Powys
108 D5 **Llanynghenedl** IOA
110 F8 **Llanynys** Denbgs
68 B3 **Llanyre** Powys
95 H5 **Llanystumdwy** Gwynd
53 H3 **Llanywern** Powys
49 H4 **Llawhaden** Pembks
81 K5 **Llawryglyn** Powys
97 M2 **Llay** Wrexhm
53 H6 **Llechrhyd** Caerph
65 H5 **Llechryd** Cerdgn
66 E1 **Lledrod** Cerdgn
94 E5 **Lleyn Peninsula** Gwynd
94 F4 **Llithfaen** Gwynd

111 G6 **Lloc** Flints
68 D6 **Llowes** Powys
52 F6 **Llwydcoed** Rhondd
82 B1 **Llwydiarth** Powys
66 B3 **Llwyncelyn** Cerdgn
65 L4 **Llwyndafydd** Cerdgn
80 D2 **Llwyngwril** Gwynd
97 K5 **Llwynmawr** Wrexhm
36 F2 **Llwynypia** Rhondd
97 L7 **Llynclys** Shrops
108 E5 **Llynfaes** IOA
49 H3 **Llys-y-fran** Pembks
110 B6 **Llysfaen** Conwy
68 C6 **Llyswen** Powys
36 E5 **Llysworney** V Glam
52 D3 **Llywel** Powys
176 C3 **Loan** Falk
177 J5 **Loanhead** Mdloth
147 G4 **Loaningfoot** D & G
163 J3 **Loans** S Ayrs
10 C7 **Lobhillcross** Devon
233 c8 **Loch Baghasdail** W Isls
233 c6 **Loch Euphoirt** W Isls
184 B6 **Loch Katrine Pier** Stirlg
183 L8 **Loch Lomond**
219 L7 **Loch Maree Hotel** Highld
233 c6 **Loch nam Madadh** W Isls
202 E1 **Loch Ness** Highld
200 B8 **Lochailort** Highld
190 D7 **Lochaline** Highld
144 C4 **Lochans** D & G
155 H6 **Locharbriggs** D & G
182 D4 **Lochavich** Ag & B
183 G2 **Lochawe** Ag & B
233 c8 **Lochboisdale** W Isls
181 J3 **Lochbuie** Ag & B
210 D6 **Lochcarron** Highld
181 L2 **Lochdon** Ag & B
181 L2 **Lochdonhead** Ag & B
172 D3 **Lochead** Ag & B
184 D3 **Lochearnhead** Stirlg
186 F2 **Lochee** C Dund
191 K2 **Locheilside Station** Highld
212 F6 **Lochend** Highld
233 C6 **Locheport** W Isls
154 F7 **Lochfoot** D & G
172 F1 **Lochgair** Ag & B
186 C8 **Lochgelly** Fife
172 E2 **Lochgilphead** Ag & B
183 H6 **Lochgoilhead** Ag & B
186 D5 **Lochieheads** Fife
215 G2 **Lochill** Moray
214 B7 **Lochindorb Lodge** Highld
224 D4 **Lochinver** Highld
211 L2 **Lochluichart** Highld
155 J5 **Lochmaben** D & G
233 C6 **Lochmaddy** W Isls
186 C7 **Lochore** Fife
172 F7 **Lochranza** N Ayrs
197 H4 **Lochside** Abers
155 G6 **Lochside** D & G
213 J4 **Lochside** Highld
152 F6 **Lochton** S Ayrs
196 E4 **Lochty** Angus
187 H5 **Lochty** Fife
190 F5 **Lochuisge** Highld
174 C6 **Lochwinnoch** Rens
155 J3 **Lochwood** D & G
5 G4 **Lockengate** Cnwll
155 K5 **Lockerbie** D & G
40 C6 **Lockeridge** Wilts
28 F6 **Lockerley** Hants
38 A8 **Locking** N Som
112 F3 **Locking Stumps** Warrtn
126 B2 **Lockington** E R Yk
99 G6 **Lockleywood** Shrops

17 G2 **Locks Heath** Hants
45 H6 **Locksbottom** Gt Lon
134 C2 **Lockton** N York
87 L3 **Loddington** Leics
88 B7 **Loddington** Nhants
7 G6 **Loddiswell** Devon
93 H4 **Loddon** Norfk
76 D3 **Lode** Cambs
85 L7 **Lode Heath** Solhll
13 L4 **Loders** Dorset
30 F6 **Lodsworth** W Susx
123 L5 **Lofthouse** Leeds
131 L5 **Lofthouse** N York
123 L5 **Lofthouse Gate** Wakefd
142 F4 **Loftus** R & Cl
164 C5 **Logan** E Ayrs
176 C6 **Loganlea** W Loth
99 G5 **Loggerheads** Staffs
197 H4 **Logie** Angus
186 F4 **Logie** Fife
214 C4 **Logie** Moray
205 K4 **Logie Coldstone** Abers
197 G4 **Logie Pert** Angus
194 F6 **Logierait** P & K
217 H8 **Logierieve** Abers
49 K3 **Login** Carmth
75 L2 **Lolworth** Cambs
209 L4 **Lonbain** Highld
125 K2 **Londesborough** E R Yk
44 F4 **London** Gt Lon
4 F6 **London Apprentice** Cnwll
59 K7 **London Colney** Herts
132 D3 **Londonderry** N York
102 F5 **Londonthorpe** Lincs
219 K5 **Londubh** Highld
219 J6 **Lonemore** Highld
38 D6 **Long Ashton** N Som
84 D8 **Long Bank** Worcs
102 D4 **Long Bennington** Lincs
14 B4 **Long Bredy** Dorset
73 J2 **Long Buckby** Nhants
102 B6 **Long Clawson** Leics
99 J7 **Long Compton** Staffs
56 F2 **Long Compton** Warwks
58 B6 **Long Crendon** Bucks
15 J1 **Long Crichel** Dorset
44 D6 **Long Ditton** Surrey
115 H7 **Long Duckmanton** Derbys
101 J5 **Long Eaton** Derbys
112 C7 **Long Green** Ches
55 J2 **Long Green** Worcs
57 H5 **Long Hanborough** Oxon
72 E2 **Long Itchington** Warwks
86 F7 **Long Lawford** Warwks
26 C6 **Long Load** Somset
58 E5 **Long Marston** Herts
124 D1 **Long Marston** N York
71 L5 **Long Marston** Warwks
138 F3 **Long Marton** Cumb
77 J5 **Long Melford** Suffk
39 K3 **Long Newnton** Gloucs
178 B5 **Long Newton** E Loth
130 F7 **Long Preston** N York
126 E3 **Long Riston** E R Yk
92 E5 **Long Stratton** Norfk
74 B5 **Long Street** M Keyn
30 C3 **Long Sutton** Hants
104 C7 **Long Sutton** Lincs
26 C6 **Long Sutton** Somset
78 B2 **Long Thurlow** Suffk
84 B1 **Long Waste** Wrekin

101 J7 **Long Whatton** Leics
41 K2 **Long Wittenham** Oxon
151 G2 **Longbenton** N Tyne
56 D3 **Longborough** Gloucs
85 H7 **Longbridge** Birm
27 K4 **Longbridge Deverill** Wilts
26 F8 **Longburton** Dorset
100 E2 **Longcliffe** Derbys
7 J4 **Longcombe** Devon
40 F3 **Longcot** Oxon
83 J3 **Longden** Shrops
85 J2 **Longdon** Staffs
70 E7 **Longdon** Worcs
85 J2 **Longdon Green** Staffs
84 B1 **Longdon upon Tern** Wrekin
11 K6 **Longdown** Devon
3 J4 **Longdowns** Cnwll
45 L6 **Longfield** Kent
100 E5 **Longford** Derbys
55 J4 **Longford** Gloucs
98 F5 **Longford** Shrops
99 G8 **Longford** Wrekin
186 E2 **Longforgan** P & K
178 E6 **Longformacus** Border
158 E3 **Longframlington** Nthumb
15 K3 **Longham** Dorset
91 L1 **Longham** Norfk
217 L6 **Longhaven** Abers
158 F4 **Longhirst** Nthumb
55 G4 **Longhope** Gloucs
234 b7 **Longhope** Ork
158 E4 **Longhorsley** Nthumb
169 J6 **Longhoughton** Nthumb
100 E5 **Longlane** Derbys
27 J3 **Longleat Safari Park** Wilts
55 J4 **Longlevens** Gloucs
122 F6 **Longley** Calder
195 L7 **Longleys** P & K
216 E2 **Longmanhill** Abers
30 C5 **Longmoor Camp** Hants
214 F3 **Longmorn** Moray
113 K6 **Longmoss** Ches
167 J4 **Longnewton** Border
141 J4 **Longnewton** S on T
55 H5 **Longney** Gloucs
177 L3 **Longniddry** E Loth
83 J4 **Longnor** Shrops
114 C8 **Longnor** Staffs
29 H3 **Longparish** Hants
121 J3 **Longridge** Lancs
176 C5 **Longridge** W Loth
175 L4 **Longriggend** N Lans
2 E5 **Longrock** Cnwll
99 L2 **Longsdon** Staffs
217 K5 **Longside** Abers
76 B3 **Longstanton** Cambs
29 G4 **Longstock** Hants
75 K4 **Longstowe** Cambs
28 C2 **Longstreet** Wilts
89 H4 **Longthorpe** C Pete
138 B3 **Longthwaite** Cumb
99 K4 **Longton** C Stke
121 G5 **Longton** Lancs
148 C2 **Longtown** Cumb
53 L3 **Longtown** Herefs
236 d7 **Longueville** Jersey
83 K5 **Longville in the Dale** Shrops
58 C6 **Longwick** Bucks
158 D4 **Longwitton** Nthumb
146 C3 **Longwood** D & G
57 G7 **Longworth** Oxon
178 C5 **Longyester** E Loth

217 J3 **Lonmay** Abers
208 D5 **Lonmore** Highld
5 K5 **Looe** Cnwll
33 K3 **Loose** Kent
58 D7 **Loosley Row** Bucks
216 B4 **Lootcherbrae** Abers
26 B8 **Lopen** Somset
98 C6 **Loppington** Shrops
46 C7 **Lords Wood** Medway
195 J6 **Lornty** P & K
101 H3 **Loscoe** Derbys
214 F1 **Lossiemouth** Moray
113 G6 **Lostock Gralam** Ches
113 G6 **Lostock Green** Ches
121 H5 **Lostock Hall** Lancs
5 H4 **Lostwithiel** Cnwll
227 G6 **Lothbeg** Highld
122 E2 **Lothersdale** N York
227 G6 **Lothmore** Highld
101 K8 **Loughborough** Leics
51 H6 **Loughor** Swans
45 H2 **Loughton** Essex
74 B6 **Loughton** M Keyn
84 B6 **Loughton** Shrops
103 H8 **Lound** Lincs
116 B4 **Lound** Notts
93 K4 **Lound** Suffk
101 G8 **Lount** Leics
118 D4 **Louth** Lincs
122 B5 **Love Clough** Lancs
30 B8 **Lovedean** Hants
28 E7 **Lover** Wilts
115 L2 **Loversall** Donc
61 G6 **Loves Green** Essex
49 J5 **Loveston** Pembks
26 E5 **Lovington** Somset
124 C6 **Low Ackworth** Wakefd
144 B2 **Low Barbeth** D & G
130 C5 **Low Bentham** N York
130 B4 **Low Biggins** Cumb
138 E6 **Low Borrowbridge** Cumb
114 E3 **Low Bradfield** Sheff
122 F2 **Low Bradley** N York
116 C2 **Low Burnham** N Linc
133 L8 **Low Catton** E R Yk
148 D3 **Low Crosby** Cumb
141 J5 **Low Dinsdale** Darltn
124 E5 **Low Eggborough** N York
132 C3 **Low Ellington** N York
151 G3 **Low Fell** Gatesd
174 E2 **Low Gartachorrans** Stirlg
132 C5 **Low Grantley** N York
26 B5 **Low Ham** Somset
132 D7 **Low Harrogate** N York
148 E5 **Low Hesket** Cumb
134 B6 **Low Hutton** N York
137 G3 **Low Lorton** Cumb
116 D7 **Low Marnham** Notts
142 E7 **Low Mill** N York
151 H5 **Low Moorsley** Sundld
134 D6 **Low Mowthorpe** N York
129 J3 **Low Newton** Cumb
149 G3 **Low Row** Cumb
140 B7 **Low Row** N York
144 B2 **Low Salchrie** D & G
125 L7 **Low Santon** N Linc
92 E4 **Low Tharston** Norfk
176 D2 **Low Torry** Fife
141 J5 **Low Worsall** N York
137 K6 **Low Wray** Cumb
102 A3 **Lowdham** Notts
25 J4 **Lower Aisholt** Somset
14 E2 **Lower Ansty** Dorset

55 J3 **Lower Apperley** Gloucs
11 J7 **Lower Ashton** Devon
42 C4 **Lower Assendon** Oxon
121 G4 **Lower Bartle** Lancs
41 L5 **Lower Basildon** W Berk
31 L6 **Lower Beeding** W Susx
88 E5 **Lower Benefield** Nhants
71 H2 **Lower Bentley** Worcs
72 F4 **Lower Boddington** Nhants
30 D3 **Lower Bourne** Surrey
72 C6 **Lower Brailes** Warwks
199 L2 **Lower Breakish** Highld
70 E3 **Lower Broadheath** Worcs
70 C4 **Lower Brockhampton Manor** Herefs
69 K6 **Lower Bullingham** Herefs
28 D7 **Lower Burgate** Hants
75 H5 **Lower Caldecote** Beds
55 H7 **Lower Cam** Gloucs
68 B7 **Lower Chapel** Powys
27 L5 **Lower Chicksgrove** Wilts
28 F2 **Lower Chute** Wilts
45 G3 **Lower Clapton** Gt Lon
85 G7 **Lower Clent** Worcs
123 J8 **Lower Cumberworth** Kirk
74 F2 **Lower Dean** Beds
210 C3 **Lower Diabaig** Highld
20 B4 **Lower Dicker** E Susx
83 G6 **Lower Down** Shrops
133 G6 **Lower Dunsforth** N York
70 B5 **Lower Egleton** Herefs
74 D6 **Lower End** M Keyn
35 H5 **Lower Eythorne** Kent
38 D5 **Lower Failand** N Som
30 B4 **Lower Farringdon** Hants
43 H6 **Lower Feltham** Gt Lon
30 C3 **Lower Froyle** Hants
7 L2 **Lower Gabwell** Devon
222 D4 **Lower Gledfield** Highld
26 C3 **Lower Godney** Somset
75 G7 **Lower Gravenhurst** Beds
32 F5 **Lower Green** Kent
33 G3 **Lower Green** Kent
43 H6 **Lower Halliford** Surrey
46 E6 **Lower Halstow** Kent
15 J4 **Lower Hamworthy** Poole
34 F4 **Lower Hardres** Kent
58 C5 **Lower Hartwell** Bucks
68 F4 **Lower Hergest** Herefs
57 J3 **Lower Heyford** Oxon
113 G3 **Lower Irlam** Salfd
160 A2 **Lower Killeyan** Ag & B
97 M1 **Lower Kinnerton** Ches

38 C7 **Lower Langford** N Som
187 G6 **Lower Largo** Fife
100 A5 **Lower Leigh** Staffs
23 K4 **Lower Loxhore** Devon
54 E5 **Lower Lydbrook** Gloucs
69 H2 **Lower Lye** Herefs
37 K3 **Lower Machen** Newpt
25 J4 **Lower Merridge** Somset
73 G6 **Lower Middleton Cheney** Nhants
71 H5 **Lower Moor** Worcs
38 F3 **Lower Morton** S Glos
60 C6 **Lower Nazeing** Essex
37 J6 **Lower Penarth** V Glam
84 F4 **Lower Penn** Staffs
113 H6 **Lower Peover** Ches
71 L5 **Lower Quinton** Warwks
78 C6 **Lower Raydon** Suffk
25 G4 **Lower Roadwater** Somset
39 L4 **Lower Seagry** Wilts
74 E6 **Lower Shelton** Beds
42 C4 **Lower Shiplake** Oxon
72 F3 **Lower Shuckburgh** Warwks
56 D4 **Lower Slaughter** Gloucs
35 H6 **Lower Standen** Kent
39 L4 **Lower Stanton St Quintin** Wilts
46 D5 **Lower Stoke** Medway
38 F2 **Lower Stone** Gloucs
91 L5 **Lower Stow Bedon** Norfk
106 F5 **Lower Street** Norfk
78 D4 **Lower Street** Suffk
59 H3 **Lower Sundon** Beds
16 F1 **Lower Swanwick** Hants
56 D3 **Lower Swell** Gloucs
100 A5 **Lower Tean** Staffs
7 G2 **Lower Town** Devon
64 D6 **Lower Town** Pembks
72 D5 **Lower Tysoe** Warwks
11 K8 **Lower Upcott** Devon
29 K7 **Lower Upham** Hants
25 H4 **Lower Vexford** Somset
26 B2 **Lower Weare** Somset
71 G6 **Lower Westmancote** Worcs
27 H3 **Lower Whatley** Somset
112 E5 **Lower Whitley** Ches
29 M4 **Lower Wield** Hants
20 C5 **Lower Willingdon** E Susx
113 J7 **Lower Withington** Ches
28 C4 **Lower Woodford** Wilts
14 B3 **Lower Wraxhall** Dorset
87 K3 **Lowesby** Leics
93 L5 **Lowestoft** Suffk
137 G3 **Loweswater** Cumb
31 L4 **Lowfield Heath** W Susx
88 E7 **Lowick** Nhants
168 F2 **Lowick** Nthumb
129 G3 **Lowick Green** Cumb
71 L2 **Lowsonford** Warwks
138 D3 **Lowther** Cumb
135 G2 **Lowthorpe** E R Yk
25 J7 **Lowton** Somset

11 L2 **Loxbeare** Devon
31 G4 **Loxhill** Surrey
23 K4 **Loxhore** Devon
72 C4 **Loxley** Warwks
26 A1 **Loxton** N Som
31 H5 **Loxwood** W Susx
229 J6 **Loyal Lodge** Highld
87 K6 **Lubenham** Leics
24 E3 **Luccombe** Somset
17 H6 **Luccombe Village** IOW
169 H4 **Lucker** Nthumb
6 B2 **Luckett** Cnwll
77 J7 **Lucking Street** Essex
39 J4 **Luckington** Wilts
24 E4 **Luckwell Bridge** Somset
69 J2 **Lucton** Herefs
233 b9 **Ludag** W Isls
118 D3 **Ludborough** Lincs
6 F5 **Ludbrook** Devon
49 K5 **Ludchurch** Pembks
122 F5 **Luddenden** Calder
122 F5 **Luddenden Foot** Calder
46 A6 **Luddesdown** Kent
125 J7 **Luddington** N Linc
71 L4 **Luddington** Warwks
89 G6 **Luddington in the Brook** Nhants
117 K4 **Ludford** Lincs
83 K8 **Ludford** Shrops
58 A4 **Ludgershall** Bucks
28 E2 **Ludgershall** Wilts
2 E5 **Ludgvan** Cnwll
107 H8 **Ludham** Norfk
83 K7 **Ludlow** Shrops
26 B8 **Ludney** Somset
27 K6 **Ludwell** Wilts
151 J6 **Ludworth** Dur
9 J6 **Luffincott** Devon
178 B3 **Luffness** E Loth
164 C5 **Lugar** E Ayrs
178 D4 **Luggate Burn** E Loth
175 K4 **Luggiebank** N Lans
174 D7 **Lugton** E Ayrs
69 K6 **Lugwardine** Herefs
209 J8 **Luib** Highld
69 H6 **Lulham** Herefs
86 B2 **Lullington** Derbys
27 H2 **Lullington** Somset
38 D7 **Lulsgate Bottom** N Som
70 D4 **Lulsley** Worcs
122 F6 **Lumb** Calder
122 C5 **Lumb** Lancs
124 D2 **Lumby** N York
175 H4 **Lumloch** E Duns
206 B4 **Lumphanan** Abers
186 C8 **Lumphinnans** Fife
205 K2 **Lumsden** Abers
197 H6 **Lunan** Angus
196 D6 **Lunanhead** Angus
186 A2 **Luncarty** P & K
126 B2 **Lund** E R Yk
125 G4 **Lund** N York
186 E1 **Lundie** Angus
184 F6 **Lundie** Stirlg
187 G6 **Lundin Links** Fife
187 G6 **Lundin Mill** Fife
235 d4 **Lunna** Shet
33 J2 **Lunsford** Kent
20 E4 **Lunsford's Cross** E Susx
111 K2 **Lunt** Sefton
12 F2 **Luppitt** Devon
7 G5 **Lupridge** Devon
123 L6 **Lupset** Wakefd
129 L4 **Lupton** Cumb
30 F6 **Lurgashall** W Susx
11 L2 **Lurley** Devon
7 J4 **Luscombe** Devon
183 L8 **Luss** Ag & B

208 D3 **Lusta** Highld
11 H8 **Lustleigh** Devon
69 J2 **Luston** Herefs
197 G3 **Luthermuir** Abers
186 E4 **Luthrie** Fife
12 D2 **Luton** Devon
7 K1 **Luton** Devon
59 H4 **Luton** Luton
46 C6 **Luton** Medway
59 J4 **Luton Airport** Luton
87 G6 **Lutterworth** Leics
6 E4 **Lutton** Devon
7 G4 **Lutton** Devon
104 C7 **Lutton** Lincs
89 G6 **Lutton** Nhants
24 F4 **Luxborough** Somset
5 G4 **Luxulyan** Cnwll
231 J7 **Lybster** Highld
83 G6 **Lydbury North** Shrops
21 K2 **Lydd** Kent
21 L2 **Lydd Airport** Kent
35 H5 **Lydden** Kent
35 K5 **Lydden** Kent
88 C4 **Lyddington** Rutlnd
25 H5 **Lydeard St Lawrence** Somset
10 D7 **Lydford** Devon
26 E5 **Lydford on Fosse** Somset
122 D5 **Lydgate** Calder
83 G5 **Lydham** Shrops
40 C3 **Lydiard Millicent** Wilts
40 C4 **Lydiard Tregoze** Swindn
111 K2 **Lydiate** Sefton
85 H7 **Lydiate Ash** Worcs
27 H5 **Lydlinch** Dorset
54 F7 **Lydney** Gloucs
49 J7 **Lydstep** Pembks
85 G6 **Lye** Dudley
32 F6 **Lye Green** E Susx
71 L2 **Lye Green** Warwks
27 J3 **Lye's Green** Wilts
41 H2 **Lyford** Oxon
34 F6 **Lymbridge Green** Kent
13 J4 **Lyme Regis** Dorset
34 F6 **Lyminge** Kent
16 C4 **Lymington** Hants
18 D5 **Lyminster** W Susx
113 G4 **Lymm** Warrtn
34 F7 **Lympne** Kent
25 M1 **Lympsham** Somset
12 C5 **Lympstone** Devon
92 D3 **Lynch Green** Norfk
203 J5 **Lynchat** Highld
16 C2 **Lyndhurst** Hants
88 C3 **Lyndon** Rutlnd
166 B2 **Lyne** Border
43 G7 **Lyne** Surrey
206 E4 **Lyne of Skene** Abers
98 C6 **Lyneal** Shrops
56 F4 **Lyneham** Oxon
40 A5 **Lyneham** Wilts
40 A5 **Lyneham Airport** Wilts
234 b7 **Lyness** Ork
106 C8 **Lyng** Norfk
25 M5 **Lyng** Somset
23 L2 **Lynmouth** Devon
214 F7 **Lynn of Shenval** Moray
34 C3 **Lynsted** Kent
23 L2 **Lynton** Devon
14 C2 **Lyon's Gate** Dorset
69 G4 **Lyonshall** Herefs
15 H4 **Lytchett Matravers** Dorset
15 H4 **Lytchett Minster** Dorset
231 K3 **Lyth** Highld

120 E5 **Lytham** Lancs
120 D5 **Lytham St Anne's** Lancs
143 H5 **Lythe** N York
230 F3 **Lythmore** Highld

M

3 K4 **Mabe Burnthouse** Cnwll
155 G7 **Mabie** D & G
119 G4 **Mablethorpe** Lincs
113 K6 **Macclesfield** Ches
216 D2 **Macduff** Abers
161 J7 **Macharioch** Ag & B
37 K3 **Machen** Caerph
162 A3 **Machrie** N Ayrs
161 G5 **Machrihanish** Ag & B
180 E8 **Machrins** Ag & B
81 G4 **Machynlleth** Powys
51 G5 **Machynys** Carmth
100 F5 **Mackworth** Derbys
177 L4 **Macmerry** E Loth
10 D6 **Maddaford** Devon
185 K3 **Madderty** P & K
176 C3 **Maddiston** Falk
99 H4 **Madeley** Staffs
76 B3 **Madingley** Cambs
69 H6 **Madley** Herefs
70 E5 **Madresfield** Worcs
2 E5 **Madron** Cnwll
65 L3 **Maen-y-groes** Cerdgn
49 J3 **Maenclochog** Pembks
36 F5 **Maendy** V Glam
95 L4 **Maentwrog** Gwynd
99 H5 **Maer** Staffs
36 F2 **Maerdy** Rhondd
97 L7 **Maesbrook** Shrops
97 L7 **Maesbury** Shrops
97 L7 **Maesbury Marsh** Shrops
65 K5 **Maesllyn** Cerdgn
36 D3 **Maesteg** Brdgnd
51 H3 **Maesybont** Carmth
37 J2 **Maesycwmmer** Caerph
215 H5 **Maggieknockater** Moray
60 D3 **Maggots End** Essex
20 C4 **Magham Down** E Susx
111 K2 **Maghull** Sefton
38 B3 **Magor** Mons
27 J4 **Maiden Bradley** Wilts
38 E6 **Maiden Head** N Som
14 B3 **Maiden Newton** Dorset
49 G7 **Maiden Wells** Pembks
32 B6 **Maidenbower** W Susx
7 L3 **Maidencombe** Torbay
13 H4 **Maidenhayne** Devon
42 E4 **Maidenhead** W & M
163 G2 **Maidens** S Ayrs
118 D5 **Maidenwell** Lincs
73 H4 **Maidford** Nhants
73 K7 **Maids Moreton** Bucks
33 K3 **Maidstone** Kent
87 L7 **Maidwell** Nhants
37 L3 **Maindee** Newpt
196 E4 **Mains of Balhall** Angus
197 G2 **Mains of Balnakettle** Abers
214 D7 **Mains of Dalvey** Highld

197 H2 **Mains of Haulkerton** Abers
141 H2 **Mainsforth** Dur
147 G4 **Mainsriddle** D & G
82 F6 **Mainstone** Shrops
55 J4 **Maisemore** Gloucs
101 G4 **Makeney** Derbys
7 G7 **Malborough** Devon
44 E6 **Malden** Surrey
61 K6 **Maldon** Essex
131 G6 **Malham** N York
199 L6 **Mallaig** Highld
199 L5 **Mallaigvaig** Highld
177 G5 **Malleny Mills** C Edin
108 E7 **Malltraeth** IOA
81 J2 **Mallwyd** Gwynd
39 L3 **Malmesbury** Wilts
24 C2 **Malmsmead** Somset
98 C3 **Malpas** Ches
4 D7 **Malpas** Cnwll
37 L3 **Malpas** Newpt
115 K3 **Maltby** Rothm
141 L5 **Maltby** S on T
118 F5 **Maltby le Marsh** Lincs
62 B4 **Malting Green** Essex
34 B6 **Maltman's Hill** Kent
134 C5 **Malton** N York
70 D5 **Malvern Hills**
70 E5 **Malvern Link** Worcs
70 D6 **Malvern Wells** Worcs
145 H4 **Malzie** D & G
70 C1 **Mamble** Worcs
53 L7 **Mamhilad** Mons
3 K6 **Manaccan** Cnwll
82 C3 **Manafon** Powys
232 d5 **Manais** W Isls
11 H8 **Manaton** Devon
118 E4 **Manby** Lincs
86 D4 **Mancetter** Warwks
113 J3 **Manchester** Manch
113 J5 **Manchester Airport** Manch
111 K7 **Mancot** Flints
201 L5 **Mandally** Highld
179 G7 **Manderston House** Border
90 C5 **Manea** Cambs
85 K4 **Maney** Birm
140 F4 **Manfield** N York
38 F5 **Mangotsfield** S Glos
232 d5 **Manish** W Isls
112 D6 **Manley** Ches
53 J7 **Manmoel** Caerph
188 C7 **Mannel** Ag & B
31 K5 **Manning's Heath** W Susx
40 C8 **Manningford Bohune** Wilts
40 C8 **Manningford Bruce** Wilts
123 H4 **Manningham** Brad
15 K2 **Mannington** Dorset
62 D2 **Manningtree** Essex
207 H4 **Mannofield** C Aber
45 H3 **Manor Park** Gt Lon
49 H7 **Manorbier** Pembks
49 H7 **Manorbier Newton** Pembks
167 K3 **Manorhill** Border
64 C7 **Manorowen** Pembks
69 H5 **Mansell Gamage** Herefs
69 H5 **Mansell Lacy** Herefs
164 C6 **Mansfield** E Ayrs
101 K1 **Mansfield** Notts
115 K8 **Mansfield Woodhouse** Notts
27 J7 **Manston** Dorset
124 B4 **Manston** Leeds
35 J2 **Manston Airport** Kent
15 J2 **Manswood** Dorset

88 F1 **Manthorpe** Lincs
116 F2 **Manton** N Linc
88 C3 **Manton** Rutlnd
40 D6 **Manton** Wilts
60 D3 **Manuden** Essex
26 F6 **Maperton** Somset
102 B1 **Maplebeck** Notts
42 A5 **Mapledurham** Oxon
30 B2 **Mapledurwell** Hants
31 K6 **Maplehurst** W Susx
45 K7 **Maplescombe** Kent
100 D3 **Mapleton** Derbys
101 H4 **Mapperley** Derbys
101 L4 **Mapperley Park** C Nott
13 L3 **Mapperton** Dorset
71 J2 **Mappleborough Green** Warwks
126 F2 **Mappleton** E R Yk
123 L7 **Mapplewell** Barns
14 E2 **Mappowder** Dorset
4 C5 **Marazanvose** Cnwll
2 F5 **Marazion** Cnwll
98 E4 **Marbury** Ches
90 B4 **March** Cambs
165 J6 **March** S Lans
41 J2 **Marcham** Oxon
98 E6 **Marchamley** Shrops
100 C6 **Marchington** Staffs
98 A3 **Marchwiel** Wrexhm
16 D1 **Marchwood** Hants
36 E6 **Marcross** V Glam
69 K5 **Marden** Herefs
33 J4 **Marden** Kent
40 C8 **Marden** Wilts
33 K5 **Marden Thorn** Kent
53 L5 **Mardy** Mons
103 L1 **Mareham le Fen** Lincs
118 C7 **Mareham on the Hill** Lincs
18 E3 **Marehill** W Susx
19 M2 **Maresfield** E Susx
126 E5 **Marfleet** C KuH
98 A2 **Marford** Wrexhm
36 B3 **Margam** Neath
27 J7 **Margaret Marsh** Dorset
61 G7 **Margaretting** Essex
61 G7 **Margaretting Tye** Essex
35 K1 **Margate** Kent
162 D3 **Margnaheglish** N Ayrs
145 M5 **Margrie** D & G
142 E4 **Margrove Park** R & Cl
91 G2 **Marham** Norfk
9 G4 **Marhamchurch** Cnwll
89 G3 **Marholm** C Pete
24 B6 **Mariansleigh** Devon
46 F5 **Marine Town** Kent
206 D4 **Marionburgh** Abers
209 H2 **Marishader** Highld
6 C3 **Maristow** Devon
163 H2 **Maritime Centre** N Ayrs
155 J5 **Marjoriebanks** D & G
26 B2 **Mark** Somset
33 G6 **Mark Cross** E Susx
32 E5 **Markbeech** Kent
119 G5 **Markby** Lincs
86 E3 **Market Bosworth** Leics
89 G2 **Market Deeping** Lincs
98 F5 **Market Drayton** Shrops
87 K6 **Market Harborough** Leics
28 A1 **Market Lavington** Wilts

88 C1 **Market Overton** Rutlnd
117 J4 **Market Rasen** Lincs
118 C5 **Market Stainton** Lincs
125 K3 **Market Weighton** E R Yk
92 B7 **Market Weston** Suffk
86 F2 **Markfield** Leics
53 J7 **Markham** Caerph
116 B6 **Markham Moor** Notts
186 E6 **Markinch** Fife
132 D6 **Markington** N York
178 C3 **Markle** E Loth
61 L4 **Marks Tey** Essex
38 F7 **Marksbury** BaNES
59 H5 **Markyate** Herts
40 D6 **Marlborough** Wilts
71 K4 **Marlcliff** Warwks
7 K3 **Marldon** Devon
79 G3 **Marlesford** Suffk
92 D2 **Marlingford** Norfk
48 D5 **Marloes** Pembks
42 D3 **Marlow** Bucks
42 D3 **Marlow Bottom** Bucks
32 D4 **Marlpit Hill** Kent
27 H7 **Marnhull** Dorset
113 L4 **Marple** Stockp
115 K1 **Marr** Donc
140 D7 **Marrick** N York
122 F7 **Marsden** Kirk
151 J3 **Marsden** S Tyne
57 K7 **Marsh Baldon** Oxon
118 E2 **Marsh Chapel** Lincs
57 M4 **Marsh Gibbon** Bucks
12 D4 **Marsh Green** Devon
32 D4 **Marsh Green** Kent
115 H5 **Marsh Lane** Derbys
24 F3 **Marsh Street** Somset
59 K6 **Marshalswick** Herts
106 E7 **Marsham** Norfk
35 J3 **Marshborough** Kent
83 J5 **Marshbrook** Shrops
37 K4 **Marshfield** Newpt
39 H5 **Marshfield** S Glos
8 F6 **Marshgate** Cnwll
90 D2 **Marshland St James** Norfk
13 J3 **Marshwood** Dorset
140 D6 **Marske** N York
142 D3 **Marske-by-the-Sea** R & Cl
69 G3 **Marston** Herefs
102 E4 **Marston** Lincs
57 K6 **Marston** Oxon
99 L6 **Marston** Staffs
27 L1 **Marston** Wilts
85 L6 **Marston Green** Solhll
26 E6 **Marston Magna** Somset
40 C2 **Marston Meysey** Wilts
100 C5 **Marston Montgomery** Derbys
74 E6 **Marston Moretaine** Beds
100 E6 **Marston on Dove** Derbys
73 G6 **Marston St Lawrence** Nhants
87 K6 **Marston Trussell** Nhants
54 D4 **Marstow** Herefs
58 F5 **Marsworth** Bucks
40 F7 **Marten** Wilts
113 J4 **Marthall** Ches
107 J8 **Martham** Norfk
28 B7 **Martin** Hants
35 J5 **Martin** Kent
103 J1 **Martin** Lincs

118 C7 **Martin** Lincs
70 F3 **Martin Hussingtree** Worcs
23 L2 **Martinhoe** Devon
14 C5 **Martinstown** Dorset
78 F5 **Martlesham** Suffk
78 F5 **Martlesham Heath** Suffk
49 H5 **Martletwy** Pembks
70 D3 **Martley** Worcs
26 C7 **Martock** Somset
113 J7 **Marton** Ches
126 F3 **Marton** E R Yk
116 D5 **Marton** Lincs
142 B4 **Marton** Middsb
132 F6 **Marton** N York
134 B3 **Marton** N York
82 F3 **Marton** Shrops
72 E2 **Marton** Warwks
132 E5 **Marton-le-Moor** N York
29 K5 **Martyr Worthy** Hants
234 b5 **Marwick** Ork
23 H4 **Marwood** Devon
6 D1 **Mary Tavy** Devon
212 D4 **Marybank** Highld
212 E3 **Maryburgh** Highld
207 G5 **Maryculter** Abers
179 G6 **Marygold** Border
216 F5 **Maryhill** Abers
175 G4 **Maryhill** C Glas
197 H3 **Marykirk** Abers
44 F4 **Marylebone** Gt Lon
121 H8 **Marylebone** Wigan
214 F6 **Marypark** Moray
147 H7 **Maryport** Cumb
144 D7 **Maryport** D & G
10 C7 **Marystow** Devon
197 H5 **Maryton** Angus
206 B6 **Marywell** Abers
207 H5 **Marywell** Abers
197 G7 **Marywell** Angus
132 C4 **Masham** N York
130 C4 **Masongill** N York
115 J6 **Mastin Moor** Derbys
60 E5 **Matching Green** Essex
60 E5 **Matching Tye** Essex
158 C7 **Matfen** Nthumb
33 H5 **Matfield** Kent
38 D3 **Mathern** Mons
70 D5 **Mathon** Herefs
48 E2 **Mathry** Pembks
106 D5 **Matlask** Norfk
100 F1 **Matlock** Derbys
100 F2 **Matlock Bath** Derbys
55 J5 **Matson** Gloucs
116 B4 **Mattersey** Notts
42 B8 **Mattingley** Hants
92 C2 **Mattishall** Norfk
92 C2 **Mattishall Burgh** Norfk
163 L4 **Mauchline** E Ayrs
217 H5 **Maud** Abers
236 d6 **Maufant** Jersey
56 D3 **Maugersbury** Gloucs
237 e3 **Maughold** IOM
212 C6 **Mauld** Highld
74 F6 **Maulden** Beds
138 F4 **Maulds Meaburn** Cumb
132 E3 **Maunby** N York
69 L4 **Maund Bryan** Herefs
25 G5 **Maundown** Somset
93 K2 **Mautby** Norfk
85 J1 **Mavesyn Ridware** Staffs
118 E7 **Mavis Enderby** Lincs
147 J5 **Mawbray** Cumb
121 G7 **Mawdesley** Lancs
36 C4 **Mawdlam** Brdgnd
3 J6 **Mawgan** Cnwll

4 D3 **Mawgan Porth** Cnwll
3 J3 **Mawla** Cnwll
3 K5 **Mawnan** Cnwll
3 K5 **Mawnan Smith** Cnwll
89 G2 **Maxey** C Pete
86 B6 **Maxstoke** Warwks
34 F5 **Maxted Street** Kent
167 J4 **Maxton** Border
35 J6 **Maxton** Kent
155 G6 **Maxwell Town** D & G
9 H6 **Maxworthy** Cnwll
99 J3 **May Bank** Staffs
163 H7 **Maybole** S Ayrs
43 G8 **Maybury** Surrey
33 G7 **Mayfield** E Susx
177 K5 **Mayfield** Mdloth
100 D4 **Mayfield** Staffs
31 G1 **Mayford** Surrey
20 C3 **Maynard's Green** E Susx
93 J4 **Maypole Green** Norfk
77 K3 **Maypole Green** Suffk
39 G8 **Meadgate** BaNES
58 D6 **Meadle** Bucks
151 G6 **Meadowfield** Dur
9 K8 **Meadwell** Devon
147 K5 **Mealrigg** Cumb
123 K3 **Meanwood** Leeds
26 C3 **Meare** Somset
25 M6 **Meare Green** Somset
25 L6 **Meare Green** Somset
174 F7 **Mearns** E Rens
74 B2 **Mears Ashby** Nhants
86 D2 **Measham** Leics
129 J4 **Meathop** Cumb
6 D3 **Meavy** Devon
88 B5 **Medbourne** Leics
115 L7 **Meden Vale** Notts
42 D4 **Medmenham** Bucks
150 E4 **Medomsley** Dur
30 A4 **Medstead** Hants
99 M1 **Meerbrook** Staffs
60 C2 **Meesden** Herts
10 E3 **Meeth** Devon
107 G6 **Meeting House Hill** Norfk
50 C2 **Meidrim** Carmth
82 D2 **Meifod** Powys
195 L7 **Meigle** P & K
164 F6 **Meikle Carco** D & G
175 J7 **Meikle Earnock** S Lans
173 H6 **Meikle Kilmory** Ag & B
195 G8 **Meikle Obney** P & K
216 D7 **Meikle Wartle** Abers
195 J7 **Meikleour** P & K
50 F4 **Meinciau** Carmth
99 L4 **Meir** C Stke
75 L5 **Melbourn** Cambs
101 G7 **Melbourne** Derbys
125 H2 **Melbourne** E R Yk
27 K7 **Melbury Abbas** Dorset
14 B2 **Melbury Bubb** Dorset
14 B2 **Melbury Osmond** Dorset
74 E2 **Melchbourne** Beds
14 E2 **Melcombe Bingham** Dorset
10 E6 **Meldon** Devon
158 E5 **Meldon** Nthumb
75 L5 **Meldreth** Cambs
184 F7 **Meldrum** Stirlg
182 B5 **Melfort** Ag & B
196 E5 **Melgund Castle** Angus
110 E5 **Meliden** Denbgs
97 G3 **Melin-y-wig** Denbgs
138 D3 **Melkinthorpe** Cumb
149 J3 **Melkridge** Nthumb
39 K7 **Melksham** Wilts
130 B5 **Melling** Lancs

111 L2 **Melling** Sefton
92 C8 **Mellis** Suffk
219 K3 **Mellon Charles** Highld
219 K3 **Mellon Udrigle** Highld
121 J4 **Mellor** Lancs
113 M4 **Mellor** Stockp
121 J4 **Mellor Brook** Lancs
27 G2 **Mells** Somset
149 G7 **Melmerby** Cumb
131 K3 **Melmerby** N York
132 E4 **Melmerby** N York
229 J3 **Melness** Highld
13 L3 **Melplash** Dorset
167 H3 **Melrose** Border
234 D7 **Melsetter** Ork
140 F5 **Melsonby** N York
123 G7 **Meltham** Kirk
126 B5 **Melton** E R Yk
79 G4 **Melton** Suffk
106 C6 **Melton Constable** Norfk
102 C8 **Melton Mowbray** Leics
126 D7 **Melton Ross** N Linc
219 H4 **Melvaig** Highld
83 G1 **Melverley** Shrops
230 C3 **Melvich** Highld
13 H2 **Membury** Devon
217 H2 **Memsie** Abers
196 C5 **Memus** Angus
109 H6 **Menai Bridge** IOA
92 F6 **Mendham** Suffk
26 D2 **Mendip Hills**
78 D2 **Mendlesham** Suffk
78 D2 **Mendlesham Green** Suffk
5 L4 **Menheniot** Cnwll
164 F7 **Mennock** D & G
123 H2 **Menston** Brad
185 H7 **Menstrie** Clacks
58 E4 **Mentmore** Bucks
200 C7 **Meoble** Highld
83 J2 **Meole Brace** Shrops
29 L7 **Meonstoke** Hants
45 M6 **Meopham** Kent
90 B7 **Mepal** Cambs
75 G7 **Meppershall** Beds
113 G5 **Mere** Ches
27 J5 **Mere** Wilts
120 F6 **Mere Brow** Lancs
122 C4 **Mereclough** Lancs
33 H3 **Mereworth** Kent
86 B6 **Meriden** Solhll
208 F7 **Merkadale** Highld
48 F7 **Merrion** Pembks
26 C8 **Merriott** Somset
31 G2 **Merrow** Surrey
43 J2 **Merry Hill** Herts
84 F4 **Merryhill** Wolves
5 L3 **Merrymeet** Cnwll
34 E6 **Mersham** Kent
32 B3 **Merstham** Surrey
18 B5 **Merston** W Susx
17 G5 **Merstone** IOW
4 D6 **Merther** Cnwll
67 L6 **Merthyr Cynog** Powys
36 D5 **Merthyr Mawr** Brdgnd
53 G6 **Merthyr Tydfil** Myr Td
53 G7 **Merthyr Vale** Myr Td
10 D3 **Merton** Devon
44 E6 **Merton** Gt Lon
91 K4 **Merton** Norfk
57 L4 **Merton** Oxon
24 B7 **Meshaw** Devon
61 L4 **Messing** Essex
116 E2 **Messingham** N Linc
93 G7 **Metfield** Suffk
6 B3 **Metherell** Cnwll
103 H1 **Metheringham** Lincs
186 F7 **Methil** Fife

186 F7 **Methilhill** Fife
124 B5 **Methley** Leeds
217 G6 **Methlick** Abers
185 L3 **Methven** P & K
91 G4 **Methwold** Norfk
91 G4 **Methwold Hythe** Norfk
93 H5 **Mettingham** Suffk
106 E5 **Metton** Norfk
4 F6 **Mevagissey** Cnwll
115 J2 **Mexborough** Donc
231 K2 **Mey** Highld
94 D6 **Meyllteyrn** Gwynd
56 C7 **Meysey Hampton** Gloucs
232 d2 **Miabhig** W Isls
232 d2 **Miavaig** W Isls
54 D3 **Michaelchurch** Herefs
69 G7 **Michaelchurch Escley** Herefs
37 J5 **Michaelston-le-Pit** V Glam
37 K4 **Michaelstone-y-Fedw** Newpt
5 G1 **Michaelstow** Cnwll
29 K4 **Micheldever** Hants
29 K3 **Micheldever Station** Hants
29 G6 **Michelmersh** Hants
78 D3 **Mickfield** Suffk
112 C7 **Mickle Trafford** Ches
115 K3 **Micklebring** Donc
143 G5 **Mickleby** N York
124 C4 **Micklefield** Leeds
31 K2 **Mickleham** Surrey
100 F5 **Mickleover** C Derb
140 B3 **Mickleton** Dur
71 L5 **Mickleton** Gloucs
124 B5 **Mickletown** Leeds
132 C4 **Mickley** N York
77 J3 **Mickley Green** Suffk
150 D3 **Mickley Square** Nthumb
217 H2 **Mid Ardlaw** Abers
206 C5 **Mid Beltie** Abers
176 E5 **Mid Calder** W Loth
231 K7 **Mid Clyth** Highld
18 B4 **Mid Lavant** W Susx
212 C6 **Mid Mains** Highld
235 d3 **Mid Yell** Shet
234 C4 **Midbea** Ork
57 J3 **Middle Aston** Oxon
57 H3 **Middle Barton** Oxon
26 C8 **Middle Chinnock** Somset
58 B3 **Middle Claydon** Bucks
55 M6 **Middle Duntisbourne** Gloucs
115 H6 **Middle Handley** Derbys
172 F1 **Middle Kames** Ag & B
71 J5 **Middle Littleton** Worcs
100 C4 **Middle Mayfield** Staffs
117 H4 **Middle Rasen** Lincs
7 K2 **Middle Rocombe** Devon
46 D5 **Middle Stoke** Medway
2 a2 **Middle Town** IOS
72 D5 **Middle Tysoe** Warwks
28 F4 **Middle Wallop** Hants
28 E5 **Middle Winterslow** Wilts
28 C4 **Middle Woodford** Wilts
155 L6 **Middlebie** D & G
194 D3 **Middlebridge** P & K
131 K3 **Middleham** N York
39 J6 **Middlehill** Wilts

83 K5 **Middlehope** Shrops
14 C2 **Middlemarsh** Dorset
141 L4 **Middlesbrough** Middsb
129 L2 **Middleshaw** Cumb
131 K5 **Middlesmoor** N York
141 G2 **Middlestone** Dur
123 K6 **Middlestown** Wakefd
167 K2 **Middlethird** Border
188 B7 **Middleton** Ag & B
114 D8 **Middleton** Derbys
100 F2 **Middleton** Derbys
77 K6 **Middleton** Essex
29 H3 **Middleton** Hants
69 K1 **Middleton** Herefs
123 L5 **Middleton** Leeds
174 D7 **Middleton** N Ayrs
123 G2 **Middleton** N York
134 B3 **Middleton** N York
88 B5 **Middleton** Nhants
90 F1 **Middleton** Norfk
158 D5 **Middleton** Nthumb
186 B6 **Middleton** P & K
113 K1 **Middleton** Rochdl
83 K7 **Middleton** Shrops
79 J2 **Middleton** Suffk
50 E7 **Middleton** Swans
85 L4 **Middleton** Warwks
73 G6 **Middleton Cheney** Nhants
79 J2 **Middleton Moor** Suffk
69 K2 **Middleton on the Hill** Herefs
125 L2 **Middleton on the Wolds** E R Yk
141 J5 **Middleton One Row** Darltn
132 E4 **Middleton Quernhow** N York
84 C6 **Middleton Scriven** Shrops
141 J5 **Middleton St George** Darltn
57 K4 **Middleton Stoney** Oxon
141 G6 **Middleton Tyas** N York
139 L3 **Middleton-in-Teesdale** Dur
18 C5 **Middleton-on-Sea** W Susx
82 F2 **Middletown** Powys
113 G7 **Middlewich** Ches
5 L2 **Middlewood** Cnwll
78 D3 **Middlewood Green** Suffk
163 M3 **Middleyard** E Ayrs
26 B5 **Middlezoy** Somset
39 H7 **Midford** BaNES
41 K6 **Midgham** W Berk
122 F5 **Midgley** Calder
123 K7 **Midgley** Wakefd
114 E2 **Midhopestones** Sheff
30 E6 **Midhurst** W Susx
167 H4 **Midlem** Border
173 H6 **Midpark** Ag & B
26 F1 **Midsomer Norton** BaNES
229 J4 **Midtown** Highld
205 K4 **Migvie** Abers
26 F7 **Milborne Port** Somset
14 F3 **Milborne St Andrew** Dorset
26 F7 **Milborne Wick** Somset
158 E6 **Milbourne** Nthumb
39 L3 **Milbourne** Wilts
138 F2 **Milburn** Cumb
38 F3 **Milbury Heath** S Glos
132 F6 **Milby** N York

72 E7 **Milcombe** Oxon	28 D3 **Milston** Wilts	83 G3 **Minsterley** Shrops	151 H3 **Monkton** S Tyne
77 L5 **Milden** Suffk	73 H5 **Milthorpe** Nhants	55 H5 **Minsterworth** Gloucs	39 H7 **Monkton Combe** BaNES
91 G8 **Mildenhall** Suffk	76 C2 **Milton** Cambs	14 C2 **Minterne Magna** Dorset	27 J4 **Monkton Deverill** Wilts
40 E6 **Mildenhall** Wilts	148 F3 **Milton** Cumb	117 K6 **Minting** Lincs	39 J7 **Monkton Farleigh** Wilts
19 H4 **Mile Oak** Br & H	144 F4 **Milton** D & G	217 J5 **Mintlaw** Abers	25 K6 **Monkton Heathfield** Somset
46 F5 **Mile Town** Kent	154 E7 **Milton** D & G	167 H5 **Minto** Border	13 J3 **Monkton Wyld** Dorset
105 L8 **Mileham** Norfk	100 F7 **Milton** Derbys	83 H5 **Minton** Shrops	151 J4 **Monkwearmouth** Sundld
113 J2 **Miles Platting** Manch	231 L5 **Milton** Highld	136 D4 **Mirehouse** Cumb	30 A5 **Monkwood** Hants
176 E2 **Milesmark** Fife	209 L5 **Milton** Highld	123 J6 **Mirfield** Kirk	85 G4 **Monmore Green** Wolves
168 D3 **Milfield** Nthumb	212 D7 **Milton** Highld	55 L6 **Miserden** Gloucs	54 D5 **Monmouth** Mons
101 G4 **Milford** Derbys	212 E4 **Milton** Highld	37 G4 **Miskin** Rhondd	69 G5 **Monnington on Wye** Herefs
99 L7 **Milford** Staffs	223 G6 **Milton** Highld	116 B3 **Misson** Notts	145 H6 **Monreith** D & G
30 F3 **Milford** Surrey	174 C5 **Milton** Inver	87 G6 **Misterton** Leics	236 b3 **Mont Saint** Guern
48 F6 **Milford Haven** Pembks	46 A5 **Milton** Kent	116 C3 **Misterton** Notts	26 D7 **Montacute** Somset
16 C4 **Milford on Sea** Hants	215 L2 **Milton** Moray	13 L2 **Misterton** Somset	83 H1 **Montford** Shrops
54 E6 **Milkwall** Gloucs	37 M7 **Milton** N Som	62 D2 **Mistley** Essex	83 H1 **Montford Bridge** Shrops
122 F6 **Mill Bank** Calder	116 B6 **Milton** Notts	44 F6 **Mitcham** Gt Lon	206 B2 **Montgarrie** Abers
113 L4 **Mill Brow** Stockp	72 F7 **Milton** Oxon	54 C6 **Mitchel Troy** Mons	164 A4 **Montgarswood** E Ayrs
42 C4 **Mill End** Bucks	41 J3 **Milton** Oxon	54 F4 **Mitcheldean** Gloucs	82 E4 **Montgomery** Powys
60 B2 **Mill End** Herts	195 H5 **Milton** P & K	4 D5 **Mitchell** Cnwll	163 J2 **Montgreenan** N Ayrs
76 F5 **Mill Green** Cambs	49 H6 **Milton** Pembks	155 G3 **Mitchellslacks** D & G	197 H5 **Montrose** Angus
61 G7 **Mill Green** Essex	26 C6 **Milton** Somset	158 F5 **Mitford** Nthumb	28 F3 **Monxton** Hants
103 L7 **Mill Green** Lincs	184 B6 **Milton** Stirlg	3 J2 **Mithian** Cnwll	114 D7 **Monyash** Derbys
77 L6 **Mill Green** Suffk	174 D4 **Milton** W Duns	73 H7 **Mixbury** Oxon	206 D3 **Monymusk** Abers
78 B3 **Mill Green** Suffk	14 F3 **Milton Abbas** Dorset	113 H5 **Mobberley** Ches	185 H3 **Monzie** P & K
78 D3 **Mill Green** Suffk	9 K8 **Milton Abbot** Devon	100 A4 **Mobberley** Staffs	175 J4 **Moodiesburn** N Lans
44 E2 **Mill Hill** Gt Lon	177 H5 **Milton Bridge** Mdloth	82 B5 **Mochdre** Powys	186 E4 **Moonzie** Fife
99 J5 **Mill Meece** Staffs	58 F3 **Milton Bryan** Beds	145 H5 **Mochrum** D & G	123 L3 **Moor Allerton** Leeds
185 H4 **Mill of Drummond** P & K	26 F4 **Milton Clevedon** Somset	33 J4 **Mockbeggar** Kent	15 J2 **Moor Crichel** Dorset
174 D2 **Mill of Haldane** W Duns	6 D3 **Milton Combe** Devon	136 F3 **Mockerkin** Cumb	122 F5 **Moor End** Calder
78 C1 **Mill Street** Suffk	9 K3 **Milton Damerel** Devon	6 F5 **Modbury** Devon	133 H7 **Moor Monkton** N York
236 a5 **Millais** Jersey	74 E4 **Milton Ernest** Beds	99 L5 **Moddershall** Staffs	118 D8 **Moorby** Lincs
30 D5 **Milland** W Susx	98 C2 **Milton Green** Ches	109 G4 **Moelfre** IOA	15 K4 **Moordown** Bmouth
217 J5 **Millbreck** Abers	41 J3 **Milton Hill** Oxon	97 J6 **Moelfre** Powys	112 E5 **Moore** Halton
216 F5 **Millbrex** Abers	74 C6 **Milton Keynes** M Keyn	155 J2 **Moffat** D & G	125 G7 **Moorends** Donc
30 D3 **Millbridge** Surrey	40 D7 **Milton Lilbourne** Wilts	75 G5 **Mogerhanger** Beds	101 J3 **Moorgreen** Notts
74 E6 **Millbrook** Beds	73 K4 **Milton Malsor** Nhants	86 C1 **Moira** Leics	123 H3 **Moorhead** Brad
29 G8 **Millbrook** C Sotn	184 D1 **Milton Morenish** P & K	199 G3 **Moi-chlach** Highld	148 B4 **Moorhouse** Cumb
6 B5 **Millbrook** Cnwll	206 B5 **Milton of Auchinhove** Abers	34 D4 **Molash** Kent	116 C7 **Moorhouse** Notts
236 c7 **Millbrook** Jersey	186 E7 **Milton of Balgonie** Fife	111 H8 **Mold** Flints	32 D3 **Moorhouse Bank** Surrey
206 F4 **Millbuie** Abers	174 E1 **Milton of Buchanan** Stirlg	123 H7 **Moldgreen** Kirk	26 B4 **Moorlinch** Somset
212 E4 **Millbuie** Highld	175 H3 **Milton of Campsie** E Duns	60 E3 **Molehill Green** Essex	142 E4 **Moorsholm** R & Cl
163 K4 **Millburn** S Ayrs	213 G6 **Milton of Leys** Highld	126 C3 **Molescroft** E R Yk	27 H7 **Moorside** Dorset
21 G2 **Millcorner** E Susx	205 J6 **Milton of Tullich** Abers	88 F7 **Molesworth** Cambs	5 K3 **Moorswater** Cnwll
222 E7 **Millcraig** Highld	27 J5 **Milton on Stour** Dorset	24 C5 **Molland** Devon	124 C7 **Moorthorpe** Wakefd
100 C2 **Milldale** Staffs	46 E6 **Milton Regis** Kent	111 L7 **Mollington** Ches	123 K3 **Moortown** Leeds
114 C6 **Miller's Dale** Derbys	56 E4 **Milton-under-Wychwood** Oxon	72 F5 **Mollington** Oxon	117 H2 **Moortown** Lincs
177 J4 **Millerhill** Mdloth	25 H6 **Milverton** Somset	175 J4 **Mollinsburn** N Lans	223 G5 **Morangie** Highld
175 H5 **Millerston** N Lans	72 C2 **Milverton** Warwks	197 J1 **Mondynes** Abers	199 L6 **Morar** Highld
68 F5 **Millhalf** Herefs	99 L6 **Milwich** Staffs	78 F3 **Monewden** Suffk	89 G5 **Morborne** Cambs
175 K7 **Millheugh** S Lans	182 D7 **Minard** Ag & B	185 M2 **Moneydie** P & K	11 H4 **Morchard Bishop** Devon
173 G4 **Millhouse** Ag & B	55 K7 **Minchinhampton** Gloucs	154 D4 **Moniaive** D & G	13 K4 **Morcombelake** Dorset
114 E2 **Millhouse Green** Barns	24 F3 **Minehead** Somset	187 H2 **Monifieth** Angus	88 D4 **Morcott** Rutlnd
155 K5 **Millhousebridge** D & G	97 L3 **Minera** Wrexhm	196 E8 **Monikie** Angus	97 L6 **Morda** Shrops
115 G5 **Millhouses** Sheff	40 A3 **Minety** Wilts	186 E5 **Monimail** Fife	15 H4 **Morden** Dorset
174 D6 **Milliken Park** Rens	95 K5 **Minffordd** Gwynd	124 D5 **Monk Fryston** N York	44 E6 **Morden** Gt Lon
125 J1 **Millington** E R Yk	190 D3 **Mingarrypark** Highld	29 L1 **Monk Sherborne** Hants	69 L6 **Mordiford** Herefs
128 E4 **Millom** Cumb	118 D8 **Miningsby** Lincs	78 E2 **Monk Soham** Suffk	141 H2 **Mordon** Dur
173 K7 **Millport** N Ayrs	5 L2 **Minions** Cnwll	60 F3 **Monk Street** Essex	83 G5 **More** Shrops
130 C2 **Millthrop** Cumb	163 J6 **Minishant** S Ayrs	31 K6 **Monk's Gate** W Susx	24 E6 **Morebath** Devon
207 G5 **Milltimber** C Aber	81 J2 **Minllyn** Gwynd	44 E1 **Monken Hadley** Gt Lon	168 B4 **Morebattle** Border
205 G4 **Milltown** Abers	145 J2 **Minnigaff** D & G	70 B5 **Monkhide** Herefs	129 J6 **Morecambe** Lancs
205 K3 **Milltown** Abers	216 E3 **Minnonie** Abers	148 C3 **Monkhill** Cumb	40 C3 **Moredon** Swindn
156 C6 **Milltown** D & G	132 F6 **Minskip** N York	84 B5 **Monkhopton** Shrops	220 E3 **Morefield** Highld
23 J4 **Milltown** Devon	16 C1 **Minstead** Hants	69 J3 **Monkland** Herefs	35 G7 **Morehall** Kent
206 C5 **Milltown of Campfield** Abers	30 D7 **Minsted** W Susx	23 G7 **Monkleigh** Devon	7 H5 **Moreleigh** Devon
215 G6 **Milltown of Edinvillie** Moray	46 F5 **Minster** Kent	36 E6 **Monknash** V Glam	184 D1 **Morenish** P & K
206 C5 **Milltown of Learney** Abers	35 J2 **Minster** Kent	10 E4 **Monkokehampton** Devon	136 D3 **Moresby** Cumb
186 B6 **Milnathort** P & K	56 F5 **Minster Lovell** Oxon	77 L5 **Monks Eleigh** Suffk	29 K6 **Morestead** Hants
175 G4 **Milngavie** W Duns		113 J6 **Monks Heath** Ches	
122 D7 **Milnrow** Rochdl		34 F6 **Monks Horton** Kent	
129 K3 **Milnthorpe** Cumb		86 F6 **Monks Kirby** Warwks	
208 B4 **Milovaig** Highld		159 H7 **Monkseaton** N Tyne	
84 B8 **Milson** Shrops		25 G4 **Monksilver** Somset	
34 B3 **Milstead** Kent		118 F7 **Monksthorpe** Lincs	
		53 M7 **Monkswood** Mons	
		12 F2 **Monkton** Devon	
		47 M6 **Monkton** Kent	
		163 J4 **Monkton** S Ayrs	

14 F4	**Moreton** Dorset	
60 E6	**Moreton** Essex	
69 K2	**Moreton** Herefs	
58 B6	**Moreton** Oxon	
111 J4	**Moreton** Wirral	
98 E7	**Moreton Corbet** Shrops	
69 L5	**Moreton Jeffries** Herefs	
72 C4	**Moreton Morrell** Warwks	
69 K5	**Moreton on Lugg** Herefs	
73 H5	**Moreton Pinkney** Nhants	
98 F5	**Moreton Say** Shrops	
55 H6	**Moreton Valence** Gloucs	
56 D2	**Moreton-in-Marsh** Gloucs	
11 H7	**Moretonhampstead** Devon	
94 E4	**Morfa Nefyn** Gwynd	
178 C4	**Morham** E Loth	
138 E3	**Morland** Cumb	
113 J5	**Morley** Ches	
101 H4	**Morley** Derbys	
123 K5	**Morley** Leeds	
113 J5	**Morley Green** Ches	
92 C4	**Morley St Botolph** Norfk	
177 H4	**Morningside** C Edin	
175 L7	**Morningside** N Lans	
92 F5	**Morningthorpe** Norfk	
158 F5	**Morpeth** Nthumb	
197 H4	**Morphie** Abers	
100 C8	**Morrey** Staffs	
51 J6	**Morriston** Swans	
106 B4	**Morston** Norfk	
23 G3	**Mortehoe** Devon	
115 J4	**Morthen** Rothm	
41 M7	**Mortimer** W Berk	
41 M7	**Mortimer West End** Hants	
44 E5	**Mortlake** Gt Lon	
148 C4	**Morton** Cumb	
101 H1	**Morton** Derbys	
116 D3	**Morton** Lincs	
103 H7	**Morton** Lincs	
102 B3	**Morton** Notts	
97 L7	**Morton** Shrops	
92 D1	**Morton on the Hill** Norfk	
132 E2	**Morton-on-Swale** N York	
2 D4	**Morvah** Cnwll	
5 K4	**Morval** Cnwll	
200 E2	**Morvich** Highld	
84 C5	**Morville** Shrops	
6 C2	**Morwellham Quay** Devon	
9 G2	**Morwenstow** Cnwll	
115 H5	**Mosborough** Sheff	
163 L2	**Moscow** E Ayrs	
85 J6	**Moseley** Birm	
85 G4	**Moseley** Wolves	
70 E3	**Moseley** Worcs	
188 B7	**Moss** Ag & B	
124 F7	**Moss** Donc	
112 D3	**Moss Bank** St Hel	
120 F2	**Moss Edge** Lancs	
213 K4	**Moss-side** Highld	
205 K2	**Mossat** Abers	
235 d4	**Mossbank** Shet	
136 D2	**Mossbay** Cumb	
163 K4	**Mossblown** S Ayrs	
167 K6	**Mossburnford** Border	
154 B7	**Mossdale** D & G	
153 K2	**Mossdale** E Ayrs	
175 K6	**Mossend** N Lans	
113 L2	**Mossley** Tamesd	
156 D3	**Mosspaul Hotel** Border	
215 H3	**Mosstodloch** Moray	
121 H7	**Mossy Lea** Lancs	
145 L5	**Mossyard** D & G	
13 L2	**Mosterton** Dorset	
113 K2	**Moston** Manch	
111 G5	**Mostyn** Flints	
27 J6	**Motcombe** Dorset	
6 F6	**Mothecombe** Devon	
138 B2	**Motherby** Cumb	
175 K6	**Motherwell** N Lans	
44 E6	**Motspur Park** Gt Lon	
45 H5	**Mottingham** Gt Lon	
28 F6	**Mottisfont** Hants	
16 E5	**Mottistone** IOW	
113 M3	**Mottram in Longdendale** Tamesd	
113 K5	**Mottram St Andrew** Ches	
236 c3	**Mouilpied** Guern	
112 D7	**Mouldsworth** Ches	
194 E4	**Moulin** P & K	
19 J4	**Moulsecoomb** Br & H	
41 L4	**Moulsford** Oxon	
74 C6	**Moulsoe** M Keyn	
222 E7	**Moultavie** Highld	
112 F7	**Moulton** Ches	
104 A7	**Moulton** Lincs	
141 G6	**Moulton** N York	
73 L2	**Moulton** Nhants	
77 G2	**Moulton** Suffk	
37 G6	**Moulton** V Glam	
103 M8	**Moulton Chapel** Lincs	
104 A6	**Moulton Seas End** Lincs	
93 H3	**Moulton St Mary** Norfk	
5 J3	**Mount** Cnwll	
3 J3	**Mount Ambrose** Cnwll	
61 L2	**Mount Bures** Essex	
3 J2	**Mount Hawke** Cnwll	
177 H6	**Mount Lothian** Mdloth	
101 G3	**Mount Pleasant** Derbys	
77 G5	**Mount Pleasant** Suffk	
122 F5	**Mount Tabor** Calder	
123 G4	**Mountain** Brad	
53 G7	**Mountain Ash** Rhondd	
176 F8	**Mountain Cross** Border	
20 E2	**Mountfield** E Susx	
212 E3	**Mountgerald House** Highld	
4 D4	**Mountjoy** Cnwll	
60 F8	**Mountnessing** Essex	
38 D2	**Mounton** Mons	
87 H2	**Mountsorrel** Leics	
30 F3	**Mousehill** Surrey	
2 E6	**Mousehole** Cnwll	
155 J7	**Mouswald** D & G	
168 B5	**Mowhaugh** Border	
87 J5	**Mowsley** Leics	
206 F7	**Mowtie** Abers	
213 J7	**Moy** Highld	
202 C8	**Moy** Highld	
200 D2	**Moye** Highld	
64 F5	**Moylgrove** Pembks	
161 H2	**Muasdale** Ag & B	
54 D3	**Much Birch** Herefs	
70 B5	**Much Cowarne** Herefs	
54 C2	**Much Dewchurch** Herefs	
60 C4	**Much Hadham** Herts	
120 F6	**Much Hoole** Lancs	
54 F2	**Much Marcle** Herefs	
84 B4	**Much Wenlock** Shrops	
207 G6	**Muchalls** Abers	
26 B6	**Muchelney** Somset	
26 C6	**Muchelney Ham** Somset	
5 K4	**Muchlarnick** Cnwll	
106 D4	**Muckleburgh Collection** Norfk	
99 G5	**Mucklestone** Staffs	
118 E5	**Muckton** Lincs	
23 J4	**Muddiford** Devon	
20 B3	**Muddles Green** E Susx	
16 A4	**Mudeford** Dorset	
26 E7	**Mudford** Somset	
26 E7	**Mudford Sock** Somset	
175 G3	**Mugdock** Stirlg	
209 G6	**Mugeary** Highld	
100 F4	**Mugginton** Derbys	
206 B3	**Muir of Fowlis** Abers	
214 E3	**Muir of Miltonduff** Moray	
212 E4	**Muir of Ord** Highld	
195 G8	**Muir of Thorn** P & K	
216 D4	**Muirden** Abers	
196 F8	**Muirdrum** Angus	
216 D5	**Muiresk** Abers	
186 E1	**Muirhead** Angus	
186 E6	**Muirhead** Fife	
175 J4	**Muirhead** N Lans	
164 D4	**Muirkirk** E Ayrs	
175 J2	**Muirmill** Stirlg	
192 B1	**Muirshearlich** Highld	
217 J6	**Muirtack** Abers	
185 J5	**Muirton** P & K	
212 C4	**Muirton Mains** Highld	
195 J7	**Muirton of Ardblair** P & K	
139 K7	**Muker** N York	
92 E4	**Mulbarton** Norfk	
215 H4	**Mulben** Moray	
181 J1	**Mull** Ag & B	
3 H7	**Mullion** Cnwll	
3 H7	**Mullion Cove** Cnwll	
119 G6	**Mumby** Lincs	
70 B4	**Munderfield Row** Herefs	
70 B4	**Munderfield Stocks** Herefs	
107 G5	**Mundesley** Norfk	
91 H5	**Mundford** Norfk	
93 G4	**Mundham** Norfk	
61 K7	**Mundon Hill** Essex	
137 K2	**Mungrisdale** Cumb	
213 G4	**Munlochy** Highld	
174 B8	**Munnoch** N Ayrs	
70 B6	**Munsley** Herefs	
83 K6	**Munslow** Shrops	
11 G7	**Murchington** Devon	
57 L5	**Murcott** Oxon	
231 H2	**Murkle** Highld	
200 F6	**Murlaggan** Highld	
187 G1	**Murroes** Angus	
89 L3	**Murrow** Cambs	
58 D3	**Mursley** Bucks	
196 D5	**Murthill** Angus	
195 H8	**Murthly** P & K	
139 G3	**Murton** Cumb	
151 J5	**Murton** Dur	
179 K8	**Murton** Nthumb	
133 K8	**Murton** York	
13 H4	**Musbury** Devon	
177 K4	**Musselburgh** E Loth	
102 D5	**Muston** Leics	
135 H4	**Muston** N York	
44 F3	**Muswell Hill** Gt Lon	
146 C5	**Mutehill** D & G	
93 K6	**Mutford** Suffk	
185 H4	**Muthill** P & K	
231 H5	**Mybster** Highld	
52 B3	**Myddfai** Carmth	
98 C7	**Myddle** Shrops	
66 B4	**Mydroilyn** Cerdgn	
4 C8	**Mylor** Cnwll	
4 C8	**Mylor Bridge** Cnwll	
49 K2	**Mynachlog ddu** Pembks	
83 H5	**Myndtown** Shrops	
38 C2	**Mynydd-bach** Mons	
51 J6	**Mynydd-Bach** Swans	
206 E5	**Myrebird** Abers	
157 G3	**Myredykes** Border	
30 E1	**Mytchett** Surrey	
122 E5	**Mytholm** Calder	
122 F5	**Mytholmroyd** Calder	
132 F6	**Myton-on-Swale** N York	

N

232 d4	**Na Buirgh** W Isls	
219 J5	**Naast** Highld	
124 F2	**Naburn** York	
34 F4	**Nackington** Kent	
78 F6	**Nacton** Suffk	
135 G7	**Nafferton** E R Yk	
25 K5	**Nailsbourne** Somset	
38 C6	**Nailsea** N Som	
86 E3	**Nailstone** Leics	
55 J7	**Nailsworth** Gloucs	
213 K3	**Nairn** Highld	
111 G7	**Nannerch** Flints	
87 G1	**Nanpantan** Leics	
4 F5	**Nanpean** Cnwll	
5 G3	**Nanstallon** Cnwll	
95 K2	**Nant Peris** Gwynd	
36 E2	**Nant-y-moel** Brdgnd	
65 L3	**Nanternis** Cerdgn	
50 F2	**Nantgaredig** Carmth	
96 F1	**Nantglyn** Denbgs	
68 B2	**Nantmel** Powys	
95 K4	**Nantmor** Gwynd	
98 F3	**Nantwich** Ches	
53 J6	**Nantyglo** Blae G	
42 D2	**Naphill** Bucks	
72 F3	**Napton on the Hill** Warwks	
49 J4	**Narberth** Pembks	
87 G4	**Narborough** Leics	
91 H2	**Narborough** Norfk	
95 H3	**Nasareth** Gwynd	
87 K7	**Naseby** Nhants	
73 L7	**Nash** Bucks	
37 M4	**Nash** Newpt	
69 L1	**Nash** Shrops	
30 A3	**Nash's Green** Hants	
88 F4	**Nassington** Nhants	
139 H6	**Nateby** Cumb	
120 F2	**Nateby** Lancs	
6 E5	**National Shire Horse Centre** Devon	
87 H3	**National Space Science Centre** C Leic	
129 L2	**Natland** Cumb	
78 B5	**Naughton** Suffk	
56 C4	**Naunton** Gloucs	
70 F6	**Naunton** Worcs	
71 G4	**Naunton Beauchamp** Worcs	
103 G2	**Navenby** Lincs	
45 K1	**Navestock** Essex	
60 E8	**Navestock Side** Essex	
227 J5	**Navidale House Hotel** Highld	
213 J2	**Navity** Highld	
133 K3	**Nawton** N York	
77 L7	**Nayland** Suffk	
60 C6	**Nazeing** Essex	
235 d5	**Neap** Shet	

100 B4 **Near Cotton** Staffs
137 K7 **Near Sawrey** Cumb
44 E3 **Neasden** Gt Lon
141 H5 **Neasham** Darltn
51 L6 **Neath** Neath
30 C4 **Neatham** Hants
107 H7 **Neatishead** Norfk
66 D2 **Nebo** Cerdgn
96 C2 **Nebo** Conwy
95 H3 **Nebo** Gwynd
108 F4 **Nebo** IOA
91 K1 **Necton** Norfk
224 D3 **Nedd** Highld
78 B5 **Nedging** Suffk
78 B4 **Nedging Tye** Suffk
92 F6 **Needham** Norfk
78 C4 **Needham Market** Suffk
75 L1 **Needingworth** Cambs
84 C7 **Neen Savage** Shrops
84 B8 **Neen Sollars** Shrops
84 B6 **Neenton** Shrops
94 E4 **Nefyn** Gwynd
174 E6 **Neilston** E Rens
37 H2 **Nelson** Caerph
122 C3 **Nelson** Lancs
165 G1 **Nemphlar** S Lans
38 D7 **Nempnett Thrubwell** BaNES
149 K6 **Nenthead** Cumb
167 K2 **Nenthorn** Border
97 K1 **Nercwys** Flints
170 E7 **Nereabolls** Ag & B
175 H6 **Nerston** S Lans
168 E3 **Nesbit** Nthumb
123 G1 **Nesfield** N York
111 J6 **Ness Botanic Gardens** Ches
98 B8 **Nesscliffe** Shrops
111 J6 **Neston** Ches
39 K6 **Neston** Wilts
84 B5 **Netchwood** Shrops
113 J6 **Nether Alderley** Ches
167 H2 **Nether Blainslie** Border
102 B7 **Nether Broughton** Notts
14 C3 **Nether Cerne** Dorset
26 E7 **Nether Compton** Dorset
206 F2 **Nether Crimond** Abers
215 H2 **Nether Dallachy** Moray
11 L5 **Nether Exe** Devon
165 H7 **Nether Fingland** S Lans
196 B7 **Nether Handwick** Angus
115 H3 **Nether Haugh** Rothm
116 C6 **Nether Headon** Notts
101 G3 **Nether Heage** Derbys
73 J3 **Nether Heyford** Nhants
165 K6 **Nether Howcleugh** S Lans
129 K6 **Nether Kellet** Lancs
217 K5 **Nether Kinmundy** Abers
115 K7 **Nether Langwith** Notts
115 G7 **Nether Moor** Derbys
114 E6 **Nether Padley** Derbys
133 J8 **Nether Poppleton** York
133 G2 **Nether Silton** N York
25 J4 **Nether Stowey** Somset

28 F4 **Nether Wallop** Hants
136 F6 **Nether Wasdale** Cumb
56 E4 **Nether Westcote** Gloucs
86 B5 **Nether Whitacre** Warwks
165 G5 **Nether Whitecleuch** S Lans
58 B5 **Nether Winchendon** Bucks
28 D2 **Netheravon** Wilts
216 F3 **Netherbrae** Abers
175 L8 **Netherburn** S Lans
13 L3 **Netherbury** Dorset
123 L2 **Netherby** N York
155 K5 **Nethercleuch** D & G
54 E7 **Netherend** Gloucs
20 E2 **Netherfield** E Susx
20 E3 **Netherfield Road** E Susx
28 C5 **Netherhampton** Wilts
13 K2 **Netherhay** Dorset
146 C6 **Netherlaw** D & G
207 G6 **Netherley** Abers
155 H5 **Nethermill** D & G
217 G5 **Nethermuir** Abers
123 H6 **Netheroyd Hill** Kirk
174 F7 **Netherplace** E Rens
86 C2 **Netherseal** Derbys
123 H8 **Netherthong** Kirk
196 E5 **Netherton** Angus
7 K2 **Netherton** Devon
85 G6 **Netherton** Dudley
175 K7 **Netherton** N Lans
168 E7 **Netherton** Nthumb
195 J6 **Netherton** P & K
84 D6 **Netherton** Shrops
175 G3 **Netherton** Stirlg
123 K6 **Netherton** Wakefd
136 D5 **Nethertown** Cumb
231 L1 **Nethertown** Highld
100 C8 **Nethertown** Staffs
165 L1 **Netherurd** Border
158 D4 **Netherwitton** Nthumb
204 B2 **Nethy Bridge** Highld
16 F2 **Netley** Hants
29 G8 **Netley Marsh** Hants
42 B3 **Nettlebed** Oxon
26 F2 **Nettlebridge** Somset
13 M4 **Nettlecombe** Dorset
59 G6 **Nettleden** Herts
117 G6 **Nettleham** Lincs
33 H3 **Nettlestead** Kent
33 H3 **Nettlestead Green** Kent
17 H4 **Nettlestone** IOW
151 K6 **Nettlesworth** Dur
117 J2 **Nettleton** Lincs
39 J3 **Nettleton** Wilts
28 C4 **Netton** Wilts
64 F6 **Nevern** Pembks
88 B5 **Nevill Holt** Leics
147 G2 **New Abbey** D & G
217 G2 **New Aberdour** Abers
45 G7 **New Addington** Gt Lon
29 L5 **New Alresford** Hants
195 K6 **New Alyth** P & K
45 L6 **New Ash Green** Kent
102 D3 **New Balderton** Notts
45 L6 **New Barn** Kent
44 F2 **New Barnet** Gt Lon
169 G5 **New Bewick** Nthumb
86 F7 **New Bilton** Warwks
104 A2 **New Bolingbroke** Lincs
116 F7 **New Boultham** Lincs
74 B6 **New Bradwell** M Keyn
115 G7 **New Brampton** Derbys
151 G6 **New Brancepeth** Dur

111 J3 **New Brighton** Wirral
92 C5 **New Buckenham** Norfk
216 F4 **New Byth** Abers
92 E2 **New Costessey** Norfk
124 B6 **New Crofton** Wakefd
45 G5 **New Cross** Gt Lon
26 B7 **New Cross** Somset
164 C6 **New Cumnock** E Ayrs
217 G5 **New Deer** Abers
43 H4 **New Denham** Bucks
73 K3 **New Duston** Nhants
133 J7 **New Earswick** York
115 K2 **New Edlington** Donc
214 F3 **New Elgin** Moray
126 E3 **New Ellerby** E R Yk
45 H5 **New Eltham** Gt Lon
71 J3 **New End** Worcs
89 H4 **New England** C Pete
89 H4 **New Fletton** C Pete
16 C2 **New Forest** Hants
154 B6 **New Galloway** D & G
187 G5 **New Gilston** Fife
2 a1 **New Grimsby** IOS
159 H6 **New Hartley** Nthumb
43 H7 **New Haw** Surrey
105 L4 **New Holkham** Norfk
126 D5 **New Holland** N Linc
115 J7 **New Houghton** Derbys
105 J6 **New Houghton** Norfk
130 B2 **New Hutton** Cumb
66 B6 **New Inn** Carmth
53 L7 **New Inn** Torfn
82 F7 **New Invention** Shrops
165 G2 **New Lanark** S Lans
156 C5 **New Langholm** D & G
104 C2 **New Leake** Lincs
217 J4 **New Leeds** Abers
123 L8 **New Lodge** Barns
121 G5 **New Longton** Lancs
144 E3 **New Luce** D & G
44 E6 **New Malden** Gt Lon
142 D3 **New Marske** R & Cl
57 K6 **New Marston** Oxon
206 E8 **New Mill** Abers
2 E4 **New Mill** Cnwll
123 H8 **New Mill** Kirk
4 D5 **New Mills** Cnwll
113 M4 **New Mills** Derbys
82 C4 **New Mills** Powys
16 B4 **New Milton** Hants
62 D2 **New Mistley** Essex
49 H3 **New Moat** Pembks
116 A7 **New Ollerton** Notts
217 G3 **New Pitsligo** Abers
163 J4 **New Prestwick** S Ayrs
65 L3 **New Quay** Cerdgn
93 G2 **New Rackheath** Norfk
68 E3 **New Radnor** Powys
150 D3 **New Ridley** Nthumb
21 L2 **New Romney** Kent
115 L2 **New Rossington** Donc
185 J7 **New Sauchie** Clacks
124 B6 **New Sharlston** Wakefd
151 J4 **New Silksworth** Sundld
102 F5 **New Somerby** Lincs
175 K6 **New Stevenston** N Lans
75 H5 **New Town** Beds
27 L2 **New Town** Dorset
27 M7 **New Town** Dorset
19 M2 **New Town** E Susx
53 H7 **New Tredegar** Caerph
164 F2 **New Trows** S Lans

90 C2 **New Walsoken** Cambs
118 C1 **New Waltham** NE Lin
177 L4 **New Winton** E Loth
103 L2 **New York** Lincs
123 J2 **Newall** Leeds
234 e4 **Newark** Ork
102 D2 **Newark-on-Trent** Notts
175 K6 **Newarthill** N Lans
177 J5 **Newbattle** Mdloth
147 L3 **Newbie** D & G
138 C2 **Newbiggin** Cumb
148 F5 **Newbiggin** Cumb
138 F2 **Newbiggin** Cumb
139 K2 **Newbiggin** Dur
131 J3 **Newbiggin** N York
159 H5 **Newbiggin-by-the-Sea** Nthumb
139 G6 **Newbiggin-on-Lune** Cumb
195 L7 **Newbigging** Angus
196 C8 **Newbigging** Angus
187 H1 **Newbigging** Angus
165 K1 **Newbigging** S Lans
115 G6 **Newbold** Derbys
86 F7 **Newbold on Avon** Warwks
72 B5 **Newbold on Stour** Warwks
72 C3 **Newbold Pacey** Warwks
86 F3 **Newbold Verdon** Leics
89 H3 **Newborough** C Pete
108 E7 **Newborough** IOA
100 C7 **Newborough** Staffs
78 F6 **Newbourne** Suffk
176 F4 **Newbridge** C Edin
37 K2 **Newbridge** Caerph
2 D5 **Newbridge** Cnwll
155 G6 **Newbridge** D & G
28 F7 **Newbridge** Hants
16 E5 **Newbridge** IOW
70 E6 **Newbridge Green** Worcs
67 L3 **Newbridge on Wye** Powys
149 L2 **Newbrough** Nthumb
11 J4 **Newbuildings** Devon
217 H3 **Newburgh** Abers
207 J1 **Newburgh** Abers
186 D4 **Newburgh** Fife
121 G7 **Newburgh** Lancs
133 H4 **Newburgh Priory** N York
150 F2 **Newburn** N u Ty
27 G2 **Newbury** Somset
41 J6 **Newbury** W Berk
45 J3 **Newbury Park** Gt Lon
138 E3 **Newby** Cumb
122 B2 **Newby** Lancs
142 B5 **Newby** N York
130 D5 **Newby** N York
129 H3 **Newby Bridge** Cumb
148 E4 **Newby East** Cumb
148 C4 **Newby West** Cumb
132 E3 **Newby Wiske** N York
54 C5 **Newcastle** Mons
82 E6 **Newcastle** Shrops
158 F7 **Newcastle Airport** Nthumb
65 J6 **Newcastle Emlyn** Carmth
151 G3 **Newcastle upon Tyne** N u Ty
99 J4 **Newcastle-under-Lyme** Staffs
156 E5 **Newcastleton** Border
65 H6 **Newchapel** Pembks
32 C5 **Newchapel** Surrey

17 G5	**Newchurch** IOW	
34 E7	**Newchurch** Kent	
38 C2	**Newchurch** Mons	
68 E4	**Newchurch** Powys	
100 D7	**Newchurch** Staffs	
177 J4	**Newcraighall** C Edin	
31 K3	**Newdigate** Surrey	
42 E6	**Newell Green** Br For	
33 L7	**Newenden** Kent	
55 G3	**Newent** Gloucs	
150 F7	**Newfield** Dur	
223 H6	**Newfield** Highld	
48 E3	**Newgale** Pembks	
59 M6	**Newgate Street** Herts	
98 E4	**Newhall** Ches	
177 H3	**Newhaven** C Edin	
19 L5	**Newhaven** E Susx	
143 H5	**Newholm** N York	
175 L6	**Newhouse** N Lans	
19 L2	**Newick** E Susx	
46 E6	**Newington** Kent	
35 G7	**Newington** Kent	
41 L2	**Newington** Oxon	
126 D4	**Newland** C KuH	
54 D6	**Newland** Gloucs	
125 G5	**Newland** N York	
24 C4	**Newland** Somset	
70 E5	**Newland** Worcs	
177 K6	**Newlandrig** Mdloth	
156 E4	**Newlands** Border	
150 D4	**Newlands** Nthumb	
215 G4	**Newlands of Dundurcas** Moray	
2 E5	**Newlyn** Cnwll	
4 C5	**Newlyn East** Cnwll	
207 G2	**Newmachar** Abers	
175 L6	**Newmains** N Lans	
77 K5	**Newman's Green** Suffk	
76 F2	**Newmarket** Suffk	
232 f2	**Newmarket** W Isls	
167 G7	**Newmill** Border	
215 K4	**Newmill** Moray	
196 C4	**Newmill of Inshewan** Angus	
123 L7	**Newmillerdam** Wakefd	
177 G5	**Newmills** C Edin	
176 D2	**Newmills** Fife	
54 D6	**Newmills** Mons	
186 B2	**Newmiln** P & K	
164 B2	**Newmilns** E Ayrs	
61 G6	**Newney Green** Essex	
55 G5	**Newnham** Gloucs	
30 B2	**Newnham** Hants	
75 J6	**Newnham** Herts	
34 C3	**Newnham** Kent	
73 H3	**Newnham** Nhants	
70 B2	**Newnham** Worcs	
9 J7	**Newport** Cnwll	
23 J5	**Newport** Devon	
125 K4	**Newport** E R Yk	
76 D7	**Newport** Essex	
39 G2	**Newport** Gloucs	
227 K4	**Newport** Highld	
16 F5	**Newport** IOW	
37 L3	**Newport** Newpt	
64 E6	**Newport** Pembks	
99 H8	**Newport** Wrekin	
74 C5	**Newport Pagnell** M Keyn	
187 G2	**Newport-on-Tay** Fife	
4 C4	**Newquay** Cnwll	
4 D3	**Newquay Airport** Cnwll	
216 D7	**Newseat** Abers	
121 G4	**Newsham** Lancs	
140 E5	**Newsham** N York	
132 E3	**Newsham** N York	
159 H6	**Newsham** Nthumb	
125 H5	**Newsholme** E R Yk	
167 H3	**Newstead** Border	
101 K3	**Newstead** Notts	
169 H4	**Newstead** Nthumb	
215 K5	**Newtack** Moray	
124 C4	**Newthorpe** N York	
101 J4	**Newthorpe** Notts	
182 F7	**Newton** Ag & B	
75 J5	**Newton** Beds	
167 J5	**Newton** Border	
36 C5	**Newton** Brdgnd	
90 B1	**Newton** Cambs	
76 B5	**Newton** Cambs	
112 B7	**Newton** Ches	
98 D1	**Newton** Ches	
128 F5	**Newton** Ches	
101 H2	**Newton** Derbys	
53 M2	**Newton** Herefs	
69 K4	**Newton** Herefs	
212 F4	**Newton** Highld	
213 H5	**Newton** Highld	
213 J2	**Newton** Highld	
121 K1	**Newton** Lancs	
103 H5	**Newton** Lincs	
177 J4	**Newton** Mdloth	
214 E2	**Newton** Moray	
215 H2	**Newton** Moray	
88 C6	**Newton** Nhants	
91 J1	**Newton** Norfk	
102 B4	**Newton** Notts	
150 C3	**Newton** Nthumb	
175 H6	**Newton** S Lans	
165 H3	**Newton** S Lans	
25 H4	**Newton** Somset	
100 B7	**Newton** Staffs	
77 K6	**Newton** Suffk	
176 E3	**Newton** W Loth	
87 G7	**Newton** Warwks	
7 K2	**Newton Abbot** Devon	
147 L4	**Newton Arlosh** Cumb	
141 G3	**Newton Aycliffe** Dur	
141 K2	**Newton Bewley** Hartpl	
74 D4	**Newton Blossomville** M Keyn	
74 E2	**Newton Bromswold** Beds	
86 D2	**Newton Burgoland** Leics	
117 H4	**Newton by Toft** Lincs	
6 A3	**Newton Ferrers** Cnwll	
6 E6	**Newton Ferrers** Devon	
232 c5	**Newton Ferry** W Isls	
92 E4	**Newton Flotman** Norfk	
87 J4	**Newton Harcourt** Leics	
113 K2	**Newton Heath** Manch	
124 C2	**Newton Kyme** N York	
58 D2	**Newton Longville** Bucks	
174 F7	**Newton Mearns** E Rens	
141 G5	**Newton Morrell** N York	
186 B5	**Newton of Balcanquhal** P & K	
187 H6	**Newton of Balcormo** Fife	
133 H7	**Newton on Ouse** N York	
116 D6	**Newton on Trent** Lincs	
12 E4	**Newton Poppleford** Devon	
57 L3	**Newton Purcell** Oxon	
86 C3	**Newton Regis** Warwks	
138 C2	**Newton Reigny** Cumb	
231 L5	**Newton Row** Highld	
100 F7	**Newton Solney** Derbys	
11 K5	**Newton St Cyres** Devon	
92 F1	**Newton St Faith** Norfk	
39 G7	**Newton St Loe** BaNES	
9 K3	**Newton St Petrock** Devon	
29 H4	**Newton Stacey** Hants	
145 J3	**Newton Stewart** D & G	
28 E4	**Newton Toney** Wilts	
23 H6	**Newton Tracey** Devon	
142 C5	**Newton under Roseberry** R & Cl	
125 H2	**Newton upon Derwent** E R Yk	
30 B5	**Newton Valence** Hants	
155 K3	**Newton Wamphray** D & G	
120 F4	**Newton with Scales** Lancs	
169 J4	**Newton-by-the-Sea** Nthumb	
132 C2	**Newton-le-Willows** N York	
112 E3	**Newton-le-Willows** St Hel	
134 C2	**Newton-on-Rawcliffe** N York	
158 F2	**Newton-on-the-Moor** Nthumb	
216 B7	**Newtongarry Croft** Abers	
177 J5	**Newtongrange** Mdloth	
207 G6	**Newtonhill** Abers	
177 J5	**Newtonloan** Mdloth	
196 F4	**Newtonmill** Angus	
203 H5	**Newtonmore** Highld	
98 F3	**Newtown** Ches	
99 K1	**Newtown** Ches	
147 J5	**Newtown** Cumb	
148 E3	**Newtown** Cumb	
164 F7	**Newtown** D & G	
12 D3	**Newtown** Devon	
24 B6	**Newtown** Devon	
54 F7	**Newtown** Gloucs	
29 L8	**Newtown** Hants	
70 B5	**Newtown** Herefs	
70 C6	**Newtown** Herefs	
202 B4	**Newtown** Highld	
16 E4	**Newtown** IOW	
158 C3	**Newtown** Nthumb	
168 F4	**Newtown** Nthumb	
15 K4	**Newtown** Poole	
82 C5	**Newtown** Powys	
98 B7	**Newtown** Shrops	
98 C6	**Newtown** Shrops	
25 L8	**Newtown** Somset	
112 E1	**Newtown** Wigan	
70 F4	**Newtown** Worcs	
87 G2	**Newtown Linford** Leics	
174 D6	**Newtown of Beltrees** Rens	
167 J3	**Newtown St Boswells** Border	
195 L7	**Newtyle** Angus	
182 D5	**Newyork** Ag & B	
49 G6	**Neyland** Pembks	
25 H7	**Nicholashayne** Devon	
51 G7	**Nicholaston** Swans	
132 D7	**Nidd** N York	
207 H5	**Nigg** C Aber	
223 H6	**Nigg** Highld	
24 D6	**Nightcott** Somset	
40 C4	**Nine Elms** Swindn	
149 K4	**Ninebanks** Nthumb	
70 B2	**Nineveh** Worcs	
20 E3	**Ninfield** E Susx	
16 E5	**Ningwood** IOW	
167 K4	**Nisbet** Border	
179 G7	**Nisbet Hill** Border	
16 G6	**Niton** IOW	
174 F6	**Nitshill** C Glas	
98 D3	**No Man's Heath** Ches	
86 C2	**No Man's Heath** Warwks	
117 H8	**Nocton** Lincs	
57 K5	**Noke** Oxon	
48 E4	**Nolton** Pembks	
48 E4	**Nolton Haven** Pembks	
11 J3	**Nomansland** Devon	
28 E7	**Nomansland** Wilts	
98 C6	**Noneley** Shrops	
35 H4	**Nonington** Kent	
129 L3	**Nook** Cumb	
44 D6	**Norbiton** Gt Lon	
98 E3	**Norbury** Ches	
100 C4	**Norbury** Derbys	
44 F6	**Norbury** Gt Lon	
83 G5	**Norbury** Shrops	
99 H7	**Norbury** Staffs	
70 F2	**Norchard** Worcs	
90 D4	**Nordelph** Norfk	
84 C4	**Nordley** Shrops	
93 K2	**Norfolk Broads** Norfk	
179 J8	**Norham** Nthumb	
123 G6	**Norland Town** Calder	
112 E6	**Norley** Ches	
16 D3	**Norleywood** Hants	
12 D2	**Norman's Green** Devon	
117 G4	**Normanby** Lincs	
125 K7	**Normanby** N Linc	
134 B3	**Normanby** N York	
142 C4	**Normanby** R & Cl	
117 J3	**Normanby le Wold** Lincs	
30 F2	**Normandy** Surrey	
101 G5	**Normanton** C Derb	
102 D4	**Normanton** Leics	
102 F4	**Normanton** Lincs	
102 B2	**Normanton** Notts	
124 B6	**Normanton** Wakefd	
86 D2	**Normanton le Heath** Leics	
101 K7	**Normanton on Soar** Notts	
101 L6	**Normanton on the Wolds** Notts	
116 C7	**Normanton on Trent** Notts	
115 K5	**North Anston** Rothm	
42 E6	**North Ascot** Br For	
57 J3	**North Aston** Oxon	
29 H7	**North Baddesley** Hants	
191 L4	**North Ballachulish** Highld	
26 E5	**North Barrow** Somset	
105 L5	**North Barsham** Norfk	
46 C3	**North Benfleet** Essex	
18 C5	**North Bersted** W Susx	
178 C2	**North Berwick** E Loth	
17 H1	**North Boarhunt** Hants	
11 H7	**North Bovey** Devon	
27 J1	**North Bradley** Wilts	
10 C8	**North Brentor** Devon	
27 G4	**North Brewham** Somset	

23 G4 **North Buckland** Devon
93 H2 **North Burlingham** Norfk
26 F6 **North Cadbury** Somset
116 F6 **North Carlton** Lincs
115 L4 **North Carlton** Notts
125 K4 **North Cave** E R Yk
56 A6 **North Cerney** Gloucs
19 K2 **North Chailey** E Susx
28 D7 **North Charford** Hants
169 H5 **North Charlton** Nthumb
44 E6 **North Cheam** Gt Lon
27 G6 **North Cheriton** Somset
13 K4 **North Chideock** Dorset
125 K3 **North Cliffe** E R Yk
116 D6 **North Clifton** Notts
118 E4 **North Cockerington** Lincs
182 C1 **North Connel** Ag & B
36 C4 **North Cornelly** Brdgnd
191 G5 **North Corry** Highld
118 E2 **North Cotes** Lincs
93 K5 **North Cove** Suffk
141 G6 **North Cowton** N York
74 D5 **North Crawley** M Keyn
105 K5 **North Creake** Norfk
25 L6 **North Curry** Somset
125 L1 **North Dalton** E R Yk
124 B1 **North Deighton** N York
34 B4 **North Downs**
125 G3 **North Duffield** N York
218 C6 **North Duntulm** Highld
35 G5 **North Elham** Kent
106 B7 **North Elmham** Norfk
124 D7 **North Elmsall** Wakefd
17 J3 **North End** C Port
61 G4 **North End** Essex
28 C7 **North End** Hants
74 D2 **North End** Nhants
18 D5 **North End** W Susx
219 H5 **North Erradale** Highld
87 J3 **North Evington** C Leic
61 K7 **North Fambridge** Essex
126 B5 **North Ferriby** E R Yk
135 H8 **North Frodingham** E R Yk
15 M1 **North Gorley** Hants
79 G3 **North Green** Suffk
134 C6 **North Grimston** N York
17 K2 **North Hayling** Hants
5 L1 **North Hill** Cnwll
43 H4 **North Hillingdon** Gt Lon
57 J6 **North Hinksey** Oxon
31 K3 **North Holmwood** Surrey
7 G5 **North Huish** Devon
116 F7 **North Hykeham** Lincs
117 H2 **North Kelsey** Lincs
213 G5 **North Kessock** Highld
126 E6 **North Killingholme** N Linc
132 F3 **North Kilvington** N York
87 H6 **North Kilworth** Leics
103 J3 **North Kyme** Lincs
135 K5 **North Landing** E R Yk

58 D6 **North Lee** Bucks
57 H5 **North Leigh** Oxon
116 C5 **North Leverton with Habblesthorpe** Notts
71 J5 **North Littleton** Worcs
92 C6 **North Lopham** Norfk
88 D3 **North Luffenham** Rutlnd
30 D7 **North Marden** W Susx
58 C4 **North Marston** Bucks
177 K6 **North Middleton** Mdloth
144 C4 **North Milmain** D & G
24 B5 **North Molton** Devon
41 K3 **North Moreton** Oxon
18 B5 **North Mundham** W Susx
102 D2 **North Muskham** Notts
125 L3 **North Newbald** E R Yk
72 E6 **North Newington** Oxon
40 C8 **North Newnton** Wilts
25 L5 **North Newton** Somset
39 H2 **North Nibley** Gloucs
142 B4 **North Ormesby** Middsb
118 C3 **North Ormsby** Lincs
132 E2 **North Otterington** N York
117 H3 **North Owersby** Lincs
13 L1 **North Perrott** Somset
25 L5 **North Petherton** Somset
9 H6 **North Petherwin** Cnwll
91 J3 **North Pickenham** Norfk
71 G4 **North Piddle** Worcs
7 H7 **North Pool** Devon
13 M3 **North Poorton** Dorset
176 F3 **North Queensferry** C Edin
24 B5 **North Radworthy** Devon
103 G3 **North Rauceby** Lincs
118 E5 **North Reston** Lincs
123 K1 **North Rigton** N York
113 K7 **North Rode** Ches
234 e3 **North Ronaldsay Airport** Ork
90 F1 **North Runcton** Norfk
116 D7 **North Scarle** Lincs
191 H7 **North Shian** Ag & B
151 J2 **North Shields** N Tyne
46 F3 **North Shoebury** Sthend
120 D3 **North Shore** Bpool
89 K4 **North Side** C Pete
118 F3 **North Somercotes** Lincs
132 D4 **North Stainley** N York
45 L4 **North Stifford** Thurr
39 G6 **North Stoke** BaNES
41 L3 **North Stoke** Oxon
18 D4 **North Stoke** W Susx
34 D3 **North Street** Kent
41 M6 **North Street** W Berk
169 J3 **North Sunderland** Nthumb
9 J3 **North Tamerton** Cnwll
10 F4 **North Tawton** Devon
175 K1 **North Third** Stirlg
118 D2 **North Thoresby** Lincs

28 E2 **North Tidworth** Wilts
10 D3 **North Town** Devon
26 E3 **North Town** Somset
42 E4 **North Town** W & M
92 C2 **North Tuddenham** Norfk
107 G6 **North Walsham** Norfk
29 K3 **North Waltham** Hants
30 B2 **North Warnborough** Hants
60 D7 **North Weald Bassett** Essex
116 C4 **North Wheatley** Notts
38 E8 **North Widcombe** BaNES
117 K4 **North Willingham** Lincs
115 H8 **North Wingfield** Derbys
102 F7 **North Witham** Lincs
26 F8 **North Wootton** Dorset
105 G7 **North Wootton** Norfk
26 E3 **North Wootton** Somset
39 J5 **North Wraxall** Wilts
142 F6 **North York Moors National Park**
58 F4 **Northall** Bucks
141 J7 **Northallerton** N York
29 H8 **Northam** C Sotn
23 G5 **Northam** Devon
73 L3 **Northampton** Nhants
70 E2 **Northampton** Worcs
59 L7 **Northaw** Herts
13 H1 **Northay** Somset
89 H3 **Northborough** C Pete
35 J4 **Northbourne** Kent
29 K4 **Northbrook** Hants
30 F5 **Northchapel** W Susx
58 F6 **Northchurch** Herts
9 J6 **Northcott** Devon
57 J7 **Northcourt** Oxon
35 K2 **Northdown** Kent
72 E4 **Northend** Warwks
113 J4 **Northenden** Manch
85 H7 **Northfield** Birm
207 G4 **Northfield** C Aber
126 C5 **Northfield** E R Yk
88 E2 **Northfields** Lincs
45 M5 **Northfleet** Kent
21 G2 **Northiam** E Susx
75 G5 **Northill** Beds
29 K4 **Northington** Hants
104 B2 **Northlands** Lincs
56 C5 **Northleach** Gloucs
12 F3 **Northleigh** Devon
10 D5 **Northlew** Devon
57 H7 **Northmoor** Oxon
196 C5 **Northmuir** Angus
17 K2 **Northney** Hants
43 J4 **Northolt** Gt Lon
111 H7 **Northop** Flints
111 J7 **Northop Hall** Flints
116 E3 **Northorpe** Lincs
103 K5 **Northorpe** Lincs
123 G5 **Northowram** Calder
15 H5 **Northport** Dorset
106 F5 **Northrepps** Norfk
232 d5 **Northton** W Isls
157 L2 **Northumberland National Park** Nthumb
25 H5 **Northway** Somset
112 F6 **Northwich** Ches
70 E3 **Northwick** Worcs
91 H4 **Northwold** Norfk

43 H3 **Northwood** Gt Lon
16 F4 **Northwood** IOW
98 C6 **Northwood** Shrops
55 G5 **Northwood Green** Gloucs
124 E7 **Norton** Donc
19 M5 **Norton** E Susx
55 J3 **Norton** Gloucs
134 C5 **Norton** N York
73 H2 **Norton** Nhants
115 L6 **Norton** Notts
68 F2 **Norton** Powys
141 K3 **Norton** S on T
84 D4 **Norton** Shrops
77 L2 **Norton** Suffk
18 C4 **Norton** W Susx
39 K4 **Norton** Wilts
70 F4 **Norton** Worcs
71 J5 **Norton** Worcs
27 K3 **Norton Bavant** Wilts
99 K6 **Norton Bridge** Staffs
85 H2 **Norton Canes** Staffs
69 H5 **Norton Canon** Herefs
102 E2 **Norton Disney** Lincs
25 J6 **Norton Fitzwarren** Somset
16 D5 **Norton Green** IOW
38 E7 **Norton Hawkfield** BaNES
60 F6 **Norton Heath** Essex
99 G5 **Norton in Hales** Shrops
72 B2 **Norton Lindsey** Warwks
77 L2 **Norton Little Green** Suffk
38 E7 **Norton Malreward** BaNES
27 H1 **Norton St Philip** Somset
26 C7 **Norton sub Hamdon** Somset
93 J4 **Norton Subcourse** Norfk
69 G5 **Norton Wood** Herefs
86 D3 **Norton-Juxta-Twycross** Leics
132 F5 **Norton-le-Clay** N York
102 C1 **Norwell** Notts
116 B8 **Norwell Woodhouse** Notts
92 F2 **Norwich** Norfk
92 E2 **Norwich Airport** Norfk
92 F2 **Norwich Cathedral** Norfk
235 e1 **Norwick** Shet
185 J8 **Norwood** Clacks
43 J5 **Norwood Green** Gt Lon
31 L3 **Norwood Hill** Surrey
6 E6 **Noss Mayo** Devon
132 D4 **Nosterfield** N York
210 D8 **Nostie** Highld
56 C4 **Notgrove** Gloucs
36 C5 **Nottage** Brdgnd
6 B4 **Notter** Cnwll
101 L5 **Nottingham** C Nott
123 L7 **Notton** Wakefd
39 K6 **Notton** Wilts
70 E2 **Noutard's Green** Worcs
83 H2 **Nox** Shrops
42 A3 **Nuffield** Oxon
133 H7 **Nun Monkton** N York
125 K2 **Nunburnholme** E R Yk
86 D5 **Nuneaton** Warwks
57 K7 **Nuneham Courtenay** Oxon
45 G5 **Nunhead** Gt Lon
126 E1 **Nunkeeling** E R Yk

27 G3 **Nunney** Somset
133 K4 **Nunnington** N York
127 G8 **Nunsthorpe** NE Lin
142 C4 **Nunthorpe** Middsb
124 F1 **Nunthorpe** York
142 C5 **Nunthorpe Village** Middsb
28 D6 **Nunton** Wilts
132 E5 **Nunwick** N York
29 G7 **Nursling** Hants
17 L2 **Nutbourne** W Susx
18 E3 **Nutbourne** W Susx
32 B3 **Nutfield** Surrey
101 K4 **Nuthall** Notts
76 B7 **Nuthampstead** Herts
31 K6 **Nuthurst** W Susx
32 D7 **Nutley** E Susx
231 L3 **Nybster** Highld
18 B6 **Nyetimber** W Susx
30 D6 **Nyewood** W Susx
11 G4 **Nymet Rowland** Devon
11 G5 **Nymet Tracey** Devon
55 J7 **Nympsfield** Gloucs
18 C5 **Nyton** W Susx

O

34 B3 **Oad Street** Kent
87 J4 **Oadby** Leics
10 D5 **Oak Cross** Devon
100 B4 **Oakamoor** Staffs
176 E5 **Oakbank** W Loth
37 J2 **Oakdale** Caerph
25 J6 **Oake** Somset
84 F3 **Oaken** Staffs
121 H2 **Oakenclough** Lancs
84 C2 **Oakengates** Wrekin
150 F7 **Oakenshaw** Dur
123 H5 **Oakenshaw** Kirk
100 F1 **Oaker Side** Derbys
66 B3 **Oakford** Cerdgn
24 E6 **Oakford** Devon
88 C2 **Oakham** Rutlnd
30 C4 **Oakhanger** Hants
26 F3 **Oakhill** Somset
76 B2 **Oakington** Cambs
55 H4 **Oakle Street** Gloucs
74 E4 **Oakley** Beds
57 M5 **Oakley** Bucks
176 D1 **Oakley** Fife
29 K2 **Oakley** Hants
92 E7 **Oakley** Suffk
55 K7 **Oakridge** Gloucs
39 M2 **Oaksey** Wilts
86 D2 **Oakthorpe** Leics
101 G5 **Oakwood** C Derb
31 J4 **Oakwoodhill** Surrey
122 F3 **Oakworth** Brad
34 D3 **Oare** Kent
24 C3 **Oare** Somset
40 D7 **Oare** Wilts
103 G5 **Oasby** Lincs
26 B6 **Oath** Somset
196 D5 **Oathlaw** Angus
43 H7 **Oatlands Park** Surrey
182 B2 **Oban** Ag & B
83 G7 **Obley** Shrops
195 G8 **Obney** P & K
26 F7 **Oborne** Dorset
78 D1 **Occold** Suffk
231 J7 **Occumster** Highld
163 L5 **Ochiltree** E Ayrs
101 H5 **Ockbrook** Derbys
31 H1 **Ockham** Surrey
190 B3 **Ockle** Highld
31 J4 **Ockley** Surrey
69 L5 **Ocle Pychard** Herefs
26 D7 **Odcombe** Somset
39 H7 **Odd Down** BaNES
71 G3 **Oddingley** Worcs

56 E3 **Oddington** Gloucs
57 K5 **Oddington** Oxon
74 D3 **Odell** Beds
30 C2 **Odiham** Hants
123 H4 **Odsal** Brad
75 K6 **Odsey** Herts
28 D6 **Odstock** Wilts
86 E3 **Odstone** Leics
72 D2 **Offchurch** Warwks
71 J5 **Offenham** Worcs
113 K4 **Offerton** Gt Man
19 L3 **Offham** E Susx
33 H2 **Offham** Kent
18 D4 **Offham** W Susx
75 J2 **Offord Cluny** Cambs
75 J2 **Offord Darcy** Cambs
78 C5 **Offton** Suffk
12 F3 **Offwell** Devon
40 D6 **Ogbourne Maizey** Wilts
40 D6 **Ogbourne St Andrew** Wilts
40 D5 **Ogbourne St George** Wilts
158 E6 **Ogle** Nthumb
112 C5 **Oglet** Lpool
36 D5 **Ogmore** V Glam
36 E3 **Ogmore Vale** Brdgnd
36 D5 **Ogmore-by-Sea** V Glam
14 F1 **Okeford Fitzpaine** Dorset
10 E5 **Okehampton** Devon
87 L8 **Old** Nhants
207 H4 **Old Aberdeen** C Aber
29 L5 **Old Alresford** Hants
154 D3 **Old Auchenbrack** D & G
101 K4 **Old Basford** C Nott
30 A2 **Old Basing** Hants
169 G5 **Old Bewick** Nthumb
118 E8 **Old Bolingbroke** Lincs
123 J2 **Old Bramhope** Leeds
115 G6 **Old Brampton** Derbys
146 D2 **Old Bridge of Urr** D & G
92 C5 **Old Buckenham** Norfk
41 J8 **Old Burghclere** Hants
133 H3 **Old Byland** N York
115 L2 **Old Cantley** Donc
127 G8 **Old Clee** NE Lin
25 G3 **Old Cleeve** Somset
115 L8 **Old Clipstone** Notts
152 F3 **Old Dailly** S Ayrs
102 A7 **Old Dalby** Leics
217 J5 **Old Deer** Abers
115 K3 **Old Edlington** Donc
126 E3 **Old Ellerby** E R Yk
79 G7 **Old Felixstowe** Suffk
89 H4 **Old Fletton** C Pete
54 E4 **Old Forge** Herefs
2 a1 **Old Grimsby** IoS
60 B4 **Old Hall Green** Herts
60 D5 **Old Harlow** Essex
105 G4 **Old Hunstanton** Norfk
89 K7 **Old Hurst** Cambs
130 B2 **Old Hutton** Cumb
4 D7 **Old Kea** Cnwll
174 E4 **Old Kilpatrick** W Duns
59 L4 **Old Knebworth** Herts
121 K4 **Old Langho** Lancs
104 C3 **Old Leake** Lincs
134 C5 **Old Malton** N York
124 C4 **Old Micklefield** Leeds
72 C2 **Old Milverton** Warwks
78 C3 **Old Newton** Suffk
68 E3 **Old Radnor** Powys

216 D8 **Old Rayne** Abers
21 K2 **Old Romney** Kent
19 G4 **Old Shoreham** W Susx
39 H4 **Old Sodbury** S Glos
102 F5 **Old Somerby** Lincs
73 L6 **Old Stratford** Nhants
84 F6 **Old Swinford** Dudley
132 F3 **Old Thirsk** N York
130 B3 **Old Town** Cumb
20 C5 **Old Town** E Susx
2 b2 **Old Town** IoS
113 J3 **Old Trafford** Traffd
75 G5 **Old Warden** Beds
89 G7 **Old Weston** Cambs
231 L5 **Old Wick** Highld
43 G5 **Old Windsor** W & M
34 E4 **Old Wives Lees** Kent
43 G8 **Old Woking** Surrey
224 D2 **Oldany** Highld
71 K2 **Oldberrow** Warwks
85 H5 **Oldbury** Sandw
84 C5 **Oldbury** Shrops
86 C5 **Oldbury** Warwks
39 J3 **Oldbury on the Hill** Gloucs
38 E2 **Oldbury-on-Severn** S Glos
53 L3 **Oldcastle** Mons
115 L4 **Oldcotes** Notts
70 E2 **Oldfield** Worcs
27 H2 **Oldford** Somset
113 L1 **Oldham** Oldham
178 F4 **Oldhamstocks** E Loth
38 F6 **Oldland** S Glos
216 F8 **Oldmeldrum** Abers
6 B2 **Oldmill** Cnwll
37 M8 **Oldmixon** N Som
228 C4 **Oldshoremore** Highld
133 H4 **Oldstead** N York
148 E3 **Oldwall** Cumb
50 F6 **Oldwalls** Swans
100 C8 **Olive Green** Staffs
165 L4 **Oliver** Border
29 J6 **Oliver's Battery** Hants
235 c3 **Ollaberry** Shet
209 H6 **Ollach** Highld
113 H6 **Ollerton** Ches
116 A7 **Ollerton** Notts
98 F7 **Ollerton** Shrops
74 C4 **Olney** M Keyn
231 H3 **Olrig House** Highld
85 K6 **Olton** Solhll
38 E3 **Olveston** S Glos
70 E2 **Ombersley** Worcs
116 B7 **Ompton** Notts
237 d5 **Onchan** IOM
100 B2 **Onecote** Staffs
83 J7 **Onibury** Shrops
191 K4 **Onich** Highld
52 C6 **Onllwyn** Neath
99 H4 **Onneley** Staffs
31 G2 **Onslow Village** Surrey
112 E6 **Onston** Ches
219 H6 **Opinan** Highld
215 G3 **Orbliston** Moray
208 D5 **Orbost** Highld
119 G7 **Orby** Lincs
25 K6 **Orchard Portman** Somset
28 B3 **Orcheston** Wilts
54 C3 **Orcop** Herefs
54 C3 **Orcop Hill** Herefs
216 C3 **Ord** Abers
206 C3 **Ordhead** Abers
205 K5 **Ordie** Abers
215 H3 **Ordiequish** Moray
150 B3 **Ordley** Nthumb
116 B5 **Ordsall** Notts
21 G4 **Ore** E Susx
79 J4 **Orford** Suffk

112 E4 **Orford** Warrtn
15 H4 **Organford** Dorset
34 D7 **Orlestone** Kent
69 J2 **Orleton** Herefs
70 C2 **Orleton** Worcs
74 C1 **Orlingbury** Nhants
142 C4 **Ormesby** R & Cl
93 K1 **Ormesby St Margaret** Norfk
93 K1 **Ormesby St Michael** Norfk
219 K4 **Ormiscaig** Highld
177 L4 **Ormiston** E Loth
189 L4 **Ormsaigmore** Highld
172 C4 **Ormsary** Ag & B
120 F8 **Ormskirk** Lancs
171 G2 **Oronsay** Ag & B
234 b6 **Orphir** Ork
45 J6 **Orpington** Gt Lon
111 K3 **Orrell** Sefton
112 D2 **Orrell** Wigan
146 D5 **Orroland** D & G
45 M4 **Orsett** Thurr
84 E1 **Orslow** Staffs
102 C4 **Orston** Notts
138 F5 **Orton** Cumb
88 B7 **Orton** Nhants
84 F4 **Orton** Staffs
89 H4 **Orton Longueville** C Pete
89 H4 **Orton Waterville** C Pete
86 C3 **Orton-on-the-Hill** Leics
75 L4 **Orwell** Cambs
121 J4 **Osbaldeston** Lancs
124 F1 **Osbaldwick** York
86 E3 **Osbaston** Leics
97 L7 **Osbaston** Shrops
17 G4 **Osborne House** IOW
103 H5 **Osbournby** Lincs
112 D7 **Oscroft** Ches
208 E6 **Ose** Highld
101 H8 **Osgathorpe** Leics
117 H3 **Osgodby** Lincs
124 F4 **Osgodby** N York
135 G3 **Osgodby** N York
209 H6 **Oskaig** Highld
189 L7 **Oskamull** Ag & B
100 D4 **Osmaston** Derbys
14 D5 **Osmington** Dorset
14 E6 **Osmington Mills** Dorset
123 L4 **Osmondthorpe** Leeds
141 K7 **Osmotherley** N York
57 J6 **Osney** Oxon
34 D3 **Ospringe** Kent
123 K6 **Ossett** Wakefd
116 C8 **Ossington** Notts
44 D5 **Osterley** Gt Lon
133 K4 **Oswaldkirk** N York
121 L5 **Oswaldtwistle** Lancs
97 L6 **Oswestry** Shrops
32 F2 **Otford** Kent
33 K3 **Otham** Kent
26 B5 **Othery** Somset
123 J2 **Otley** Leeds
78 E4 **Otley** Suffk
172 F2 **Otter Ferry** Ag & B
29 J6 **Otterbourne** Hants
131 G7 **Otterburn** N York
157 M4 **Otterburn** Nthumb
8 F6 **Otterham** Cnwll
25 K3 **Otterhampton** Somset
232 c5 **Otternish** W Isls
43 G7 **Ottershaw** Surrey
235 d3 **Otterswick** Shet
12 E5 **Otterton** Devon
6 C2 **Ottery** Devon
12 E4 **Ottery St Mary** Devon

34 F6 **Ottinge** Kent
127 G5 **Ottringham** E R Yk
147 K6 **Oughterside** Cumb
114 F3 **Oughtibridge** Sheff
113 G4 **Oughtrington** Warrtn
133 H5 **Oulston** N York
147 M5 **Oulton** Cumb
106 D6 **Oulton** Norfk
99 K5 **Oulton** Staffs
93 L5 **Oulton** Suffk
93 L5 **Oulton Broad** Suffk
106 D6 **Oulton Street** Norfk
88 F6 **Oundle** Nhants
84 F5 **Ounsdale** Staffs
149 G7 **Ousby** Cumb
77 G3 **Ousden** Suffk
125 K6 **Ousefleet** E R Yk
151 G4 **Ouston** Dur
120 E3 **Out Rawcliffe** Lancs
137 K7 **Outgate** Cumb
139 H6 **Outhgill** Cumb
71 K2 **Outhill** Warwks
123 G6 **Outlane** Kirk
90 D3 **Outwell** Norfk
32 B4 **Outwood** Surrey
99 H8 **Outwoods** Staffs
123 L5 **Ouzlewell Green** Leeds
75 L1 **Over** Cambs
26 E7 **Over Compton** Dorset
114 D7 **Over Haddon** Derbys
129 L5 **Over Kellet** Lancs
57 H4 **Over Kiddington** Oxon
56 F3 **Over Norton** Oxon
113 H6 **Over Peover** Ches
133 G2 **Over Silton** N York
25 J4 **Over Stowey** Somset
26 B7 **Over Stratton** Somset
28 F4 **Over Wallop** Hants
86 B5 **Over Whitacre** Warwks
57 H3 **Over Worton** Oxon
71 G6 **Overbury** Worcs
14 D6 **Overcombe** Dorset
26 C4 **Overleigh** Somset
111 L6 **Overpool** Ches
225 J4 **Overscaig Hotel** Highld
86 C1 **Overseal** Derbys
34 E3 **Oversland** Kent
74 B2 **Overstone** Nhants
106 F4 **Overstrand** Norfk
72 F6 **Overthorpe** Nhants
207 G3 **Overton** C Aber
29 K2 **Overton** Hants
129 J7 **Overton** Lancs
133 H7 **Overton** N York
69 K1 **Overton** Shrops
50 F7 **Overton** Swans
123 K7 **Overton** Wakefd
98 A4 **Overton** Wrexhm
130 C4 **Overtown** Lancs
175 L7 **Overtown** N Lans
58 C4 **Oving** Bucks
18 B5 **Oving** W Susx
19 K5 **Ovingdean** Br & H
150 D3 **Ovingham** Nthumb
140 E4 **Ovington** Dur
77 H6 **Ovington** Essex
29 K5 **Ovington** Hants
91 K3 **Ovington** Norfk
150 D3 **Ovington** Nthumb
28 F7 **Ower** Hants
14 E5 **Owermoigne** Dorset
115 G4 **Owlerton** Sheff
42 D7 **Owlsmoor** Br For
58 C6 **Owlswick** Bucks
117 H1 **Owmby** Lincs
117 G4 **Owmby** Lincs
29 K6 **Owslebury** Hants

124 E7 **Owston** Donc
87 L3 **Owston** Leics
116 D2 **Owston Ferry** N Linc
127 G4 **Owstwick** E R Yk
127 H5 **Owthorne** E R Yk
102 A5 **Owthorpe** Notts
91 G3 **Oxborough** Norfk
13 L3 **Oxbridge** Dorset
118 D6 **Oxcombe** Lincs
61 G3 **Oxen End** Essex
129 G3 **Oxen Park** Cumb
129 L2 **Oxenholme** Cumb
122 F4 **Oxenhope** Brad
26 C3 **Oxenpill** Somset
55 L2 **Oxenton** Gloucs
40 F8 **Oxenwood** Wilts
57 K6 **Oxford** Oxon
43 J2 **Oxhey** Herts
72 C5 **Oxhill** Warwks
84 F3 **Oxley** Wolves
61 L5 **Oxley Green** Essex
90 C6 **Oxlode** Cambs
167 L5 **Oxnam** Border
106 F7 **Oxnead** Norfk
43 J7 **Oxshott** Surrey
114 F2 **Oxspring** Barns
32 C3 **Oxted** Surrey
178 B7 **Oxton** Border
124 D2 **Oxton** N York
101 M3 **Oxton** Notts
51 G7 **Oxwich** Swans
50 F7 **Oxwich Green** Swans
221 K2 **Oykel Bridge Hotel** Highld
206 D1 **Oyne** Abers
51 H7 **Oystermouth** Swans

P

232 g2 **Pabail** W Isls
86 D1 **Packington** Leics
196 C6 **Padanaram** Angus
58 B2 **Padbury** Bucks
44 F4 **Paddington** Gt Lon
46 B7 **Paddlesworth** Kent
35 G6 **Paddlesworth** Kent
33 H4 **Paddock Wood** Kent
122 B4 **Padiham** Lancs
132 B7 **Padside** N York
4 E2 **Padstow** Cnwll
41 L7 **Padworth** W Berk
18 B6 **Pagham** W Susx
46 F2 **Paglesham** Essex
7 K4 **Paignton** Torbay
86 F6 **Pailton** Warwks
68 D5 **Painscastle** Powys
150 D3 **Painshawfield** Nthumb
134 C7 **Painsthorpe** E R Yk
55 K6 **Painswick** Gloucs
34 D3 **Painter's Forstal** Kent
174 E5 **Paisley** Rens
93 L5 **Pakefield** Suffk
77 L2 **Pakenham** Suffk
42 E5 **Paley Street** W & M
85 H4 **Palfrey** Wsall
92 D7 **Palgrave** Suffk
14 E4 **Pallington** Dorset
163 L5 **Palmerston** E Ayrs
146 E4 **Palnackie** D & G
145 J3 **Palnure** D & G
115 J7 **Palterton** Derbys
41 L8 **Pamber End** Hants
41 L8 **Pamber Green** Hants
41 L7 **Pamber Heath** Hants
55 L2 **Pamington** Gloucs
15 J3 **Pamphill** Dorset
76 C5 **Pampisford** Cambs
187 J1 **Panbride** Angus
9 H4 **Pancrasweek** Devon

53 M4 **Pandy** Mons
110 B8 **Pandy Tudur** Conwy
61 H3 **Panfield** Essex
41 M5 **Pangbourne** W Berk
19 J4 **Pangdean** W Susx
123 L1 **Pannal** N York
132 D8 **Pannal Ash** N York
205 J6 **Pannanich Wells Hotel** Abers
97 L7 **Pant** Shrops
95 H3 **Pant Glas** Gwynd
36 E4 **Pant-ffrwyth** Brdgnd
81 L8 **Pant-y-dwr** Powys
111 H8 **Pant-y-mwyn** Flints
111 G6 **Pantasaph** Flints
81 H4 **Pantglas** Powys
117 K5 **Panton** Lincs
93 H2 **Panxworth** Norfk
234 c1 **Papa Westray Airport** Ork
136 F2 **Papcastle** Cumb
231 L5 **Papigoe** Highld
178 D4 **Papple** E Loth
101 K3 **Papplewick** Notts
75 K3 **Papworth Everard** Cambs
75 J2 **Papworth St Agnes** Cambs
5 G5 **Par** Cnwll
121 G7 **Parbold** Lancs
26 E4 **Parbrook** Somset
96 D5 **Parc** Gwynd
38 B3 **Parc Seymour** Newpt
136 F3 **Pardshaw** Cumb
79 G3 **Parham** Suffk
206 E5 **Park** Abers
154 F4 **Park** D & G
149 H3 **Park** Nthumb
42 B3 **Park Corner** Oxon
34 D6 **Park Farm** Kent
17 G2 **Park Gate** Hants
123 J3 **Park Gate** Leeds
44 D4 **Park Royal** Gt Lon
59 J6 **Park Street** Herts
54 E6 **Parkend** Gloucs
33 G4 **Parkers Green** Kent
111 J6 **Parkgate** Ches
155 H4 **Parkgate** D & G
31 K3 **Parkgate** Surrey
174 E4 **Parkhall** W Duns
22 F6 **Parkham** Devon
207 G3 **Parkhill House** Abers
51 G7 **Parkmill** Swans
151 K5 **Parkside** Dur
175 L6 **Parkside** N Lans
15 J4 **Parkstone** Poole
60 C6 **Parracombe** Devon
23 L3 **Parracombe** Devon
89 L2 **Parson Drove** Cambs
62 B3 **Parson's Heath** Essex
174 F5 **Partick** C Glas
113 G3 **Partington** Traffd
118 F7 **Partney** Lincs
136 D3 **Parton** Cumb
19 G2 **Partridge Green** W Susx
100 D2 **Parwich** Derbys
73 L6 **Passenham** Nhants
30 D4 **Passfield** Hants
107 G5 **Paston** Norfk
19 J4 **Patcham** Br & H
18 E4 **Patching** W Susx
38 E4 **Patchway** S Glos
132 B6 **Pateley Bridge** N York
185 M5 **Path of Condie** P & K
186 E8 **Pathhead** Fife
177 K5 **Pathhead** Mdloth
163 K7 **Patna** E Ayrs
40 B8 **Patney** Wilts
132 C2 **Patrick Brompton** N York

113 H2 **Patricroft** Salfd
127 H6 **Patrington** E R Yk
35 G4 **Patrixbourne** Kent
137 L4 **Patterdale** Cumb
84 E4 **Pattingham** Staffs
73 J4 **Pattishall** Nhants
61 K3 **Pattiswick Green** Essex
2 E5 **Paul** Cnwll
28 C5 **Paul's Dene** Wilts
73 K5 **Paulerspury** Bucks
126 E5 **Paull** E R Yk
26 F1 **Paulton** BaNES
158 D3 **Pauperhaugh** Nthumb
74 E4 **Pavenham** Beds
25 L3 **Pawlett** Somset
71 L6 **Paxford** Gloucs
179 J7 **Paxton** Border
12 E3 **Payhembury** Devon
122 C1 **Paythorne** Lancs
19 L5 **Peacehaven** E Susx
114 D3 **Peak District National Park**
114 C5 **Peak Forest** Derbys
89 H3 **Peakirk** C Pete
190 E1 **Peanmeanach** Highld
31 L5 **Pease Pottage** W Susx
39 G8 **Peasedown St John** BaNES
41 J5 **Peasemore** W Berk
79 H2 **Peasenhall** Suffk
31 H3 **Peaslake** Surrey
112 D3 **Peasley Cross** St Hel
21 H2 **Peasmarsh** E Susx
187 G5 **Peat Inn** Fife
217 H2 **Peathill** Abers
87 H5 **Peatling Magna** Leics
87 H5 **Peatling Parva** Leics
77 J7 **Pebmarsh** Essex
71 K5 **Pebworth** Worcs
122 E5 **Pecket Well** Calder
98 D2 **Peckforton** Ches
45 G5 **Peckham** Gt Lon
86 F4 **Peckleton** Leics
34 F7 **Pedlinge** Kent
85 G6 **Pedmore** Dudley
26 B4 **Pedwell** Somset
166 C2 **Peebles** Border
237 b4 **Peel** IOM
35 G6 **Peene** Kent
59 J2 **Pegsdon** Beds
159 G5 **Pegswood** Nthumb
35 K2 **Pegwell** Kent
209 H7 **Peinchorran** Highld
208 F3 **Peinlich** Highld
62 B5 **Peldon** Essex
85 H3 **Pelsall** Wsall
151 G4 **Pelton** Dur
5 K5 **Pelynt** Cnwll
51 G5 **Pemberton** Carmth
112 D2 **Pemberton** Wigan
50 E5 **Pembrey** Carmth
69 H3 **Pembridge** Herefs
49 G7 **Pembroke** Pembks
49 G6 **Pembroke Dock** Pembks
48 E4 **Pembrokeshire Coast National Park** Pembks
33 G5 **Pembury** Kent
51 L4 **Pen Rhiwfawr** Neath
80 F6 **Pen-bont Rhydybeddau** Cerdgn
49 J3 **Pen-ffordd** Pembks
65 H6 **Pen-rhiw** Pembks
54 D6 **Pen-twyn** Mons
97 K7 **Pen-y-bont** Powys
97 G7 **Pen-y-bont-fawr** Powys
65 G6 **Pen-y-bryn** Pembks

54 C6 **Pen-y-clawdd** Mons
37 G3 **Pen-y-coedcae** Rhondd
48 E3 **Pen-y-cwn** Pembks
111 G7 **Pen-y-felin** Flints
97 H7 **Pen-y-Garnedd** Powys
94 D5 **Pen-y-graig** Gwynd
97 J3 **Pen-y-stryt** Denbgs
54 D6 **Penallt** Mons
49 J7 **Penally** Pembks
54 E3 **Penalt** Herefs
37 J6 **Penarth** V Glam
65 J4 **Penbryn** Cerdgn
66 B7 **Pencader** Carmth
177 L5 **Pencaitland** E Loth
108 D6 **Pencarnisiog** IOA
66 C5 **Pencarreg** Carmth
53 H3 **Pencelli** Powys
51 G6 **Penclawdd** Swans
36 E4 **Pencoed** Brdgnd
69 L4 **Pencombe** Herefs
54 E4 **Pencraig** Herefs
97 G6 **Pencraig** Powys
2 C4 **Pendeen** Cnwll
52 E6 **Penderyn** Rhondd
50 B4 **Pendine** Carmth
113 H2 **Pendlebury** Salfd
121 L3 **Pendleton** Lancs
55 H2 **Pendock** Worcs
8 D8 **Pendoggett** Cnwll
13 M1 **Pendomer** Somset
37 G5 **Pendoylan** V Glam
81 G4 **Penegoes** Powys
37 J2 **Pengam** Caerph
37 K5 **Pengam** Cardif
45 G6 **Penge** Gt Lon
8 E7 **Pengelly** Cnwll
4 F6 **Pengrugla** Cnwll
3 K2 **Penhallow** Cnwll
3 J4 **Penhalvean** Cnwll
40 D3 **Penhill** Swindn
38 B3 **Penhow** Newpt
177 H6 **Penicuik** Mdloth
209 G6 **Penifiler** Highld
161 J4 **Peninver** Ag & B
114 E2 **Penistone** Barns
152 F3 **Penkill** S Ayrs
85 G2 **Penkridge** Staffs
9 G5 **Penlean** Cnwll
98 B4 **Penley** Wrexhm
36 F5 **Penllyn** V Glam
96 C3 **Penmachno** Conwy
37 J2 **Penmaen** Caerph
51 G7 **Penmaen** Swans
109 K6 **Penmaenmawr** Conwy
95 M8 **Penmaenpool** Gwynd
37 G6 **Penmark** V Glam
95 J4 **Penmorfa** Gwynd
109 G6 **Penmynydd** IOA
42 F2 **Penn** Bucks
42 F2 **Penn Street** Bucks
80 F4 **Pennal** Gwynd
216 F2 **Pennan** Abers
81 J4 **Pennant** Powys
83 G4 **Pennerley** Shrops
122 E4 **Pennines**
128 F4 **Pennington** Cumb
53 H3 **Pennorth** Powys
129 G3 **Penny Bridge** Cumb
104 B6 **Penny Hill** Lincs
181 L2 **Pennycross** Ag & B
181 H3 **Pennyghael** Ag & B
163 H7 **Pennyglen** S Ayrs
11 L5 **Pennymoor** Devon
65 H5 **Penparc** Cerdgn
53 L6 **Penperlleni** Mons
5 J5 **Penpoll** Cnwll
3 H4 **Penponds** Cnwll
154 E4 **Penpont** D & G
65 K5 **Penrhiw-pal** Cerdgn

37 G2 **Penrhiwceiber** Rhondd
65 K6 **Penrhiwllan** Cerdgn
94 F5 **Penrhos** Gwynd
54 B5 **Penrhos** Mons
110 A5 **Penrhyn Bay** Conwy
109 H6 **Penrhyn Castle** Gwynd
95 K5 **Penrhyndeudraeth** Gwynd
50 F7 **Penrice** Swans
161 L1 **Penrioch** N Ayrs
138 D2 **Penrith** Cumb
4 D2 **Penrose** Cnwll
138 B2 **Penruddock** Cumb
3 K4 **Penryn** Cnwll
50 E2 **Pensarn** Carmth
110 A5 **Pensarn** Conwy
70 C2 **Pensax** Worcs
27 H5 **Penselwood** Somset
38 F7 **Pensford** BaNES
71 G5 **Pensham** Worcs
151 H4 **Penshaw** Sundld
32 F4 **Penshurst** Kent
5 L2 **Pensilva** Cnwll
4 F6 **Pentewan** Cnwll
109 H7 **Pentir** Gwynd
4 C4 **Pentire** Cnwll
77 J5 **Pentlow** Essex
91 G2 **Pentney** Norfk
29 G3 **Penton Mewsey** Hants
156 D6 **Pentonbridge** Cumb
109 G5 **Pentraeth** IOA
36 F2 **Pentre** Rhondd
98 A8 **Pentre** Shrops
108 F6 **Pentre Berw** IOA
83 G7 **Pentre Hodrey** Shrops
110 F8 **Pentre Llanrhaeadr** Denbgs
36 E5 **Pentre Meyrick** V Glam
52 E2 **Pentre-bach** Powys
97 J2 **Pentre-celyn** Denbgs
81 J3 **Pentre-celyn** Powys
51 J6 **Pentre-chwyth** Swans
65 L6 **Pentre-cwrt** Carmth
51 H3 **Pentre-Gwenlais** Carmth
96 C1 **Pentre-tafarn-y-fedw** Conwy
53 G7 **Pentrebach** Myr Td
97 J3 **Pentredwr** Denbgs
95 J5 **Pentrefelin** Gwynd
96 D3 **Pentrefoelas** Conwy
65 K4 **Pentregat** Cerdgn
101 G3 **Pentrich** Derbys
28 B7 **Pentridge Hill** Dorset
37 J2 **Pentwynmaur** Caerph
37 H4 **Pentyrch** Cardif
5 G5 **Penwithick** Cnwll
51 H2 **Penybanc** Carmth
68 C2 **Penybont** Powys
97 L4 **Penycae** Wrexhm
97 L1 **Penyffordd** Flints
36 F3 **Penygraig** Rhondd
51 H3 **Penygroes** Carmth
95 H2 **Penygroes** Gwynd
108 F4 **Penysarn** IOA
52 F6 **Penywaun** Rhondd
2 E5 **Penzance** Cnwll
2 E5 **Penzance Heliport** Cnwll
71 G4 **Peopleton** Worcs
98 F7 **Peplow** Shrops
163 J2 **Perceton** N Ayrs
206 B6 **Percie** Abers
217 H2 **Percyhorner** Abers
236 b3 **Perelle** Guern

24 E3 **Periton** Somset
44 D4 **Perivale** Gt Lon
12 D4 **Perkins Village** Devon
115 M7 **Perlethorpe** Notts
3 K4 **Perranarworthal** Cnwll
3 K1 **Perranporth** Cnwll
2 F5 **Perranuthnoe** Cnwll
3 K4 **Perranwell** Cnwll
3 K2 **Perranzabuloe** Cnwll
85 J5 **Perry Barr** Birm
39 L3 **Perry Green** Wilts
99 J6 **Pershall** Staffs
71 G5 **Pershore** Worcs
74 F2 **Pertenhall** Beds
186 B3 **Perth** P & K
98 A5 **Perthy** Shrops
69 L6 **Perton** Herefs
84 F4 **Perton** Staffs
6 D1 **Peter Tavy** Devon
59 J4 **Peter's Green** Herts
89 H4 **Peterborough** C Pete
69 G6 **Peterchurch** Herefs
206 F5 **Peterculter** C Aber
217 L5 **Peterhead** Abers
151 K6 **Peterlee** Dur
10 C3 **Peters Marland** Devon
30 C6 **Petersfield** Hants
44 D5 **Petersham** Gt Lon
37 G5 **Peterston-super-Ely** V Glam
37 K4 **Peterstone Wentlooge** Newpt
54 E3 **Peterstow** Herefs
34 F4 **Petham** Kent
9 H6 **Petherwin Gate** Cnwll
10 D3 **Petrockstow** Devon
21 H3 **Pett** E Susx
78 E3 **Pettaugh** Suffk
196 C5 **Petterden** Angus
165 J2 **Pettinain** S Lans
79 G4 **Pettistree** Suffk
24 E3 **Petton** Devon
45 J6 **Petts Wood** Gt Lon
177 H2 **Pettycur** Fife
207 G1 **Pettymuk** Abers
31 G6 **Petworth** W Susx
20 D5 **Pevensey** E Susx
40 D7 **Pewsey** Wilts
71 G3 **Phepson** Worcs
22 D6 **Philham** Devon
166 F4 **Philiphaugh** Border
2 F4 **Phillack** Cnwll
4 D7 **Philleigh** Cnwll
176 B3 **Philpstoun** W Loth
30 C1 **Phoenix Green** Hants
203 G6 **Phoines** Highld
26 C6 **Pibsbury** Somset
136 E3 **Pica** Cumb
115 K1 **Pickburn** Donc
134 C3 **Pickering** N York
86 C6 **Pickford** Covtry
132 E3 **Pickhill** N York
83 J4 **Picklescott** Shrops
113 G6 **Pickmere** Ches
25 J5 **Pickney** Somset
121 K6 **Pickup Bank** Bl w D
87 L2 **Pickwell** Leics
88 E2 **Pickworth** Lincs
103 H5 **Pickworth** Lincs
206 E3 **Pictillum** Abers
112 B7 **Picton** Ches
141 K5 **Picton** N York
19 L5 **Piddinghoe** E Susx
74 B4 **Piddington** M Keyn
57 M5 **Piddington** Oxon
14 D3 **Piddlehinton** Dorset
14 D3 **Piddletrenthide** Dorset

89 K7 **Pidley** Cambs
140 F4 **Piercebridge** Darltn
234 c3 **Pierowall** Ork
45 L2 **Pilgrims Hatch** Essex
116 E3 **Pilham** Lincs
6 A3 **Pillaton** Cnwll
72 C5 **Pillerton Hersey** Warwks
72 C5 **Pillerton Priors** Warwks
115 G2 **Pilley** Barns
16 D3 **Pilley** Hants
120 E2 **Pilling** Lancs
38 D4 **Pilning** S Glos
114 C8 **Pilsbury** Derbys
13 K3 **Pilsdon** Dorset
114 E7 **Pilsley** Derbys
101 H1 **Pilsley** Derbys
93 H2 **Pilson Green** Norfk
19 L2 **Piltdown** E Susx
23 J5 **Pilton** Devon
88 E6 **Pilton** Nhants
88 D3 **Pilton** Rutlnd
26 E3 **Pilton** Somset
15 G1 **Pimperne** Dorset
59 L3 **Pin Green** Herts
103 L7 **Pinchbeck** Lincs
12 C4 **Pinhoe** Devon
72 B2 **Pinley Green** Warwks
152 E4 **Pinminnoch** S Ayrs
152 E4 **Pinmore** S Ayrs
12 E5 **Pinn** Devon
43 J3 **Pinner** Gt Lon
43 J3 **Pinner Green** Gt Lon
71 G5 **Pinvin** Worcs
152 E5 **Pinwherry** S Ayrs
101 J2 **Pinxton** Derbys
69 K5 **Pipe and Lyde** Herefs
99 G4 **Pipe Gate** Shrops
213 K4 **Piperhill** Highld
88 B6 **Pipewell** Nhants
30 F1 **Pirbright** Surrey
167 K4 **Pirnie** Border
161 L1 **Pirnmill** N Ayrs
59 J2 **Pirton** Herts
70 F5 **Pirton** Worcs
42 B3 **Pishill** Oxon
94 F4 **Pistyll** Gwynd
194 C3 **Pitagowan** P & K
217 J2 **Pitblae** Abers
185 M3 **Pitcairngreen** P & K
223 H6 **Pitcalnie** Highld
206 D1 **Pitcaple** Abers
196 B4 **Pitcarity** Angus
58 C7 **Pitch Green** Bucks
30 E4 **Pitch Place** Surrey
55 J6 **Pitchcombe** Gloucs
58 C4 **Pitchcott** Bucks
83 K3 **Pitchford** Shrops
214 E6 **Pitchroy** Moray
26 F5 **Pitcombe** Somset
178 E8 **Pitcox** E Loth
206 D3 **Pitfichie** Abers
216 D5 **Pitglassie** Abers
223 H3 **Pitgrudy** Highld
196 E5 **Pitkennedy** Angus
186 E5 **Pitlessie** Fife
194 E5 **Pitlochry** P & K
216 C8 **Pitmachie** Abers
203 H5 **Pitmain** Highld
217 G8 **Pitmedden** Abers
217 G8 **Pitmedden Garden** Abers
25 K7 **Pitminster** Somset
196 F5 **Pitmuies** Angus
206 C3 **Pitmunie** Abers
26 C5 **Pitney** Somset
186 C3 **Pitroddie** P & K
187 G5 **Pitscottie** Fife
46 C3 **Pitsea** Essex
73 L2 **Pitsford** Nhants
58 F5 **Pitstone** Bucks
25 G7 **Pitt** Devon

197 H2 **Pittarrow** Abers
187 J6 **Pittenweem** Fife
186 D7 **Pitteuchar** Fife
151 H6 **Pittington** Dur
206 D1 **Pittodrie House Hotel** Abers
28 E5 **Pitton** Wilts
217 H2 **Pittulie** Abers
151 G5 **Pity Me** Dur
31 K2 **Pixham** Surrey
175 L5 **Plains** N Lans
83 K4 **Plaish** Shrops
101 G2 **Plaistow** Derbys
45 H4 **Plaistow** Gt Lon
31 G5 **Plaistow** W Susx
28 F7 **Plaitford** Hants
108 C6 **Plas Cymyran** IOA
33 G2 **Platt** Kent
151 G5 **Plawsworth** Dur
33 G3 **Plaxtol** Kent
42 G5 **Play Hatch** Oxon
21 H2 **Playden** E Susx
78 F5 **Playford** Suffk
55 H2 **Playley Green** Gloucs
83 H3 **Plealey** Shrops
175 L2 **Plean** Stirlg
186 D5 **Pleasance** Fife
121 J5 **Pleasington** Bl w D
115 J8 **Pleasley** Derbys
236 d2 **Pleinheaume** Guern
236 a5 **Plemont** Jersey
112 C7 **Plemstall** Ches
61 G5 **Pleshey** Essex
210 C7 **Plockton** Highld
83 H6 **Plowden** Shrops
83 G3 **Plox Green** Shrops
34 B5 **Pluckley** Kent
34 B5 **Pluckley Thorne** Kent
147 K6 **Plumbland** Cumb
113 G6 **Plumley** Ches
148 E7 **Plumpton** Cumb
19 K3 **Plumpton** E Susx
73 H5 **Plumpton** Nhants
73 K5 **Plumpton End** Nhants
19 K3 **Plumpton Green** E Susx
45 J4 **Plumstead** Gt Lon
106 D5 **Plumstead** Norfk
101 L6 **Plumtree** Notts
102 C5 **Plungar** Leics
34 C7 **Plurenden** Kent
14 D3 **Plush** Dorset
65 K4 **Plwmp** Cerdgn
6 C5 **Plymouth** C Plym
6 D4 **Plymouth Airport** C Plym
6 D5 **Plympton** C Plym
6 D5 **Plymstock** C Plym
12 D2 **Plymtree** Devon
133 K3 **Pockley** N York
125 J2 **Pocklington** E R Yk
26 D6 **Podimore** Somset
74 D3 **Podington** Beds
99 H5 **Podmore** Staffs
103 J6 **Pointon** Lincs
15 L4 **Pokesdown** Bmouth
224 B6 **Polbain** Highld
6 A4 **Polbathic** Cnwll
176 D5 **Polbeth** W Loth
3 H5 **Poldark Mine** Cnwll
88 F6 **Polebrook** Nhants
20 C5 **Polegate** E Susx
86 C3 **Polesworth** Warwks
224 C6 **Polglass** Highld
4 F5 **Polgooth** Cnwll
154 C2 **Polgown** D & G
18 E5 **Poling** W Susx
18 E4 **Poling Corner** W Susx
5 H5 **Polkerris** Cnwll
142 F6 **Pollington** E R Yk
190 F3 **Polloch** Highld

175 G6 **Pollokshaws** C Glas
175 G5 **Pollokshields** C Glas
4 F6 **Polmassick** Cnwll
176 C3 **Polmont** Falk
200 B8 **Polnish** Highld
5 K5 **Polperro** Cnwll
5 H5 **Polruan** Cnwll
78 B6 **Polstead** Suffk
182 B7 **Poltalloch** Ag & B
12 C3 **Poltimore** Devon
177 J5 **Polton** Mdloth
178 F7 **Polwarth** Border
9 H7 **Polyphant** Cnwll
4 E1 **Polzeath** Cnwll
177 H6 **Pomathorn** Mdloth
45 G2 **Ponders End** Gt Lon
89 J5 **Pondersbridge** Cambs
3 K4 **Ponsanooth** Cnwll
7 G2 **Ponsworthy** Devon
82 C2 **Pont Robert** Powys
51 G2 **Pont-ar-gothi** Carmth
67 L7 **Pont-faen** Powys
52 D6 **Pont-Nedd-Fechan** Neath
36 C2 **Pont-rhyd-y-fen** Neath
96 B2 **Pont-y-pant** Conwy
236 e8 **Pontac** Jersey
50 F3 **Pontantwn** Carmth
51 K5 **Pontardawe** Neath
51 H5 **Pontarddulais** Swans
66 B8 **Pontarsais** Carmth
97 L1 **Pontblyddyn** Flints
124 C6 **Pontefract** Wakefd
158 F7 **Ponteland** Nthumb
81 G7 **Ponterwyd** Cerdgn
83 H3 **Pontesbury** Shrops
83 H3 **Pontesford** Shrops
97 K5 **Pontfadog** Wrexhm
64 E7 **Pontfaen** Pembks
65 K4 **Pontgarreg** Cerdgn
50 F4 **Ponthenry** Carmth
37 M2 **Ponthir** Torfn
65 J5 **Ponthirwaun** Cerdgn
37 J2 **Pontllanfraith** Caerph
51 H5 **Pontlliw** Swans
95 G3 **Pontlyfni** Gwynd
37 L2 **Pontnewydd** Torfn
150 E4 **Pontop** Dur
67 G2 **Pontrhydfendigaid** Cerdgn
81 G8 **Pontrhydygroes** Cerdgn
54 B3 **Pontrilas** Herefs
20 D3 **Ponts Green** E Susx
66 B5 **Pontshaen** Cerdgn
54 F4 **Pontshill** Herefs
53 G5 **Pontsticill** Powys
65 L6 **Pontwelly** Carmth
50 F4 **Pontyates** Carmth
51 G4 **Pontyberem** Carmth
97 L2 **Pontybodkin** Flints
37 G4 **Pontyclun** Rhondd
36 D3 **Pontycymer** Brdgnd
53 L7 **Pontypool** Torfn
37 G3 **Pontypridd** Rhondd
37 K2 **Pontywaun** Caerph
3 H3 **Pool** Cnwll
123 J2 **Pool** Leeds
185 L7 **Pool of Muckhart** Clacks
77 H6 **Pool Street** Essex
15 J4 **Poole** Poole
39 M2 **Poole Keynes** Gloucs
219 K5 **Poolewe** Highld
138 C3 **Pooley Bridge** Cumb
99 K1 **Poolfold** Staffs
55 G3 **Poolhill** Gloucs
45 G4 **Poplar** Gt Lon
16 F4 **Porchfield** IOW
92 F3 **Poringland** Norfk

3 J5 **Porkellis** Cnwll
24 D3 **Porlock** Somset
24 D2 **Porlock Weir** Somset
191 H7 **Port Appin** Ag & B
171 H5 **Port Askaig** Ag & B
173 J5 **Port Bannatyne** Ag & B
147 M3 **Port Carlisle** Cumb
170 E6 **Port Charlotte** Ag & B
173 G4 **Port Driseach** Ag & B
50 F7 **Port Einon** Swans
160 C1 **Port Ellen** Ag & B
206 E2 **Port Elphinstone** Abers
237 a6 **Port Erin** IOM
8 D8 **Port Gaverne** Cnwll
174 C4 **Port Glasgow** Inver
219 H6 **Port Henderson** Highld
8 D8 **Port Isaac** Cnwll
144 D6 **Port Logan** D & G
189 K1 **Port Mor** Highld
232 g2 **Port nan Giuran** W Isls
232 c5 **Port nan Long** W Isls
232 g1 **Port Nis** W Isls
184 D6 **Port of Menteith** Stirlg
232 g1 **Port of Ness** W Isls
8 C3 **Port Quin** Cnwll
191 H7 **Port Ramsay** Ag & B
237 c6 **Port Soderick** IOM
237 b7 **Port St Mary** IOM
36 B3 **Port Talbot** Neath
170 D7 **Port Wemyss** Ag & B
145 H6 **Port William** D & G
210 B7 **Port-an-Eorna** Highld
172 C6 **Portachoillan** Ag & B
172 F4 **Portavadie** Ag & B
38 D5 **Portbury** N Som
17 H2 **Portchester** Hants
152 B7 **Portencalzie** D & G
173 K8 **Portencross** N Ayrs
14 B5 **Portesham** Dorset
215 K2 **Portessie** Moray
48 F4 **Portfield Gate** Pembks
10 B7 **Portgate** Devon
215 J2 **Portgordon** Moray
227 H5 **Portgower** Highld
4 C4 **Porth** Cnwll
36 F3 **Porth** Rhondd
3 K5 **Porth Navas** Cnwll
3 K6 **Porthallow** Cnwll
5 K5 **Porthallow** Cnwll
36 C5 **Porthcawl** Brdgnd
4 D2 **Porthcothan** Cnwll
2 C6 **Porthcurno** Cnwll
64 A7 **Porthgain** Pembks
2 C6 **Porthgwarra** Cnwll
37 G6 **Porthkerry** V Glam
3 H6 **Porthoustock** Cnwll
95 K5 **Porthmadog** Gwynd
3 K6 **Porthoustock** Cnwll
5 G5 **Porthpean** Cnwll
3 J2 **Porthtowan** Cnwll
51 G3 **Porthyrhyd** Carmth
183 J8 **Portincaple** Ag & B
236 a5 **Portinfer** Jersey
125 J4 **Portington** E R Yk
182 D5 **Portinnisherrich** Ag & B
137 H3 **Portinscale** Cumb
38 C5 **Portishead** N Som
215 K2 **Portknockie** Moray
14 D7 **Portland** Dorset
207 H6 **Portlethen** Abers
146 F4 **Portling** D & G
4 E7 **Portloe** Cnwll
223 K4 **Portmahomack** Highld
95 K5 **Portmeirion** Gwynd

4 F6 **Portmellon** Cnwll
191 H6 **Portnacroish** Ag & B
232 g2 **Portnaguran** W Isls
170 D7 **Portnahaven** Ag & B
208 E7 **Portnalong** Highld
177 J4 **Portobello** C Edin
85 G4 **Portobello** Wolves
28 D4 **Porton** Wilts
144 B4 **Portpatrick** D & G
3 H3 **Portreath** Cnwll
209 G5 **Portree** Highld
4 D8 **Portscatho** Cnwll
17 J3 **Portsea** C Port
230 C3 **Portskerra** Highld
38 D3 **Portskewett** Mons
19 H4 **Portslade** Br & H
19 H5 **Portslade-by-Sea** Br & H
144 B3 **Portslogan** D & G
17 J3 **Portsmouth** C Port
122 D5 **Portsmouth** Calder
182 F3 **Portsonachan Hotel** Ag & B
216 B2 **Portsoy** Abers
29 H8 **Portswood** C Sotn
189 K3 **Portuairk** Highld
85 J8 **Portway** Worcs
6 A5 **Portwrinkle** Cnwll
145 K7 **Portyerrock** D & G
77 H5 **Poslingford** Suffk
166 B3 **Posso** Border
10 F8 **Postbridge** Devon
58 B7 **Postcombe** Oxon
34 F6 **Postling** Kent
93 G2 **Postwick** Norfk
206 B6 **Potarch** Abers
58 F3 **Potsgrove** Beds
113 L5 **Pott Shrigley** Ches
59 G6 **Potten End** Herts
134 F4 **Potter Brompton** N York
107 J8 **Potter Heigham** Norfk
117 H7 **Potterhanworth** Lincs
117 H7 **Potterhanworth Booths** Lincs
39 M8 **Potterne** Wilts
39 M8 **Potterne Wick** Wilts
59 L7 **Potters Bar** Herts
59 J6 **Potters Crouch** Herts
87 G4 **Potters Marston** Leics
73 L6 **Potterspury** Nhants
207 H3 **Potterton** Abers
141 L6 **Potto** N York
75 J5 **Potton** Beds
9 G4 **Poughill** Cnwll
11 K3 **Poughill** Devon
15 M2 **Poulner** Hants
39 L7 **Poulshot** Wilts
56 C7 **Poulton** Gloucs
120 D3 **Poulton-le-Fylde** Lancs
20 B2 **Pound Green** E Susx
77 G4 **Pound Green** Suffk
32 B5 **Pound Hill** W Susx
51 H6 **Poundffald** Swans
57 M3 **Poundon** Bucks
7 G2 **Poundsgate** Devon
9 G5 **Poundstock** Cnwll
145 K5 **Pouton** D & G
31 L3 **Povey Cross** Surrey
168 F6 **Powburn** Nthumb
12 C5 **Powderham** Devon
13 M3 **Powerstock** Dorset
147 K2 **Powfoot** D & G
147 M4 **Powhill** Cumb
70 E4 **Powick** Worcs
185 L7 **Powmill** P & K
14 E5 **Poxwell** Dorset
43 G5 **Poyle** Slough
19 H4 **Poynings** W Susx

26 F7 **Poyntington** Dorset
113 L5 **Poynton** Ches
98 E8 **Poynton Green** Wrekin
3 G5 **Praa Sands** Cnwll
45 J7 **Pratt's Bottom** Gt Lon
3 H4 **Praze-an-Beeble** Cnwll
98 D5 **Prees** Shrops
98 E6 **Prees Green** Shrops
120 E2 **Preesall** Lancs
65 L5 **Pren-gwyn** Cerdgn
168 E6 **Prendwick** Nthumb
95 K4 **Prenteg** Gwynd
112 C3 **Prescot** Knows
25 H8 **Prescott** Devon
195 J3 **Presnerb** Angus
110 E5 **Prestatyn** Denbgs
113 K6 **Prestbury** Ches
55 L4 **Prestbury** Gloucs
69 G2 **Presteigne** Powys
26 F4 **Prestleigh** Somset
179 G6 **Preston** Border
19 J4 **Preston** Br & H
7 K2 **Preston** Devon
14 D5 **Preston** Dorset
178 D3 **Preston** E Loth
126 F4 **Preston** E R Yk
56 B7 **Preston** Gloucs
59 K3 **Preston** Herts
34 D3 **Preston** Kent
35 H3 **Preston** Kent
121 H4 **Preston** Lancs
169 H4 **Preston** Nthumb
88 C3 **Preston** Rutlnd
25 H4 **Preston** Somset
77 L4 **Preston** Suffk
7 K4 **Preston** Torbay
40 B5 **Preston** Wilts
71 L2 **Preston Bagot** Warwks
58 A3 **Preston Bissett** Bucks
25 H6 **Preston Bowyer** Somset
98 D7 **Preston Brockhurst** Shrops
112 E5 **Preston Brook** Halton
29 L3 **Preston Candover** Hants
73 H4 **Preston Capes** Nhants
71 L2 **Preston Green** Warwks
98 C8 **Preston Gubbals** Shrops
72 B4 **Preston on Stour** Warwks
112 E5 **Preston on the Hill** Halton
69 H6 **Preston on Wye** Herefs
129 L3 **Preston Patrick** Cumb
26 D7 **Preston Plucknett** Somset
84 C1 **Preston upon the Weald Moors** Wrekin
69 L5 **Preston Wynne** Herefs
131 K2 **Preston-under-Scar** N York
177 K4 **Prestonpans** E Loth
113 J1 **Prestwich** Bury
163 J4 **Prestwick** S Ayrs
163 J4 **Prestwick Airport** S Ayrs
58 E7 **Prestwood** Bucks
90 E6 **Prickwillow** Cambs
26 D2 **Priddy** Somset
129 L5 **Priest Hutton** Lancs

164 B2 **Priestland** E Ayrs
82 F4 **Priestweston** Shrops
179 G6 **Primrosehill** Border
168 B4 **Primsidemill** Border
58 D7 **Princes Risborough** Bucks
72 E1 **Princethorpe** Warwks
6 E2 **Princetown** Devon
72 F4 **Priors Hardwick** Warwks
72 F3 **Priors Marston** Warwks
55 K3 **Priors Norton** Gloucs
40 C3 **Priory Vale** Swindn
39 G7 **Priston** BaNES
46 E3 **Prittlewell** Sthend
30 B6 **Privett** Hants
4 E6 **Probus** Cnwll
178 C3 **Prora** E Loth
147 K6 **Prospect** Cumb
3 H5 **Prospidnick** Cnwll
216 F2 **Protstonhill** Abers
150 D3 **Prudhoe** Nthumb
38 F7 **Publow** BaNES
60 C4 **Puckeridge** Herts
26 B7 **Puckington** Somset
39 G5 **Pucklechurch** S Glos
111 K6 **Puddington** Ches
11 J3 **Puddington** Devon
14 E4 **Puddletown** Dorset
123 J4 **Pudsey** Leeds
18 E3 **Pulborough** W Susx
98 A2 **Pulford** Ches
14 D2 **Pulham** Dorset
92 E6 **Pulham Market** Norfk
92 E6 **Pulham St Mary** Norfk
74 F7 **Pulloxhill** Beds
176 E4 **Pumpherston** W Loth
66 E6 **Pumsaint** Carmth
49 G2 **Puncheston** Pembks
14 A5 **Puncknowle** Dorset
20 C2 **Punnett's Town** E Susx
17 J2 **Purbrook** Hants
45 K4 **Purfleet** Thurr
25 L3 **Puriton** Somset
61 K7 **Purleigh** Essex
44 F7 **Purley** Gt Lon
42 A5 **Purley** W Berk
27 G7 **Purse Caundle** Dorset
13 K2 **Purtington** Somset
55 G7 **Purton** Gloucs
54 F6 **Purton** Gloucs
40 C3 **Purton** Wilts
40 C3 **Purton Stoke** Wilts
73 K5 **Pury End** Nhants
41 G2 **Pusey** Oxon
70 B6 **Putley** Herefs
70 B6 **Putley Green** Herefs
55 H6 **Putloe** Gloucs
44 E5 **Putney** Gt Lon
236 d3 **Putron Village** Guern
30 F2 **Puttenham** Surrey
73 L6 **Puxley** Nhants
38 B7 **Puxton** N Som
50 F5 **Pwll** Carmth
50 C3 **Pwll Trap** Carmth
97 H2 **Pwll-glas** Denbgs
36 C2 **Pwll-y-glaw** Neath
68 B7 **Pwllgloyw** Powys
94 F5 **Pwllheli** Gwynd
38 D2 **Pwllmeyric** Mons
101 H3 **Pye Bridge** Derbys
60 D5 **Pye Corner** Herts
19 J3 **Pyecombe** W Susx
36 C4 **Pyle** Brdgnd
25 H5 **Pyleigh** Somset
26 E4 **Pylle** Somset

90 C6 **Pymoor** Cambs
13 L4 **Pymore** Dorset
43 H8 **Pyrford** Surrey
42 B2 **Pyrton** Oxon
88 C8 **Pytchley** Nhants
9 J4 **Pyworthy** Devon

Q

103 L6 **Quadring** Lincs
58 C4 **Quainton** Bucks
25 J4 **Quantock Hills** Somset
28 F3 **Quarley** Hants
101 G4 **Quarndon** Derbys
174 C5 **Quarrier's Village** Inver
103 H4 **Quarrington** Lincs
151 H7 **Quarrington Hill** Dur
85 G6 **Quarry Bank** Dudley
214 E2 **Quarrywood** Moray
173 L6 **Quarter** N Ayrs
175 J7 **Quarter** S Lans
84 D5 **Quatford** Shrops
84 D6 **Quatt** Shrops
150 F6 **Quebec** Dur
55 J5 **Quedgeley** Gloucs
90 E7 **Queen Adelaide** Cambs
26 E6 **Queen Camel** Somset
38 F6 **Queen Charlton** BaNES
184 B6 **Queen Elizabeth Forest Park** Stirlg
27 H5 **Queen Oak** Dorset
33 H4 **Queen Street** Kent
17 K5 **Queen's Bower** IOW
46 E5 **Queenborough** Kent
70 F6 **Queenhill** Worcs
123 G4 **Queensbury** Brad
111 K7 **Queensferry** Flints
175 H5 **Queenslie** C Glas
175 J3 **Queenzieburn** N Lans
60 E3 **Quendon** Essex
87 J2 **Queniborough** Leics
56 C7 **Quenington** Gloucs
85 J4 **Queslett** Birm
5 L3 **Quethiock** Cnwll
92 B6 **Quidenham** Norfk
28 C5 **Quidhampton** Wilts
73 L4 **Quinton** Nhants
4 D4 **Quintrell Downs** Cnwll
10 C8 **Quither** Devon
179 G5 **Quixwood** Border
9 K5 **Quoditch** Devon
87 H1 **Quorn** Leics
165 J2 **Quothquan** S Lans
234 c6 **Quoyburray** Ork
234 b5 **Quoyloo** Ork

R

165 L3 **Rachan Mill** Border
109 J7 **Rachub** Gwynd
24 D7 **Rackenford** Devon
18 E3 **Rackham** W Susx
93 G1 **Rackheath** Norfk
155 H7 **Racks** D & G
234 a7 **Rackwick** Ork
100 F5 **Radbourne** Derbys
113 H1 **Radcliffe** Bury
159 G2 **Radcliffe** Nthumb
101 M5 **Radcliffe on Trent** Notts
73 J7 **Radclive** Bucks
213 H3 **Raddery** Highld
187 G5 **Radernie** Fife

72 D2 **Radford Semele** Warwks
59 K7 **Radlett** Herts
57 K7 **Radley** Oxon
60 F6 **Radley Green** Essex
42 C2 **Radnage** Bucks
27 G1 **Radstock** BaNES
73 H6 **Radstone** Nhants
72 D5 **Radway** Warwks
74 E3 **Radwell** Beds
75 J7 **Radwell** Herts
76 E6 **Radwinter** Essex
37 H4 **Radyr** Cardif
214 C3 **Rafford** Moray
102 A8 **Ragdale** Leics
54 B6 **Raglan** Mons
116 D6 **Ragnall** Notts
213 J8 **Raigbeg** Highld
70 F4 **Rainbow Hill** Worcs
112 C2 **Rainford** St Hel
45 K4 **Rainham** Gt Lon
46 D6 **Rainham** Medway
112 C4 **Rainhill** St Hel
112 D4 **Rainhill Stoops** St Hel
113 L6 **Rainow** Ches
132 E4 **Rainton** N York
101 L2 **Rainworth** Notts
134 D7 **Raisthorpe** N York
186 D3 **Rait** P & K
118 D5 **Raithby** Lincs
118 E7 **Raithby** Lincs
30 D5 **Rake** W Susx
203 H5 **Ralia** Highld
208 B5 **Ramasaig** Highld
3 J4 **Rame** Cnwll
6 B6 **Rame** Cnwll
14 B3 **Rampisham** Dorset
128 F6 **Rampside** Cumb
76 B2 **Rampton** Cambs
116 D5 **Rampton** Notts
122 B6 **Ramsbottom** Bury
40 F6 **Ramsbury** Wilts
227 K3 **Ramscraigs** Highld
30 B6 **Ramsdean** Hants
41 L8 **Ramsdell** Hants
57 G5 **Ramsden** Oxon
46 B2 **Ramsden Bellhouse** Essex
89 K6 **Ramsey** Cambs
62 E2 **Ramsey** Essex
237 e3 **Ramsey** IOM
89 K6 **Ramsey Forty Foot** Cambs
89 J6 **Ramsey Heights** Cambs
61 M6 **Ramsey Island** Essex
89 K5 **Ramsey Mereside** Cambs
89 J6 **Ramsey St Mary's** Cambs
35 K2 **Ramsgate** Kent
131 L5 **Ramsgill** N York
157 J2 **Ramshope** Nthumb
100 B4 **Ramshorn** Staffs
30 F5 **Ramsnest Common** Surrey
118 B5 **Ranby** Lincs
116 A5 **Ranby** Notts
117 J5 **Rand** Lincs
55 J6 **Randwick** Gloucs
174 D5 **Ranfurly** Rens
100 D7 **Rangemore** Staffs
39 G3 **Rangeworthy** S Glos
163 L6 **Rankinston** E Ayrs
121 K5 **Rann** Bl w D
193 G5 **Rannoch Station** P & K
24 E3 **Ranscombe** Somset
116 A4 **Ranskill** Notts
99 J7 **Ranton** Staffs
99 J7 **Ranton Green** Staffs
93 H1 **Ranworth** Norfk
185 G7 **Raploch** Stirlg

234 C4 **Rapness** Ork
146 D5 **Rascarrel** D & G
173 K2 **Rashfield** Ag & B
71 G2 **Rashwood** Worcs
133 G5 **Raskelf** N York
123 H6 **Rastrick** Calder
200 E2 **Ratagan** Highld
87 G3 **Ratby** Leics
86 D4 **Ratcliffe Culey** Leics
101 J6 **Ratcliffe on Soar** Notts
87 J1 **Ratcliffe on the Wreake** Leics
217 J3 **Rathen** Abers
186 F3 **Rathillet** Fife
130 F7 **Rathmell** N York
176 F4 **Ratho** C Edin
215 K2 **Rathven** Moray
72 E5 **Ratley** Warwks
35 H4 **Ratling** Kent
83 H4 **Ratlinghope** Shrops
231 J2 **Rattar** Highld
7 H4 **Rattery** Devon
77 L3 **Rattlesden** Suffk
20 C5 **Ratton Village** E Susx
195 J7 **Rattray** P & K
88 E8 **Raunds** Nhants
115 J3 **Ravenfield** Rothm
136 F7 **Ravenglass** Cumb
93 H4 **Raveningham** Norfk
143 K6 **Ravenscar** N York
74 F4 **Ravensden** Beds
101 K2 **Ravenshead** Notts
123 J6 **Ravensthorpe** Kirk
73 J1 **Ravensthorpe** Nhants
86 E2 **Ravenstone** Leics
74 B4 **Ravenstone** M Keyn
139 G6 **Ravenstonedale** Cumb
165 H1 **Ravenstruther** S Lans
140 E5 **Ravensworth** N York
125 G6 **Rawcliffe** E R Yk
133 J8 **Rawcliffe** York
123 J3 **Rawdon** Leeds
34 B3 **Rawling Street** Kent
115 H3 **Rawmarsh** Rothm
46 C2 **Rawreth** Essex
12 F2 **Rawridge** Devon
122 B6 **Rawtenstall** Lancs
78 C6 **Raydon** Suffk
46 D2 **Rayleigh** Essex
61 H4 **Rayne** Essex
44 E6 **Raynes Park** Gt Lon
76 E2 **Reach** Cambs
122 B4 **Read** Lancs
42 B5 **Reading** Readg
34 B8 **Reading Street** Kent
35 K2 **Reading Street** Kent
138 E4 **Reagill** Cumb
223 G3 **Rearquhar** Highld
87 J2 **Rearsby** Leics
230 D3 **Reay** Highld
47 L6 **Reculver** Kent
25 H7 **Red Ball** Somset
15 K4 **Red Hill** Bmouth
71 K4 **Red Hill** Warwks
77 G1 **Red Lodge** Suffk
49 L5 **Red Roses** Carmth
159 G3 **Red Row** Nthumb
109 G5 **Red Wharf Bay** IOA
49 J6 **Redberth** Pembks
59 J5 **Redbourn** Herts
116 F2 **Redbourne** N Linc
54 D6 **Redbrook** Gloucs
98 D4 **Redbrook** Wrexhm
34 C7 **Redbrook Street** Kent
213 L5 **Redburn** Nthumb
142 D3 **Redcar** R & Cl
146 E2 **Redcastle** D & G
212 E4 **Redcastle** Highld
176 C3 **Redding** Falk

176 C3 **Reddingmuirhead** Falk
71 J2 **Redditch** Worcs
77 J4 **Rede** Suffk
92 F6 **Redenhall** Norfk
157 L5 **Redesmouth** Nthumb
197 J3 **Redford** Abers
196 F7 **Redford** Angus
30 E6 **Redford** W Susx
166 E6 **Redfordgreen** Border
186 A2 **Redgorton** P & K
92 C7 **Redgrave** Suffk
206 E4 **Redhill** Abers
59 M2 **Redhill** Herts
38 D7 **Redhill** N Som
32 B3 **Redhill** Surrey
93 J6 **Redisham** Suffk
38 E5 **Redland** Bristl
234 b5 **Redland** Ork
78 E1 **Redlingfield** Suffk
78 E1 **Redlingfield Green** Suffk
27 G5 **Redlynch** Somset
28 D7 **Redlynch** Wilts
70 D2 **Redmarley** Worcs
55 H2 **Redmarley D'Abitot** Gloucs
141 J3 **Redmarshall** S on T
102 D5 **Redmile** Leics
131 K2 **Redmire** N York
197 J2 **Redmyre** Abers
98 A6 **Rednal** Shrops
167 J3 **Redpath** Border
219 H7 **Redpoint** Highld
3 J3 **Redruth** Cnwll
186 C1 **Redstone** P & K
38 B4 **Redwick** Newpt
38 D3 **Redwick** S Glos
141 G3 **Redworth** Darltn
75 L7 **Reed** Herts
93 J3 **Reedham** Norfk
125 J6 **Reedness** E R Yk
117 H6 **Reepham** Lincs
106 D7 **Reepham** Norfk
140 C7 **Reeth** N York
86 C7 **Reeves Green** Solhll
224 B5 **Reiff** Highld
31 L2 **Reigate** Surrey
135 H4 **Reighton** N York
207 G2 **Reisque** Abers
231 L5 **Reiss** Highld
2 F5 **Relubbus** Cnwll
214 B5 **Relugas** Moray
42 C4 **Remenham** Wokham
42 C4 **Remenham Hill** Wokham
101 L7 **Rempstone** Notts
56 A6 **Rendcomb** Gloucs
79 H2 **Rendham** Suffk
174 F5 **Renfrew** Rens
74 F4 **Renhold** Beds
115 J6 **Renishaw** Derbys
169 J5 **Rennington** Nthumb
174 D3 **Renton** W Duns
149 G6 **Renwick** Cumb
93 J1 **Repps** Norfk
100 F6 **Repton** Derbys
213 H5 **Resaurie** Highld
4 F7 **Rescassa** Cnwll
190 E4 **Resipole** Highld
3 H3 **Reskadinnick** Cnwll
213 G2 **Resolis** Highld
52 C7 **Resolven** Neath
183 J6 **Rest and be thankful** Ag & B
179 H6 **Reston** Border
196 E6 **Reswallie** Angus
116 B5 **Retford** Notts
61 J7 **Rettendon** Essex
103 M1 **Revesby** Lincs
16 F4 **Rew Street** IOW

12 B3 **Rewe** Devon
93 K7 **Reydon** Suffk
92 B3 **Reymerston** Norfk
49 J5 **Reynalton** Pembks
50 F7 **Reynoldston** Swans
6 A1 **Rezare** Cnwll
67 H5 **Rhandirmwyn** Carmth
67 L2 **Rhayader** Powys
212 D5 **Rheindown** Highld
111 G7 **Rhes-y-cae** Flints
97 H1 **Rhewl** Denbgs
97 J4 **Rhewl** Denbgs
224 D4 **Rhicarn** Highld
228 C5 **Rhiconich** Highld
222 F6 **Rhicullen** Highld
52 E6 **Rhigos** Rhondd
220 D3 **Rhireavach** Highld
223 H2 **Rhives** Highld
37 J4 **Rhiwbina** Cardif
37 K3 **Rhiwderyn** Newpt
109 H7 **Rhiwlas** Gwynd
33 H4 **Rhoden Green** Kent
34 F6 **Rhodes Minnis** Kent
48 C3 **Rhodiad-y-brenin** Pembks
146 C3 **Rhonehouse** D & G
37 G6 **Rhoose** V Glam
65 L7 **Rhos** Carmth
51 L5 **Rhos** Neath
110 B5 **Rhos-on-Sea** Conwy
96 E5 **Rhos-y-gwaliau** Gwynd
108 E3 **Rhosbeirio** IOA
108 C6 **Rhoscolyn** IOA
48 F6 **Rhoscrowther** Pembks
111 H7 **Rhosesmor** Flints
68 D5 **Rhosgoch** Powys
65 H6 **Rhoshill** Pembks
94 D6 **Rhoshirwaun** Gwynd
80 D3 **Rhoslefain** Gwynd
97 L3 **Rhosllanerchrugog** Wrexhm
108 F6 **Rhosmeirch** IOA
108 D6 **Rhosneigr** IOA
50 E7 **Rhossili** Swans
95 H2 **Rhostryfan** Gwynd
97 L3 **Rhostyllen** Wrexhm
108 F4 **Rhosybol** IOA
97 L4 **Rhosymedre** Wrexhm
174 B2 **Rhu** Ag & B
110 F6 **Rhuallt** Denbgs
173 H4 **Rhubodach** Ag & B
110 E6 **Rhuddlan** Denbgs
172 C8 **Rhunahaorine** Ag & B
95 L4 **Rhyd** Gwynd
95 K3 **Rhyd-Ddu** Gwynd
96 D5 **Rhyd-uchaf** Gwynd
80 E6 **Rhyd-y pennau** Cerdgn
94 F5 **Rhyd-y-clafdy** Gwynd
110 C6 **Rhyd-y-foel** Conwy
109 H7 **Rhyd-y-groes** Gwynd
50 F1 **Rhydargaeau** Carmth
66 D6 **Rhydcymerau** Carmth
65 K5 **Rhydlewis** Cerdgn
66 B5 **Rhydowen** Cerdgn
51 K4 **Rhydyfro** Neath
110 D5 **Rhyl** Denbgs
53 H6 **Rhymney** Caerph
186 B4 **Rhynd** P & K
215 L8 **Rhynie** Abers
223 J5 **Rhynie** Highld
84 D8 **Ribbesford** Worcs
121 H4 **Ribbleton** Lancs
121 J4 **Ribchester** Lancs
126 F8 **Riby** Lincs
124 F3 **Riccall** N York
156 F3 **Riccarton** Border
163 K3 **Riccarton** E Ayrs

69 J1 **Richards Castle** Herefs
44 D5 **Richmond** Gt Lon
140 F6 **Richmond** N York
115 H4 **Richmond** Sheff
236 b3 **Richmond Fort** Guern
99 L7 **Rickerscote** Staffs
38 C8 **Rickford** N Som
7 H7 **Rickham** Devon
92 C7 **Rickinghall** Suffk
60 D2 **Rickling** Essex
60 E3 **Rickling Green** Essex
43 H2 **Rickmansworth** Herts
167 H4 **Riddell** Border
10 F3 **Riddlecombe** Devon
123 G3 **Riddlesden** Brad
15 H5 **Ridge** Dorset
59 K7 **Ridge** Herts
27 L5 **Ridge** Wilts
86 C4 **Ridge Lane** Warwks
38 D7 **Ridgehill** N Som
115 H5 **Ridgeway** Derbys
77 G6 **Ridgewell** Essex
19 M2 **Ridgewood** E Susx
74 E7 **Ridgmont** Beds
150 C3 **Riding Mill** Nthumb
107 H6 **Ridlington** Norfk
88 B3 **Ridlington** Rutlnd
158 A5 **Ridsdale** Nthumb
133 J3 **Rievaulx** N York
133 J3 **Rievaulx Abbey** N York
148 B2 **Rigg** D & G
175 K4 **Riggend** N Lans
213 K4 **Righoul** Highld
118 F6 **Rigsby** Lincs
165 G3 **Rigside** S Lans
121 J5 **Riley Green** Lancs
5 L2 **Rilla Mill** Cnwll
134 D5 **Rillington** N York
122 B2 **Rimington** Lancs
26 E6 **Rimpton** Somset
127 H5 **Rimswell** E R Yk
49 G3 **Rinaston** Pembks
84 D4 **Rindleford** Shrops
146 C4 **Ringford** D & G
92 D2 **Ringland** Norfk
19 L3 **Ringmer** E Susx
6 F6 **Ringmore** Devon
7 L2 **Ringmore** Devon
215 G5 **Ringorm** Moray
93 J5 **Ringsfield** Suffk
93 J6 **Ringsfield Corner** Suffk
59 G5 **Ringshall** Bucks
78 C4 **Ringshall** Suffk
78 C4 **Ringshall Stocks** Suffk
88 E7 **Ringstead** Nhants
105 H4 **Ringstead** Norfk
15 L2 **Ringwood** Hants
35 K5 **Ringwould** Kent
20 B4 **Ripe** E Susx
101 H3 **Ripley** Derbys
15 M3 **Ripley** Hants
132 D7 **Ripley** N York
31 H1 **Ripley** Surrey
30 A6 **Riplington** Hants
132 D5 **Ripon** N York
103 H6 **Rippingale** Lincs
35 J5 **Ripple** Kent
70 F6 **Ripple** Worcs
122 F6 **Ripponden** Calder
160 B2 **Risabus** Ag & B
69 K4 **Risbury** Herefs
77 H2 **Risby** Suffk
37 K3 **Risca** Caerph
126 E3 **Rise** E R Yk
103 K6 **Risegate** Lincs
74 F3 **Riseley** Beds
42 B7 **Riseley** Wokham

78 E2 **Rishangles** Suffk
121 L4 **Rishton** Lancs
122 F6 **Rishworth** Calder
101 J5 **Risley** Derbys
112 F3 **Risley** Warrtn
132 C5 **Risplith** N York
35 J6 **River** Kent
30 F6 **River** W Susx
212 E4 **Riverford** Highld
32 F3 **Riverhead** Kent
121 J7 **Rivington** Lancs
73 L4 **Roade** Nhants
176 B7 **Roadmeetings** S Lans
164 B5 **Roadside** E Ayrs
231 H4 **Roadside** Highld
25 G4 **Roadwater** Somset
208 D5 **Roag** Highld
153 G2 **Roan of Craigoch**
S Ayrs
60 D2 **Roast Green** Essex
37 J5 **Roath** Cardif
166 F6 **Roberton** Border
165 H4 **Roberton** S Lans
20 E2 **Robertsbridge**
E Susx
123 J6 **Roberttown** Kirk
49 J4 **Robeston Wathen**
Pembks
155 M7 **Robgill Tower** D & G
143 K6 **Robin Hood's Bay**
N York
10 E2 **Roborough** Devon
6 D4 **Roborough** Devon
112 B4 **Roby** Knows
100 C5 **Rocester** Staffs
48 E3 **Roch** Pembks
122 D7 **Rochdale** Rochdl
4 F4 **Roche** Cnwll
46 C6 **Rochester** Medway
157 L3 **Rochester** Nthumb
46 E3 **Rochford** Essex
70 B2 **Rochford** Worcs
4 E2 **Rock** Cnwll
169 J5 **Rock** Nthumb
70 D1 **Rock** Worcs
111 K4 **Rock Ferry** Wirral
12 C4 **Rockbeare** Devon
28 C7 **Rockbourne** Hants
148 C3 **Rockcliffe** Cumb
146 E4 **Rockcliffe** D & G
7 L4 **Rockend** Torbay
223 K5 **Rockfield** Highld
54 C5 **Rockfield** Mons
24 B2 **Rockford** Devon
38 F2 **Rockhampton** S Glos
82 F7 **Rockhill** Shrops
88 C5 **Rockingham** Nhants
92 B4 **Rockland All Saints**
Norfk
93 G3 **Rockland St Mary**
Norfk
92 B4 **Rockland St Peter**
Norfk
116 B6 **Rockley** Notts
40 D6 **Rockley** Wilts
173 L1 **Rockville** Ag & B
42 D3 **Rockwell End** Bucks
55 J6 **Rodborough** Gloucs
40 C4 **Rodbourne** Swindn
39 L4 **Rodbourne** Wilts
14 B5 **Rodden** Dorset
27 J2 **Rode** Somset
99 J2 **Rode Heath** Ches
232 d5 **Rodel** W Isls
83 L1 **Roden** Wrekin
24 F4 **Rodhuish** Somset
83 L1 **Rodington** Wrekin
83 L1 **Rodington Heath**
Wrekin
55 H5 **Rodley** Gloucs
39 L2 **Rodmarton** Gloucs
19 L4 **Rodmell** E Susx
34 B3 **Rodmersham** Kent

34 B3 **Rodmersham Green**
Kent
26 C2 **Rodney Stoke**
Somset
100 D4 **Rodsley** Derbys
59 K6 **Roe Green** Herts
75 K7 **Roe Green** Herts
132 E6 **Roecliffe** N York
44 E5 **Roehampton** Gt Lon
31 K5 **Roffey** W Susx
226 C7 **Rogart** Highld
30 D6 **Rogate** W Susx
37 L3 **Rogerstone** Newpt
232 d5 **Roghadal** W Isls
38 C3 **Rogiet** Mons
41 L2 **Roke** Oxon
151 J3 **Roker** Sundld
93 J1 **Rollesby** Norfk
87 K4 **Rolleston** Leics
102 C3 **Rolleston** Notts
100 E6 **Rolleston** Staffs
126 F2 **Rolston** E R Yk
33 L6 **Rolvenden** Kent
33 L6 **Rolvenden Layne**
Kent
140 C2 **Romaldkirk** Dur
37 M3 **Roman**
Amphitheatre
Caerleon Newpt
39 H7 **Roman Baths &**
Pump Room BaNES
132 E2 **Romanby** N York
177 G8 **Romanno Bridge**
Border
24 B7 **Romansleigh** Devon
208 F4 **Romesdal** Highld
15 K1 **Romford** Dorset
45 K3 **Romford** Gt Lon
113 L4 **Romiley** Stockp
29 G6 **Romsey** Hants
84 D6 **Romsley** Shrops
85 G7 **Romsley** Worcs
172 C7 **Ronachan** Ag & B
150 B6 **Rookhope** Dur
17 G5 **Rookley** IOW
26 A2 **Rooks Bridge**
Somset
25 H5 **Rooks Nest** Somset
132 C3 **Rookwith** N York
127 G4 **Roos** E R Yk
75 G3 **Roothams Green**
Beds
29 M5 **Ropley** Hants
29 L5 **Ropley Dean** Hants
103 G5 **Ropsley** Lincs
217 K4 **Rora** Abers
82 F4 **Rorrington** Shrops
215 J4 **Rosarie** Moray
3 K1 **Rose** Cnwll
24 C6 **Rose Ash** Devon
61 L3 **Rose Green** Essex
77 L6 **Rose Green** Suffk
77 L5 **Rose Green** Suffk
18 B5 **Rose Green** W Susx
122 C4 **Rose Hill** Lancs
175 L7 **Rosebank** S Lans
49 J2 **Rosebush** Pembks
142 F7 **Rosedale Abbey**
N York
225 K7 **Rosehall** Highld
217 H2 **Rosehearty** Abers
214 E2 **Roseisle** Moray
20 C5 **Roselands** E Susx
49 G5 **Rosemarket** Pembks
213 H3 **Rosemarkie** Highld
25 J7 **Rosemary Lane**
Devon
195 J7 **Rosemount** P & K
4 E3 **Rosenannon** Cnwll
177 J6 **Rosewell** Mdloth
141 K3 **Roseworth** S on T
138 D4 **Rosgill** Cumb
208 D5 **Roskhill** Highld

148 B6 **Rosley** Cumb
177 H5 **Roslin** Mdloth
86 B1 **Rosliston** Derbys
174 B2 **Rosneath** Ag & B
146 B6 **Ross** D & G
54 E4 **Ross-on-Wye** Herefs
98 A2 **Rossett** Wrexhm
132 D8 **Rossett Green**
N York
115 L2 **Rossington** Donc
174 E4 **Rossland** Rens
231 J7 **Roster** Highld
113 H5 **Rostherne** Ches
137 H4 **Rosthwaite** Cumb
100 C4 **Roston** Derbys
176 F2 **Rosyth** Fife
158 D2 **Rothbury** Nthumb
87 J1 **Rotherby** Leics
32 F7 **Rotherfield** E Susx
42 B4 **Rotherfield Greys**
Oxon
42 B4 **Rotherfield**
Peppard Oxon
115 H3 **Rotherham** Rothm
73 K3 **Rotherthorpe**
Nhants
30 B1 **Rotherwick** Hants
215 G4 **Rothes** Moray
173 J5 **Rothesay** Ag & B
216 E6 **Rothiebrisbane**
Abers
215 M5 **Rothiemay** Moray
204 B4 **Rothiemurchus**
Lodge Highld
216 D7 **Rothienorman** Abers
87 H2 **Rothley** Leics
216 D7 **Rothmaise** Abers
123 L5 **Rothwell** Leeds
117 J2 **Rothwell** Lincs
88 B7 **Rothwell** Nhants
196 B3 **Rottal Lodge** Angus
19 K5 **Rottingdean** Br & H
136 D5 **Rottington** Cumb
155 H6 **Roucan** D & G
34 F3 **Rough Common**
Kent
105 K7 **Rougham** Norfk
77 K3 **Rougham Green**
Suffk
205 H3 **Roughpark** Abers
118 C8 **Roughton** Lincs
106 F5 **Roughton** Norfk
84 D5 **Roughton** Shrops
60 F5 **Roundbush Green**
Essex
13 K1 **Roundham** Somset
123 L3 **Roundhay** Leeds
40 A7 **Roundway** Wilts
196 C6 **Roundyhill** Angus
71 H4 **Rous Lench** Worcs
13 H4 **Rousdon** Devon
57 J3 **Rousham** Oxon
173 L6 **Routenburn** N Ayrs
126 D3 **Routh** E R Yk
129 K2 **Row** Cumb
61 J4 **Row Green** Essex
156 D6 **Rowanburn** D & G
183 L7 **Rowardennan**
Hotel Stirlg
183 L7 **Rowardennan**
Lodge Stirlg
114 A4 **Rowarth** Derbys
38 C8 **Rowberrow** Somset
39 L7 **Rowde** Wilts
109 L6 **Rowen** Conwy
149 H3 **Rowfoot** Nthumb
62 B4 **Rowhedge** Essex
72 B2 **Rowington** Warwks
114 E6 **Rowland** Derbys
17 K1 **Rowland's Castle**
Hants
150 E4 **Rowland's Gill** Gatesd
30 D3 **Rowledge** Surrey

150 D5 **Rowley** Dur
126 B4 **Rowley** E R Yk
86 D6 **Rowley Green** Covtry
85 H6 **Rowley Regis** Sandw
54 A3 **Rowlstone** Herefs
31 H4 **Rowly** Surrey
17 H3 **Rowner** Hants
71 J1 **Rowney Green**
Worcs
29 G7 **Rownhams** Hants
136 E4 **Rowrah** Cumb
58 D4 **Rowsham** Bucks
114 E7 **Rowsley** Derbys
103 H2 **Rowston** Lincs
112 C8 **Rowton** Ches
98 E8 **Rowton** Wrekin
167 L4 **Roxburgh** Border
125 L6 **Roxby** N Linc
75 G4 **Roxton** Beds
61 G6 **Roxwell** Essex
192 D1 **Roy Bridge** Highld
177 H4 **Royal Botanic**
Gardens C Edin
60 C6 **Roydon** Essex
105 H7 **Roydon** Norfk
92 D7 **Roydon** Norfk
60 C6 **Roydon Hamlet**
Essex
124 B7 **Royston** Barns
75 L6 **Royston** Herts
122 D8 **Royton** Oldham
236 e6 **Rozel** Jersey
97 L4 **Ruabon** Wrexhm
188 D6 **Ruaig** Ag & B
4 D7 **Ruan Lanihorne**
Cnwll
3 J7 **Ruan Major** Cnwll
3 J7 **Ruan Minor** Cnwll
54 F4 **Ruardean** Gloucs
54 F5 **Ruardean Hill** Gloucs
54 F5 **Ruardean Woodside**
Gloucs
85 H7 **Rubery** Birm
233 c9 **Rubha Ban** W Isls
69 J6 **Ruckhall** Herefs
34 D7 **Ruckinge** Kent
83 K4 **Ruckley** Shrops
141 L6 **Rudby** N York
150 E2 **Rudchester** Nthumb
101 L6 **Ruddington** Notts
27 J2 **Rudge** Somset
38 F3 **Rudgeway** S Glos
31 H5 **Rudgwick** W Susx
61 K7 **Rudley Green** Essex
39 J6 **Rudloe** Wilts
37 J3 **Rudry** Caerph
135 H6 **Rudston** E R Yk
99 L2 **Rudyard** Staffs
167 J5 **Ruecastle** Border
120 F7 **Rufford** Lancs
124 D1 **Rufforth** York
87 G7 **Rugby** Warwks
100 B8 **Rugeley** Staffs
25 K6 **Ruishton** Somset
43 H3 **Ruislip** Gt Lon
215 J4 **Rumbach** Moray
185 L7 **Rumbling Bridge**
P & K
93 H7 **Rumburgh** Suffk
4 D2 **Rumford** Cnwll
176 C3 **Rumford** Falk
37 K5 **Rumney** Cardif
112 D5 **Runcorn** Halton
18 B5 **Runcton** W Susx
90 E2 **Runcton Holme**
Norfk
30 E3 **Runfold** Surrey
92 E3 **Runhall** Norfk
93 K2 **Runham** Norfk
25 H6 **Runnington** Somset
143 G4 **Runswick** N York
195 L3 **Runtaleave** Angus
46 C2 **Runwell** Essex

42 D5 **Ruscombe** Wokham
62 E5 **Rush Green** Essex
45 K3 **Rush Green** Gt Lon
70 B7 **Rushall** Herefs
92 E6 **Rushall** Norfk
28 C1 **Rushall** Wilts
77 K3 **Rushbrooke** Suffk
83 K5 **Rushbury** Shrops
60 A2 **Rushden** Herts
74 D2 **Rushden** Nhants
91 K7 **Rushford** Norfk
20 D3 **Rushlake Green** E Susx
93 K6 **Rushmere** Suffk
30 E4 **Rushmoor** Surrey
70 F1 **Rushock** Worcs
113 J3 **Rusholme** Manch
112 E8 **Rushton** Ches
88 B6 **Rushton** Nhants
113 L8 **Rushton Spencer** Staffs
70 E4 **Rushwick** Worcs
141 G2 **Rushyford** Dur
184 D7 **Ruskie** Stirlg
103 H3 **Ruskington** Lincs
129 H2 **Rusland** Cumb
31 K4 **Rusper** W Susx
54 F5 **Ruspidge** Gloucs
31 L4 **Russ Hill** Surrey
42 B3 **Russell's Water** Oxon
32 F5 **Rusthall** Kent
18 E5 **Rustington** W Susx
134 E3 **Ruston** N York
135 G6 **Ruston Parva** E R Yk
143 H5 **Ruswarp** N York
167 K4 **Rutherford** Border
175 H6 **Rutherglen** S Lans
4 F3 **Ruthernbridge** Cnwll
97 H2 **Ruthin** Denbgs
207 H4 **Ruthrieston** C Aber
215 L5 **Ruthven** Abers
195 L6 **Ruthven** Angus
203 H5 **Ruthven** Highld
195 L6 **Ruthven House** Angus
4 E4 **Ruthvoes** Cnwll
147 J2 **Ruthwell** D & G
98 B7 **Ruyton-XI-Towns** Shrops
158 C7 **Ryal** Nthumb
13 K4 **Ryall** Dorset
70 F6 **Ryall** Worcs
33 H2 **Ryarsh** Kent
137 K6 **Rydal** Cumb
17 H4 **Ryde** IOW
21 H2 **Rye** E Susx
21 H2 **Rye Foreign** E Susx
70 D7 **Rye Street** Worcs
88 F2 **Ryhall** Rutlnd
124 B7 **Ryhill** Wakefd
151 K4 **Ryhope** Sundld
117 G5 **Ryland** Lincs
101 K5 **Rylands** Notts
131 H7 **Rylstone** N York
14 B1 **Ryme Intrinseca** Dorset
124 E3 **Ryther** N York
150 E3 **Ryton** Gatesd
84 D3 **Ryton** Shrops
86 E8 **Ryton-on-Dunsmore** Warwks

S

122 B3 **Sabden** Lancs
60 B4 **Sacombe** Herts
151 G5 **Sacriston** Dur
141 H4 **Sadberge** Darltn
161 K3 **Saddell** Ag & B
87 J5 **Saddington** Leics
90 E1 **Saddle Bow** Norfk
19 H4 **Saddlescombe** W Susx
76 D6 **Saffron Walden** Essex
49 H6 **Sageston** Pembks
91 K3 **Saham Hills** Norfk
91 K3 **Saham Toney** Norfk
98 C1 **Saighton** Ches
179 J5 **St Abbs** Border
178 E5 **St Agnes** Border
3 J2 **St Agnes** Cnwll
59 J6 **St Albans** Herts
4 C5 **St Allen** Cnwll
236 c3 **St Andrew** Guern
37 H6 **St Andrew's Major** V Glam
187 H4 **St Andrews** Fife
13 L4 **St Andrews Well** Dorset
155 J4 **St Ann's** D & G
6 B2 **St Ann's Chapel** Cnwll
6 F6 **St Ann's Chapel** Devon
120 D5 **St Anne's** Lancs
3 K6 **St Anthony** Cnwll
20 D5 **St Anthony's Hill** E Susx
38 D2 **St Arvans** Mons
110 E6 **St Asaph** Denbgs
36 F6 **St Athan** V Glam
236 b7 **St Aubin** Jersey
4 F5 **St Austell** Cnwll
138 D5 **St Bees** Cumb
5 G5 **St Blazey** Cnwll
167 J3 **St Boswells** Border
236 b7 **St Brelade** Jersey
236 b7 **St Brelade's Bay** Jersey
4 F2 **St Breock** Cnwll
5 H1 **St Breward** Cnwll
54 E6 **St Briavels** Gloucs
36 D5 **St Bride's Major** V Glam
37 H6 **St Brides super-Ely** V Glam
37 L4 **St Brides Wentlooge** Newpt
6 C4 **St Budeaux** C Plym
2 D6 **St Buryan** Cnwll
183 G6 **St Catherines** Ag & B
55 J7 **St Chloe** Gloucs
50 C3 **St Clears** Carmth
5 K3 **St Cleer** Cnwll
4 D6 **St Clement** Cnwll
236 e8 **St Clement** Jersey
9 G7 **St Clether** Cnwll
173 H5 **St Colmac** Ag & B
4 E3 **St Columb Major** Cnwll
4 D4 **St Columb Minor** Cnwll
4 E4 **St Columb Road** Cnwll
217 K2 **St Combs** Abers
93 G6 **St Cross South Elmham** Suffk
197 J4 **St Cyrus** Abers
185 K4 **St David's** P & K
48 C3 **St David's** Pembks
3 J3 **St Day** Cnwll
3 H3 **St Dennis** Cnwll
65 G5 **St Dogmaels** Cerdgn
6 B3 **St Dominick** Cnwll
36 E6 **St Donats** V Glam
4 F1 **St Endellion** Cnwll
4 D4 **St Enoder** Cnwll
4 D6 **St Erme** Cnwll
6 B4 **St Erney** Cnwll
2 F4 **St Erth** Cnwll
3 G4 **St Erth Praze** Cnwll
4 D2 **St Ervan** Cnwll
4 F6 **St Ewe** Cnwll
37 H5 **St Fagans** Cardif
37 H5 **St Fagans Welsh Life Museum** Cardif
217 K4 **St Fergus** Abers
184 F3 **St Fillans** P & K
49 J7 **St Florence** Pembks
8 F5 **St Gennys** Cnwll
110 D6 **St George** Conwy
37 H5 **St George's** V Glam
38 B7 **St Georges** N Som
6 A4 **St Germans** Cnwll
23 H7 **St Giles in the Wood** Devon
9 K6 **St Giles-on-the-Heath** Cnwll
81 L8 **St Harmon** Powys
140 F2 **St Helen Auckland** Dur
92 E1 **St Helena** Norfk
17 J5 **St Helens** IOW
112 D3 **St Helens** St Hel
44 E6 **St Helier** Gt Lon
236 d7 **St Helier** Jersey
2 F5 **St Hilary** Cnwll
36 F5 **St Hilary** V Glam
59 K3 **St Ippollitts** Herts
48 E6 **St Ishmael's** Pembks
4 E2 **St Issey** Cnwll
5 L3 **St Ive** Cnwll
75 K1 **St Ives** Cambs
2 F3 **St Ives** Cnwll
93 G7 **St James South Elmham** Suffk
73 L3 **St James's End** Nhants
6 B5 **St John** Cnwll
236 c5 **St John** Jersey
237 b5 **St John's** IOM
23 H5 **St John's Chapel** Devon
149 M7 **St John's Chapel** Dur
90 D2 **St John's Fen End** Norfk
165 J3 **St John's Kirk** S Lans
154 B6 **St John's Town of Dalry** D & G
44 F4 **St John's Wood** Gt Lon
32 F3 **St Johns** Kent
43 G8 **St Johns** Surrey
70 E4 **St Johns** Worcs
237 d3 **St Jude's** IOM
2 C5 **St Just** Cnwll
4 D8 **St Just-in-Roseland** Cnwll
216 E7 **St Katherines** Abers
3 K6 **St Keverne** Cnwll
5 G1 **St Kew** Cnwll
5 G2 **St Kew Highway** Cnwll
5 K4 **St Keyne** Cnwll
62 A6 **St Lawrence** Essex
17 G6 **St Lawrence** IOW
236 c6 **St Lawrence** Jersey
35 K2 **St Lawrence** Kent
58 E6 **St Leonards** Bucks
15 L2 **St Leonards** Dorset
20 F4 **St Leonards** E Susx
2 C6 **St Levan** Cnwll
37 H6 **St Lythans** V Glam
5 G2 **St Mabyn** Cnwll
186 C3 **St Madoes** P & K
93 G6 **St Margaret South Elmham** Suffk
35 K5 **St Margaret's at Cliffe** Kent
234 C7 **St Margaret's Hope** Ork
69 G7 **St Margarets** Herefs
60 B5 **St Margarets** Herts
237 C6 **St Marks** IOM
5 K5 **St Martin** Cnwll
236 d3 **St Martin** Guern
236 e6 **St Martin** Jersey
186 B2 **St Martin's** P & K
97 L5 **St Martins** Shrops
236 b6 **St Mary** Jersey
29 H2 **St Mary Bourne** Hants
36 F6 **St Mary Church** V Glam
45 J6 **St Mary Cray** Gt Lon
21 L1 **St Mary in the Marsh** Kent
234 c6 **St Mary's** Ork
21 L1 **St Mary's Bay** Kent
46 D5 **St Mary's Hoo** Medway
7 L3 **St Marychurch** Torbay
54 C5 **St Maughans Green** Mons
3 L5 **St Mawes** Cnwll
4 D3 **St Mawgan** Cnwll
6 B3 **St Mellion** Cnwll
37 K4 **St Mellons** Cardif
4 D2 **St Merryn** Cnwll
4 F5 **St Mewan** Cnwll
4 F7 **St Michael Caerhays** Cnwll
25 L5 **St Michael Church** Somset
4 D7 **St Michael Penkevil** Cnwll
93 H6 **St Michael South Elmham** Suffk
120 F3 **St Michael's on Wyre** Lancs
34 B7 **St Michaels** Kent
69 L2 **St Michaels** Worcs
4 F1 **St Minver** Cnwll
187 H6 **St Monans** Fife
5 J3 **St Neot** Cnwll
75 H3 **St Neots** Cambs
64 C7 **St Nicholas** Pembks
37 H5 **St Nicholas** V Glam
47 L6 **St Nicholas at Wade** Kent
185 G8 **St Ninians** Stirlg
93 J4 **St Olaves** Norfk
62 D5 **St Osyth** Essex
236 b6 **St Ouen** Jersey
54 D3 **St Owens Cross** Herefs
59 K4 **St Paul's Walden** Herts
45 J6 **St Pauls Cray** Gt Lon
236 b6 **St Peter** Jersey
236 d3 **St Peter Port** Guern
236 b3 **St Peter's** Guern
35 K2 **St Peter's** Kent
5 J3 **St Pinnock** Cnwll
163 J5 **St Quivox** S Ayrs
236 d2 **St Sampson** Guern
236 c3 **St Saviour** Guern
236 d7 **St Saviour** Jersey
4 E5 **St Stephen** Cnwll
4 E5 **St Stephen's Coombe** Cnwll
9 J7 **St Stephens** Cnwll
6 B4 **St Stephens** Cnwll
8 E8 **St Teath** Cnwll
5 G1 **St Tudy** Cnwll
48 F7 **St Twynnells** Pembks
5 J5 **St Veep** Cnwll
197 G7 **St Vigeans** Angus
4 F3 **St Wenn** Cnwll
54 D3 **St Weonards** Herefs
71 K6 **Saintbury** Gloucs
191 L6 **Salachail** Ag & B
7 H7 **Salcombe** Devon
12 F5 **Salcombe Regis** Devon
61 M5 **Salcott** Essex
113 H3 **Sale** Traffd
71 G3 **Sale Green** Worcs
118 F5 **Saleby** Lincs

20 F2 **Salehurst** E Susx
80 F6 **Salem** Cerdgn
95 J2 **Salem** Gwynd
190 C7 **Salen** Ag & B
190 D4 **Salen** Highld
74 D6 **Salford** Beds
56 F3 **Salford** Oxon
113 J2 **Salford** Salfd
71 J4 **Salford Priors**
    Warwks
32 B4 **Salfords** Surrey
93 G1 **Salhouse** Norfk
185 L8 **Saline** Fife
28 C5 **Salisbury** Wilts
28 C5 **Salisbury Cathedral**
    Wilts
28 B3 **Salisbury Plain** Wilts
148 F7 **Salkeld Dykes** Cumb
106 D7 **Salle** Norfk
118 D6 **Salmonby** Lincs
56 B4 **Salperton** Gloucs
175 L5 **Salsburgh** N Lans
99 L6 **Salt** Staffs
123 H3 **Saltaire** Brad
6 B4 **Saltash** Cnwll
223 G7 **Saltburn** Highld
142 E3 **Saltburn-by-the-**
    Sea R & Cl
102 D7 **Saltby** Leics
163 G2 **Saltcoats** N Ayrs
19 K5 **Saltdean** Br & H
136 D3 **Salterbeck** Cumb
122 D2 **Salterforth** Lancs
28 C4 **Salterton** Wilts
118 F3 **Saltfleet** Lincs
118 F4 **Saltfleetby All**
    Saints Lincs
118 F3 **Saltfleetby St**
    Clement Lincs
118 F4 **Saltfleetby St**
    Peter Lincs
39 G6 **Saltford** BaNES
106 C4 **Salthouse** Norfk
125 J5 **Saltmarshe** E R Yk
111 L8 **Saltney** Flints
133 L4 **Salton** N York
23 G6 **Saltrens** Devon
34 F7 **Saltwood** Kent
18 F5 **Salvington** W Susx
70 F3 **Salwarpe** Worcs
13 L3 **Salwayash** Dorset
71 J3 **Sambourne** Warwks
99 G7 **Sambrook** Wrekin
121 H4 **Samlesbury** Lancs
25 H7 **Sampford Arundel**
    Somset
25 G3 **Sampford Brett**
    Somset
10 F5 **Sampford**
    Courtenay Devon
25 H7 **Sampford Moor**
    Somset
25 G8 **Sampford Peverell**
    Devon
6 D2 **Sampford Spiney**
    Devon
234 d5 **Samsonlane** Ork
178 B4 **Samuelston** E Loth
170 E4 **Sanaigmore** Ag & B
2 D5 **Sancreed** Cnwll
125 L3 **Sancton** E R Yk
124 B3 **Sand Hills** Leeds
125 J3 **Sand Hole** E R Yk
133 L7 **Sand Hutton** N York
199 L5 **Sandaig** Highld
123 L6 **Sandal Magna**
    Wakefd
199 G7 **Sandavore** Highld
234 d4 **Sanday Airport** Ork
99 H1 **Sandbach** Ches
173 K3 **Sandbank** Ag & B
15 K5 **Sandbanks** Poole
216 B2 **Sandend** Abers

45 G7 **Sanderstead** Gt Lon
139 G4 **Sandford** Cumb
11 J4 **Sandford** Devon
15 H5 **Sandford** Dorset
15 M3 **Sandford** Hants
17 G6 **Sandford** IOW
38 B8 **Sandford** N Som
164 E2 **Sandford** S Lans
26 F7 **Sandford Orcas**
    Dorset
57 H3 **Sandford St Martin**
    Oxon
57 K7 **Sandford-on-**
    Thames Oxon
35 G7 **Sandgate** Kent
217 H2 **Sandhaven** Abers
144 D5 **Sandhead** D & G
57 K6 **Sandhills** Oxon
30 F4 **Sandhills** Surrey
150 B2 **Sandhoe** Nthumb
182 E7 **Sandhole** Ag & B
125 J4 **Sandholme** E R Yk
42 D7 **Sandhurst** Br For
55 J4 **Sandhurst** Gloucs
33 K7 **Sandhurst** Kent
132 F3 **Sandhutton** N York
101 J5 **Sandiacre** Derbys
119 G5 **Sandilands** Lincs
28 C7 **Sandleheath** Hants
57 J7 **Sandleigh** Oxon
27 H6 **Sandley** Dorset
235 b5 **Sandness** Shet
61 H6 **Sandon** Essex
75 K7 **Sandon** Herts
99 L6 **Sandon** Staffs
99 L6 **Sandon Bank** Staffs
17 H5 **Sandown** IOW
5 K4 **Sandplace** Cnwll
59 K6 **Sandridge** Herts
105 H6 **Sandringham** Norfk
143 H5 **Sandsend** N York
125 H8 **Sandtoft** N Linc
34 B5 **Sandway** Kent
35 J2 **Sandwich** Kent
235 c7 **Sandwick** Shet
232 g2 **Sandwick** W Isls
136 D4 **Sandwith** Cumb
75 H5 **Sandy** Beds
39 L6 **Sandy Lane** Wilts
11 G6 **Sandy Park** Devon
155 L4 **Sandyford** D & G
7 K2 **Sandygate** Devon
237 d3 **Sandygate** IOM
146 F4 **Sandyhills** D & G
129 J6 **Sandylands** Lancs
228 F3 **Sangobeg** Highld
228 F3 **Sangomore** Highld
70 E2 **Sankyn's Green**
    Worcs
189 K3 **Sanna Bay** Highld
232 g2 **Sanndabhaig** W Isls
162 C1 **Sannox** N Ayrs
164 F7 **Sanquhar** D & G
136 F6 **Santon Bridge**
    Cumb
91 J6 **Santon Downham**
    Suffk
86 F5 **Sapcote** Leics
70 C2 **Sapey Common**
    Herefs
91 K7 **Sapiston** Suffk
55 L7 **Sapperton** Gloucs
103 G5 **Sapperton** Lincs
104 B6 **Saracen's Head** Lincs
231 L6 **Sarclet** Highld
17 G2 **Sarisbury** Hants
94 D6 **Sarn** Gwynd
81 K4 **Sarn** Powys
82 E5 **Sarn** Powys
65 K4 **Sarnau** Cerdgn
82 E1 **Sarnau** Powys
69 H4 **Sarnesfield** Herefs
51 H3 **Saron** Carmth

109 G7 **Saron** Gwynd
59 H7 **Sarratt** Herts
47 L6 **Sarre** Kent
56 F4 **Sarsden** Oxon
150 E6 **Satley** Dur
23 L6 **Satterleigh** Devon
129 H2 **Satterthwaite** Cumb
206 D3 **Sauchen** Abers
186 C2 **Saucher** P & K
197 G3 **Sauchieburn** Abers
55 H6 **Saul** Gloucs
116 C4 **Saundby** Notts
49 K6 **Saundersfoot**
    Pembks
58 C7 **Saunderton** Bucks
23 G4 **Saunton** Devon
118 E7 **Sausthorpe** Lincs
123 K6 **Savile Town** Kirk
73 G2 **Sawbridge** Warwks
60 D5 **Sawbridgeworth**
    Herts
134 E3 **Sawdon** N York
122 B2 **Sawley** Lancs
132 C6 **Sawley** N York
76 C5 **Sawston** Cambs
89 H6 **Sawtry** Cambs
102 D8 **Saxby** Leics
117 G4 **Saxby** Lincs
126 B6 **Saxby All Saints**
    N Linc
102 B7 **Saxelbye** Leics
78 C3 **Saxham Street** Suffk
116 E6 **Saxilby** Lincs
106 B5 **Saxlingham** Norfk
92 F4 **Saxlingham Green**
    Norfk
92 F4 **Saxlingham**
    Nethergate Norfk
92 E4 **Saxlingham Thorpe**
    Norfk
79 H2 **Saxmundham** Suffk
76 F3 **Saxon Street** Cambs
102 B4 **Saxondale** Notts
78 F2 **Saxtead** Suffk
78 F2 **Saxtead Green** Suffk
78 F2 **Saxtead Little Green**
    Suffk
106 D6 **Saxthorpe** Norfk
124 D3 **Saxton** N York
19 H3 **Sayers Common**
    W Susx
133 K5 **Scackleton** N York
137 H5 **Scaftell Pike** Cumb
116 A3 **Scaftworth** Notts
134 C5 **Scagglethorpe**
    N York
180 E8 **Scalasaig** Ag & B
125 K5 **Scalby** E R Yk
134 F2 **Scalby** N York
73 L1 **Scaldwell** Nhants
148 D3 **Scaleby** Cumb
148 D3 **Scalebyhill** Cumb
137 K2 **Scales** Cumb
129 G5 **Scales** Cumb
102 C7 **Scalford** Leics
142 F4 **Scaling** N York
235 c6 **Scalloway** Shet
118 C5 **Scamblesby** Lincs
191 G2 **Scamodale** Highld
134 D4 **Scampston** N York
116 F5 **Scampton** Lincs
212 F6 **Scaniport** Highld
123 G7 **Scapegoat Hill** Kirk
135 G2 **Scarborough** N York
4 E5 **Scarcewater** Cnwll
115 J7 **Scarcliffe** Derbys
124 B3 **Scarcroft** Leeds
231 J2 **Scarfskerry** Highld
140 D5 **Scargill** Dur
188 D7 **Scarinish** Ag & B
120 E7 **Scarisbrick** Lancs
91 L2 **Scarning** Norfk
102 B4 **Scarrington** Notts

118 C1 **Scartho** Lincs
235 c4 **Scatsta Airport** Shet
116 F1 **Scawby** N Linc
115 K1 **Scawsby** Donc
115 K1 **Scawthorpe** Donc
133 H3 **Scawton** N York
19 K2 **Scayne's Hill** W Susx
53 H3 **Scethrog** Powys
123 H8 **Scholes** Kirk
124 B3 **Scholes** Leeds
115 H3 **Scholes** Rothm
112 E1 **Scholes** Wigan
123 K7 **Scissett** Kirk
64 C7 **Scleddau** Pembks
115 L5 **Scofton** Notts
92 D7 **Scole** Norfk
186 B3 **Scone** P & K
209 H7 **Sconser** Highld
186 F6 **Scoonie** Fife
103 H2 **Scopwick** Lincs
220 C3 **Scoraig** Highld
126 C2 **Scorborough** E R Yk
3 J3 **Scorrier** Cnwll
121 G2 **Scorton** Lancs
141 G7 **Scorton** N York
158 C5 **Scot's Gap** Nthumb
148 D4 **Scotby** Cumb
140 F6 **Scotch Corner** N York
129 K7 **Scotforth** Lancs
117 G6 **Scothern** Lincs
186 C6 **Scotlandwell** P & K
231 G4 **Scotscalder Station**
    Highld
206 B2 **Scotsmill** Abers
174 F5 **Scotstoun** C Glas
150 F3 **Scotswood** N u Ty
116 E2 **Scotter** Lincs
116 E2 **Scotterthorpe** Lincs
116 E2 **Scotton** Lincs
140 F7 **Scotton** N York
132 E7 **Scotton** N York
92 B4 **Scoulton** Norfk
228 B6 **Scourie** Highld
228 B6 **Scourie More** Highld
235 C7 **Scousburgh** Shet
231 G2 **Scrabster** Highld
167 K5 **Scraesburgh** Border
104 C4 **Scrane End** Lincs
87 J3 **Scraptoft** Leics
93 K1 **Scratby** Norfk
133 L7 **Scrayingham** N York
103 H4 **Scredington** Lincs
118 F7 **Scremby** Lincs
179 L8 **Scremerston**
    Nthumb
102 B3 **Screveton** Notts
132 E7 **Scriven** N York
115 M4 **Scrooby** Notts
100 D6 **Scropton** Derbys
103 L2 **Scrub Hill** Lincs
195 K5 **Scruschloch** Angus
132 D2 **Scruton** N York
229 J4 **Scullomie** Highld
105 L6 **Sculthorpe** Norfk
125 K7 **Scunthorpe** N Linc
107 J6 **Sea Palling** Norfk
13 L3 **Seaborough** Dorset
35 G7 **Seabrook** Kent
151 J3 **Seaburn** Sundld
124 B4 **Seacroft** Leeds
209 G5 **Seafield** Highld
176 D5 **Seafield** W Loth
20 A6 **Seaford** E Susx
111 K3 **Seaforth** Sefton
101 L8 **Seagrave** Leics
151 K5 **Seaham** Dur
169 J3 **Seahouses** Nthumb
32 F2 **Seal** Kent
30 E2 **Seale** Surrey
142 B5 **Seamer** N York
134 F3 **Seamer** N York
173 L8 **Seamill** N Ayrs
117 H1 **Searby** Lincs

47 H6 **Seasalter** Kent
136 E6 **Seascale** Cumb
137 H7 **Seathwaite** Cumb
137 H4 **Seatoller** Cumb
5 L5 **Seaton** Cnwll
136 E2 **Seaton** Cumb
13 G4 **Seaton** Devon
126 E2 **Seaton** E R Yk
35 G3 **Seaton** Kent
159 H6 **Seaton** Nthumb
88 C4 **Seaton** Rutlnd
142 B2 **Seaton Carew** Hartpl
159 H6 **Seaton Delaval** Nthumb
125 J3 **Seaton Ross** E R Yk
159 H6 **Seaton Sluice** Nthumb
13 K4 **Seatown** Dorset
142 C7 **Seave Green** N York
17 J4 **Seaview** IOW
147 K4 **Seaville** Cumb
26 B7 **Seavington St Mary** Somset
26 B7 **Seavington St Michael** Somset
148 C6 **Sebergham** Cumb
86 C3 **Seckington** Warwks
130 C2 **Sedbergh** Cumb
38 D2 **Sedbury** Gloucs
131 G2 **Sedbusk** N York
71 H6 **Sedgeberrow** Worcs
102 D5 **Sedgebrook** Lincs
141 J2 **Sedgefield** Dur
105 H5 **Sedgeford** Norfk
27 K5 **Sedgehill** Wilts
85 G5 **Sedgley** Dudley
129 L3 **Sedgwick** Cumb
20 F3 **Sedlescombe** E Susx
58 D5 **Sedrup** Bucks
39 L7 **Seend** Wilts
39 L7 **Seend Cleeve** Wilts
42 F3 **Seer Green** Bucks
93 G4 **Seething** Norfk
111 K2 **Sefton** Sefton
99 K7 **Seighford** Staffs
109 H7 **Seion** Gwynd
84 E4 **Seisdon** Staffs
97 K5 **Selattyn** Shrops
30 C5 **Selborne** Hants
124 F4 **Selby** N York
30 F7 **Selham** W Susx
45 G6 **Selhurst** Gt Lon
167 G4 **Selkirk** Border
54 E3 **Sellack** Herefs
235 d2 **Sellafirth** Shet
34 E6 **Sellindge** Kent
34 D4 **Selling** Kent
39 L7 **Sells Green** Wilts
85 J6 **Selly Oak** Birm
20 B4 **Selmeston** E Susx
45 G7 **Selsdon** Gt Lon
18 B6 **Selsey** W Susx
130 E4 **Selside** N York
55 J7 **Selsley** Gloucs
35 G5 **Selsted** Kent
101 J2 **Selston** Notts
24 E3 **Selworthy** Somset
78 B5 **Semer** Suffk
39 K7 **Semington** Wilts
27 K6 **Semley** Wilts
31 G1 **Send** Surrey
37 H3 **Senghenydd** Caerph
2 C6 **Sennen** Cnwll
2 C6 **Sennen Cove** Cnwll
52 E3 **Sennybridge** Powys
133 G4 **Sessay** N York
90 F2 **Setchey** Norfk
177 L4 **Seton Mains** E Loth
130 F6 **Settle** N York
134 C5 **Settrington** N York
25 J5 **Seven Ash** Somset
25 J3 **Seven Kings** Gt Lon
52 C6 **Seven Sisters** Neath

61 M3 **Seven Star Green** Essex
71 K7 **Seven Wells** Gloucs
56 B4 **Sevenhampton** Gloucs
40 E3 **Sevenhampton** Swindn
32 F3 **Sevenoaks** Kent
32 F3 **Sevenoaks Weald** Kent
38 D4 **Severn Beach** S Glos
70 F5 **Severn Stoke** Worcs
34 D6 **Sevington** Kent
76 E6 **Sewards End** Essex
59 G4 **Sewell** Beds
135 J5 **Sewerby** E R Yk
3 J5 **Seworgan** Cnwll
102 E7 **Sewstern** Leics
232 g1 **Sgiogarstaigh** W Isls
58 A6 **Shabbington** Bucks
86 D3 **Shackerstone** Leics
30 F3 **Shackleford** Surrey
232 f1 **Shader** W Isls
151 H6 **Shadforth** Dur
93 J6 **Shadingfield** Suffk
34 C7 **Shadoxhurst** Kent
91 L6 **Shadwell** Norfk
76 B6 **Shaftenhoe End** Herts
27 K6 **Shaftesbury** Dorset
124 B7 **Shafton** Barns
40 F7 **Shalbourne** Wilts
30 B3 **Shalden** Hants
7 L2 **Shaldon** Devon
16 E5 **Shalfleet** IOW
61 H3 **Shalford** Essex
31 G3 **Shalford** Surrey
61 H3 **Shalford Green** Essex
34 E4 **Shalmsford Street** Kent
73 J7 **Shalstone** Bucks
31 G3 **Shamley Green** Surrey
196 D4 **Shandford** Angus
174 B2 **Shandon** Ag & B
223 J6 **Shandwick** Highld
87 K4 **Shangton** Leics
17 H6 **Shanklin** IOW
138 E4 **Shap** Cumb
15 H3 **Shapwick** Dorset
26 B4 **Shapwick** Somset
101 H6 **Shardlow** Derbys
85 G3 **Shareshill** Staffs
124 B6 **Sharlston** Wakefd
74 E3 **Sharnbrook** Beds
86 F5 **Sharnford** Leics
121 G4 **Sharoe Green** Lancs
132 E3 **Sharow** N York
59 H2 **Sharpenhoe** Beds
158 B2 **Sharperton** Nthumb
54 F7 **Sharpness** Gloucs
106 C5 **Sharrington** Norfk
84 E7 **Shatterford** Worcs
6 D3 **Shaugh Prior** Devon
99 G3 **Shavington** Ches
122 D8 **Shaw** Oldham
41 J6 **Shaw** W Berk
39 K7 **Shaw** Wilts
132 C6 **Shaw Mills** N York
232 e2 **Shawbost** W Isls
98 E7 **Shawbury** Shrops
87 G7 **Shawell** Leics
29 J6 **Shawford** Hants
154 F6 **Shawhead** D & G
175 K7 **Shawsburn** S Lans
147 H2 **Shearington** D & G
87 J5 **Shearsby** Leics
25 L5 **Shearston** Somset
10 C3 **Shebbear** Devon
99 H7 **Shebdon** Staffs
230 E3 **Shebster** Highld
175 G6 **Sheddens** E Rens
29 K8 **Shedfield** Hants

100 C1 **Sheen** Derbys
123 H6 **Sheepridge** Kirk
123 L4 **Sheepscar** Leeds
55 K6 **Sheepscombe** Gloucs
6 E3 **Sheepstor** Devon
10 C4 **Sheepwash** Devon
86 D3 **Sheepy Magna** Leics
86 D3 **Sheepy Parva** Leics
60 E5 **Sheering** Essex
46 F5 **Sheerness** Kent
43 H7 **Sheerwater** Surrey
30 C6 **Sheet** Hants
115 G4 **Sheffield** Sheff
115 H4 **Sheffield City Airport** Sheff
75 G6 **Shefford** Beds
228 B4 **Sheigra** Highld
83 L3 **Sheinton** Shrops
83 H7 **Shelderton** Shrops
85 L6 **Sheldon** Birm
114 D7 **Sheldon** Derbys
12 E2 **Sheldon** Devon
34 D4 **Sheldwich** Kent
92 D6 **Shelfanger** Norfk
102 A4 **Shelford** Notts
168 D2 **Shellacres** Border
123 J7 **Shelley** Kirk
78 B6 **Shelley** Suffk
40 F2 **Shellingford** Oxon
60 F6 **Shellow Bowells** Essex
70 D2 **Shelsley Beauchamp** Worcs
70 C2 **Shelsley Walsh** Worcs
74 F2 **Shelton** Beds
92 F5 **Shelton** Norfk
102 C4 **Shelton** Notts
99 J5 **Shelton Under Harley** Staffs
83 G4 **Shelve** Shrops
69 K6 **Shelwick** Herefs
45 L2 **Shenfield** Essex
72 D6 **Shenington** Oxon
59 K7 **Shenley** Herts
74 B7 **Shenley Brook End** M Keyn
74 B7 **Shenley Church End** M Keyn
69 H6 **Shenmore** Herefs
145 H3 **Shennanton** D & G
85 K3 **Shenstone** Staffs
84 F8 **Shenstone** Worcs
86 E4 **Shenton** Leics
59 L4 **Shephall** Herts
44 E4 **Shepherd's Bush** Gt Lon
35 H5 **Shepherdswell** Kent
123 J8 **Shepley** Kirk
43 H6 **Shepperton** Surrey
76 B5 **Shepreth** Cambs
101 J8 **Shepshed** Leics
26 B7 **Shepton Beauchamp** Somset
26 F3 **Shepton Mallet** Somset
27 G7 **Shepton Montague** Somset
33 K3 **Shepway** Kent
151 K7 **Sheraton** Dur
26 F7 **Sherborne** Dorset
56 D5 **Sherborne** Gloucs
26 E1 **Sherborne** Somset
29 L1 **Sherborne St John** Hants
72 C3 **Sherbourne** Warwks
151 H6 **Sherburn** Dur
134 E4 **Sherburn** N York
151 H6 **Sherburn Hill** Dur
124 D4 **Sherburn in Elmet** N York
31 H2 **Shere** Surrey
105 L6 **Shereford** Norfk

28 F6 **Sherfield English** Hants
42 B8 **Sherfield on Loddon** Hants
7 H6 **Sherford** Devon
133 K6 **Sheriff Hutton** N York
84 D2 **Sheriffhales** Shrops
106 E4 **Sheringham** Norfk
74 C5 **Sherington** M Keyn
105 H6 **Shernborne** Norfk
27 L4 **Sherrington** Wilts
39 J3 **Sherston** Wilts
101 K4 **Sherwood** C Nott
101 L2 **Sherwood Forest** Notts
175 H5 **Shettleston** C Glas
121 H8 **Shevington** Wigan
6 B5 **Sheviock** Cnwll
123 G5 **Shibden Head** Brad
16 F5 **Shide** IOW
168 B2 **Shidlaw** Nthumb
200 E2 **Shiel Bridge** Highld
210 C4 **Shieldaig** Highld
155 H5 **Shieldhill** D & G
176 B3 **Shieldhill** Falk
165 J2 **Shieldhill House Hotel** S Lans
175 K7 **Shields** N Lans
190 D3 **Shielfoot** Highld
196 C5 **Shielhill** Angus
173 L4 **Shielhill** Inver
84 D2 **Shifnal** Shrops
169 J7 **Shilbottle** Nthumb
141 G3 **Shildon** Dur
174 E6 **Shillford** E Rens
24 F6 **Shillingford** Devon
41 L2 **Shillingford** Oxon
11 K6 **Shillingford Abbot** Devon
11 K7 **Shillingford St George** Devon
14 F1 **Shillingstone** Dorset
75 G7 **Shillington** Beds
56 E6 **Shilton** Oxon
86 E6 **Shilton** Warwks
92 D6 **Shimpling** Norfk
77 J4 **Shimpling** Suffk
77 K4 **Shimpling Street** Suffk
151 H6 **Shincliffe** Dur
151 H4 **Shiney Row** Sundld
42 B6 **Shinfield** Wokham
225 L5 **Shinness** Highld
33 G3 **Shipbourne** Kent
91 L3 **Shipdham** Norfk
38 C8 **Shipham** Somset
7 K3 **Shiphay** Torbay
42 C5 **Shiplake** Oxon
123 H3 **Shipley** Brad
31 J6 **Shipley** W Susx
32 B5 **Shipley Bridge** Surrey
93 H5 **Shipmeadow** Suffk
41 J2 **Shippon** Oxon
72 B6 **Shipston on Stour** Warwks
56 B4 **Shipton** Gloucs
133 H7 **Shipton** N York
83 L5 **Shipton** Shrops
28 E3 **Shipton Bellinger** Hants
13 L4 **Shipton Gorge** Dorset
17 L3 **Shipton Green** W Susx
39 K3 **Shipton Moyne** Gloucs
57 J5 **Shipton-on-Cherwell** Oxon
56 F4 **Shipton-under-Wychwood** Oxon
125 K2 **Shiptonthorpe** E R Yk

42 B2 **Shirburn** Oxon
120 E7 **Shirdley Hill** Lancs
115 K7 **Shirebrook** Derbys
115 G3 **Shiregreen** Sheff
38 D5 **Shirehampton** Bristl
159 H4 **Shiremoor** N Tyne
38 C2 **Shirenewton** Mons
115 K5 **Shireoaks** Notts
101 H2 **Shirland** Derbys
29 H8 **Shirley** C Sotn
100 E4 **Shirley** Derbys
45 G6 **Shirley** Gt Lon
85 K7 **Shirley** Solhll
29 L8 **Shirrell Heath** Hants
172 E2 **Shirvan** Ag & B
23 J4 **Shirwell** Devon
162 B4 **Shiskine** N Ayrs
69 H3 **Shobdon** Herefs
11 K5 **Shobrooke** Devon
102 B7 **Shoby** Leics
98 C3 **Shocklach** Ches
46 F3 **Shoeburyness** Sthend
35 K4 **Sholden** Kent
16 F1 **Sholing** C Sotn
9 G2 **Shop** Cnwll
78 F2 **Shop Street** Suffk
45 G4 **Shoreditch** Gt Lon
25 K6 **Shoreditch** Somset
45 K7 **Shoreham** Kent
19 G5 **Shoreham Airport** W Susx
19 H5 **Shoreham-by-Sea** W Susx
29 L6 **Shorley** Hants
46 B5 **Shorne** Kent
20 A3 **Shortgate** E Susx
4 C6 **Shortlanesend** Cnwll
74 F5 **Shortstown** Beds
16 F5 **Shorwell** IOW
27 G1 **Shoscombe** BaNES
92 F4 **Shotesham** Norfk
46 C2 **Shotgate** Essex
78 F7 **Shotley** Suffk
150 D4 **Shotley Bridge** Dur
78 F7 **Shotley Gate** Suffk
78 F7 **Shotley Street** Suffk
34 D4 **Shottenden** Kent
71 L4 **Shottery** Warwks
72 E5 **Shotteswell** Warwks
79 G5 **Shottisham** Suffk
100 F3 **Shottle** Derbys
100 F3 **Shottlegate** Derbys
151 K6 **Shotton** Dur
111 J7 **Shotton** Flints
176 B6 **Shotts** N Lans
111 K6 **Shotwick** Ches
214 F4 **Shougle** Moray
90 F2 **Shouldham** Norfk
90 F2 **Shouldham Thorpe** Norfk
70 E3 **Shoulton** Worcs
83 H1 **Shrawardine** Shrops
70 E2 **Shrawley** Worcs
72 B2 **Shrewley** Warwks
83 J2 **Shrewsbury** Shrops
28 B3 **Shrewton** Wilts
18 C5 **Shripney** W Susx
40 E3 **Shrivenham** Oxon
92 B5 **Shropham** Norfk
69 L6 **Shucknall** Herefs
76 E5 **Shudy Camps** Cambs
55 L4 **Shurdington** Gloucs
42 D5 **Shurlock Row** W & M
230 H4 **Shurrery** Highld
230 F4 **Shurrery Lodge** Highld
25 J3 **Shurton** Somset
86 B5 **Shustoke** Warwks
99 K7 **Shut Heath** Staffs
13 G3 **Shute** Devon
72 E6 **Shutford** Oxon
70 F7 **Shuthonger** Gloucs

73 K4 **Shutlanger** Nhants
86 B3 **Shuttington** Warwks
115 J6 **Shuttlewood** Derbys
122 B6 **Shuttleworth** Bury
232 e2 **Siabost** W Isls
232 f1 **Siadar** W Isls
87 K6 **Sibbertoft** Nhants
72 D6 **Sibford Ferris** Oxon
72 D6 **Sibford Gower** Oxon
77 H7 **Sible Hedingham** Essex
60 F3 **Sibley's Green** Essex
104 B3 **Sibsey** Lincs
89 G4 **Sibson** Cambs
86 D4 **Sibson** Leics
231 K5 **Sibster** Highld
116 B6 **Sibthorpe** Notts
102 C4 **Sibthorpe** Notts
79 H1 **Sibton** Suffk
77 K3 **Sicklesmere** Suffk
124 B2 **Sicklinghall** N York
12 E4 **Sidbury** Devon
84 C6 **Sidbury** Shrops
38 B8 **Sidcot** N Som
45 J5 **Sidcup** Gt Lon
113 J7 **Siddington** Ches
56 B7 **Siddington** Gloucs
106 F4 **Sidestrand** Norfk
12 E4 **Sidford** Devon
18 B6 **Sidlesham** W Susx
20 E4 **Sidley** E Susx
12 E5 **Sidmouth** Devon
126 E2 **Sigglesthorne** E R Yk
36 F6 **Sigingstone** V Glam
41 L7 **Silchester** Hants
87 H1 **Sileby** Leics
128 D3 **Silecroft** Cumb
92 D4 **Silfield** Norfk
103 H4 **Silk Willoughby** Lincs
114 F1 **Silkstone** Barns
114 F1 **Silkstone Common** Barns
151 J4 **Silksworth** Sundld
147 K4 **Silloth** Cumb
134 E2 **Silpho** N York
122 F2 **Silsden** Brad
74 F7 **Silsoe** Beds
27 H5 **Silton** Dorset
61 K4 **Silver End** Essex
177 G6 **Silverburn** Mdloth
129 K4 **Silverdale** Lancs
99 J3 **Silverdale** Staffs
216 E2 **Silverford** Abers
73 J5 **Silverstone** Nhants
12 B2 **Silverton** Devon
84 B7 **Silvington** Shrops
157 L7 **Simonburn** Nthumb
25 H7 **Simons Burrow** Devon
24 B4 **Simonsbath** Somset
122 B4 **Simonstone** Lancs
168 C1 **Simprim** Border
74 C7 **Simpson** M Keyn
48 F4 **Simpson Cross** Pembks
179 G7 **Sinclair's Hill** Border
163 L6 **Sinclairston** E Ayrs
132 E3 **Sinderby** N York
113 G4 **Sinderland Green** Traffd
42 C6 **Sindlesham** Wokham
101 G6 **Sinfin** C Derb
120 E3 **Singleton** Lancs
18 B3 **Singleton** W Susx
46 A6 **Singlewell** Kent
205 K3 **Sinnarhard** Abers
134 B3 **Sinnington** N York
70 E3 **Sinton** Worcs
70 E3 **Sinton Green** Worcs
33 K5 **Sissinghurst** Kent
39 G5 **Siston** S Glos
3 H5 **Sithney** Cnwll
34 B3 **Sittingbourne** Kent

84 E5 **Six Ashes** Staffs
76 E3 **Six Mile Bottom** Cambs
236 C6 **Six Rues** Jersey
117 K4 **Sixhills** Lincs
34 F5 **Sixmile Cottages** Kent
27 M7 **Sixpenny Handley** Dorset
129 K3 **Sizergh Castle** Cumb
234 d6 **Skaill** Ork
164 B6 **Skares** E Ayrs
207 G6 **Skateraw** Abers
178 F4 **Skateraw** E Loth
208 F5 **Skeabost** Highld
140 F6 **Skeeby** N York
87 L3 **Skeffington** Leics
127 J6 **Skeffling** E R Yk
101 J1 **Skegby** Notts
116 C7 **Skegby** Notts
119 H8 **Skegness** Lincs
223 H3 **Skelbo** Highld
223 H3 **Skelbo Street** Highld
124 D7 **Skelbrooke** Donc
104 B5 **Skeldyke** Lincs
116 F6 **Skellingthorpe** Lincs
124 E7 **Skellow** Donc
123 J7 **Skelmanthorpe** Kirk
112 C1 **Skelmersdale** Lancs
173 L5 **Skelmorlie** N Ayrs
229 L4 **Skelpick** Highld
154 E5 **Skelston** D & G
148 D7 **Skelton** Cumb
125 H5 **Skelton** E R Yk
132 E5 **Skelton** N York
142 E4 **Skelton** R & Cl
133 J7 **Skelton** York
137 K6 **Skelwith Bridge** Cumb
118 F7 **Skendleby** Lincs
206 E4 **Skene House** Abers
54 C4 **Skenfrith** Mons
135 G7 **Skerne** E R Yk
229 K3 **Skerray** Highld
228 C5 **Skerricha** Highld
129 K6 **Skerton** Lancs
86 E5 **Sketchley** Leics
51 J6 **Sketty** Swans
51 K6 **Skewen** Neath
133 K5 **Skewsby** N York
230 E3 **Skiall** Highld
126 C4 **Skidby** E R Yk
232 g1 **Skigersta** W Isls
24 F6 **Skilgate** Somset
102 E7 **Skillington** Lincs
147 K4 **Skinburness** Cumb
176 B2 **Skinflats** Falk
208 C5 **Skinidin** Highld
172 F6 **Skipness** Ag & B
135 J8 **Skipsea** E R Yk
122 E1 **Skipton** N York
132 E4 **Skipton-on-Swale** N York
125 G3 **Skipwith** N York
126 E3 **Skirlaugh** E R Yk
165 L2 **Skirling** Border
42 C3 **Skirmett** Bucks
134 B7 **Skirpenbeck** E R Yk
149 G7 **Skirwith** Cumb
231 L2 **Skirza** Highld
199 K2 **Skulamus** Highld
208 F6 **Skye** Highld
61 L4 **Skye Green** Essex
204 B1 **Skye of Curr** Highld
122 E5 **Slack** Calder
216 F5 **Slacks of Cairnbanno** Abers
55 K6 **Slad** Gloucs
23 H3 **Slade** Devon
24 C6 **Slade** Somset
45 K5 **Slade Green** Kent
115 K4 **Slade Hooton** Rothm
149 H4 **Slaggyford** Nthumb

130 D8 **Slaidburn** Lancs
123 G7 **Slaithwaite** Kirk
150 B4 **Slaley** Nthumb
176 B4 **Slamannan** Falk
58 F4 **Slapton** Bucks
7 J6 **Slapton** Devon
73 J5 **Slapton** Nhants
31 L5 **Slaugham** W Susx
39 J5 **Slaughterford** Wilts
87 L5 **Slawston** Leics
30 D4 **Sleaford** Hants
103 H4 **Sleaford** Lincs
138 E4 **Sleagill** Cumb
84 B1 **Sleapford** Wrekin
222 E3 **Sleasdairidh** Highld
134 E6 **Sledmere** E R Yk
140 B5 **Sleightholme** Dur
143 H5 **Sleights** N York
231 K3 **Slickly** Highld
162 B5 **Sliddery** N Ayrs
209 G7 **Sligachan** Highld
173 K1 **Sligrachan** Ag & B
55 H7 **Slimbridge** Gloucs
99 J6 **Slindon** Staffs
18 C4 **Slindon** W Susx
31 J5 **Slinfold** W Susx
133 L4 **Slingsby** N York
59 H4 **Slip End** Beds
75 K6 **Slip End** Herts
88 D7 **Slipton** Nhants
100 B8 **Slitting Mill** Staffs
182 B7 **Slockavullin** Ag & B
146 B2 **Slogarie** D & G
11 H7 **Sloncombe** Devon
119 G7 **Sloothby** Lincs
43 G4 **Slough** Slough
25 L7 **Slough Green** Somset
210 D6 **Slumbay** Highld
129 K6 **Slyne** Lancs
167 K3 **Smailholm** Border
19 G3 **Small Dole** W Susx
85 K6 **Small Heath** Birm
34 B8 **Small Hythe** Kent
107 G7 **Smallburgh** Norfk
101 H4 **Smalley** Derbys
32 B5 **Smallfield** Surrey
13 H3 **Smallridge** Devon
92 B7 **Smallworth** Norfk
29 G2 **Smannell** Hants
34 B6 **Smarden** Kent
34 B6 **Smarden Bell** Kent
32 F5 **Smart's Hill** Kent
190 D2 **Smearisary** Highld
12 F1 **Smeatharpe** Devon
34 E6 **Smeeth** Kent
87 K5 **Smeeton Westerby** Leics
227 L2 **Smerral** Highld
84 F5 **Smestow** Staffs
85 H6 **Smethwick** Sandw
101 G8 **Smisby** Derbys
76 F6 **Smith's Green** Essex
148 D2 **Smithfield** Cumb
219 J6 **Smithstown** Highld
213 H5 **Smithton** Highld
228 F3 **Smoo** Highld
61 L4 **Smythe's Green** Essex
154 E5 **Snade** D & G
83 G3 **Snailbeach** Shrops
76 F2 **Snailwell** Cambs
134 E3 **Snainton** N York
124 F6 **Snaith** E R Yk
132 D3 **Snape** N York
79 H3 **Snape** Suffk
79 H3 **Snape Street** Suffk
45 H3 **Snaresbrook** Gt Lon
86 D2 **Snarestone** Leics
117 K6 **Snarford** Lincs
34 D8 **Snargate** Kent
34 D8 **Snave** Kent
143 J5 **Sneaton** N York

117 H5 **Snelland** Lincs
100 D4 **Snelston** Derbys
92 B5 **Snetterton** Norfk
105 G5 **Snettisham** Norfk
158 C2 **Snitter** Nthumb
117 G3 **Snitterby** Lincs
72 B3 **Snitterfield** Warwks
83 L7 **Snitton** Shrops
46 B7 **Snodland** Kent
60 C2 **Snow End** Herts
95 K2 **Snowdon** Gwynd
96 C6 **Snowdonia**
        National Park
71 K7 **Snowshill** Gloucs
17 J1 **Soake** Hants
29 L7 **Soberton** Hants
29 L8 **Soberton Heath**
        Hants
141 J5 **Sockburn** Darltn
90 E8 **Soham** Cambs
232 C5 **Solas** W Isls
29 M4 **Soldridge** Hants
46 A6 **Sole Street** Kent
34 E5 **Sole Street** Kent
85 L7 **Solihull** Solhll
69 H4 **Sollers Dilwyn** Herefs
54 E2 **Sollers Hope** Herefs
48 D3 **Solva** Pembks
156 B6 **Solwaybank** D & G
87 L2 **Somerby** Leics
117 H1 **Somerby** Lincs
101 H2 **Somercotes** Derbys
15 M4 **Somerford** Dorset
40 A2 **Somerford Keynes**
        Gloucs
17 M3 **Somerley** W Susx
93 K4 **Somerleyton** Suffk
100 C5 **Somersal Herbert**
        Derbys
118 D6 **Somersby** Lincs
89 L7 **Somersham** Cambs
78 C5 **Somersham** Suffk
57 J3 **Somerton** Oxon
26 C5 **Somerton** Somset
77 J4 **Somerton** Suffk
19 G5 **Sompting** W Susx
42 C5 **Sonning** Wokham
42 B4 **Sonning Common**
        Oxon
15 M3 **Sopley** Hants
39 J3 **Sopworth** Wilts
145 J5 **Sorbie** D & G
231 G3 **Sordale** Highld
189 H4 **Sorisdale** Ag & B
164 B4 **Sorn** E Ayrs
231 K3 **Sortat** Highld
136 F3 **Sosgill** Cumb
117 K5 **Sotby** Lincs
117 J8 **Sots Hole** Lincs
93 J6 **Sotterly** Suffk
111 H7 **Soughton** Flints
58 E3 **Soulbury** Bucks
139 H5 **Soulby** Cumb
57 K2 **Souldern** Oxon
74 E3 **Souldrop** Beds
215 H4 **Sound Muir** Moray
38 F5 **Soundwell** S Glos
10 D6 **Sourton** Devon
128 F3 **Soutergate** Cumb
91 J2 **South Acre** Norfk
35 H6 **South Alkham** Kent
7 J7 **South Allington**
        Devon
185 J8 **South Alloa** Falk
30 E7 **South Ambersham**
        W Susx
115 K5 **South Anston** Rothm
34 D6 **South Ashford** Kent
16 D3 **South Baddesley**
        Hants
124 F1 **South Bank** York
26 E5 **South Barrow**
        Somset

44 F7 **South Beddington**
        Gt Lon
46 C3 **South Benfleet**
        Essex
18 C5 **South Bersted**
        W Susx
124 F7 **South Bramwith**
        Donc
7 G4 **South Brent** Devon
27 G4 **South Brewham**
        Somset
159 G3 **South Broomhill**
        Nthumb
93 H3 **South Burlingham**
        Norfk
26 F6 **South Cadbury**
        Somset
116 F6 **South Carlton** Lincs
115 L5 **South Carlton** Notts
125 L4 **South Cave** E R Yk
40 B2 **South Cerney** Gloucs
19 K3 **South Chailey** E Susx
169 H5 **South Charlton**
        Nthumb
27 G6 **South Cheriton**
        Somset
140 F2 **South Church** Dur
125 K4 **South Cliffe** E R Yk
116 D7 **South Clifton** Notts
118 E4 **South Cockerington**
        Lincs
36 C4 **South Cornelly**
        Brdgnd
93 K7 **South Cove** Suffk
105 K5 **South Creake** Norfk
87 K2 **South Croxton** Leics
126 B2 **South Dalton** E R Yk
19 K4 **South Downs**
125 G4 **South Duffield**
        N York
118 D4 **South Elkington**
        Lincs
124 D7 **South Elmsall**
        Wakefd
219 H7 **South Erradale**
        Highld
46 E2 **South Fambridge**
        Essex
126 B6 **South Ferriby** N Linc
126 C5 **South Field** E R Yk
15 M1 **South Gorley** Hants
151 G2 **South Gosforth**
        N u Ty
46 B2 **South Green** Essex
33 L2 **South Green** Kent
92 C2 **South Green** Norfk
177 G4 **South Gyle** C Edin
61 H8 **South Hanningfield**
        Essex
30 C7 **South Harting**
        W Susx
17 K3 **South Hayling** Hants
58 E7 **South Heath** Bucks
151 J6 **South Hetton** Dur
124 B7 **South Hiendley**
        Wakefd
5 M2 **South Hill** Cnwll
57 K7 **South Hinksey** Oxon
31 K3 **South Holmwood**
        Surrey
45 K4 **South Hornchurch**
        Gt Lon
7 G7 **South Huish** Devon
116 F8 **South Hykeham**
        Lincs
151 J4 **South Hylton** Sundld
117 H2 **South Kelsey** Lincs
213 G5 **South Kessock**
        Highld
126 E2 **South Killingholme**
        N Linc
132 F3 **South Kilvington**
        N York

87 H6 **South Kilworth**
        Nhants
124 C7 **South Kirkby** Wakefd
103 K3 **South Kyme** Lincs
56 F5 **South Lawn** Oxon
57 H6 **South Leigh** Oxon
116 C5 **South Leverton**
        Notts
71 J5 **South Littleton**
        Worcs
92 C7 **South Lopham** Norfk
88 D3 **South Luffenham**
        Rutlnd
19 L4 **South Malling** E Susx
40 D3 **South Marston**
        Swindn
32 B3 **South Merstham**
        Surrey
124 D4 **South Milford** N York
7 G7 **South Milton** Devon
59 L7 **South Mimms** Herts
23 L6 **South Molton** Devon
150 F5 **South Moor** Dur
41 K3 **South Moreton** Oxon
18 B5 **South Mundham**
        W Susx
125 L4 **South Newbald**
        E R Yk
57 H2 **South Newington**
        Oxon
28 C4 **South Newton** Wilts
101 H2 **South Normanton**
        Derbys
45 G6 **South Norwood**
        Gt Lon
45 L4 **South Ockendon**
        Thurr
118 E6 **South Ormsby** Lincs
132 E3 **South Otterington**
        N York
117 H3 **South Owersby**
        Lincs
31 L2 **South Park** Surrey
13 L2 **South Perrott**
        Dorset
26 B7 **South Petherton**
        Somset
9 J8 **South Petherwin**
        Cnwll
91 J3 **South Pickenham**
        Norfk
6 B4 **South Pill** Cnwll
7 H7 **South Pool** Devon
13 M3 **South Poorton**
        Dorset
176 F3 **South Queensferry**
        C Edin
24 B5 **South Radworthy**
        Devon
103 G4 **South Rauceby** Lincs
105 L7 **South Raynham**
        Norfk
118 E5 **South Reston** Lincs
90 F2 **South Runcton**
        Norfk
116 D8 **South Scarle** Notts
191 H7 **South Shian** Ag & B
151 J2 **South Shields** S Tyne
120 D4 **South Shore** Bpool
132 D6 **South Stainley**
        N York
39 H7 **South Stoke** BaNES
102 F6 **South Stoke** Lincs
41 L4 **South Stoke** Oxon
18 D4 **South Stoke** W Susx
34 E3 **South Street** Kent
47 J6 **South Street** Kent
176 D7 **South Tarbrax** S Lans
10 F6 **South Tawton** Devon
118 E6 **South Thoresby**
        Lincs
93 H2 **South Walsham**
        Norfk

30 B3 **South**
        Warnborough Hants
45 L2 **South Weald** Essex
42 B2 **South Weston** Oxon
9 H6 **South Wheatley**
        Cnwll
38 E8 **South Widcombe**
        BaNES
87 H4 **South Wigston** Leics
34 D6 **South**
        Willesborough Kent
117 K5 **South Willingham**
        Lincs
151 K7 **South Wingate** Dur
101 G2 **South Wingfield**
        Derbys
102 F8 **South Witham** Lincs
61 J7 **South Woodham**
        Ferrers Essex
105 G7 **South Wootton**
        Norfk
39 J7 **South Wraxall** Wilts
10 F6 **South Zeal** Devon
43 J4 **Southall** Gt Lon
55 L3 **Southam** Gloucs
72 E3 **Southam** Warwks
29 H8 **Southampton** C Sotn
29 J7 **Southampton**
        Airport Hants
45 H6 **Southborough**
        Gt Lon
33 G5 **Southborough** Kent
15 L4 **Southbourne**
        Bmouth
17 L2 **Southbourne** W Susx
92 B3 **Southburgh** Norfk
134 F8 **Southburn** E R Yk
46 E3 **Southchurch** Sthend
9 G5 **Southcott** Cnwll
10 E5 **Southcott** Devon
11 H8 **Southcott** Devon
58 D5 **Southcourt** Bucks
19 L5 **Southease** E Susx
161 H7 **Southend** Ag & B
46 E3 **Southend Airport**
        Essex
46 E3 **Southend-on-Sea**
        Sthend
36 D5 **Southerndown**
        V Glam
147 G4 **Southerness** D & G
12 D4 **Southerton** Devon
90 E5 **Southery** Norfk
175 L4 **Southfield** Falk
45 L5 **Southfleet** Kent
44 F2 **Southgate** Gt Lon
51 G7 **Southgate** Swans
75 H6 **Southill** Beds
29 J2 **Southington** Hants
12 F4 **Southleigh** Devon
62 A7 **Southminster** Essex
41 H2 **Southmoor** Oxon
196 C5 **Southmuir** Angus
75 H2 **Southoe** Cambs
78 E2 **Southolt** Suffk
88 F3 **Southorpe** C Pete
14 C4 **Southover** Dorset
123 G5 **Southowram** Calder
120 D6 **Southport** Sefton
106 F5 **Southrepps** Norfk
117 J7 **Southrey** Lincs
56 D7 **Southrop** Gloucs
30 A3 **Southrope** Hants
17 J3 **Southsea** C Port
140 E2 **Southside** Dur
93 L3 **Southtown** Norfk
148 D6 **Southwaite** Cumb
44 F4 **Southwark** Gt Lon
31 J6 **Southwater** W Susx
102 B2 **Southwell** Notts
17 J2 **Southwick** Hants
88 E5 **Southwick** Nhants
151 J4 **Southwick** Sundld

19 H5 **Southwick** W Susx
27 J1 **Southwick** Wilts
93 K7 **Southwold** Suffk
122 F6 **Sowerby** Kirk
132 F4 **Sowerby** N York
122 F5 **Sowerby Bridge** Calder
123 G6 **Sowood** Calder
6 D3 **Sowton** Devon
12 C4 **Sowton** Devon
122 F6 **Soyland Town** Calder
76 F6 **Spain's End** Essex
103 L7 **Spalding** Lincs
125 H4 **Spaldington** E R Yk
89 G8 **Spaldwick** Cambs
116 D7 **Spalford** Notts
103 H5 **Spanby** Lincs
106 C8 **Sparham** Norfk
129 G3 **Spark Bridge** Cumb
26 E6 **Sparkford** Somset
85 K6 **Sparkhill** Birm
6 E4 **Sparkwell** Devon
114 C5 **Sparrowpit** Derbys
33 H6 **Sparrows Green** E Susx
29 H5 **Sparsholt** Hants
41 G3 **Sparsholt** Oxon
133 L2 **Spaunton** N York
25 K4 **Spaxton** Somset
201 K8 **Spean Bridge** Highld
28 F6 **Spearywell** Hants
58 D7 **Speen** Bucks
41 J6 **Speen** W Berk
135 J4 **Speeton** N York
112 C5 **Speke** Lpool
32 F5 **Speldhurst** Kent
60 D4 **Spellbrook** Herts
99 J1 **Spen Green** Ches
42 B6 **Spencers Wood** Wokham
131 L2 **Spennithorne** N York
151 G7 **Spennymoor** Dur
70 F4 **Spetchley** Worcs
15 G3 **Spetisbury** Dorset
93 H7 **Spexhall** Suffk
215 H2 **Spey Bay** Moray
204 C1 **Speybridge** Highld
215 G6 **Speyview** Moray
118 E7 **Spilsby** Lincs
115 J5 **Spinkhill** Derbys
222 F4 **Spinningdale** Highld
115 L3 **Spital Hill** Donc
178 B3 **Spittal** E Loth
231 H5 **Spittal** Highld
179 L7 **Spittal** Nthumb
49 G3 **Spittal** Pembks
205 G7 **Spittal of Glenmuick** Abers
195 H3 **Spittal of Glenshee** P & K
167 J5 **Spittal-on-Rule** Border
195 H7 **Spittalfield** P & K
92 F1 **Spixworth** Norfk
10 E4 **Splatt** Devon
19 L2 **Splayne's Green** E Susx
37 K5 **Splottlands** Cardif
124 B1 **Spofforth** N York
101 H5 **Spondon** C Derb
92 D4 **Spooner Row** Norfk
91 J2 **Sporle** Norfk
178 E4 **Spott** E Loth
178 D7 **Spottiswoode** Border
73 K1 **Spratton** Nhants
30 D3 **Spreakley** Surrey
11 G5 **Spreyton** Devon
6 D5 **Spriddlestone** Devon
117 G5 **Spridlington** Lincs
175 G5 **Springburn** C Glas
148 B2 **Springfield** D & G
61 H6 **Springfield** Essex

186 E5 **Springfield** Fife
154 E7 **Springholm** D & G
163 J2 **Springside** N Ayrs
116 E4 **Springthorpe** Lincs
151 H4 **Springwell** Sundld
126 F4 **Sproatley** E R Yk
113 G7 **Sproston Green** Ches
115 K2 **Sprotbrough** Donc
78 D5 **Sproughton** Suffk
168 A3 **Sprouston** Border
92 F2 **Sprowston** Norfk
102 D7 **Sproxton** Leics
133 J3 **Sproxton** N York
98 D2 **Spurstow** Ches
14 A4 **Spyway** Dorset
84 D7 **Stableford** Shrops
114 F4 **Stacey Bank** Sheff
130 F6 **Stackhouse** N York
49 G7 **Stackpole** Pembks
6 D5 **Staddiscombe** C Plym
57 L7 **Stadhampton** Oxon
233 b7 **Stadhlaigearraidh** W Isls
148 F6 **Staffield** Cumb
218 D7 **Staffin** Highld
99 L7 **Stafford** Staffs
74 E5 **Stagsden** Beds
136 E2 **Stainburn** Cumb
123 K2 **Stainburn** N York
102 E7 **Stainby** Lincs
123 L7 **Staincross** Barns
140 E3 **Staindrop** Dur
43 G6 **Staines** Surrey
124 F7 **Stainforth** Donc
130 F6 **Stainforth** N York
120 D4 **Staining** Lancs
123 G6 **Stainland** Calder
143 J5 **Stainsacre** N York
138 C2 **Stainton** Cumb
129 L3 **Stainton** Cumb
115 K3 **Stainton** Donc
140 D4 **Stainton** Dur
141 L4 **Stainton** Middsb
117 H6 **Stainton by Langworth** Lincs
117 K3 **Stainton le Vale** Lincs
128 F5 **Stainton with Adgarley** Cumb
143 K7 **Staintondale** N York
163 K5 **Stair** E Ayrs
144 E4 **Stair Haven** D & G
143 G4 **Staithes** N York
159 G5 **Stakeford** Nthumb
17 K2 **Stakes** Hants
27 G7 **Stalbridge** Dorset
27 G7 **Stalbridge Weston** Dorset
107 H7 **Stalham** Norfk
34 C4 **Stalisfield Green** Kent
26 E7 **Stallen** Dorset
126 F7 **Stallingborough** NE Lin
120 E2 **Stalmine** Lancs
113 L2 **Stalybridge** Tamesd
77 G6 **Stambourne** Essex
77 G6 **Stambourne Green** Essex
88 E3 **Stamford** Lincs
169 J5 **Stamford** Nthumb
112 C7 **Stamford Bridge** Ches
133 L7 **Stamford Bridge** E R Yk
45 G3 **Stamford Hill** Gt Lon
158 D7 **Stamfordham** Nthumb
58 F3 **Stanbridge** Beds
122 F3 **Stanbury** Brad
175 K5 **Stand** N Lans
176 C4 **Standburn** Falk

85 G3 **Standeford** Staffs
33 L5 **Standen** Kent
27 J2 **Standerwick** Somset
30 D4 **Standford** Hants
147 J7 **Standingstone** Cumb
121 H7 **Standish** Wigan
57 H7 **Standlake** Oxon
29 H6 **Standon** Hants
60 C4 **Standon** Herts
99 J5 **Standon** Staffs
176 B6 **Stane** N Lans
105 M7 **Stanfield** Norfk
75 H6 **Stanford** Beds
34 F6 **Stanford** Kent
70 C4 **Stanford Bishop** Herefs
70 C2 **Stanford Bridge** Worcs
41 L6 **Stanford Dingley** W Berk
41 G2 **Stanford in the Vale** Oxon
46 B4 **Stanford le Hope** Thurr
87 H7 **Stanford on Avon** Nhants
101 K7 **Stanford on Soar** Notts
70 C2 **Stanford on Teme** Worcs
115 J6 **Stanfree** Derbys
142 E4 **Stanghow** R & Cl
89 H4 **Stanground** C Pete
105 J5 **Stanhoe** Norfk
165 L4 **Stanhope** Border
150 C6 **Stanhope** Dur
88 D6 **Stanion** Nhants
101 H4 **Stanley** Derbys
150 F4 **Stanley** Dur
186 B2 **Stanley** P & K
99 L3 **Stanley** Staffs
150 E7 **Stanley Crook** Dur
55 M3 **Stanley Pontlarge** Gloucs
19 K4 **Stanmer** Br & H
44 D2 **Stanmore** Gt Lon
29 J5 **Stanmore** Hants
157 J7 **Stannersburn** Nthumb
77 K3 **Stanningfield** Suffk
158 F6 **Stannington** Nthumb
114 F4 **Stannington** Sheff
158 F5 **Stannington Station** Nthumb
69 G3 **Stansbatch** Herefs
77 H4 **Stansfield** Suffk
77 J5 **Stanstead** Suffk
60 C5 **Stanstead Abbotts** Herts
77 J5 **Stanstead Street** Suffk
45 L7 **Stansted** Kent
60 E4 **Stansted Airport** Essex
60 E3 **Stansted Mountfitchet** Essex
71 J7 **Stanton** Gloucs
158 E4 **Stanton** Nthumb
100 C4 **Stanton** Staffs
91 L8 **Stanton** Suffk
101 G6 **Stanton by Bridge** Derbys
101 J5 **Stanton by Dale** Derbys
38 E7 **Stanton Drew** BaNES
40 D3 **Stanton Fitzwarren** Swindn
57 H6 **Stanton Harcourt** Oxon
114 E8 **Stanton in Peak** Derbys

83 K7 **Stanton Lacy** Shrops
114 E8 **Stanton Lees** Derbys
83 L5 **Stanton Long** Shrops
101 M6 **Stanton on the Wolds** Notts
39 G7 **Stanton Prior** BaNES
40 C7 **Stanton St Bernard** Wilts
57 L6 **Stanton St John** Oxon
39 K4 **Stanton St Quintin** Wilts
77 L2 **Stanton Street** Suffk
86 F2 **Stanton under Bardon** Leics
98 E7 **Stanton upon Hine Heath** Shrops
38 E7 **Stanton Wick** BaNES
61 M3 **Stanway** Essex
56 B2 **Stanway** Gloucs
43 H5 **Stanwell** Surrey
74 E1 **Stanwick** Nhants
148 D4 **Stanwix** Cumb
233 b8 **Staoinebrig** W Isls
143 G7 **Stape** N York
99 G3 **Stapeley** Ches
100 E7 **Stapenhill** Staffs
35 H4 **Staple** Kent
25 H3 **Staple** Somset
25 G7 **Staple Cross** Devon
20 F2 **Staple Cross** E Susx
25 K7 **Staple Fitzpaine** Somset
32 B7 **Staplefield** W Susx
76 C4 **Stapleford** Cambs
60 A5 **Stapleford** Herts
102 D8 **Stapleford** Leics
102 E2 **Stapleford** Lincs
101 J5 **Stapleford** Notts
28 B4 **Stapleford** Wilts
45 K2 **Stapleford Abbotts** Essex
25 K6 **Staplegrove** Somset
25 K6 **Staplehay** Somset
33 K5 **Staplehurst** Kent
34 E3 **Staplestreet** Kent
69 G2 **Stapleton** Herefs
86 E4 **Stapleton** Leics
141 G5 **Stapleton** N York
83 J3 **Stapleton** Shrops
26 C7 **Stapleton** Somset
25 J8 **Stapley** Somset
75 G3 **Staploe** Beds
70 C6 **Staplow** Herefs
186 E6 **Star** Fife
65 H7 **Star** Pembks
38 C8 **Star** Somset
132 E7 **Starbeck** N York
131 H5 **Starbotton** N York
12 C6 **Starcross** Devon
72 D1 **Stareton** Warwks
60 D2 **Starlings Green** Essex
92 F6 **Starston** Norfk
140 D4 **Startforth** Dur
39 L4 **Startley** Wilts
35 J4 **Statenborough** Kent
26 A5 **Stathe** Somset
102 C6 **Stathern** Leics
75 G2 **Staughton Green** Cambs
54 D5 **Staunton** Gloucs
55 H3 **Staunton** Gloucs
69 G3 **Staunton Green** Herefs
69 G3 **Staunton on Arrow** Herefs
69 G5 **Staunton on Wye** Herefs
129 H3 **Staveley** Cumb
138 C7 **Staveley** Cumb
115 H6 **Staveley** Derbys
132 E6 **Staveley** N York

7 J3 **Staverton** Devon
55 K4 **Staverton** Gloucs
73 G3 **Staverton** Nhants
39 J7 **Staverton** Wilts
26 A4 **Stawell** Somset
25 G6 **Stawley** Somset
231 L5 **Staxigoe** Highld
134 F4 **Staxton** N York
120 E2 **Staynall** Lancs
131 K5 **Stean** N York
73 G6 **Steane** Nhants
133 J3 **Stearsby** N York
25 L3 **Steart** Somset
61 G3 **Stebbing** Essex
61 H4 **Stebbing Green** Essex
61 G3 **Stebbing Park** Essex
30 E6 **Stedham** W Susx
156 F4 **Steele Road** Border
185 L8 **Steelend** Fife
69 K3 **Steen's Bridge** Herefs
30 C6 **Steep** Hants
122 F5 **Steep Lane** Calder
61 M7 **Steeple** Essex
27 K1 **Steeple Ashton** Wilts
57 J3 **Steeple Aston** Oxon
76 F6 **Steeple Bumpstead** Essex
58 B3 **Steeple Claydon** Bucks
89 G7 **Steeple Gidding** Cambs
28 B4 **Steeple Langford** Wilts
75 K6 **Steeple Morden** Cambs
122 F2 **Steeton** Brad
208 D3 **Stein** Highld
34 F5 **Stelling Minnis** Kent
26 B7 **Stembridge** Somset
4 F4 **Stenalees** Cnwll
154 D4 **Stenhouse** D & G
176 B2 **Stenhousemuir** Falk
218 D7 **Stenscholl** Highld
178 D4 **Stenton** E Loth
232 f2 **Steornabhagh** W Isls
49 K6 **Stepaside** Pembks
45 G4 **Stepney** Gt Lon
74 E7 **Steppingley** Beds
175 H5 **Stepps** N Lans
79 H3 **Sternfield** Suffk
40 B8 **Stert** Wilts
76 F3 **Stetchworth** Cambs
59 L3 **Stevenage** Herts
163 H2 **Stevenston** N Ayrs
29 K2 **Steventon** Hants
41 J3 **Steventon** Oxon
76 E6 **Steventon End** Essex
74 E4 **Stevington** Beds
74 E6 **Stewartby** Beds
175 H7 **Stewartfield** S Lans
163 K1 **Stewarton** E Ayrs
58 D3 **Stewkley** Bucks
25 L7 **Stewley** Somset
19 G4 **Steyning** W Susx
48 F6 **Steynton** Pembks
9 G3 **Stibb** Cnwll
10 C2 **Stibb Cross** Devon
40 E7 **Stibb Green** Wilts
106 B6 **Stibbard** Norfk
88 F4 **Stibbington** Cambs
167 L2 **Stichill** Border
4 F5 **Sticker** Cnwll
104 B1 **Stickford** Lincs
10 F6 **Sticklepath** Devon
60 D2 **Stickling Green** Essex
104 B2 **Stickney** Lincs
106 A4 **Stiffkey** Norfk
233 b7 **Stilligarry** W Isls
124 F3 **Stillingfleet** N York
133 J6 **Stillington** N York
141 J3 **Stillington** S on T

89 H5 **Stilton** Cambs
55 G7 **Stinchcombe** Gloucs
14 D4 **Stinsford** Dorset
83 G4 **Stiperstones** Shrops
217 L6 **Stirling** Abers
185 G8 **Stirling** Stirlg
75 H2 **Stirtloe** Cambs
131 H8 **Stirton** N York
61 J3 **Stisted** Essex
3 J4 **Stithians** Cnwll
86 D7 **Stivichall** Covtry
117 K7 **Stixwould** Lincs
112 B6 **Stoak** Ches
166 B2 **Stobo** Border
15 H5 **Stoborough** Dorset
167 G7 **Stobs Castle** Border
158 F3 **Stobswood** Nthumb
61 H7 **Stock** Essex
38 C7 **Stock** N Som
71 H3 **Stock Green** Worcs
71 H3 **Stock Wood** Worcs
29 G4 **Stockbridge** Hants
164 F3 **Stockbriggs** S Lans
46 D7 **Stockbury** Kent
41 H6 **Stockcross** W Berk
88 B4 **Stockerston** Leics
54 F2 **Stocking** Herefs
60 D3 **Stocking Pelham** Herts
86 D5 **Stockingford** Warwks
13 G2 **Stockland** Devon
25 K3 **Stockland Bristol** Somset
11 K4 **Stockleigh English** Devon
11 K4 **Stockleigh Pomeroy** Devon
39 M6 **Stockley** Wilts
26 B7 **Stocklinch** Somset
113 K4 **Stockport** Stockp
114 E2 **Stocksbridge** Sheff
150 D3 **Stocksfield** Nthumb
69 K3 **Stockton** Herefs
93 H5 **Stockton** Norfk
84 C4 **Stockton** Shrops
72 E2 **Stockton** Warwks
27 M4 **Stockton** Wilts
84 D1 **Stockton** Wrekin
112 E4 **Stockton Heath** Warrtn
70 C2 **Stockton on Teme** Worcs
133 K7 **Stockton on the Forest** York
141 K4 **Stockton-on-Tees** S on T
38 F6 **Stockwood** Bristl
14 B2 **Stockwood** Dorset
35 G4 **Stodmarsh** Kent
106 C5 **Stody** Norfk
224 C3 **Stoer** Highld
26 E8 **Stoford** Somset
28 B4 **Stoford** Wilts
25 H4 **Stogumber** Somset
25 J3 **Stogursey** Somset
86 D7 **Stoke** Covtry
22 C6 **Stoke** Devon
29 H2 **Stoke** Hants
17 K3 **Stoke** Hants
46 D5 **Stoke** Medway
13 L3 **Stoke Abbott** Dorset
88 B5 **Stoke Albany** Nhants
78 D1 **Stoke Ash** Suffk
101 M4 **Stoke Bardolph** Notts
70 B2 **Stoke Bliss** Worcs
73 L4 **Stoke Bruerne** Nhants
77 G5 **Stoke by Clare** Suffk
12 B3 **Stoke Canon** Devon
29 J4 **Stoke Charity** Hants
6 A2 **Stoke Climsland** Cnwll

70 B4 **Stoke Cross** Herefs
43 J8 **Stoke D'Abernon** Surrey
88 E6 **Stoke Doyle** Nhants
88 C4 **Stoke Dry** Rutlnd
69 L6 **Stoke Edith** Herefs
28 B6 **Stoke Farthing** Wilts
91 G4 **Stoke Ferry** Norfk
7 K6 **Stoke Fleming** Devon
7 J4 **Stoke Gabriel** Devon
38 F4 **Stoke Gifford** S Glos
86 E4 **Stoke Golding** Leics
74 B5 **Stoke Goldington** M Keyn
58 E3 **Stoke Hammond** Bucks
92 F3 **Stoke Holy Cross** Norfk
70 B5 **Stoke Lacy** Herefs
57 K3 **Stoke Lyne** Oxon
58 D6 **Stoke Mandeville** Bucks
45 G3 **Stoke Newington** Gt Lon
55 K3 **Stoke Orchard** Gloucs
42 F4 **Stoke Poges** Bucks
69 K3 **Stoke Prior** Herefs
71 G2 **Stoke Prior** Worcs
23 K4 **Stoke Rivers** Devon
42 B4 **Stoke Row** Oxon
25 M6 **Stoke St Gregory** Somset
25 K6 **Stoke St Mary** Somset
26 F3 **Stoke St Michael** Somset
83 L6 **Stoke St Milborough** Shrops
26 C7 **Stoke sub Hamdon** Somset
58 B7 **Stoke Talmage** Oxon
27 H5 **Stoke Trister** Somset
98 F6 **Stoke upon Tern** Shrops
14 E2 **Stoke Wake** Dorset
78 B7 **Stoke-by-Nayland** Suffk
99 K3 **Stoke-on-Trent** C Stke
99 K4 **Stoke-upon-Trent** C Stke
15 G5 **Stokeford** Dorset
116 C6 **Stokeham** Notts
7 L2 **Stokeinteignhead** Devon
42 C2 **Stokenchurch** Bucks
7 J7 **Stokenham** Devon
83 H6 **Stokesay Castle** Shrops
93 J2 **Stokesby** Norfk
142 B5 **Stokesley** N York
25 K3 **Stolford** Somset
26 F2 **Ston Easton** Somset
60 F7 **Stondon Massey** Essex
58 C5 **Stone** Bucks
39 G2 **Stone** Gloucs
21 J1 **Stone** Kent
115 K4 **Stone** Rothm
99 K5 **Stone** Staffs
84 F7 **Stone** Worcs
26 B2 **Stone Allerton** Somset
35 H4 **Stone Cross** Kent
33 G3 **Stone Street** Kent
93 H6 **Stone Street** Suffk
38 B7 **Stonebridge** N Som
86 B6 **Stonebridge** Solhll
101 H2 **Stonebroom** Derbys
33 J6 **Stonecrouch** Kent
126 D4 **Stoneferry** C KuH

172 E4 **Stonefield Castle Hotel** Ag & B
33 H7 **Stonegate** E Susx
133 K4 **Stonegrave** N York
207 G7 **Stonehaven** Abers
28 C3 **Stonehenge** Wilts
6 C5 **Stonehouse** C Plym
112 D7 **Stonehouse** Ches
146 E2 **Stonehouse** D & G
55 J6 **Stonehouse** Gloucs
175 K8 **Stonehouse** S Lans
86 D8 **Stoneleigh** Warwks
62 E3 **Stones Green** Essex
102 D7 **Stonesby** Leics
57 H4 **Stonesfield** Oxon
215 G2 **Stonewells** Moray
114 E6 **Stoney Middleton** Derbys
86 F4 **Stoney Stanton** Leics
27 G5 **Stoney Stoke** Somset
26 F4 **Stoney Stratton** Somset
83 H2 **Stoney Stretton** Shrops
233 b8 **Stoneybridge** W Isls
176 D5 **Stoneyburn** W Loth
87 H3 **Stoneygate** C Leic
144 C4 **Stoneykirk** D & G
207 G3 **Stoneywood** C Aber
175 L2 **Stoneywood** Falk
78 D3 **Stonham Aspal** Suffk
85 J3 **Stonnall** Staffs
42 B3 **Stonor** Oxon
87 K4 **Stonton Wyville** Leics
115 J7 **Stony Houghton** Derbys
73 L6 **Stony Stratford** M Keyn
23 K5 **Stoodleigh** Devon
24 E7 **Stoodleigh** Devon
18 D2 **Stopham** W Susx
59 J3 **Stopsley** Luton
232 f2 **Stornoway** W Isls
232 g2 **Stornoway Airport** W Isls
18 E3 **Storrington** W Susx
125 H2 **Storwood** E R Yk
214 F1 **Stotfield** Moray
75 J7 **Stotfold** Beds
84 C6 **Stottesdon** Shrops
87 J3 **Stoughton** Leics
31 G2 **Stoughton** Surrey
17 L1 **Stoughton** W Susx
200 B6 **Stoul** Highld
70 F4 **Stoulton** Worcs
27 H6 **Stour Provost** Dorset
27 J6 **Stour Row** Dorset
84 F6 **Stourbridge** Dudley
15 G1 **Stourpaine** Dorset
70 E1 **Stourport-on-Severn** Worcs
84 F6 **Stourton** Staffs
72 C6 **Stourton** Warwks
27 H5 **Stourton** Wilts
27 G7 **Stourton Caundle** Dorset
235 c7 **Stove** Shet
93 J6 **Stoven** Suffk
167 G1 **Stow** Border
116 E5 **Stow** Lincs
90 F3 **Stow Bardolph** Norfk
91 L4 **Stow Bedon** Norfk
75 G1 **Stow Longa** Cambs
61 K7 **Stow Maries** Essex
76 D3 **Stow-cum-Quy** Cambs
56 D3 **Stow-on-the-Wold** Gloucs
90 E3 **Stowbridge** Norfk
82 F8 **Stowe** Shrops

100 A6 **Stowe by Chartley** Staffs
27 G6 **Stowell** Somset
38 E7 **Stowey** BaNES
10 C5 **Stowford** Devon
23 K3 **Stowford** Devon
10 C7 **Stowford** Devon
77 L2 **Stowlangtoft** Suffk
78 C3 **Stowmarket** Suffk
34 F6 **Stowting** Kent
34 F6 **Stowting Common** Kent
78 C3 **Stowupland** Suffk
204 B3 **Straanruie** Moray
206 D6 **Strachan** Abers
182 F6 **Strachur** Ag & B
197 G4 **Stracthro Hospital** Angus
92 F8 **Stradbroke** Suffk
77 H4 **Stradishall** Suffk
90 F3 **Stradsett** Norfk
102 E3 **Stragglethorpe** Lincs
177 H5 **Straiton** Mdloth
153 H2 **Straiton** S Ayrs
207 G2 **Straloch** Abers
195 G4 **Straloch** P & K
100 B5 **Stramshall** Staffs
237 C5 **Strang** IOM
113 J2 **Strangeways** Salfd
54 E3 **Strangford** Herefs
144 C3 **Stranraer** D & G
42 A7 **Stratfield Mortimer** W Berk
42 B7 **Stratfield Saye** Hants
42 B7 **Stratfield Turgis** Hants
45 H3 **Stratford** Gt Lon
79 H3 **Stratford St Andrew** Suffk
78 C7 **Stratford St Mary** Suffk
28 C6 **Stratford Tony** Wilts
72 B4 **Stratford-upon-Avon** Warwks
219 J5 **Strath** Highld
224 D4 **Strathan** Highld
229 J3 **Strathan** Highld
164 D1 **Strathan** Highld
175 G3 **Strathaven** S Lans
175 G3 **Strathblane** Stirlg
220 F2 **Strathcanaird** Highld
210 E6 **Strathcarron** Highld
181 K2 **Strathcoil** Ag & B
205 H3 **Strathdon** Abers
187 G4 **Strathkinness** Fife
176 C4 **Strathloanhead** W Loth
202 F6 **Strathmashie House** Highld
186 C5 **Strathmiglo** Fife
212 D3 **Strathpeffer** Highld
194 E5 **Strathtay** P & K
162 D3 **Strathwhillan** N Ayrs
230 B3 **Strathy** Highld
230 B3 **Strathy Inn** Highld
184 C4 **Strathyre** Stirlg
9 G4 **Stratton** Cnwll
14 C4 **Stratton** Dorset
56 A7 **Stratton** Gloucs
57 L3 **Stratton Audley** Oxon
40 D3 **Stratton St Margaret** Swindn
92 E5 **Stratton St Michael** Norfk
106 F7 **Stratton Strawless** Norfk
26 F2 **Stratton-on-the-Fosse** Somset
187 J5 **Stravithie** Fife
19 K3 **Streat** E Susx
44 F5 **Streatham** Gt Lon
59 H3 **Streatley** Beds
41 L4 **Streatley** W Berk

12 F5 **Street** Devon
26 C4 **Street** Somset
86 F6 **Street Ashton** Warwks
97 M5 **Street Dinas** Shrops
34 F4 **Street End** Kent
18 A5 **Street End** W Susx
26 F4 **Street on the Fosse** Somset
85 K2 **Streethay** Staffs
141 H7 **Streetlam** N York
76 E5 **Streetly End** Cambs
186 C1 **Strelitz** P & K
101 K4 **Strelley** Notts
133 K7 **Strensall** York
25 L3 **Stretcholt** Somset
7 J6 **Strete** Devon
113 H3 **Stretford** Traffd
76 C6 **Strethall** Essex
90 D8 **Stretham** Cambs
18 B4 **Strettington** W Susx
101 H1 **Stretton** Derbys
88 D1 **Stretton** Rutlnd
84 F2 **Stretton** Staffs
100 E7 **Stretton** Staffs
112 F5 **Stretton** Warrtn
70 B5 **Stretton Grandison** Herefs
72 B6 **Stretton on Fosse** Warwks
69 J6 **Stretton Sugwas** Herefs
86 F7 **Stretton under Fosse** Warwks
83 L4 **Stretton Westwood** Shrops
86 E8 **Stretton-on-Dunsmore** Warwks
217 H4 **Strichen** Abers
25 J3 **Stringston** Somset
74 C3 **Strixton** Nhants
38 E2 **Stroat** Gloucs
210 D7 **Stromeferry** Highld
234 b6 **Stromness** Ork
183 L5 **Stronachlachar** Stirlg
173 H3 **Stronafian** Ag & B
224 F5 **Stronchrubie** Highld
173 L3 **Strone** Ag & B
192 B1 **Strone** Highld
201 J8 **Stronenaba** Highld
183 G2 **Stronmilchan** Ag & B
234 d5 **Stronsay Airport** Ork
191 G4 **Strontian** Highld
46 B6 **Strood** Medway
55 J6 **Stroud** Gloucs
30 B6 **Stroud** Hants
46 E3 **Stroud Green** Essex
55 J6 **Stroud Green** Gloucs
102 E6 **Stroxton** Lincs
208 E6 **Struan** Highld
194 C4 **Struan** P & K
93 H3 **Strumpshaw** Norfk
175 K7 **Strutherhill** S Lans
186 F5 **Struthers** Fife
212 B6 **Struy** Highld
217 H5 **Stuartfield** Abers
17 G2 **Stubbington** Hants
122 B6 **Stubbins** N York
102 E3 **Stubton** Lincs
28 D8 **Stuckton** Hants
59 G5 **Studham** Beds
148 A4 **Studholme** Cumb
15 J6 **Studland** Dorset
71 J2 **Studley** Warwks
39 L6 **Studley** Wilts
132 D5 **Studley Roger** N York
132 D5 **Studley Royal** N York
90 D7 **Stuntney** Cambs
77 G5 **Sturmer** Essex
27 H8 **Sturminster Common** Dorset

15 H3 **Sturminster Marshall** Dorset
27 H8 **Sturminster Newton** Dorset
35 G3 **Sturry** Kent
116 F2 **Sturton** N Linc
116 E5 **Sturton by Stow** Lincs
116 C5 **Sturton le Steeple** Notts
92 D7 **Stuston** Suffk
124 D3 **Stutton** N York
78 D7 **Stutton** Suffk
113 J5 **Styal** Ches
215 H3 **Stynie** Moray
115 L4 **Styrrup** Notts
183 K6 **Succoth** Ag & B
70 C4 **Suckley** Worcs
88 D6 **Sudborough** Nhants
79 J4 **Sudbourne** Suffk
102 F4 **Sudbrook** Lincs
38 D3 **Sudbrook** Mons
117 G6 **Sudbrooke** Lincs
100 D6 **Sudbury** Derbys
44 D3 **Sudbury** Gt Lon
77 K6 **Sudbury** Suffk
70 F2 **Suddington** Worcs
134 F2 **Suffield** N York
106 F6 **Suffield** Norfk
99 H6 **Sugnall** Staffs
69 J6 **Sugwas Pool** Herefs
199 J3 **Suisnish** Highld
237 d3 **Sulby** IOM
73 G5 **Sulgrave** Nhants
73 H5 **Sulgrave Manor** Nhants
41 M5 **Sulham** W Berk
41 M6 **Sulhamstead** W Berk
235 C4 **Sullom** Shet
235 c4 **Sullom Voe** Shet
37 J6 **Sully** V Glam
235 c8 **Sumburgh Airport** Shet
132 C6 **Summerbridge** N York
4 D5 **Summercourt** Cnwll
105 J5 **Summerfield** Norfk
140 F4 **Summerhouse** Darltn
18 B4 **Summersdale** W Susx
122 B7 **Summerseat** Bury
57 K6 **Summertown** Oxon
43 J6 **Sunbury** Surrey
154 E5 **Sundaywell** D & G
170 E5 **Sunderland** Ag & B
147 L7 **Sunderland** Cumb
129 J7 **Sunderland** Lancs
151 J4 **Sunderland** Sundld
151 G7 **Sunderland Bridge** Dur
166 E4 **Sundhope** Border
32 E3 **Sundridge** Kent
42 F6 **Sunningdale** W & M
42 F6 **Sunninghill** W & M
57 J7 **Sunningwell** Oxon
150 E7 **Sunniside** Dur
150 F3 **Sunniside** Gatesd
101 G6 **Sunnyhill** C Derb
121 K6 **Sunnyhurst** Bl w D
185 G7 **Sunnylaw** Stirlg
57 J6 **Sunnymead** Oxon
44 D6 **Surbiton** Gt Lon
103 L6 **Surfleet** Lincs
93 G3 **Surlingham** Norfk
61 L4 **Surrex** Essex
106 E5 **Sustead** Norfk
116 D2 **Susworth** Lincs
9 J3 **Sutcombe** Devon
9 J3 **Sutcombemill** Devon
118 E6 **Sutterby** Lincs
103 M5 **Sutterton** Lincs
75 J5 **Sutton** Beds
89 G4 **Sutton** C Pete

90 C7 **Sutton** Cambs
7 G7 **Sutton** Devon
20 A5 **Sutton** E Susx
44 E7 **Sutton** Gt Lon
35 J5 **Sutton** Kent
124 D5 **Sutton** N York
107 H7 **Sutton** Norfk
102 C5 **Sutton** Notts
84 D6 **Sutton** Shrops
99 H7 **Sutton** Staffs
79 G5 **Sutton** Suffk
18 D3 **Sutton** W Susx
45 K6 **Sutton at Hone** Kent
87 L5 **Sutton Bassett** Nhants
39 L5 **Sutton Benger** Wilts
101 K7 **Sutton Bonington** Notts
104 D7 **Sutton Bridge** Lincs
86 E4 **Sutton Cheney** Leics
85 K4 **Sutton Coldfield** Birm
41 J2 **Sutton Courtenay** Oxon
116 B5 **Sutton cum Lound** Notts
132 D5 **Sutton Grange** N York
31 G1 **Sutton Green** Surrey
132 D4 **Sutton Howgrave** N York
101 J2 **Sutton in Ashfield** Notts
84 C3 **Sutton Maddock** Shrops
26 A4 **Sutton Mallet** Somset
27 M5 **Sutton Mandeville** Wilts
26 F6 **Sutton Montis** Somset
119 G5 **Sutton on Sea** Lincs
100 E5 **Sutton on the Hill** Derbys
116 D7 **Sutton on Trent** Notts
29 J4 **Sutton Scotney** Hants
89 L2 **Sutton St Edmund** Lincs
104 C8 **Sutton St James** Lincs
69 K5 **Sutton St Nicholas** Herefs
125 G2 **Sutton upon Derwent** E R Yk
33 L4 **Sutton Valence** Kent
27 K3 **Sutton Veny** Wilts
27 K7 **Sutton Waldron** Dorset
112 D5 **Sutton Weaver** Ches
38 E8 **Sutton Wick** BaNES
41 J2 **Sutton Wick** Oxon
122 F2 **Sutton-in-Craven** N York
126 E4 **Sutton-on-Hull** C KuH
133 J6 **Sutton-on-the-Forest** N York
72 C6 **Sutton-under-Brailes** Warwks
133 G3 **Sutton-under-Whitestonecliffe** N York
118 E6 **Swaby** Lincs
100 F8 **Swadlincote** Derbys
91 J2 **Swaffham** Norfk
76 D3 **Swaffham Bulbeck** Cambs
76 E2 **Swaffham Prior** Cambs
107 G6 **Swafield** Norfk
141 L6 **Swainby** N York

92 F4 **Swainsthorpe** Norfk
39 H6 **Swainswick** BaNES
72 E6 **Swalcliffe** Oxon
47 J6 **Swalecliffe** Kent
117 K2 **Swallow** Lincs
116 F7 **Swallow Beck** Lincs
27 L6 **Swallowcliffe** Wilts
42 B7 **Swallowfield** Wokham
113 G6 **Swan Green** Ches
15 J6 **Swanage** Dorset
58 D3 **Swanbourne** Bucks
126 B5 **Swanland** E R Yk
45 K6 **Swanley** Kent
45 K6 **Swanley Village** Kent
29 L7 **Swanmore** Hants
86 E1 **Swannington** Leics
106 D8 **Swannington** Norfk
116 F7 **Swanpool Garden Suburb** Lincs
45 L5 **Swanscombe** Kent
51 J6 **Swansea** Swans
51 H7 **Swansea Airport** Swans
106 F7 **Swanton Abbot** Norfk
92 B1 **Swanton Morley** Norfk
106 B6 **Swanton Novers** Norfk
101 H2 **Swanwick** Derbys
17 G1 **Swanwick** Hants
103 H4 **Swarby** Lincs
92 E3 **Swardeston** Norfk
101 G6 **Swarkestone** Derbys
158 E2 **Swarland** Nthumb
29 K4 **Swarraton** Hants
129 G4 **Swarthmoor** Cumb
103 J5 **Swaton** Lincs
75 L2 **Swavesey** Cambs
16 C3 **Sway** Hants
103 G7 **Swayfield** Lincs
29 H7 **Swaythling** C Sotn
11 K5 **Sweetham** Devon
32 E7 **Sweethaws** E Susx
8 F5 **Sweets** Cnwll
5 H4 **Sweetshouse** Cnwll
79 H2 **Swefling** Suffk
86 D2 **Swepstone** Leics
57 G2 **Swerford** Oxon
113 J7 **Swettenham** Ches
78 E4 **Swilland** Suffk
124 B4 **Swillington** Leeds
23 K5 **Swimbridge** Devon
23 J5 **Swimbridge Newland** Devon
56 F5 **Swinbrook** Oxon
132 C7 **Swincliffe** N York
116 E8 **Swinderby** Lincs
55 L3 **Swindon** Gloucs
84 F5 **Swindon** Staffs
40 D4 **Swindon** Swindn
126 E4 **Swine** E R Yk
125 H6 **Swinefleet** E R Yk
74 F2 **Swineshead** Beds
103 L4 **Swineshead** Lincs
227 M2 **Swiney** Highld
87 H7 **Swinford** Leics
35 G6 **Swingfield Minnis** Kent
35 H6 **Swingfield Street** Kent
77 L5 **Swingleton Green** Suffk
169 J4 **Swinhoe** Nthumb
131 K2 **Swinithwaite** N York
100 C3 **Swinscoe** Staffs
137 H3 **Swinside** Cumb
103 G7 **Swinstead** Lincs
179 H8 **Swinton** Border
132 C4 **Swinton** N York
134 B5 **Swinton** N York
115 J2 **Swinton** Rothm

113 H2 **Swinton** Salfd
87 G2 **Swithland** Leics
212 E2 **Swordale** Highld
200 B6 **Swordland** Highld
229 M3 **Swordly** Highld
99 J5 **Swynnerton** Staffs
13 M5 **Swyre** Dorset
81 L3 **Sychtyn** Powys
55 L5 **Syde** Gloucs
45 G5 **Sydenham** Gt Lon
58 B7 **Sydenham** Oxon
6 B2 **Sydenham Damerel** Devon
105 K6 **Syderstone** Norfk
14 C3 **Sydling St Nicholas** Dorset
41 J8 **Sydmonton** Hants
102 C3 **Syerston** Notts
95 K3 **Sygun Copper Mine** Gwynd
124 F6 **Sykehouse** Donc
235 d4 **Symbister** Shet
163 J3 **Symington** S Ayrs
165 J3 **Symington** S Lans
54 E5 **Symonds Yat** Herefs
13 K4 **Symondsbury** Dorset
229 L6 **Syre** Highld
56 B4 **Syreford** Gloucs
73 J6 **Syresham** Nhants
87 J2 **Syston** Leics
102 F4 **Syston** Lincs
70 E2 **Sytchampton** Worcs
74 B2 **Sywell** Nhants

T

57 J4 **Tackley** Oxon
92 D4 **Tacolneston** Norfk
124 D2 **Tadcaster** N York
114 C7 **Taddington** Derbys
56 C2 **Taddington** Gloucs
41 L7 **Tadley** Hants
75 K5 **Tadlow** Cambs
72 E6 **Tadmarton** Oxon
44 E8 **Tadworth** Surrey
37 H4 **Taff's Well** Cardif
36 B3 **Taibach** Neath
231 J3 **Tain** Highld
223 G5 **Tain** Highld
232 e4 **Tairbeart** W Isls
60 E4 **Takeley** Essex
60 E4 **Takeley Street** Essex
80 E5 **Tal-y-bont** Cerdgn
109 L7 **Tal-y-Bont** Conwy
95 K7 **Tal-y-bont** Gwynd
109 J7 **Tal-y-bont** Gwynd
109 M7 **Tal-y-Cafn** Conwy
54 B5 **Tal-y-coed** Mons
12 D3 **Talaton** Devon
48 E5 **Talbenny** Pembks
12 E3 **Taleford** Devon
81 K4 **Talerddig** Powys
65 L4 **Talgarreg** Cerdgn
68 D7 **Talgarth** Powys
208 E7 **Talisker** Highld
99 J2 **Talke** Staffs
148 F4 **Talkin** Cumb
166 A5 **Talla Linnfoots** Border
219 L7 **Talladale** Highld
153 J3 **Tallaminnock** S Ayrs
98 C4 **Tallarn Green** Wrexhm
147 K7 **Tallentire** Cumb
66 E7 **Talley** Carmth
88 F2 **Tallington** Lincs
229 J3 **Talmine** Highld
50 D1 **Talog** Carmth
66 D4 **Talsarn** Cerdgn
95 K5 **Talsarnau** Gwynd
4 E3 **Talskiddy** Cnwll

109 G6 **Talwrn** IOA
53 H4 **Talybont-on-Usk** Powys
95 H2 **Talysarn** Gwynd
6 C4 **Tamerton Foliot** C Plym
86 B3 **Tamworth** Staffs
65 J5 **Tan-y-groes** Cerdgn
32 C3 **Tandridge** Surrey
150 F4 **Tanfield** Dur
150 F4 **Tanfield Lea** Dur
28 F2 **Tangley** Hants
18 B4 **Tangmere** W Susx
233 b9 **Tangusdale** W Isls
234 c6 **Tankerness** Ork
115 G2 **Tankersley** Barns
47 J6 **Tankerton** Kent
231 K6 **Tannach** Highld
206 E8 **Tannachie** Abers
196 D5 **Tannadice** Angus
85 J8 **Tanner's Green** Worcs
78 F2 **Tannington** Suffk
175 J6 **Tannochside** N Lans
100 F1 **Tansley** Derbys
88 F5 **Tansor** Nhants
150 F4 **Tantobie** Dur
142 B5 **Tanton** N York
71 K1 **Tanworth in Arden** Warwks
232 d5 **Taobh Tuath** W Isls
42 E4 **Taplow** Bucks
172 B7 **Tarbert** Ag & B
172 E5 **Tarbert** Ag & B
232 e4 **Tarbert** W Isls
183 K6 **Tarbet** Ag & B
228 B5 **Tarbet** Highld
200 B6 **Tarbet** Highld
163 K4 **Tarbolton** S Ayrs
176 D7 **Tarbrax** S Lans
71 H2 **Tardebigge** Worcs
196 D1 **Tarfside** Angus
205 K4 **Tarland** Abers
120 F6 **Tarleton** Lancs
55 L7 **Tarlton** Gloucs
26 B2 **Tarnock** Somset
112 D8 **Tarporley** Ches
24 D5 **Tarr** Somset
25 H5 **Tarr** Somset
15 H2 **Tarrant Crawford** Dorset
27 L8 **Tarrant Gunville** Dorset
15 H1 **Tarrant Hinton** Dorset
15 H2 **Tarrant Keyneston** Dorset
15 H1 **Tarrant Launceston** Dorset
15 H2 **Tarrant Monkton** Dorset
15 H2 **Tarrant Rawston** Dorset
15 H2 **Tarrant Rushton** Dorset
19 L5 **Tarring Neville** E Susx
70 B6 **Tarrington** Herefs
199 J4 **Tarskavaig** Highld
217 G7 **Tarves** Abers
194 F4 **Tarvie** P & K
112 C7 **Tarvin** Ches
92 E4 **Tasburgh** Norfk
100 D7 **Tasley** Shrops
118 D5 **Tathwell** Lincs
32 D2 **Tatsfield** Surrey
98 C2 **Tattenhall** Ches
105 K6 **Tatterford** Norfk
105 K6 **Tattersett** Norfk
103 K2 **Tattershall** Lincs
103 L1 **Tattershall Thorpe** Lincs
78 D6 **Tattingstone** Suffk

78 D6 **Tattingstone White Horse** Suffk
13 J2 **Tatworth** Somset
215 J4 **Tauchers** Moray
25 K6 **Taunton** Somset
92 E2 **Taverham** Norfk
49 K5 **Tavernspite** Pembks
6 C2 **Tavistock** Devon
10 F5 **Taw Green** Devon
23 J5 **Tawstock** Devon
114 A5 **Taxal** Derbys
194 C4 **Tay Forest Park** P & K
182 F3 **Taychreggan Hotel** Ag & B
161 H1 **Tayinloan** Ag & B
55 G4 **Taynton** Gloucs
56 E5 **Taynton** Oxon
182 E2 **Taynuilt** Ag & B
187 G2 **Tayport** Fife
172 C2 **Tayvallich** Ag & B
117 J4 **Tealby** Lincs
151 G3 **Team Valley** Gatesd
199 K4 **Teangue** Highld
212 F2 **Teanord** Highld
138 E6 **Tebay** Cumb
59 G3 **Tebworth** Beds
11 J6 **Tedburn St Mary** Devon
55 L2 **Teddington** Gloucs
44 D6 **Teddington** Gt Lon
70 C3 **Tedstone Delamere** Herefs
70 C3 **Tedstone Wafer** Herefs
141 J5 **Teesside Airport** S on T
73 K1 **Teeton** Nhants
27 M5 **Teffont Evias** Wilts
27 M5 **Teffont Magna** Wilts
65 H7 **Tegryn** Pembks
88 C1 **Teigh** Rutlnd
7 K2 **Teigngrace** Devon
12 B7 **Teignmouth** Devon
166 F7 **Teindside** Border
84 C2 **Telford** Wrekin
27 J1 **Tellisford** Somset
19 L5 **Telscombe** E Susx
193 L5 **Tempar** P & K
155 J5 **Templand** D & G
5 J2 **Temple** Cnwll
177 J6 **Temple** Mdloth
66 C4 **Temple Bar** Cerdgn
38 F8 **Temple Cloud** BaNES
35 H5 **Temple Ewell** Kent
71 K4 **Temple Grafton** Warwks
56 C3 **Temple Guiting** Gloucs
124 F5 **Temple Hirst** N York
115 H7 **Temple Normanton** Derbys
197 K1 **Temple of Fiddes** Abers
212 E7 **Temple Pier** Highld
138 E2 **Temple Sowerby** Cumb
27 G6 **Templecombe** Somset
11 K3 **Templeton** Devon
49 J5 **Templeton** Pembks
150 E5 **Templetown** Dur
75 H4 **Tempsford** Beds
90 E4 **Ten Mile Bank** Norfk
69 L2 **Tenbury Wells** Worcs
49 J7 **Tenby** Pembks
62 D3 **Tendring** Essex
62 D3 **Tendring Green** Essex
62 D3 **Tendring Heath** Essex
34 B7 **Tenterden** Kent
61 J5 **Terling** Essex

98 F6 **Ternhill** Shrops
155 G6 **Terregles** D & G
133 K5 **Terrington** N York
104 E7 **Terrington St Clement** Norfk
90 D2 **Terrington St John** Norfk
33 J3 **Teston** Kent
29 G8 **Testwood** Hants
39 K2 **Tetbury** Gloucs
98 B6 **Tetchill** Shrops
9 J5 **Tetcott** Devon
118 D6 **Tetford** Lincs
118 D2 **Tetney** Lincs
58 B7 **Tetsworth** Oxon
84 F4 **Tettenhall** Wolves
101 J1 **Teversal** Notts
76 C3 **Teversham** Cambs
156 D2 **Teviothead** Border
59 L5 **Tewin** Herts
55 K2 **Tewkesbury** Gloucs
34 C3 **Teynham** Kent
123 H3 **Thackley** Brad
18 F3 **Thakeham** W Susx
58 B6 **Thame** Oxon
44 D6 **Thames Ditton** Surrey
45 J4 **Thamesmead** Gt Lon
34 F4 **Thanington** Kent
165 J2 **Thankerton** S Lans
92 E5 **Tharston** Norfk
41 K6 **Thatcham** W Berk
60 F2 **Thaxted** Essex
56 B7 **The Beeches** Gloucs
209 H7 **The Braes** Highld
178 E4 **The Brunt** E Loth
237 d4 **The Bungalow** IOM
55 K5 **The Butts** Gloucs
42 C2 **The City** Bucks
28 E5 **The Common** Wilts
83 J6 **The Corner** Shrops
174 C7 **The Den** N Ayrs
5 G5 **The Eden Project** Cnwll
34 B5 **The Forstal** Kent
34 D6 **The Forstal** Kent
128 E3 **The Green** Cumb
61 J4 **The Green** Essex
143 G6 **The Green** N York
151 M7 **The Headland** Hartpl
128 E3 **The Hill** Cumb
58 E6 **The Lee** Bucks
237 d2 **The Lhen** IOM
215 G2 **The Lochs** Moray
33 K7 **The Moor** Kent
51 J7 **The Mumbles** Swans
175 H7 **The Murray** S Lans
206 D5 **The Neuk** Abers
55 K4 **The Reddings** Gloucs
185 G3 **The Ross** P & K
21 H1 **The Stocks** Kent
39 L8 **The Strand** Wilts
132 D3 **Theakston** N York
125 K6 **Thealby** N Linc
26 C3 **Theale** Somset
41 M6 **Theale** W Berk
126 D3 **Thearne** E R Yk
79 J2 **Theberton** Suffk
87 J6 **Theddingworth** Leics
118 F4 **Theddlethorpe All Saints** Lincs
119 G4 **Theddlethorpe St Helen** Lincs
92 B7 **Thelnetham** Suffk
92 E7 **Thelveton** Norfk
112 F4 **Thelwall** Warrtn
106 C7 **Themelthorpe** Norfk
73 G6 **Thenford** Nhants
75 L6 **Therfield** Herts
91 K6 **Thetford** Norfk
91 J5 **Thetford Forest Park** Norfk
60 D7 **Theydon Bois** Essex

39 J5 **Thickwood** Wilts
118 C7 **Thimbleby** Lincs
141 K7 **Thimbleby** N York
111 J5 **Thingwall** Wirral
133 G4 **Thirkleby** N York
133 G3 **Thirlby** N York
178 C8 **Thirlestane** Border
137 J4 **Thirlspot** Cumb
132 C3 **Thirn** N York
132 F3 **Thirsk** N York
120 E3 **Thistleton** Lancs
102 E8 **Thistleton** Rutlnd
90 F7 **Thistley Green** Suffk
134 C7 **Thixendale** N York
158 B6 **Thockrington** Nthumb
90 B3 **Tholomas Drove** Cambs
133 G6 **Tholthorpe** N York
216 B6 **Thomastown** Abers
91 K4 **Thompson** Norfk
46 B6 **Thong** Kent
131 J3 **Thoralby** N York
117 K3 **Thoresway** Lincs
117 K3 **Thorganby** Lincs
125 G3 **Thorganby** N York
142 E7 **Thorgill** N York
93 J8 **Thorington** Suffk
78 B7 **Thorington Street** Suffk
131 H8 **Thorlby** N York
60 D4 **Thorley** Herts
16 D5 **Thorley Street** IOW
133 G5 **Thormanby** N York
141 K4 **Thornaby-on-Tees** S on T
106 C5 **Thornage** Norfk
73 L7 **Thornborough** Bucks
132 D4 **Thornborough** N York
123 J4 **Thornbury** Brad
9 K3 **Thornbury** Devon
70 B3 **Thornbury** Herefs
38 F3 **Thornbury** S Glos
87 J7 **Thornby** Nhants
100 A2 **Thorncliff** Staffs
13 J2 **Thorncombe** Dorset
78 D1 **Thorndon** Suffk
10 E8 **Thorndon Cross** Devon
125 D7 **Thorne** Donc
26 D7 **Thorne** Somset
25 H7 **Thorne St Margaret** Somset
124 B3 **Thorner** Leeds
89 K3 **Thorney** C Pete
116 E6 **Thorney** Notts
26 B6 **Thorney** Somset
16 A3 **Thorney Hill** Hants
25 L6 **Thornfalcon** Somset
26 E8 **Thornford** Dorset
149 K2 **Thorngrafton** Nthumb
126 F5 **Thorngumbald** E R Yk
105 H4 **Thornham** Norfk
78 D1 **Thornham Magna** Suffk
92 D8 **Thornham Parva** Suffk
88 F4 **Thornhaugh** C Pete
29 J8 **Thornhill** C Sotn
154 F3 **Thornhill** D & G
114 D5 **Thornhill** Derbys
123 K6 **Thornhill** Kirk
184 E7 **Thornhill** Stirlg
135 H6 **Thornholme** E R Yk
15 G2 **Thornicombe** Dorset
168 D3 **Thornington** Nthumb
150 E7 **Thornley** Dur
151 J6 **Thornley** Dur

174 F6 **Thornliebank** E Rens
77 G4 **Thorns** Suffk
114 A4 **Thornsett** Derbys
137 H3 **Thornthwaite** Cumb
132 B7 **Thornthwaite** N York
196 C6 **Thornton** Angus
123 G4 **Thornton** Brad
73 L7 **Thornton** Bucks
125 H2 **Thornton** E R Yk
186 E7 **Thornton** Fife
120 D3 **Thornton** Lancs
86 F3 **Thornton** Leics
118 C7 **Thornton** Lincs
141 L4 **Thornton** Middsb
179 K8 **Thornton** Nthumb
126 D6 **Thornton Curtis** N Linc
44 F6 **Thornton Heath** Gt Lon
111 J5 **Thornton Hough** Wirral
130 D5 **Thornton in Lonsdale** N York
134 C3 **Thornton le Dale** N York
117 H3 **Thornton le Moor** Lincs
131 H2 **Thornton Rust** N York
132 B3 **Thornton Steward** N York
132 C3 **Thornton Watlass** N York
122 D2 **Thornton-in-Craven** N York
132 F2 **Thornton-le-Beans** N York
133 L6 **Thornton-le-Clay** N York
132 F2 **Thornton-le-Moor** N York
112 C6 **Thornton-le-Moors** Ches
132 F3 **Thornton-le-Street** N York
175 G7 **Thorntonhall** S Lans
178 F4 **Thorntonloch** E Loth
178 D8 **Thornydykes** Border
137 L3 **Thornythwaite** Cumb
102 C4 **Thoroton** Notts
124 C2 **Thorp Arch** Leeds
100 D3 **Thorpe** Derbys
126 B2 **Thorpe** E R Yk
131 J6 **Thorpe** N York
102 C3 **Thorpe** Notts
43 G6 **Thorpe** Surrey
92 E7 **Thorpe Abbotts** Norfk
102 C7 **Thorpe Arnold** Leics
124 D7 **Thorpe Audlin** Donc
134 D5 **Thorpe Bassett** N York
46 E3 **Thorpe Bay** Sthend
88 C4 **Thorpe by Water** Rutlnd
86 C2 **Thorpe Constantine** Staffs
93 G2 **Thorpe End** Norfk
62 E4 **Thorpe Green** Essex
77 L4 **Thorpe Green** Suffk
115 G3 **Thorpe Hesley** Rothm
124 F7 **Thorpe in Balne** Donc
116 E5 **Thorpe in the Fallows** Lincs
87 L5 **Thorpe Langton** Leics
125 K2 **Thorpe le Street** E R Yk
43 G6 **Thorpe Lea** Surrey

88 B7 **Thorpe Malsor** Nhants
73 G5 **Thorpe Mandeville** Nhants
106 F5 **Thorpe Market** Norfk
77 L4 **Thorpe Morieux** Suffk
116 E7 **Thorpe on the Hill** Lincs
43 G6 **Thorpe Park** Surrey
115 K5 **Thorpe Salvin** Rothm
87 K2 **Thorpe Satchville** Leics
92 F2 **Thorpe St Andrew** Norfk
104 D1 **Thorpe St Peter** Lincs
141 J3 **Thorpe Thewles** S on T
103 J2 **Thorpe Tilney** Lincs
133 G7 **Thorpe Underwood** N York
88 E7 **Thorpe Waterville** Nhants
124 E4 **Thorpe Willoughby** N York
62 E4 **Thorpe-le-Soken** Essex
79 K3 **Thorpeness** Suffk
62 C4 **Thorrington** Essex
11 L4 **Thorverton** Devon
92 D7 **Thrandeston** Suffk
88 E7 **Thrapston** Nhants
98 C4 **Threapwood** Ches
100 B4 **Threapwood** Staffs
163 J7 **Threave** S Ayrs
146 C3 **Threave Castle** D & G
32 B5 **Three Bridges** W Susx
33 L5 **Three Chimneys** Kent
68 D6 **Three Cocks** Powys
51 H6 **Three Crosses** Swans
20 D2 **Three Cups Corner** E Susx
33 H6 **Three Leg Cross** E Susx
15 K2 **Three Legged Cross** Dorset
42 B6 **Three Mile Cross** Wokham
176 E3 **Three Miletown** W Loth
21 G3 **Three Oaks** E Susx
103 H5 **Threekingham** Lincs
167 H2 **Threepwood** Border
137 J3 **Threlkeld** Cumb
131 J6 **Threshfield** N York
93 K2 **Thrigby** Norfk
101 H8 **Thringstone** Leics
132 D2 **Thrintoft** N York
76 B5 **Thriplow** Cambs
60 B3 **Throcking** Herts
150 E2 **Throckley** N u Ty
71 H4 **Throckmorton** Worcs
15 L4 **Throop** Bmouth
158 C2 **Thropton** Nthumb
176 B1 **Throsk** Stirlg
154 F5 **Throughgate** D & G
11 G6 **Throwleigh** Devon
34 C4 **Throwley Forstal** Kent
101 J6 **Thrumpton** Notts
231 L6 **Thrumster** Highld
127 H8 **Thrunscoe** NE Lin
55 K7 **Thrupp** Gloucs
60 D6 **Thrushesbush** Essex
87 J1 **Thrussington** Leics
28 F3 **Thruxton** Hants
69 J7 **Thruxton** Herefs
115 J3 **Thrybergh** Rothm
101 H6 **Thulston** Derbys
46 C3 **Thundersley** Essex

87 H2	Thurcaston	Leics
115 J4	Thurcroft	Rothm
106 E5	Thurgarton	Norfk
102 B3	Thurgarton	Notts
114 F2	Thurgoland	Barns
87 G4	Thurlaston	Leics
72 F1	Thurlaston	Warwks
25 K7	Thurlbear	Somset
102 E1	Thurlby	Lincs
89 G1	Thurlby	Lincs
119 G6	Thurlby	Lincs
74 F3	Thurleigh	Beds
7 G7	Thurlestone	Devon
76 F4	Thurlow	Suffk
25 L5	Thurloxton	Somset
114 E2	Thurlstone	Barns
93 J4	Thurlton	Norfk
87 H2	Thurmaston	Leics
87 J3	Thurnby	Leics
93 J1	Thurne	Norfk
33 K2	Thurnham	Kent
88 F6	Thurning	Nhants
106 C6	Thurning	Norfk
115 J1	Thurnscoe	Barns
148 B5	Thursby	Cumb
106 B5	Thursford	Norfk
30 E4	Thursley	Surrey
231 G2	Thurso	Highld
111 H5	Thurstaston	Wirral
77 L2	Thurston	Suffk
148 B4	Thurstonfield	Cumb
123 H7	Thurstonland	Kirk
93 G4	Thurton	Norfk
100 E5	Thurvaston	Derbys
92 B3	Thuxton	Norfk
139 K7	Thwaite	N York
78 D2	Thwaite	Suffk
129 H2	Thwaite Head	Cumb
93 G4	Thwaite St Mary	Norfk
135 G5	Thwing	E R Yk
185 L3	Tibbermore	P & K
154 E3	Tibbers	D & G
55 H4	Tibberton	Gloucs
70 F3	Tibberton	Worcs
99 G7	Tibberton	Wrekin
166 C5	Tibbie Shiels Inn	Border
92 D5	Tibenham	Norfk
101 H1	Tibshelf	Derbys
134 E7	Tibthorpe	E R Yk
33 H7	Ticehurst	E Susx
29 L5	Tichborne	Hants
88 E2	Tickencote	Rutlnd
38 C6	Tickenham	N Som
115 L3	Tickhill	Donc
83 J5	Ticklerton	Shrops
101 G7	Ticknall	Derbys
126 D3	Tickton	E R Yk
40 F8	Tidcombe	Wilts
57 M6	Tiddington	Oxon
72 B4	Tiddington	Warwks
33 G7	Tidebrook	E Susx
6 A4	Tideford	Cnwll
38 E2	Tidenham	Gloucs
114 D6	Tideswell	Derbys
41 M5	Tidmarsh	W Berk
72 C6	Tidmington	Warwks
48 F5	Tiers Cross	Pembks
73 K4	Tiffield	Nhants
196 E4	Tigerton	Angus
233 D6	Tigh a Ghearraidh	W Isls
7 H4	Tigharry	Devon
74 F2	Tilbrook	Cambs
45 M5	Tilbury	Thurr
77 H6	Tilbury Green	Essex
86 C7	Tile Hill	Covtry
42 A5	Tilehurst	Readg
30 E3	Tilford	Surrey
31 L4	Tilgate	W Susx
26 E4	Tilham Street	Somset
185 J7	Tillicoultry	Clacks
164 F1	Tillietudlem	S Lans
62 B7	Tillingham	Essex
69 J5	Tillington	Herefs
30 F6	Tillington	W Susx
69 J5	Tillington Common	Herefs
206 D4	Tillybirloch	Abers
205 K5	Tillycairn	Abers
206 C3	Tillyfourie	Abers
207 G2	Tillygreig	Abers
186 B6	Tillyrie	P & K
35 J4	Tilmanstone	Kent
104 F8	Tilney All Saints	Norfk
104 E8	Tilney High End	Norfk
90 D2	Tilney St Lawrence	Norfk
28 B2	Tilshead	Wilts
98 D5	Tilstock	Shrops
98 C3	Tilston	Ches
98 E1	Tilstone Fearnall	Ches
59 C3	Tilsworth	Beds
87 L3	Tilton on the Hill	Leics
39 J2	Tiltups End	Gloucs
103 J2	Timberland	Lincs
113 K8	Timbersbrook	Ches
24 E3	Timberscombe	Somset
132 B8	Timble	N York
156 B7	Timpanheck	D & G
113 H4	Timperley	Traffd
38 F8	Timsbury	BaNES
29 G6	Timsbury	Hants
232 d2	Timsgarry	W Isls
232 d2	Timsgearraidh	W Isls
77 J1	Timworth	Suffk
77 J2	Timworth Green	Suffk
14 E4	Tincleton	Dorset
149 G3	Tindale	Cumb
140 F2	Tindale Crescent	Dur
58 A2	Tingewick	Bucks
123 K5	Tingley	Leeds
59 G2	Tingrith	Beds
235 c6	Tingwall Airport	Shet
9 K7	Tinhay	Devon
115 H4	Tinsley	Sheff
32 B5	Tinsley Green	W Susx
8 E6	Tintagel	Cnwll
8 D6	Tintagel Castle	Cnwll
54 D7	Tintern Abbey	Mons
54 D7	Tintern Parva	Mons
26 D7	Tintinhull	Somset
114 A3	Tintwistle	Derbys
155 H5	Tinwald	D & G
88 E3	Tinwell	Rutlnd
85 G5	Tipton	Sandw
12 E4	Tipton St John	Devon
61 L5	Tiptree	Essex
61 L5	Tiptree Heath	Essex
67 J6	Tirabad	Powys
188 C7	Tiree Airport	Ag & B
172 C6	Tiretigan	Ag & B
55 J3	Tirley	Gloucs
53 H7	Tirphil	Caerph
138 D2	Tirril	Cumb
27 L5	Tisbury	Wilts
100 D3	Tissington	Derbys
22 C6	Titchberry	Devon
17 G2	Titchfield	Hants
88 E7	Titchmarsh	Nhants
105 J4	Titchwell	Norfk
102 B5	Tithby	Notts
69 G3	Titley	Herefs
32 D3	Titsey	Surrey
99 K5	Tittensor	Staffs
105 L7	Tittleshall	Norfk
70 E1	Titton	Worcs
98 D1	Tiverton	Ches
24 E8	Tiverton	Devon
92 E6	Tivetshall St Margaret	Norfk
92 E6	Tivetshall St Mary	Norfk
24 E3	Tivington	Somset
99 L7	Tixall	Staffs
88 E4	Tixover	Rutlnd
189 L5	Tobermory	Ag & B
181 L5	Toberonochy	Ag & B
233 b7	Tobha Mor	W Isls
216 D7	Tocher	Abers
215 L2	Tochieneal	Moray
40 B4	Tockenham	Wilts
121 K6	Tockholes	Bl w D
38 E3	Tockington	S Glos
133 G8	Tockwith	N York
27 J7	Todber	Dorset
158 E3	Todburn	Nthumb
59 G3	Toddington	Beds
56 B2	Toddington	Gloucs
72 B7	Todenham	Gloucs
196 C8	Todhills	Angus
148 C3	Todhills	Cumb
122 D5	Todmorden	Calder
115 J5	Todwick	Rothm
75 L4	Toft	Cambs
88 F1	Toft	Lincs
235 c3	Toft	Shet
140 E2	Toft Hill	Dur
93 J4	Toft Monks	Norfk
117 H4	Toft next Newton	Lincs
105 L6	Toftrees	Norfk
159 G2	Togston	Nthumb
199 J3	Tokavaig	Highld
42 B5	Tokers Green	Oxon
232 g2	Tolastadh	W Isls
124 E8	Toll Bar	Donc
25 H5	Tolland	Somset
27 L7	Tollard Royal	Wilts
14 B3	Toller Fratrum	Dorset
14 B3	Toller Porcorum	Dorset
13 M3	Toller Whelme	Dorset
133 H6	Tollerton	N York
101 L5	Tollerton	Notts
62 A6	Tollesbury	Essex
61 L5	Tolleshunt D'Arcy	Essex
61 L5	Tolleshunt Knights	Essex
61 L5	Tolleshunt Major	Essex
235 c8	Tolob	Shet
14 E4	Tolpuddle	Dorset
232 g2	Tolsta	W Isls
44 D6	Tolworth	Gt Lon
213 J8	Tomatin	Highld
201 K3	Tomchrasky	Highld
201 H5	Tomdoun	Highld
226 A7	Tomich	Highld
211 L8	Tomich	Highld
212 E5	Tomich	Highld
222 F7	Tomich	Highld
204 E2	Tomintoul	Moray
212 D6	Tomnacross	Highld
204 F1	Tomnavoulin	Moray
33 G4	Tonbridge	Kent
36 D4	Tondu	Brdgnd
25 H6	Tonedale	Somset
123 J4	Tong	Brad
34 C4	Tong	Kent
84 E3	Tong	Shrops
84 E2	Tong Norton	Shrops
123 J4	Tong Street	Brad
101 H7	Tonge	Leics
30 E2	Tongham	Surrey
146 C4	Tongland	D & G
229 J4	Tongue	Highld
37 H4	Tongwynlais	Cardif
52 B7	Tonna	Neath
60 B5	Tonwell	Herts
36 F3	Tonypandy	Rhondd
36 F3	Tonyrefail	Rhondd
57 K7	Toot Baldon	Oxon
60 E7	Toot Hill	Essex
40 C4	Toothill	Swindn
44 F5	Tooting	Gt Lon
44 F5	Tooting Bec	Gt Lon
132 F4	Topcliffe	N York
92 F5	Topcroft	Norfk
92 F5	Topcroft Street	Norfk
77 G6	Toppesfield	Essex
92 E4	Toprow	Norfk
12 C5	Topsham	Devon
162 A4	Torbeg	N Ayrs
223 G2	Torboll	Highld
213 G6	Torbreck	Highld
7 J3	Torbryan	Devon
192 B2	Torcastle	Highld
7 J7	Torcross	Devon
212 F4	Tore	Highld
172 D5	Torinturk	Ag & B
116 D5	Torksey	Lincs
39 H5	Tormarton	S Glos
161 M3	Tormore	N Ayrs
213 J4	Tornagrain	Highld
206 C4	Tornaveen	Abers
212 E8	Torness	Highld
140 F2	Toronto	Dur
181 L1	Torosay Castle	Ag & B
147 L6	Torpenhow	Cumb
176 C4	Torphichen	W Loth
206 C5	Torphins	Abers
6 C5	Torpoint	Cnwll
7 L3	Torquay	Torbay
177 L8	Torquhan	Border
209 J5	Torran	Highld
175 H4	Torrance	E Duns
163 J1	Torranyard	N Ayrs
210 D3	Torridon	Highld
210 D3	Torridon House	Highld
199 J2	Torrin	Highld
161 K3	Torrisdale	Ag & B
229 K3	Torrisdale	Highld
227 G5	Torrish	Highld
129 K6	Torrisholme	Lancs
226 A7	Torrobull	Highld
207 H4	Torry	C Aber
176 D2	Torryburn	Fife
84 E8	Tortan	Worcs
236 b4	Torteval	Guern
155 H6	Torthorwald	D & G
39 G2	Tortworth	S Glos
209 H5	Torvaig	Highld
137 J7	Torver	Cumb
175 L2	Torwood	Falk
167 G2	Torwoodlee	Border
116 A4	Torworth	Notts
209 L6	Toscaig	Highld
75 J3	Toseland	Cambs
130 E7	Tosside	N York
77 L2	Tostock	Suffk
208 C4	Totaig	Highld
208 F5	Tote	Highld
209 H3	Tote	Highld
16 D5	Totland	IOW
114 F5	Totley	Sheff
7 J4	Totnes	Devon
101 J5	Toton	Notts
188 F5	Totronald	Ag & B
208 F2	Totscore	Highld
45 G3	Tottenham	Gt Lon
90 F2	Tottenhill	Norfk
44 E2	Totteridge	Gt Lon
59 G4	Totternhoe	Beds
122 B7	Tottington	Bury
29 G8	Totton	Hants

25 J5 **Toulton** Somset
223 J5 **Toulvaddie** Highld
33 K3 **Tovil** Kent
150 E6 **Tow Law** Dur
173 K5 **Toward** Ag & B
173 J5 **Toward Quay** Ag & B
73 K5 **Towcester** Nhants
2 E4 **Towednack** Cnwll
58 B6 **Towersey** Oxon
205 K3 **Towie** Abers
90 B4 **Town End** Cambs
128 F2 **Town End** Cumb
19 L3 **Town Littleworth**
 E Susx
91 H6 **Town Street** Suffk
168 B4 **Town Yetholm**
 Border
174 D3 **Townend** W Duns
114 D2 **Townhead** Barns
155 H4 **Townhead** D & G
146 C3 **Townhead of**
 Greenlaw D & G
176 F1 **Townhill** Fife
41 K8 **Towns End** Hants
3 G5 **Townshend** Cnwll
133 K7 **Towthorpe** York
124 D3 **Towton** N York
110 D5 **Towyn** Conwy
111 K4 **Toxteth** Lpool
32 E3 **Toy's Hill** Kent
118 E8 **Toynton All Saints**
 Lincs
163 K5 **Trabboch** E Ayrs
163 L5 **Trabbochburn** E Ayrs
213 K3 **Tradespark** Highld
65 J4 **Traethsaith** Cerdgn
52 E3 **Trallong** Powys
101 G2 **Tramway Museum**
 Derbys
177 L4 **Tranent** E Loth
111 J4 **Tranmere** Wirral
230 C5 **Trantelbeg** Highld
230 C5 **Trantlemore** Highld
51 J2 **Trapp** Carmth
178 D4 **Traprain** E Loth
166 E3 **Traquair** Border
23 K6 **Traveller's Rest**
 Devon
122 D3 **Trawden** Lancs
96 A5 **Trawsfynydd** Gwynd
80 E5 **Tre Taliesin** Cerdgn
65 L5 **Tre-groes** Cerdgn
36 F3 **Trealaw** Rhondd
120 F4 **Treales** Lancs
108 C5 **Trearddur Bay** IOA
208 F4 **Treaslane** Highld
8 D7 **Trebarwith** Cnwll
4 E1 **Trebetherick** Cnwll
24 F4 **Treborough** Somset
5 M1 **Trebullett** Cnwll
6 A1 **Treburley** Cnwll
52 D3 **Trecastle** Powys
64 D7 **Trecwn** Pembks
52 F7 **Trecynon** Rhondd
9 G8 **Tredaule** Cnwll
53 H6 **Tredegar** Blae G
55 K3 **Tredington** Gloucs
72 C5 **Tredington** Warwks
38 B2 **Tredunhock** Mons
2 D6 **Treen** Cnwll
115 H4 **Treeton** Rothm
64 D7 **Trefasser** Pembks
53 H2 **Trefecca** Powys
81 L5 **Trefeglwys** Powys
49 G3 **Treffgarne** Pembks
48 E3 **Treffgarne Owen**
 Pembks
37 G3 **Trefforest** Rhondd
66 D3 **Trefilan** Cerdgn
64 B7 **Trefin** Pembks
110 E7 **Trefnant** Denbgs
97 K6 **Trefonen** Shrops
94 F4 **Trefor** Gwynd

8 E7 **Trefrew** Cnwll
109 L8 **Trefriw** Conwy
9 H7 **Tregadillett** Cnwll
54 B6 **Tregare** Mons
66 F3 **Tregaron** Cerdgn
109 H7 **Tregarth** Gwynd
9 H7 **Tregeare** Cnwll
97 J5 **Tregeiriog** Wrexhm
108 D3 **Tregele** IOA
3 K6 **Tregidden** Cnwll
48 D2 **Treglemais** Pembks
9 G5 **Tregole** Cnwll
4 E3 **Tregonetha** Cnwll
4 E6 **Tregony** Cnwll
68 E6 **Tregoyd** Powys
82 C4 **Tregynon** Powys
37 G3 **Trehafod** Rhondd
6 B4 **Trehan** Cnwll
37 H2 **Treharris** Myr Td
52 E7 **Treherbert** Rhondd
6 A1 **Trekenner** Cnwll
8 D7 **Treknow** Cnwll
110 F5 **Trelawnyd** Flints
65 J7 **Trelech** Carmth
48 C2 **Treleddyd-fawr**
 Pembks
37 H2 **Trelewis** Myr Td
8 C8 **Trelights** Cnwll
5 G1 **Trelill** Cnwll
4 C7 **Trelissick Garden**
 Cnwll
54 D6 **Trelleck** Mons
110 F5 **Trelogan** Flints
4 E3 **Trelow** Cnwll
95 K4 **Tremadog** Gwynd
8 F7 **Tremail** Cnwll
65 H5 **Tremain** Cerdgn
9 G6 **Tremaine** Cnwll
5 K3 **Tremar** Cnwll
6 B4 **Trematon** Cnwll
110 F6 **Tremeirchion** Denbgs
4 D3 **Trenance** Cnwll
4 E2 **Trenance** Cnwll
9 G5 **Trencreek** Cnwll
3 H5 **Trenear** Cnwll
9 G7 **Treneglos** Cnwll
26 E7 **Trent** Dorset
23 K2 **Trentishoe** Devon
36 E5 **Treoes** V Glam
36 E2 **Treorchy** Rhondd
5 G1 **Trequite** Cnwll
36 F5 **Trerhyngyll** V Glam
5 M4 **Trerulefoot** Cnwll
2 a1 **Tresco Heliport** IOS
3 G5 **Trescowe** Cnwll
4 C4 **Tresean** Cnwll
39 H3 **Tresham** Gloucs
4 D6 **Tresillian** Cnwll
9 G5 **Treskinnick Cross**
 Cnwll
9 G7 **Tresmeer** Cnwll
8 F6 **Tresparrett** Cnwll
194 C4 **Tressait** P & K
235 C5 **Tresta** Shet
235 e3 **Tresta** Shet
116 C5 **Treswell** Notts
8 E6 **Trethevey** Cnwll
2 C6 **Trethewey** Cnwll
5 G5 **Trethurgy** Cnwll
54 D4 **Tretire** Herefs
53 J4 **Tretower** Powys
97 K2 **Treuddyn** Flints
9 G8 **Trevague** Cnwll
8 E6 **Trevalga** Cnwll
98 B2 **Trevalyn** Wrexhm
4 D3 **Trevarrian** Cnwll
4 C4 **Treveal** Cnwll
8 E8 **Treveighan** Cnwll
3 J2 **Trevellas Downs**
 Cnwll
5 K3 **Trevelmond** Cnwll
3 K5 **Treverva** Cnwll
2 C6 **Trevescan** Cnwll

4 E5 **Treviscoe** Cnwll
4 D2 **Trevone** Cnwll
97 L4 **Trevor** Denbgs
8 E7 **Trewalder** Cnwll
9 J8 **Trewarlett** Cnwll
8 E7 **Trewarmett** Cnwll
9 G7 **Treween** Cnwll
9 G8 **Trewint** Cnwll
4 D7 **Trewithian** Cnwll
4 F5 **Trewoon** Cnwll
30 D7 **Treyford** W Susx
122 F6 **Triangle** Calder
151 J7 **Trimdon** Dur
151 J7 **Trimdon Colliery** Dur
151 J7 **Trimdon Grange** Dur
107 G5 **Trimingham** Norfk
78 F6 **Trimley** Suffk
50 F5 **Trimsaran** Carmth
23 H3 **Trimstone** Devon
194 B4 **Trinafour** P & K
58 F5 **Tring** Herts
196 F4 **Trinity** Angus
236 d6 **Trinity** Jersey
185 K4 **Trinity Gask** P & K
25 J4 **Triscombe** Somset
191 L2 **Trislaig** Highld
4 D5 **Trispen** Cnwll
158 F4 **Tritlington** Nthumb
194 F7 **Trochry** P & K
65 K5 **Troedyraur** Cerdgn
53 G7 **Troedyrhiw** Myr Td
236 c6 **Trois Bois** Jersey
3 H4 **Troon** Cnwll
163 H3 **Troon** S Ayrs
123 L3 **Tropical World**
 Roundhay Park
 Leeds
184 B5 **Trossachs** Stirlg
91 K8 **Troston** Suffk
70 F4 **Trotshill** Worcs
33 H2 **Trottiscliffe** Kent
30 D7 **Trotton** W Susx
157 L4 **Troughend** Nthumb
137 L6 **Troutbeck** Cumb
137 L7 **Troutbeck Bridge**
 Cumb
115 H5 **Troway** Derbys
39 J8 **Trowbridge** Wilts
101 J4 **Trowell** Notts
92 F3 **Trowse Newton**
 Norfk
27 H3 **Trudoxhill** Somset
25 K6 **Trull** Somset
208 C3 **Trumpan** Highld
70 B6 **Trumpet** Herefs
76 C4 **Trumpington** Cambs
107 G5 **Trunch** Norfk
4 C6 **Truro** Cnwll
4 C6 **Truro Cathedral**
 Cnwll
11 K7 **Trusham** Devon
100 E5 **Trusley** Derbys
119 G5 **Trusthorpe** Lincs
84 F5 **Trysull** Staffs
57 H7 **Tubney** Oxon
7 J5 **Tuckenhay** Devon
84 E6 **Tuckhill** Shrops
3 H3 **Tuckingmill** Cnwll
27 L5 **Tuckingmill** Wilts
15 L4 **Tuckton** Bmouth
77 G1 **Tuddenham** Suffk
78 E5 **Tuddenham** Suffk
33 G4 **Tudeley** Kent
151 G2 **Tudhoe** Dur
94 D5 **Tudweiliog** Gwynd
55 J5 **Tuffley** Gloucs
29 J3 **Tufton** Hants
49 H2 **Tufton** Pembks
87 L4 **Tugby** Leics
83 L6 **Tugford** Shrops
169 J4 **Tughall** Nthumb
185 H7 **Tullibody** Clacks
212 F8 **Tullich** Highld

223 J6 **Tullich** Highld
194 F5 **Tulliemet** P & K
216 F7 **Tulloch** Abers
184 C4 **Tulloch** Stirlg
192 F1 **Tulloch Station**
 Highld
182 D7 **Tullochgorm** Ag & B
185 L1 **Tullybeagles Lodge**
 P & K
206 B2 **Tullynessle** Abers
44 F5 **Tulse Hill** Gt Lon
51 G3 **Tumble** Carmth
103 L1 **Tumby** Lincs
103 L2 **Tumby Woodside**
 Lincs
194 B5 **Tummel Bridge** P & K
33 G5 **Tunbridge Wells** Kent
155 L6 **Tundergarth** D & G
99 K3 **Tunstall** C Stke
127 H4 **Tunstall** E R Yk
34 B3 **Tunstall** Kent
130 B5 **Tunstall** Lancs
140 F7 **Tunstall** N York
93 J2 **Tunstall** Norfk
99 H6 **Tunstall** Staffs
79 H4 **Tunstall** Suffk
151 J4 **Tunstall** Sundld
114 C6 **Tunstead** Derbys
107 G7 **Tunstead** Norfk
114 B5 **Tunstead Milton**
 Derbys
30 A2 **Tunworth** Hants
87 K5 **Tur Langton** Leics
42 B8 **Turgis Green** Hants
56 C4 **Turkdean** Gloucs
39 J7 **Turleigh** Wilts
69 G7 **Turnastone** Herefs
152 E2 **Turnberry** S Ayrs
100 F3 **Turnditch** Derbys
32 C6 **Turner's Hill** W Susx
14 F4 **Turners Puddle**
 Dorset
177 G4 **Turnhouse** C Edin
14 F7 **Turnworth** Dorset
216 D4 **Turriff** Abers
121 L7 **Turton Bottoms**
 Bl w D
89 L4 **Turves** Cambs
74 D4 **Turvey** Beds
42 C3 **Turville** Bucks
73 H6 **Turweston** Bucks
166 D5 **Tushielaw Inn**
 Border
98 D3 **Tushingham cum**
 Grindley Ches
100 E6 **Tutbury** Staffs
38 D2 **Tutshill** Gloucs
106 F6 **Tuttington** Norfk
116 C7 **Tuxford** Notts
234 b5 **Twatt** Ork
235 c5 **Twatt** Shet
175 J3 **Twechar** E Duns
179 K7 **Tweedmouth**
 Nthumb
165 L4 **Tweedsmuir** Border
3 K3 **Twelveheads** Cnwll
113 H7 **Twemlow Green**
 Ches
103 J7 **Twenty** Lincs
39 J7 **Twerton** BaNES
44 D5 **Twickenham** Gt Lon
55 J4 **Twigworth** Gloucs
19 H2 **Twineham** W Susx
77 J6 **Twinstead** Essex
24 C5 **Twitchen** Devon
114 F8 **Two Dales** Derbys
86 D3 **Twycross** Leics
86 C3 **Twycross Zoo** Leics
58 A3 **Twyford** Bucks
29 J6 **Twyford** Hants
87 K2 **Twyford** Leics
106 B7 **Twyford** Norfk
42 C5 **Twyford** Wokham

146 B4 Twynholm D & G
70 F7 Twyning Gloucs
70 F6 Twyning Green
    Gloucs
51 L2 Twynllanan Carmth
88 D7 Twywell Nhants
97 K4 Ty'n-dwr Denbgs
109 L7 Ty'n-y-Groes Conwy
96 F4 Ty-nant Conwy
69 H6 Tyberton Herefs
51 H4 Tycroes Carmth
97 H8 Tycrwyn Powys
104 D8 Tydd Gote Lincs
90 B1 Tydd St Giles Cambs
104 C8 Tydd St Mary Lincs
76 E7 Tye Green Essex
113 G2 Tyldesley Wigan
34 F3 Tyler Hill Kent
36 F2 Tylorstown Rhondd
37 G4 Tyn-y-nant Rhondd
183 K2 Tyndrum Stirlg
151 J2 Tynemouth N Tyne
178 D3 Tyninghame E Loth
154 E4 Tynron D & G
38 D6 Tyntesfield Somset
66 F1 Tynygraig Cerdgn
74 C5 Tyringham M Keyn
36 D5 Tythegston Brdgnd
113 K6 Tytherington Ches
38 F3 Tytherington S Glos
27 K3 Tytherington Wilts
13 H2 Tytherleigh Devon
39 L5 Tytherton Lucas
    Wilts
5 H5 Tywardreath Cnwll
80 D4 Tywyn Gwynd

U

79 G1 Ubbeston Green
    Suffk
38 D8 Ubley BaNES
141 G6 Uckerby N York
19 M2 Uckfield E Susx
70 F6 Uckinghall Worcs
55 K3 Uckington Gloucs
83 L2 Uckington Shrops
175 J6 Uddingston S Lans
165 G3 Uddington S Lans
21 H2 Udimore E Susx
207 G1 Udny Green Abers
207 G1 Udny Station Abers
25 G8 Uffculme Devon
88 F3 Uffington Lincs
40 F3 Uffington Oxon
83 K2 Uffington Shrops
89 G3 Ufford C Pete
79 G4 Ufford Suffk
72 E3 Ufton Warwks
41 M6 Ufton Nervet W Berk
161 K4 Ugadale Ag & B
7 G5 Ugborough Devon
93 J7 Uggeshall Suffk
143 H5 Ugglebarnby N York
114 E4 Ughill Sheff
60 E3 Ugley Essex
60 E3 Ugley Green Essex
143 G5 Ugthorpe N York
188 F5 Uig Ag & B
208 C4 Uig Highld
208 F2 Uig Highld
232 d2 Uig W Isls
209 G5 Uigshader Highld
180 E4 Uisken Ag & B
231 K7 Ulbster Highld
137 L3 Ulcat Row Cumb
118 F6 Ulceby Lincs
126 D7 Ulceby N Linc
126 E7 Ulceby Skitter N Linc
33 L4 Ulcombe Kent
147 M7 Uldale Cumb

55 H7 Uley Gloucs
159 G4 Ulgham Nthumb
220 E3 Ullapool Highld
71 K2 Ullenhall Warwks
124 D3 Ulleskelf N York
87 G6 Ullesthorpe Leics
115 J4 Ulley Rothm
69 L4 Ullingswick Herefs
208 E6 Ullinish Lodge Hotel
    Highld
136 E3 Ullock Cumb
138 B3 Ullswater Cumb
128 E2 Ulpha Cumb
135 J7 Ulrome E R Yk
235 d3 Ulsta Shet
129 G4 Ulverston Cumb
15 J6 Ulwell Dorset
209 J4 Umachan Highld
23 J6 Umberleigh Devon
224 F2 Unapool Highld
156 E5 Under Burnmouth
    Border
32 F3 Under River Kent
129 K2 Underbarrow Cumb
123 J4 Undercliffe Brad
83 K2 Underdale Shrops
101 J3 Underwood Notts
38 C3 Undy Mons
237 c5 Union Mills IOM
115 G6 Unstone Derbys
14 C2 Up Cerne Dorset
12 B2 Up Exe Devon
112 D1 Up Holland Lancs
30 D8 Up Marden W Susx
26 E7 Up Mudford Somset
30 B2 Up Nately Hants
29 H5 Up Somborne Hants
14 C3 Up Sydling Dorset
28 C1 Upavon Wilts
46 D6 Upchurch Kent
24 B5 Upcott Devon
24 E6 Upcott Somset
106 D8 Upgate Norfk
14 B2 Uphall Dorset
176 E4 Uphall W Loth
11 K3 Upham Devon
29 K7 Upham Hants
69 H2 Uphampton Herefs
70 E2 Uphampton Worcs
37 L8 Uphill N Som
174 E7 Uplawmoor E Rens
55 H3 Upleadon Gloucs
142 D4 Upleatham R & Cl
13 L4 Uploders Dorset
24 F7 Uplowman Devon
13 H4 Uplyme Devon
45 K3 Upminster Gt Lon
12 F2 Upottery Devon
75 G7 Upper & Lower
    Stondon Beds
83 J6 Upper Affcot Shrops
222 E4 Upper Ardchronie
    Highld
84 D7 Upper Arley Worcs
41 L5 Upper Basildon
    W Berk
19 G4 Upper Beeding
    W Susx
88 E5 Upper Benefield
    Nhants
71 H2 Upper Bentley Worcs
230 C4 Upper Bighouse
    Highld
72 F4 Upper Boddington
    Nhants
72 C6 Upper Brailes
    Warwks
199 L2 Upper Breakish
    Highld
70 E4 Upper Broadheath
    Worcs
102 B7 Upper Broughton
    Notts

41 K6 Upper Bucklebury
    W Berk
28 D7 Upper Burgate Hants
75 H5 Upper Caldecote
    Beds
73 G3 Upper Catesby
    Nhants
67 L6 Upper Chapel Powys
27 L5 Upper Chicksgrove
    Wilts
28 F2 Upper Chute Wilts
45 G3 Upper Clapton Gt Lon
29 G3 Upper Clatford Hants
55 M5 Upper Coberley
    Gloucs
83 K3 Upper Cound Shrops
123 J8 Upper
    Cumberworth Kirk
215 H2 Upper Dallachy
    Moray
35 K4 Upper Deal Kent
74 F2 Upper Dean Beds
114 E1 Upper Denby Kirk
20 B4 Upper Dicker E Susx
230 E3 Upper Dounreay
    Highld
62 F2 Upper Dovercourt
    Essex
184 E6 Upper Drumbane
    Stirlg
133 G6 Upper Dunsforth
    N York
30 F3 Upper Eashing
    Surrey
213 J2 Upper Eathie Highld
70 B5 Upper Egleton
    Herefs
100 B2 Upper Elkstone
    Staffs
100 C4 Upper Ellastone
    Staffs
30 B4 Upper Farringdon
    Hants
55 H6 Upper Framilode
    Gloucs
30 C3 Upper Froyle Hants
26 C3 Upper Godney
    Somset
75 G7 Upper Gravenhurst
    Beds
76 E7 Upper Green Essex
41 G7 Upper Green W Berk
30 D2 Upper Hale Surrey
43 H6 Upper Halliford
    Surrey
88 C3 Upper Hambleton
    Rutlnd
34 F3 Upper Harbledown
    Kent
32 E6 Upper Hartfield
    E Susx
55 L4 Upper Hatherley
    Gloucs
123 H6 Upper Heaton Kirk
133 L7 Upper Helmsley
    N York
68 F4 Upper Hergest
    Herefs
73 J3 Upper Heyford
    Nhants
57 J3 Upper Heyford Oxon
69 J4 Upper Hill Herefs
123 J6 Upper Hopton Kirk
100 A1 Upper Hulme Staffs
40 D2 Upper Inglesham
    Swindn
51 H6 Upper Killay Swans
183 G2 Upper Kinchrackine
    Ag & B
40 F4 Upper Lambourn
    W Berk
85 H3 Upper Landywood
    Staffs

38 C7 Upper Langford
    N Som
115 K7 Upper Langwith
    Derbys
187 G6 Upper Largo Fife
100 A5 Upper Leigh Staffs
85 J2 Upper Longdon
    Staffs
231 J7 Upper Lybster Highld
54 E5 Upper Lydbrook
    Gloucs
69 H2 Upper Lye Herefs
84 E8 Upper Milton Worcs
40 A3 Upper Minety Wilts
215 H4 Upper Mulben Moray
83 L5 Upper Netchwood
    Shrops
100 B5 Upper Nobut Staffs
18 C3 Upper Norwood
    W Susx
133 H8 Upper Poppleton
    York
71 L5 Upper Quinton
    Warwks
28 F6 Upper Ratley Hants
70 B2 Upper Rochford
    Worcs
145 L3 Upper Ruscoe D & G
70 C2 Upper Sapey Herefs
39 L4 Upper Seagry Wilts
74 E5 Upper Shelton Beds
106 D4 Upper Sheringham
    Norfk
173 L5 Upper Skelmorlie
    N Ayrs
56 D4 Upper Slaughter
    Gloucs
54 F6 Upper Soudley
    Gloucs
35 H6 Upper Standen Kent
154 E5 Upper Stepford
    D & G
92 F3 Upper Stoke Norfk
73 J3 Upper Stowe Nhants
28 D7 Upper Street Hants
107 G8 Upper Street Norfk
93 H1 Upper Street Norfk
77 H4 Upper Street Suffk
78 D4 Upper Street Suffk
59 H3 Upper Sundon Beds
56 D3 Upper Swell Gloucs
92 E4 Upper Tasburgh
    Norfk
100 A5 Upper Tean Staffs
100 E1 Upper Town Derbys
69 L5 Upper Town Herefs
38 D7 Upper Town N Som
77 K2 Upper Town Suffk
51 G3 Upper Tumble
    Carmth
72 D5 Upper Tysoe Warwks
187 J1 Upper Victoria Angus
72 F5 Upper Wardington
    Oxon
19 L3 Upper Wellingham
    E Susx
92 F7 Upper Weybread
    Suffk
29 L4 Upper Wield Hants
58 C5 Upper Winchendon
    Bucks
28 C4 Upper Woodford
    Wilts
39 J5 Upper Wraxall Wilts
148 D4 Upperby Cumb
208 E4 Uppergien Highld
113 M1 Uppermill Oldham
123 H8 Upperthong Kirk
30 F6 Upperton W Susx
231 L1 Uppertown Highld
88 C4 Uppingham Rutlnd
83 L2 Uppington Shrops
133 G3 Upsall N York

168 C1 **Upsettlington** Border
60 C7 **Upshire** Essex
35 G3 **Upstreet** Kent
58 C5 **Upton** Bucks
89 G4 **Upton** C Pete
89 H7 **Upton** Cambs
112 B7 **Upton** Ches
5 L2 **Upton** Cnwll
12 E2 **Upton** Devon
7 G7 **Upton** Devon
14 E5 **Upton** Dorset
15 J4 **Upton** Dorset
29 G1 **Upton** Hants
29 G7 **Upton** Hants
86 D4 **Upton** Leics
116 E4 **Upton** Lincs
93 H2 **Upton** Norfk
102 B2 **Upton** Notts
116 C6 **Upton** Notts
41 K3 **Upton** Oxon
43 G5 **Upton** Slough
24 F5 **Upton** Somset
26 C6 **Upton** Somset
124 D7 **Upton** Wakefd
27 K5 **Upton** Wilts
111 J4 **Upton** Wirral
54 F3 **Upton Bishop** Herefs
39 G6 **Upton Cheyney**
S Glos
84 B5 **Upton Cressett**
Shrops
5 L2 **Upton Cross** Cnwll
30 B2 **Upton Grey** Hants
11 J4 **Upton Hellions**
Devon
27 L4 **Upton Lovell** Wilts
83 K2 **Upton Magna** Shrops
27 G4 **Upton Noble** Somset
11 L5 **Upton Pyne** Devon
27 K2 **Upton Scudamore**
Wilts
71 G4 **Upton Snodsbury**
Worcs
55 K5 **Upton St Leonards**
Gloucs
70 F6 **Upton upon Severn**
Worcs
71 G2 **Upton Warren** Worcs
18 C3 **Upwaltham** W Susx
90 C3 **Upwell** Norfk
60 D3 **Upwick Green** Herts
89 J6 **Upwood** Cambs
40 B8 **Urchfont** Wilts
113 H3 **Urmston** Traffd
215 G2 **Urquhart** Moray
142 C6 **Urra** N York
212 D4 **Urray** Highld
197 H5 **Usan** Angus
151 G6 **Ushaw Moor** Dur
54 B7 **Usk** Mons
117 H3 **Usselby** Lincs
151 H4 **Usworth** Sundld
112 D8 **Utkinton** Ches
122 F3 **Utley** Brad
11 J5 **Uton** Devon
118 D3 **Utterby** Lincs
100 C5 **Uttoxeter** Staffs
43 H4 **Uxbridge** Gt Lon
235 d2 **Uyeasound** Shet
49 G5 **Uzmaston** Pembks

V

236 d2 **Vale** Guern
80 F7 **Vale of Rheidol**
Railway Cerdgn
108 C5 **Valley** IOA
209 H2 **Valtos** Highld
232 d2 **Valtos** W Isls
46 B3 **Vange** Essex
235 d3 **Vatsetter** Shet

208 D5 **Vatten** Highld
53 G6 **Vaynor** Myr Td
236 b3 **Vazon Bay** Guern
68 D7 **Velindre** Powys
12 D4 **Venn Ottery** Devon
9 K3 **Venngreen** Devon
17 G6 **Ventnor** IOW
16 E4 **Venton** Devon
29 G1 **Vernham Dean** Hants
41 G8 **Vernham Street**
Hants
15 K2 **Verwood** Dorset
4 E7 **Veryan** Cnwll
128 E5 **Vickerstown** Cumb
4 F4 **Victoria** Cnwll
235 d4 **Vidlin** Shet
215 G2 **Viewfield** Moray
175 J6 **Viewpark** N Lans
45 M7 **Vigo** Kent
236 a5 **Ville la Bas** Jersey
236 c3 **Villiaze** Guern
20 C3 **Vines Cross** E Susx
43 G6 **Virginia Water**
Surrey
9 K6 **Virginstow** Devon
27 G2 **Vobster** Somset
235 c4 **Voe** Shet
69 G7 **Vowchurch** Herefs

W

140 E3 **Wackerfield** Dur
92 E5 **Wacton** Norfk
70 F5 **Wadborough** Worcs
58 C5 **Waddesdon** Bucks
7 K4 **Waddeton** Devon
117 G3 **Waddingham** Lincs
121 L2 **Waddington** Lancs
116 F8 **Waddington** Lincs
4 F2 **Wadebridge** Cnwll
13 H1 **Wadeford** Somset
88 E6 **Wadenhoe** Nhants
60 B4 **Wadesmill** Herts
33 H6 **Wadhurst** E Susx
114 F7 **Wadshelf** Derbys
115 K3 **Wadworth** Donc
104 D2 **Wainfleet All Saints**
Lincs
9 G5 **Wainhouse Corner**
Cnwll
46 C6 **Wainscott** Medway
122 F5 **Wainstalls** Calder
139 H5 **Waitby** Cumb
118 C2 **Waithe** Lincs
123 L6 **Wakefield** Wakefd
88 D4 **Wakerley** Nhants
61 L3 **Wakes Colne** Essex
93 K8 **Walberswick** Suffk
18 C4 **Walberton** W Susx
146 D2 **Walbutt** D & G
26 D3 **Walcombe** Somset
103 H5 **Walcot** Lincs
83 L2 **Walcot** Shrops
40 D4 **Walcot** Swindn
92 D7 **Walcot Green** Norfk
87 H6 **Walcote** Leics
103 J2 **Walcott** Lincs
107 H6 **Walcott** Norfk
124 E6 **Walden Stubbs**
N York
46 C7 **Walderslade** Medway
17 L1 **Walderton** W Susx
13 L4 **Walditch** Dorset
151 G5 **Waldridge** Dur
79 G5 **Waldringfield** Suffk
20 B2 **Waldron** E Susx
115 J5 **Wales** Rothm
26 E6 **Wales** Somset
117 J3 **Walesby** Lincs
116 B7 **Walesby** Notts
83 H8 **Walford** Herefs

54 E4 **Walford** Herefs
98 C8 **Walford Heath**
Shrops
99 G3 **Walgherton** Ches
74 B1 **Walgrave** Nhants
122 C5 **Walk Mill** Lancs
113 G2 **Walkden** Salfd
151 H3 **Walker** N u Ty
69 K5 **Walker's Green**
Herefs
166 E3 **Walkerburn** Border
116 C3 **Walkeringham** Notts
116 C3 **Walkerith** Lincs
59 M3 **Walkern** Herts
186 D6 **Walkerton** Fife
16 B4 **Walkford** Dorset
6 D2 **Walkhampton** Devon
126 B3 **Walkington** E R Yk
115 G4 **Walkley** Sheff
71 J2 **Walkwood** Worcs
150 A4 **Wall** Nthumb
85 K3 **Wall** Staffs
153 C2 **Wallacetown** S Ayrs
163 J5 **Wallacetown** S Ayrs
19 L4 **Wallands Park** E Susx
111 J3 **Wallasey** Wirral
41 L3 **Wallingford** Oxon
44 F6 **Wallington** Gt Lon
17 H2 **Wallington** Hants
75 K7 **Wallington** Herts
15 K4 **Wallisdown** Poole
235 D5 **Walls** Shet
151 H2 **Wallsend** N Tyne
177 K4 **Wallyford** E Loth
35 K5 **Walmer** Kent
121 G5 **Walmer Bridge** Lancs
85 K5 **Walmley** Birm
93 H8 **Walpole** Suffk
104 E8 **Walpole Cross Keys**
Norfk
90 D2 **Walpole Highway**
Norfk
104 D8 **Walpole St Andrew**
Norfk
90 C1 **Walpole St Peter**
Norfk
85 H4 **Walsall** Wsall
122 D6 **Walsden** Calder
78 B1 **Walsham le Willows**
Suffk
132 F8 **Walshford** N York
90 C2 **Walsoken** Norfk
165 K1 **Walston** S Lans
59 K3 **Walsworth** Herts
34 E5 **Waltham** Kent
118 C2 **Waltham** NE Lin
60 C7 **Waltham Abbey**
Essex
29 K7 **Waltham Chase**
Hants
60 B7 **Waltham Cross** Herts
102 D7 **Waltham on the**
Wolds Leics
42 D5 **Waltham St**
Lawrence W & M
148 F3 **Walton** Cumb
115 G7 **Walton** Derbys
124 C2 **Walton** Leeds
87 H6 **Walton** Leics
74 C7 **Walton** M Keyn
68 F3 **Walton** Powys
26 C4 **Walton** Somset
79 G7 **Walton** Suffk
17 M2 **Walton** W Susx
123 L6 **Walton** Wakefd
98 E8 **Walton** Wrekin
55 K2 **Walton Cardiff**
Gloucs
49 H3 **Walton East** Pembks
31 L1 **Walton on the Hill**
Surrey
62 F4 **Walton on the Naze**
Essex

101 L8 **Walton on the**
Wolds Leics
38 B6 **Walton Park** N Som
48 E5 **Walton West**
Pembks
38 B5 **Walton-in-Gordano**
N Som
121 H5 **Walton-le-Dale** Lancs
43 J6 **Walton-on-Thames**
Surrey
99 L7 **Walton-on-the-Hill**
Staffs
100 E8 **Walton-on-Trent**
Derbys
141 G4 **Walworth** Darltn
45 G4 **Walworth** Gt Lon
48 E5 **Walwyn's Castle**
Pembks
13 H2 **Wambrook** Somset
30 F2 **Wanborough** Surrey
40 E4 **Wanborough** Swindn
44 E5 **Wandsworth** Gt Lon
93 K7 **Wangford** Suffk
87 H2 **Wanlip** Leics
165 G6 **Wanlockhead** D & G
20 C5 **Wannock** E Susx
88 F4 **Wansford** C Pete
135 G7 **Wansford** E R Yk
33 K4 **Wanshurst Green**
Kent
45 H3 **Wanstead** Gt Lon
27 G3 **Wanstrow** Somset
55 G7 **Wanswell** Gloucs
41 H3 **Wantage** Oxon
72 E2 **Wappenbury** Warwks
73 J5 **Wappenham** Nhants
20 C3 **Warbleton** E Susx
41 L2 **Warborough** Oxon
89 K7 **Warboys** Cambs
120 D3 **Warbreck** Bpool
9 G6 **Warbstow** Cnwll
113 G4 **Warburton** Traffd
139 H4 **Warcop** Cumb
150 A2 **Warden** Nthumb
72 F5 **Wardington** Oxon
98 E2 **Wardle** Ches
122 D6 **Wardle** Rochdl
151 H3 **Wardley** Gatesd
88 B4 **Wardley** Rutlnd
114 D6 **Wardlow** Derbys
90 C6 **Wardy Hill** Cambs
60 B5 **Ware** Herts
15 H5 **Wareham** Dorset
34 D7 **Warehorne** Kent
169 H4 **Warenford** Nthumb
60 C5 **Wareside** Herts
75 J4 **Waresley** Cambs
42 E6 **Warfield** Br For
7 K6 **Warfleet** Devon
42 C5 **Wargrave** Wokham
105 M4 **Warham All Saints**
Norfk
105 M4 **Warham St Mary**
Norfk
168 C2 **Wark** Nthumb
157 L6 **Wark** Nthumb
23 K6 **Warkleigh** Devon
88 C7 **Warkton** Nhants
72 F6 **Warkworth** Nhants
159 G2 **Warkworth** Nthumb
132 E2 **Warlaby** N York
5 J3 **Warleggan** Cnwll
122 F5 **Warley Town** Calder
32 C2 **Warlingham** Surrey
147 L2 **Warmanbie** D & G
124 B6 **Warmfield** Wakefd
99 G1 **Warmingham** Ches
88 F5 **Warmington** Nhants
72 E5 **Warmington** Warwks
27 K3 **Warminster** Wilts
38 F5 **Warmley** S Glos
115 K2 **Warmsworth** Donc
14 E5 **Warmwell** Dorset

29 L6 **Warnford** Hants
31 J5 **Warnham** W Susx
18 D4 **Warningcamp** W Susx
31 L6 **Warninglid** W Susx
113 K7 **Warren** Ches
48 F7 **Warren** Pembks
42 M4 **Warren Row** W & M
34 C4 **Warren Street** Kent
165 J2 **Warrenhill** S Lans
74 C4 **Warrington** M Keyn
112 E4 **Warrington** Warrtn
177 H4 **Warriston** C Edin
16 F2 **Warsash** Hants
100 C2 **Warslow** Staffs
115 K7 **Warsop** Notts
125 K1 **Warter** E R Yk
132 C4 **Warthermaske** N York
133 K7 **Warthill** N York
20 D4 **Wartling** E Susx
102 B7 **Wartnaby** Leics
120 E5 **Warton** Lancs
129 K5 **Warton** Lancs
86 C3 **Warton** Warwks
148 E4 **Warwick** Cumb
72 C2 **Warwick** Warwks
72 C2 **Warwick Castle** Warwks
234 c4 **Wasbister** Ork
137 G5 **Wasdale Head** Cumb
5 G2 **Washaway** Cnwll
7 J5 **Washbourne** Devon
78 D6 **Washbrook** Suffk
11 L2 **Washfield** Devon
140 D6 **Washfold** N York
25 G3 **Washford** Somset
11 J3 **Washford Pyne** Devon
117 G7 **Washingborough** Lincs
151 H4 **Washington** Sundld
18 F3 **Washington** W Susx
72 C3 **Wasperton** Warwks
133 H4 **Wass** N York
25 G3 **Watchet** Somset
40 E3 **Watchfield** Oxon
138 D7 **Watchgate** Cumb
11 H8 **Water** Devon
125 J3 **Water End** E R Yk
76 E6 **Water End** Essex
89 G4 **Water Newton** Cambs
85 L5 **Water Orton** Warwks
73 J7 **Water Stratford** Bucks
76 C2 **Waterbeach** Cambs
18 B4 **Waterbeach** W Susx
155 M6 **Waterbeck** D & G
14 E5 **Watercombe** Dorset
100 B3 **Waterfall** Staffs
175 G7 **Waterfoot** S Lans
60 A5 **Waterford** Herts
8 F8 **Watergate** Cnwll
164 B6 **Waterhead** E Ayrs
177 H7 **Waterheads** Border
100 B3 **Waterhouses** Staffs
33 H3 **Wateringbury** Kent
199 K2 **Waterloo** Highld
175 L7 **Waterloo** N Lans
195 G8 **Waterloo** P & K
49 G6 **Waterloo** Pembks
111 K2 **Waterloo** Sefton
17 J1 **Waterlooville** Hants
138 C3 **Watermillock** Cumb
57 L6 **Waterperry** Oxon
25 G6 **Waterrow** Somset
98 F8 **Waters Upton** Wrekin
18 D3 **Watersfield** W Susx
121 K5 **Waterside** Bl w D
163 K7 **Waterside** E Ayrs
163 L2 **Waterside** E Ayrs
175 J4 **Waterside** E Duns

208 B5 **Waterstein** Highld
57 M6 **Waterstock** Oxon
48 F6 **Waterston** Pembks
43 J2 **Watford** Herts
73 H2 **Watford** Nhants
132 B6 **Wath** N York
132 E4 **Wath** N York
115 H2 **Wath upon Dearne** Rothm
90 E2 **Watlington** Norfk
42 B2 **Watlington** Oxon
231 J5 **Watten** Highld
92 B8 **Wattisfield** Suffk
78 B4 **Wattisham** Suffk
13 L4 **Watton** Dorset
126 C1 **Watton** E R Yk
91 K4 **Watton** Norfk
60 A4 **Watton-at-Stone** Herts
175 K4 **Wattston** N Lans
37 J3 **Wattsville** Caerph
206 C6 **Waulkmill** Abers
51 H6 **Waunarlwydd** Swans
80 E6 **Waunfawr** Cerdgn
95 J2 **Waunfawr** Gwynd
74 C6 **Wavendon** M Keyn
147 L5 **Waverbridge** Cumb
112 C8 **Waverton** Ches
147 L5 **Waverton** Cumb
126 D3 **Wawne** E R Yk
107 J7 **Waxham** Norfk
11 K3 **Way Village** Devon
13 K2 **Wayford** Somset
13 L3 **Waytown** Dorset
25 H4 **Weacombe** Somset
56 F7 **Weald** Oxon
44 D7 **Wealdstone** Gt Lon
123 K2 **Weardley** Leeds
26 B2 **Weare** Somset
23 G6 **Weare Giffard** Devon
149 L6 **Wearhead** Dur
26 B5 **Wearne** Somset
105 K7 **Weasenham All Saints** Norfk
105 K7 **Weasenham St Peter** Norfk
113 J2 **Weaste** Salfd
112 E6 **Weaverham** Ches
134 E5 **Weaverthorpe** N York
71 H2 **Webheath** Worcs
216 F7 **Wedderlairs** Abers
86 D5 **Weddington** Warwks
40 B8 **Wedhampton** Wilts
26 C2 **Wedmore** Somset
85 H4 **Wednesbury** Sandw
85 G4 **Wednesfield** Wolves
58 D4 **Weedon** Bucks
73 J3 **Weedon** Nhants
73 H5 **Weedon Lois** Nhants
85 K3 **Weeford** Staffs
9 H5 **Week St Mary** Cnwll
29 J5 **Weeke** Hants
88 C7 **Weekley** Nhants
126 D3 **Weel** E R Yk
62 D4 **Weeley** Essex
62 D4 **Weeley Heath** Essex
194 D6 **Weem** P & K
71 J4 **Weethley** Warwks
91 H5 **Weeting** Norfk
127 H6 **Weeton** E R Yk
120 E4 **Weeton** Lancs
123 K2 **Weeton** N York
123 K3 **Weetwood** Leeds
122 C5 **Weir** Lancs
6 C3 **Weir Quay** Devon
92 C2 **Welborne** Norfk
102 F2 **Welbourn** Lincs
133 L6 **Welburn** N York
141 J6 **Welbury** N York
102 F5 **Welby** Lincs
22 C7 **Welcombe** Devon
87 J7 **Welford** Nhants
41 H5 **Welford** W Berk

71 K4 **Welford-on-Avon** Warwks
87 L5 **Welham** Leics
116 B5 **Welham** Notts
59 L6 **Welham Green** Herts
30 C3 **Well** Hants
118 F6 **Well** Lincs
132 D3 **Well** N York
59 K3 **Well Head** Herts
70 E6 **Welland** Worcs
196 D8 **Wellbank** Angus
72 C4 **Wellesbourne** Warwks
45 J5 **Welling** Gt Lon
74 C2 **Wellingborough** Nhants
105 L7 **Wellingham** Norfk
103 G2 **Wellingore** Lincs
136 F6 **Wellington** Cumb
69 K5 **Wellington** Herefs
25 H7 **Wellington** Somset
84 B2 **Wellington** Wrekin
70 C6 **Wellington Heath** Herefs
39 H8 **Wellow** BaNES
16 E5 **Wellow** IOW
116 A7 **Wellow** Notts
26 D3 **Wells** Somset
105 L4 **Wells-next-the-sea** Norfk
61 G4 **Wellstye Green** Essex
185 K3 **Welltree** P & K
176 E2 **Wellwood** Fife
90 D5 **Welney** Norfk
98 A6 **Welsh Frankton** Shrops
54 D4 **Welsh Newton** Herefs
36 F5 **Welsh St Donats** V Glam
98 C5 **Welshampton** Shrops
82 B3 **Welshpool** Powys
148 C6 **Welton** Cumb
126 B5 **Welton** E R Yk
117 G5 **Welton** Lincs
73 H2 **Welton** Nhants
119 G7 **Welton le Marsh** Lincs
118 C4 **Welton le Wold** Lincs
127 H6 **Welwick** E R Yk
59 L5 **Welwyn** Herts
59 L5 **Welwyn Garden City** Herts
98 D6 **Wem** Shrops
25 L4 **Wembdon** Somset
44 D3 **Wembley** Gt Lon
6 D6 **Wembury** Devon
10 F3 **Wembworthy** Devon
173 L4 **Wemyss Bay** Inver
76 D7 **Wendens Ambo** Essex
57 K4 **Wendlebury** Oxon
91 L2 **Wendling** Norfk
58 E6 **Wendover** Bucks
3 H5 **Wendron** Cnwll
75 K5 **Wendy** Cambs
93 J7 **Wenhaston** Suffk
89 J7 **Wennington** Cambs
45 K4 **Wennington** Gt Lon
130 C5 **Wennington** Lancs
100 E1 **Wensley** Derbys
131 K2 **Wensley** N York
124 D6 **Wentbridge** Wakefd
83 H5 **Wentnor** Shrops
90 C7 **Wentworth** Cambs
115 G2 **Wentworth** Rothm
37 H6 **Wenvoe** V Glam
69 H4 **Weobley** Herefs
69 H4 **Weobley Marsh** Herefs
18 E4 **Wepham** W Susx
90 F3 **Wereham** Norfk

89 H3 **Werrington** C Pete
9 J7 **Werrington** Cnwll
112 B6 **Wervin** Ches
120 F4 **Wesham** Lancs
101 G2 **Wessington** Derbys
91 H1 **West Acre** Norfk
7 G6 **West Alvington** Devon
24 D6 **West Anstey** Devon
118 C6 **West Ashby** Lincs
17 M2 **West Ashling** W Susx
27 K1 **West Ashton** Wilts
140 F3 **West Auckland** Dur
134 F3 **West Ayton** N York
25 J5 **West Bagborough** Somset
112 D5 **West Bank** Halton
117 K5 **West Barkwith** Lincs
143 K5 **West Barnby** N York
178 E3 **West Barns** E Loth
105 L5 **West Barsham** Norfk
13 L4 **West Bay** Dorset
106 D5 **West Beckham** Norfk
43 H5 **West Bedfont** Surrey
62 A3 **West Bergholt** Essex
14 A5 **West Bexington** Dorset
91 G1 **West Bilney** Norfk
19 J4 **West Blatchington** Br & H
151 J3 **West Boldon** S Tyne
123 H4 **West Bowling** Brad
34 E6 **West Brabourne** Kent
91 K2 **West Bradenham** Norfk
121 L2 **West Bradford** Lancs
26 E4 **West Bradley** Somset
123 K7 **West Bretton** Wakefd
101 L5 **West Bridgford** Notts
85 H5 **West Bromwich** Sandw
166 E6 **West Buccleuch Hotel** Border
23 K5 **West Buckland** Devon
131 J3 **West Burton** N York
116 D1 **West Butterwick** N Linc
43 H7 **West Byfleet** Surrey
144 D8 **West Cairngaan** D & G
93 K2 **West Caister** Norfk
176 D5 **West Calder** W Loth
26 E6 **West Camel** Somset
14 E5 **West Chaldon** Dorset
41 G3 **West Challow** Oxon
7 H7 **West Charleton** Devon
159 G3 **West Chevington** Nthumb
18 E3 **West Chiltington** W Susx
26 C8 **West Chinnock** Somset
31 H2 **West Clandon** Surrey
35 J5 **West Cliffe** Kent
26 D8 **West Coker** Somset
26 E3 **West Compton** Somset
14 B4 **West Compton Abbas** Dorset
125 G3 **West Cottingwith** N York
124 F6 **West Cowick** E R Yk
51 H7 **West Cross** Swans
148 B5 **West Curthwaite** Cumb
18 B3 **West Dean** W Susx
28 E6 **West Dean** Wilts
89 G2 **West Deeping** Lincs

111 L3 **West Derby** Lpool
90 F4 **West Dereham** Norfk
23 H3 **West Down** Devon
43 H4 **West Drayton** Gt Lon
116 B6 **West Drayton** Notts
231 J2 **West Dunnet** Highld
126 C5 **West Ella** E R Yk
74 E4 **West End** Beds
29 J8 **West End** Hants
38 C6 **West End** N Som
93 K2 **West End** Norfk
42 F7 **West End** Surrey
27 M6 **West End** Wilts
42 A7 **West End Green** Hants
33 J3 **West Farleigh** Kent
73 G4 **West Farndon** Nhants
97 M7 **West Felton** Shrops
19 M4 **West Firle** E Susx
40 E7 **West Grafton** Wilts
30 C1 **West Green** Hants
28 E6 **West Grimstead** Wilts
31 K6 **West Grinstead** W Susx
124 E5 **West Haddlesey** N York
73 J1 **West Haddon** Nhants
41 K3 **West Hagbourne** Oxon
84 F7 **West Hagley** Worcs
101 H4 **West Hallam** Derbys
125 L6 **West Halton** N Linc
45 H4 **West Ham** Gt Lon
115 H6 **West Handley** Derbys
41 H2 **West Hanney** Oxon
61 H7 **West Hanningfield** Essex
28 C5 **West Harnham** Wilts
38 E8 **West Harptree** BaNES
30 C7 **West Harting** W Susx
25 L7 **West Hatch** Somset
27 L5 **West Hatch** Wilts
187 J1 **West Haven** Angus
85 J7 **West Heath** Birm
227 H5 **West Helmsdale** Highld
41 H3 **West Hendred** Oxon
134 E4 **West Heslerton** N York
38 B7 **West Hewish** N Som
12 D4 **West Hill** Devon
32 C6 **West Hoathly** W Susx
15 G5 **West Holme** Dorset
45 M3 **West Horndon** Essex
26 E3 **West Horrington** Somset
31 H2 **West Horsley** Surrey
35 H6 **West Hougham** Kent
15 K4 **West Howe** Bmouth
185 M3 **West Huntingtower** P & K
25 L3 **West Huntspill** Somset
34 F7 **West Hythe** Kent
41 J4 **West Ilsley** W Berk
17 L3 **West Itchenor** W Susx
40 C6 **West Kennett** Wilts
173 L8 **West Kilbride** N Ayrs
45 L7 **West Kingsdown** Kent
39 J5 **West Kington** Wilts
111 H4 **West Kirby** Wirral
134 D4 **West Knapton** N York
14 D5 **West Knighton** Dorset
27 K5 **West Knoyle** Wilts
26 B7 **West Lambrook** Somset

35 J5 **West Langdon** Kent
191 L5 **West Laroch** Highld
30 E7 **West Lavington** W Susx
28 A2 **West Lavington** Wilts
140 E5 **West Layton** N York
101 K7 **West Leake** Notts
11 G4 **West Leigh** Devon
7 H4 **West Leigh** Devon
25 H5 **West Leigh** Somset
91 J1 **West Lexham** Norfk
133 K6 **West Lilling** N York
176 F7 **West Linton** Border
39 H5 **West Littleton** S Glos
41 H3 **West Lockinge** Oxon
14 F6 **West Lulworth** Dorset
134 E5 **West Lutton** N York
26 E5 **West Lydford** Somset
25 L5 **West Lyng** Somset
104 F7 **West Lynn** Norfk
33 H2 **West Malling** Kent
70 D5 **West Malvern** Worcs
30 C8 **West Marden** W Susx
116 B6 **West Markham** Notts
127 G8 **West Marsh** NE Lin
122 D1 **West Marton** N York
27 K7 **West Melbury** Dorset
29 M6 **West Meon** Hants
62 B5 **West Mersea** Essex
84 E7 **West Midlands Safari Park** Worcs
13 L3 **West Milton** Dorset
46 E5 **West Minster** Kent
43 J6 **West Molesey** Surrey
25 K5 **West Monkton** Somset
15 K2 **West Moors** Dorset
15 G4 **West Morden** Dorset
167 J2 **West Morriston** Border
26 E7 **West Mudford** Somset
133 L4 **West Ness** N York
126 F3 **West Newton** E R Yk
105 H6 **West Newton** Norfk
25 L5 **West Newton** Somset
44 F5 **West Norwood** Gt Lon
7 J2 **West Ogwell** Devon
27 J7 **West Orchard** Dorset
40 C6 **West Overton** Wilts
15 K3 **West Parley** Dorset
33 H3 **West Peckham** Kent
151 G4 **West Pelton** Dur
26 D4 **West Pennard** Somset
4 B4 **West Pentire** Cnwll
75 G2 **West Perry** Cambs
24 D3 **West Porlock** Somset
14 D2 **West Pulham** Dorset
9 K2 **West Putford** Devon
25 H3 **West Quantoxhead** Somset
11 K4 **West Raddon** Devon
151 H5 **West Rainton** Dur
117 H4 **West Rasen** Lincs
105 L7 **West Raynham** Norfk
141 K6 **West Rounton** N York
90 F7 **West Row** Suffk
105 K6 **West Rudham** Norfk
106 E4 **West Runton** Norfk
178 B5 **West Saltoun** E Loth
11 J4 **West Sandford** Devon
235 d3 **West Sandwick** Shet
131 K3 **West Scrafton** N York
14 D4 **West Stafford** Dorset

116 C3 **West Stockwith** Notts
17 M2 **West Stoke** W Susx
27 H6 **West Stour** Dorset
35 H3 **West Stourmouth** Kent
77 J1 **West Stow** Suffk
40 C7 **West Stowell** Wilts
78 B1 **West Street** Suffk
132 D4 **West Tanfield** N York
5 J3 **West Taphouse** Cnwll
172 E5 **West Tarbert** Ag & B
18 F5 **West Tarring** W Susx
158 F3 **West Thirston** Nthumb
17 L3 **West Thorney** W Susx
101 L7 **West Thorpe** Notts
45 L4 **West Thurrock** Thurr
46 A4 **West Tilbury** Thurr
29 M5 **West Tisted** Hants
117 J5 **West Torrington** Lincs
17 K3 **West Town** Hants
38 C6 **West Town** N Som
28 F5 **West Tytherley** Hants
90 C2 **West Walton** Norfk
90 C2 **West Walton Highway** Norfk
28 F7 **West Wellow** Hants
6 D6 **West Wembury** Devon
186 E7 **West Wemyss** Fife
76 E5 **West Wickham** Cambs
45 G6 **West Wickham** Gt Lon
49 H6 **West Williamston** Pembks
90 F1 **West Winch** Norfk
28 E5 **West Winterslow** Wilts
17 L3 **West Wittering** W Susx
131 K2 **West Witton** N York
157 M5 **West Woodburn** Nthumb
41 H7 **West Woodhay** W Berk
30 C4 **West Worldham** Hants
18 F5 **West Worthing** W Susx
76 E4 **West Wratting** Essex
9 H2 **West Youlstone** Cnwll
35 G3 **Westbere** Kent
102 D4 **Westborough** Lincs
15 K4 **Westbourne** Bmouth
17 L2 **Westbourne** W Susx
35 J2 **Westbrook** Kent
41 H6 **Westbrook** W Berk
73 J7 **Westbury** Bucks
83 G2 **Westbury** Shrops
27 K2 **Westbury** Wilts
27 K2 **Westbury Leigh** Wilts
55 G5 **Westbury on Severn** Gloucs
38 E5 **Westbury-on-Trym** Bristl
26 D2 **Westbury-sub-Mendip** Somset
120 E4 **Westby** Lancs
46 E3 **Westcliff-on-Sea** Sthend
27 G4 **Westcombe** Somset
56 E4 **Westcote** Gloucs
58 B5 **Westcott** Bucks
12 C2 **Westcott** Devon
31 J2 **Westcott** Surrey
40 E7 **Westcourt** Wilts

20 B5 **Westdean** E Susx
8 E7 **Westdowns** Cnwll
212 F7 **Wester Drumashie** Highld
176 D4 **Wester Ochiltree** W Loth
187 J6 **Wester Pitkierie** Fife
220 C5 **Wester Ross** Highld
231 G5 **Westerdale** Highld
142 E6 **Westerdale** N York
78 E5 **Westerfield** Suffk
18 C5 **Westergate** W Susx
32 D3 **Westerham** Kent
150 F2 **Westerhope** N u Ty
7 K4 **Westerland** Devon
39 G4 **Westerleigh** S Glos
197 G6 **Westerton** Angus
26 F2 **Westfield** BaNES
136 D2 **Westfield** Cumb
21 G3 **Westfield** E Susx
230 F3 **Westfield** Highld
175 J4 **Westfield** N Lans
92 B2 **Westfield** Norfk
176 C4 **Westfield** W Loth
195 J6 **Westfields of Rattray** P & K
150 A7 **Westgate** Dur
125 J8 **Westgate** N Linc
35 J2 **Westgate on Sea** Kent
93 J7 **Westhall** Suffk
14 C6 **Westham** Dorset
20 D5 **Westham** E Susx
26 B3 **Westham** Somset
18 B4 **Westhampnett** W Susx
26 C3 **Westhay** Somset
69 L5 **Westhide** Herefs
206 F4 **Westhill** Abers
69 J4 **Westhope** Herefs
83 J6 **Westhope** Shrops
103 L6 **Westhorpe** Lincs
78 C2 **Westhorpe** Suffk
112 F1 **Westhoughton** Bolton
130 D5 **Westhouse** N York
101 H2 **Westhouses** Derbys
31 K2 **Westhumble** Surrey
6 F5 **Westlake** Devon
23 G5 **Westleigh** Devon
25 G7 **Westleigh** Devon
79 J2 **Westleton** Suffk
77 J2 **Westley** Suffk
76 E3 **Westley Waterless** Cambs
58 C6 **Westlington** Bucks
148 D3 **Westlinton** Cumb
35 H3 **Westmarsh** Kent
19 K3 **Westmeston** E Susx
60 B3 **Westmill** Herts
44 F4 **Westminster** Gt Lon
196 B5 **Westmuir** Angus
147 K6 **Westnewton** Cumb
151 J2 **Westoe** S Tyne
39 G6 **Weston** BaNES
99 G3 **Weston** Ches
12 E3 **Weston** Devon
12 F5 **Weston** Devon
30 B6 **Weston** Hants
59 L3 **Weston** Herts
103 M7 **Weston** Lincs
123 H2 **Weston** N York
73 H5 **Weston** Nhants
116 C7 **Weston** Notts
83 L5 **Weston** Shrops
97 L6 **Weston** Shrops
99 L6 **Weston** Staffs
41 H5 **Weston** W Berk
69 L6 **Weston Beggard** Herefs
87 L5 **Weston by Welland** Nhants
29 J4 **Weston Colley** Hants

76 E4 **Weston Colville** Cambs
30 B3 **Weston Corbett** Hants
99 L4 **Weston Coyney** C Stke
73 L3 **Weston Favell** Nhants
76 F4 **Weston Green** Cambs
84 D2 **Weston Heath** Shrops
99 H7 **Weston Jones** Staffs
92 D1 **Weston Longville** Norfk
98 B7 **Weston Lullingfields** Shrops
30 B3 **Weston Patrick** Hants
97 L5 **Weston Rhyn** Shrops
71 K6 **Weston Subedge** Gloucs
58 D6 **Weston Turville** Bucks
54 F4 **Weston under Penyard** Herefs
72 D1 **Weston under Wetherley** Warwks
100 F4 **Weston Underwood** Derbys
74 C4 **Weston Underwood** M Keyn
38 C5 **Weston-in-Gordano** N Som
57 K4 **Weston-on-the-Green** Oxon
37 L7 **Weston-Super-Mare** N Som
84 E2 **Weston-under-Lizard** Staffs
98 E6 **Weston-under-Redcastle** Shrops
101 H6 **Weston-upon-Trent** Derbys
39 J3 **Westonbirt** Gloucs
59 G2 **Westoning** Beds
26 A4 **Westonzoyland** Somset
134 B6 **Westow** N York
26 B7 **Westport** Somset
176 B3 **Westquarter** Falk
234 c3 **Westray Airport** Ork
41 K4 **Westridge Green** W Berk
176 B5 **Westrigg** W Loth
40 D2 **Westrop** Swindn
178 D7 **Westruther** Border
90 B4 **Westry** Cambs
148 B6 **Westward** Cumb
23 G5 **Westward Ho!** Devon
34 D5 **Westwell** Kent
56 E6 **Westwell** Oxon
34 C5 **Westwell Leacon** Kent
76 B2 **Westwick** Cambs
12 C3 **Westwood** Devon
35 K2 **Westwood** Kent
39 J8 **Westwood** Wilts
116 C2 **Westwoodside** N Linc
148 E4 **Wetheral** Cumb
124 B2 **Wetherby** Leeds
78 B3 **Wetherden** Suffk
78 D2 **Wetheringsett** Suffk
61 H2 **Wethersfield** Essex
78 D2 **Wetherup Street** Suffk
99 L3 **Wetley Rocks** Staffs
98 F1 **Wettenhall** Ches
100 C2 **Wetton** Staffs
134 E7 **Wetwang** E R Yk
99 H5 **Wetwood** Staffs

40 F8 **Wexcombe** Wilts
106 D4 **Weybourne** Norfk
92 F7 **Weybread** Suffk
92 F7 **Weybread Street** Suffk
43 H7 **Weybridge** Surrey
13 H3 **Weycroft** Devon
231 H3 **Weydale** Highld
28 F3 **Weyhill** Hants
14 D6 **Weymouth** Dorset
74 B7 **Whaddon** Bucks
75 L5 **Whaddon** Cambs
55 J5 **Whaddon** Gloucs
39 K7 **Whaddon** Wilts
28 D6 **Whaddon** Wilts
115 K7 **Whaley** Derbys
114 A5 **Whaley Bridge** Derbys
115 K7 **Whaley Thorns** Derbys
231 K7 **Whaligoe** Highld
121 L4 **Whalley** Lancs
158 E6 **Whalton** Nthumb
104 A7 **Whaplode** Lincs
89 K2 **Whaplode Drove** Lincs
72 E4 **Wharf** Warwks
130 E5 **Wharfe** N York
120 F4 **Wharles** Lancs
114 F3 **Wharncliffe Side** Sheff
134 D6 **Wharram-le-Street** N York
69 K4 **Wharton** Herefs
140 E6 **Washton** N York
129 L4 **Whasset** Cumb
72 C5 **Whatcote** Warwks
86 B4 **Whateley** Warwks
78 B5 **Whatfield** Suffk
13 J2 **Whatley** Somset
27 G3 **Whatley** Somset
20 F3 **Whatlington** E Susx
34 F5 **Whatsole Street** Kent
101 G2 **Whatstandwell** Derbys
102 D3 **Whatton** Notts
145 J5 **Whauphill** D & G
93 K5 **Wheatacre** Norfk
59 K5 **Wheathampstead** Herts
84 B6 **Wheathill** Shrops
30 C4 **Wheatley** Hants
57 L6 **Wheatley** Oxon
151 J6 **Wheatley Hill** Dur
115 L1 **Wheatley Hills** Donc
84 F2 **Wheaton Aston** Staffs
24 E4 **Wheddon Cross** Somset
99 H2 **Wheelock** Ches
121 J6 **Wheelton** Lancs
125 G2 **Wheldrake** York
56 D7 **Whelford** Gloucs
59 G6 **Whelpley Hill** Bucks
60 A4 **Whempstead** Herts
133 K5 **Whenby** N York
77 J3 **Whepstead** Suffk
78 E6 **Wherstead** Suffk
29 H3 **Wherwell** Hants
114 C6 **Wheston** Derbys
33 H4 **Whetsted** Kent
87 G4 **Whetstone** Leics
128 D3 **Whicham** Cumb
72 C7 **Whichford** Warwks
150 F3 **Whickham** Gatesd
11 G6 **Whiddon Down** Devon
196 D7 **Whigstreet** Angus
73 J2 **Whilton** Nhants
12 D3 **Whimple** Devon
107 H6 **Whimpwell Green** Norfk

92 B2 **Whinburgh** Norfk
146 C4 **Whinnie Liggate** D & G
217 K7 **Whinnyfold** Abers
17 G4 **Whippingham** IOW
59 G4 **Whipsnade** Beds
59 G4 **Whipsnade Wild Animal Park** Beds
12 B4 **Whipton** Devon
116 E7 **Whisby** Lincs
88 B2 **Whissendine** Rutlnd
105 L7 **Whissonsett** Norfk
183 J8 **Whistlefield** Ag & B
183 G8 **Whistlefield Inn** Ag & B
42 C5 **Whistley Green** Wokhm
112 C3 **Whiston** Knows
74 B3 **Whiston** Nhants
115 H4 **Whiston** Rothm
84 F2 **Whiston** Staffs
100 B3 **Whiston** Staffs
128 D3 **Whitbeck** Cumb
70 D3 **Whitbourne** Herefs
151 J3 **Whitburn** S Tyne
176 C5 **Whitburn** W Loth
143 J5 **Whitby** N York
178 F6 **Whitchester** Border
38 F6 **Whitchurch** BaNES
58 D4 **Whitchurch** Bucks
37 J4 **Whitchurch** Cardif
6 D2 **Whitchurch** Devon
29 J2 **Whitchurch** Hants
54 D4 **Whitchurch** Herefs
41 M5 **Whitchurch** Oxon
48 D3 **Whitchurch** Pembks
98 D4 **Whitchurch** Shrops
13 K4 **Whitchurch Canonicorum** Dorset
41 M5 **Whitchurch Hill** Oxon
14 D5 **Whitcombe** Dorset
83 H5 **Whitcot** Shrops
82 F6 **Whitcott Keysett** Shrops
25 H7 **White Ball** Somset
121 H3 **White Chapel** Lancs
61 L3 **White Colne** Essex
3 H6 **White Cross** Cnwll
70 E7 **White End** Worcs
14 D3 **White Lackington** Dorset
71 G4 **White Ladies Aston** Worcs
61 J4 **White Notley** Essex
118 E6 **White Pit** Lincs
60 E5 **White Roding** Essex
69 L6 **White Stone** Herefs
42 D5 **White Waltham** W & M
86 B5 **Whiteacre Heath** Warwks
202 D3 **Whitebridge** Highld
54 D6 **Whitebrook** Mons
207 H2 **Whitecairns** Abers
45 G4 **Whitechapel** Gt Lon
54 E6 **Whitecliffe** Gloucs
177 K4 **Whitecraig** E Loth
144 E4 **Whitecrook** D & G
176 C3 **Whitecross** Falk
222 F4 **Whiteface** Highld
161 L2 **Whitefarland** N Ayrs
163 H7 **Whitefaulds** S Ayrs
113 J1 **Whitefield** Bury
25 G5 **Whitefield** Somset
206 D1 **Whiteford** Abers
112 F7 **Whitegate** Ches
234 d5 **Whitehall** Ork
136 D4 **Whitehaven** Cumb
30 C5 **Whitehill** Hants
216 C2 **Whitehills** Abers
206 C3 **Whitehouse** Abers
172 D6 **Whitehouse** Ag & B

178 D3 **Whitekirk** E Loth
26 B7 **Whitelackington** Somset
17 G6 **Whiteley Bank** IOW
214 B4 **Whitemire** Moray
101 K4 **Whitemoor** C Nott
4 F4 **Whitemoor** Cnwll
235 c6 **Whiteness** Shet
28 E6 **Whiteparish** Wilts
206 F2 **Whiterashes** Abers
231 L5 **Whiterow** Highld
214 C3 **Whiterow** Moray
55 J6 **Whiteshill** Gloucs
20 B3 **Whitesmith** E Susx
13 H1 **Whitestaunton** Somset
11 K6 **Whitestone Cross** Devon
121 K2 **Whitewell** Lancs
35 J5 **Whitfield** Kent
73 H6 **Whitfield** Nhants
149 K4 **Whitfield** Nthumb
38 F3 **Whitfield** S Glos
13 G4 **Whitford** Devon
111 G5 **Whitford** Flints
125 J6 **Whitgift** E R Yk
99 K6 **Whitgreave** Staffs
145 J6 **Whithorn** D & G
162 D4 **Whiting Bay** N Ayrs
124 B4 **Whitkirk** Leeds
49 L4 **Whitland** Carmth
167 G6 **Whitlaw** Border
163 J5 **Whitletts** S Ayrs
124 E6 **Whitley** N York
42 B6 **Whitley** Readg
115 G3 **Whitley** Sheff
39 K6 **Whitley** Wilts
159 J7 **Whitley Bay** N Tyne
150 B4 **Whitley Chapel** Nthumb
123 J6 **Whitley Lower** Kirk
55 H6 **Whitminster** Gloucs
99 J4 **Whitmore** Staffs
25 G7 **Whitnage** Devon
72 D2 **Whitnash** Warwks
68 F5 **Whitney-on-Wye** Herefs
147 M4 **Whitrigglees** Cumb
28 C7 **Whitsbury** Hants
179 H7 **Whitsome** Border
38 B4 **Whitson** Newpt
47 J6 **Whitstable** Kent
9 H5 **Whitstone** Cnwll
168 F6 **Whittingham** Nthumb
83 H5 **Whittingslow** Shrops
115 G6 **Whittington** Derbys
56 A4 **Whittington** Gloucs
130 B4 **Whittington** Lancs
91 G4 **Whittington** Norfk
97 L6 **Whittington** Shrops
85 L2 **Whittington** Staffs
84 F6 **Whittington** Staffs
86 C4 **Whittington** Warwks
70 F4 **Whittington** Worcs
121 H6 **Whittle-le-Woods** Lancs
73 K5 **Whittlebury** Nhants
89 J4 **Whittlesey** Cambs
76 C5 **Whittlesford** Cambs
125 L5 **Whitton** N Linc
158 D3 **Whitton** Nthumb
68 F2 **Whitton** Powys
141 J3 **Whitton** S on T
83 L8 **Whitton** Shrops
150 D4 **Whittonstall** Nthumb
41 J8 **Whitway** Hants
115 K6 **Whitwell** Derbys
59 K4 **Whitwell** Herts
17 G6 **Whitwell** IOW
141 G7 **Whitwell** N York
88 D2 **Whitwell** Rutlnd

106 D7 **Whitwell Street** Norfk
133 L6 **Whitwell-on-the-Hill** N York
86 E1 **Whitwick** Leics
122 D6 **Whitworth** Lancs
98 D5 **Whixall** Shrops
133 G7 **Whixley** N York
140 E4 **Whorlton** Dur
141 L6 **Whorlton** N York
69 L3 **Whyle** Herefs
32 C2 **Whyteleafe** Surrey
123 H4 **Wibsey** Brad
86 F6 **Wibtoft** Warwks
70 D3 **Wichenford** Worcs
34 B4 **Wichling** Kent
15 L4 **Wick** Bmouth
231 L5 **Wick** Highld
39 G5 **Wick** S Glos
36 E6 **Wick** V Glam
18 D5 **Wick** W Susx
71 G5 **Wick** Worcs
231 L5 **Wick Airport** Highld
38 A7 **Wick St Lawrence** N Som
76 E1 **Wicken** Cambs
73 L6 **Wicken** Nhants
60 D2 **Wicken Bonhunt** Essex
117 H5 **Wickenby** Lincs
77 L6 **Wicker Street Green** Suffk
115 J3 **Wickersley** Rothm
46 C2 **Wickford** Essex
17 H1 **Wickham** Hants
41 H6 **Wickham** W Berk
61 K5 **Wickham Bishops** Essex
78 D2 **Wickham Green** Suffk
79 G4 **Wickham Market** Suffk
78 C2 **Wickham Skeith** Suffk
77 J7 **Wickham St Paul** Essex
78 C1 **Wickham Street** Suffk
35 G3 **Wickhambreaux** Kent
77 H4 **Wickhambrook** Suffk
71 J6 **Wickhamford** Worcs
93 J3 **Wickhampton** Norfk
92 C3 **Wicklewood** Norfk
106 E5 **Wickmere** Norfk
39 G3 **Wickwar** S Glos
60 E2 **Widdington** Essex
159 G3 **Widdrington** Nthumb
159 G4 **Widdrington Station** Nthumb
159 G7 **Wide Open** N Tyne
7 G1 **Widecombe in the Moor** Devon
5 L4 **Widegates** Cnwll
9 G4 **Widemouth Bay** Cnwll
61 H6 **Widford** Essex
60 C5 **Widford** Herts
42 E2 **Widmer End** Bucks
101 M6 **Widmerpool** Notts
45 H6 **Widmore** Gt Lon
112 D5 **Widnes** Halton
13 G3 **Widworthy** Devon
112 E1 **Wigan** Wigan
26 C7 **Wigborough** Somset
12 E4 **Wiggaton** Devon
90 E2 **Wiggenhall St Germans** Norfk
90 E2 **Wiggenhall St Mary Magdalen** Norfk
90 E2 **Wiggenhall St Mary the Virgin** Norfk
76 F6 **Wiggens Green** Essex
58 F6 **Wigginton** Herts

57 H2 **Wigginton** Oxon
86 B3 **Wigginton** Staffs
133 J7 **Wigginton** York
130 F7 **Wigglesworth** N York
148 B4 **Wiggonby** Cumb
124 D2 **Wighill** N York
105 M4 **Wighton** Norfk
84 F4 **Wightwick** Wolves
69 H2 **Wigmore** Herefs
46 D6 **Wigmore** Medway
116 E7 **Wigsley** Notts
88 F6 **Wigsthorpe** Nhants
87 H4 **Wigston** Leics
86 F5 **Wigston Parva** Leics
115 L5 **Wigthorpe** Notts
103 L5 **Wigtoft** Lincs
148 A5 **Wigton** Cumb
145 J4 **Wigtown** D & G
123 L3 **Wike** Leeds
88 B5 **Wilbarston** Nhants
125 H1 **Wilberfoss** E R Yk
90 C7 **Wilburton** Cambs
74 C2 **Wilby** Nhants
92 B5 **Wilby** Norfk
78 F1 **Wilby** Suffk
40 C7 **Wilcot** Wilts
98 B8 **Wilcott** Shrops
113 M7 **Wildboarclough** Ches
75 G4 **Wilden** Beds
84 E8 **Wilden** Worcs
175 L7 **Wildmanbridge** S Lans
85 G7 **Wildmoor** Worcs
116 D3 **Wildsworth** Lincs
98 F4 **Wilkesley** Ches
223 K4 **Wilkhaven** Highld
176 F5 **Wilkieston** W Loth
12 D1 **Willand** Devon
111 K6 **Willaston** Ches
99 G3 **Willaston** Ches
74 C6 **Willen** M Keyn
86 D7 **Willenhall** Covtry
85 H4 **Willenhall** Wsall
126 C4 **Willerby** E R Yk
134 F4 **Willerby** N York
71 K6 **Willersey** Gloucs
68 F5 **Willersley** Herefs
34 D6 **Willesborough** Kent
34 D6 **Willesborough Lees** Kent
44 E3 **Willesden** Gt Lon
39 J3 **Willesley** Wilts
25 H5 **Willett** Somset
84 C4 **Willey** Shrops
86 F6 **Willey** Warwks
30 F2 **Willey Green** Surrey
72 F5 **Williamscot** Oxon
59 L2 **Willian** Herts
60 F6 **Willingale** Essex
20 C5 **Willingdon** E Susx
76 B1 **Willingham** Cambs
116 E5 **Willingham by Stow** Lincs
76 F4 **Willingham Green** Cambs
75 G4 **Willington** Beds
100 F6 **Willington** Derbys
150 F7 **Willington** Dur
33 K3 **Willington** Kent
72 C6 **Willington** Warwks
151 H2 **Willington Quay** N Tyne
125 H4 **Willitoft** E R Yk
25 H4 **Williton** Somset
119 G6 **Willoughby** Lincs
73 G2 **Willoughby** Warwks
87 H5 **Willoughby Waterleys** Leics
101 M7 **Willoughby-on-the-Wolds** Notts
116 F3 **Willoughton** Lincs
61 H4 **Willows Green** Essex

26 B6 **Willtown** Somset
71 L3 **Wilmcote** Warwks
13 G3 **Wilmington** Devon
20 B5 **Wilmington** E Susx
45 K5 **Wilmington** Kent
113 J5 **Wilmslow** Ches
121 K4 **Wilpshire** Lancs
123 G3 **Wilsden** Brad
103 G4 **Wilsford** Lincs
40 C8 **Wilsford** Wilts
28 C4 **Wilsford** Wilts
123 G8 **Wilshaw** Kirk
132 B6 **Wilsill** N York
101 H7 **Wilson** Leics
176 C7 **Wilsontown** S Lans
74 F5 **Wilstead** Beds
88 F2 **Wilsthorpe** Lincs
58 E5 **Wilstone** Herts
54 E3 **Wilton** Herefs
134 D3 **Wilton** N York
142 C4 **Wilton** R & Cl
28 C5 **Wilton** Wilts
40 E7 **Wilton** Wilts
167 G6 **Wilton Dean** Border
76 E6 **Wimbish** Essex
76 E7 **Wimbish Green** Essex
44 E6 **Wimbledon** Gt Lon
90 B5 **Wimblington** Cambs
113 G8 **Wimboldsley** Ches
15 J3 **Wimborne Minster** Dorset
28 B8 **Wimborne St Giles** Dorset
90 E3 **Wimbotsham** Norfk
75 L4 **Wimpole** Cambs
72 B5 **Wimpstone** Warwks
27 G5 **Wincanton** Somset
176 E4 **Winchburgh** W Loth
56 A3 **Winchcombe** Gloucs
21 H3 **Winchelsea** E Susx
29 J5 **Winchester** Hants
33 J5 **Winchet Hill** Kent
30 C1 **Winchfield** Hants
42 F2 **Winchmore Hill** Bucks
44 F2 **Winchmore Hill** Gt Lon
113 L7 **Wincle** Ches
115 G3 **Wincobank** Sheff
137 L7 **Windermere** Cumb
72 D6 **Winderton** Warwks
212 E5 **Windhill** Highld
42 F7 **Windlesham** Surrey
4 D2 **Windmill** Cnwll
20 D4 **Windmill Hill** E Susx
25 L7 **Windmill Hill** Somset
56 D5 **Windrush** Gloucs
216 D3 **Windsole** Abers
42 F5 **Windsor** W & M
42 F5 **Windsor Castle** W & M
77 K4 **Windsor Green** Suffk
55 L7 **Windsoredge** Gloucs
72 C1 **Windy Arbour** Warwks
186 E7 **Windygates** Fife
31 L7 **Wineham** W Susx
127 G5 **Winestead** E R Yk
92 D6 **Winfarthing** Norfk
17 G5 **Winford** IOW
38 D7 **Winford** N Som
68 F5 **Winforton** Herefs
14 F5 **Winfrith Newburgh** Dorset
58 E4 **Wing** Bucks
88 C3 **Wing** Rutlnd
151 J7 **Wingate** Dur
115 G7 **Wingerworth** Derbys
59 G3 **Wingfield** Beds
92 F7 **Wingfield** Suffk
27 J1 **Wingfield** Wilts
35 H3 **Wingham** Kent

35 G5 **Wingmore** Kent
58 E4 **Wingrave** Bucks
102 B2 **Winkburn** Notts
42 E6 **Winkfield** Br For
42 E6 **Winkfield Row** Br For
100 B3 **Winkhill** Staffs
10 F4 **Winkleigh** Devon
132 C5 **Winksley** N York
150 F3 **Winlaton** Gatesd
231 K5 **Winless** Highld
120 F2 **Winmarleigh** Lancs
29 J5 **Winnall** Hants
42 C6 **Winnersh** Wokham
112 F6 **Winnington** Ches
38 B8 **Winscombe** N Som
112 F7 **Winsford** Ches
24 E4 **Winsford** Somset
23 H4 **Winsham** Devon
13 J2 **Winsham** Somset
100 F7 **Winshill** Staffs
51 K6 **Winshwen** Swans
149 G7 **Winskill** Cumb
30 A2 **Winslade** Hants
39 J7 **Winsley** Wilts
58 C3 **Winslow** Bucks
56 C6 **Winson** Gloucs
28 F8 **Winsor** Hants
129 J2 **Winster** Cumb
100 E1 **Winster** Derbys
140 E4 **Winston** Dur
78 E3 **Winston** Suffk
55 L6 **Winstone** Gloucs
10 D3 **Winswell** Devon
14 D5 **Winterborne Came** Dorset
14 F2 **Winterborne Clenston** Dorset
14 F2 **Winterborne Houghton** Dorset
15 G3 **Winterborne Kingston** Dorset
14 D5 **Winterborne Monkton** Dorset
14 F2 **Winterborne Stickland** Dorset
14 F3 **Winterborne Whitechurch** Dorset
15 G3 **Winterborne Zelston** Dorset
38 F4 **Winterbourne** S Glos
41 J6 **Winterbourne** W Berk
14 C4 **Winterbourne Abbas** Dorset
40 C5 **Winterbourne Bassett** Wilts
28 D4 **Winterbourne Dauntsey** Wilts
28 D5 **Winterbourne Earls** Wilts
28 D4 **Winterbourne Gunner** Wilts
40 C6 **Winterbourne Monkton** Wilts
14 C4 **Winterbourne Steepleton** Dorset
28 B3 **Winterbourne Stoke** Wilts
131 H7 **Winterburn** N York
125 L6 **Winteringham** N Linc
99 H2 **Winterley** Ches
28 E5 **Winterslow** Wilts
125 L6 **Winterton** N Linc
107 K8 **Winterton-on-Sea** Norfk
102 D2 **Winthorpe** Notts
15 K4 **Winton** Bmouth
139 H5 **Winton** Cumb
134 D3 **Wintringham** N York
89 G7 **Winwick** Cambs
87 J8 **Winwick** Nhants
112 E3 **Winwick** Warrtn

100 F2 **Wirksworth** Derbys
111 J4 **Wirral**
98 D4 **Wirswall** Ches
90 C2 **Wisbech** Cambs
90 B2 **Wisbech St Mary** Cambs
31 H6 **Wisborough Green** W Susx
49 K6 **Wiseman's Bridge** Pembks
116 B4 **Wiseton** Notts
175 L7 **Wishaw** N Lans
85 L5 **Wishaw** Warwks
43 H8 **Wisley Gardens** Surrey
117 K6 **Wispington** Lincs
93 H7 **Wissett** Suffk
62 A2 **Wissington** Suffk
83 H6 **Wistanstow** Shrops
98 F6 **Wistanswick** Shrops
99 G2 **Wistaston** Ches
49 H4 **Wiston** Pembks
165 J3 **Wiston** S Lans
18 F3 **Wiston** W Susx
89 K7 **Wistow** Cambs
124 F4 **Wistow** N York
121 L3 **Wiswell** Lancs
90 C7 **Witcham** Cambs
15 J2 **Witchampton** Dorset
90 C7 **Witchford** Cambs
26 C6 **Witcombe** Somset
61 K5 **Witham** Essex
27 H3 **Witham Friary** Somset
88 F1 **Witham on the Hill** Lincs
118 C5 **Withcall** Lincs
19 J4 **Withdean** Br & H
33 H7 **Witherenden Hill** E Susx
11 J3 **Witheridge** Devon
86 D4 **Witherley** Leics
118 F5 **Withern** Lincs
127 H5 **Withernsea** E R Yk
126 F3 **Withernwick** E R Yk
92 F7 **Withersdale Street** Suffk
76 F5 **Withersfield** Essex
129 J3 **Witherslack** Cumb
129 J3 **Witherslack Hall** Cumb
4 F3 **Withiel** Cnwll
24 F5 **Withiel Florey** Somset
56 B5 **Withington** Gloucs
69 L5 **Withington** Herefs
113 J3 **Withington** Manch
83 L2 **Withington** Shrops
100 B5 **Withington** Staffs
11 K3 **Withleigh** Devon
85 H8 **Withybed Green** Worcs
86 E6 **Withybrook** Warwks
24 F3 **Withycombe** Somset
32 E6 **Withyham** E Susx
24 D4 **Withypool** Somset
38 E6 **Withywood** Bristl
30 F4 **Witley** Surrey
78 E4 **Witnesham** Suffk
57 G6 **Witney** Oxon
88 F3 **Wittering** C Pete
21 H1 **Wittersham** Kent
85 J5 **Witton** Birm
93 G2 **Witton** Norfk
107 H6 **Witton** Norfk
151 G5 **Witton Gilbert** Dur
140 E2 **Witton le Wear** Dur
140 F2 **Witton Park** Dur
25 G5 **Wiveliscombe** Somset
30 A4 **Wivelrod** Hants
19 K2 **Wivelsfield** E Susx
19 K2 **Wivelsfield Green** E Susx
62 C4 **Wivenhoe** Essex
106 C4 **Wiveton** Norfk
62 E3 **Wix** Essex
71 K4 **Wixford** Warwks
77 G6 **Wixoe** Essex
58 F2 **Woburn** Beds
58 F2 **Woburn Abbey** Beds
74 D7 **Woburn Sands** M Keyn
43 G8 **Woking** Surrey
42 D6 **Wokingham** Wokham
135 G5 **Wold Newton** E R Yk
118 C3 **Wold Newton** NE Lin
32 C3 **Woldingham** Surrey
49 G3 **Wolf's Castle** Pembks
165 K3 **Wolfclyde** S Lans
105 G6 **Wolferton** Norfk
186 B2 **Wolfhill** P & K
48 F3 **Wolfsdale** Pembks
84 F6 **Wollaston** Dudley
74 C2 **Wollaston** Nhants
83 G2 **Wollaston** Shrops
101 K4 **Wollaton** C Nott
98 F6 **Wollerton** Shrops
85 G6 **Wollescote** Dudley
100 A7 **Wolseley Bridge** Staffs
150 D7 **Wolsingham** Dur
99 J3 **Wolstanton** Staffs
86 E7 **Wolston** Warwks
57 J6 **Wolvercote** Oxon
85 G4 **Wolverhampton** Wolves
84 E5 **Wolverhampton Business Airport** Staffs
84 E7 **Wolverley** Worcs
41 K8 **Wolverton** Hants
74 B6 **Wolverton** M Keyn
72 B3 **Wolverton** Warwks
27 H5 **Wolverton** Wilts
54 C7 **Wolvesnewton** Mons
86 E6 **Wolvey** Warwks
86 E6 **Wolvey Heath** Warwks
141 K3 **Wolviston** S on T
133 K3 **Wombleton** N York
84 F5 **Wombourne** Staffs
115 H2 **Wombwell** Barns
35 G4 **Womenswold** Kent
124 E6 **Womersley** N York
31 G3 **Wonersh** Surrey
12 B4 **Wonford** Devon
29 K4 **Wonston** Hants
42 E3 **Wooburn** Bucks
42 E3 **Wooburn Green** Bucks
71 J4 **Wood Bevington** Warwks
106 C6 **Wood Dalling** Norfk
43 J4 **Wood End** Gt Lon
60 B3 **Wood End** Herts
71 K1 **Wood End** Warwks
118 C8 **Wood Enderby** Lincs
44 F2 **Wood Green** Gt Lon
85 G3 **Wood Hayes** Wolves
106 B6 **Wood Norton** Norfk
107 H7 **Wood Street** Norfk
30 F2 **Wood Street** Surrey
89 J7 **Wood Walton** Cambs
20 D2 **Wood's Corner** E Susx
33 H6 **Wood's Green** E Susx
115 J3 **Woodall** Rothm
93 G1 **Woodbastwick** Norfk
101 M3 **Woodborough** Notts
40 C7 **Woodborough** Wilts
12 F4 **Woodbridge** Devon
78 F5 **Woodbridge** Suffk
12 C5 **Woodbury** Devon
12 C5 **Woodbury Salterton** Devon
55 J7 **Woodchester** Gloucs
34 C7 **Woodchurch** Kent
24 E3 **Woodcombe** Somset
44 F7 **Woodcote** Gt Lon
41 M4 **Woodcote** Oxon
84 D1 **Woodcote** Wrekin
38 D2 **Woodcroft** Gloucs
76 F3 **Woodditton** Cambs
57 K5 **Woodeaton** Oxon
190 F4 **Woodend** Highld
73 H5 **Woodend** Nhants
176 C4 **Woodend** W Loth
17 M2 **Woodend** W Susx
60 E3 **Woodend Green** Essex
28 D7 **Woodfalls** Wilts
9 G3 **Woodford** Cnwll
39 G2 **Woodford** Gloucs
45 H2 **Woodford** Gt Lon
88 D7 **Woodford** Nhants
113 K5 **Woodford** Stockp
45 H2 **Woodford Bridge** Gt Lon
73 G4 **Woodford Halse** Nhants
45 H2 **Woodford Wells** Gt Lon
85 H6 **Woodgate** Birm
25 H7 **Woodgate** Devon
18 C5 **Woodgate** W Susx
71 H2 **Woodgate** Worcs
28 D7 **Woodgreen** Hants
131 J2 **Woodhall** N York
117 K8 **Woodhall Spa** Lincs
58 B4 **Woodham** Bucks
43 H7 **Woodham** Surrey
61 J7 **Woodham Ferrers** Essex
61 K6 **Woodham Mortimer** Essex
61 K6 **Woodham Walter** Essex
216 E6 **Woodhead** Abers
26 A6 **Woodhill** Somset
159 H4 **Woodhorn** Nthumb
123 K4 **Woodhouse** Leeds
87 G1 **Woodhouse** Leics
115 H4 **Woodhouse** Sheff
124 B6 **Woodhouse** Wakefd
87 G2 **Woodhouse Eaves** Leics
177 H5 **Woodhouselee** Mdloth
156 D6 **Woodhouselees** D & G
100 D8 **Woodhouses** Staffs
89 K7 **Woodhurst** Cambs
19 K5 **Woodingdean** Br & H
123 K5 **Woodkirk** Leeds
207 G2 **Woodland** Abers
7 J3 **Woodland** Devon
6 F5 **Woodland** Devon
140 D2 **Woodland** Dur
34 F6 **Woodland** Kent
152 E3 **Woodland** S Ayrs
206 E6 **Woodlands** Abers
124 E8 **Woodlands** Donc
15 K2 **Woodlands** Dorset
16 C1 **Woodlands** Hants
132 E8 **Woodlands** N York
25 J4 **Woodlands** Somset
42 E5 **Woodlands Park** W & M
7 H6 **Woodleigh** Devon
42 C5 **Woodley** Wokham
55 L3 **Woodmancote** Gloucs
56 A6 **Woodmancote** Gloucs
39 H2 **Woodmancote** Gloucs
17 L2 **Woodmancote** W Susx
19 H3 **Woodmancote** W Susx
29 K3 **Woodmancott** Hants
126 C3 **Woodmansey** E R Yk
30 E6 **Woodmansgreen** W Susx
32 B2 **Woodmansterne** Surrey
12 C5 **Woodmanton** Devon
35 J4 **Woodnesborough** Kent
88 F5 **Woodnewton** Nhants
121 G4 **Woodplumpton** Lancs
92 B3 **Woodrising** Norfk
99 H7 **Woodseaves** Staffs
115 K5 **Woodsetts** Rothm
14 E4 **Woodsford** Dorset
42 F6 **Woodside** Br For
187 G5 **Woodside** Fife
45 G6 **Woodside** Gt Lon
195 K8 **Woodside** P & K
57 H5 **Woodstock** Oxon
89 H4 **Woodston** C Pete
93 G5 **Woodton** Norfk
22 F6 **Woodtown** Devon
69 K2 **Woofferton** Shrops
26 D3 **Wookey** Somset
26 D2 **Wookey Hole** Somset
14 F5 **Wool** Dorset
23 G3 **Woolacombe** Devon
35 H5 **Woolage Green** Kent
54 E7 **Woolaston** Gloucs
54 E7 **Woolaston Common** Gloucs
25 M3 **Woolavington** Somset
30 E6 **Woolbeding** W Susx
12 E5 **Woolbrook** Devon
24 F5 **Woolcotts** Somset
168 E4 **Wooler** Nthumb
22 E7 **Woolfardisworthy** Devon
11 J3 **Woolfardisworthy** Devon
176 D6 **Woolfords** S Lans
41 L6 **Woolhampton** W Berk
69 L7 **Woolhope** Herefs
14 E2 **Woolland** Dorset
39 H6 **Woolley** BaNES
89 G8 **Woolley** Cambs
123 L7 **Woolley** Wakefd
59 L4 **Woolmer Green** Herts
71 G2 **Woolmere Green** Worcs
13 K2 **Woolminstone** Somset
77 L3 **Woolpit** Suffk
83 J4 **Woolstaston** Shrops
102 D5 **Woolsthorpe** Lincs
102 F7 **Woolsthorpe-by-Colsterworth** Lincs
16 E1 **Woolston** C Sotn
97 L7 **Woolston** Shrops
83 H6 **Woolston** Shrops
25 H4 **Woolston** Somset
26 F5 **Woolston** Somset
112 F4 **Woolston** Warrtn
7 H3 **Woolston Green** Devon
55 L3 **Woolstone** Gloucs
74 C6 **Woolstone** M Keyn
40 F3 **Woolstone** Oxon
112 B4 **Woolton** Lpool
41 H7 **Woolton Hill** Hants
78 E6 **Woolverstone** Suffk
27 H2 **Woolverton** Somset
45 H4 **Woolwich** Gt Lon

69 G4 **Woonton** Herefs
99 G4 **Woore** Shrops
92 F8 **Wootten Green** Suffk
74 E5 **Wootton** Beds
35 G5 **Wootton** Kent
126 D7 **Wootton** N Linc
73 L3 **Wootton** Nhants
57 H4 **Wootton** Oxon
57 J7 **Wootton** Oxon
100 C4 **Wootton** Staffs
40 B4 **Wootton Bassett** Wilts
17 G4 **Wootton Bridge** IOW
24 E3 **Wootton Courtenay** Somset
13 J4 **Wootton Fitzpaine** Dorset
40 D7 **Wootton Rivers** Wilts
29 L2 **Wootton St Lawrence** Hants
71 L2 **Wootton Wawen** Warwks
70 F4 **Worcester** Worcs
44 E6 **Worcester Park** Gt Lon
84 F6 **Wordsley** Dudley
84 D4 **Worfield** Shrops
136 D2 **Workington** Cumb
115 L5 **Worksop** Notts
126 C7 **Worlaby** N Linc
41 J5 **World's End** W Berk
29 M8 **Worlds End** Hants
19 J2 **Worlds End** W Susx
38 A7 **Worle** N Som
98 F2 **Worleston** Ches
93 J5 **Worlingham** Suffk
11 H3 **Worlington** Devon
91 G8 **Worlington** Suffk
78 F2 **Worlingworth** Suffk
132 D6 **Wormald Green** N York
54 B2 **Wormbridge** Herefs
90 F2 **Wormegay** Norfk
54 C3 **Wormelow Tump** Herefs
114 C6 **Wormhill** Derbys
61 M2 **Wormingford** Essex
57 M6 **Worminghall** Bucks
71 J7 **Wormington** Gloucs
186 F3 **Wormit** Fife
72 F4 **Wormleighton** Warwks
60 B6 **Wormley** Herts
30 F4 **Wormley** Surrey
34 B3 **Wormshill** Kent
69 H5 **Wormsley** Herefs
30 F2 **Worplesdon** Surrey
114 F3 **Worrall** Sheff
115 G2 **Worsbrough** Barns
115 G2 **Worsbrough Bridge** Barns
115 G2 **Worsbrough Dale** Barns
113 H2 **Worsley** Salfd
107 G7 **Worstead** Norfk
122 C4 **Worsthorne** Lancs
6 E5 **Worston** Devon
122 B3 **Worston** Lancs
35 J4 **Worth** Kent
15 H6 **Worth Matravers** Dorset
92 C7 **Wortham** Suffk
83 G3 **Worthen** Shrops
98 B4 **Worthenbury** Wrexhm
106 B8 **Worthing** Norfk
18 F5 **Worthing** W Susx
101 H7 **Worthington** Leics
114 F2 **Wortley** Barns
123 K4 **Wortley** Leeds
131 H2 **Worton** N York
39 L8 **Worton** Wilts

92 F6 **Wortwell** Norfk
58 B5 **Wotton Underwood** Bucks
39 H2 **Wotton-under-Edge** Gloucs
74 C6 **Woughton on the Green** M Keyn
46 B7 **Wouldham** Kent
84 D5 **Woundale** Shrops
62 E2 **Wrabness** Essex
23 H4 **Wrafton** Devon
117 J6 **Wragby** Lincs
124 C6 **Wragby** Wakefd
7 G4 **Wrangaton** Devon
104 C3 **Wrangle** Lincs
25 H7 **Wrangway** Somset
25 L6 **Wrantage** Somset
126 C8 **Wrawby** N Linc
38 C6 **Wraxall** N Som
26 E4 **Wraxall** Somset
130 B6 **Wray** Lancs
43 G5 **Wraysbury** W & M
130 C4 **Wrayton** Lancs
120 E4 **Wrea Green** Lancs
148 D5 **Wreay** Cumb
30 D3 **Wrecclesham** Surrey
151 G3 **Wrekenton** Gatesd
134 B8 **Wrelton** N York
98 E3 **Wrenbury** Ches
92 E4 **Wreningham** Norfk
93 K6 **Wrentham** Suffk
83 H3 **Wrentnall** Shrops
125 C6 **Wressle** E R Yk
126 B8 **Wressle** N Linc
75 J5 **Wrestlingworth** Beds
91 G4 **Wretton** Norfk
97 M3 **Wrexham** Wrexhm
84 E7 **Wribbenhall** Worcs
99 H3 **Wrinehill** Staffs
38 C7 **Wrington** N Som
27 G1 **Writhlington** BaNES
61 G6 **Writtle** Essex
84 B2 **Wrockwardine** Wrekin
116 B2 **Wroot** N Linc
123 H3 **Wrose** Brad
33 G2 **Wrotham** Kent
40 C4 **Wroughton** Swindn
17 G6 **Wroxall** IOW
72 B1 **Wroxall** Warwks
83 L2 **Wroxeter** Shrops
107 G8 **Wroxham** Norfk
72 E6 **Wroxton** Oxon
100 D4 **Wyaston** Derbys
104 B4 **Wyberton East** Lincs
75 H3 **Wyboston** Beds
99 G3 **Wybunbury** Ches
71 G2 **Wychbold** Worcs
85 L1 **Wychnor** Staffs
30 C4 **Wyck** Hants
56 D4 **Wyck Rissington** Gloucs
140 E4 **Wycliffe** Dur
122 D3 **Wycoller** Lancs
102 C7 **Wycomb** Leics
42 E3 **Wycombe Marsh** Bucks
60 B2 **Wyddial** Herts
34 E5 **Wye** Kent
123 H5 **Wyke** Brad
27 H6 **Wyke** Dorset
26 F4 **Wyke Champflower** Somset
14 C6 **Wyke Regis** Dorset
134 E3 **Wykeham** N York
86 D7 **Wyken** Covtry
84 D4 **Wyken** Shrops
98 B7 **Wykey** Shrops
150 E3 **Wylam** Nthumb
85 K5 **Wylde Green** Birm
28 A4 **Wylye** Wilts
101 L7 **Wymeswold** Leics
74 D2 **Wymington** Beds

102 D8 **Wymondham** Leics
92 D3 **Wymondham** Norfk
14 B3 **Wynford Eagle** Dorset
71 G5 **Wyre Piddle** Worcs
101 L6 **Wysall** Notts
85 J7 **Wythall** Worcs
57 J6 **Wytham** Oxon
113 J4 **Wythenshawe** Manch
89 K8 **Wyton** Cambs
126 E4 **Wyton** E R Yk
78 C2 **Wyverstone** Suffk
78 B2 **Wyverstone Street** Suffk

Y

109 G7 **Y Felinheli** Gwynd
65 G5 **Y Ferwig** Cerdgn
95 G5 **Y Ffor** Gwynd
97 G2 **Y Gyffylliog** Denbgs
96 F4 **Y Maerdy** Conwy
94 D6 **Y Rhiw** Gwynd
116 E1 **Yaddlethorpe** N Linc
141 H7 **Yafforth** N York
7 K4 **Yalberton** Torbay
33 J3 **Yalding** Kent
138 D2 **Yanwath** Cumb
56 B5 **Yanworth** Gloucs
125 J1 **Yapham** E R Yk
18 D5 **Yapton** W Susx
38 B8 **Yarborough** N Som
118 E3 **Yarburgh** Lincs
13 G2 **Yarcombe** Devon
24 B6 **Yard** Devon
85 K6 **Yardley** Birm
73 L5 **Yardley Gobion** Nhants
74 C3 **Yardley Hastings** Nhants
85 K7 **Yardley Wood** Birm
69 L6 **Yarkhill** Herefs
26 D3 **Yarley** Somset
26 F5 **Yarlington** Somset
141 K5 **Yarm** S on T
16 D4 **Yarmouth** IOW
27 K1 **Yarnbrook** Wilts
99 K6 **Yarnfield** Staffs
23 J6 **Yarnscombe** Devon
57 J5 **Yarnton** Oxon
69 J2 **Yarpole** Herefs
166 E4 **Yarrow** Border
166 E4 **Yarrow Feus** Border
166 F4 **Yarrowford** Border
88 F4 **Yarwell** Nhants
39 G4 **Yate** S Glos
42 D7 **Yateley** Hants
40 B6 **Yatesbury** Wilts
41 K5 **Yattendon** W Berk
69 H2 **Yatton** Herefs
54 F2 **Yatton** Herefs
38 B7 **Yatton** N Som
39 K5 **Yatton Keynell** Wilts
17 H5 **Yaverland** IOW
92 B2 **Yaxham** Norfk
89 H5 **Yaxley** Cambs
92 D8 **Yaxley** Suffk
69 H5 **Yazor** Herefs
43 J4 **Yeading** Gt Lon
123 J3 **Yeadon** Leeds
129 K5 **Yealand Conyers** Lancs
129 K4 **Yealand Redmayne** Lancs
6 E5 **Yealmpton** Devon
133 J5 **Yearsley** N York
98 B8 **Yeaton** Shrops
100 D4 **Yeaveley** Derbys
168 D4 **Yeavering** Nthumb
134 D4 **Yedingham** N York

57 G6 **Yelford** Oxon
75 J3 **Yelling** Cambs
87 H7 **Yelvertoft** Nhants
6 D3 **Yelverton** Devon
93 G3 **Yelverton** Norfk
27 G7 **Yenston** Somset
11 H5 **Yeoford** Devon
9 J7 **Yeolmbridge** Cnwll
26 D7 **Yeovil** Somset
26 D7 **Yeovil Marsh** Somset
26 D6 **Yeovilton** Somset
26 D6 **Yeovilton Fleet Air Arm Museum** Somset
234 b5 **Yesnaby** Ork
14 B1 **Yetminster** Dorset
12 D5 **Yettington** Devon
185 L6 **Yetts o' Muckhart** Clacks
85 H4 **Yew Tree** W Mids
74 E2 **Yielden** Beds
176 B7 **Yieldshields** S Lans
43 H4 **Yiewsley** Gt Lon
37 G2 **Ynysboeth** Rhondd
37 J2 **Ynysddu** Caerph
36 F3 **Ynyshir** Rhondd
51 K5 **Ynystawe** Swans
37 G2 **Ynysybwl** Rhondd
83 H2 **Yockleton** Shrops
125 J5 **Yokefleet** E R Yk
174 F5 **Yoker** C Glas
124 F1 **York** York
124 F1 **York Minster** York
42 E7 **York Town** Surrey
34 E3 **Yorkletts** Kent
54 F6 **Yorkley** Gloucs
131 G4 **Yorkshire Dales National Park**
114 E8 **Youlgreave** Derbys
134 B7 **Youlthorpe** E R Yk
133 G6 **Youlton** N York
61 H4 **Young's End** Essex
100 C8 **Yoxall** Staffs
79 H2 **Yoxford** Suffk
96 C3 **Ysbyty Ifan** Conwy
67 G1 **Ysbyty Ystwyth** Cerdgn
111 G7 **Ysceifiog** Flints
52 B6 **Ystalyfera** Powys
36 F2 **Ystrad** Rhondd
66 C4 **Ystrad Aeron** Cerdgn
66 F2 **Ystrad Meurig** Cerdgn
37 H2 **Ystrad Mynach** Caerph
52 E5 **Ystradfellte** Powys
52 C6 **Ystradgynlais** Powys
36 F5 **Ystradowen** V Glam
217 G7 **Ythanbank** Abers
216 C6 **Ythanwells** Abers
217 G7 **Ythsie** Abers

Z

11 G4 **Zeal Monachorum** Devon
27 H5 **Zeals** Wilts
2 E4 **Zennor** Cnwll
101 J7 **Zouch** Notts